Scripture and Communty

Collected Essays on the Jains

HARVARD UNIVERSITY
CENTER FOR THE STUDY OF WORLD RELIGIONS

Studies in World Religions

Studies in World Religions publishes monographs, translations, and collections of essays on the comparative study of religion, on religious traditions, and on methodological issues in the study of the world's religions, as well as proceedings of conferences and colloquia sponsored by Harvard's Center for the Study of World Religions.

Number 6
Scripture and Community
Essays on the Jains

by
Kendall W. Folkert

edited by
John E. Cort

SCRIPTURE AND COMMUNITY

Collected Essays on the Jains

by
Kendall W. Folkert

edited by
John E. Cort

Scholars Press
Atlanta, Georgia

Scripture and Community
Collected Essays on the Jains

by
Kendall W. Folkert

edited by
John E. Cort

Center for the Study of World Religions
Harvard University

A list of publishers from whom permission has been given to reprint in this volume articles previously published elsewhere may be found on page 451.

On front cover: Young man being initiated as a Śvetāmbara Jain mendicant. Koba, Gujarat, February 1987. Photograph by John E. Cort.

On back cover: Kendall W. Folkert.
Spring 1985. Photograph by Thomas A. Zwicker.

Cover Design by Darwin Melnyk.

Library of Congress Cataloging in Publication Data
Folkert, Kendall W. 1942–1985.
Scripture and community: essays on the Jains/ by Kendall W. Folkert; edited by John E. Cort.
p. cm. — (Studies in world religions; no. 6)
ISBN 1–55540–858–3 (pbk.)
1. Jainism. I. Cort, John. II. Title. III. Series.
BL1355.F65 1993
294.4—dc20 93–15811
CIP

Printed in the United States of America
on acid-free paper

Kendall W. Folkert. Spring 1985
Photograph by Thomas A. Zwicker

CONTENTS

PART II: A Jain Approach to Non-Jains: The 363-Account

PART III: Four Jain Philosophical Compendia

FOREWORD

William A. Graham

The following volume of published articles together with the unpublished *Nachlaß* of Kendall Wayne Folkert (March 5, 1942 - October 29, 1985) represents a welcome set of materials for students of both the Jain tradition and the comparative study of religion. It represents also a substantial labor of love and scholarly service on the part of its editor, John E. Cort, who as a Jain specialist, a comparativist scholar of religion, and as a friend and working colleague of Ken Folkert is peculiarly well suited to the difficult task that he has accomplished in such exemplary fashion here.

John Cort's important introduction leaves little to be added by way of foreword, but as Ken Folkert's colleague and friend of longest standing among scholars of religion, I would like to preface John's lucid remarks with a few comments about Ken's life and work.

Associate Professor of Religion at Central Michigan University at his death and a native Michiganer, Ken received his A. B. in religion from Western Michigan University in 1964. As a Fulbright Scholar in 1964-65 in Göttingen, where he and I first became friends, he studied history of religion with Carsten Colpe. Ken returned to the States in 1965 to study at Harvard Divinity School, and he received the S.T.B. degree *cum laude* there in 1968. In this period, in 1966, he began his study of Sanskrit with Daniel H. H. Ingalls and returned to the history of religion under the tutelage of first Wilfred Cantwell Smith and then also John Braisted Carman, who became, with Dan Ingalls, a mentor also in Indian studies for Ken. Ken was married to Ruth Zwagerman in June 1967, and is survived by her and two sons, Kendall W. Folkert II and Gregory D. Folkert. He was active as a teaching fellow and in administrative work at the Center for the Study of World Religions throughout his doctoral studies. He spent one year (1972) with Ruth and two-year-old Kendall as a Fulbright-Hayes Fellow working at Banaras Hindu University and with Pandit Ambika Datta Upadhyaya in Banaras. This work led to his thesis, "Two Jaina Approaches to Non-Jainas: Patterns and Implications," upon the completion of which he was awarded the Ph.D. degree in 1975.

His fulltime teaching career was all too brief. From 1975 until his death, he taught in the religion department at Central Michigan and was active in faculty affairs at the University. He was the author of several published articles, including the new Jain chapter in Charles J. Adams, *A Reader's Guide to the Great Religions* (2nd. ed., 1977); "Jainism," in the *Penguin Handbook of Living Religions*; and "Jain Religious Life at Ancient Mathurā: The Heritage of Late-Victorian Interpretation," in a volume on ancient Mathurā edited by Doris Srinivasan. Although, as the present collection assembled so ably by John Cort shows, his most important work lay well begun but unfinished at his death, many Asianists and religionists will have known Ken from the stimulating papers he delivered at meetings of the American Oriental Society and the American Academy of Religion. Others will have known him from his lively and helpful participation in conferences, workshops, and seminars across the country.

Ken was not always an easy companion, but he was always an engaged and engaging one. He did not suffer fools gladly, but his charity with his ideas and assistance to others was unstinting. His pleasure in collaborative ventures was, I would like to think, ahead of his time. He loved conversation, and my lasting images of Ken are of him in full, intense cry, seated or pacing, in Göttingen, Leningrad, Cambridge, Mt. Pleasant, or Pune, punctuating his lively commentaries on almost anything and everything with a wave of the ubiquitous cigarette, a bark of infectious laughter, or a cascade of hot coffee from a cup that ran afoul of his emphatic gestures. Always involved, whether in writing letters to newspapers, preaching in local churches, or working to circumvent bureaucratic mentalities or conservative politicians, Ken was intense about things he believed in or loved. Chief among the latter were his family, his friends, his work, and India. His many leadership roles in the life of his community, university, and the scholarly world have been sorely missed since his death by those who knew him. Among both South Asianists and religionists, the loss of his highly promising work in Gujarat will be especially felt by those of us who saw emerging in it a new perspective on both Jain practice and piety and on Western scholarly study of religion more generally.

The publication of these articles and essays is both a fitting tribute to a lost friend and fellow scholar and a genuine contribution to the ongoing task of interpreting faithfully and creatively the history of religion around the globe and across the centuries. It will sadden its readers by reminding how much unrealized promise lay in Ken Folkert's unfinished work, but it will also gladden them to see in that work, even in incomplete form, that his brief career did leave us all with much to think about, much to think "with," much to think "toward": an unfinished agenda that beckons to colleagues and successors with promises of rewarding trajectories of inquiry still to be followed. Ken would be pleased if even some part of that agenda could be realized.

Cambridge, Massachussetts
July 1991

INTRODUCTION: KENDALL FOLKERT AND THE STUDY OF THE JAINS

John E. Cort

When Kendall Folkert began his doctoral dissertation with the statement, "Almost every more recent study of the Jainas begins with a section on the history of Jaina studies" (see chapter 2), he clearly enunciated a theme that would be central to all his subsequent work. Folkert's studies constantly oscillated between on the one hand the historical, and later ethnographical, study of the Jain tradition, and on the other the historiographical study of the history of Jain studies in the West. He had an abiding interest in understanding the Jain tradition, both in its own right and within the broader contexts of Indian society and comparative religions. At the same time, his approach to the previous scholarship on which he based much of his own attempt to understand the Jains in some instances treated this scholarship as second-level discourse on the Jains, and in other instances as primary-level discourse on the history of Western thought. But these two foci were not separated into discrete areas of inquiry; the two always went hand in hand as essential and mutually interactive elements of the broader effort at understanding. This dual focus, on both the Jains and on Western attempts to understand the Jains (and also on both India and Western attempts to understand India), was evident from the very first words of his 1973 doctoral dissertation prospectus:

> There appears to exist, among scholars of Comparative Religion and related fields, a general image of Indian Religion and Philosophy as 'tolerant' or 'assimilative.' The notion seems to be that Indian thinkers, rather than dogmatically rejecting opposing views, tend rather to find a *modus vivendi*, a way of co-existing with those views or of assimilating them in one form or another into their own formal systems.
>
> It is difficult to assess this description of Indian thought, or to locate precisely where in the mass of Indian religious and philosophical literature the sources for such an analysis might lie. Further, it is almost impossible to examine the history and literature of the period when Indian philosophical and religious schools were developing most vigorously without concluding that this characterization is a fiction.

Folkert's concerns with both the Jains themselves and the ways in which scholarship has understood and presented the Jains were by no means restricted to his scholarship. In addition to being a first-class scholar, Folkert was also a committed teacher of comparative religion. Increasingly his scholarship came to be informed by the labor involved in trying to present information on any religious tradition to American undergraduate students, in his case students at a large Midwestern state university. Interaction with students and the presuppositions they brought to his classes led him to a deeper understanding of the intellectual and cultural presuppositions that scholars bring to their studies and that therefore underlie much of Western scholarship. His study of the phenomenon of scripture within comparative religions was informed by, and in turn informed, his efforts at teaching with and about scriptures in courses on comparative religion (see chapter 6).

At the time of his death he was engaged in writing an essay for a joint project on teaching comparative religion sponsored by Harvard University, the University of Chicago, and the Graduate Theological Union. In this essay, published posthumously in a volume of essays related to the project, edited by John B. Carman and Steven P. Hopkins, he expressed his deep misgivings about the current condition of comparative studies of religion. He felt that the field of comparative religion was in fact in a state of malaise that was due to "our field's frequently passive acquiesence in the perpetuation of *impedimenta* from the last century: 'world religions' and 'comparative religion' are the *Paradebeispiele* [exemplary models] of such impedimenta." Folkert goes on to argue that the study of religion needs to develop a distinctive anthropology (in the older sense of the word as the study of what it means to be human, rather than in the more recent sense of a particular discipline within the social sciences), placed firmly within the realm of the humanities, which keeps the physical and moral nature of the human being at the center of all comparative studies. In his words, "studying religion is—and has been—a demanding process of inquiry into the fundamental character of human being." This essay was left unfinished, and much that was in it was still in the process of being thought through by Folkert, and so the reader is frustrated at not having a polished thesis to which to respond. But it showed the fundamental nature of the questions that informed Folkert's teaching, and that also informed his scholarship, as seen in the essays in the present volume.

Part of Folkert's interest in the ways in which the presuppositions behind Jain scholarship have shaped our understandings of the Jains was due to the fact that he, like most other Western Jain scholars, was to a large extent self-trained as a Jain scholar. Western presentations of the Jains, especially before 1979 when P. S. Jaini published his ground-breaking *The Jaina Path of Purification* (and Folkert talked of "pre-Jaini" and "post-Jaini" phases in Western Jain scholarship), gave one at best a severely incomplete picture of a complex and varied historical tradition of great antiquity. Further, as he was to note in many places, Jain scholarship in the West had been driven by issues and concerns that were often external to the material at hand, and so presented that material in a very idiosyncratic manner. Anyone who has looked directly at Jain material, whether it be textual or ethnographic, is almost instantly struck by the disjunction between the vitality and diversity of the material at hand and the aridity and static nature of the previous scholarly presentations of the Jains. Most recent Western scholars have had to rebuild their models of the Jains from the ground up. But Folkert was equally interested in exploring the reasons behind the idiosyncracies and inadequacies of the existing scholarly models. Some of these reasons could be traced to professional reasons; for example, the deeply philological bent of much European Jain scholarship is due to the fact that scholars have been more interested in the Prakrit and Apabhramsa languages in which Jain texts have been written than in the contents of those texts. Folkert, however, was also interested in uncovering as much as possible the cultural presuppositions that underlay previous scholarship, such as Protestant models of the Bible underlying scholarly understandings of scripture in comparative religion.

In this effort to uncover the intellectual underpinnings of Western scholarly models, Folkert was a very contemporary scholar. But at the same time he chose not to cloak his scholarship in the latest academic jargon, and so it is possible for the casual reader to miss the profoundly radical thrust to much of Folkert's scholarship. One will not find in his writings the vocabulary of post-modernism or deconstruction—and in this he perhaps reflects his Harvard background, as religion scholars trained at Harvard oftentimes have a deep-seated suspicion of intellectual jargon—but his intentions were largely the same. (One can also make the same statement about Wilfred Cantwell Smith, one of Folkert's principle teachers at Harvard.) Folkert saw clearly that the model of the Jains as presented in Western scholarship was just that, a creation of Western scholarship. He saw that to understand that intellectual model, one had to understand the intellects that created the model, and the cultural and academic presuppositions that informed those intellects. At the same time, however, Folkert realized that Jainism as portrayed in Western scholarship was not a purely Western creation; rather, it was an interpretation of an extremely complex historical tradition, an interpretation that was also itself interacting with that tradition. Radical and total deconstruction of Western Jain scholarship as an Orientalist fabrication was not only inadequate, it was wrong, a case of throwing out the baby with the bath water. For all of the problems with the Western academic understanding of the Jains, there were also great strengths in that understanding, some of which were not to be found within the tradition itself, and so the scholar's task of appropriating previous scholarship into his or her own understanding of the Jains was a growing and changing enterprise that required constant attention and reassessment. The reader of these essays will learn much about the Jains. But that reader will also learn much about Western scholarship, and the culture in which that scholarship has been embedded.

The reader will also find a great number of unanswered questions. Folkert was an intuitively brilliant scholar, who could quickly penetrate beneath the surface of any given issue to expose the underlying problems of interpretation and understanding, and develop a thesis to explain those underlying problems. But he did not always follow through those initial insights and perform the lengthy, detailed research needed to confirm (or deny) and modify those theses. In those cases where Folkert carried out such research, as in chapters 5, 7, 8, and Part II, the reader will encounter a mind that is finely tuned to details and nuances. Many of the other papers are either short conference presentations or proposals for future research. In these the reader will find a problem painted in broad strokes, and some possible answers painted in equally broad strokes. These essays are also enlightening and fruitful, not only because they give us a glimpse into the workings of his mind, but more so because they open up many avenues of future research. In those areas where my own research has touched upon Folkert's, I have found his suggestions insightful and challenging.[1] In other areas I have found in his writings ideas and theses that would amply reward further research, and I am sure that other scholars will find these essays equally rewarding.

Folkert's scholarship can be divided into three general concerns: the problem of inter-religious attitudes, the category of scripture, and patterns of lay-monastic interaction. These were not discrete, separate concerns, however; they grew organically one from the other, and earlier concerns always underlay later concerns.

---

1 Two instances in which I have built upon and extended Folkert's ideas are Cort 1990 and 1991b.

Folkert's work on the Jains started with a basic issue in comparative religion: how does one religious tradition view other religious traditions? (This work is found in parts II and III, and chapter 8.) Given that at the heart of all religious systems are an interrelated set of axiomatic claims to truth and salvation, the attitudes of most religions toward all other religions are characterized by yes/no, saved/unsaved evaluations. But many scholars had posited that within the Hindu tradition there was a different approach, one based upon tolerance and inclusion rather than judgment and exclusion. The Jains were offered as a special instance of this broader Indian paradigm, in which the Jain moral principle of *ahiṃsā* ("non-harm") was extended into the arena of logic and judgment. G. B. Burch (1964) and A. B. Dhruva (1933) both characterized the interrelated Jain logical tools of *syādvāda* ("doctrine of maybe") and *anekāntavāda* ("doctrine of non-absolutism") as "intellectual *ahiṃsā*." Burch presented these logical tools as a way to acknowledge the validity of all judgments. Folkert proposed to take a fresh look at the ways in which the Jains presented other contemporary religious systems and to adjudge the accuracy of Burch's assessment. Folkert, as he indicated in his dissertation prospectus, was less sanguine concerning this assessment:

> Jaina philosophy's particular aspect, then, which makes it the focus of this thesis, is this: a claim to be able to see fairly and completely the mutual relationships of Indian schools of thought, and to be able to judge and evaluate them impartially. Implicit in this is, of course, a claim to superiority, in that the Jaina philosophy, by recognizing the limitations of any one viewpoint and by using its relativistic logic, claims to be able to see all sides of a given problem; and this is by definition superior to any absolute, exclusive claim. In addition, however, to the strictly epistemological and logical apparatus there is the further claim that this judgment and evaluation is done within the framework of *ahiṃsā*. These two aspects combine to give Jaina thought the particular outlook which makes it the subject of this thesis.

But Folkert's research into this issue raised a host of other issues. An issue that presented itself almost immediately was that of textual or scriptural authority. Folkert found himself dealing extensively with texts that belong to the Śvetāmbara canon, and that, according to the prevailing academic model, have been denied as authoritative by the Digambaras. Upon investigation, however, Folkert discovered that the actual situation was not nearly as cut and dried as one might think from reading the scholarly accounts of Jain literature, and that the situation of the relationships of the Śvetāmbaras and Digambaras to the texts that scholarship termed the Jain canon was in fact quite complicated (see chapters 3-6).

Folkert was led in two directions in his further research on scripture. On the one hand, there was the continuing effort to understand the ways in which the Jains, both Śvetāmbara and Digambara, understood their own and the other's textual traditions, and how these understandings changed over time. On the other hand, Folkert was led into an investigation of the presuppositions behind the Western academic understanding of Jain canon and scripture, and one of his first conference papers was on this very topic (chapter 3). Here he found himself looking less at the non-Western data and more at the Western models for understanding. The problems presented by scripture and canon as categories within comparative religion are similar to the problems presented by most comparative categories. The categories themselves are derived from the Christian tradition and then projected upon other traditions. Oftentimes the Christian origins of the categories are obscured by the fact of a relatively neat fit in its first few applications, usually in the Jewish and Muslim contexts. As the categories themselves become increasingly reified as intellectual categories, they oftentimes become not a model *of* the phenomenon under investigation, but a model *for* our understanding of the phenomenon.[2] Instead of being a tool to help us understand widely diverse cultural phenomena, those phenomena are understood only through the comparative categories, and contradictory evidence is oftentimes not even perceived.[3]

Preliminary results from Folkert's research into the Jains' own understandings of their texts and scriptures are found in chapters 4 and 5. The latter chapter also presents the first results from his investigations into the presuppositions behind Western academic understandings of the Jain scriptures in particular, and scripture as a comparative category in general. He was continuing research on this topic at the time of his death, and some of the directions his research was leading him are indicated in chapter 6. It is not customary to publish grant

---

2 The distinction between model of and model for is from Geertz (1973:93). I have applied this distinction to the understanding of the Jains in Cort 1990.

3 For two recent explorations of the applicability and limitations of comparative categories (scripture and saint), see Levering 1989 and Kieckhefer and Bond 1988. Folkert contributed an essay (see chapter 5) to the Levering volume, but also had come to question the applicability of 'saint' as a comparative category. In a 1983 statement evaluating an N.E.H. Fellowship, he wrote the following:

> I have been pressed to rethink the ways in which one judges religious traditions and their specific features to be 'comparable,' and what academic objectives are attainable by such comparison. Through working with Jains in India, I have been particularly struck, for example, by a need to examine more carefully the role of 'exemplary persons' in religious cultures. On the surface, this category resembles that of 'saints' in Occidental culture; but since comparative religion as an academic discipline has been almost exclusively a Protestant-secular enterprise, insufficient attention has been paid to the status, role, and varying nature of such figures in communal religious life. Hence, where 'scripture' is an extant category whose nature needs reconsideration, the role of 'saints' represents an area where categorical structuring needs to be done.

From his observations on scripture and saint as comparative categories, Folkert had come to have a deep distrust of most contemporary approaches to comparative studies as being too lackadaisical. On this, see his aforementioned article in the volume edited by Carman and Hopkins on teaching the introductory course on religion.

proposals, as has been done here with both chapter 6 and chapter 12. But in this case I think that they serve an essential funtion in this volume, for it is only in these documents that we can see the points which Folkert's thinking had reached on key elements of his research. They also have the virtue of presenting Folkert's thinking in broad, somewhat speculative strokes, whereas his finished writings oftentimes are more concerned with specific details. Folkert's work on the nineteenth century background to academic understandings of scripture also led him into the specific instance of the problems behind the scholarly interpretation of the Jain *stūpa* and other archaeological findings at Mathurā. Folkert anticipated two monographs emerging from his work in the area of scripture. The first was to have been on Jain scripture and canon, and would have included chapters 4, 5, and 7, in addition to some of his work on the *Pratikramaṇa Sūtras* described in chapter 6. The second monograph was to have been on the problems presented by scripture as a phenomenological category for the comparative study of religion.

Folkert's interest in monastic practice grew from two sources. One of these was a text he translated as part of his dissertation, the *Ṣaḍdarśanasamuccaya* of Rājaśekhara. As he relates in chapter 10, Folkert had been led by previous scholarship on the Jains to expect that one of the major issues behind the Śvetāmbara-Digambara split would be a disagreement over which texts were authoritative. But he found no mention of this in Rājaśekhara's discussion of sectarian differences. Instead he found listed a number of aspects of monastic practice, aspects described by Schubring (1962:70) as "irrelevant matters of praxis." Folkert, however, was led to consider whether it was the data that was insignificant, or our scholarly models that were inadequate. Folkert concluded that centuries of Western, Christian preoccupation with theological debates over matters of doctrine, creed, and texts had led to the unconscious scholarly presupposition that such matters must lie behind all important religious sectarian disputes, and that therefore these presuppositions made it difficult for Western scholars to perceive details of monastic practice as possible or serious sources of disagreement. Here the specifically Protestant nature of much of Western academia's presuppositions is also apparent, for the sorts of differences listed by Rājaśekhara would not appear all that unusual or irrelevant to a scholar of Catholic monasticism.

The other source of Folkert's interest in monastic practice was his study of Jain scriptures. In attempting to understand the Jains' own understanding of their texts, he was led to focus on a set of ancient texts that contain the six obligatory rituals (*āvaśyaka*) that lie at the heart of the daily Śvetāmbara Jain mendicant practice. These texts are largely the same in both the Śvetāmbara and Digambara traditions (see Leumann 1934), and so predate the separation into two distinct sects in the early centuries C.E. These texts include the *Pratikramaṇa Sūtras* discussed in chapter 6.[4]

Folkert's discovery of the central importance of the *Pratikramaṇa Sūtras* underscores the importance of a scholar doing fieldwork even on such a seemingly library-oriented topic as the Jain scriptures. As Folkert notes in his discussion of these texts in chapter 6, "in line with the nineteenth-century perspectives [of previous scholarship] ...these texts have hardly been touched by scholars." The only discussion of the *pratikramaṇa* texts was by R. Williams (1963:203-7), and his discussion is, quite frankly, almost unintelligible. Williams' discussion was based on medieval Jain textual presentations of the ritual. But, as Folkert points out in a portion of his grant proposal not included in chapter 6, ritual manuals such as this in and of themselves "would not show the text's full character, or allow other scholars to understand readily its place in Jain religious life." He goes on to observe,

> The situation may be compared to translating a Christian liturgy and hymnal into an Asian language: neither the technical material (e.g., the specific ritual language) nor the poetic passages (e.g., the words of the hymns) would be fully understood without annotation as to meaning, accompanying actions, and sources of the material....A bare translation of [a passage from the *Lutheran Book of Worship*] would never show its multiple associations in actual practice. These include: New Testament sources for the actual words used, and the nature of these sources; the rich history of Christian interpretation (and dispute) over the meaning of certain phrases; the general place of this piece of ritual literature in the church's larger ritual; and the specific actions performed while the passage is said.

Folkert was engaged in his study of the *Pratikramaṇa Sūtras* with Muni Jambūvijay at the time of his death. He was working on a translation of the various textual layers (there is a layer common to all performances of *pratikramaṇa*, and slightly different portions for the five separate types of *pratikramaṇa*: morning, evening, fortnightly, four-monthly, and annual). He was also engaged in participant-observation of the rituals themselves, as indicated in chapter 13. He envisaged as a final product a book of translations of the texts themselves, accompanied by extensive annotations based on both fieldwork and historical textual studies. The text was to be in parallel parts, with plain translation on the left, and annotation on the right. He also felt that such a book would need to be

[4] The *Pratikramaṇa Sūtras* were also the subject of Folkert's last conference paper, entitled "Canon and the Process of Canonization: The Jains and the *Pañc-Pratikramaṇa Sūtras*." This was read as part of a panel on "Scripture and Sacred Texts in Comparative Perspective" at the 1983 Annual Meeting of the American Academy of Religion. I did not discover a text of this presentation among his papers, and other participants in the panel recall that his presentation consisted of some of the material found in chapter 5 combined with an extemporaneous description of the *Pratikramaṇa Sūtras*. The abstract of this paper is incorporated into chapter 4.

accompanied by extensive photographs, of the various stylized ritual acts, and the implements used in the ritual.

Simultaneous with this research Folkert was engaged in the study described in the last part of chapter 12, on lay-mendicant interaction among the Śvetāmbar Mūrtipūjak Jains. His interest in this issue was one of long standing, as he felt that understanding this interaction was central to explaining the survival and vitality of the Jain tradition in the face of pressures of absorption into Hinduism, especially in light of the near-total disappearance of Buddhism in India. His interest in this issue was further piqued in the course of spending time with Muni Jambūvijay while studying the *Pratikramaṇa Sūtras*. Muni Jambūvijay is known to the world of Western Jain scholarship as the greatest Jain monk-scholar alive today, as a person who has done excellent critical editions of a number of important texts. But he is known to his followers in India for his great charisma, especially in terms of enabling his devotees to perform fasts of a length which they would otherwise be incapable. Jambūvijay's devotees come to him for advice on a wide variety of spiritual, personal, family, business, and community issues, and he frequently will take time out from a scholarly discussion to address these concerns, allowing Folkert to see clearly the nature of the monk-devotee relationship. Folkert thus found that his two simultaneous research interests, of textual study of the *Pratikramaṇa Sūtras* with Muni Jambūvijay and fieldwork observation of lay-mendicant interaction, were eminently complimentary activities. Further, Jambūvijay in observance of his monastic code of conduct was constantly travelling from village to village except for the four months of the rainy season retreat. But it was quickly evident that these travels were not random. A Jain monk does not 'wander.' Each journey is for a specific purpose: to visit a famous pilgrimage temple, to consult a manuscript collection, to grace with his presence a lay temple ritual, or to fulfill some other pastoral duty to his devotees. During the time of Folkert's fieldwork Jambūvijay was staying in an area of several dozen villages with Jain inhabitants in northern Gujarat. At the same time Jambūvijay stressed that he did not like to stay too long in any given area, as a monk then developed relationships with the local laity of a strength that went against the spirit of nonattachment that lies at the heart of a monk's life. He therefore preferred to shift regions every five or six years. Earlier parts of his monastic career had been spent in the area around Pune, in southern Rajasthan, and in Kacch in far western Gujarat. But the area he was in when Folkert was doing his fieldwork was his favorite, for it was the area in which he, his father (who was also his initiating guru, Muni Bhuvanvijay), and his mother (who travelled with him as a *sādhvī*, Manoharśrī) had originally lived before becoming mendicants. It is also the area around his favorite pilgrimage temple, that of Śaṅkheśvara Pārśvanātha in the town of Shankheshvar.

Like most scholars of religion, Ken was trained as a textual scholar. His first two extended trips to India had been spent largely in Banaras and Pune, where he was able to work in libraries and with scholars. But in each of these trips he had made visits to consult with Muni Jambūvijay, first in Rajasthan and then in northern Gujarat, and had also come into contact with families in Ahmedabad, Bombay, and elsewhere who were devotees of Jambūvijay. His next-to-last trip to India, for several months in early 1985, had been much more extensively devoted to fieldwork, in part due to the changing nature of his research interests, but also in significant part due to his collaboration with Thomas Zwicker. Tom was a doctoral student in anthropology at the University of Pennsylvania, who was in Gujarat conducting fieldwork on everyday Jain merchant ethics. In large part because of the earlier contacts with Muni Jambūvijay developed by Folkert, Tom had chosen for his area of research the same area in which Jambūvijay was travelling. As a result Tom and Ken became an informal research team. Through Tom's ethnographic experience Ken was fully exposed to fieldwork, and for the first time experienced all the joys of total cultural immersion that can be found in fieldwork. When Ken returned to India in September 1985, after a summer visit back to the United States, he continued his collaboration with Tom. By this time it was an even larger research team, as I had arrived in Gujarat in August to pursue the fieldwork for my own dissertation, a religious ethnography of contemporary Śvetāmbar Mūrtipūjak belief and practice. My research was centered in the town of Patan, just a few miles to the east of the area of Tom and Ken's research. All of us also spent extensive time in Ahmedabad, both to use the libraries there and to conduct related research among the much larger communities of laity and mendicants to be found in the big city.

The nature and fruits of such collaborative research are clearly seen in chapter 13, which was edited from Folkert's fieldwork journal. This collaborative venture was cut short, however, when Ken and Tom were killed in a traffic accident on the evening of October 29, 1985, while returning to Ahmedabad from a visit to north Gujarat. I stayed on in Gujarat with my wife Cynthia until April 1987 to finish my research. I am sure that the direction and shape of that research would have been drastically different, and the results much richer, had I been able to continue our collaboration.

The following collection of essays is edited from the published and unpublished writings of Ken Folkert. His dissertation was never published, so much of this volume is taken from his dissertation. It was accepted for publication in the Harvard Dissertations in Religion Series, published by Scholars Press. But Ken withdrew the dissertation from publication, in large part because he felt that it was of too detailed and technical a nature to be of interest to a broader audience, but also pending his new translation of Haribhadra's *Ṣaḍdarśanasamuccaya*, since in the dissertation he had included the translation of K. Satchidananda Murty. He later considered publishing just the translations from the dissertation as a separate book in India, but as far as I have been able to ascertain from his papers he never commenced his translation of Haribhadra's text.

The portions of his dissertation included in this volume (Parts II and III, chapter 8, and parts of 2) have undergone extensive editing, to make them more accessible to a larger audience. Other chapters were articles requested for specific volumes (chapters 1 and 7, and parts of 2). The rest were parts of his ongoing research projects, either as unpublished conference papers, or as published articles. The chapters derived from the conference papers have been edited from Folkert's hand-written presentation texts, and occasionally filled in with passages from his dissertation as indicated in his notes. Because Folkert several times used the same material to address different issues, the reader will find several short passages repeated in more than one chapter. But I think that the contexts are sufficiently different that the repetitions will not be overly noticeable, and I decided to include a small amount of repetition rather than break the integrity of the individual chapters. I have also sought to standardize the entire volume in terms of style, which has resulted in an extensive amount of detailed editing, so the reader will not find the texts of any of the previously published articles identical with the texts found here. But I have made sure not to alter Folkert's distinctive authorial voice, for it is his voice as much as the content that provides the unity to this volume. In line with Folkert's later usage, I have used the contemporary "Jain" rather than the classicist "Jaina" throughout the book, except in case of direct translation. Finally, I have added a small number of footnotes, indicated as mine by the notation "[Editor's note.]" With one or two exceptions, I have refrained from commenting on the content of Folkert's material, and restricted my notes to giving subsequent bibliographic references that directly relate to the material at hand. I have been very fortunate in this project to have the invaluable assistance of Lisa Hammer, staff assistant at the Center for the Study of World Religions of Harvard University. Lisa started this project as a typist, but quickly assumed many editorial responsibilities. She also prepared the index. To her is due much of the credit for the order and coherence of this volume. I would also like to thank three successive directors of the Center for the Study of World Religions at Harvard University, all of whom were both generous and enthusiastic in their support of the editing of this volume: John B. Carman, M. David Eckel, and Lawrence E. Sullivan.

Before his death, I knew Ken Folkert as a friend and colleague. After working at the editing of this volume for several years, I can say that I probably know his thoughts better than those of any other person except myself. But I cannot claim to have penetrated fully his thinking, and there is much contained in these pages that continues to challenge me, much that continues to be new, much that deserves to be read. While this editorial work has oftentimes been a painful task, it has also been a great privilege. The esteem and respect felt for Ken by his friends and colleagues is seen in that three books have been dedicated to his memory. This book I want to dedicate to those who have faced the greatest challenges posed by Ken's tragic and sudden death: his wife, Ruth Folkert Magnell, and his sons Kendall W. Folkert II and Gregory D. Folkert.

Published Works of Kendall W. Folkert

"The Jainas." In *A Reader's Guide to the Great Religions*, 2nd ed., 231-46. Ed. Charles J. Adams. New York: The Free Press, 1977.

Following entries in *Abingdon Dictionary of Living Religions*. Ed. Keith Crim. Nashville: Abingdon, 1981. Reprinted as *The Perennial Dictionary of World Religions*. New York: Harper & Row, 1989.

"Ādinātha," 4.
"Ājīvikas," 19-20.
"Cārvāka," 157-58.
"Digambara," 223.
"Jainism," 369-72.
"Jīva," 382-83.
"Kaivalya," 397.
"Mahāvīra," 451-52.
"Śvetāmbara," 728.
"Tīrthaṅkara," 762.

"Jainism." In *A Handbook of Living Religions*, 256-77. Ed. John R. Hinnells. London: Penguin, 1984.

Following entries in *The World Book Encyclopedia* (1988 Edition). Chicago: World Book, 1987.

"Jainism," volume 11, 22.
"Lamaism," volume 12, 51-52.
"Sikhism," volume 17, 455-56.

"Jain Religious Life at Ancient Mathurā: The Heritage of Late-Victorian Interpretation." In *Mathurā: The Cultural Heritage*, 103-112. Ed. Doris Meth Srinivasan. Delhi: Manohar and American Institute for Indian Studies, 1989.

"The 'Canons' of 'Scripture.'" In *Rethinking Scripture: Essays from a Comparative Perspective*, 170-79. Ed. Miriam Levering. Albany: State University of New York Press, 1989.

"Notes on Paryuṣaṇ in Samī and Veḍ." Ed. John E. Cort. In *Center for the Study of World Religions Bulletin* 16:2 (1990), 54-73.

"A Thematic Course in the Study of Religion." Ed. John E. Cort. In *Tracing Common Themes: Comparative Courses in the Study of Religion*, 19-36. Ed. John B. Carman and Steven P. Hopkins. Atlanta: Scholars Press, 1991.

Book reviews and notes:

John Braisted Carman, *The Theology of Rāmānuja*. In *Religious Studies Review* 2:1 (1976), 31.

Edward C. Dimock, Jr. et al., *The Literature of India*. In *Religious Studies Review* 2:1 (1976), 31-32.

David R. Kinsley, *The Sword and the Flute*. In *Religious Studies Review* 2:2 (1976), 24.

Lawrence A. Babb, *The Divine Hierarchy*. In *Religious Studies Review* 2:3 (1976), 45.

Charlotte Vaudeville, *Kabīr*. In *Religious Studies Review* 2:3 (1976), 46.

Paul R. Brass, *Language, Religion and Politics in North India*; and G. R. Thursby, *Hindu-Muslim Relations in British India*. In *Religious Studies Review* 3:4 (1977), 241-42.

David M. Miller and Dorothy C. Wertz, *Hindu Monastic Life*. In *Religious Studies Review* 3:4 (1977), 242.

Jean Varenne, *Yoga and the Hindu Tradition*. In *Religious Studies Review* 3:4 (1977), 242.

K. C. Bhattacharyya, *Search for the Absolute in Neo-Vedanta*. In *Religious Studies Review* 4:3 (1978), 203.

Bardwell L. Smith, *Hinduism*. In *Religious Studies Review* 4:3 (1978), 203-4.

Padmanabh S. Jaini, *The Jaina Path of Purification*. In *Journal of Asian Studies* 39 (1980), 829-31.

LIST OF ILLUSTRATIONS

Part I

SCRIPTURE, COMMUNITY, AND THE HISTORY OF JAIN STUDIES

1

INTRODUCTION TO JAINISM*

Jains have been present in India's religious life for at least 2,500 years and continue to be a visible and active community, holding tenaciously to a rigorous discipline whose roots pre-date the Buddha. The community at present includes only some three million persons (roughly one-half of one percent of India's population), and its relative size has been small throughout its history. Yet the influence of the Jains on Indian culture and the continuity of their history have been such that Jainism is commonly regarded as one of India's major indigenous religious traditions.

At the core of Jainism lies an ascetic ideal. Jains take their name from the term 'Jina,' which means 'conqueror.' 'Jina' is an honorific term, not a proper name (cf. 'Buddha'); it is given by Jains to twenty-four great teachers. The message and example of these teacher-conquerors was that the human being, without supernatural aid, is capable of conquering the bondage of physical existence and achieving freedom from rebirth; and that this conquest is to be achieved only by the most rigorous renunciation of all physical comforts and social constraints. These teachers are also called Tīrthaṅkaras, a title meaning 'crossing-maker,'

* "Jainism." In *A Handbook of Living Religions*, 256-77. Ed. J. R. Hinnells. Harmondsworth: Viking/Penguin, 1984.

which points to their role as teachers and exemplars for others who seek the same goal.[1]

Though relatively small in numbers, Jainism is not monolithic. Regional and linguistic divisions, and differences in religious practice, have been present in Jainism since at least the early centuries C.E. Jains are, by and large, divided into Śvetāmbaras (so named because their monks and nuns are 'white-clad'), Digambaras (so named because their male ascetics are 'sky-clad,' i.e., nude), and several reform movements which have arisen in recent centuries. It is also important to note that, while Jainism has an ascetic basis, the majority of those who call themselves Jains are lay persons whose religious life is not monastic.

PRIMARY SOURCES FOR THE STUDY OF JAINISM

Sources for study are best treated as three categories of literature: (1) early scriptures, (2) later Sanskrit writings, and (3) more recent literature. The first category comprises the oldest texts of Jainism, which were composed in various Prakrits (early Indian vernacular languages). By the fifth century C.E., the Śvetāmbara Jains had assembled a collection of forty-five extant texts into a 'canon' (Jaini 1979:47-77; a complete list is found in Appendix below), commonly called the *Siddhānta*.[2] This canon's oldest and most venerated texts are the *Aṅgas*, which present early accounts of Jain monastic discipline and contain sermons and dialogues of Vardhamāna Mahāvīra (sixth century B.C.E.), the last of the twenty-four Tīrthaṅkaras.

Not all Jains, however, regard these forty-five texts as normative. In the sixteenth century C.E. a reform movement called the Sthānakavāsīs produced a canon of texts that contains only thirty-two of the forty-five texts in the *Siddhānta*; and the Digambara Jains, while not repudiating most of the dogmatic content of the *Siddhānta*, hold that the language and form of this canon are not authentic. The Digambaras preserve two very old Prakrit texts that pre-date the compilation of the Śvetāmbara canon. These earliest Digambara texts, the *Ṣaṭkhaṇḍāgama* ('Scripture in Six Parts') and the *Kaṣāyaprābhṛta* ('Treatise on the Stain of Passion'), were supplemented by commentaries and writings which, together with the older texts, give the Digambaras their own body of normative literature, called the *Anuyoga* ('Expositions').

The second category of primary source literature, written in Sanskrit largely from 700 C.E. onward, signals a major change in Jainism. Alongside commen-

---

1 The term "Tīrthaṅkara" is variously translated as "ford-maker," "crossing-maker," etc. Perhaps more apt than any translation is Louis Renou's (1953:112) comparison of the image to the Latin *pontifes*, literally "bridge-maker."

2 On the Śvetāmbara 'canon,' see chapters 4 and 5.

taries on older texts, this large body of literature contains new didactic texts, philosophical writings, and narrative and technical works. An important feature of this literature is that much of it deals with the lay community, and includes writings (resembling the Hindu *Purāṇas*) that give a Jain view of world prehistory and of the origins of basic human institutions and everyday religious activity.

These Sanskrit sources thus point beyond themselves to a major development in Jainism: the systematization of lay life, including religious discipline and temple, home, and life-cycle rituals. These sources are, therefore, important for understanding the full range of Jain religious life. (For the reader's guidance, a list of major works in several categories is provided in Appendix B below.)

The third area of primary source material, of more recent origin, consists of works in modern Indian languages (including early forms of such languages as Gujarati, Hindi, Kannada, and Marathi) and, over the last century, in English. The vernacular works cover a range of popular religious material, including recastings of Sanskrit narratives. There are also works written in the last few decades that are directed towards Jain renewal and contemporary problems (Sangave 1980:291-92).

Jain writings in English were often directed towards European and American audiences, and include efforts at presenting ancient Jain texts and ideas to the Western world. Notable in this connection, though many more examples could be cited, is the work of J. L. Jaini, a Digambara layman, whose *Outlines of Jainism* and many other works present something of a modern apologetic for Jainism.

JAIN HISTORY

It is common to refer to Vardhamāna Mahāvīra, who lived from 599 to 527 B.C.E. (the traditional dating), as the 'founder' of Jainism, and to regard Jain history as beginning with him. However, Jains hold that the universe is eternal and uncreated and, as do Hindus, conceive of time in vast, cyclic terms. A full cycle of time consists of two main periods of some 600 million years, each subdivided into six parts. One of these main periods is a period of ascent, in which all conditions improve; the other is a time of descent, in which knowledge, behavior, human stature, etc., all decline. In each main half-cycle there appear twenty-four great teachers, the Jinas or Tīrthaṅkaras referred to above.

In the current cycle of cosmic time (which is a period of decline), twenty-four such teachers are thus held to have lived. The last of these was Vardhamāna Mahāvīra. His predecessor in the series was a man named Pārśva, whom the Jains place in the ninth century B.C.E., and for whose life there is some (but very little) historical evidence. Modern accounts of Jain history thus begin with Mahāvīra, but Jain literature and religious life include all twenty-four Tīrthaṅkaras.

Mahāvīra was born Vardhamāna Jñātṛputra in northeastern India, near modern Patna. (Jñātṛputra is his clan-name; 'Mahāvīra' is an honorific title meaning 'great hero.') At thirty years of age, he abandoned his life as a member of the warrior (Kṣatriya) class, and took up the life of a possessionless mendicant. For more than twelve years Mahāvīra devoted himself to renunciation and detachment from all physical needs and comforts. At the end of this time, having reached complete understanding of the nature of the universe and absolute detachment from worldly desires, he began teaching others. By Jain accounts, he had assembled a following of several hundred thousand by the time of his death at the age of seventy-two.

Leadership of the Jains thereafter passed to Mahāvīra's senior disciples, and under these men and their successors the movement began to spread from northeastern India into eastern and northwestern population centres. The Jains, like the Buddhists, benefited from the support for monastic ideals of the Mauryan dynasty (third century B.C.E.), and the growth and geographical spread of Jainism accelerated, carrying it into central and southern India.

In the period after Mahāvīra's death, divisions emerged within Jainism, in particular the Śvetāmbara-Digambara schism mentioned above. The two groups disagreed largely over monastic practice. The Digambaras maintained that an ascetic who had truly renounced the world would also renounce clothing, and go naked, as Mahāvīra apparently had done. The Śvetāmbaras maintained, however, that Mahāvīra's life and teachings did not make nudity an absolute requirement, and that the wearing of simple white garments would be a sufficient act of renunciation. From this particular disagreement have come the names that characterize this lasting division within Jainism.

Other areas of disagreement also arose, no less significant than the matter of clothing, but often more technical and less subject to popular debate. These included the question of scriptures, as detailed earlier; there were also disagreements over other particulars of monastic life, and differing versions of the life story of Mahāvīra, plus a significant and lasting disagreement concerning the status of women (P. S. Jaini 1991). Śvetāmbaras admit women to full monastic vows, but Digambaras do not, arguing that women are not capable of attaining liberation and must await rebirth as males in order to pursue full ascetic careers.

All these differences were accentuated (and may well have been partly caused) by the fact that the two groups were concentrated in different regions and subcultures of India during Jainism's period of growth. The Digambaras were the principal Jains in southern and central India, while the Śvetāmbaras concentrated in the north and west. Thus it is appropriate to think of the Śvetāmbara-Digambara division as being in many ways like the difference between Orthodox and Roman Catholic Christians.

Internal divisions notwithstanding, the Jains entered a period of growth and influence by the fifth century C.E.. In central and southern India, the Digambaras won royal patronage and were a notable cultural force, especially in such matters as the development of vernacular literatures. A few centuries later the Śvetāmbaras played much the same role in the north, and even more so in western India.

This was the period, as noted above, that gave a coherent and lasting pattern to the Jain lay community. As Jainism had moved into diverse regions and had grown in numbers, the absorption of lay persons into the movement required that the lay Jain be given a distinctive identity. Thus narrative texts and models of lay discipline are prominent in this period's literature.

By the eleventh and twelfth centuries C.E. Jainism was beginning to retreat geographically into its present area of concentration, the area in western India from Rajasthan in the north through Karnataka in the south. A rising tide of Hindu theistic religion in south and central India, with accompanying royal patronage, led to the Jains falling into disfavor in those regions. The Digambaras gradually retreated to the north and west, leaving behind only a shadow of their earlier presence in the central and southern regions. In the Śvetāmbara-dominated areas less contraction occurred, although the Śvetāmbaras also declined in influence as new Hindu movements gained a following. The Śvetāmbaras also experienced the increasing presence of Islam in India from the twelfth century onwards. Thus the growth of Jainism was deflected in the northwest as well as in the Digambara regions.

By 1500 C.E., Jainism had largely reached its current geographic status, and from this time onwards began to see various movements of reform and renewal. Prominent among these was a fifteenth- and sixteenth-century Śvetāmbara movement called the Sthānakavāsīs. Still active today, its members are recognizable by their practice of wearing a cloth or mask over the mouth and nose. This group produced, as noted, its own canon of scripture; and it objected to the veneration of images as practised by Jains, as well as to the entire complex of temple-cultus and activity that had developed in Jainism by that time. Other movements followed, notably a similar Digambara group, known as the Tāraṇapanthas, which originated in the sixteenth century, and the eighteenth-century Śvetāmbara Terāpantha movement.

Jainism has thus passed through periods of formative, largely monastic life (from Mahāvīra to the early centuries C.E.); of spread, growth, and engagement with laity (early centuries C.E. to twelfth century); and of contraction, reform, and redevelopment.

SCHOLARLY STUDY OF THE JAINS

The Jains came to the notice of Western scholarship largely through the efforts of Albrecht Weber, Georg Bühler, and Hermann Jacobi. Weber and Bühler combined efforts in the 1880s to present to scholars a comprehensive account of the Jain scriptures, and Jacobi pioneered the translation of Jain Prakrit texts into European languages. A number of other scholars, too numerous to catalogue here (see Schubring 1962:1-13), contributed to early Jain studies, but the work of the three just mentioned was formative. This is so for two reasons. First, it was not uncommon for nineteenth-century scholars of India to portray Jainism as subordinate to Buddhism or as a schismatic offshoot. Some scholarly attempts were made to show that Vardhamāna Mahāvīra and Siddhārtha Gautama, the Buddha, were one and the same, the Jain schismatics having altered the founder's portrait just enough to make it appear that they had their own unique origin (Jacobi 1884b:ix-xlvii). It was Jacobi who put this notion to rest by his tireless translation and assembling of evidence, and since his time the Jains have been accorded appropriate recognition.

The second formative dimension of the work of Weber, Bühler, and Jacobi was that their interests, typical for the nineteenth century, were heavily textual and historical. Given this, they were drawn first to the Śvetāmbara tradition, which appeared to preserve the oldest and most complete set of texts. As a result, the Western world's earliest complete picture of Jainism was drawn from Śvetāmbara sources, while the Digambaras were portrayed in a secondary light.

The effect of this early focus on the Śvetāmbaras and on Jain texts is still felt. Subsequent Jain scholarship, by such eminent figures as Helmuth von Glasenapp, Ernst Leumann, Walther Schubring, and Ludwig Alsdorf, remained textual and historical in focus, with an emphasis on the Śvetāmbaras. Such work still represents the dominant approach to the study of the Jains. More comprehensive, topical, and social-structural study of Jainism is rare. Efforts to portray the Jains as a living, practising community, such as those of Mrs. Sinclair Stevenson early in this century, and of V. A. Sangave in the 1950s, only partly fill this gap. By and large it must simply be said that Jain scholarship, perhaps more than any other part of the study of India, has remained where it began: in an almost exclusively textual and historical mode.

BASIC TEACHINGS

As noted, Jainism teaches that the human being can conquer the limitations of physical existence and attain immortality by means of rigorous ascetic discipline. Jainism bases its teaching on a fundamental division of all existing things into two classes: *jīva*, i.e., that which is sentient; and *ajīva*, that which is not. Every living thing consists of a *jīva* (often translated as 'soul,' but better understood as a 'sentient essence') and of *ajīva*, i.e., a nonsentient, material component that has become associated with the *jīva*. This association with *ajīva* prevents the *jīva* from realizing its true nature, which is immortal, omniscient, and absolutely complete in itself.

There is an infinite number of *jīva*s, and each is an eternal and discrete entity, not linked to other *jīva*s in any fashion. The *jīva*s neither emanate from a common source nor in any way merge with one another upon liberation. There is no 'supreme *jīva*' or supreme deity/creator, and the Tīrthaṅkaras, or Jinas, are not regarded as divine. They are venerated, but this is in virtue of their status as teachers and models of renunciation.

Jains also hold that each *jīva* has eternally been associated with *ajīva*, i.e., that there was no 'fall' of the *jīva* into an impure state. The association of the *jīva* with *ajīva* is beginningless, like the universe; yet the condition is not unchangeable. The association of the two is understood to be the work of karma, a concept that the Jains share with the larger Hindu tradition, but which they understand in a unique fashion. In the Jain view, karma is a subtle form of matter that clings to the *jīva*, obscuring (but not actually altering) the innate capacities of the *jīva*. This obscuring of its faculties causes the *jīva* to be reborn into an infinite series of physical existences, another basic premise that Jainism shares with Hinduism as a whole.

There is only one way in which the *jīva* can be set free of this karmic bondage and resultant physical rebirth, and that way involves the ascetic life. The goal of ascetic discipline is to stop any further association of the *jīva* with karma, and to hasten the decay of such karma as has previously obscured the *jīva*. When the *jīva* is at last rid of all karmic association, it is held to be freed of rebirth and to rise to the uppermost reaches of the universe, the *siddha-loka* (see Figure 1), to abide there eternally in its innate perfection: total knowledge and self-containment.

An interesting dimension of the Jain consideration of *jīva* and *ajīva* is the system of philosophical analysis known as *anekāntavāda*, the teaching of 'non-onesidedness,' which Jain philosophers developed as a way of dealing with the multiple dimensions of reality. Jain metaphysics considers the soul to be both essentially unchanging and yet capable of various qualitative alterations, and seeks to synthesize conflicting analyses of reality (e.g., either as permanent or as constantly changing). In the Jain view, any philosophical system that holds reality to be ultimately reducible to one ontological dimension (e.g., to permanence, or to constant change) is an *ekāntavāda*, a 'onesided view,' and is condemned to error by its very failure to take account of the several equally important dimensions of being. Therefore the Jains insist on 'non-onesidedness.'

These core teachings contain certain key elements related to basic Jain values. The first such matter is the nature of the *jīva*. Jains infer the existence of the *jīva* from its function as 'knower' and agent of activity in living things, and argue that the innate nature of the *jīva* must be whole and complete or else there would be an inconsistency in its existence, even though it has been eternally associated with karma. Therefore the *jīva* is held to be innately omniscient and eternal. It is this capacity for omniscience that gives authority to Jain teachings, for the Tīrthaṅkaras are held to have attained omniscience in virtue of their ascetic detachment from all physical things. There being no supernatural agency, there can be no divine revelation; the truth of a Tīrthaṅkara's teaching ultimately rests on the Jain conviction that all *jīva*s are capable of total knowledge (Tatia 1951:61-64). The work of a Tīrthaṅkara is to show the way, to 'make a crossing,' based upon his attainment, which is, properly speaking, the recovery of the true nature of his own *jīva*, not the discovery of something new.

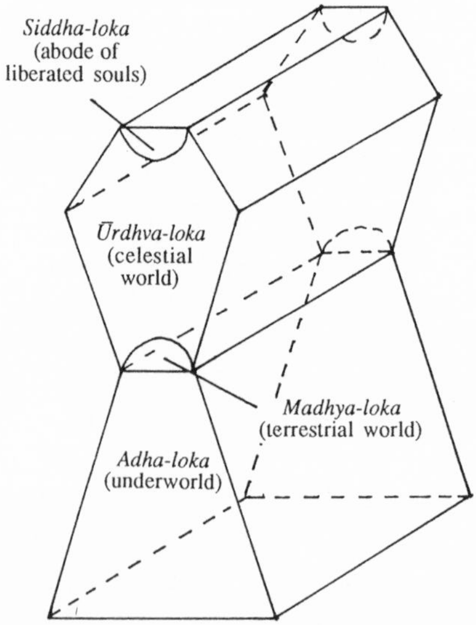

Figure I: Jain *pratīka,* symbol of Jain faith. This was officially adopted in 1975 at the celebration of the 2,500th anniversary of Mahāvīra's nirvāṇa. The symbol clearly reflects the archaic view of the universe (see Figure II).

A second key element in Jain teachings is the nature of *ajīva* and the working of karma (see Tatia 1951:220-60). All insentient existents are included in the category of *ajīva*, particularly space, time, and matter, the latter conceived of as atoms. It is important to note that the actual existence of *ajīva* is not denied by Jains, and that matter is therefore real and eternal. Karma, then, as a subtle form of matter, is not an illusion or result of perceptual error. It is real, and must be dealt with in a physical way, like components of worldly existence.

Dissolution of the association of the *jīva* with karma thus requires the cultivation of actual and extreme detachment from all that is not-*jīva*. No purely 'spiritual' or 'mental' exercise will suffice. Therefore Jain monastic life has always had, and has today, a quality of concreteness and actual physical rigor to it.

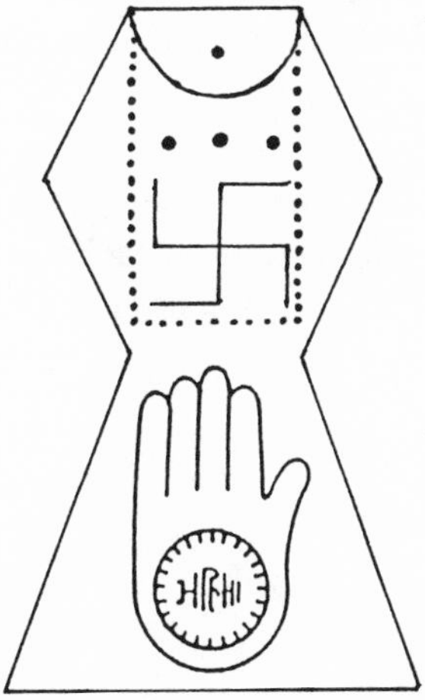

Figure II: The archaic view of the universe, representing in rough outline the human form, and its four levels of abode. Humans dwell in the *Madhya-loka*. The celestial world and underworld comprise many internal levels corresponding to the type of celestial or infernal being.

A third key element is the practice of *ahiṃsā*, 'non-injury.' As Jainism evolved, *ahiṃsā* came more and more to the fore as a key component of detachment from *ajīva*, from the material world of karma. For Jains, *ahiṃsā* has come to embody one's willingness to separate oneself altogether not merely from acts of injury or killing, but also from the entire mechanism of aggression, possession, and consumption that characterizes life in this world. Thus *ahiṃsā* has come to be a hallmark of the Jain commitment to detachment. It is not only an ethical goal, but also a metaphysical truth for Jains that non-injury is part of the path to liberation.

The central place given to this teaching has resulted in a number of characteristic Jain practices, including the monastic practice of carrying a small broom or whisk with which to brush away gently any living creatures before one sits or lies down; the Sthānakavāsī practice of wearing a mask stems from a desire to prevent even the accidental ingestion of invisible creatures. The concern for *ahiṃsā* has also involved the entire community, monastic and lay, in a characteristic insistence upon vegetarian diet, and opposition to animal slaughter in general, as important dimensions of non-injury. Jain lay persons are enjoined to engage only in occupations that minimize the destruction of living beings. Therefore most Jains are members of mercantile or professional classes.

The achievement of such detachment, in total reliance upon one's innate capacities, is an arduous task. The Jain lay person has no expectation of final liberation. Living outside of monastic orders means that release from physical existence can come only in some future life. Moreover, even the ascetic is understood to live many lifetimes of renunciation before achieving total conquest. The casting of this rigorous teaching into day-to-day practice dominates the history of Jainism and its concrete everyday life.

CHARACTERISTIC JAIN PRACTICES

In matters of religious practice Jainism presents an interesting case. Since Jain teachings give absolute centrality to the ascetic ideal, monastic practice is the most direct outcome of the teachings. At the same time, one cannot quickly and sharply draw a line between monastic and lay religious practice in Jainism, and treat the former as orthopraxis and the latter as the 'little' tradition in Jainism. Such a bifurcation fails because there is a body of lay Jain practice that is modeled on the monastic life, and because Jainism has regularly sought to link together monk and lay person, ascetic and lay life.

Therefore, Jain religious practices are best seen as being of two basic types: first, those practices—monastic and lay—that are most informed by the ascetic ideal; and second, those practices—largely of lay persons—that are less directly linked to asceticism and which are thus more representative of popular religious practice.

The more ascetic model is framed by a vision of the complete path to liberation as consisting of fourteen stages, called *guṇasthāna*s (P. S. Jaini 1979:272-73; Tatia 1951:268-80). These stages trace the progression of the *jīva* from a state of total karmic bondage to its final release and the regaining of its full capacities. Only at the fourth *guṇasthāna* is the *jīva* sufficiently free of bondage to enable one to live as a pious lay person, and the monastic path proper begins at the sixth *guṇasthāna*. Therefore the formal orthopraxis of Jainism assumes a continuity between the lay and monastic careers.

Monastic Asceticism

Entry to the sixth *guṇasthāna* is marked by the taking of monastic vows. Jains have always taken the specifics of monastic practice with great seriousness; as noted above, differences over monastic practice have led to divisions within Jainism. Despite these differences, however, there is a basic set of monastic practices that is widely shared (Deo 1956:139ff.). The aspirant to monastic orders must be physically and morally fit, and will have prepared for entry into orders by studying under a chosen preceptor who is already in orders. When the aspirant is ready, a formal ceremony of initiation is conducted.

In this ceremony, the new ascetic takes five great vows (*mahāvrata*s): vows to observe *ahiṃsā*, and to avoid lying, stealing, sexual intercourse, and ownership of any possessions. He or she will be given a new name, usually the name of the preceptor's monastic lineage.[3]

If the aspirant is entering a Digambara order, he gives up all his possessions and clothing, and is given a small whisk of peacock feathers as his only possession. A Śvetāmbara initiate is given three pieces of cloth to wear, a whisk made of wool, and a begging-bowl and staff. The Sthānakavāsīs and Terāpanthīs add a face-mask to this set of items. Thereafter, the new monk or nun is expected to join with at least two or three others and to live a life of increasingly rigorous discipline. Such a small group of ascetics generally remains relatively mobile eight months of the year, spending periods of time in various temples, study centers, and places of pilgrimage, or simply in wandering. They beg for all their food and accept no possessions beyond those given them at their initiation. During the four remaining months, specifically in the rainy season (late June to early October), monks and nuns congregate in various towns and villages, to be with their preceptors and the leaders of their larger monastic groups. Here the monks and nuns are instructed, formally confess their transgressions of monastic discipline to their superiors, and in turn instruct and assist the lay community that hosts them for this period of time.

In the course of this day-to-day life, the monk or nun engages in study, meditation, and physical discipline designed to further the continuing dissocia-

---

3 Beginning early in the history of the movement, Jain ascetics formed themselves into monastic lineages, called *gaccha*s, whose members follow the monastic example of a series of leaders. Major *gaccha*s to be found today among the Śvetāmbara Mūrtipūjakas are the Kharatara, Tapā, and Añcala *gacchas*. For details of monastic organization, see Deo 1956:337-38. and Mehta 1975:76-77.

tion of the *jīva* from the bonds of karma and to advance it along the subsequent *guṇasthāna*s. As noted above, many lifetimes of monastic discipline are required to traverse these stages, and as the Jain ascetic reaches old age, he or she may choose to die voluntarily, undertaking a ritual death by fasting, which is called *sallekhanā*. Performed under the close supervision of one's preceptor, this ideally passionless death ensures that one will not void one's spiritual progress by clinging to material existence at the end of one lifetime. It is a powerful sign of Jainism's dedication to the conquest of material existence by renunciation.

Lay Asceticism

As noted in the introduction, Jainism passed through a period of change from ca. 500 to 1300 C.E. particularly in respect of its lay community. While there is evidence for the presence of lay persons in Jainism from early on, their role vis-à-vis the monastic orders probably remained somewhat fluid until the early centuries C.E. Growth in Hindu popular piety and Jainism's growing presence among new populations in the Deccan and western India led to the development of a distinctive lay Jain religious identity during this period.

One of the foci of this development was the ordering of lay discipline modeled on the monastic orders. To further this, some forty texts and manuals of lay discipline, called *śrāvakācāra*s, were produced (R. Williams 1963:xxvii-xxx). A basic pattern of lay requirements emerged from these texts, consisting of a set of prescribed disciplines that leads the Jain lay person through eleven stages of heightened renunciation.

These eleven stages, known as *pratimā*s, are essentially a lay version of the monastic career, and all Jain lay persons are expected to reach at least some point of progression through these stages. The stages are: (1) right views; (2) taking vows; (3) practicing equanimity through meditation; (4) fasting on certain holy days; (5) purity of nourishment; (6) sexual continence by day; (7) absolute continence; (8) abandoning household activity; (9) abandoning possessions; (10) renouncing all concern for the householder's life; and (11) renouncing all connections with one's family (Jaini 1979:186). Linked to the *pratimā*s is a collection of some twelve vows. These are also modeled on monastic requirements, and involve restraint in diet, travel, clothing, and the like. These vows are taken at the second *pratimā*, and full practice of them is attained as one moves through the stages. There is even a final vow, recommended but not obligatory, that is a lay version of the ascetic death by starvation.

The *pratimā*s clearly carry the lay person along a path of increasing ascetic rigor, leading at the eleventh stage to virtual ascetic renunciation. There is nothing here of the Hindu or Buddhist notion that the lay person can find salvation through alternative disciplines or devotional religion. The lay discipline of the

Jains can have only one of two results: (1) rebirth in circumstances that permit an ascetic life, brought about by partial progression through the stages; or (2) full ascetic renunciation in one's present life. In neither case will the lay vows and stages themselves lead to liberation.

There is, therefore, remarkable consistency between Jainism's basic ascetic teaching and this view of lay life. Arising as it did in Jainism's period of greatest growth and change, it represents a major effort to bind together the lay and monastic community.

Daily Religious Life

Notwithstanding the significance of formal lay discipline, a great many Jains do not practice the ascetic model of lay piety, but rather participate in the Jain tradition by means of other religious activities that are often the more visible features of Jainism. These include temple worship, pilgrimage, observance of holidays, and participation in Jain 'rites of passage.' Many of these would appear to have only a tenuous connection with the ascetic core of Jainism, yet the ascetic model has at least penetrated these to some extent, and long historical association has woven them into a whole that is largely consonant with Jainism's basic teachings.

Temple Worship

The most visible non-ascetic practice is the temple cult. Although Jainism teaches no supreme deity or creator, there is an extraordinary profusion of Jain temples to be found in India, so that few Jain communities, however small, are likely to be without one or more. The cult itself centers on veneration of images of the Tīrthaṅkaras. Evidence of such a cult of images is as old as Mauryan times (third century B.C.E.), and votive slabs from the early centuries C.E., found at Mathurā, show images of Tīrthaṅkaras in standardized forms identical to those in later temples: seated in deep meditation or standing erect, arms and hands held at the side, in an attitude of immobile bodily discipline (cf. the great statue of Bāhubali [Gommaṭeśvara] at Śravaṇa-Beḷgoḷa in Karnataka).

The seated image came to dominate Jain iconography, and at least one such image is the focal point of each Jain temple. This image is offered *pūjā* ('worship,' i.e., homage shown by acts of symbolic hospitality) by lay persons according to their private patterns of temple attendance. Jains are enjoined to perform *pūjā* especially in the early morning, after bathing and before breakfasting. The ceremony itself has at least four parts though it may be more elaborate:

1. The worshiper approaches the image, reciting a litany of homage, named the *Pañca-namaskāra-māntra*, then forms a diagram with rice grains. The form of the diagram is shown in the center drawing (dotted-rectangle area) of

Figure 2. Jains interpret the *svastika* as representing the four possible levels of rebirth: divine, human, nether world, and animal/vegetable; the three dots are the religious virtues of insight, knowledge, and conduct; and the crescent represents the abode of liberated *jīva*s (P. S. Jaini 1979:108-200). The text of the litany (translated into English) is as follows:

—Homage to the Jinas!
—Homage to the souls that have
attained release!
—Homage to the leaders of the
Jain orders!
—Homage to the preceptors!
—Homage to all the Jain
mendicants in the world!
—This fivefold salutation,
—destroyer of all sin,
—is of all auspicious things
—the most auspicious!

Thereafter the worshiper offers the image a symbolic bath, or actually shower-bathes a small adjacent image.

2. The name of the Tīrthaṅkara whose image is present is invoked, and an offering of eight substances, each representing a religious virtue, is made.
3. The names of all twenty-four Tīrthaṅkaras are recited.
4. Lighted lamps are waved before the image.

Many Jains do not perform temple *pūjā* daily, often choosing to perform much the same act in a home shrine. The temples more commonly draw the entire community to them on festival occasions, particularly those that celebrate events in the lives of the Tīrthaṅkaras. On such occasions elaborate *pūjā* ceremonies are staged, often including decorations and renewal of a temple's images.

This act of worship is related to ascetic Jainism in that its stated purpose is to focus the lay person's desires on detachment from material existence as represented by the Tīrthaṅkara's image, and thus to reduce karmic bondage. But it is doubtful that its significance ends there. It is also fruitful to see *pūjā* in Jainism as a particularly lay institution, one that gives the lay community a sense of identity that it cannot easily obtain from the ascetic ideals of Jainism. The temple cult is largely the province of lay persons. Monks and nuns are not to serve as temple officiants, nor is their presence during *pūjā* even welcomed. Temple officiants, who may assist with *pūjā* and who care for the images and the temple itself, are most often chosen from the lay community. This remains true despite the fact that ascetics have often attached themselves to temples for purposes of study and teaching, and in some regions have become almost a class of temple specialists.

Briefly put, the temple-cultus in Jainism, while penetrated by the ascetic ideal and orthodox Jain teachings, is also kept apart from asceticism by being—at least ideally—outside the domain of monastic control. Thus the Jain lay person, while being drawn towards the rigorous ideals of an ascetic tradition, also has an institutional arena in his or her religious life in which lay control is dominant.

Pilgrimage and Holidays

Pilgrimage to holy places is an important act for Jains, and is closely related to the purposes of temple *pūjā*. Pilgrimage sites are associated with events, especially the attainment of final liberation, in the lives of Tīrthaṅkaras and other great Jain saints, and pious lay persons have endowed such sites with great complexes of temples and shrines. Among major sites of pilgrimage are Sameta Śikhara and Pāvāpurī (in Bihar) and Mt. Girnār (in Gujarat), all of which are sites where Tīrthaṅkaras attained liberation, as well as Śatruñjaya (in Gujarat), Mt. Ābū (in Rajasthan), and Śravaṇa-Beḷgoḷa (in Karnataka), which are sites of major temples and monuments celebrating the asceticism of Tīrthaṅkaras and other Jain saints.

Jains also celebrate a complex calendar of holidays whose principle festivals are, like pilgrimage rites, linked to major events in the lives of the Tīrthaṅkaras, especially Ṛṣabha (the first Tīrthaṅkara), Mahāvīra, and his predecessor Pārśva. The events are: (1) descent into the mother's womb; (2) birth; (3) ascetic renunciation; (4) attainment of omniscience; (5) physical death and final liberation. Many of these events are particularly celebrated by pilgrimage to sites associated with the Tīrthaṅkaras, and the birth date and death/liberation date of Mahāvīra (in Caitra [March/April] and Kārttika [October/November], respectively) are widely celebrated by all Jain communities. A wide range of other celebrations and monthly fast-days are also observed (Sangave 1980:233-38). Notable among these is Akṣayatṛtīya ('the immortal third,' celebrated on the third day of the waxing moon in Vaiśākh [April/May], commemorating the first giving of alms to the first Tīrthaṅkara, Ṛṣabha, and emphasizing the virtue of alms-giving to ascetics in general.

But perhaps the most significant holiday period is Paryuṣaṇa, held for eight days (by Śvetāmbaras) or ten days (by Digambaras) in the month of Bhadrapāda

(August/September), while the monks and nuns are in their rainy season retreat (Sangave 1980:233-35). In this period, lay persons particularly seek to perform fasting and austerities on the ascetic model, and spend time with monastic ascetics and lay persons together for a protracted period. It also serves the lay community itself, for on the final day of Paryuṣaṇa, known as Saṃvatsarī, lay persons make a general confession for the transgressions of the past year, not only to their monastic confessors, but also to each other. Letters are written and visits paid for the purpose of asking and extending forgiveness. Persons will often return to home villages and towns for these holidays and the accompanying activities. Thus Paryuṣaṇa, while it emphasizes the lay person's efforts to participate in ascetic activities, also serves to bind together the lay community and strengthen its identity.

Rites of Passage

As one would expect in a tradition whose fundamental basis is ascetic and which counsels absolute detachment from social values and material existence, the oldest Jain teachings do not establish norms in the area of religious life to do with life-cycle rites, an area of great importance for communal identity in a social setting. In the period after 500 C.E., when Jainism was growing vigorously, the problem became critical. Various efforts at defining the Jain relationship to Hindu day-to-day religious culture came to full fruition in the eighth century C.E. in Jinasena's *Ādipurāṇa*, a Jain *Purāṇa*, or 'account of ancient things.' In it, Jinasena sought to establish a Jain version of the Hindu *saṃskāra*s, or life-cycle rites.

In this case, however, the ideal has not fully penetrated day-to-day practice. Jinasena's vision of the life-cycle rites extends to fifty-three 'sacraments,' of which the first twenty-two cover the life-cycle of the lay householder, while the remaining thirty-one sacramental stages trace one's life through post-householder ascetic renunciation, rebirths on the ascetic path, and, finally, absolute liberation. But Jains, by and large, use a series of life-cycle rites only somewhat different from its Hindu counterpart. Sixteen sacraments, from prenatal observances up to funeral rites, are usually observed, with some variation between Śvetāmbara and Digambara communities (Sangave 1980:243-52).

Yet one significant difference remains between the Jain and Hindu rites, in that most Jains do not observe the rites of *śrāddha*, the post-funeral rites that Hindus observe in order to effect the transition of the deceased's soul from one existence to the next. These rites have been sharply decried by Jain teachers as being contrary to Jain views concerning the *jīva* and the workings of karma (P. S. Jaini 1979:302-4). Jains therefore cremate their dead ceremonially, but there the formal life-cycle rites end.

Hence, even where Hindu practice appears to have been adopted by Jains, at least one characteristic sign of Jain orthodoxy remains, enough perhaps to mark a distinctive identity even in this area where the Jain lay community most resembles its larger Hindu context.

TWENTIETH-CENTURY TRENDS IN JAINISM

In the first half of the twentieth century, the Jain community appeared to be shrinking as a percentage of India's population. In the 1881 census, Jains had represented 0.48 percent of India's total population; by 1941 this figure stood at 0.37 percent. By the 1970s, however, this trend had reversed itself, so that the population percentage represented by Jains now has nearly returned to its level of a century ago, and the equivalent percentage represents a growth in actual numbers of nearly two million (from ca. 1.2 million in 1881 to ca. 3.2 million in the 1971 census).

This growth notwithstanding, the Jain community remains a very small part of India's total population, and continues to face the problem of maintaining its distinctive identity in the midst of the rapid change and vast population of modern-day India. This is not to say that the problem is insoluble. The community has shown considerable strength in recent times, particularly in the recovery of its classical ideals, and the monastic orders contained more than 5,500 monks and nuns as of 1977 (P. S. Jaini 1979:247).

Nineteenth-century Western Indology exerted on the Jains much the same force as it did on the Hindu tradition, creating a strong interest in ancient sources, history, and, especially, in sacred literature. In addition to the efforts of those European scholars who took a particular interest in Jainism, the Jains themselves undertook to collect and publish their own ancient literature, a task that is still under way today. Underwritten by donations from lay persons, Jain publishing houses in Calcutta and Bombay produced printed editions of the Śvetāmbara *Siddhānta*. Digambaras set out to publish the normative texts of their tradition as well. In this connection, it is noteworthy that this undertaking, once launched, has been carried forward almost exclusively at Jain initiative and effort, despite some early reluctance in parts of the community to see sacred texts printed. European scholars have edited and translated scattered texts, but no comprehensive publication of Jain texts has been done by anyone but the Jains themselves.

In addition to publishing houses, Jains established numerous centers for research and study, and such centers became the focal points for the unearthing of a great treasure of manuscripts contained in Jain temple libraries. Since medieval times it has been held to be meritorious for a Jain to commission the copying of a text, and Jain libraries, carefully preserved and catalogued, were discovered to contain great literary reserves, including non-Jain texts.

The renewed availability of this classical heritage also stimulated efforts to place Jain teachings into modern vernacular languages, and led to attempts to relate contemporary religious and social issues to the norms established in older models. While modern Jain thinkers have often struggled with such relatively archaic teachings as those concerning karma or Jain cosmology (see Figure 1), Jainism's ethics, especially its emphasis on *ahiṃsā*, have proved to be a continuing source of inspiration capable of bringing classical norms into modern-day contexts.

Twentieth-century Jains have been moved by their ethical heritage, and by the fundamentally egalitarian concept of the *jīva*, to engage in a wide range of charitable undertakings and social concerns. It may well be that these classical Jain perspectives are significantly responsible for the community's disproportionate effect on Indian life in recent times. Perhaps nowhere is this more the case than in the life of Mohandas K. Gandhi who, though a Hindu, was significantly influenced by a Jain layman, Raychandbhai Mehta, and whose early efforts in labor reform in Ahmedabad brought him into a curious and apparently formative relationship with Jain mill-owners in that city.

At the same time, Jainism faces critical pressures in maintaining its distinctive day-to-day religious life. Jains have tended to live in cities and big towns in large numbers, so much so that the urban population of Jains already approached 50 percent early in this century (Sangave 1980:39). This is in large measure due to their traditional occupational role in India, as merchants and professionals in law, education, and related fields. In the twentieth century, however, the relatively urban character of the Jain community poses particular challenges, for it is in India's urban centers that the impact of rapid change and non-Indian cultural and social forces is greatest.

The Jains do bring strengths to this situation. Though their community has, over the centuries, adapted itself to a caste-like social structure, the Jain 'castes' tend to be agents more of familial and social stability than of hierarchical distinction, and considerable occupational flexibility obtains within them. Jains have, therefore, been relatively able to engage in the newer occupations brought by technology without the accompanying religious and social strains that affect Hindu society. The Jains are a comparatively wealthy subculture, and are thus able to underwrite the educational and institutional costs involved in preserving and transmitting their tradition.

But the homogeneous culture of the late-twentieth-century world stands in stark contrast to the archaic asceticism of Jainism's core. Just as Jainism faced the problem of forming and maintaining a distinctive community over a millennium ago, it now appears to face the same problem again, in a new context. This threatens to undercut the extraordinary goal of Jainism, the goal of looking far beyond one's present life, and seizing upon the absolutely human endeavor to recover one's original being.

APPENDIX

A. The Śvetāmbara Siddhānta

The texts listed below were all written in Prakrit. Following the common practice, the Sanskritized forms for their titles are given here with the Prakrit title in parantheses. An asterisk indicates that the work is available in translation into a European language; all translations are found in the Bibliography.

Aṅgas (Aṅgas):
- *1. *Ācārāṅga* (*Āyāraṅga*)
- *2. *Sūtrakṛtāṅga* (*Sūyagaḍaṅga*)
- 3. *Sthānāṅga* (*Ṭhāṇaṅga*)
- 4. *Samavāyāṅga* (*Samavāyaṅga*)
- *5. *Vyākhyāprajñapti* (*Viyāhapannatti*) or *Bhagavatī* (*Bhagavaī*)
- *6. *Jñātṛdharmakathā* (*Nāyādhammakahāo*)
- *7. *Upāsakadaśāḥ* (*Uvāsagadasāo*)
- *8. *Antakṛddaśāḥ* (*Antagaḍadasāo*)
- *9. *Anuttaraupapātikadaśāḥ* (*Aṇuttarovavāiyadasāo*)
- 10. *Praśnavyākaraṇa* (*Paṇhāvāgaraṇāiṃ*)
- *11. *Vipākaśruta* (*Vivāgasūya*)
- 12. *Dṛṣṭivāda* (*Diṭṭhivāya*) (extinct)

Upāṅgas (Uvaṅgas):
- 1. *Aupapātika* (*Uvavāia*)
- 2. *Rājapraśnīya* (*Rāyapaseṇaïjja*)
- 3. *Jīvājīvābhigama* (*Jīvājīvābhigama*)
- 4. *Prajñāpanā* (*Pannavaṇā*)
- 5. *Sūryaprajñapti* (*Sūrapannatti*)
- 6. *Jambūdvīpaprajñapti* (*Jambuddīvapannatti*)
- 7. *Candraprajñapti* (*Candapannatti*)
- *8. *Nirayāvalī* (*Nirayāvalī*)
- 9. *Kalpāvataṃsikāḥ* (*Kappāvaḍiṃsiyāo*)
- 10. *Puṣpikāḥ* (*Puppiyāo*)
- 11. *Puṣpacūlikāḥ* (*Pupphacūlaō*)
- 12. *Vṛṣṇidaśāḥ* (*Vaṇhidasāo*)
- 12a. *Dvīpasāgaraprajñapti* (*Dīvasāgarapannatti*)

Chedasūtras (Cheyasuttas):

*1. *Ācāradaśāḥ (Āyāradasāo)* or *Daśāśrutaskanda (Dasāsuyakkhanda)*
*2. *Bṛhatkalpa (Bihākappa)*
*3. *Vyavahāra (Vavahāra)*
4. *Niśītha (Nisīha)*
*5. *Mahāniśītha (Mahānisīha)*
6. *Pañcakalpa (Pañcakappa)* (extinct)
6a. *Jītakalpa (Jīyakappa)*

Mūlasūtras (Mūlasuttas):

*1. *Daśavaikālika (Dasaveyāliya)*
*2. *Uttarādhyayana (Uttarajjhāyā)*
3. *Āvaśyaka (Āvassaya)*
4. *Piṇḍaniryukti (Piṇḍanijjutti)*
4a. *Oghaniryukti (Ohanijjutti)*
4b. *Pākṣi (Pakkhi)*

Prakīrṇakas (Païṇṇas):

*1. *Catuḥśaraṇa (Caüsarana)*
2. *Āturapratyākhyāna (Āurapaccakkhāṇa)*
3. *Bhaktaparijñā (Bhattaparinnā)*
4. *Saṃstāraka (Saṃthāra)*
5. *Taṇḍulavaicārika (Tandulaveyāliya)*
*6. *Candravedhyaka (Candāvejjhaya)*
7. *Devendrastava (Devindatthaya)*
8. *Gaṇividyā (Gaṇivijjā)*
9. *Mahāpratyākhyāna (Mahāpaccakkhāṇa)*
10. *Vīrastava (Vīratthaya)*

Cūlikāsūtras (Cūliyāsuttas):

1. *Nandī (Nandī)*
*2. *Anuyogadvāra (Aṇuogadārāiṃ)*

B. Major Sanskrit Works

What follows is a highly limited selection of works by major authors, divided according to subject matter. An asterisk indicates that the work is available in translation into European languages. See Bibliography for full citations of both original texts and translations. The most comprehensive account of this literature in general is contained in Winternitz 1933. The literature concerning lay disciplines is best surveyed in Williams 1963.

1. Narrative literature, including Jain *Purāṇas*:
   Ādipurāṇa, Jinasena (Digambara), eighth century C.E.
   Uttarapurāṇa, Guṇabhadra (Digambara), ninth century C.E.
   **Triṣaṣṭiśalākāpuruṣacaritra*, Hemacandra (Śvetāmbara), twelfth century C.E.

2. Writings on lay discipline:
   **Ratnakaraṇḍa*, Samantabhadra (Digambara), fifth century C.E.
   Śrāvakācāra, Amitagati (Digambara), eleventh century C.E.
   **Dharmabindu*, Haribhadra (Śvetāmbara), eighth century C.E.
   **Yogaśāstra*, Hemacandra (Śvetāmbara), twelfth century C.E.

3. Didactic and philosophical writings:
   **Tattvārthādhigamasūtra*, Umāsvāti (claimed by both Digambaras and Śvetāmbaras), second century C.E.(?)
   Āptamīmāṃsā, Samantabhadra (Digambara), fifth century C.E.
   **Pramāṇamīmāṃsā*, Hemacandra (Śvetāmbara), twelfth century C.E.
   **Anyayogavyavacchedikā*, Hemacandra (Śvetāmbara), twelfth century C.E.
   **Syādvādamañjarī* (a commentary on the foregoing), Malliṣeṇa (Śvetāmbara), thirteenth century C.E.

2

JAIN STUDIES*

INTRODUCTION

The Jains present a formidable challenge to one who sets out to learn something of them. Throughout their 2,500 year history the Jains have been prodigious authors, producing a vast and complex literature in various Prakrits and Sanskrit, and showing an extraordinary respect—even love, perhaps—for the written word. They not only produced a vast literature, they also preserved it. The libraries (*bhaṇḍāra*s) attached to Jain temples, large and small, contain countless carefully kept books and manuscripts, including a great many writings by non-Jains. The copying of texts by scribes was often commissioned by lay Jains, such an act being deemed meritorious or even simply auspicious. To see one of the catalogues of such a library, wherein are recorded the occasions upon which such copies were made, is to glimpse a remarkable attitude toward literary products of every kind, and perhaps to gain something of an insight into the firmness of purpose that has maintained the Jain community for so long.

---

*Edited from the following three works:

Two Jaina Approaches to Non-Jainas: Patterns and Implications. Harvard University Ph.D. dissertation, 1975. Pp. 1-13.

"The Jainas." In *A Reader's Guide to the Great Religions*, 231-46. Ed. Charles J. Adams. New York: The Free Press, 1977.

Review of Padmanabh S. Jaini, *The Jaina Path of Purification*. In *Journal of Asian Studies* 39 (1980), 829-31.

This ancient tradition and its vast literature have been studied far more than is often realized by students of religion. As an object of study the Jains occupy an ambiguous position between being treated as a separate arena of study—as is Indian Buddhism—and being treated as a portion of the larger Hindu tradition. This ambiguity has been a part of Jain studies from the beginning, and it makes the sources of information on the Jains a very diffuse lot, since there exist not only studies that treat the Jains alone, but also countless portions of larger studies of Hinduism that attempt to treat the Jains in some way.

The Jain teachings prescribe a rigorous course of ascetic practices, centering on *ahiṃsā* (non-injury) as the sole means of dissipating the karma that materially accumulates on the individual *jīva*s (souls) and binds them to earthly existence. When finally freed, each *jīva* attains its innate nature, which is pure knowledge and bliss, and abides in that state. This is *mokṣa*, and it is finally attainable only by practices that require leading the life of a homeless ascetic. The Jain layperson is not expected to attain release in this life; this will come only in a future birth, after lifetimes of increasing ascetic practice. There is no deity; Jains do, however, venerate the Tīrthaṅkaras and some saints, and a temple cultus exists around these figures, who are not seen as intervening in any way in the lives of the devotee.

Given this set of teachings, the Jains are often characterized as austere or somber—in Louis Renou's (1953:111) words, "Buddhism's darker reflection"—and their position is often portrayed as somehow less vital or less compelling than that of Buddhism or other segments of the Indian tradition. It is not possible to argue these points here, but the person who seeks information concerning the Jains is likely to confront such characterizations with almost monotonous regularity.

JAIN STUDIES IN THE NINETEENTH AND TWENTIETH CENTURIES

Almost every more recent study of the Jains begins with a section on the history of Jain studies. Perhaps the authors of those accounts felt something of the same need that is felt here, namely, that although those scholars who have worked on Jain literature and history have performed herculean tasks, they and their work are hardly known to the academic world in general; or if the scholars are well-known, it is not because of their contributions to the Western understanding of the Jains. Thus it seems almost necessary to recount the story of Jain studies lest the remainder of any particular study be peopled with scholars and works that mean nothing to the reader.

There is something of necessity in these studies, too, for they cover a great deal of ground and rely on the previous work of a great many scholars. Yet there is another reason for including in this work a brief introduction to Jain studies. That is the fact that the general attitude of Western scholars toward the Jains has certain peculiar aspects to it, at least some of which are related to the course of the Western encounter with the Jains. Other accounts of the history of Jain studies are not duplicated here. Rather, certain problems are pointed out that have to do not with the Jain tradition alone, but with the scholar's perception of it.

The course of Jain studies in the West has been marked by spurts of activity and periods where little progress is visible. The present period has been one of the latter sort.[1] More recent comprehensive accounts of the Jains tend to be reworkings of older material. The generation of European scholars of the Jains—Jacobi, Hoernle, Guérinot, Leumann, von Glasenapp, Schubring, Alsdorf—has not yet generated its like replacements.[2] America has never been active in Jain scholarship. Another index to the lowered level of Western interest in the Jains is the fact that less and less of the Jain study done in India is being published in English, though a large amount of research and study continues to be done there. In 1965, Ludwig Alsdorf summed up the situation thus (Alsdorf 1965:2):

> Je crois être obligé de dire qu'il nous faut constater après les grandes découvertes du début ainsi que des décennies suivantes une certain récession des études jaina dans l'indologie occidentale du présent. Cette récession forme un regrettable contraste avec le net essor de ces études en Inde, où les jainas eux-mêmes se sont ouverts de plus en plus à la recherche occidentale, y collaborent et mettent à sa disposition un matériel nouveau, resté longtemps caché, et ceci dans une large mesure qu'on n'aurait pas osé espérer autrefois. Il n'y a pas là pour nous, me semble-t-il, seulement une obligation morale, mais aussi une attirante perspective.[3]

In speaking of "the grand discoveries" that preceded the present state of affairs, Alsdorf also might well have spoken of the fitful progress of early Jain studies, which made the subsequent great achievements seem even greater. The

---

1 [Editor's note.] This sentence was written in 1975. The last decade has seen a renewed interest in Jain studies.

2 It must be stated that European study of the Jains does continue, in the work of both Colette Caillat and R. Williams, who have produced important monographs, and in the primarily linguistic studies of such scholars as Jozef Deleu, F. R. Hamm, and Klaus Bruhn.

3 [Editor's Translation.] I am obliged to say that it behooves us to recognize that, after the grand discoveries at the outset and in the following decades, there is a certain decline in Jaina studies in present-day Western Indology. This decline stands in regrettable contrast to the distinct vigor of such studies in India, where the Jainas themselves are increasingly receptive to Western research, collaborating in it and employing to this purpose new material, which for a long time lay hidden, and this in a significant measure that one would not have dared otherwise hope. From this we have, it seems to me, not only a moral obligation, but also an engaging perspective.

earliest efforts in the field have been chronicled by Walther Schubring, Ernst Windisch, and Helmuth von Glasenapp, among others, and Alsdorf has updated those accounts.[4] Suffice it here to say that Mackenzie, Colebrooke, and H. H. Wilson included the Jains in their accounts of India and its inhabitants, Mackenzie's and Colebrooke's articles in *Asiatic Researches* 9 (1807)[5] marking in Schubring's (1935:1) words "das Geburtsjahr der Jaina Wissenschaft" ("the birthyear of Jaina Studies").

However, it was twenty years before any comprehensive accounts, by W. Franklin (1827) and H. H. Wilson (1828-32) appeared, and twenty more years before the first texts came out in Western editions in 1847.[6] Yet ten more years passed before another text appeared, this one from Albrecht Weber (1858). No account, however brief, of the beginnings of Jain studies could be complete without reference to Weber, and his work and its effects are examined in detail below. In 1865-66 he presented another piece of textual work, this time on the *Bhagavatī Sūtra,* a canonical text (Weber 1865-66), and in 1883-85 he published his monumental "Über die heiligen Schriften der Jaina,"[7] based on manuscripts collected at Berlin in the 1870s.[8]

These manuscripts were collected in India largely under the guidance of Georg Bühler, who must also be mentioned as one of the prime movers behind the increased study of the Jains.[9] Weber's descriptive catalogue of these manuscripts[10] stands alongside his account of the Jain scriptures as a truly epic piece of work, and together they helped to unleash a flood of activity. The 1880s were the period when Jacobi, Pullé, Leumann, and Hoernle added their products

---

4 See Schubring 1935:1-7 (1962:1-13); Windisch 1917-20:29ff.; von Glasenapp 1925:2-5; and Alsdorf 1965:25-50.

5 Note that some scholars give the year of publication as 1809. This is because the same numbers of *Asiatic Researches* were published in different years in Calcutta and London. The London editions bear later dates.

6 See Böhtlingk and Rieu's translation of Hemacandra's *Abhidhānacintāmaṇi*, and Stevenson's translation of the *Kalpa Sūtra* and *Navatattva*

7 This was translated by H. Weir Smyth as "Weber's *Sacred Literature of the Jains,*" in *Indian Antiquary* from 1888 to 1892. Smyth's translation was then reprinted, with consecutive pagination, in 1893. Smyth preserved in brackets the pagination of the German original. Because there are three differently paginated possible sources, this study cites Weber by page number of the Bombay reprint, with original page number in brackets. The translation is used because it was updated and edited with the aid of Ernst Leumann, whose additional notes are often of value.

8 Weber was truly performing a pioneering work, and on many points there is now much better information. Hiralal Rasikdas Kapadia, *A History of the Canonical Literature of the Jainas* (1941), incorporates many of the later discoveries, is conversant with major European scholarship on the texts, and has the virtue of presenting an Indian approach to the texts as scripture, though the reader may find the style of the whole to be a bit trying at times.

9 See Schubring 1935:4-5 (1962:4-5) for an account of Bühler's work.

10 Because of its being part of a larger catalogue of all manuscripts at Berlin, the portion completed by Weber is often wrongly cited and/or catalogued in libraries. The specific portion in question is volume 2, parts 1-3.

to the flow of Jain scholarship, and from this point until the 1920s there continued a high level of activity.

To give a more detailed account of this early work would merely duplicate the work of Windisch and the others cited above. What is of more interest—and is in fact worth a lengthy study by itself—is the peculiar character taken on by most of the study of the Jains, given the problems that it faced. Several matters should at least by mentioned. The first is the fact that until Hermann Jacobi's arguments convinced the Indological community otherwise, the relationship of the Jain tradition to the Buddhist was generally conceived in such a way as to subordinate the former, either into a predecessor's or schismatic role.[11] In a sense, then, up to Jacobi's time there was no "Jainology" as a field that could be readily delimited.

Another matter worthy of note is the strong linguistic orientation that dominates European study of the Jains. While this is to some extent true of all European—particularly German—Indology, the Jains were particularly subject to study by linguists. The reason for this is the nature of Jain literature. This reason can be broken down into two sub-headings: (1) the language in which the Jains wrote, and (2) the content of the literature as scholars perceived it.

In the first case, linguistic interest in the Jains was heightened by the fact that their older literature is preserved in various Prakrits. That of the canonical (Śvetāmbara) texts is Ardhamāgadhī; of later Śvetāmbara texts, Jain-Māhārāṣṭrī; of older Digambara texts, Jain-Śauraseni; of some later texts of both groups, Apabhramśa.[12] The logicians and philosophers of both groups (less so, however, the Digambaras) wrote commentaries and independent works in Sanskrit, but not in large numbers until the eighth and ninth centuries C.E.

The designation of two of these Prakrits as Jain versions of a language known from other sources indicates the somewhat peculiar position of Jain literature. Its linguistic nonconformity was one of the features that drew European scholars to the Jain tradition. Ludwig Alsdorf (1965:12-18) has summarized some of the early, fairly intense debates concerning the place of the Prakrits mentioned above in the general pattern of Indic languages, and Alsdorf's account goes on to show that the debate is not yet over. For the purposes of this study, the above designations will serve, with the reminder that only a fraction of the Jain Prakrit literature has really been explored.

These linguistic factors, though they played a role in stimulating early interest, now prove to be something of a burden. Despite the efforts of the scholars, very few critical editions of Jain texts exist, and the student today

11 For a summary of the points at issue, and of the arguments of Jacobi and his opponents, see von Glasenapp 1925:3-4.

12 For a more complete account, see Schubring 1935:14-17.

confronts a mass of partially explored literature in several Prakrits. This has undoubtedly been a factor in lowering the level of Jain study.

The second factor mentioned above—the scholars' perceptions of the content of the literature—also played a role in the early linguistic orientation as well as in the present situation. The first scholars of Jain literature were singularly unimpressed by the Jains' presentation of their teachings as found in the older literature, particularly in comparison with Buddhist texts. While they were interested in the language itself, their reaction to the whole is well represented by Alsdorf (1965:2-3):

> On ne peut certes nier que, vis-à-vis du jainisme, le bouddhisme représente une participation plus importante de l'Inde à la civilisation de l'humanité. La doctrine du Bouddha est sans aucun doute d'une spiritualité plus haute et nous attire dans son ensemble davantage. Elle a pu devenir une religion mondiale tandis que le jainisme restait limité a l'Inde, où après une ère d'epanouissement et de suprématie spirituelle—en particulier dans le Sud—il ne compte plus guère que deux millions d'adeptes. A cela s'ajoute que, a quelques exceptions près, les textes anciens du jainisme ne soutiennent pas la comparaison sous l'angle littéraire avec les textes analogues du bouddhisme, tant leur forme est littéralement rébarbative. Sans aller aussi loin qu'Albrecht Weber qui qualifait le canon jaina de "document littéraire véritablement grandiose par son abondance massive ainsi que par sa monotonie et sa pauvreté spirituelle" on devra reconnaître avec Winternitz que les textes du jainisme font rarement preuve de cet intérêt humaine propre à tant de textes bouddhiques.[13]

That is a relatively mild judgement, by a scholar thoroughly familiar with the Jain texts who is an enthusiastic student of the Jains. Persons less inclined to charitable judgement made extraordinary pronouncements concerning the Jain tradition. The most grotesque of these is from the pen of E. Washburn Hopkins who, though not noted for tactful statements in general, quite outdid himself on the Jains (Hopkins 1898:296-97):

> Of all the great religious sects of India, that of Nātaputta [Mahāvīra] is perhaps the least interesting. . . . The Jains offered to the world but one great moral truth, withal a negative truth, 'not to harm,' nor was this verity invented by them. . . . Of all the sects the Jains are the most colorless, the most insipid. They have no literature

---

13 [Editor's Translation.] One certainly cannot deny that in contrast to Jainism Buddhism represents a more important contribution of India to world civilization. Without doubt the doctrine of the Buddha possesses a loftier spirituality, and is more appealing. It has developed into a world religion, whereas Jainism has remained limited to India, where after a period of blossoming and spiritual ascendancy—especially in the South—it cannot count more than two million followers. In addition, with only a few exceptions the ancient texts of Jainism do not bear comparison from the literary point of view with the analogous Buddhist texts, since their form is quite literally formidable. Without going further than Albrecht Weber, who described the Jaina canon as a "literature remarkable not less for its immensity than for its monotony and intellectual poverty" (Weber 1883-85:12[240]), one should recognize with Winternitz (1933:426) that Jaina texts rarely prove to be of the same human interest as do Buddhist texts.

> worthy of the name. . . . A religion in which the chief points insisted upon are that one should deny God, worship man, and nourish vermin, has indeed no right to exist; nor has it had as a system much influence on the history of thought.

Hopkins's remarks, if they illustrate more than his temperament, serve to show what the paucity of information on the Jains and the negative attitude of that time toward their literature were capable of generating. Unfortunately, a less extreme version of Hopkins's assessment is all too often the first account of the Jains that beginning students of India encounter.[14]

More comprehensive accounts of the Jains began to appear early in this century, notably Margaret (Mrs. Sinclair) Stevenson's *The Heart of Jainism* (1915), J. L. Jaini's, *Outlines of Jainism* (1915), and Helmuth von Glasenapp's *Der Jainismus* (1925). The first two of these studies share one major feature: they rely heavily on field observation and participation, and hardly at all on the work of the Western linguist-Indologists. In fact, they mark a de facto division that persists for the most part in Jain studies. Those whose primary focus is the literature of the Jains tend to stay within linguistic boundaries, while those who wish to portray the religious life of the Jains tend to pay little attention to the linguistic scholarship in the field.

Mrs. Stevenson's work, largely based on her own tireless observations of Jains among whom she lived in India, is useful in its emphasis on daily life and the state of the community early in this century, but weak on history and literature. Despite its colonialisms and theological framework (namely, the heart of Jainism is empty, lacking the love and trust that can only obtain where there is faith in a compassionate God), and its occasionally dense recitals of utterly unexplained detail, it is an adequate introduction. Yet is has serious flaws, and is generally repudiated by Jains. J. L. Jaini's slim volume has the virtue of being an exposition of Jain thought by a Jain. However, it is more a compact presentation of Jain philosophy (including a selection of texts in translation) than a general introduction.

Helmuth von Glasenapp's *Der Jainismus* marks something of an exception and high-water mark in scholarly portrayals of the Jains, for it draws heavily on the whole spectrum of Jain material available at the time of its composition, material that had increased spectacularly in volume in the first quarter of this century. One need only examine the sources cited in Georg Bühler's *Über die indische Secte der Jaina*, a brief tract that dates to 1887 (or the sources noted in the 1903 English edition), and then compare them with those at von Glasenapp's disposal to see the great change that had occurred.

Von Glasenapp was himself aware of the linguistic bent of the earlier work, especially its focus on the Śvetāmbara canonical texts, and made a conscious

---

14 See, for example, Basham 1963:289, 297, and Renou 1953:111-33.

effort at breaking out of that mold. At the same time, he attributed a good deal of the earlier work's character to the fact that little material was available outside the canonical texts (von Glasenapp 1925:4). This particular issue and its relationship to still another peculiarity of Western study of the Jains, namely, the virtual exclusion of the Digambaras, will be taken up again below.

For the moment, let it be noted that von Glasenapp's work is exceptional in that it bridged the growing gap between the Jain studies of the linguists and those of the field observer/participant. However, it is not without significance that the work done in the years after von Glasenapp tended to return to the linguistic orientation of the earlier scholars, and for the most part has remained in that mold.

One particular consequence of this is a genuine weakness in Western study of Jain analytical thought, or Jain 'philosophy.' General treatments of Jain thought still tend to rely largely on Umāsvāti's *Tattvārthādhigamasūtra* and perhaps one or two later Jain thinkers. Monographic studies and serious assessments by Western scholars are rare, and the quality of the general accounts varies widely. Almost every account of the Jains that is available in Europe or America must be subjected to serious scrutiny simply in terms of what sources the author actually uses to discuss Jain thought and its major figures.

These general characteristics of Jain studies produce two specific problems. The first is intimately related to the linguistic bent of previous scholarship and the weakness in philosophical study. In sum, it is the problem of the relationship between the older Prakrit materials and the later, largely Sanskrit philosophical texts. Scholars take widely varying stances on the issue, ranging from the view that the two linguistic and literary areas are almost discrete entities united by little more than a common religious tradition, to the view that there are important and meaningful direct connections between the two spheres.

The second problem arises from the same basic source, but has slightly different causes and overtones. In brief, it is the severe imbalance in Western scholarship in favor of the Śvetāmbara Jains and away from the Digambaras. This occasionally poses real difficulties, since it means that where Digambara materials are included it is often only possible to make very tentative judgements.

The general background of this imbalance seems clear. It has two sides, both of them literary in nature. First, it is true that the Śvetāmbara communities in India were, in the beginning, more willing to permit scholars access to their libraries than were the Digambara communities. This meant that the early study of Jain literature concentrated on the Śvetāmbaras. Second, according to the version of Jain history that was first accepted and promulgated by scholars, the

Digambaras hold that the original Jain scriptures were irretrievably lost, and do not accept the Śvetāmbara canon.

These two factors appear to have combined with the linguistic interests of early Jain studies, resulting in a virtual ignorance of—and negative attitude toward—the Digambaras. This entire episode in Western Indology deserves a thorough and critical study, both for the sake of rectifying this particular imbalance, and so as to shed some light on the often unrecognized presuppositions of the study of India and their often serious consequences.

These are, then, the factors and problems in the background of any study of the Jains. No new study can be seen apart from such factors. Indeed, every new study of the Jains should be at least partially involved in clarifying these problematic areas in the Jains' encounter with Indology.

The Jaina Path of Purification

The author of an introductory volume is always vulnerable in matters of selection of material, methodological approaches, incorporation of recent scholarship, and so on; and in some areas, one must ask what makes a new introductory work worth having alongside those that already exist. In the case of Jaini's book, the latter point is easily addressed—so easily, in fact that the answer tends to blunt other potential criticism, for this book stands alone in its field.

Jaini has written a modern and scholarly general introduction to the Jains and their religion, something that has been astonishingly absent from the ranks of recent academic literature on India. Until now, those seeking a place to begin studying the Jains have not really had a good beginning point. One's choices in English have been limited to outdated volumes (e.g., Mrs. Sinclair Steventon's 1915 *The Heart of Jainism*), relatively weak recent attempts (e.g., Asim Kumar Chatterjee's 1978-84 *A Comprehensive History of Jainism*), or reasonably accurate but brief and overly general sections on the Jains within larger works on religion in India. It is no longer necessary to make such unhappy choices; Jaini's work is clearly at the head of the field.

While Jaini's book will be useful for anyone interested in the Jains, it was intended to be usable as a college-level textbook. Undergraduates may find it moderately difficult, but the book is true to its original goal, for one of its great strengths is its clear and careful expository style. It commands the technical detail of Jainism, but is not unwilling to generalize. It is an admirable synthesis of the salient points in contemporary critical scholarship, yet its tone throughout is sympathetic to the ideals of Jainism. It is, in sum, an unusually satisfying introduction, and its bibliography and glossary are strong contributions to its value.

All of that is enough, in many ways, to make criticism very nearly gratuitous. This book was so badly needed, and has accomplished its basic objectives so well, that one is tempted to let it go at that. The book generally does not break new scholarly ground, but Jaini has accomplished a most important task. At the same time, given its incorporation of more recent scholarship, the book poses—at least implicitly—an important question: is our understanding of the Jains at a point where the basic framework is in place, and what remains is only the filling in of empty or sketchy areas? The question arises because this book is really a relatively standard portrayal of the Jains, and a book as well done as this one is bound to reinforce that standard view. Is that view fully satisfactory?

Here the author of an introductory volume is particularly vulnerable. But Jaini's own approach in the opening chapter implies that one ought perhaps to be somewhat restless about doing business as usual. Jaini begins with two chapters on the early history of Jainism; all books on the Jains seem to begin this way. But Jaini gives this potentially routine opening a creative dimension, for he immediately takes account of the fact that the sources of Jain history are shaped by subsequent divisions within the tradition. He does not openly say so, but his approach implies that authors who present only a single version of Jain origins are not being true to the nature of the sources. This implication is correct. The Śvetāmbara and Digambara versions of the beginnings of Jainism—i.e., the career of Mahāvīra, his ascetic praxis, his nature of enlightenment, and the early development of the tradition—are different and not readily reconcilable. Jaini has taken care to show that there are such differences, and to weave an account of them into a unified telling of the origins of Jainism.

Thus there is at the start a promise of some reappraisal of the standard approach to the Jains, but from that point onward (and even before the end of the second chapter) some of the promise fades, and matters are pursued in somewhat familiar form. A case in point is the very clear, detailed discussion of the Jain 'scriptures' in the second chapter. Understanding 'scripture' in Jainism is intimately tied to understanding the Śvetāmbara-Digambara division, since the two subtraditions ostensibly disagree over 'scripture' to the point where each denies the validity of the other's sacred texts. Having seen some earlier creative handling of the two subtraditions' differing views of Mahāvīra, one waits for more of the same here, but there is little sign of it. There is an excellent presentation of the standard view, but no more.

This leads to a larger question. At the end of the second chapter, Jaini points out that there is a remarkable unity in Jain doctrines over the whole course of the tradition's history, so much so that "it is possible to consider [the doctrines] as a coherent whole, with little reference to questions of interpretation or chronology" (Jaini 1979:88). This is an important point, for it permits the greater part of the rest of the book to be written in a more or less ahistorical manner, focusing on Jain teachings, and to leave historical development for the last chapter. The exposition is very good, particularly in its attention to the lay community and the Jain understanding of karma. But this rather ahistorical, nondevelopmental view of the teachings of Jainism is very much the conventional view, and one wonders: have we here a dog that did not bark? The Jain tradition has certainly not been static and unchanging. The history of the movement, both in terms of its geographical spread and in terms of its developing identity vis-à-vis the larger Hindu tradition, merits anything but an ahistorical treatment. That such a varied history should be overarched by unchanging ideas has become part of the usual view of the Jains; but one suspects that there is a dog here somewhere that should be making noise, especially given Jaini's approach in the opening chapter.

An ahistorical approach can be accepted as a necessary choice in an introduction, but some important questions have been left unaddressed. I expect this excellent volume will open the door to some serious reappraisal of the usual treatment of the Jains; if it had attempted to incorporate such reappraisal, consideration of length would have meant that we might have had to forgo some of the contributions it does make.

3

SCRIPTURE AS A PHENOMENOLOGICAL CATEGORY*

We are all familiar enough by now with academics who open their papers by quoting Humpty Dumpty's famous exchange with Alice in *Through the Looking Glass*. Nonetheless, it is appropriate to attend Humpty Dumpty's major statement one more time: "When *I* use a word . . . it means just what I choose it to mean—neither more nor less."

So it is, it seems, with 'scripture.' My colleague has been concerned to point out that the senses in which the Bible is 'scripture,' and needs to be treated as 'scripture,' may be in need of examination and evaluation.[1] In this paper I would

---

* Paper read at joint meeting of the Midwest section of the Society of Biblical Literature and the Middle West Branch of the American Oriental Society, February 1976.

1 [Editor's note.] The paper preceding Folkert's was "The Bible as Scripture," by Stanley D. Walters, also of Central Michigan University. Following is the abstract of his paper:

> The scholarly study of the Bible during the past two centuries or so has concentrated heavily on literary and philological studies. Without denigrating in any way that work, the present paper wishes to inquire to what extent the scholar and teacher in Biblical studies is obliged to consider the Bible not just as literature but as sacred text. Approaches in the wider discipline of the study of religion open the way for academicians to recognize dimensions of the Bible's origin and use which are best subsumed under the category 'scripture' and which are likely to be overlooked by literary or historical approaches. This paper suggests that the academic study of the Bible needs to consider it as scripture just as the academic study of the Quran must do so in order to be true to the assertion of the text and to the full history of its use.

like to point to some wider contexts, both methodological and historical, in which the question of 'scripture' as a category may need to be examined.

The methodological considerations should, perhaps, come first; but I prefer to leave them for later, because the specific historical instances will, I hope, make the questions of method more immediately perceptible. However, this much should be said at the outset: what we now have is less a category than a generally agreed-upon usage that renders 'scripture' as equivalent to 'sacred text.' We shall consider here whether it would not be more helpful to take 'scripture' quite literally, as meaning 'written,' in a sense in which the 'written' form itself is important to the religious value of the material, and under which a number of other headings—book, inscription, etc.—should be included.

No sacred text, perhaps, falls solely under this heading, least of all the Bible. But some texts clearly tend in this direction, at least at some point in the history of their use. This includes the Bible. Others do not, though they do not altogether avoid it, either. Let us look first at two specific, historical cases of texts that exemplify both sides of the question. One of these is *not* 'scriptural,' the other is.

The first instance comes from the Hindu tradition, and it particularly illustrates the need for a clear category of 'scripture.' This is so because both the linguists and the students of religion who undertook the presentation of the Hindu textual material to the Western world chose, rather unreflectively, to present the Veda, the Bhagavadgītā, and like texts, as the Hindu 'scriptures,' or 'sacred books,' or the like—and one can still find them being so presented.

The particular instance of the Veda provides the best example possible of the problem. According to the Hindu view, the Veda consists solely of sound; sound, moreover, is eternal. Particular recitations or statements of the Veda do no more—*nor less*—than to make audible the eternally existent sounds that make it up. Therefore, the *ṛṣis*—those who first enunciated the Veda, in ancient times—are held to have heard the Veda. A specific, though surmountable, obstacle already rears its head, then, when we speak of the *ṛṣis* as "seers"—though in this instance, we deal more with a symptom than with something that is necessarily a problem.

However, when the Veda is presented as 'scripture,' we do not have a problem. It is true that the Veda exists in written form, nor is there at present any great Hindu objection to this (though our knowledge on this point in the older tradition is admittedly limited). But, as anyone who has ever cracked his brain over Sanskrit knows, the written form of that language is distinctly subordinated to the spoken form. Sanskrit writes all of its *saṃdhi*, or changes produced by the juxtaposition of sounds; the implication clearly is that the written language must be perfect reproduction of the spoken form.

Moreover, the audible language was subject, long before any widespread reduction of it to writing, to a most rigorous analysis in terms of sound. This was not primarily (or even at all, as those might be tempted to say who have puzzled over the ancient grammars from Pāṇini onward) in terms of 'grammar,' in the sense truest to its etymology. 'Syntax,' in its truest sense, was, of course, a concern, for closely tied to the study of the Veda was a concern for how the arrangement and modification of sounds came about, and—most significant—what these had to do with the process of perception of those sounds, particularly the perception of 'meaning' in those sounds.

To call the Veda 'scripture' is clearly a Humpty-Dumpty-ism. In the long run, the written form of the Veda is arbitrary, so long as it performs one crucial task: to make possible the precise rendition of its sounds. To call the Veda a 'sacred book' is to go one step further from accuracy. *As book*, it has no value. It must be *used*, as 'word,' to be efficacious. At the same time, as a further illustration of the problem, I would hasten to add that this understanding of the Veda is not necessarily uniform throughout the tradition; but it *is* the position against which other arguments range themselves.

The second instance that I wish to raise, more briefly, is that of the Qur'ān. Scholars are becoming more careful about this text, and rightly so; but the temptation (and often, the practice) in the past has been to see it, too, as 'scripture' or 'sacred book' in a rather unreflective way. If the Veda can teach us something in one way, the Qur'ān is admirably suited to teaching a different lesson, which I shall seek to cover quickly.

First, the Qur'ān perhaps testifies most eloquently to the need for a 'scripture' category. The identification of this revelation from God with its written form appears to be present even in the text itself, and was certainly brought to the fore in later Islamic debates over the relationship between the written Qur'ān and God. The power of the inscription, of calligraphy, in Islam is well-known, and it is consistent with the Muslim view of the Qur'ān.

Second, the Qur'ān illustrates a particular danger inherent in calling it 'scripture' in any way derived from the Christian use of the term. For, if there is a parallel between Islam and Christianity on this point, it is not a parallel between the Bible and the Qur'ān, but between Jesus Christ and the Qur'ān.[2] The Islamic debates over the nature of the Qur'ān and its relationship to God can almost be recast, without changing the lines of argument, into debates over the nature of Christ and his relationship to God. Is the Qur'ān eternal? Is it uncreated—i.e., "begotten, not made"? These and like questions echo throughout the history of Islam, and they extend to its *written* form. The matter even reaches

2 [Editor's note.] This comparison was made by Wilfred Cantwell Smith in his lectures at Harvard University, from whom Folkert would have heard it. See Smith 1957:17-18.

into the history of Islamic expansion. With some justification, it has been said that while Christians go about the world translating the Bible into various languages, Muslims have gone about the world teaching people Arabic.

Neither of these two specific examples really contains startlingly new information. But the methodological implications of this material do deserve our attention, both as they apply to the Christian scriptures and to such things as the Veda and Qur'ān in non-Christian traditions.

Gerardus van der Leeuw's treatment of such matters can serve as a model for a brief look at these implications, if not in every case as a normative statement. Chapters 58-64 of van der Leeuw's *Religion in Essence and Manifestation* (1986:403-446) are devoted to the general rubric of "The Written Word." This series of chapters culminates in a brief essay (chapter 64) on "The Written Word." In these seven chapters, van der Leeuw discusses and catalogues a variety of roles of "the Word" in the religious life of humankind. Van der Leeuw as a phenomenologist (albeit in a sense that he himself more or less defined) treats the matter of 'scripture' within the larger context of the religious phenomenon of 'the word'—implying, if not explicitly stating, a difference between intelligible sound, the 'word,' and unintelligeble sound (such as music) which also can claim a place in a complete phenomenology. (The line, one might add, is not always altogether clear.)

In this schema, the 'scripture,' the *written word*, occupies only one category of 'word.' Within this 'written' category, van der Leeuw proceeds from 'inscription,' where the written form is regarded as possessing its own particular power in virtue of being written, to 'sacred book,' wherein the written word is not so much a power unto itself as it is a power to reveal something beyond it. He then proceeds through creed, doctrine, and law.

One may well wish to quibble with the internal arrangement of this section on 'the written word,' and with the logic and evidence used to tie it together. But the simple existence of such a set of categories within a heading that is only one of seven headings under which van der Leeuw feels compelled to treat 'the word' is itself instructive. Perhaps most instructive is the way in which the Bible, and the Christian uses of it, fall into a number of categories, both within the section on 'written word' and outside of it. The immediate conclusion to be drawn from this seems clear: a self-conscious understanding of the Bible in the Christian church demands that one take account of the several uses and significances that this 'word' has had.

To narrow the point a bit: the Bible has at times been, and still is, *scripture*, if by that we mean a particular religious use attached to the word *as written*. That there is need of such a category in phenomenology is clear, as witnessed by, in particular, the Muslim understanding of the Qur'ān. But the Christian 'word' has certainly not only, or even essentially, been 'scripture' from that point of view. Therefore, we do two kinds of violence when we speak of the 'Hindu scripture' or of any other sort of 'scripture.' First, since such notions have commonly rested on some idea of comparableness between our Bible and the texts of other traditions, the first element in the comparison is awry. Our Bible is not solely 'scripture.' Second, in applying the comparison, we err seriously. The others are not, in many cases, 'scripture' in the phenomenological sense.

But beyond the clarification of such points—which would themselves be a significant contribution to the study of sacred texts—there lie, I think, even greater rewards. Principally, they have to do with this point: the general use of 'scripture' to equal 'sacred text' can have the effect of shutting us off from the great richness and variety that 'the word' encompasses. The narrower category of 'scripture' would be helpful. We would benefit by seeing the many other dimensions of the sacred texts that we now see all too often in one dimension, for we would be forced, if we narrowed 'scripture,' to become aware of such phenomena as the recited or chanted word (*vide* the Veda and the Bible in places). In short, we should look not only for literary types, but also, wherever possible, for the actual use of the 'word' in scripture.

This little essay has been just that: an essay into an area of phenomena shared by students of both Biblical materials and other sacred texts from other traditions. I expect that there is much to be shared; but we now need a more self-conscious effort to make sure (1) that we appreciated our own materials, *and* (2) that, when we make presumptions of comparableness, we make them with care.

4

SCRIPTURE AND CONTINUITY IN THE JAIN TRADITION*

I.

The Jain author Rājaśekhara, as part of his *Ṣaḍdarśanasamuccaya* (ca. 1350 C.E.), presents the following piquant description of the Śvetāmbara-Digambara division within the Jain tradition:

20. There are two wings to the Jain doctrine:
    Śvetāmbara and Digambara;
    The Śvetāmbaras were discussed above,
    and now the Digambaras are told.

21. There are four divisions among Digambaras,
    all following the vow of nakedness:
    The Kāṣṭhasaṅgha, Mūlasaṅgha,
    and the Māthura and Gopyaka Saṅghas.

22. In the Kāṣṭhasaṅgha, the broom is ordained
    to be made of the yak's tail.

* Paper read at a conference on the study of religion in honor of Wilfred Cantwell Smith at the Center for the Study of World Religions, Harvard University, June 1979.

In the Mūlasaṅgha, the brush is made
of peacock feathers.

23. The broom has never been an issue
in the Māthura Saṅgha.
The Gopyas sweep with peacock feathers;
their greeting is "*dharma lābha*" ["may you attain dharma"].

24. The rest greet with "*dharma vṛddhi*" ["may your dharma increase"].
The Gopyas declare release for women;
The three Saṅghas other than the Gopya
declare that women cannot attain it.

25. Neither the other three nor the Gopyas
hold that an omniscient takes food;
There is no release for one wearing monk's garb,
though he keep the vow well.

26. There are thirty-two obstacles
and fourteen impurities in mendicancy;
How to avoid them
is found in their *āgama*.

27. For the rest, they are like the Śvetāmbaras
in matters of conduct, deity, and teacher;
They accept the logic-treatises
composed by the Śvetāmbaras.

28. Theirs are mostly of the same nature,
illuminated by knowledge of the *syādvāda*;
The *Paramāṣṭasahasrī*,
that moon to the *nyāya*-lotuses;

29. The *Siddhāntasāra* and the other logic-books
are very difficult;
Each word of them is capable
of imparting victory.

30. These divisions in Jain practice, etc.,
will presently be obscured in the Kali-age;
And then these present things, taught here,
will have to be learned from the Jain *āgama*.[1]

---

1 [Editor's note.] Folkert's translation.

For our immediate purposes, what is of interest in Rājaśekhara's account is its attention to the tradition's major divisions and even the subdivisions within those divisions, and its simultaneous attitude that in matters of doctrine, the divisions within the tradition are not of great consequence. We are interested here in the larger problem of continuity within religious traditions, and the Jains present us with an interesting puzzle. On the one hand, we routinely accept the notion that the Jains are fundamentally divided, primarily into two great movements, the Digambara and the Śvetāmbara. Beyond that, a closer examination of the tradition reveals that Rājaśekhara's mention of further subdivisions of Digambara is not an anachronism. One need plunge only briefly into a variety of studies to have the point amply demonstrated. The eventual number of subdivisions is indeed large, large enough for Śvetāmbara sources to assign the number 84 to them (84 being the Jain equivalent of "eleventy-'leven"). Moreover, in the *Kalpa Sūtra* translated by Hermann Jacobi, we find a *therāvalī* that indicates that divisions and even subdivisions are a very early feature of the tradition, textual evidence soundly confirmed by J. G. Bühler's interpretation of inscriptions at Mathurā.

On the other hand, the Jains present to us a remarkable unity and continuity in matters of doctrine. It is indeed notable that, given the persistent presence of divisions and subdivisions within the tradition, one is even hard-pressed to find major doctrinal differences between the Śvetāmbaras and Digambaras. Rājaśekhara is not significantly overstating matters in verses 27 and 28. As P. S Jaini (1979:88) has put it:

> [The Śvetāmbaras and Digambaras] have been very alike . . . in their remarkable unwillingness to depart from their basic doctrines and practices. . . . The basic Jain doctrines thus show extraordinary uniformity through the centuries; indeed, it is possible to consider them as a coherent whole, with little reference to questions of interpretation or chronology.

Beyond the major divisions, neither the subdivisions nor the rise of the more modern divisions (e.g., the Sthānakavāsīs) can be adequately accounted for in doctrinal terms. How is one, then, to account for such tenacious unity and such persistent division within the same tradition?

Only the beginnings of a full inquiry can be presented here, and those beginnings themselves will be rather narrowly focused. In large measure, it develops that we must discuss some modes of Western scholarship. At the same time, this narrower discussion may succeed in raising and framing some larger issues and topics that lie beyond the scope of this study.

Specifically, the following pages examine the question of the Jain scriptures. This is an appropriate place to begin because, while there is doctrinal unity, scholars have also presumed that the major division in the tradition has involved sharp and fundamental disagreement over 'scriptures.' In brief, it is held that the Śvetāmbaras have established and preserved a canon of scripture that the Digambaras do not accept.

It is noteworthy that Rājaśekhara makes no mention of this matter. As we shall see, Jain accounts of the Śvetāmbara-Digambara split also do not show great concern on this point. Nonetheless, Western scholars have consistently raised it. And it would appear that such radical disagreement over scripture as is assumed to exist would be a fundamental barrier to doctrinal unity. Yet such does not appear to be the case. This being so, it is proper to inquire into our perspective in this matter of 'scripture,' as a means of inquiring whether a part of the conundrum posed by doctrinal continuity in a tradition characterized by division and subdivision cannot be preliminarily understood by clarifying some of our own methods of study.

Our goal is twofold: first, to examine some of the ways in which our vision of the Śvetāmbara Jain canon of scripture has come into being (a task that, as my studies have evolved, has proven to have its own revealing and interesting dimensions) and to suggest an alternative view; and second, to see briefly how the Digambaras, presumed not to share this 'canon' of scripture, nonetheless participate fully and without basic disagreement in the fundamental doctrines of the tradition. Finally, we shall briefly examine further courses of study that may be indicated if we are to better understand the intriguing matter of continuity within the Jain tradition as a whole.

II.

As noted above, it is commonly held that the Śvetāmbaras have established and preserved the canon of Jain scriptures. (See above in chapter 1 for the list of the canonical texts that is commonly given.) There is a rough progression in age in the list, the *Aṅga*s containing the oldest material for the most part, and *Nandī* and *Aṇuyogadvārā* being among the youngest portions of the corpus. In general the oldest parts of the *Aṅga*s appear to have been fixed ca. 300 B.C.E., while the youngest material may have been added as much as a millenium later.

The total number of texts, their division into classes, the names of the classes, and even the particular texts within the classes are all problematic points. (Some of the common variations are indicated by the numbers 4a, 4b, and the like.) Yet this particular list is given by virtually every scholar of the Jains, and is perhaps the single most pervasive symptom of several tendencies within Jain studies concerning the canon of scripture.

When one begins to trace this list through the major Occidental studies of the Jains, it turns out to have a single source, George Bühler. Scholar after scholar gives the above texts, grouped and numbered generally as above, and cites Bühler.[2] Bühler (1882:579) himself accounted for the list in a report to the Kaiserliche Akademie at Vienna, in a footnote to a recounting of the list:

> [Die] Liste wurde für mich im Jahre 1871 von einem gelehrten Yati angefertigt und ist später von verschiedenen Jaina Gelehrten, unter denen ich den Śrîpûj des Kharatara Gaccha Jinamuktisûri nennen kann, geprüft and für richtig erklärt.[3]

Bühler's list is not the only version of what comprised the Śvetāmbara scriptures in the late nineteenth century. However, it is not Bühler's list itself, or its source, that is really at issue. Rather, it is the effect on subsequent study that the list was to exert. There is no doubting the fact that Bühler's list is a reasonably standard account of the Śvetāmbara scriptures as they were regarded at that time and place. However, the alacrity with which virtually every scholarly account of the Jains took up Bühler's list served in all likelihood to obscure the fact that the Śvetāmbara scriptures were not a uniformly regarded entity, and it led to a general unwillingness on the part of European scholars to rate other, differing accounts as highly as Bühler's, though the other accounts do not suffer measurably when compared with Bühler's in terms of source authority.[4]

It might be argued that such a problem is minor and typical of the earlier stages of all Indian studies,[5] except that Bühler's list had a secondary effect that cannot be overlooked. While in India, Bühler collected manuscripts and sent them to Berlin in the 1870s, and Albrecht Weber relied on those manuscripts and on Bühler in his pioneering study, *Über die heiligen Schriften der Jaina* (Weber 1883-85). The Foreword to part three of Weber's second volume in his Catalogue of manuscripts in the Royal Library at Berlin (Weber 1886-92) testifies clearly to the close relationship between Bühler's work and Weber's notion of the extent of the Jain scriptures. Weber's examination of the Śvetāmbara canon has never been duplicated, nor has its basic scope been seriously

2 See Jacobi 1879:14, Hoernle 1885-90:II:vii, Charpentier 1922:9ff., and other standard accounts of the Jains.

3 [Editor's translation.] "The list was prepared for me in 1871 by a learned Yati [monk], and later was checked and explained by other Jain scholars, including Jinamuktisūri, the Śrīpūj of the Kharatara Gaccha."

The only secondary reference to Bühler's statement of his actual source that I have been able to find occurs in A. Guérinot (1906:57). There the year of the *Sitzungsbericht* is wrongly given as 1881. In those of Bühler's writings that I have been able to consult, I have not found any other statement concerning the source of his list, or any recurrence of the above remarks.

4 The most difficult such account to handle, and one which did give Weber and others pause, is that of Mitra (1876:67-68). Cf. Weber 1893:7 [226-27].

5 What is not taken up here is the fact that the conclusions of Bühler, Weber et al., were in turn picked up by Indian scholars, even by Jains, and re-introduced into the Indian tradition. Thus these "minor" early problems often bore complex fruit not merely in Western circles, but also in Indian traditions.

challenged by any later scholar. *Über die heiligen Schriften der Jaina* thus had the effect of firmly setting Bühler's list into place.

Had this vision of the Śvetāmbara canon remained limited to the time and place of its origin, it might yet have been an acceptable and useful source and guide. However, the next use to which it was put has had extremely serious consequences for Jain studies. This use was the extension of the nineteenth century version of the canon back into the history of the Jain tradition and into the Western vision of the growth of the Jain scriptures.

The Jains themselves point to three significant councils at which their texts were at issue.[6] The first is placed at Mathurā, ca. 350 C.E., under the leadership of Skandila. The second is placed at Valabhī, in Saurashtra, at about the same time, under Nāgārjuna. The third council is again placed at Valabhī, ca. 500 C.E., under Devarddhigaṇī. The function of the first two councils apparently was to commit to writing the texts subscribed to by the Śvetāmbara monastic groups (*gaccha*s) represented at each. The third council appears to have produced a uniform version of those texts, noting certain important variants, and to have seen that copies were made and delivered to major Jain centers.

Early Occidental scholarship tended to the view that the corpus given in Bühler's list was the result of the Valabhī council of C.E. 500.[7] After Weber and others had made accessible a large number of Jain texts, it became apparent that there were problems involved in this view. The crux of the difficulties lay in the lists of texts given in Jain sources, notably in the *Nandī* and *Anuyogadvāra Sūtra*, the "appendices" to the canon.[8] These lists give the *Aṅga*s as in Bühler's list, as a separate class of works, and then go on to list sixty or more additional texts, ordering them quite differently from what is shown in the table, and giving numerous titles that are not in Bühler's list.

The issue for scholars then became one of solving the discrepancies between these lists and Bühler's. The general solution most often put forth was that considerable alterations, losses, etc., after the third council were partly responsible for the discrepancies, and that some of the texts given in the earlier lists were actually only the titles of portions of larger texts found in Bühler's list. Both of these proposed solutions have been found true in part. Yet the problem has not

---

6 This brief summary of the councils is based on Kapadia 1941:61-67. European scholars did not all accept the historicity of all three councils, but most of them had not had access to enough sources even to know of the work of all three. In general, the actuality of all three is now accepted.

A much earlier Jain council at Pāṭaliputra (fourth century B.C.E.), which is supposed to have fixed certain materials in standard oral form, is more difficult to assess, because it is part and parcel of the conflicting histories of the beginnings of the Śvetāmbara-Digambara division. Even the Jain sources concerning the three later councils do not tend to relate the work of the Pāṭaliputra council to these later assemblies.

7 See, for example, Jacobi 1879:14ff.

8 For these lists, see Kapadia 1941:24ff.

really been solved, because texts have been discovered that are named in the older lists but are not in Bühler's in any form, and to blame all of the differences on loss or mutilation hardly seems reasonable.

The matter stands basically at that point at present. The problem, if not actively dismissed, is at least ignored. In the absence of a solution to the problem, Bühler's list is accepted as defining the shape and limits of the canon, and the presumption is still active that the third council gave the canon that shape.[9]

The point to be made out of all this is that Bühler's list transmitted to European scholarship more than a certain number of texts arranged in a certain order. It also transmitted the notion of a fixed 'canon,' with all the nuances borne by the term. This is the backdrop to the probem of the disagreement between lists of texts. The idea of a 'canon' as the Christian tradition understands it is such that one cannot easily account for significant variations in the materials that make it up. Since Bühler's list must have seemed to be unimpeachable evidence, the solution to the discrepancies lay in the directions noted: assumption of corruptions, losses, and mistakes in identity, and the general acceptance of Bühler's list as dating to the third council.

It is not possible here to present fully the alternatives to this either-or approach. However, it must be pointed out that there are alternatives available, and that the notion of the Jain canon as fixed has had serious and perhaps unwarranted consequences. Perhaps the most useful alternative lies in the approach to the materials that is found in the Jain lists themselves.[10] There, two major divisions are presented: *aṅgapaviṭṭha* and *anaṅgapaviṭṭha* (or *aṅgabāhira*). The referent of both terms is not specific texts or scriptures, but the class of knowledge that the Jains term *suyanāṇa*.[11] Some of this knowledge is contained in the *aṅgas* (*aṅgapaviṭṭha*), some not therein (*anaṅgapaviṭṭha*). The latter class is further subdivided into *āvassaya* (having to do with six essential observances for Jains) and *āvassayavairitta* (not associated with the six observances). The

---

9 See Schubring (1959:669): "Die fur die Shvetāmbaras verbindlichen Werke . . . stammen in ihren ältesten Teilen aus dem 3. bis 2.Jh. vChr. Zum Kanon wurden sie in einem Konzil auf Kathiawar (Gujarat) Ende des 6.Jh. gesammelt. Dieser Siddhânta oder Âgama umfasst 45 Texte."
[Editor's translation.] "The authoritative texts of the Śvetāmbaras . . . in their oldest portions date from the 3rd to 2nd century B.C.E. The canon was collected at a council in Kathiawar (Gujarat) in the 6th century C.E. These Siddhānta or Āgama comprise 45 texts."

10 The following is according to Kapadia 1941:20ff.

11 Kapadia (1941:20) translates this as "scriptural knowledge." *Tattvārthādhigamasūtra* I.9 and other sources testify to this as a reasonable translation, though the term gained the sense of being 'transmitted' knowledge in later philosophical discussions. While the two English terms appear to be quite different, it is likely that the later Jain interpretation of the term may imply nothing more than a change in the scope of the sources of knowledge. In other words, 'scripture' is 'transmission' of a specific sort. The later usage seems to imply something more on the order of the *śabda-pramāṇa* of other Indian schools of thought.

latter is again subdivided, into *kāliya* (to be studied at specific times) and *ukkāliya* (to be studied at any time).[12] Schematically:

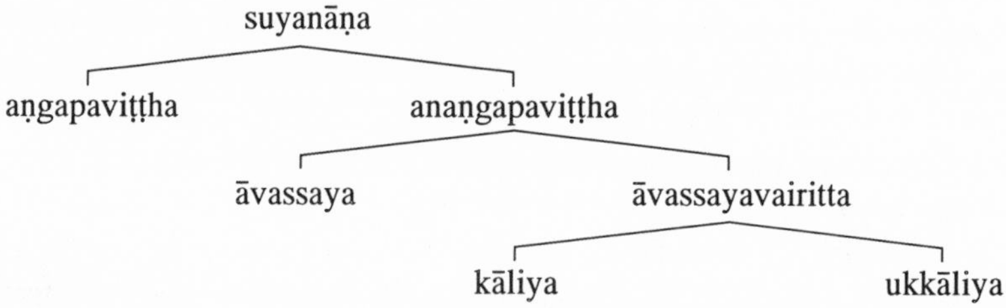

This scheme is then used to classify various texts, and it is the scheme followed in the lists of texts that Weber and others found so different from Bühler's list.

There are two striking features here. First, the scheme is based, as noted, on distinctions in types of things that one must know, and not on a distinction among texts per se. Second, the scheme shows a steady progression outward from the knowledge most directly derived from Mahāvīra (the *Aṅga*s), through the essentials of monastic praxis, to knowledge that may be handled incidentally. As was noted above, the *aṅgapaviṭṭha* material, i.e., the *Aṅga*s themselves, are uniformly given in various lists, while the *anaṅgapaviṭṭha* material shows variations. However, when a scheme like this is one's frame of reference, the variation is not necessarily a grave problem.

This is quite different from what the West has come to think of as 'canonical.' It is quite clear that the approach of Jain scholars has been fixed on a notion of 'canon' as implying a certain set of texts, and that this has excluded the broader, original sense of 'canon' as a standard or norm, a sense that could properly apply to the Jain scheme outlined above. But when the narrower sense of canon is applied to the discrepancies pointed out earlier, it leads to difficulties. Either something is part of 'the canon' or it is not, in the narrower view. A body of scriptures that is not limited in terms of texts and books themselves does not, in the narrower view, appear to be a canon.[13]

It cannot be said that European (and even Indian) scholars were unaware of the alternative classification as given. Yet even those who knew of it turned to the model provided by Bühler's list. As noted, it is not the case that the latter is a non-Jain product; however, it must be regarded as distinctly possible that the two models, rather than merely being in conflict with each other, reflect a change in the Jain view of the scriptures.

---

12 The exact meaning of these terms is not clear. See Kapadia 1941:24, 26ff.

13 These general statements point to one central fact: scholars of the Jains have failed to reflect seriously on what the term 'canon' might mean, or even what their own version of it might be.

Sources indicate that the later model—forty-five texts—begins to show up in the thirteenth century C.E.;[14] but later sources still use the older model. Yet the studies that have been made of the Jain scriptures simply do not take up the possibility that between the third council, ca. 500 C.E., and the time when the later model begins to appear the Jains may have held a very different view of the scriptures than is implied by Bühler's list and the Western understanding of it. This possibility, by itself, should help us in clarifying the matter of doctrinal continuity in the Jain tradition.[15]

III.

Given some new insight into the canon, we now turn to the presumed status of the Digambaras, who are held to reject the canon of the Śvetāmbaras and to have elevated certain other works to authoritative status. The Digambaras do, however, preserve lists of works that they hold are now lost, in which are given the titles and summaries of the contents of twelve *Aṅga*s and fourteen *Prakīrṇaka*s. The *Aṅga* titles correspond to those given above and the titles of a number of *Prakīrṇaka*s correspond to the titles of some of the non-*Aṅga* Śvetāmbara texts. There is also a certain amount of correspondence between the Digambara descriptions of contents and the texts as preserved by the Śvetāmbaras.

In point of fact, the exact nature and sources of the Digambara rejection of the Śvetāmbara texts have not been thoroughly explored. The reason usually given for the rejection comes from the version of the Digambara-Śvetāmbara schism in which a council is held in the north to fix the tradition while

---

14 Kapadia 1941:30, 58.

15 It is very interesting to think of such movements as the intra-Śvetāmbara 'reform' movements, the Loṅkā (or Lumpāka), ca. 1500, and the Sthānakavāsī, ca. 1700, in a different framework than that of the 'fixed canon.' A major part of these 'reforms' was the rejection of the practice of doing *pūjā* to temple-housed *Tīrthaṅkara* images, and this rejection is often linked to an appeal to the scriptures on the part of the reformers. The Sthānakavāsīs are often portrayed as having rejected a part of the Śvetāmbara canon because they felt that only those parts of the *Siddhānta* that did not mention image worship were the true teachings. (The Sthānakavāsī canon consists of thirty-two texts, all of which are contained in Bühler's list. The *Aṅga*s and *Upāṅga*s are given in the same way, but the other classes of texts are very differently ordered, the *Prakīrṇaka*s and three other texts not being included at all.) This so-called rejection, is, however, clearly not based on the matter of image veneration, since the texts retained by the Sthānakavāsīs include texts that refer to images.

What is genuinely exciting is the possibility that, in classifying and limiting the number of canonical texts, the Sthānakavāsīs were not 'rejecting' a firmly held, previously existing Śvetāmbara canon, but were rather breaking new ground, i.e., presenting a new alternative in a situation where a 'fixed canon' of the sort that one could reject was not really present. Alternatively, the Sthānakavāsī canon might be another version of the process of beginning to fix a set of scriptures, and not a 'rejection.' Thus it might develop that clarifying our view of the canon might also assist us in better understanding the genesis of the most recent set of divisions within the Jain tradition.

Bhadrabāhu and a portion of the Jain monastic community are in the south because of famine in the north. The council at Pāṭaliputra is held to fix the tradition because it is feared that few monks will survive the famine. Further, those in the north have taken to wearing white garb, while those in the south continue to practice nakedness. The latter, upon their return north, reject both the form in which the tradition has been fixed and the practice of wearing clothing.[16]

It should be noted first of all that this is a Digambara version of the events leading to the schism, and is not the only Digambara version.[17] Without entering into a full-fledged discussion, one can at least note that the Śvetāmbara account of the schism is totally different. Neither it nor the bulk of the Digambara accounts make the matter of the scriptures of any real import, if they mention it at all. Later accounts of the division, Śvetāmbara and Digambara alike, do not raise the matter of 'canon.'[18] It would appear that the issue is far more complicated than most current accounts have it. When matters are reduced to their essentials, all that has been accomplished is the discovery that the Śvetāmbaras put forth a *Siddhānta* that consists of admittedly old texts and that the Digambaras claim that these particular texts are not genuine, but are only substitutes that bear the same titles as original teachings that have been lost. The Digambara claim has simply not been taken seriously.

It is true that the Digambaras present a number of texts, divided into four *anuyoga*s ("disciplines"), that are said to contain authoritative teachings. The four disciplines are *prathamānuyoga*, *karaṇānuyoga*, *dravyānuyoga*, and *caraṇānuyoga*, which might be translated as world history, cosmography, philosophy, and ethics. The exact number of texts in each does not appear firmly fixed. The headings inlude such works as the *Tattvārthādhigamasūtra* and its major Digambara commentaries, some of the works of Kundakunda, Vaṭṭakera's *Mūlācāra*, the *Ṣaṭkhaṇḍāgama*, and the like.

It should be noted that a number of these texts antedate the council held ca. 500 C.E, and this point alone would seem to make it rash to regard these Digambara texts as secondary "substitutes" for a canon.[19] In fact, the various points that are often raised when the textual traditions of the Śvetāmbaras and Digambaras are compared all weaken in the face of specific pieces of evidence. It appears that only when a number of poorly documented claims are lumped together, and then viewed by persons who rely on a narrow notion of 'canon' for a framework,

---

16 Charpentier (1922:13-15) presents a curious conflated version, blending together several accounts of the schism.

17 See C. J. Shah 1932:67-74, 221-23.

18 For a full discussion of the standard later accounts, with notes on the earlier versions, see Jacobi 1884a.

19 For examples of such treatment, see Kapadia 1941:57-58, and others.

does there arise a nebulous picture of the Digambaras as being somehow outside the Jain mainstream.

One must at the very least remain open to other possibilities. Over the *aṅgapaviṭṭha* material there is clearly some disagreement between the two groups, although Bühler himself reported that Digambara Jains with whom he had been in contact (1) did not regard the *Aṅga*s as lost, but held that theirs and the Śvetāmbaras' were merely different, and (2) used some texts that, even so, conformed to the Śvetāmbara texts that Bühler knew.[20] Where the *anaṅga-paviṭṭha* materials are concerned, several specific points must be kept in mind. First, there has been no thorough study of the Digambara classifications of texts. The division into four *anuyoga*s is also found in some Śvetāmbara sources, and the Digambaras make use of some of the headings in the older Śvetāmbara classification outlined above. In fact, they preserve some *āvassaya* material that is the same as that preserved by the Śvetāmbaras.[21] In sum, past scholarship seems not only to have obscured possible alternative Śvetāmbara visions of the scriptures, but also to have failed to examine in any depth the Digambara vision. In effect, the Digambaras have been judged solely in light of their relationship to the Śvetāmbara canon—itself perhaps poorly understood—and hardly ever on their own merits.

It will perhaps be most effective to close this argument by presenting a suggestion for a different assessment of the Digambara and Śvetāmbara relationships to the development of a canon. K. K. Dixit has proposed a possible account whose general direction avoids the complications and drawbacks that accompany the notion of a 'fixed canon' and the Digambara rejection of it. In his words (1971:79):

> What seems to have happened is that in the times of Ṣaṭkhaṇḍāgama [prior to the third council] the Jain authors had devised to compose such texts as would render superfluous a study of the old Āgamic texts like Bhagavatī, Prajñāpanā, Jīvābhigama, and this was true of the Śvetāmbara as well as Digambara authors. Thus a Śvetāmbara student could feel that his theoretical needs were fully satisfied by the texts like Anuyogadvāra, Nandī, Āvaśyaniryukti, Tattvārthasūtra along with Bhāṣya, [and] a Digambara student could feel that the same was done by the texts like Ṣaṭkhaṇḍāgama, Kaṣāyaprābhṛta, Mūlācāra, Tattvārthasūtra along with Sarvārthasiddhi. The only difference—in its own way remarkable—was that the Śvetāmbara camp thought it proper also to preserve the wordings of the old Āgamic texts while its Digambara counterpart refused to shoulder such a responsibility. All this accounts for the so striking a similarity that obtains between the theoretical views of the Śvetāmbaras and Digambaras in spite of the fact that the former uphold and the latter repudiate the authority of the now current Āgamic texts.

---

20 Bühler 1878a:28-29.

21 Leumann 1934:1-19.

Dixit's suggestion is based on his observation of shifts in the formulation and discussion of certain theoretical issues in Jain thought, and not on textual analysis in linguistic terms, etc. Yet its thrust is almost strikingly reasonable compared with the snarl that results from the Western view of the canon. Some possible documentation for it exists in an analysis of the composition of the Digambara texts put forth by J. P. Jain (1964:106-110). Yet no Western scholar has made any such approach to the Digambaras or to the problem as a whole.

IV.

At this juncture we can observe that at least some of the foreground clutter that obscures our sense of unity and diversity in the Jain tradition may have been cleared away. All that we have here is a prolegomena to an actual study of the problem. Nonetheless, some distinct conclusions and some urgent tasks for the future can be identified.

First, if the study of Jain 'scriptures' can be brought outside of the narrow idea of canon, then each text and its contents can be far more adequately judged, and one step toward understanding Jain doctrinal unity will have been taken. There is the further benefit of being able to do justice to the Digambara texts by themselves.

Second, it is clear that we must re-assess the development of the Śvetāmbara-Digambara split. The matter of the canon may be something of a separable issue, one created more by our scholarship than by the Jains themselves; but our investigation of it points up the fact that although the Jains are divided, our usual categories for handling such divisions may be seriously inadequate. If it is puzzling, it is that they should be divided in practice, and it may develop that our image of this division in praxis is also faulty.

Finally, we must attend to the least familiar category of material that Rājaśekhara presents in his verses: the internal subdivisions. These small units are older than the Śvetāmbara-Digambara split, they are persistent, and they are, by all accounts, the basic form in which "Jainism" has existed throughout its history. Perhaps our understanding of the Jain tradition would be clearer, and our concerns over continuity and division within it more creatively shaped, if we were to concentrate on the small divisions within the tradition and make them part and parcel of our understanding of the Jains, and if we were less willing to treat the Śvetāmbara-Digambara split as informing all of Jain history.

5

THE 'CANONS' OF 'SCRIPTURE': TEXT, RITUAL, AND SYMBOL*

The study that led to this essay began as an inquiry into some peculiar features of the way that occidental scholarship has treated the Jain textual tradition. But unraveling that matter came to involve ever broader consideration of the study of 'scripture' as a problem in itself. This has led me to make the order of presentation what it is, namely, to begin with the general and to move to the specific; students of the Jains are not encouraged to skip ahead to section III, nor others to skip over it.

I.

> It is sometimes difficult to say what is
> a Sacred Book, and what is not.
> —F. Max Müller (1889:538)

---

* Paper written for the 1984 N.E.H. summer seminar at Harvard University under Wilfred Cantwell Smith on "Scripture: Its Nature and Evolving Role." A shorter, slightly different version was published as "The 'Canons' of 'Scripture,'" in Miriam Levering (ed.), *Rethinking Scripture* (Albany: SUNY Press, 1989), 170-79. I have incorporated some of Levering's editorial changes in this version. In the course of working on this paper, Folkert became so sensitized to the provisional nature of many of our scholarly categories that he enclosed many terms in single quotation marks. Since these marks can easily clutter the text, I have retained them in this chapter only in the first usage.

Given Max Müller's own tendency to sprinkle his lectures and writings with biblical quotations, one's instinct is to append, "He who has ears to hear, let him hear!" to the above declaration. But this was—alas—no parable or saying that only the audience could not appreciate or grasp. Unfortunately, Müller himself did not take the statement seriously, nor were several of its possible significations a part of his thinking. There is translation, there is the critical study of texts, there is study of the Bible, and more. But these are not, singly or together, what is needed.

This statement represents both an ironic and complex state of affairs—ironic because the very roots of the modern discipline of studying religion are bound up in the study of texts and scriptures; complex because a discussion of studying scripture can be an entrée to consideration of the entire history of the discipline. For, among other things that bear on the matter, the study of religion sits (uneasily) bestride the bifurcation of the study of human communities into 'history,' with its focus on textual documentation, and 'social science,' with its—sometimes relentless—discounting of literary evidence. Yet scripture, it seems, has suffered an unhappy and peculiar fate in that situation: it has been taken for granted, both negatively and positively.

It is this condition of being taken for granted that especially wants exploration and rectification. To accomplish that, without essaying a review of the entire history of the study of religion, let us return to Max Müller, with whose words we began. Müller's role in the first great period of the study of literature and languages from non-European cultures, including the genesis of The Sacred Books of the East,[1] makes it appropriate to propose him as a bellwether for the study of scriptures, and to see what can be learned by examining his view of the subject. I say that he might be "proposed" as a bellwether because our purpose here in looking at Müller's notion of scripture is not the production of a definitive history of recent conceptions of it, nor even an essay on Müller himself.

The problem, rather, is that scripture, in being so taken for granted as it has been, seems to have no history as a clear category or concept in that study of religion. Therefore, Müller's views are offered as an exemplar, albeit an influential one, and are presented in the spirit of challenge referred to above. The challenge has two dimensions. The first, but not necessarily prior, is to spur students of religion into re-examining the areas of the discipline with which they are most familiar, on this point: how have scholars in various specialties spoken of scripture? The second, but not necessarily secondary, dimension of the

---

1 See Nirad Chaudhuri 1974:367 where Müller is quoted as viewing, in the last year of his life (1900), the Ṛg Veda and The Sacred Books of the East as constituting his life's work.

challenge is directed toward persons now working in the study of religion: do Müller's notions resemble current writing, teaching, and scholarly discourse?

A premise that I expect has been clear from the outset is that the notion of scripture exemplified by Müller is unsatisfactory and incomplete. The question is whether it is typical, both for the past and the present. The challenge, both historical and immediate, is to address the adequacy of our views of scripture. If, in the end, more questions are raised than answered, that too will be satisfactory. There has been enough of taking scripture for granted.

What, then, are the exemplary features of Max Müller's general view of scripture, especially as concerns taking if for granted? On the positive side, i.e., in the sense that scripture is simply said to exist, we can speak of Müller's case of a broad and unreflective generic notion of scripture, involving an unwavering focus on the study of 'original' texts. With respect to taking scripture negatively for granted, we can see an ultimate devaluation of scripture in favor of other foci for understanding religion. Let us examine these two more specifically.

The Genus Scripture

Müller's generic notion of scripture has two major dimensions, both of which worked to make his declaration that "it is sometimes difficult to say what is a 'Sacred Book'" very nearly a rhetorical flourish. At a first and most general level, he expressed no significant, detectable doubt about what constituted the 'Sacred Books' of the world's religious traditions. Second, and at a more fundamental level, he seems never to have doubted that such a phenomenon as Sacred Books existed as an entity that might be compared across religious and cultural boundaries. This two-part general perception pre-existed the time of the statement in question, and one does not find an occasion where Müller grappled explicitly with the issues involved.

Müller dealt with the subject of scriptures generally on three principal occasions: in his *Introduction to the Science of Religion* (Müller 1873), comprising four lectures delivered in 1870; in the "Preface to the Sacred Books of the East," published as part of the first volume of the series in 1879 (Müller 1879:a) (and which largely reflects the proposal for the series, which dates to 1876 [Müller 1879:b]); and in his *Natural Religion*, the Gifford Lectures (at Glasgow) for 1888 (Müller 1889). From first to last, his vision of the material in question underwent no significant change, either as to its limits or its basic character.

In 1870, in the second lecture on the Science of Religion, Müller declared that "Sacred Books" come from three basic sources—India, the Near East, and China—and represent eight religions—Brāhmaṇic Hinduism, Buddhism, Zoroastrianism, Judaism, Christianity, Islam, Confucianism, and Taoism. "With these eight religions," he said, "the library of the Sacred Books of the whole human race is complete . . ." (Müller 1873:106). Within the traditions, Müller identified the specific "Sacred Books" as the Veda, the Zend Avesta, the Tripiṭaka, the Old Testament, the New Testament, the Qur'an, the five classics (*ching*) and four books (*shu*) from the Confucian tradition, and the Tao Te Ching (Müller 1873:107-116). By 1888-89, in the lectures on *Natural Religion*, neither of these basic sets had been altered, except for the loose inclusion of the Jains and the Śvetāmbara Jain canon, or Siddhānta, into the same category with the Buddhists (a category that Müller conceived of as a non-Brāhmaṇic entity), and the addition of more detailed accounts of some of the literature (Müller 1889:539-49). The account written to propose the inauguration of The Sacred Books of the East, which falls between these, does not reflect any interim period where the notion of eight religions and their sacred books was cast into any serious doubt (Müller 1879b:xl-xli).

Müller's notion that this was "the library of the Sacred Books of the whole human race" appears to have sprung from several sources, and these should be reviewed briefly. A first (and, though apparently obvious, certainly not to be taken for granted) source is the state of the information concerning literature and cultures that was available to Müller, along with the framework through which he viewed it. Characterizing this matter briefly is not easy to do, but one can point to two principal contributing factors. The first is something that exists everywhere and nowhere in Müller's work, and that persons living in the 1980s may need to make an active effort to recall: how relatively new and exhilirating was the notion in Müller's day that one could put together a factual and documented image of the entire world. Yet—and here is the second factor—that image of the world was seen by Müller through a powerful lens: his participation in the German romantic view of the East—the Morgenland.[2] Highly revealing in this respect are the opening words of Müller's *Natural Religion* lecture on "Sacred Books" (Müller 1889:538): "All Sacred Books came to us from the East: not one of them has been conceived, composed, or written down in Europe."

It is valuable to note that in Müller's view, "the Sacred Books of the East" did not therefore, mean "of the Orient" or "of Asia"; and also to note that "the East" included the domain of biblical literature. In all of this, Müller participates fully in the stream of German romantic orientalism.

This framework also helps to account for the surprising (at first glance) lack of concern for historical survival of texts and cultural data.[3] Yet Müller's

---

2 See Chaudhuri 1974:123ff. for an excellent portrayal of this dimension of Müller's views.

3 The proposal for The Sacred Books of the East discusses this point, but only very briefly. There, in something of a departure from both his earlier and later phraseology, Müller spoke of "the great and

worldview, including his view of 'the East,' is not the only determinant of the limits of the 'library.' There is another, and it is revealed in his choice of adjectives in the line from the proposal for The Sacred Books of the East: "the great and original religions." In this phrase almost surely lies the explanation for another prominent usage: "book religions." Müller uses the latter characterization from the beginning to speak of the eight religions in question (Müller 1873:102-3, 122, et passim). But when one looks for some principle underlying this phrase, one is disappointed. The phrase itself is borrowed from what Müller knew of Islam, and receives no systematic discussion at all, save in a context to which we shall return.

What Müller meant by "book religions" was almost surely what he called in the *Proposal* (1879b:xli) "great and original." It seems correct to see this as the equivalent for Müller of such usages as "world religions" that have become more common in the study of religion; and while such a conception is closely related to the framework in which Müller set his view of the world, it is not tantamount to it. The notion of "great and original" was also tied to what Müller saw to be the nature of languages and language families. In the lectures on the Science of Religion, the discussion of religions and their Sacred Books is firmly set within one of Müller's premier discussions of the language families of the world, such that one can see that the set of "book religions," i.e., "great and original religions," was delimited by its having sprung from what Müller saw as linguistic fountainheads (Müller 1873:215-16). The choice of religions was not, therefore, random nor altogether influenced by Müller's world view.

We have before us, then, one dimension of Müller's generic view of scripture and a sense of its sources: Sacred Books represent a delimited body of literature from specific religions, fixed from early on in Müller's thinking. The second part of the generic assumption—that an entity existed that might be compared across religious boundaries—now requires attention. Up to now, obviously, we have looked at Müller's declaration from 1888 as if it had been (and in a way that was, from the content of his lectures, certainly part of the intended meaning), "It is sometimes difficult to say which religions have Sacred Books, and which do not." Now it is necessary to look more closely at the original phraseology, namely, "what is a Sacred Book, and what is not."

original religions" which profess to be founded on Sacred Books, and have preserved them in manuscript (Müller 1879b:xli). But the possibility that other materials might exist that ought to be included in the 'library' is not treated seriously. There is brief mention of possible material from Egypt, Babylon, and Assyria (Müller 1978b:xl-xli), but European religious literature is dismissed with virtually no discussion (although there is a sidelong glance at the Edda) (Müller 1879b:xl): "Neither Greeks, nor Romans, nor Germans, nor Celts, nor Slaves [*sic*] have left us anything that deserves the name of Sacred Books."

Again, the declaration is curious. Either it is a description of fact or a flourish, and one must opt for the latter, for outside of the very prominent framework of religions and their texts, it is difficult to find in Müller's work an effort to evolve a generic statement that would apply to texts themselves. Only in his lecture on Sacred Books in *Natural Religion* does something like a systematic statement emerge, and it is worth quoting at length. Speaking of the selection of material for The Sacred Books of the East, Müller (1889:538-39) said:

> It was suggested that those books only should be considered as sacred which professed to be revealed, or to be directly communicated by the Deity to the great teachers of mankind. But it was soon found that very few, if any, of the books themselves put forward that claim. Such a claim was generally advanced and formulated by a later generation, and chiefly by theologians, in support of that infallible authority which they wished to secure for the books on which their teaching was founded. But even that was by no means a general rule, and we should have had to exclude the Sacred Books of the Buddhists, of the followers of Confucius and Lao-tze, possibly even the Old Testament, as looked upon in early times by the Jews themselves, if we had kept to that definition. So we agreed to treat as Sacred Books all those which had been formally recognised by religious communities as constituting the highest authority in matters of religion, which had received a kind of canonical sanction, and might therefore be appealed to for deciding any disputed points of faith, morality, or ceremonial.
>
> We should not treat the Homeric poems, for instance, as Sacred Books, because, though Herodotus tells us that Homer and Hesiod made the gods of the Greeks—whatever that may mean—neither the Odyssey nor the Iliad was ever intended to teach religion. There are many books which have exercised a far greater influence on religious faith and moral conduct than the Bibles of the world. Such are, for instance, the *Imitatio Christi* by Thomas à Kempis, Bunyan's *Pilgrim's Progress*, Dante's *Divina Comedia*, or in Southern India the *Kural*. But none of these works received any canonical sanction; their doctrines were not binding, and might be accepted or rejected without peril.

When one examines the history of Müller's thinking, especially the strong formation of the library of texts from the eight religions that reaches back to his lectures on the Science of Religion, one is obliged to discount significantly the first part of the quoted passage. The concern over 'revealed' books comes after the fact, and is a prologue to the fundamental notion of the genus that comes midway in the passage and that is illustrated by the examples in the final paragraph. In essence, once the prefatory considerations are removed, the definition serves Müller principally for thinking about Sacred Books within a tradition; yet not even then is the nature of the texts themselves drawn into the discussion.

For even this definition and its uses were not fully developed by Müller, nor are his choices as Sacred Books documented according to the definition. There is simply no resolution for this problem, save one: Müller treated as Sacred Books the oldest texts for which he could see any religious sanction within a tradition, and the specifics of that sanctioning were simply not dealt with. This is visible in his characterization of the Veda within the Hindu tradition, again worth quoting at length (Müller 1873:108-111):

> The hymns of the Rigveda, which are the real bible of the ancient faith of the Vedic Rishis, are only 1,028 in number, consisting of about 10,580 verses. The commentary, however, on these hymns, of which I have published five goodsized quarto volumes, is estimated at 100,000 lines, consisting of 32 syllables each, that is at 3,200,000 syllables. There are, besides, the three minor Vedas, the Yajurveda, the Sāmaveda, the Atharvaveda, which, though of less importance for religious doctrines, are indispensable for a right appreciation of the sacrificial and ceremonial system of the worshippers of the ancient Vedic gods.
>
> To each of these four Vedas belong collections of so-called *Brāhmaṇas*, scholastic treatises of a later time, it is true, but nevertheless written in archaic Sanskrit, and reckoned by every orthodox Hindu as part of his revealed literature. Their bulk is much larger than that of the ancient Vedic hymn-books.
>
> And all this constitutes the text only for numberless treatises, essays, manuals, glosses, &c., forming an uninterrupted chain of theological literature, extending over more than three thousand years, and receiving new links even at the present time . . .
>
> Nor can we exclude the sacred law-books, nor the ancient epic poems, the Mahābhārata and Rāmāyana, nor the more modern, yet sacred literature of India, the Purānas and Tantras, if we wish to gain an insight into the religious belief of millions of human beings, who, though they all acknowledge the Veda as their supreme authority in matters of faith, are yet unable to understand one single line of it, and in their daily life depend entirely for spiritual food on the teaching conveyed to them by these more recent and more popular books.

What leaps out at one is that Müller knew full well the intricacies of the textual tradition in question, and the range of the materials involved. Yet is it the Veda to which, in all of his accounts of Sacred Books, Müller gives the status of Sacred Book without dealing with the other Hindu candidates for that status. The genus scripture, then, so far as one can actually extend it to the matter of texts qua texts, is presumably based on antiquity buttressed by a loose notion of authoritative status within a community, the latter presumably consciously granted.

This focus on antiquity brings us one further step in piecing together Müller's views, thus raising the point that his generic notion of scripture rested in the value of original texts, and their original meaning, as the prime objective in the study of scripture. Here Müller seems fully in the stream of nineteenth-century historiography: in an era nearly obsessed with the question of origins, he saw the search for beginnings as the key to understanding the progression of human history.[4]

The most telling index of this concern and its effect on his notion of scriptures is his relative disregard of the value of commentaries and other intervening literature that might stand, as it were, between the scholar and the text. Though he had used and published Sāyana's commentary on the Ṛg Veda, his own view was that Sāyana and other commentators had been necessary for scholars to begin to understand the original texts, but that a scholar should not hesitate to ignore the commentators when they were, in the former's view, wrong.[5] In Müller's view, the critical scholar could expect that "like an old precious medal, the ancient religion, after the rust of ages has been removed, will come out in all its purity and brightness" (Müller 1873:67). It was, then, the original text, critically and historically studied, and the meaning that emerged from this effort that ultimately counted.

With the forgoing in mind, it is worth noting, finally, the term Sacred Book. The generic and presumably comparable entity in question is called by a cacophany of names. Within the first ten pages of the printed version of the 1888 lecture, Müller speaks of: Sacred Books, Bibles, sacred writings, sacred literature, canons, sacred book, religious literature, and religious classics (Müller 1889:538-47). All of this polyonymony is, moreover, utterly unsystematic. One might allow that the phrase "what is a Sacred Book" has a generic sense because of the use of upper case letters to begin the crucial terms (a point, incidentally, that would have been lost on Müller's original audience, since the phrase first occurred in a lecture); but this is almost surely a product of some minor reification in Müller's own thinking, given the strong influence of The Sacred Books of the East in his writings. Surrounded as it is by a sea of other terminology, one has to conclude that Sacred Book has a fundamentally undefined referent, as do all of the other terms used as would-be synonyms for it, except in one respect: the subject was assumed to be 'books.'

The foregoing, then, are components of Müller's generic view. All of them, singly and together, point to what I have called taking scripture positively for granted. As noted above, there are two other headings in Müller's view that also point toward the same sort of taking scripture for granted: Müller's view of the Bible, and his focus on texts. In some ways, these have been foreshadowed in the preceding review, and are part of the generic notion. Yet each also

---

4 Chaudhuri (1974:89) quotes Müller as saying, "My interest in all religions is chiefly historical; I want to see what has been, in order to understand what is."

5 See especially a report by Müller on translation procedures for The Sacred Books of the East, quoted in Chaudhuri 1974:354; see also Müller 1873:26-27.

contributes a distinctive flavor to the whole, and we shall want to take brief note of them.

The Christian Bible

It is tempting simply to surmise that the Christian, and specifically, Protestant view of the Bible from the seventeenth and eighteenth centuries onward is the basic source and model for a major part of our image(s) of scripture in the comparative study of religion. Ascertaining whether that is true or not would require two sorts of study—of the history of the Bible itself, and of a wide range of scholarly writings in the period. What seems to be true is that some—but not all—of the terminology used by Christians to speak of the Bible were used as models for thinking about scriptures.[6] In Müller's case, we can see several of these possibilities in a concrete setting.

Müller's view of the Bible was described above as being basically Protestant and relatively insular. At first glance, this would seem to be contradicted by some features of his work that both imply and directly express a kind of egalitarianism with regard to the relationship of Christian scriptures to those of other traditions. Such is certainly the case for his model of the 'library of Sacred Books'; and in his Science of Religion lectures he expressed himself as follows, setting a tone that he would often revert to on subsequent occasions (Müller 1873:281): "Let us but treat our own sacred books with neither more nor less mercy than the sacred books of any other nation . . ." This apparent act of seeing the Christian Bible on the same level with other scriptures provoked some degree of opposition. According to Müller's most thorough biographer, Nirad C. Chaudhuri, such opposition came to a head at the time when The Sacred Books of the East began to appear (Chaudhuri 1974:350):

> The Christian and Judaic scriptures, though eastern in their origin, were excluded [from the series] for fear of offending orthodoxy, and even the publication of the others gave offence to many English Christians.

One should not doubt that Müller fully intended that scriptures should be regarded as equals in the eyes of scholars; yet side by side with this intent there existed the elements mentioned earlier as comprising his view of the Bible. On those occasions when Müller spoke directly of it, he was clearly disposed to regard it in terms that reflect a sense of its superiority to other scriptures, terms

---

6 A degree of difference, in Müller's own day, on the point of models and terminology can be seen in a curious spot: the polemical exchanges between supporters of Müller and of his opponent for the Boden Professorship of Sanskrit at Oxford, Monier-Williams, in 1860. The Monier-Williams camp argued that their candidate was familiar with the "real Bible" of India, namely, the *Puraṇa*s and epics, while Müller's Hindu "Bible," the Veda, was only a relic of long-past religiosity. Müller lost the election for the professorship but not, by all accounts, on those grounds. See Chaudhuri 1974:220ff.

that are characteristic of his German Lutheran background.[7] On the matter of the Bible and The Sacred Books of the East he wrote, in a letter to one of his supporters (Chaudhuri 1974:355):

> Of one thing I feel very certain, that this translation of The Sacred Books of the East, which some of the good people here consider most objectionable, will do a great deal towards lifting Christianity into its highest historical position. I look forward to the time when those who objected to my including the Old and New Testaments among The Sacred Books of the East will implore me to do so.

His view of the general nature and status of the Bible can also be seen in two characteristic ways. First, indirectly, there is his view of scripture as the "highest authority in matters of religion," as expressed in his broadest generic definition. Second, and more direct, is his notion of the text itself in a comparative setting. In the "Preface to the Sacred Books of the East," he wrote (Müller 1879:xv-xvi):

> . . . mixed up with real treasures of thought, we meet in the sacred books with . . . many passages and whole chapters which either never had any life or meaning at all, or if they had, have, in the form in which they have come down to us, completely lost it. We must try to imagine what the Old Testament would have been, if it had not been kept distinct from the Talmud; or the New Testament, if it had been mixed up not only with the spurious gospels, but with the records of the wranglings of the early Councils, if we wish to understand, to some extent at least, the wild confusion of sublime truth with vulgar stupidity that meets us in the pages of the Veda, the Avesta, and the Tripiṭaka. The idea of keeping the original and genuine tradition separate from apocryphal accretions was an idea of later growth, that could spring up only after the earlier tendency of preserving whatever could be preserved of sacred or halfsacred lore, had done its work, and wrought its own destruction.

Here one certainly sees, if a broad generalization be allowed, a Protestant-flavored notion of the Bible as an almost pristine source, of religious value throughout, and closed off from all that does not belong to it.

By and large, Müller was unsystematic in his dealings with the Bible, and in the end, one has the sense that for Müller the Bible and a general perception of its status and nature is in the background at all times, but that it was absorbed into his work at a variety of levels and in uneven fashion. The shared terminology for scriptures discussed earlier may indicate this; and perhaps such a shadowy presence for the Bible, especially in Protestant modes, is the very essence of its relationship to the matter of scripture. Moreover, the Bible is also present in something of the same direct and indirect, resolved and unresolved relationship to the third heading in Müller's views: the primacy of texts.

---

7 See Chaudhuri's account (1974:69ff.) for a balanced portrayal of formative Christian ideas in Müller's life.

The Ultimate Devaluation of Scripture

With this heading, we come to the taking of scripture negatively for granted. Rather than try to grasp this potentially curious formulation at the outset, let us look at two ways in which this sort of 'taking for granted' occurs in Müller's work, and then try to summarize what it may say about the study of scripture. The two chief points that lead to such an evaluation are (1) Müller's view of scripture qua text, and (2) Müller's valuation of scripture vis-à-vis other dimensions of religion.

We have already looked at some features of Müller's views of scripture as a thing in itself. His generic conception of it was, in part, closely related to his view of languages and language families as the basic sources of 'great and original' religions, or 'book religions.' As was pointed out earlier, the latter notion especially shows little or no reflection or development.[8] The key point here is that, beyond the incipient secondary status for scripture that lies in its existence being conceived in terms of theories of language, there is a fundamental capacity for the devaluation of scriptures in that their existence—the fact of it—is not reflected upon with care in Müller's work.

The farthest that Müller ever went in assessing the actual process by which a scripture, as text, might come into existence was to speculate unsystematically about how traditions might have accidentally and unselectively retained various sorts of sayings, poetry, tales, and wisdom. Intrinsic qualities, circumstantial memories, and reverence for antiquity all combine in his loose notion of how some sort of process of 'scripturalization' would occur (Müller 1879:xiiff.), the principal force bonding it all together seeming to be, in Müller's mind, an association with the founder or some great teacher to whom truths were attributed and whose image it was deemed vital to preserve or enhance (Müller 1873:124ff.). The final step, as we have seen, was the community's selection of a text as an ultimately authoritative source; but at that point Müller is already far away from the underlying issue that the item in question came to exist, and in what ways this occurred.

Müller's view of scripture qua text, then, can very nearly be said to be a non-view. Sacred Books appear simply to be, and that they exist is not a significant matter. Hence there is, in the end, no difference between a 'book religion' and a 'non-book religion' that has essentially to do with the book itself. Müller neither sought nor laid a foundation for the phenomenon of the Sacred Book itself, and in that sense it is perhaps not surprising that he should ultimately have taken a view of scripture that virtually discounted the phenomenon altogether in his ultimate view of what religion was about.

---

8 See Müller 1889:552ff., especially 561-63, for a discussion that exemplifies this point.

We can see two facets to this actual devaluation of scripture. The first one appears in the way that Müller denigrated the actual texts. We have seen him speak of a "wild confusion of sublime truth and vulgar stupidity" in the very Sacred Books that he appeared so to love. Elsewhere, in perhaps the single context where one might see an inkling of a notion of the significance of the scripture itself, he said (Müller 1889:564):

> Sacred Books often become a kind of fetish, requiring an implicit and unquestioning faith; their historical or natural origin is often completely forgotten, and the old ideas of what is true and divine are almost absorbed in the one idea of what is written and orthodox.

Another telling image that occurs regularly is the notion that scriptures are especially to be studied for the sake of "any grains of truth that may be hidden beneath an accumulation of rubbish" (Müller 1889:571), an image with which Müller in fact justified the publication of The Sacred Books of the East, warning his readers that the texts themselves were bound to be a disappointment (Müller 1879:ixff.).

If one were to suggest a single basis for this part of Müller's thinking, the following would suggest itself strongly. Müller's view of scriptures was that they were a pristine source of truth that had been covered with 'rubbish' by subsequent mishandling. This putative mishandling we have already seen in the blaming of 'theologians' for advancing self-interested claims to the divine inspiration of texts; but more often it is set into the following sort of framework (Müller 1879:xv):

> . . . we must remember that those who handed down the ancestral treasures of ancient wisdom, would often feel inclined to add what seemed useful to themselves, and what they knew could be preserved in one way only, namely, if it was allowed to form part of the tradition that had to be handed down, as a sacred trust, from generation to generation. The priestly influence was at work, even before there were priests by profession, and when the priesthood had once become professional, its influence may account for much that would otherwise seem inexplicable in the sacred codes of the ancient world.

Is this simple anticlericalism? Perhaps, but it is more basically the case that Müller's view involves a sharp separation of 'scriptures,' both essentially and in terms of the goals of studying them, from other forms of religious life. In a way, to the extent that 'scriptures' had value for him, they had it in that they could, if studied correctly, take one back behind the accretions of institutions and priests and ritual. That this was part of Müller's perspective, not only as a romantic idealist but also in a general way, emerges from his reaction to post-Tractarian Oxford. Chaudhuri summarizes Müller's autobiographical recollections as follows (Chaudhuri 1974:102):

> . . . the practice and profession of religion at Oxford baffled Müller. . . . He was puzzled to see men whose learning and character he sincerely admired, absorbed in subjects which, to his mind, seemed merely childish. He expected he would hear from them some new views on the date of the gospels, the meaning of revelation, the historical value of revelation, or the early history of the Church. But of all this he heard not a word. Nothing but discussions on the validity of the Anglican orders, on vestments, genuflexion and candles, on the altar being made of wood or stone, of consecrated wine being mixed with water, of the priest turning his back on the congregation, etc.

It seems correct to offer the separation of scripture from other phenomena as the key to Müller's 'negative taking for granted.' Given that, it was not a large step for Müller to reach his own ultimate valuation of scripture, namely that it was altogether subordinate to what he viewed as 'true religion,' i.e., 'natural religion.' Hence, in the only case where he professes to be discussing the subject of scripture in and of itself, namely, in the final lecture on *Natural Religion*, entitled "Sacred Books," the ultimate outcome is this: "We must all have our own bookless religion, if the Sacred Books, whatever they be, are to find a safe and solid foundation within ourselves" (Müller 1889:569).

Müller's idealist view of religion, centering on natural religion, needs no elaboration here. But it is important to stress that, for the scholar whose name is so extraordinarily connected with Sacred Books, it eventually became possible to see scriptures as expressions *only*, as corroded vessels of a more fundamental truth. They are useful, but must ultimately be seen beyond by scholars, for along with their utility comes a capacity to obscure the basic nature of religion.

Summary

The preceding cannot pass for a full study of Müller, but it should suffice to raise a series of points about the conceptualization of scripture that can serve as measures of the present and past state of affairs. For the sake of clarity, I shall list briefly several key items that emerge from Müller's views:

a) a notion of great or world religions;
b) the influence of world-views;
c) terminology that is used unreflectively;
d) a concern for original texts and meanings;
e) a denigration of interim interpretations;
f) a somewhat indefinite but notable presence of images of the Bible;
g) a separation of scripture from other religious forms;
h) an ultimate disinterest in the fact of scripture's existence.

Having described in Müller what I clearly take to be a state of disarray in the study of scripture, I should like to point out the dimension of challenge mentioned at the outset. Is Müller typical of the past and/or present? Some effort at a judgement on that point, and at alternative approaches to scripture is the objective of the next section.

II.

A poem should not mean
But be.
—Archibald MacLeish (1952:41)
"Ars Poetica"

MacLeish's words seem especially apt at this point, though what follows uses them as a point of departure, and does not pretend to interpret them. If the foregoing survey of Max Müller suggests anything by way of a single summation that can be of use in constructive directions, it could be this: where scripture has been studied, its 'meaning' is what has been sought; and if the meaning of scripture has been devalued by scholars, the material has been disregarded. The end result, thus, is that the 'being' of scripture is left unexamined, so that the introduction of something like genuine study of scripture into the study of religion requires that this imbalance be redressed.

Such a separation into meaning and being is not meant to ignore the fact that the being of anything has, and has had, meaning most clearly in a historical sense. Ultimately, the question of scripture should in fact be brought round to the sense in which humans attach meaning to its very presence. But for now, let us take MacLeish's opposition of terms to reflect propositional, content-based meaning for scriptures, as opposed to such states of being in which we find it.

We can use the features that have been delineated in our survey of Max Müller as an outline for surveying what might result from a conscious effort to pay attention to the being of scripture. First, in place of the 'generic' assumption of a class of scriptures, alternately polyonymously and homonymously denoted,[9] what must be studied seriously is *that* scripture exists, and whether a genuinely comparable phenomenon is involved. That is no small task, but an immediate first step would be to tackle the terminological morass. For example, it may well be that Christians and biblical scholars use polyonymony for the Bible with impunity. But that is itself a religious datum, and deserves study in its own right;

[9] I could not resist these sesquipedalian terms, particularly as polyonymony was a favorite of Müller, used by him to describe the linguistic symptom (cause?) of polytheism.

it is no longer useful to use the same aggregate of terms to describe any scripture from any cultural matrix.

Therefore, where the existent status of a piece of scripture is such that its written-ness is of major importance, let us call it scripture; where the entity is appropriately treated qua book, let it be called a sacred book; and so on. If a neutral generic term is required, some debate is in order, presuming some caution about the ultimate existence of a genus. So as to make a start (and to be able to stop writing scripture), I should like to suggest 'text' (without quotation marks) as the most likely candidate, both in terms of etymology and association.[10]

Finally, a most fundamental task is to bring to light and to use with great care the proper name(s) within each tradition for the entity in question. Such a process has been steadily underway for other matters; it has taught us both to be careful and to understand more clearly such matters as *nirvāṇa, dharma, kāmi*, and even, perhaps, *tanakh*. If there are reasons why such an approach should not be taken, they need to be debated. In all of these, and surely other, ways the forms of a given text's being can begin to be addressed.

Second, as has already been hinted, the Christian Bible and its role in this matter needs to be reassessed,[11] again from the perspective of examining the fact and modes of its existence. A case in point is the existence and nature of biblical studies; and this may be as appropriate a point as any to state that, from this perspective, no confusion could be more damaging than the confusion of biblical studies with the study of texts. What wants studying is the existence of modern biblical scholarship as one of the loci of the Bible's being;[12] and one of the virtues of this perspective should be to bring more clearly into view a great and fascinating variety of other loci—something to which we shall return shortly.

Third, textual study must take on a different meaning and range than the term has signified until now. Two cases in point, of the many that might be examined in this connection, are the modern critical edition and the commentary traditions. (Also, in a very direct way, this problem-area is one of the matters that ought to be re-examined with respect to the Bible, in light of the Christian religious insistence on the text by itself, and its original meaning.)

---

10 No existing term will have no prior associations, and it is a problem to me that the term text should have been used here to describe an approach to scripture that is less than complete. However, text has the sense of "structured unit," or "internal structure" at its etymological base, and thus offers what I think is a creditable generic option.

11 This is already occurring within biblical studies, a point that ought not be overlooked. As an example, I should cite several of the chapters in Freedman and O'Connor 1983. A number of other authors and publications could be cited.

12 Wilfred Cantwell Smith, whose work on scripture has been of enormous aid to and influence on me, first enunciated this in his essay, "The Study of Religion and the Study of the Bible" (Smith 1971).

As to the critical edition, we need to examine seriously the possibility that such a text-form has no being, or that its being is a very special, new thing. Paul Ricoeur (1979:271) has observed that a critically edited text no longer is a sacred text, but rather a scholar's text. That very judgement needs to be reflected upon, especially in reference to recent times, but it points to the heart of the problem. Directly related to this is the fact that the most egregrious lacuna in the study of text-forms is this: we do not take seriously the history of the form itself, and too often simply assume, for example, a continuity between the Tripiṭaka of the Pali Text Society and that of the Buddhists a millenium ago. One wonders—one is obliged by the state of scholarship to wonder—what the state of the text-form itself over that millenium could reveal; and one wonders at our failure to take seriously the impact of modern, European-inspired text-editions on recent religious history.

As to the commentary traditions, Holmes Welch, in discussing the matter of translations of Chinese texts, made the following observations (Welch 1957:12):

> Until this century no Chinese, if he decided to read the *Analects* of Confucius, would ignore the Commentary. He would turn to it after reading every clause—if he had not already learnt it by heart. Written hundreds or many hundreds of years after the original text, the Commentary explained what each clause meant, sometimes each word in each clause, even where the meaning was already clear. After consulting it our Chinese reader might have to turn to the Subcommentary. This was a higher stratum of trot, written hundreds or many hundreds of years after the Commentary. It explained what the Commentary had failed to explain in the text, or what was clear in the text and had been garbled by the Commentary, or difficulties not in the text but raised by the Commentary itself. All this could only work like compound interest: it has left a vast accumulation. On every one of the major classics hundreds of commentaries and subcommentaries have been written, often running to several times the length of the classic itself.

One simply has to ask, and not only for the Chinese tradition, what a full awareness of the role and place of commentaries would do for our sense of the being of any text.

Finally, and in relation to our review of Max Müller's taking scripture negatively for granted, we need to deal with the difficult problem of the discounting or subordination of texts in favor of other forms or loci for understanding religious traditions. Here, ultimately, is the question of whether texts have meaning in and of themselves, and if so, how; or whether they must finally be seen as symbols, or as parts of social-structuring mechanisms; or, in another dimension of devaluation, whether they must be discounted as products of the 'great' tradition, not fully valuable as evidence for the study of religion or culture—a perspective that Müller was closer to than one might have thought. To begin to tackle this difficult matter, I wish to take us back to a particular feature of Müller's view of texts, and then to suggest a way of looking at texts that may be of use in a search for a way beyond the 'negative taking for granted' that has happened to scripture.

The element in Müller's view is the separation of texts from other forms of religious activity. This, I would suggest, springs not from the nature of texts at all, but from recent scholarly use of them, a mode of use that is consistent with, if not informed by—and an informer of—the Christian use of its text in recent times, which also reflects a would-be separation of it from a wide range of visible and apparently universal religious behavior.

By way of contrast, it is most intriguing to try to see texts not as separate from—or in opposition to—myth, ritual, and symbol, and the institutional structures that are associated with such forms of religiosity, but rather as related to them in various ways, even as they are related to each other. This emphatically means that texts must not be seen as being subsumed in other forms, any more than they should be separated from them.

To make this possible view of texts concrete, I should like to propose a typology for understanding the way in which texts exist within the context of the full range of religious activity. The proposed typology is the following: that texts can be seen as occurring in two general forms, which can be called Canon I and Canon II. The obvious paucity of terminological genius is regrettable, but the prosaic choice does have a rationale. "Canon" is used because of the way in which its basic meaning (that of law/rule, fundamental axiom, principle, or standard) lends itself to the understanding of textual status. It is important to understand that Canon I and Canon II each can and do occur within single religious traditions, the two even existing simultaneously at times, and perhaps even being simultaneous dimensions of the same text. In both Canon I and Canon II the underlying etymologically true sense of 'canon' is active; but the ways in which Canons I and II are actually present in a tradition are significantly different, and the failure to perceive this difference is the major cause of confusion in dealing with 'scriptures.'

What, then, is meant by these terms? Canon I denotes normative texts, oral or written, that are present in a religious tradition principally by the force of a vector or vectors. Canon II refers to normative texts that are more independently and distinctively present within a tradition, i.e., as pieces of literature more or less as such are currently thought of, and which themselves often function as vectors.

Further explanation is clearly in order, though types of material will be explained by example, below. By 'vector' is meant the means or mode by which something is carried; in this usage I wish to approximate the biological sense in which the word vector is otherwise used, despite the common association of it with mathematics. By way of example: the mosquito is spoken of as the vector of malaria. The intended sense, moreover, is not merely that of 'carrying'; otherwise 'tradition' might be made to do. Rather, what is intended is a virtually organic relationship between carrier and thing carried, so that the two operate in more than a purely mechanical relationship. Thus the place of Canon I in a tradition is largely due to its being vectored by some other form of religious activity; such a text cannot be fully perceived without reference to its vector and to the relationship between the two. The same is true of religious activities that are being vectored by a Canon II text.

The most common vector of Canon I is ritual activity, but other significant vectors are also to be found. Canon II most commonly serves as a vector of religious authority, but is also often a vector of ritual iconolatry and individualist piety. By giving careful attention to both the vectors and the activity or form of Canon, some significant new insights into textual status may be possible. At the very least, what this approach can accomplish is to bring texts into relationship with ritual (Canon I) and symbol (Canon II).

Clearly a word of caution is in order. The proposed typology does not presume a causal or developmental relationship between Canons I and II, nor am I ready to assert that it solves the full problem of relating texts to traditions in a satisfactory way. In particular, it is not proposed by way of arguing that propositional, content-related 'meaning' is not also an essential part of the status of texts. Finally, the preceding paragraphs may strike one as the sort of terminological obfuscation better left to working groups at academic conventions. The latter issue is best dealt with by testing the approach, and to that end, we turn now to consideration of two text-situations: the Jain tradition, and the Christian.

III.

To show clearly the utility of the typology, it will be used here to explore two blocs of scriptural material. This process will also enable us to see some of the subtypes that can be found within each larger category of Canon. The first example will be the normative texts of the Jain tradition; the second will be the Christian Bible.[13]

From almost the earliest scholarly efforts to portray the Jains up to the most recent, it has been held that the Jains have a specific, clearly delimited body of scripture consisting of some 45 texts in various fixed categories. It has been

13 See the appendix to this chapter for a discussion of Jñāna-pañcamī omitted from the last draft of the chapter.

assumed that this bloc of scripture dates to the period around 500 C.E., when it was edited into a collection; and it is further assumed that individual parts of this bloc existed as scripture throughout some six to eight preceding centuries. It is also widely held that one community of Jains, the Śvetāmbaras, accept this scripture while another community, the Digambaras, reject it out of hand. Such has been the general portrait of the Jain scriptures since the 1870s; yet there are several nagging problems associated with it that refuse to go away.

The first problem is that texts from the sixth century C.E. (after or contemporary with the editing of the collection) do not, when they describe the Jains' normative literature, list the same texts as are given in the current portrait, nor restrict themselves to 45 titles, nor use the same categories for the texts. Bedeviled by these inconsistencies, scholars have generally chalked up the variations to loss of texts, alterations, or other accidental causes; but no satisfying accounting for the differences has been put forward.

The second problem is that when one asks contemporary Jains what their scriptures are, one receives widely varying answers, responses that vary not because of ignorance, but because there does not appear to be a wholly accepted body of scripture that is of equal value to the entire community. Moreover, it does not appear true that the Digambaras routinely reject the body of texts ostensibly accepted by the Śvetāmbaras; certainly this proposition must be significantly qualified.

Amid all of this welter, examination of the history of Jain scholarship reveals a signal fact: the 45-text body of literature was originally put forward as the 'Jain scriptures' by one scholar, George Bühler, who was relied upon on this point by all others in the nineteenth and early twentieth centuries. Bühler obtained his information from a single oral source within the Jain community; and while he found it attested by other oral sources, he also knew that it did not jibe with still other such sources, or with the older literary testimony. Yet he put it forward, and lived to see it perpetuated by other scholars.

Beyond this, a charming anomaly surfaced very early in Jain scholarship. When Hermann Jacobi was asked to make translations of Jain texts for The Sacred Books of the East, one of the first two texts so translated and published was the *Kalpa Sūtra*. Yet, as Jacobi had to admit, the *Kalpa Sūtra* that was being published as a sacred book was not in the 45-text scripture bloc.[14] Despite this,

[14] [Editor's note.] Folkert made a slight, uncharacteristic error here. When Jacobi published his critical edition of the *Kalpa Sūtra* in 1879, he wrote, "the Kalpasutra . . . does not belong to the Āgamas or sacred books of the Jainas" (Jacobi 1879:22). In fact, the *Kalpa Sūtra* is the eighth part of the *Daśāśrutaskandha*, one of the four Cheda Sūtras. This was noted by Weber in his "Uber die heiligen Schriften der Jaina" (Weber 1883-85), and the correction duly noted by Jacobi in the introduction to his English translation of the *Kalpa Sūtra* (Jacobi 1884:lii). But the *Kalpa Sūtra*, edited, translated, and understood by scholars as an independent 'scripture,' is not an independent entity in the list of 45 Āgamas.

he chose it because of its enormous popularity and value to the community, a fact that is attested by the *Kalpa Sūtra*'s overwhelming presence in manuscript collections and its dominance as a text chosen for illustration by manuscript artists. Therefore, far from being a minor matter associated with obscure texts, the problem of inconsistency in the Jain scriptures proved to be an immediate difficulty for scholars. Yet the notion of the 45-text bloc continued to be put forward.

What were Bühler and the others doing? The simplest answer, and the one that permits the best explanation of the whole range of problems involved, is this: Bühler superimposed a Canon II model of scripture onto a tradition whose literature was of the Canon I variety. This conclusion can be illuminated by reference to two critical points.

First, scriptural material of the Canon I type needs to be understood at all times in terms of its vectors. The Jain tradition exhibits both the ritual-activity-vector mentioned above, and others as well; and the place of scriptures in Jain religious life is only fully intelligible in terms of the vectors to be found in various situations. The problem of the *Kalpa Sūtra* clarifies itself at once in these terms, for the text in question is vectored by a major ritual activity. It is festively read aloud in a communal gathering during Paryuṣaṇa, the penitential/confessional period at the end of the Jain religious year, a ritual time of intense activity for the entire community. Hence the *Kalpa Sūtra* finds its prominence in the Jain community; hence it is one of the texts most frequently copied and illustrated; hence Jains speak of it as a normative text, a scripture. That it is not found in the 45-text bloc of scriptures is not even a matter of moment in the community.

One more example: the older, sixth-century accounts of the Jains' texts that are at variance with the 45-text model are also vectored by specific religious activities. They are carried largely by a ritually structured monastic course of instruction, one that leaps into view as soon as the commentaries on the texts are drawn into the picture. And so the variances between the older accounts and the 45-text model are not simply the result of happenstance; or, at least, the older model was not merely the prototype of the more recent one, with loss and confusion intervening. But the rationale for the older model will not emerge from the texts alone; its vector finally clarifies its status.

One notes also that this latter vector is discoverable only with the aid of the commentaries on the texts; and this leads to the second critical point concerning Bühler's superimposition of Canon types. Canon II scripture is, among other major features, especially characterized by being viewed as independently valid and powerful, and as such, as being absolutely closed and complete. What is in Canon II is normative, true, and binding; what is outside of it is secondary in all these respects. Therefore, for Bühler and his successors, the existence of different accounts of the range and contents of the Jain scriptures posed a problem, but this problem does not necessarily affect the Jains. In Canon I instances, the vector and its validity are at least as determinative as any limit on the scripture itself. Further, scholars who thought (and think) of scriptures in Canon II modes are likely to do what Jain scholars have done: they ignore or depreciate the commentaries. Some exoneration is called for here, since the commentaries were often not fully accessible to scholars. Yet, in their Canon II orientation, the early editors and translators did not wait for or insist on a full commentorial context before pushing ahead with publication and analysis of the scriptures. Nor need one look far ahead in the study of religion to see numerous similar cases in the handling of traditions other than the Jain.

It appears, then, that the Canon I Jain texts have been much obscured, and their role in Jain religious history and life much misunderstood, in virtue of their having been forced into a Canon II mold; it is hoped that this example has shed some light on the working of the Canons I and II typology. Yet this method of treating scripture is not necessarily of full value if it illuminates only one tradition, or if it springs only from a peculiar example of misapplied concepts in comparative religion. A greater text of its value is to turn it onto the tradition that informed the Western scholars, i.e., to test it on the Bible itself. And so we turn to our second example.

The basic thesis is simple: that the Protestant Bible is a Canon II phenomenon, and that through much of Christian religious history, and even still at present, the Bible also functions—at times even prominantly functions—as a Canon I text. The startling fact is that scholars have not only imposed Canon II models onto non-Christian traditions; they have also, as Wilfred Cantwell Smith has pointed out, forgotten the rich multi-dimensionality of the Bible's own role within Christianity. The loosely held, but dominant, Protestant model of the Bible mentioned earlier is also the dominant model for 'biblical studies,' and it is an altogether Canon II model.

How, specifically, does the adoption of Canons I and II in viewing the Bible shed light on its status as a phenomenon? To see this quickly, it is possible to look at two areas of material and evidence. The first is the use of the Bible in Christian churches, and the second is the problem of the Christian relationship to the Hebrew scriptures.

It is an interesting exercise to observe the specific status and use of the Bible in various Christian denominations. The available evidence is obvious, and significant. Two basic questions can be asked: (1) how are the Bible's contents used in the church service? and (2) what is the Bible's physical status, qua book, in the service and church building?

With respect to the first question, one observes an immediate division within Christianity between churches that use a lectionary and those that use the Bible's contents in a more random fashion. In the former case, the contents of the Bible are clearly being vectored. They are carried by the ritual pattern of the Christian year, and are even more specifically vectored by the internal rhythm of the service itself—for example, a Lesson from the Old Testament, a Psalm, a Lesson or Epistle from the New Testament, and finally, hedged by chanting and changing postures, a Gospel portion. In those churches that do not use a lectionary, such clear patterns of vectoring are not prominent; nor even would the theologies of some such churches accept any such limitation on or division within the scripture and its use. It is also clear that significant correspondence exists between churches that use a lectionary and churches whose emphasis in worship is eucharistic, i.e., the greater prominence of ritual communion is linked to a structured 'carrying' of the Bible.

With respect to the second question, it is also clear that churches differ markedly in terms of the Bible's physical presence. In some churches, an oversized Bible is prominently displayed, and is usually accompanied by the presence of Bibles in the pews. In others, nary a Bible, oversized or not, is to be found. And again, the correspondence holds: the presence of a ritual vector implies the physical absence of the Bible. Also highly revealing is the link between Bible and clergyman; here one consistently observes a range of phenomena, from no visible link at all, to the presence of the Bible on the lectern before the clergyman, to the physical holding of the Bible by the clergyman. Once more, the correspondence holds: the clergyman whose role is ritual/priestly has no Bible; the Protestant evangelist sports his aloft, elevated in his hand.

For all of this material the Canon I and II typology is most apt. The observer would conclude that the liturgical churches' Bible is clearly best understood, if one is seeking its full function in the community, as a Canon I phenomenon; and that the non-liturgical churches' Bible is of a Canon II variety. The typology can be further verified by noting that the Canon II Bible, while not being vectored by the ritual processes of eucharist and sacred calendar, is itself vectoring at least two things: (1) its physical presence as an 'icon' of sorts in churches is a clear index of those churches near-veneration of it as a sacred book; and (2) its link with clergymen is a sign of its capacity to vector authority (this latter point may be reduced to an axiom: the fewer bishops, the more Bibles).

In terms of this essay's general context, the following is clear: the Protestant churches, by and large, are those whose Bible is Canon II. And the specific patterns of use in those churches correspond to basic assumptions that provide the framework for 'Biblical Studies': (1) that the entire Bible is of equal significance in all its parts, and that the reading and study of all of it is a necessary and even salvific task (the parallel is to the random use of the whole Bible in church services); (2) that the Bible itself is the chief focus of concern, and that, though its contextual setting—rites, commentaries, and other religious acts—may be useful to the scholar, they are distinctly secondary in value (parallel: the iconization of the 'Bible' as a distinct physical object); and (3) that biblical studies itself is an absolutely distinctive and separate discipline from the tasks of theology, church history, and liturgics (parallel: that authority in the church is vectored by the Bible).

These observations concerning the Christian Bible, and the way in which biblical studies reflect only a portion of its multiple character, can be related back to the general utility of the Canon I and II typology simply by substituting into the three propositions given above the word *Siddhānta* (the most common indigenous Jain term for the 45-text scriptures discussed earlier). The result is three basic misperceptions of the Jains' normative texts, all of which cease to apply when those texts are considered in a Canon I context. Even more revealing is the fact that these misperceptions would come distressingly close to describing the modes of thought that have long governed the study of religious literature in non-Christian traditions; the reader is invited to substitute his or her own choice of non-Christian normative text in order to test the proposition.

To finish off the presentation of examples from the Christian heritage, it will be useful to cite very briefly the problem of the Hebrew scriptures, and to offer a thesis that still requires detailed exploration. It is this: the Old Testament, i.e., the Hebrew scriptures as Christians use them, had themselves undergone a process of becoming Canon II materials *within* Judaism prior to their inclusion in Christianity's body of texts. As such, the Law, Prophets, and Writings as they stand are once-removed from many of their original vectors; and the Old Testament does not contain many things that were vectored by activities once prominent in Israelite religion and now gone, e.g., liturgical materials.

This Judaic Canon II was then used, as best it could be, in various Canon I modes in Christianity prior to the Protestant Reformation—a reversal, almost, of the squeezing into molds done by scholars of non-Christian scriptures. Finally, with the rise of the Canon II Protestant Bible, those Hebrew texts underwent a second de-vectoring, so to speak, with interpretive consequences whose permutations are truly dazzling.

The foregoing proposals for new looks at both Christian and Jain scriptures in the light of Canon I and II analysis should be—and are meant to be—provocative. But they also constitute as serious as possible a typological proposal. Such a venture calls out for at least one more thing, in addition to the detailed working-out of its theses: a "Concluding Anti-Reductionist Postscript." The power, the sacredness, of the word/text is not truly seized by such functional analyses alone. Yet our approaches to the problem of scripture must be pushed onward, and a broader view with systematic force developed, if we are to escape the one-dimensional view of the Bible and of other texts that our unwitting reliance on Canon II models and modes has generated. Now to begin.

APPENDIX 1[15]

In connexion with the antiquity of the Jaina scriptures it is interesting to notice that once a year a fast is observed called Jñāna pañcamī, on which day all Jaina sacred books are not only worshipped but also dusted, freed from insects and rearranged. If only this custom prevailed with regard to all English parish registers, how many of our records might have been saved!

—Mrs. Sinclair Stevenson (1915:261-62)

The Jain tradition, in its 2,500 historically attested years, has generated a rich textual heritage that occidental scholars have only partially understood, and that we will try to grasp by means of the categories of Text and Canon. I open with Mrs. Stevenson's field-observation of the Śvetāmbara festival of Jñāna-pañcamī (the "Knowledge-Fifth," which is celebrated by Digambaras as Śruta-pañcamī, the "Śruta-knowledge-fifth") because the latter presents a good brief introduction to our approach, and because Mrs. Stevenson's field notes on the Jain scriptures can effectively punctuate and illustrate our analyses, both in this case and in others. Writing in the early twentieth century, Mrs. Stevenson could be reasonably confident that she understood the meaning and general content of basic Jain religious texts; the considerable efforts of a handful of scholars from about 1850 onwards had seen to that. But neither she nor her predecessors grasped the status, the being, of those texts within the Jain tradition, and that state of affairs still holds.

Jñāna-pañcamī, as Mrs. Stevenson saw it, was not an occasion where the meaning or content of the texts was involved, and so she notes it only as testifying to the Jains' achievements as preservers of text-libraries. But the festival actually shows quite effectively the utility of Canons I and II as ways of seeing the status of Texts (including the way in which the two Canons can be virtually simultaneous dimensions of a Text's status in certain settings), and it also makes a point about terminology. For at Jñāna-pañcamī, the Texts' vector is a ritual and calendrical event; but the Texts also serve as a vector for the authoritative knowledge (*jñāna*) that is at the heart of the Jain religious ideal. Moreover, the term sacred book is finally appropriate as a description of the

15 [Editor's note.] The following is from an earlier draft of this chapter, and was deleted by the author from the last version. I include it here, however, because it sheds light both on Folkert's model of Canon I and Canon II, and on earlier scholarly understandings of the Jain canon. The draft went on to include extensive material from chapter 3, above, on the history of the evolution of the occidental understanding of the Jain canon. I have skipped over this material and concluded with a section existing only as a hand-written draft, which evidently was to serve as the basis for a more extensive treatment of the Jain canon. For an extension and development of the argument put forward by Folkert in this chapter, see Cort 1991b.

Text-form that is concretely present. Hence, in this small example, the status of texts can be seen and accounted for even where the matter of content-related meaning is difficult to grasp or elucidate.

With this approach to Jñāna-pañcamī in mind, we can turn to three major arenas of concern in understanding Jain textual life, each of which has posed some difficulty for occidental scholarship. They are: (1) the nature of the Jain canon; (2) the status of a particular text, the *Kalpa Sūtra*; and (3) the layperson's use of the scriptures. In all three, a sense of the being of texts within the Jain tradition has been wanting, and explaining these instances should provide insight into both the tradition and our categories.

The Jain Canon

It is commonly held that the Jains have a canon of some 45 extant texts, and that this canon was established by the Śvetāmbara Jains but is rejected by the Digambaras, while preserved in modified form (containing only 32 texts) by the more recent reform movement of the Sthānakvāsīs. The oldest textual materials in this canon appear, on linguistic grounds, to have been fixed ca. 300 B.C.E., and its most recent material may have been added as much as a millenium later. But this canon is not a very tidy collection. The total number of texts, their division into classes, the names of the classes, and even the particular texts are all problematic points.

When Mrs. Stevenson inquired into the matter, she was obliged to report that the numerous sub-groups of Śvetāmbara Jains whom she encountered in Gujarat "hold different views as to the correct list of books rightly comprised in their canon," and in the end, as "one . . . list from among those that have been given to the writer," (Stevenson 1915:13) she provided a canonical listing that generally resembles, but is on several points different from, the one given above in chapter 1. Yet the list reproduced above is given by virtually every scholar of the Jains as representing the canon, with the known variations largely left out of reckoning.

One of occidental scholarship's first steps in dealing with the Jain textual tradition was to seek out the limits of the sacred library (to use Müller's phrase) of the Jain scriptures. The Jains' own collective terms for such materials are *Āgama* and *Siddhānta* ('tradition' and 'doctrine,' if any direct translation of the terms is possible), which scholars replaced with the terms "canon" and "canonical literature." No reflection on this significant matter is to be found in the writings of the early students of the Jains, yet the force with which it has shaped our perceptions of the *Āgamas* is extraordinary.

The quest for a body of canonical literature yielded results, such that it is now commonly held that the Jains have a specific, clearly delimited body of scripture consisting of some 45 texts in various fixed categories.[16]

But the truth of the matter is this: one must wonder about the reliability of the standard portrait of the Jain scriptures given in virtually every account of the Jains available today, certainly insofar as it applies to the tradition's earlier history, and even to the extent that it claims to represent the more recent tradition. Further—and here is the more striking feature of this whole matter—one cannot feel assured that this literature constitutes a canon in any way that makes the unreflective use of the term meaningful. For the scholars who transmuted *Āgama* into canon understood the literature in question to be what the term connoted for them: a specified body of text that is closed, i.e., that admits of no open-endedness or alteration. It is on the basis of this presupposition that the standard list can be insisted upon as being valid through Jain history.

And there is still more to this tale. Having discovered that the Digambara Jains do not regard the texts of the Śvetāmbaras as being authentic, scholars took the step of treating the Digambara dissent from the texts as if it were a dissent from the canon. The Digambara Jains' textual tradition has thus been characterized as a secondary canon, and has been treated as if it were a conscious imitation of the former; the Digambara textual history has thereby been relegated to a distinctly secondary position in all accounts of the Jain scriptures. We will return to the specifics of this problem of the Digambara textual tradition; for now, the point is that this common portrait of the Digambaras reveals a second characteristic of the notion of canon as scholars used it of the Jain tradition: that the act of subscribing to a canon of texts is a distinctive feature of a religious movement.

Both of these features of canon—its closed nature and its capacity to distinguish religious movements—have been described earlier as dimensions of Canon II. The best way to understand the entire scrambled history of scholarly dealings with the Jain tradition may simply be this: the superimposition of a Canon II model of textual status onto a textual history that has strong Canon I characteristics. In order to see this, and to see the tradition itself more clearly, so that we need not merely reject the standard portrait and have nothing to put in its place, let us return to the earliest Jain accounts of the *Āgama* or *Siddhānta*, and try to understand anew the process of canonization within the tradition.

---

16 [Editor's note.] Refer here to the discussion of the evolution of the standard portrait of the Jain canon in chapter 4, above.

Āgama and *Siddhānta*, as general collective terms, are supplemented in the Jain tradition by several others. Important for our understanding of the tradition are:

1) *nigganṭha-pāvayaṇa* (the teachings [*pāvayaṇa*] of the unfettered one [*nigganṭha*, i.e., *Tīrthaṅkara*]), which refers simply to the teachings themselves;
2) *duvālas-aṅga gaṇi-piḍaga* (the "basket" [*piḍaga*] of the teachers [*gaṇi*] that has twelve [*duvālas*] parts [*aṅga*]), which has reference to a Text-form, namely, the 12 *Aṅga*s;
3) *suya-ṇāṇa* (knowledge [*ṇāṇa*] gained through specific sources of transmission [*suya*]), a general term for one of five types of knowledge, that came to be applied especially to the knowledge that one gains from Texts, i.e., from things "heard" (*suya*) (Mālvaṇiā 1968:11).
4) *sutta*, the term most commonly used as a general term for Text.

Āgama itself, as a term for what is "received" (*ā-gam*), or for "tradition," is also specified by Jains when it is used of texts, though it is also used generally as we shall use it here; and the term *suya*, uncombined with *ṇāṇa*, is also at times broken down into sub-classes when applied to Texts. For example, in reference to the content or intent of the text, *suya* is spoken of as *bhāvasuya*, "essential" *suya*; while the text-materials (books, pages, etc.) are *davvasuya*, "material" *suya* (Mālvaṇiā 1968:11).

When this is all recast into a somewhat overgeneralized statement, one can say that the Jain view of their texts is roughly as follows: the Texts, or *Sutta*s, transmit *suya-ṇāṇa*, a particular kind of knowledge; the core of *suya-ṇāṇa* is contained in the *duvālasaṅga-gaṇipiḍaga*, the twelve-part vehicle composed by the teachers; this *duvālasaṅga-gaṇipiḍaga* transmits the *nigganṭha-pāvayaṇa*, the teachings of the Tīrthaṅkara. This systematic view of the status of the Texts rests, finally, on a specific image of how the Tīrthaṅkara transmits his teachings. According to tradition, a Tīrthaṅkara's instruction, the *nigganṭha-pāvayaṇa*, takes the form of a supernal sound, a *divyadhvani*, which transmits to his hearers the import, or *artha*, of the teachings. This import is then transmuted into the *gaṇi-piḍaga* by the Tīrthaṅkara's chief followers, or *gaṇadhara*s ("leaders" [*dhara*] of the "community" [*gaṇa*]).

As one might conclude from the definition of *duvālasaṅga-gaṇipiḍaga*, this vision of the nature of Texts applies primarily to the 12 *Aṅga*s, and any discussion of the Jain textual tradition needs to treat the *Aṅga*s as a special category of Text, with special problems. Drawing this line around the *Aṅga*s is, then, a necessary first step in clarifying our view of Jain texts, and is a step fully consistent with the tradition's own treatment of them.

The next step, before returning to the *Aṅga*s, is to ask: what about the rest of the texts? The answer is clear. From early on the Jains operated with two categories of texts: *Aṅga*-texts, and non-*Aṅga*-texts, or *aṅgabāhya* texts. Further, the *aṅgabāhya* texts were not simply a random collection of material that fell outside the status of *niggantha-pāvayaṇa*. They were organized according to their status within the religious life of the community. The principle of organization derived from a basic element in Jain religious practice: the *āvaśyaka*s, "essentials," i.e., six religious duties incumbent upon every Jain ascetic.

Therefore, the *aṅgabāhya* texts are found to have been organized into *āvaśyaka*-texts and non-*āvaśyaka* (*āvaśyaka-vyatirikta*) texts. This organization was further developed by applying the notion that there were certain texts that were to be studied at fixed times, and other texts that might be studied at any time (*kāliya* and *ukkāliya* texts.) This pattern of organization [which is reproduced in chapter 4, above] underlies the text-accounts from the late-fifth century, the manuscripts that so radically differ from the standard account based on Bühler.

APPENDIX 2[17]

I.

'Text' must be the term of choice, at the simplest level to cut through the welter of would-be synonymns, but more seriously, to take a first step toward a proper perception of the phenomenon, for the gravest problem in the study of scriptures has been the (unwitting?) treatment of them (1) simply as documents, and (2) if religiously, as if they were Protestant-style Bibles.

In the first instance, texts have been treated as documentary evidence for the nature of traditions, or more cautiously as the products or exponents of 'great traditions' and in that connection are often discounted in the end. (Max Müller was more modern than often is thought.)

In the second instance, presumptions are made that are unwarranted about the way texts are treated. At the simplest level, it is assumed that people meet the text by reading (alone) something written or printed. At another level, it is presumed that the text is the touchstone for all of the teachings of the tradition, and that it is the ultimate authority in matters of faith. At yet another level, it is presumed that the tradition treats the text as being of uniform value throughout, each part of it being equally important as a source and authority.

But if the truth be known, the study of religions—as opposed to the social sciences or biblical studies—has generally muddled along doing some of both, mixing the two approaches quite indiscriminately. (Max Müller and The Sacred Books of the East are an almost classic example of this.)

The study of religions must carve out its own space on this business, particularly in terms of the establishment of text as a genuine religious phenomenon, and its relationship to other phenomenon, specifically ritual and symbol.

This essay is particularly addressed toward that goal.

II.

1. The study of scripture (or, preferably, of Texts; see #2 below) actually ought to carry us back to basic debates about the nature of religious traditions. Texts cannot be regarded as 'independent' testimony to the traditions. The way

---

[17] [Editor's note.] These two short pieces are included for the clear summary they provide of Folkert's thinking on the subject of scripture. The first piece is a handwritten manuscript found among his notes for this chapter. The second is the summary observation he wrote for the 1984 N.E.H. summer seminar under Wilfred Cantwell Smith which provided the impetus for this chapter.

that we seek to understand the status, the being, of texts must be consistent with the whole of our approaches to the whole of traditions. (This is so, I believe, in W. C. Smith's work.) The heart of our past difficulties is the separation of Texts from other religious phenomena, both as phenomena and in the study of phenomena; but note: the problem is 'separation,' not the 'distinguishing' of Texts. The latter must be done.

2. The term of choice for me is Text. Scripture means something written (if not printed) and, too commonly for me to get past it, appropriated by reading—commonly by and to oneself. The field of study could, of course, be reduced to written Texts, and distinguishing such phenomena would be a positive step. But this would be too restricted, it seems to me. The phenomenon as a whole embraces a broad sense of Text: that fabric of a tradition, if you will, which has language as its primary locus, and which can be distinguished as to specific cultural loci and roles. Texts, finally, do (I think) constitute a genus, and a text's place in religious life can be diagrammed as follows:

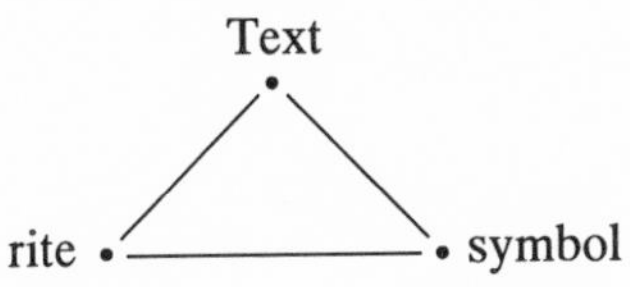

None of these can be reduced to the other two; all function in varying relationships to one another, with each sometimes primary, sometimes co-present in religious settings.

3. The notion of 'synesthetics' in connection with Texts tantalizes me. Texts (and even Scriptures) are appreciated in a whole range of ways: the sound of them, heard and said and sung; the sight of them, seen and in the making; the touch of them—all are real dimensions of the relationship between text and community, text and individual.

6

The Jain Scriptures and the History of Jainism*

THE STUDY OF 'SCRIPTURE' AS A CATEGORY IN COMPARATIVE RELIGION

This study stems from a problem in undergraduate teaching and course-conception, and deals with an area in scholarship that is in need of reconception. Within the field of comparative religion, the major subject area of the study of 'scripture' is still conceived in terms inherited from older, more sectarian models. In the study of scripture, comparative religion has had surprisingly little impact in shaping the study of religion as an academic, humanistic enterprise. Most departments of religion in public, non-sectarian universities still have courses in teaching positions designated for biblical studies. This approach contributes to keeping the study of Christianity outside of the mainstream of comparative religion, and has also seriously affected the study of non-Christian religions. This study seeks to examine this model for the study of religious texts, and to contribute to re-thinking 'scriptural' studies in the academic enterprise.

Both in the general course ("Introduction to Religion") that I teach and in my courses on specific religious traditions, the problem of placing and dealing

* Edited from six grant proposals dated between 1980 and 1984, and the abstract from "Canon and the Process of Canonization: The Jains and the *Pañc-Pratikramaṇa Sūtras*," paper given at the 1983 Annual Meeting of the American Academy of Religion.

with 'scriptures' is always prominent. It can be as simple (but also complex) as whether to have students read primary sources directly in translation (such as the Bhagavadgītā), and if so, how to teach students properly what the actual use and significance of such a text is within that particular tradition. Or the problem may take the form of having to 'teach around' an introductory textbook's assumption of a category of 'sacred texts,' as the presence of such a category almost always tempts undergraduates to think of scriptures in terms parallel to their understanding of the Christian Bible.

In addition to the above classroom-oriented concern, I have a curricular interest in the question of scriptures, with which I grappled for some years as department chair. In baldly practical terms, the problem is how, or even whether, a department of religion should offer courses in 'Biblical Studies' that are basically undergraduate versions of courses such as 'Introduction to the New Testament,' that would be found at a divinity school. The range of issues raised by this problem is enormous, having to do with student expectations at one extreme, and with fundamental questions of methodology in the study of religion at the other extreme. It is my own view that biblical studies represent a major blind spot in our understanding of the study of religion, a blind spot that also obscures our approach to Judaic studies and Christian studies. Such a view, however, is hard to sell in most college or university departments of religion.

A major failing in phenomenology of religion and comparative religion has been the unreflective assumption of 'scripture' as a universal feature of religious traditions. The classic phenomenologists and historians of religion such as Gerardus van der Leeuw and Mircea Eliade have left scripture virtually unexplored. From the nineteenth century heyday of the study of religious texts up to the present, the study of religion has unfailingly presumed that the study of 'sacred books' (cf. Max Müller's great project, The Sacred Books of the East) was an automatic entrée to the comparative study of religion.

I do not deny that great bodies of religious literature are central to religious traditions, and are highly valued by them. In other words, I do not propose to bifurcate religion into 'great'/literate and 'little'/illiterate traditions. Rather, I seek to examine not only 'scripture' itself, but also changing religious attitudes toward scripture as religious phenomena in need of far more acute study and elucidation than they have been given until now.

Three examples may serve to show the range of general and comparative concerns involved. First, mention has been made of nineteenth century Western approaches to the study of religion. It is likely (but in need of exploration) that the early scholars of comparative religion attributed to the religious literatures of non-Christian cultures the same importance and status that the Bible held in the West at that time. Two nineteenth century religious attitudes toward the Bible are notable here: (1) for Protestants, it had assumed the status of being *the* normative source of religious values and teachings; and (2) it was a written, book-form source, whose written words were to speak for themselves wherever possible, i.e., it was truly 'scripture.' It is demonstrable, but generally forgotten, that neither of these religious attitudes toward the Bible were uniformly present throughout the history of Christianity. What appears to have occurred is that a particular set of Christian attitudes toward the Bible unduly influenced the approach taken by scholars to the literature of other religions. These other literatures thus came to be (and still are) treated as 'Bibles.'

The two additional examples show this. In the study of Chinese religion it came to be, and still is, in vogue to present single texts as 'sacred books' (for example, the *Analects* of Confucius or the *Tao Te Ching*). However, the Chinese themselves have never treated these as isolated texts, or as 'Bibles.' They are not, by themselves, normative sources. They are consistently given new interpretation, both orally and by means of monumental layers of written commentary. To study Chinese religion by reading these as 'sacred books' is severely restrictive.

In the study of the Hindu tradition much the same approach was taken, for example, to the Veda. However, the Veda is not a book, strictly speaking. At best it is a missal, or hymnal; and most important, the Veda has no religious function as a book. The words of the Veda must be intoned to have any power in Hindu eyes: it is the words of the Veda that matters, not the written form.

THE JAIN SCRIPTURES AND THE STUDY OF JAINISM

The Jain scriptures have been given a standard, stereotypical scholarly treatment since the late nineteenth century, thanks to two factors. First, there has been very little study of the Jains in the Western scholarly world, despite their durable and influential presence in Indian culture for over 2,500 years. Thus the standard portrayals of Jain history, and of the major features of Jain religion (such as the scriptures), have not been significantly re-examined since early in the period of Western Indological studies. Second, a basically Christian presupposition about the nature of scriptures and sacred texts has informed most of our study of the Jain scriptures and of the history of Jainism. This presupposition has not been self-consciously examined by Western scholars.

The history of Jain scriptures has been understood very poorly, largely as the result of nineteenth-century views both of the Jains and of the phenomenon of scripture. As concerns the former point, very little attention has been paid to the Jains' actual use of their sacred texts, especially the layperson's view of them. In conformity with the view of religious movements prevalent in the nineteenth century, scholars focused on the Jain ascetic, assuming that lay practice was largely a 'lower' form of the tradition. This focus also led to a concentration on the older literature, which is dominated by ascetic concerns.

This bias was not unusual for its time, but its effects were compounded by the nineteenth-century view of scripture. In sum, scholars conceived of religious literature in other traditions on the model of the Protestant Christian view of the Bible, which can be summarized as follows:

> The sacred literature of a tradition, its canon, is a 'closed' canon. In other words, a particular set of writings, being of divine inspiration, are seen throughout the tradition's history as absolutely normative and undoubtedly true, with all other literature excluded from this status and holding a position of distinctly secondary importance.

Jain scholarship has wedged the Jain scriptures, accordingly, into this mold, disregarding in many instances the literature's own evidence to the contrary, and choosing to ignore significant areas of literature because they appear to fall outside the 'closed' canon.

The hypothesis underlying this research is that the Jains have viewed their scriptures quite differently from the way in which Western scholarship has looked at the matter, and that clarifying this point will assist our understanding of Jain history. Western scholars have treated the Jain scriptures as a closed canon, on the model of the Bible, dating from the fifth century C.E. Scholars have therefore tended to treat deviations from this closed canon as indications of 'heresy' or of sectarian tendencies. However, my own research indicates that the standard treatment may be in error.

To give these explorations a specific comparative grounding, this study will focus on clarifying a particular cultural and religious development, and the previous scholarship on it, in an area where I already have completed some research. The particular context is the Jain 'canon of scripture.' As described above, the Jain scriptures have been treated as a 'Bible' by a series of Western scholars. But my previous work leads me to conclude that prior scholarship has produced a much distorted view of the history of the Jain scriptures, and that this distorted view has also wrongly colored much of our view of the history of the movement.

In order to clarify this matter, a more exhaustive exploration of Jain accounts of their scriptures and their internal divisions must be undertaken. A series of Jain texts and commentaries need to be read and, where feasible, translated. The texts in question include 'canonical' sources themselves, such as the *Nandī Sūtra* (ca. 450 C.E.), which speak to the nature of scriptural authority in Jainism. When the Jains themselves have written about their internal divisions, they have rarely made an issue of the scriptures. I have traced this attitude through a number of texts from the eighth century C.E. up to the fourteenth century C.E. The Jains' own accounts of their canon of scripture (for example, that found in the *Nandī Sūtra*) do not indicate a closed canon of the sort assumed by Western scholarship. A particular problem to be investigated, then, is that the *Siddhānta* described in the *Nandī Sūtra* is not the same as the *Siddhānta* that European Indologists have reported and described as being the sacred texts of the Jains in studies published in the nineteenth and twentieth centuries. This discrepancy or discontinuity in Jain sacred texts is in need of exploration, so that a more accurate picture of the Jain *Siddhānta* may be given. An investigation of the history of the Jain *Siddhānta*, of which the *Nandī Sūtra* is a part, will enable us to determine better whether European and American scholars in the nineteenth and twentieth centuries have properly understood this history. Also to be studied are Jain histories and compendia of religious teachings, such as Jinasena's *Ādipurāṇa*, which adumbrate the sources of knowledge, scriptural and otherwise, to which the Jains have turned in the course of their history.

In addition to the above, more thorough consultation with Jain leaders (*ācāryas* and *munis*) is required in order to explore their knowledge of Jain attitudes toward scripture and the role that scriptures play and have played in the history of the tradition. The ways in which the texts of the Jain *Siddhānta* have been used in day-to-day fashion in more recent times need to be investigated, so as to establish a comparative viewpoint on the use of the *Siddhānta* by the Jains and the use of sacred texts in other religious traditions.

THE JAIN SCRIPTURES AND THE DIGAMBARA JAIN TRADITION

My previous research has dealt almost exclusively with the Śvetāmbara Jains. This sub-tradition was the first Jain movement to come to Western scholarly attention, and the early scholars of the Jains accepted and transmitted nineteenth-century testimony to the following effect: (1) while the Śvetāmbaras possessed a 'canon' of ancient sacred texts, this same 'canon' was totally rejected by the other main Jain sub-tradition, the Digambaras; and (2) the latter had generated a 'secondary canon' of more recent texts.

It was lacunae and opacity in our perception of that Śvetāmbara canon that first drew my attention to the Jain scriptures. Now it is necessary to turn to the matter of the actual status of the Digambara textual tradition. This requires, first of all, that whatever evidence there is for the Digambaras' own view of their scriptures needs to be collected and reviewed. Astoundingly enough, this simply has not been done by scholars.

THE LINGUISTIC CONTEXT OF JAIN SCRIPTURES

The project on which I am engaged has to do most directly with the structure and function of a canon of literature in Jain history, and with our understanding of it. This is clearly a long-term project; but two specific problems have emerged in my research to date that are directly relevant to the actual process of the formation of a canon, and that should be investigated in order for me to gain a better understanding of the Jain canon's historical standing and use once it developed.

Both specific problems fall within what I would loosely term the 'linguistic context' of Jain scriptures. By this I mean the following: (1) the significance (or lack of it) of the actual language used by the Jains to transmit their teachings, and (2) the question of whether the Jains themselves may have been aware of the changes implied by the adoption of written transmission as opposed to oral tradition.

With respect to the first point, Jain normative literature is in various Prakrits (early Indian vernaculars), and the Jains notably refused, for some centuries, to use Sanskrit. Madhav Deshpande (1979) has suggested that this use of Prakrit was a variety of "socio-linguistic self-defence," i.e., that the Jains, by sticking with the early vernacular languages, were accentuating their distinctive identity over against the Sanskritic priestly tradition of India. This is a seminal thesis, and I would like to extend it and test it in certain ways. Deshpande's thesis makes especially good sense if one is talking about a 'popular' tradition in some way. But early Jainism is not a 'popular' tradition *per se*, being basically an ascetic movement. Therefore, one must explore the sense in which the Jain ascetic authors of the normative texts felt themselves to be related to the lay community at the time that the texts were codified. For example, one dimension of the Jain development of scriptures is the sense in which this canon had a role to play in the larger life of the community, and one aspect of such a role could be the choice of language.

As concerns the second point, there are statements in early Jain literature to the effect that the possession of written texts was forbidden to monks. These statements have been described by B. J. Sandesara (1962:99) in the following words:

> One of the principal vows or Mahāvratas to be observed by the Jaina monks is *aparigraha* or absence of worldly possessions, and the books were likely to become *parigraha* or possession, and hence in some parts of the Canonical literature it is clearly stated that a monk should not possess the books, and even for copying or handling a book an atonement is prescribed.

This is something that I have discovered very recently, and it is highly intriguing. It may have been simply an extension of the Jain monastic rules against owning property, or it may have been a Jain version of the Hindu concern that sacred literature not fall into the hands of the uninitiated. For the Brahmanical priestly tradition, there is an explanation for this, in that only the initiated can properly use the power inherent in the recitation of Vedic formulae. But the Jains, having no notion of 'powerful formulae' so far as I know, would not readily have felt this concern. A third alternative may be that the linguistic nature of Prakrit is such that when written it becomes hard to read properly, a bit like unpointed Hebrew. I know of no scholar who has suggested this third alternative. In fact, the entire matter of these prohibitions has received no notice.

It seems to me that these prohibitions ought to be explored. Possible explanations for them are not unrelated to the question of the communal role of scriptures mentioned above; for example, the scriptures may have been meant, in written form, for the lay community. But this seems highly unlikely. One would have to explore the earliest layers of written commentary on such passages in order to see whether the Jains consciously voided these prohibitions, which might point toward an 'occasion' of some sort that led to the production of a written canon.

TRANSLATION AND ANNOTATION OF THE JAIN *PRATIKRAMAṆA SŪTRAS*

This particular project involves the translation of a set of Jain religious texts from Prakrit and Gujarati into English, and the writing of a set of annotations for the translation. The texts in question are collectively held in a single work known as the *Pratikramaṇa Sūtras*. The term *pratikramaṇa* refers to the general and regular religious ritual obligations of the Jains, and the *sūtra*s are the texts that accompany these rituals. These texts occupy a central niche in Jain religious literature.

Over the past year I have been exploring the Jains' normative, or sacred, literature with two objectives in mind. The first goal has been to explore the general concept of 'scripture' as a category in the comparative study of religion, looking especially for the religious and intellectual currents involved in the rise of this category in the nineteenth century. This part of the study was inspired by a need to understand and document the ways in which the concept 'scripture' in the minds of scholars influenced their reading of the history and nature of the Jains's own religious literature. The second goal has been to review intensively both the Jain literature and the Jains' own day-to-day practice to see whether

Jain scholarship can rest content with the view of the Jain scriptures formulated in the nineteenth century and still prevalent today.

This on-going research has revealed two matters. The first is that there is available within the Jain tradition itself a model for understanding the Jain scriptures that is much more intelligible and meaningful than the Protestant model summarized above. My work at present involves translating texts that bear on this point and describing this indigenous model, a task that I hope will get the classical Jain literature out of a mold that is essentially false to its role in Jain life.

The second is that Jain literature also contains a significant bloc of texts that are the direct source of 'scriptural' involvement for the lay community, and which thus offer the opportunity to obtain a complete picture of what scripture is for the Jains. By and large, the Jains do *not* 'read' their canonical literature *per se*, either in a ritual or a daily pattern. What they do use is a collection of excerpts, in the format of a missal. This collection is known as the *Pratikramaṇa Sūtras*, and it is notable that, in line with the nineteenth-century perspectives described above (and which still have considerable effect today), these texts have hardly been touched by scholars.

The *Pratikramaṇa Sūtras* is essentially a manual for Jain daily religious ritual, and consists of excerpts from canonical texts, rearranged into patterns for ritual recitation, plus devotional poetry and chants. This material is usually in Prakrit, the Jain classical language, but it is commonly transliterated into Gujarati script so that laypeople can read and pronounce the older material. This literature is accompanied by Gujarati explanations and detailed instructions for the ritual actions that are to be performed as the Prakrit passages are read or sung. The *Pratikramaṇa* material forms the major part of all the religious literature, or scripture, that the Jain layperson knows. This form of transmission is the dominant mode, and has been for the last 500 years, of 'scriptural' use by Jains.

If seen only in the context of Jain studies, this project might appear fairly specialized. However, it also has broader value to the discipline as a whole in two areas. The first is a somewhat general arena of historical conceptualization and information, and the other is a highly interesting area involving the analysis of the cultural setting and function of a tradition's normative literature.

In the more general arena, this study can help to pave the way for a wider recognition of the nature of sacred books, or 'scriptures.' It is not only the Jain canon that has suffered from being wedged into the mold described above, for it has been very common for the study of religions to focus on, or almost wholly involve, what were and are perceived to be a religion's 'scriptures' or 'Bible' in structuring books and courses about various religions. Most college bookstores have on their shelves one or more publications bearing titles like *The World*

Bible, or reprints of The Sacred Books of the East, and courses with titles such as "Sacred Books of the East" are still common at the college and university level. This still very common approach assumes that all religions—not only the Jains—resemble Protestant Christianity where sacred texts are concerned. This is patently not so, and any specific study that can negate this notion is of value, both as concerns written expositions of religious traditions and in the area of course construction.

The study of the *Pratikramaṇa Sūtras* illuminates several aspects of the broader problem of 'scripture.' It predates the modern form of the Jain 'canon,' and its relationship to the older patterns of canonization in Jain literary history clarifies our understanding of that process by filling a major gap between such older and more modern formulations of the canon. The *Pratikramaṇa Sūtras* also gives indigenous, direct testimony to the way in which Jains themselves understand and perceive the form of their scripture, something that past approaches to the canon have not been able to show. Finally, the interplay between the historical and written text and its use as ritual recitative opens up the arena of oral/aural significance for scripture in a tradition heretofore studied almost solely in terms of written texts and their propositional content.

In the arena of the cultural setting and function of normative literature very basic issues are involved in this work, issues having to do with understanding cultural processes. The basic matter is one that has been formulated in more than one way, namely the relationship between the formal literature and ideology of a tradition and the specific day-to-day practice of its members. In terms of a familiar culture, it is the question of how to understand the relationship between formal Christian theology and the actual beliefs and practices of ordinary Christian laypersons. Between the two domains there is often a considerable gap, not only in terms of practice, but even in terms of how basic ideas and beliefs are formulated.

How these two domains are linked, carry each other, and influence each other is a perennial problem in cultural studies. It may be understood in terms like Redfield's (1956) the 'great' (i.e., literate and educated) tradition versus the 'little' (i.e., popular) tradition. It may be understood in terms of 'text' and 'context,' i.e., the tradition's formal literature over against that formal material's translation into everyday cultural life. Or it may be understood in socio-economic terms: since the 'great' or 'textual' tradition is usually in the hands of a culture's elite, it may be one of the mechanisms for controlling the common majority. Other models are also available, each contributing dimensions to the understanding of this fundamental cultural process.

The Jain materials involved in this study are of special value here, for they appear to be a distinctive linking mechanism between the 'great' or 'textual' tradition (the Prakrit literature) and the 'little' or contextual tradition (the everyday religious life of the Jain layperson and the specific ways in which he or she uses or knows the 'great' tradition). As such, the proposed work has value as a case-study in which major theses about cultural workings can be tested, and so it can contribute to the discipline well beyond the specifics on Jain studies.

But the benefit to Jain studies should not be ignored. It is appropriate to stress that none of the classic expositions of Jainism discuss the *Pratikramaṇa* literature in any detail, if at all. Yet the literature plays and has played a major role in shaping the religious life of the community.

7

JAIN RELIGIOUS LIFE AT ANCIENT MATHURĀ: THE HERITAGE OF LATE-VICTORIAN INTERPRETATION*

The Jain remains found at Kaṅkālī Ṭīlā in Mathurā, and dated to Kuṣāṇa and pre-Kuṣāṇa times, are often treated as if they were self-evidently meaningful. Yet a close examination will reveal that the religious significance attributed to them is of a curious sort when all is said and done. Only some of what the evidence reveals is given much attention, and that to excess, while other dimensions of it seem to have been nearly invisible to scholars. This invisibility is above all notable, as its causes are themselves often not perceived because of their being embedded in the scholarly presuppositions that govern much of Jain studies as a whole. In sum, the patterns in interpretation of the Jain evidence from Mathurā reflect larger premises in the study of Jain history, and so long as those premises remain in force, the Mathurā evidence will be trapped in an interpretive context that conceals as much as it reveals about Jain religious life at Mathurā.

The relationship between the materials from Kaṅkālī Ṭīlā and certain modes of thinking about the Jains is so fundamental that any effort at interpreting those materials ought to involve two kinds of retrospective inquiry. First, earlier interpretations, especially those from the 1890s and early 1900s, need to be

* In *Mathurā: The Cultural Heritage*, 103-112. Ed. D. M. Srinivasan. New Delhi: Manohar, 1989.

given the most intense scrutiny before they are used, so that one is fully aware of the argumentative presuppositions about the Jains that affect (and sometimes even effect) those interpretations. Second, the nature of the actual evidence can never be taken for granted. The context and mechanics of discovery at Kaṅkālī Ṭīlā were such that one often must conduct a basic investigation into the status and character of the find-pieces involved before accepting or making generalizations about them.

These are rather drastic cautions, and their impact extends beyond the bare evidence from Mathurā. Given the problematic status of prior interpretations of the evidence, and given that the evidence itself is open to reservations, a reconsideration of the Jain presence in ancient Mathurā may be in order, one that would touch general assumptions about Mathurā and about Jain history.

One may well ask whether such far-reaching consequences are actually at stake. The answer must be that it is possible, and that an inquiry into the matter is necessary, especially because of an additional factor that is often forgotten: the discoveries at Kaṅkālī Ṭīlā came at a pivotal moment in nineteenth-century Jain studies. The magnitude assigned to the evidence from there was often other than what one might expect; and since even a slight misdirection at a critical turning becomes magnified with the passage of time and distance, it is instructive in more than just an antiquarian sense to inquire how certain perceptions of the Jain tradition were interwoven with the discoveries at Mathurā.

I.

The major finds of Jain materials at Kaṅkālī Ṭīlā occurred between 1888 and 1896, and in one sense those explorations can be understood as part of a linear chain of events in Jain studies. The site and its surroundings had been partially explored in the 1870s by Cunningham, Harding, and Growse, and Cunningham had published some results as early as 1873 (Cunningham 1873). But little attention was paid to those discoveries until the late 1880s, when Kaṅkālī Ṭīlā was re-opened by James Burgess (and explored from 1889 onward by A. A. Führer) for a specific reason: Cunningham's findings had become relevant to a debate that dominated Jain scholarship in the 1800s. That debate was over the origins of the Jain tradition, and evidence from Mathurā was wanted as ammunition for use in it.

Kaṅkālī Ṭīlā was thus given its second set of explorations not because of general interest in the site, but rather out of a particular desire for a certain sort of evidence. The foremost general factor affecting the explorations is this narrowness of purpose, and its consequences were and are manifold and damaging. It was even responsible for some of the dubious status of the evidence itself, because it established much of the immeditate context for the handling of the finds; and some of this damage is very nearly irreparable. But before such concrete and mechanical concerns can be fully understood, it is important to see how the debate over Jain origins shaped the narrow issues that evidence from Kaṅkālī Ṭīlā was expected to resolve.

The debate over origins informed early Jain studies to a degree remarkable even in an intellectual era nearly obsessed with the question of origins. Most students of the Jains have some familiarity with this debate because of the prominent (and often re-printed) publication of one part of it: Hermann Jacobi's introductions to his two volumes of translated Jain texts for the Sacred Books of the East (Jacobi 1884b and 1895a). But there was more to the debate than is revealed by Jacobi's arguments, for they actually form the pivot between a first and a second stage in the debate. The Mathurā finds occurred within the second stage, and they were used to address issues that were only nascent in the earlier debate. Thus a knowledge of Jacobi's work does not carry one into the direct context of the digs at Kaṅkālī Tīlā.

At the same time, the way in which Jacobi's arguments closed the debate's first stage left open the door for the second stage and its issues. In a linear sense, then, the re-opening of Kaṅkālī Ṭīlā is actually linked to the earlier debate, so that understanding the explorations does require a look back into the mid-1800s and earlier.

Developments before 1884

The transition from the first stage of the debate to the second occurred in 1884. Up to that time, the debate had focused on the proposition that the Jains had originated out of Buddhism. Beginning in 1858, Albrecht Weber argued that Mahāvīra and the Buddha had actually been one and the same person, and that the Jains were Buddhist schismatics who had, in breaking away ca. 350 B.C.E., altered the portrait of their founder just enough to legitimize their position (Weber 1858:1ff.) Christian Lassen theorized, in the 1860s, that the Jains' general resemblence to Buddhism and to other Indian movements pointed to the Jains' having originated as a movement in "the 1st or 2nd century after Christ" (Lassen 1873:197). In his view, ". . . no doubt can remain that the *Jainas* are descendants from the Bauddhas, but that in some points they considered it advantageous to approach the Brahmans, probably in order to escape being persecuted by them." (Lassen 1873:199)

Both of these theories rested in part on the judgement that Jain Prakrit literature was not as old as the Buddhist canonical writings, but the general line of argument pre-dated such literary judgements. Fundamentally, the question of Jain origins was pursued in the form of a via negativa whose roots lay in the earliest scholarly writings on the Jains.[1] From the beginning, the Jain tradition's own accounts of its origins were doubted, and the debate consisted of a series of negative propositions that had to be set aside in order to establish the credibility of the Jain versions of their history. The theories of Weber and Lassen were, then, links in a longer chain of arguments whose momentum and direction were established very early in the history of Jain scholarship.

Between 1879 and 1884 (the latter being the year of his first volume of translations) Jacobi undertook the refutation of the negative thesis that the Jains had arisen out of Buddhism.[2] He succeeded, and his role in the debate is largely remembered because of this accomplishment. Using newly available Jain literature (which had begun to reach scholars in significant measure in the 1870s), he was able to undermine Weber's theory and to establish Mahāvīra's historicity; and he also showed that Lassen's hypothesis did not stand up under close scrutiny.

Jacobi argued that some of the semblances that Lassen saw between the Jains and Buddhists did not actually exist, and that those that existed did not detract from the distinctiveness of Jain teachings. In sum, he took the line that where the Jains and Buddhists did resemble each other, they also resembled movements in the larger Hindu tradition, specifically in matters of general ascetic praxis, cosmology, and cultic activity (Jacobi 1884b:xix-xxv). These, in his view, were not the essential parts of the Jain tradition; hence similarities in such areas did not vitiate the Jains' own claims about their origins, even as they explained the Jains' resemblances to non-Buddhist movements.

Jacobi's presentation was convincing, and from 1884 onwards the thesis that the Jains had originated within Buddhism was in general disrepute. But the debate, and the via negativa, had one more stage to go. Jacobi's arguments had settled the matter of Jain-Buddhist relationships, but they carried with them two after-effects that shaped and dominated the second stage of the debate. First, in terms of the more linear series of debate-propositions, Jacobi's arguments suffered from being purely literary, and the reliability of Jain literature—whose antiquity, at least in terms of extant materials, even Jacobi admitted did not match the Buddhist's—remained open to some doubt. This specific question would dominate the final stage of the debate, and is its most direct link to the Mathurā explorations.

The second after-effect, which was not so much a linear debate-matter, is less visible but was eqully powerful in shaping the debate. In establishing the Jains' independence from Buddhism, Jacobi had in effect treated the Jains as a

---

1 Various accounts of these earliest writings can be found at the outset of the previously cited works by Jacobi, Lassen, and Weber.

2 See Jacobi 1879:1ff.,1880, and 1884b.

miniature Buddhism, i.e., as a parallel but distinctive ascetic movement whose history should be understood on the same model as Buddhist history. Nowhere is this more obvious than in his argument that the cultic life of both the Buddhists and the Jains was a borrowing from the larger Hindu context. He wrote, in connection with the cult of the Buddha and the Jina (Jacobi 1884b:xxi):

> . . . I believe that this worship had nothing to do with original Buddhism or Jainism, that it did not originate with the monks, but with the lay community, when the people in general felt the want of a higher cult than that of their rude deities and demons, and when the religious development of India found in the Bhakti the supreme means of salvation. Therefore instead of seeing in the Buddhists the originals, and in the Jainas the imitators, with regard to the erection of temples and worship of statues, we assume that both sects were, independently from each other, brought to adopt this practice by the perpetual and irresistible influence of the religious development of the people in India.

This after-effect is less visible in the debate because it was so readily accepted on all sides. It was not even a point of argument in the debate, because Jacobi's line of argument here was simply consistent with the ways in which scholars in general were categorizing Indian religion in the 1800s. One might compare this mode of thinking to a broad stream of ideas about Indian religion that the debate over the Jains channeled into a particular course and whose intensity was magnified by that channeling. In this way, the task of refuting negative propositions about Jain origins can be seen as heightening the nineteenth-century tendency to think of religious movements solely in terms of their abstract teachings and literature, which were the points of supposed similarity between the Jains and the Buddhists that Jacobi most seriously explored, while dismissing popular practice and cultic life as secondary.

In brief, one sees at the end of the debate's first stage two determinative patterns that would form the second stage: (1) an acceptable separation of Jain history from the Buddhist tradition, and (2) a conceptualization of the Jain tradition as a closed, essentially ascetic system, parallel to Buddhism. As the debate moved into its second stage, then, the terms in which the Jains would be discussed and which would inform the investigation of Kaṅkālī Ṭīlā had already begun to solidify into the forms that still haunt Jain studies today, forms that can be comprised in the term "Jainism."

The Debate: Stage Two

The argumentative shift that marks this stage was provided by Auguste Barth, who had actually entered the debate in the first stage, but whose distinctive contribution came after Jacobi had settled the question of the Jains' relationship to Buddhism. Barth had originally agreed with Weber and Lassen, but after Jacobi's work he formulated a new stage in the via negativa: he disputed the continuity and distinct identity of the Jain tradition prior to the fixing of the Śvetāmbara canon in the fifth century C.E.; and he was cautious to the point of scepticism about any literary evidence prior to that time (Barth 1880:256-57; 1914-27:I:286-87). Though he accepted Jacobi's proofs for the historicity of Mahāvīra and did not dispute traditional Jain chronology concerning him, he still argued (Barth 1881:90; 1914-27:I:306-7):

> . . . what we dispute, because it does not as yet appear to us to be demonstrated, is the conscious and continuous existence of the [Jain] sect beginning in that long-ago time [of Mahāvīra], and the direct transmission of a proper doctrine and tradition. This tradition appears to us, on the contrary, to have been formed much later, out of vague recollections and along the lines of the Buddhist tradition.[3]

Jacobi made an effort to counter this point of view, and his essay of 1884 concludes with a response from Barth. In Jacobi's view, Barth's principal error lay in confusing the fixing of the Jain canon with its composition, and he demonstrated by metrical analysis that the earliest Jain literature should be dated ca. 300 B.C.E. But he was obliged to carry the tradition back to Mahāvīra's time by arguing that, absent evidence to the contrary, the Jains' own accounts of their early history should be regarded as generally reliable, and he could not deny that the canon contained much that was far more recent than 300 B.C.E. (Jacobi 1884b:xxxix-xlvi). In a sense, Jacobi was hoisted by his own petard. His treatment of the Jains as an essentially ascetic order parallel to Buddhism forced the issue of this 'Jainism's' age onto the grounds of the age of its ascetic literature, and thus allowed Barth's claim that, on literary grounds, the Jains could be seen as having led for centuries "an obscure, undefined existence much like that of other ascetic groups" (Barth 1881:91; 1914-27:I:308).

One can say, then, that the second stage of the debate became an argument over the origins of 'Jainism' in terms of nineteenth-century categories focusing on literary evidence. Both Jacobi and Barth accepted the notion that the tradition's continuity and identity were to be measured by the state of its ascetic core, with Buddhism as a parallel model but not the source, and what remained to be settled was the point at which this entity came into existence.

This formulation of the question set the stage for the work of Georg Bühler who, with Barth as his opponent, would dominate the rest of the debate. Bühler was knowledgeable about the Jains. During seventeen years in India (1863-1880), he had collected and sent to Europe most of the Jain literature that Weber and Jacobi used in their work. Though he had at one time agreed with Weber and Lassen (Bühler 1887b:38-39n.16), he came to share Jacobi's view of Jain origins; and he and Jacobi (apparently working independently) had unraveled a

---

3 Folkert's translation.

major clue to Mahāvīra's historical identity by linking Vardhamāna Jñātṛputra with the Nigaṇṭha Nātaputta of Buddhist texts (Bühler 1878b:143-45 and 1887b). But Bühler had otherwise been silent through the first stage of the debate.

In 1879 he entered the debate in earnest, first through a lecture given to the Vienna Academy (Bühler 1887b), and then in a provocative article in the *Wiener Zeitschrift für die Kunde des Morgenlandes* (hereafter WZKM) (Bühler 1887a). The latter piece most clearly expresses his sense of the debate and of his role in it; even the title is significant: "On the Authenticity of the Jaina Tradition." The channeling force of the debate and the adversarial effect of its via negativa are clearly visible in the hard line that Bühler took there in commenting on the views of Weber and Barth: ". . . both distrust the Jaina tradition and consider it to be probable that the latter has been made up or, to use the proper word, has been forged according to the Buddhist scriptures" (Bühler 1887a:165).

After reviewing and complimenting Jacobi's arguments from 1884, Bühler went on to state his own purposes in entering the debate (Bühler 1887a:168-69):

> On reading [Jacobi's discussion], I could, however, not suppress a regret, that his answer to Mr. Barth is in one important point incomplete, since it furnishes no instance in which the tradition of the Jainas is proved to be trustworthy by independent, really historical sources. This feeling induced me to enter on a careful re-examination of all the ancient historical documents which refer to the Jains, and to enquire, if they furnish any data which corroborate the earlier Jaina tradition and liberate at least portions of it from the suspicion of being a deliberate forgery. The result is that I believe to be able to prove the correctness of a not inconsiderable part of the larger list of teachers and schools, preserved in the Sthavirāvali of the Kalpasūtra.

What Bühler had discovered is not well-known: that a number of inscriptions from Mathurā, unearthed by Cunningham at Kaṅkālī Ṭīlā in 1871 and dated to Kuṣāṇa times, recorded Jain donations by laypersons under the direction of ascetic preceptors, and that the inscriptions used technical terminology for Jain ascetic sub-orders (*gaṇa*s, *kula*s, *śākhā*s) that matched the terminology of the *Kalpa Sūtra* and even contained some of the same proper names for orders. This, in Bühler's view, was precisely what was needed in order to address Barth's doubts about the continuity of the early Jain tradition.

As noted before, this moment in the debate does not actually reflect a new discovery. It was a re-discovery of Sir Alexander Cunningham's evidence and the entering of it, at last, into the debate. While Cunningham had not noticed the technical terminology that so excited Bühler, he had found statues of Tīrthaṅkaras, and had noted that the inscriptions included the words Vardhamāna and Mahāvīra. From this he drew an enthusiastic conclusion, already in

1873, to the effect that there was at last "tangible evidence to vouch for the truth" (Cunningham 1873:46) of traditional Jain claims.

But no one had paid much attention until the second stage of debate, where the evidence was both needed and relevant. Literary testimony had been pushed to its limit, but a negative proposition still remained; and the issues at stake in considering Jain origins had now been so framed by the earlier discussions that Cunningham's inscriptional evidence spoke directly to the question, for it substantiated the Jain literary tradition precisely on the point of its ascetic identity and continuity—the very conception of the tradition that now governed the debate.

Being absolutely seized by the appropriateness of the evidence, Bühler did not rest content with this initial discovery. He took steps to obtain more materials, and within a year he had in hand a new inscription with which to bolster his views. He began his initial report on its discovery and translation with the following background information (Bühler 1888:141):

> Encouraged by the results of my re-examination of Sir A. Cunningham's Mathurā inscriptions I asked Dr. J. Burgess in September last [1887] to resume during the next working season the excavations at the Kaṅkālī Ṭīlā where the published documents have been found.

Burgess agreed and began working in January, 1888; and thus it is to Bühler and to the debate over Jain origins that the re-opening of Kaṅkālī Ṭīlā can be directly traced.

As finds at Kaṅkālī Ṭīlā emerged (under the direction of Burgess in 1888, and thereafter under A. A. Führer), Bühler published a spate of reports, translating and interpreting inscriptions found on the materials.[4] Including his first article in 1887 he published the following series of pieces on the same theme:

1887, WZKM I:	"On the Authenticity of the Jaina Tradition"
1888, WZKM II:	"Further Proofs of the Authenticity of the Jaina Tradition"
1889, WZKM III:	"Further Proofs for the Authenticity of the Jaina Tradition"
1890, WZKM IV:	"Further Proofs of the Authenticity of the Jaina Tradition"

The WZKM for 1890, as well as those for 1891 (V) and 1896 (X), also contained "Brief Communications" (Kleine Mitteilungen) in which Bühler summarized Führer's finds as news of them reached him at Vienna. These "Brief Communications" were also put before a wider audience through publication in *The Academy*. Beginning in 1892, Bühler published his findings in more

[4] A full listing of these publications emerges from the references in the text and in the bibliography; see also Luders 1961:40-41. Janert's edition of Luder's work first called my attention to many of the problematic dimensions of Mathurā-interpretation.

comprehensive fashion in *Epigraphia Indica*, a project that eventually ran to four reports published in volumes I and II.[5]

Bühler carried the day against Barth by means of this steady flow of pointed, though brief, pieces. As Bühler was the only scholar intimately involved with interpreting the finds, and was highly respected, his interpretation of them was widely accepted. The general accord granted to them put an end to formal argument over Jain origins by the mid-1890s, and this especially is why the Mathurā finds occupy such a pivotal point in Jain studies. Jacobi had distinguished Jain from Buddhist history on the basis of literary testimony, and now Bühler had produced evidence to substantiate the literature's claims.

The Debate and Kaṅkālī Ṭīlā: The End Result

Even with the debate established as the immediate context of the finds and their interpretation, it is important to see that in the end, the whole exceeded the sum of the parts. The finds of Kaṅkālī Ṭīlā were as forcibly used by Bühler to argue his case as had the Jains' similarities to Buddhism been used by Weber et al., to argue the contrary. Bühler did not really refute Barth; Barth was simply overwhelmed.

What the finds at Mathurā accomplished, viewed objectively, was no more than the strengthening of Jacobi's original literary chronology, which carried the Jain tradition back to ca. 300 B.C.E. None of the archaeological evidence could be claimed, after all, to be as old as the oldest Prakrit literature. The lynch-pin of Bühler's argument was the conjecture that the testimony of Kaṅkālī Ṭīlā pointed well back beyond itself, i.e., that a clearly organized ascetic tradition, attested by the technical language of the inscriptions as existing in Kuṣāṇa times and slightly before, probably implied a long history for such a tradition.

That this was a conjecture was clearly seen by Barth. In 1889, he exhaustively reviewed Jacobi's final statements on the subject of Jain origins along with Bühler's first two articles on the subject, and bitingly pronounced himself unconvinced. He did revise his original, more drastic suspicion that the fixing of the Śvetāmbara canon was the first point at which one had to deal with a truly continuous tradition. But he would not yield on his doubts about the tradition prior to the first two centuries B.C.E. (Barth 1889; 1914-27:II:40-85), and his last statement on the subject, in 1902, showed him still unrepentent (Barth 1902; 1914-27:II:373-88).

But Barth stood alone after 1890. The debate was not so much won as abandoned. Bühler seems to have felt so firmly that his evidence settled matters that after 1887 he did not again refer explicitly to Barth's views, not even to the latter's vigorous response of 1889. Nor did this occur because others had taken

5 [Editor's note.] See Bibliography for full references.

up the battle. Bühler remained, through the 1890s, the only scholar working with the materials at a primary level. His sense that the matter of Jain origins was settled by the Mathurā evidence was simply adopted wholesale.

Here, one may plausibly surmise, the via negativa of the debate finally turned back on itself. The scholarly community seems at last to have had enough of doubts about the Jains, and to have been ready to accept, almost with relief, a new position. Thus the debate's final effect was to produce an overly-enthusiastic mirror-image of the earlier scepticism at the expense, in the end, of a clear view of the evidence involved. Although the position taken by Jacobi and Bühler has proven to provide an acceptable version of early Jain history, the effort expended in establishing that view supplied more heat than light as concerns the actual evidence and its various dimensions. Though Weber, Lassen, and Barth were wrong about the Jains, they may have been proven wrong for reasons that had a damaging impact on later scholarly views of the tradition.

This is especially so because of the debate's linkage with the notion of 'Jainism,' i.e., with the idea of the tradition enunciated by Jacobi: that its non-ascetic features were secondary accretions. This latter perspective, used by both sides in the argument, assured that only certain questions were asked of the Mathurā evidence, namely, such questions as were relevant both to the tradition's ascetic dimension and to the concrete points at issue in the debate. In general, this meant that Bühler's interest in the evidence was drawn toward whatever would substantiate older Jain writings on ascetic life, and this approach shines through all of his writings on the subject.

This was so from the very beginning. Already in 1887, with only Cunningham's finds in hand, Bühler regarded the specific language of the inscriptions as showing the ascetic continuity of the tradition. As he put it, in direct response to Barth's own language: "The existence of [ascetic] titles . . . and of ancient schools at the end of the first century A.D. show [*sic*] that at [that] period the Jaina sect had possessed already for a long time 'a continuous and self-conscious existence.'" (Bühler 1887a:180) In 1890, when he had seen and dealt with sixty-six inscriptions, and could no longer be thought of as having only a partial view of the evidence, he still wrote: "In the discussion of the contents of these documents, the constitution of the order of the Jaina ascetics must naturally take the first place." (Bühler 1890a:315)

This statement itself virtually defines the terms in which the Jain tradition's history and nature would be viewed. The inscriptions and their find-context were treated almost as if they had no evidence to offer other than what related to literary/ascetic matters. Thus the debate and the intellectual currents that it channeled with particular force led to an almost unconscious limitation on interpretation of the evidence from Kaṅkālī Ṭīlā. This limitation, moreover, was of two sorts.

While the non-ascetic/literary evidence remained virtually invisible, other evidence was over-interpreted in terms of continuity and the antiquity of the tradition. The final outcome is a curiously one-dimensional picture of Jain life at ancient Mathurā.

II.

The best way to see this one-dimensionality is to look briefly at a particular piece of evidence, one that ought not show what it has regularly been taken to prove. That piece is the 'Jain *stūpa*' at Kaṅkālī Ṭīlā, and it can serve especially well as an example of the currents and pressures that shaped Mathurā-Jain interpretation. But in addition to that, it also shows the effect of a general problem mentioned at the outset: the fact that the actual evidence from Kaṅkālī Ṭīlā is still open to question.

The roots of the evidentiary problem lie, again, in the debate. The narrowness of purpose that it brought to the explorations after 1888 actually affected the handling of the evidence itself. In the first place, it led to greater emphasis being placed on the inscriptions than on the sculptural and architectural pieces. This was certainly true of Bühler's approach, though it was in part circumstantial: Bühler was in Vienna, and what Burgess and Führer could most readily send him were rubbings of the inscriptions.

But the inscriptions were what Bühler wanted, because they contained the evidence most needed in the debate over origins. This means that the earliest interpretations of the Jain remains at Kaṅkālī Ṭīlā paid little attention to the actual pieces on which the inscriptions were found. Bühler wrote his first relatively exhaustive interpretation of the finds in 1890, and even then he appears to have had in hand only brief descriptions of some pieces, though he does mention one rough sketch (Bühler 1890a:327). It was not until 1894, in volume II of *Epigraphia Indica*, that a connected account of some sculptural pieces and their inscriptions was given by him. This account was based on ten photographs that Bühler had recieved from Führer, and these appear to have been Bühler's only sustained contact with the pieces themselves (Bühler 1894b). Moreover, the peculiar circumstances of the debate, and Bühler's dominant role in it, meant that no one else was dealing with these materials.

This separation of the inscriptions from the plastic evidence from Kaṅkālī Ṭīlā is by itself a continuing problem in dealing with those materials; even today, no sustained parallel account of the two kinds of evidence exists. Why this should be so is something of a puzzle, but it may be partially explained by a set of peculiar accidents that compounded the interpretive tendencies that were afoot in the early 1890s. First, Bühler was drowned in April 1898, in a boating accident in Europe. He had not written anything on the inscriptions since 1894; and with his sudden death, the possibility of any synthetic account of the evidence from Mathurā, which he alone of scholars in Europe knew thoroughly, virtually ceased to exist.

Such chance of retrieving a full sense of the finds as might have survived Bühler's death were dealt a fatal blow by a second 'accident.' Also in 1898, A. A. Führer abruptly left the service of the Archaeological Survey of India, and his departure finally crippled sustained interpretation of the evidence by knowledgeable scholars, especially interpretation that would combine the study of the inscriptions with examination of the sculptural pieces. Führer neither left behind nor published subsequently any systematic account of his work at Kaṅkālī Ṭīlā.

Without any systematic account by Bühler, and without Führer's personal remembrance of what had been done at the site, scholars had (and still have) little or no sense of the actual find-location of most pieces of evidence, and it is an open question whether any such record was in fact kept. This has left an aura of doubt about Führer's work at Kaṅkālī Ṭīlā; but to blame Führer alone is to overlook the debate-context that surrounded the re-opening of the site.

Some of Führer's handling of the digs may even have been due to a sense on his own part that the inscriptions were the most crucial matter, overshadowing the sculpture and architecture. But a larger share of the problem arises from the fact that he served in a period when archaeological work in British India was at a low point in funding and staff. By all accounts, Führer had enormous responsibilities, virtually no help, and a miserly budget (Marshall 1904:5-7). Indeed, it appears—perhaps as one of the 'accidents' involved—that the explorations of Kaṅkālī Ṭīlā could not have occurred at a worse time in terms of the support given to them. Viewed in retrospect, Jain studies would have been better served had James Burgess turned down Bühler's request in 1887 that the site be re-opened.

But the work was done. Führer had prepared a number of plates illustrating some of his finds, but these were unaccompanied by any data. So as to ensure that at least some of the Mathurā evidence would reach a larger audience, Vincent A. Smith was asked, in 1900, to undertake the publication of Führer's plates, something that Smith himself had suggested be done, but which he did himself only because "no one else was available" (Smith 1901:iii).

The task Smith faced was formidable. He knew nothing of the site, and could not explain Führer's diagrams or drawings of it (Smith 1901:8). As concerned the plates of sculptural and architectural pieces, Führer had left these "without a word of explanatory text" (Smith 1901:iii). Smith noted that he had in some cases been unable to accept Führer's headings for the plates, that he himself had "seen most of the originals from time to time," but had been unable "to make a minute examination of the objects described," and that his assitant, P.C. Mukherji, had "to some extent" compared the plates with the originals at the Lucknow Museum and had "in a few cases . . . detected discrepancies between Dr. Führer's headings to the plates and the labels affixed to the originals in the Museum" (Smith 1901:iii).

All of this notwithstanding, Smith went forward; and so was born *The Jain Stûpa and other Antiquities of Mathurâ*, published in 1901. Smith combined Führer's plates and illustrations with a text consisting mostly of Bühler's interpretation of the inscriptions. In that sense alone, the volume is nearly a case of the blind leading the blind. Seen in retrospect, *The Jain Stûpa* should also be classed as one of the 'accidents' that affected the evidence from Mathurā. Further, despite Smith's disclaimers, and despite the fact that most of the text in the volume is either quoted or directly derived from Bühler (including those parts attributed to Führer, who simply quoted Bühler's pieces in the WZKM on all interpretive points), Smith's name has since then been repeatedly associated with the intepretation of Kaṅkālī Ṭīlā.

That critical evidence should have been in such a state, and should have been published in such a way, is one of the great problems in interpreting Jain life at Mathurā. Yet, as one of the few comprehensive publications of the evidence, *The Jain Stûpa* gained a curious life of its own, and its flaws were, and still are, largely overlooked. It would be valuable to trace, if space allowed, the volume's post-1900 life in order to undertand better its persistent influence. But one answer to why it endures, and one of the keys to its success, may be no further away than the following statement by Smith in the Introduction (Smith 1901:6):

> The discoveries [at Kaṅkālī Ṭīlā] have to a very large extent supplied corroboration to the written Jain tradition, and they offer tangible incontrovertible proof of the antiquity of the Jain religion, and of its early existence very much in its present form.

In sum, the scholars to whom was left the task of interpreting the materials from Mathurā could do, it seems, little more than adopt and continue the basic line of interpretation established by Bühler: that the basic significance of the evidence was its testimony to the age and continuity of the Jain tradition. The strength of this general approach was remarkable, for it succeeded in establishing the basic approach still taken today to the evidence.

Nowhere is this more apparent than in the matter of the *stūpa*, which is a classic example of both the one-dimensional interpretation of the finds and of the misfortunes that befell the evidence. So many factors from the debate-context affect this particular item that it deserves a major review in its own right; what follows is only a partial treatment of it for the sake of showing its exemplary status as an item whose major dimensions remained virtually invisible while those things about it that were relevant to the intellectual context of its discovery were over-interpreted.

The Discovery of the 'Jain Stūpa'

The presence of a *stūpa* at Kaṅkālī Ṭīlā was first noticed by Führer in his explorations of 1890. But both he and Bühler thought at first that it was Buddhist (Bühler 1890a:314). This is all the more notable because, in the first article in the WZKM in which Bühler discussed the *stūpa*, he also discussed the finding of a sculptured panel (J.623, State Museum, Lucknow; inscription: Luders #75) portraying in its upper quarter a frieze containing a *stūpa* flanked by two seated Tīrthaṇkaras on either side. Bühler regarded the frieze-portrait of a *stūpa* in this way: "No less interesting is the additional proof, furnished by Dr. Führer's slab, that the Jainas formerly worshipped *Stūpas*." (Bühler 1890a:328)

Bühler drew this conclusion because the frieze substantiated literary evidence in his view. Ernst Leumann had discovered references to *stūpas* in the *Rājapraśnīya* (*Rāyapaseṇaijja)*, the second Śvetāmbara *Upāṅga*; and in a manner wholly consistent with the forces operating in the debate over origins, Bühler thus accepted the frieze as indicating a Jain *stūpa*-cult even as the *stūpa* on the site was still thought of as Buddhist (Bühler 1890a:328-29).

Less than a year later, his view of the *stūpa* began to change. Führer had discovered the famous inscription (Luders #47) that refers to the installation of an image at the '*vodva stūpa*, built by the gods.' This inscriptional reference to a *stūpa* unleashed an interpretive stream. In assessing it, Bühler wrote (Bühler 1891a:61):

> The sculptures [discovered previously] left no doubt that the Jains worshipped Stūpas, which fact is also mentioned in the extracts from the Rājapasenaijja translated by Professor Leumann. . . . Yet, the assertion that there was a Jaina Stūpa at Mathurā teaches us something new that hereafter will prove very important. For, it must be kept in mind that Dr. Führer had found a Stūpa in the immediate vicinity of the two Jaina temples [at Kaṅkālī Ṭīlā]. He believed it to be Buddhistic, because he discovered close to it a seal with a Buddhist inscription. I have adopted his conjecture. . . . But the point becomes now doubtful. It can be decided only when the Stūpa has been opened, and its surroundings have been completely explored.

This cautious note about the original provenance of the *stūpa* was far outstripped, however, by Bühler's vision of its age. For he went on, in the same discussion (Bühler 1891a:61-62):

> Even more valuable is the statement that the Stūpa was *devanirmita*, 'built by the gods' i.e. so ancient that at the time, when the inscription was incised, its origin had been forgotten. On the evidence of the characters the date of the inscription has to be referred undoubtedly to the Indoscythic era . . . The Stūpa must, therefore, have

> been built several centuries before the beginning of the Christian era, as the name of its builder would certainly have been known, if it had been erected during the period when the Jainas of Mathurā carefully kept record of their donations. This period began with the first century B.C. . . . Our inscription furnishes therefore a strong argument for the assumption that one Jaina Monument at Mathurā is as old as the oldest known Buddhist Stūpas.

By late 1892, some two years after Führer's first report of a *stūpa*, Bühler had thrown all caution to the winds. Writing in *Epigraphia Indica*, in connection with the editing and translation of the inscription that refers to the *stūpa*, he put it this way (Bühler 1894a:198):

> . . . with respect to the history of the Jaina sect, we learn. . . through No. XX [the number assigned by Bühler to the inscription numbered 47 by Luders] that an ancient Jaina Stūpa existed in Mathurā, which in A.D. 167 was considered to have been built by the gods, i.e. was so ancient that its real origin had been completely forgotten.

The only new evidence to lead Bühler to his increasing conviction that the *stūpa* at Kaṅkālī Ṭīlā was Jain was an increasing number of *stūpa*-portraits on other finds. But his discussions do not even reflect a systematic consideration of that evidence. What had apparently seized his attention was the notion of *devanirmita*, which he interpreted as further testimony to the age of the Jain tradition. In the years that followed, Bühler reinforced this interpretation, especially in 1898 in an account of Jinaprabha's *Vividhatīrthakalpa* (fourteenth century C.E.), whose section on Mathurā contains a legendary account of the erection by the goddess Kuberā of a *stūpa* at Mathurā dedicated to the Tīrthaṅkara Supārśva (Bühler 1898).

This one dimension of the *stūpa*—its extraordinary age—has come to dominate virtually all discussion of it. After Bühler's death, the *stūpa* was given its ultimate push to prominence by Vincent Smith. It is not clear whether the order of *The Jain Stûpa* was at all dictated by any arrangement of the plates on Führer's part; but the volume's title, design, and organization pulled the *stūpa* into extraordinary visibility. After presenting in plates i and ii the general outlines of the mound and photographs of the excavations, Smith devoted plates iii, iv, and v to the *stūpa*-foundation remains, and plate vi (which received the longest textual accompaniment of any plate in the volume) to the sculpture-base on which the '*stūpa*'-inscription occurred.

In Smith's text, and in virtually every discussion of the *stūpa* since then, the words first used by Bühler in the 1890s echo and re-echo, which is why they have been so extensively quoted above. The notion that the *stūpa* was so old in Kuṣāṇa times that no one knew who had built it has become the one feature of it that dominates all discussion, and the *stūpa* itself has become the prime piece of

Jain evidence from Mathurā, despite the checkered history of its discovery and the doubtful state of the evidence.

Stūpa-interpretation and Mathurā-interpretation

The *stūpa* does not stand alone in having been interpreted one-dimensionally, but space prevents a review of the many other items whose interpretation-history runs parallel to what has been sketched out above. Nor is this review of the *stūpa* as complete as is needed if its full significance is to be understood. What the *stūpa* here shows is, however, critical for understanding the problems of interpretation that still exist concerning the Jain presence at Mathurā.

At the most drastic level, the faint possibility exists that the *stūpa* was Buddhist or that the foundations are those of some other circular structure. But such a totally revisionist thesis need not be adopted. There very likely was a *stūpa* at Kaṅkālī Ṭīlā, and later Jain literature does refer to a *stūpa* (or *stūpa*s) at Mathurā. But the evidence, for various reasons, is problematic enough to always sustain a faint level of doubt; and such is unfortunately the case for most of the finds. This is the first problem illustrated by the *stūpa* that must receive systematic attention in dealing with the Jain presence at Mathurā.

But serious as that problem may be, the tendencies in interpretation that the *stūpa* illustrates are even more critically important, and directly reflect major concerns in understanding the general meaning of the Jain presence at Mathurā. The first such general concern is again parallel to the interpretation of the *stūpa*: the tendency to treat the existence of the remains almost solely in terms of their ability to prove the antiquity of the Jain tradition. This approach to the materials from Kaṅkālī Ṭīlā derives most directly from the context supplied by the debate over origins, and while it is an important feature of the finds, it does not deserve the degree of attention that it still receives.

This is especially so because preoccupation with the question of antiquity has succeeded in obscuring so many other features of the evidence. The most startlingly 'invisible' dimension of the *stūpa*, as of most other materials, is that it clearly reflects a vigorous lay-cult. Moreover, this cult was clearly condoned, if not abetted, by the monastic Jains at Mathurā. Yet analysis of the finds has stayed with Jacobi and Bühler in focusing almost exclusively on their testimony in the domain of the ascetic tradition. In this connection, the *stūpa* is perhaps the most startling instance of forced interpretation. It can hardly attest any ascetic practice at all. But rather than deal with this obvious point, scholars have rested content with reading the *stūpa*'s presence in a way that must wedge it into the mold of being evidence for the antiquity of the Jains as an ascetic movement.

All of this springs, in terms of its intensity, from the debate over the origins and its entanglement with the nineteenth-century vision of cultic activity as a secondary accretion to 'Jainism.' Yet the evidence itself, had it been found outside of that setting, might open the door to far more interesting possibilities. Those possibilities can be summed up by proposing the following options for re-understanding the Jain presence at Mathurā.

First, if the religious life of the Jains as revealed at Kaṅkālī Ṭīlā is typical of the Jain tradition for Kuṣāṇa times, a major reconsideration of Jain history is indicated. The *stūpa* and other evidence indicates a variety of religious interaction between ascetic and lay Jains that would require significant re-thinking of the role of the lay-community in early Jain history. At the very least, any vestiges of the notion that Jain cultic life was an inessential borrowing from the surrounding context ought to be seriously re-evaluated. Most Jain scholars are somewhat aware of this concern; but if the evidence from Kaṅkālī Ṭīlā were liberated from its one-dimensional past interpretations, that concern might find a new impetus and new information with which to work.

Second, it is possible that one has to think in terms of a 'Mathurā-Jain tradition,' i.e., that Jain life at Mathurā was not typical. This, too, has major implications for thinking about Jain history, most especially in terms of the common supposition that the Jain tradition forms a kind of unchanging monolith. Again, scholars are aware that the period in question, from ca. 200 B.C.E., to 300 C.E., is one of extraordinary fluidity in Jain history. The Mathurā evidence, seen more clearly, could assist significantly in understanding the range of varying development in the Jain tradition at that time, and could provide useful concrete models for taking seriously the fluidity of the tradition in the face of the usual assumption about its unchanging character.

But even beyond that, the possibility of an 'untypical' Jain community at Mathurā raises the possibility that Mathurā itself has been underestimated. Certainly the interpretations of the Jain community there have given priority to the 'Jainism' involved in all of the evidence. But it may be important to think of Mathurā itself as the major force in the situation. The power of an ancient *tīrtha* to deflect and shape even an ascetic tradition that comes within its precincts has seldom appeared as a factor in interpreting the Jain remains. To cite a single instance: it may be that the ancient sacredness of Mathurā, which in essence did not derive from Jain religiosity, is the place to begin in trying to understand why the 'Jain *stūpa*' was thought of as having been built by the gods.

In the end, it appears that the Jain presence at Mathurā cannot be left in the interpretive modes that have driven it thus far. All that has been seen of it is the one dimension of the tradition's antiquity and continuity, in conceptual terms that are themselves in need of reconsideration. Until Kaṅkālī Ṭīlā is re-examined, almost literally piece by piece, both Jain history and the life of Mathurā in general will remain to a significant degree eclipsed where much clearer light could prevail.

8

"FAITH" AND "SYSTEM": *DARŚANA* IN THE JAIN TRADITION*

I. *Samyaktva, Mithyātva, and Darśana*

The use of the term *darśana* in Indian thought to designate "systems" or "viewpoints" seems to be a usage without a clear starting point. The matter is further complicated by the fact that the Buddhist tradition often made use of the term *dṛṣṭi* (*diṭṭhi*) to speak of non-Buddhist schools. A clear connection between this Buddhist usage and the wider use of *darśana* has not been established. In the Jain tradition, the history of the term *darśana* is complex, and a large part of its complex history lies in its associations with "right" and "wrong."

It is clearly not possible in an essay this size to give an account of the notions expressed by *samyaktva* and *mithyātva*, which are commonly translated as "rightness" and "wrongness."[1] Yet these terms are an important matter, because the most common use of these terms in the Jain tradition occurs in relation to the terms *dṛṣṭi* and *darśana*.[2] The already difficult problem of "right" and "wrong" is exacerbated in this relationship because the term *darśana* is also

* From dissertation, pp. 232-310. For a subsequent discussion of *darśana*, see Halbfass 1979.

1 For some important studies of the terms themselves, see Wackernagel 1930:229ff., and Foy 1900:133ff.

2 In contradistinction to the Buddhist tradition's general usage, *darśana* and *dṛṣṭi* are used as synonyms in the Jain tradition, both in Sanskrit and Prakrit texts. This is true at least of those I have consulted. Hence the terms are used interchangeably here, though *darśana* is used more often.

tual *darśana* as indeterminate knowledge, and *jñāna* as determinate knowledge. This was perhaps along the lines followed by other schools in distinguishing *nirvikalpaka* and *savikalpaka* perception, though the Jain position should be kept separate in that it approached the problem in terms of generality and particularity. The Digambaras took another tack, developing the idea that *jñāna* is related to knowledge of external objects and *darśana* to knowledge of internal ones, in particular the *jīva*.

When thinkers of both sects applied themselves to the problem, they were apparently dealing with a very old notion, according to which the *jīva* was held to possess both perceptual faculties, *darśana* and *jñāna*. The best testimony for this is the presence in the Jain karma-literature of two types of perception-obscuring karma, *jñānāvaraṇa* and *darśanāvaraṇa* karma (von Glasenapp 1942:6-7). The canonical texts also speak of two such faculties (Tatia 1951:71). It is intriguing to ponder the relationship between the *darśana* that functions in perception and that which is given above as "faith." But the problem presents immense difficulties, for Pūjyapāda's sixth century C.E. commentary on *Tattvārthādhigama Sūtra* already does not see, or express, a relationship between *darśana* as "faith" (*Tattvārthādhigama* I.2) and the specialized perceptual *darśana* (*Tattvārthādhigama* VIII.4[D]; VIII.5[Ś]).[5] For the present it seems best to admit the separation of the two, with the proviso that a full investigation into the nature of *darśana* as perception might reveal something of its sense as faith. The latter sense, then, is the one to which the discussion now turns.

To repeat, the usual point of primary reference for *darśana* as faith is the tripartite *mokṣamārga*. In this context, the term is commonly glossed as follows: Right faith is firm conviction concerning the true nature of things.[6] Further, it arises from innate causes or by being obtained from outside sources.[7] The *tattva*, true nature of things, is as follows: the *tattvas* are *jīva, ajīva, āsrava, bandha, saṃvara, nirjarā*, and *mokṣa*.[8] Once this basic statement has been made, the *Tattvārthādhigama* goes on to describe several ways of considering the seven *tattva*s and learning of them. It then turns to *jñāna*.

Packed into these few *sūtra*s is an intensely complex and lengthy process of systematization, which brought the Jains to the point of formulating the *tattva*s and the *mokṣamārga*. The *Tattvārthādhigama* statement is apparently one of the earliest formulations. *Uttarādhyayana* XXVIII seems to contain another, slightly

---

5 See S. A. Jain 1960:5, 220 for the comments on these.

Because of the sectarian variations in the text of the *Tattvārthādhigama*, it is at times necessary to specify which version is being cited. In this study, this is done by inserting Ś or D in parentheses after a citation where a variation is to be noted.

6 Tattvārthaśraddhānam samyagdarśanam. *Tattvārthādhigama Sūtra* I.2.

7 Tan nisargād adhigamād vā. *Tattvārthādhigama Sūtra* I.3.

8 Jīvājivāsravabandhasaṃvaranirjarāmokṣās tattvam. *Tattvārthādhigama Sūtra* I.4.

different early statement. *Sūtrakṛtāṅga* I.6 may be another early formulation, since it speaks of a triad of *ṇāṇa* (*jñāna*), *daṃsaṇa* (*darśana*), and *sīla* (*śīla*) in verse 2 (see Jacobi 1895b:287), but it contains no mention of anything resembling the *tattva*s. According to K. K. Dixit (1971:21), the relationship that is set up between *darśana* and the *tattva*s in the *mokṣamārga* has no clear antecedent in the older texts.

While this study cannot trace the details of the development of the *tattva*s, the fact of their development demands attention, for the formulation of the *tattva*s appears to have involved finding common ground in terminology and structure between the Jain position and the rest of Indian analytical thought. The development of the *tattva*s in itself, however, has implications for the development of *darśana* as well.

These implications can best be seen by first examining the nature of the relationship of *darśana* with *samyak* in the *mokṣamārga*, for there it is held that *samyagdarśana* consists in a particular relationship between person and *tattva*, a relationship summed up in the word *śraddhāna*. The translation of the latter term into English is a thorny problem; "belief" has generally held the field, and Jains commonly take the term thus.[9] However, it does not seem particularly felicitious to translate the gloss of one complex term by another complex term, not to mention the question of whether faith can be glossed by belief. It would seem more useful to keep in mind that *samyagdarśana* consists in the relationship just noted, and then to explore how that relationship affects *darśana*.

The first and most obvious point to make is that if there are no *tattva*s, this particular relationship can hardly obtain. I have elsewhere (chapter 16, below) shown something of the lateness of the development of the *tattva*s. Since *darśana* antedates the existence of the *tattva* formulation, it must have functioned in some other manner in earlier periods.

It is clearly the case that *darśana* (both as faith and perception) antedates the *tattva*s, and it appears to be correct to say that its function was different from that implied in its relationship to the *tattva*s. Further, the early history of *darśana* finds it intimately related to *samyak* and *mithyā*, and this relationship is formulated in terms of karma. In the early Jain texts, *darśana* is the object of a specific type of karma, a type that co-exists with the *darśanāvaraṇa* (perception-obscuring) karma; this also means that a distinction between *darśana* as faith and as perception is an early feature of Jain thought.

The specific type of karma involved is *mohanīya*, or delusive, karma, which is one of eight basic types of karma (*darśanāvaraṇa* being another). *Mohanīya* karma consists of two types, one of which is *darśanamohanīya*, the other

---

9 Translators are often careless on this point and it is not unusual to find *samyagdarśana* given as "right belief."

cāritramohanīya, of which more in a moment. *Darśanamohanīya* itself consists of three sorts, which Helmuth von Glasenapp (1942:8) describes thus:

> The *darśana-mohanīya*-k[arma] causes a disturbance of the knowledge of the religious truth inherent in the *jīva* by natural disposition. According as to whether the disturbance is an absolute or a partial one, 3 kinds of this k[arma] are to be distinguised:
>
> 1. *Mithyātva*-k[arma]. This causes complete unbelief or heterodoxy. If it realizes itself, the *jīva* does not believe in the truths as proclaimed by Mahāvīra; he believes false prophets to be saints and enjoins false doctrines.
> 2. *Samyagmithyātva- (miśra-)* k[arma]. This produces a mixed belief, i.e., if it operates the soul waves to and fro betwixt true and false; it is indifferent to the religion of the Jina and has no predilection for, nor hatred against it.
> 3. *Samyaktva*-k[arma]. This induces the correct belief. This *samyaktva* is, however, not the correct faith in its completeness, but only in a preliminary degree; it is a so-called *mithyātva*, from which the *mithyātva*-quality has been abstracted, a *mithyatva* free from poison. . . The true belief in its perfection is only obtained, when the atoms of the *samyaktva-mohanīya*-k[arma] have disappeared, even as milk which is covered by quite clear water only becomes perfectly pure after the water has been poured off.

Some of von Glasenapp's work rests on texts that are younger than the earliest systematic considerations of karma. However, the practice of arraying karma into the group of eight from which von Glasenapp's summary is drawn, a grouping determined by the effect of the types of karma on the *jīva*, is definitely not a late practice, though it may not belong to the very earliest discussions of karma (see Dixit 1971:38). It certainly antedates the *Tattvārthādhigama* and other formulations of the *mokṣamārga*.

This early setting for *darśana* is important for understanding what lies behind its role in the *mokṣamārga*, especially on two points. The first is the intimate connection of early *darśana* with karma;[10] the second is its early and consistent connection with *samyak* and *mithyā*. This connection can perhaps be placed even earlier than the eight-fold karma scheme, since *samyagdarśana* and

10 In Jain tradition, the single most powerful element governing early analytic thought is the notion of karma. K. K. Dixit has demonstrated quite convincingly that karma, as the factor that produces variation in the realm of observable phenomena, lies behind the earliest systematic Jain approaches to the analysis of these phenomena. A glance through the later Digambara scholastic literature will show how tenacious this approach to analysis was. The given factors for early Jain thought appear to have been the fundamental division of the world into *jīva* and *ajīva*; the working of karma produces the assorted phenomena in the realm of *ajīva*, which can thus best be analyzed in terms of karma. Karma also produces the various qualities of the *jīva*, and thus accounts for the different conditions of conscious beings. Von Glasenapp's analysis, despite some of its later features, shows this very nicely. This matter of karma really requires a full, new study by itself; in this study it simply must be kept in mind as a constant factor in the background.

mithyādarśana are regular features of the list of fourteen *guṇasthānas* (karmic conditions of the *jīva*) that, in one form or another, has been present in Jain analytical thought from early on (Dixit 1971:15-16). Here *mithyādarśana* gradually gives way to varieties of *samyagdarśana* in the first four of these fourteen stages on the way to omniscience (see von Glasenapp 1942:76-81).

Beyond this established antiquity for *darśana*, it is vital to see the importance of its karmic setting. This karma basis gives *samyag/mithyādarśana* a character wholly different from that which it has in the *mokṣamārga*. In its early history, *samyagdarśana* consists in the removal of karma that is preventing the *jīva* from enjoying its natural faculty of *darśana*. While the later tradition never gives up its reliance on karma altogether, the introduction of the *tattva* formulation and the notion of *tattvārthaśraddhāna* in the *mokṣamārga* put *samyagdarśana* in a very different light. In sum, it has the effect of considerably loosening *darśana*'s link with karma.

The loss of this close link with karma appears, further, to have another interesting effect: it loosens the close association of *samyak* and *mithyā* with *darśana*. This general process of loosening can be shown in two ways. The first of these has to do with terminology in the older Jain texts that deal with non-Jains; the second has to do with the quasi-independent treatment of *samyaktva* in Jain texts that are informed by the *mokṣamārga* approach to *darśana*.

In the early parts of *Sūtrakṛtāṅga* the erroneousness of non-Jain positions is apparently based on karma. *Mithyādarśana* (*micchādiṭṭhi*) is one of the terms commonly used of non-Jains, a point that could also serve to reconfirm the above conclusions concerning the early history of *darśana*. Now, if one examines the terminology in *Sūtrakṛtāṅga* for the pattern of its use of *darśana* in general, a further important discovery comes to light. This is the fact that *darśana*, whether *samyak* or *mithyā*, is not the term most commonly used of either the Jain or non-Jain positions. The Jain position is generally referred to as *dhamma*; a survey reveals the variety of terms for others that well-outnumber *mithyādarśana*.[11] The point of this observation is that *darśana* here apparently speaks more of the conditions of the *jīva* than of actual viewpoints or schools of thought.

This shows in the use of the term in the early part of *Sūtrakṛtāṅga*. Part I of *Sūtrakṛtāṅga* uses *darśana* in only four instances not covered by the above-noted instances of *mithyādarśana*. These four are I.1.1.19; I.1.2.24; I.1.2.30; and I.8.22-23. In all these cases, it is hard to say whether the term refers to a school of thought or to a state of the *jīva*; where the former seems to be the case, the reference is not to a non-Jain position. I.1.1.19 refers to *imam darişaṇam* in an apparent reference to the Jain position. I.1.2.24 speaks of the *kiriyāvāidar-*

11 See chapter 17, below.

iṣaṇam; the passage is another reference to the Jain position. I.1.2.30 uses *diṭṭhi* alone, in the sense that *diṭṭhi* by itself is not sufficient for *mokṣa*; the context makes it more likely that the term refers to a *jīva* state. I.8.22-23 speaks of men who possess *samyak-* or *mithyādarśana* (i.e., of *sammatta-* or *asammattadamsinas*); the reference is clearly to states of the *jīva*.

However, in the later portions of *Sūtrakṛtāṅga* this ambiguous state of affairs is significantly altered. Five instances of *diṭṭhi* are found in the second part of *Sūtrakṛtāṅga*, at II.1.34; II.2.80; and II.6.11, 12, and 13. These begin to show a character very different from that of the earlier uses, for here *diṭṭhi* begins to be used in a general sense. II.1.34 and II.2.80 use the term with the prefix *ṇāṇā* ("varied"), speaking of men as being possessed of various *diṭṭhis*; this is the least general of the usages, for there is still a strong sense of *diṭṭhi* as a quality of the *jīva*. But the occurences in II.6 are distinctively different. II.6.11 speaks of teachers who each put forth their own *diṭṭhi* (*sayam sayam diṭṭhi*); II.6.12 speaks of *diṭṭhi* in the same sense of "teaching" or "doctrine"; and, most strikingly, II.6.13 speaks of the way (*magga*) of the speaker's own *diṭṭhi* (*sadiṭṭhi*), i.e., of the way of the Jain *diṭṭhi*.

These instances mark a definite shift in the use of *darśana*, for here it is not so much solely a quality of the *jīva*, but also an abstract, external element. There are hints that such a reinterpretation even extends to the sense of *dhamma*. The latter is still used in the later parts of *Sūtrakṛtāṅga* as the dominant term for Jain teachings; but at several points it, too, seems subject to generalization. *Sūtrakṛtāṅga* II.1.18 speaks of non-Jains who put forth a law of their own (*māmagam dhammam*). II.6.7 has a non-Jain speak of "our law" (*amha dhamma*). II.6.42 takes the highly unusual step, not found elsewhere in *Sūtrakṛtāṅga*, of speaking of the *nigganṭha dhamma*, the Jain law; *dhamma* is elsewhere simply understood to be the Jain position, without qualification.

With respect to the Jain view of others, it is surely significant that this shift in the use of *darśana* (and even *dhamma*) occurs along the same lines as a shift noted elsewhere (chapter 17, below), where specific terms like *annautthiya* begin to replace the general terms used before. The end-product of these replacements was a *mithyādarśana* quite divorced from the workings of karma. Here there appears to be another side to the same development: the separation of *darśana* itself from the arena of karma, and the beginnings of the occurrence of *darśana* as a general term for a viewpoint, a term that needs to be qualified as *mithyā* or *samyak* before its nature is clear.

This pattern in the use of *darśana* can also bé approached from another direction, focussing on *samyaktva*, though one must adopt a via negativa in order to draw it out fully. To begin, it is commonly assumed that in the *mokṣamārga* formulation *samyak* is to be associated with all three elements, *darśana, jñāna,* and *cāritra*; and further, that this is generally true within the Jain tradition. But this does not seem actually to be the case in the *Tattvārthādhigama* statement. After *Tattvārthādhigama* I.2-8 have discussed *darśana*, I.9 takes up *jñāna* without introducing the notion that *samyak* is to be associated with it, either in verse 9 or in verses 10-35, which discuss *jñāna*. Nor is *samyak* associated with *cāritra* in the *Tattvārthādhigama*.

The same point can be made concerning the presentation of the *mokṣamārga* in *Uttarādhyayana* XXVIII. Only in that section devoted to *darśana* (verses 16-31) does *samyak* or *samyaktva* enter the discussion. Further, in the early version of *cāritramohanīya* karma (mentioned above) there is no association of *samyak* or *mithyā* with *cāritra*, though it is very prominent in the discussion of *darśanamohanīya* karma (see von Glasenapp 1942:8-11).

One does not ordinarily find that studies of Jain thought consider *samyak* to be associated only with *darśana*, and the Jain tradition itself does not hew strictly to this line. The *Svabhāṣya* on *Tattvārthādhigama*, which is followed by Siddhasenagaṇi and the subsequent Śvetāmbara tradition, begins by saying immediately that *samyak* applies to all three items. So does Pūjyapāda, who is followed by the Digambara commentary tradition. One might venture at this point to say that it is the cumulative effect of this dogmatic tradition that has led Jain and non-Jain scholars alike to present the *mokṣamārga* as consisting of "right faith, right knowledge, and right conduct." But beyond this dogmatic tradition lies another possibility, which has to do with the change that the *mokṣamārga* effects in the status of *darśana*, for this change also alters the status of *samyak*. Since *samyaktva* now consists in a relationship between *tattva* and the *darśana*-possessing *jīva*, this has the effect of elevating *samyaktva* into an independent element, a qualifier of *darśana*.

This somewhat independent status for *samyaktva* shows up in the fact that the later tradition produced a number of what it calls treatments of *samyaktva*. Yet it does not appear that these treatments reflect complete independence from *darśana*. It is almost as if the process of breaking them apart did not completely succeed.

This may show up as early as two canonical passages, which are entitled *samyaktva*: *Ācārāṅga* I.4 and *Uttarādhyayana* XXIX. The latter, which is, again, part of the later, more systematic portion of *Uttarādhyayana*, occupies itself with presenting 73 items. But very few of the specific discussions of these items make any reference to *samyaktva*. In only two of them does *samyaktva* actually make an appearance, and in both of these cases it is linked with *darśana*. In two verses (59 and 61) that actively discuss *jñāna* and *cāritra*, *samyaktva* has absolutely no place. Thus, although the title of the chapter is *samyaktva*, the term itself preserves a close connection with *darśana*.

In *Ācārāṅga* I.4 the same holds true. The one point at which *samyaktva* actually enters into the text is I.4.3.1, where it occurs as *sammattadaṃsina*. The chapter as a whole is devoted to the high value of not harming any creature. As concerns these two texts, one might hazard the guess that the titles reflect a later conception of *samyaktva* as a general category, while the texts themselves preserve an older, direct connection with *darśana*.

The text of the *sūtras* in *Tattvārthādhigama*, as pointed out above, also maintains this connection, regardless of the commentary tradition. Further, the later non-canonical tradition, despite the tendency for *samyaktva* to receive some sort of nominally separate treatment, treats *samyaktva* and *samyagdarśana* as near-synonyms. Where these supposedly separate treatments occur, the pattern of the treatment is generally such that the connection is quite unmistakable. Amitagati's *Subhāṣitaratnasandoha* (993 C.E., according to R. Williams 1963:17, 23) provides an excellent example. Chapter seven of this text deals with *samyaktva* and *mithyātva*, and chapters eight and nine with *jñāna* and *cāritra* in turn. Ernst Leumann was quick to note this pattern, and to observe the apparent identification of *samyaktva* and *darśana* in this text and elsewhere, in the face of the tendency to link *samyak* with *darśana*, *jñāna* and *cāritra*. He concluded that "*samyaktva* [wird] in allgemeinen nur dem ersten Glied jener Dreiheit gleichgestellt" (Leumann 1905:578).[12]

In his treatment of the *śrāvakācāras*, texts dealing with the standards of behavior for lay Jains, R. Williams (1963:41) also treats *samyagdarśana* and *samyaktva* as synonyms. His wide-ranging text citations, some of which will be discussed momentarily, appear to establish the point beyond reasonable doubt.

This persistent near identity between *samyaktva* and *darśana* seems puzzling unless one sees that the two were originally intimately related, and then strongly affected by the *mokṣamārga*. When *tattvārthaśraddhāna* becomes the criterion of *samyagdarśana*, *samyak* begins to have an independent role to play, while the status of *darśana* also changes radically in that it becomes a general term for a position or viewpoint, subject to rightness or wrongness. But the two continue to be closely related. Neither of them seems to achieve full independence.

This point has tremendous implications for the general history of Jain thought, and for their view of non-Jains. It also has some direct consequences having to do with the search for the meaning of *darśana*, particularly in the Jain compendia. The most direct result of the above discoveries is that such a search should also include treatments of *samyaktva*. In fact, the discussions of *samyaktva* studied by Williams proved a direct insight into the meaning of *darśana* in the compendia.

12 [Editor's translation] "*Samyaktva* [was] in general equivalent to only the first limb of the three."

In the approaches to *samyaktva* that Williams has examined, the Jain writers have considered the problem from a number of aspects. A great many authors discuss the elements that make up *samyaktva*, listing them as its *aṅga*s, *liṅga*s, *guṇa*s, etc. Also popular were lists of elements that constituted transgressions against *samyaktva*, i.e., *mithyātva*; these were referred to as *doṣa*s, *aticāra*s, etc., many of which are merely the reverse of the positive elements. There are a number of lists and groupings, and Williams (1963:41-50) has collected the more popular ones in his study. Among these sets of what will hereafter be called *darśana* marks there occur several series of marks that are of great interest here. According to Williams (1963:41), "Digambaras such as Samantabhadra, Somadeva, and Vasunandin describe it [*samyaktva*] . . . as faith in the three articles of belief: *āpta* (the Jina), *āgama* (the scriptures), and *padārtha* or *tattva* (the dogmas)." Another tripartite formula is given by Hemacandra, who says that it is "'faith in the right *deva*, the right guru, and the right *dharma*'" (Williams 1963:41).

Among negative formulations, the Digambara notion of six non-abodes of *samyaktva* can serve as an example (Williams 1963:47):

1) false divinities (*kudeva*)
2) false ascetics (*kuliṅgin*)
3) false scriptures (*kuśāstra*)
4) worship of false divinities (*kudevasevā*)
5) worship of false ascetics (*kuliṅgisevā*)
6) worship of false scriptures (*kuśāstrasevā*)

These sets of *darśana* marks are highly significant, not merely for the insights that they grant into the status of *darśana*, but also because they provide a model much like that around which the bulk of the compendia are constructed. While many of the lists produced by Williams do not exactly resemble the compendium model, the notion of *darśana* marks provides a context that gives a strikingly apt explanation for the structure of the compendia, and some of the sets of marks are virtually reproduced in the compendia.

As was noted earlier, there are very few clues in the compendia themselves that might provide some means of explaining the function or purpose of a compendium or the significance of *darśana*. However, the compendia do exhibit a set of principles around which the information about the various schools of thought is organized, and these internal principles provide a direct point of contact with the *darśana* marks. Haribhadra's *Ṣaḍdarśanasamuccaya* states as its second verse:

In this world, according to fundamental differences, there are
just six *darśana*s;

And they should be known by the wise according to differences
in *devatā* and *tattva*.

Rājaśekhara's *Ṣaḍdarśanasamuccaya* expresses its structure as follows, in verses 2 and 3:

> *Dharma* is beloved in all the world;
> let the six *darśanas* declare it.
> Among them, in mark, dress, conduct,
> deity and teacher,
>
> In *pramāṇa* and *tattva*, release and logic,
> one perceives difference.
> This is their common declaration:
> release comes through the eight-fold *yoga*.

Merutuṅga's *Ṣaḍdarśananirṇaya*, after arguing that the content of the six *darśanas* is reducible to the Jain position, sums up matters thus:

> Thus having seen the correct nature of the three principles—deity, teacher, and *dharma*—held in common by all the systems, and having left behind all the rest, which is naught but attachment to inessentials, the wise man should know, believe, and practice this triple quintessence of all knowables.

It must be admitted at once that of these three compendia, that of Merutuṅga exhibits the closest connection with any system of *darśana* marks cited by Williams, parallelling exactly the formula given by Hemacandra. Matters are not so directly clear in the case of Haribhadra and Rājaśekhara, or in other compendia such as the anonymous *Sarvasiddhāntapraveśaka* and Jinadatta's *Vivekavilāsa*. However, closer analysis of these texts against the backdrop of the *darśana* marks and with respect to other features in them should make quite clear an important discovery: the term *darśana* in the compendia is the same term as the *darśana* being discussed under the rubric of *samyaktva*, i.e., the *darśana* that is commonly translated as "faith" in the *mokṣamārga* statements.

II. *The Ṣaḍdarśanasamuccaya of Haribhadra*

Haribhadra has often been touted as both an extraordinary author and an extraordinary person. The former characterization is largely the result of his versatility, and the latter the result of what has often been proclaimed as his strikingly tolerant attitude toward non-Jain schools of thought. The question of his 'tolerance,' of course, goes to the root of a basic issue. It is important to emphasize that what will be presented here as the special characteristic of the *Ṣaḍdarśanasamuccaya*, a brief metrical work of 87 verses, dating probably from the eighth century C.E., does not depend on the author's 'tolerance' for its striking character.

Haribhadra states in verse 2 of the *Ṣaḍdarśanasamuccaya* that there are just six *darśanas*, and that they are to be known according to differences in *devatā* and *tattva*. This simple statement of purpose, viewed against the backdrop of the *darśana* marks, can be seen to have an important set of connotations, both for understanding the text and for understanding the Jain view of others.

Each section of the text begins with an immediate reference to the marks as they are found in the school under discussion. Verse 4 states that Sugata is the Buddhist *devatā*; verses 5-12 account for the *tattvas* of the four noble truths, the twelve *āyatanas*, and two *pramāṇas*. Verse 13 gives Śiva as the *devatā* of Nyāya, and verses 14-32 summarily present the sixteen categories given in the *Nyāya Sūtras*. Verse 34 observes that in Sāṃkhya some are *nirīśvara* and others *seśvara*, but that all accept the twenty-five *tattvas*, which are then summarized in verses 35-43.[13] Verses 45-46 state that for Jains, the Jina is the *devatā*; verse 47 lists the *tattvas*, which are thereafter expounded along with the Jain notion of *pramāṇa*.

After this, the matter of *darśana* marks becomes even more interesting. Verse 59 observes that Nyāya and Vaiśeṣika do not disagree on *devatā*, but that since they differ on *tattva*, this difference will be revealed; verses 60-67 very briefly present the six-fold version of the Vaiśeṣika *padārthas*. Verses 68-71 are then forced to state a prologue of sorts to the Mīmāṃsā, for here there is no *devatā* save for the Veda, and no *tattva* save, perhaps, for *dharma* and the *pramāṇas*. Thereafter, the six *pramāṇas* of the Mīmāṃsā are presented. Finally, an appendix-like section on Lokāyata is introduced, and verse 80 makes it quite plain that here it is the absence of *devatā* and *tattva* that is the feature of note.

The pattern in which the schools are presented and the way in which the facts concerning each are organized reveals the pervasive force of Haribhadra's marks. The *Ṣaḍdarśanasamuccaya* begins by presenting four schools with distinctive *devatā* and *tattva* marks, and thereafter presents three more that are not so clearly marked: Vaiśeṣika, where the *devatā* mark is the same as in Nyāya; Mīmāṃsā, where the clear existence of these marks is dubious, but where substitutes or approximations can be found; and Lokāyata, where the marks are regarded as absent. One can say that the system of marks works here to produce an intriguing conjunction of rationale and reality, in that the text

13 The verse-numbers for Sāṃkhya follow Jain's edition of the text, which is primarily based on the text preserved in Guṇaratna's commentary. In the text preserved by Somatilaka, verse 36 (Jain) precedes verses 34-35 (Jain); but since verse 36 is already discussing the *tattvas*, this rather dislocates the order in which *devatā* and *tattva* are taken up in the other sections.

produces an account of schools of thought extant in the eighth century C.E. while fitting them into a framework that accounts for their differences.

But a question may remain as to whether these are *darśana* marks in the way that they function in the discussions of *samyaktva*. Such a question is most likely to surface in connection with the use of *devatā*, the mark that seems the most strained in that it does not appear to be proper to apply it to the Buddha, or to the Jina, for that matter.

Two things need to be recalled in this connection. The first is the conception of *samyagdarśana* as *tattvārthaśraddhāna*; the second is that certain of the marks discussed by Williams are not very far removed from Haribhadra's use of *devatā*. Williams (1963:41) has cited a practice present as early as Samantabhadra (who may date to 450 C.E.) of defining *samyaktva* as "faith in . . . *āpta* (the Jina), *āgama* (the scriptures), and *padārtha* or *tattva* (the dogmas)." This pattern is present as late as Vasunandin (ca. 1100 C.E.) and would seem to be roughly equivalent to Hemacandra's triad of *deva, guru*, and *dharma*, which is directly repeated by Merutuṅga.

Understanding these particular sets of marks and the use of *devatā* by Haribhadra has to do with the *mokṣamārga* formulation, for it introduces the *tattva*s and a certain attitude toward them as requisite to *samyagdarśana*. This matter of *tattva* also entails the problem of whence a particular *tattva* should be known.

This point is raised immediately in *Tattvārthādhigama* I.3, where it is posited that *tattvārthaśraddhāna* may be inborn (the result, according to some commentators, of the effect of previous lives, and according to others, simply the result of the subsidence of *darśanamohanīyakarma*), or may result from being taught. This is an important point, showing clearly the effect of the presence of the *tattva*s and preserving both the karmic setting of *darśana* and another possible source for it. This other source raises a new problem, which may be summed up in the word *āptatva*, or the reliability of one's sources. For the Jains *āptatva* resides in the Jina, and it is not difficult to see how this general category can embrace *āgama* (as for Samantabhadra, et al.) or *guru* (as for Hemacandra).

There remains the problem of how the term *devatā* (commonly translated as "deity") should have come to be used. That Haribhadra's usage is not necessarily an aberration is testified to by Hemacandra's triad, where the word *deva* is used, and by the fact that a number of *samyaktva* discussions seem to treat the Jina and the notion of *devatā* as being generally equivalent. As an example of this equivalence, albeit negatively put, one can cite William's (1963:49) summary of the *samyaktva* flaw known as *devatā-mūḍhatā*, or foolishness concerning *devatā*:

> It is a misconception of the nature of the divinity, says Samantabhadra, to worship *devas* stained with passion and hate in order to obtain a boon. Hemacandra charac-

terizes the *ku-devas* or *a-devas* as addicted to women (symbolizing *rāga*), weapons (symbolizing *dveṣa*), and rosaries (symbolizing *moha*), and accustomed to inflict punishments or grant boons. All of these attributes are inappropriate to the Jina who is devoid of passion, hate, and delusion.

Further testimony to this effect comes from another work of Haribhadra, the *Lokatattvanirṇaya*,[14] which is an investigation and refutation of non-Jain positions on several issues. Part of its first section is devoted to the question of *devatā*. Luigi Suali (1905:266) summarizes thus:

> si passano in rassegna le principali divinità del Pantheon brahmanico con i loro attributi di violenza e di crudeltà, contrapponendole al Jina, immacolato e dedito solo al bene delle creature. Non ostante che in questa parte predomini un certo spirito polemico, tuttavia la nota fondamentale è questa: si esaminino senza preconcetti le diverse teorie, e si segua la migliore. Serenità di giudizio riassunta nel verso 40:
>
> «Onore a colui nel quale non si trova nessun difetto ma»
>
> «sono tutti le virtù, sia egli Brahma, Visṇu o Macheçvara [sic],» ma in sostanza contraddetta dall esposizione precendente e dalla discussione contenuta nella parte seconda.[15]

It is important to view these discussions with care. The negative formulation should not be taken to mean that *devatā* is an erroneous or superfluous conception alongside that of the Jina and his *āptatva*. Rather, it appears that the Jina also occupies the position called *devatā*. The important point here is not "gods" versus Jina, but *āptatva*.[16] Haribhadra's verse speaks of the need for *devatā* to be unsullied in order for a viewpoint to be acceptable. This comes through clearly in two additional verses from the passage in question, verses 32 and 38:

> The Blessed One is not of our family, nor are the others our foes;
> Nor was one of them actually seen before [by us].

---

14 This is its popular title, not the title given in the colophon. The latter is *Nṛtattvanigama*, which may or may not be a significant difference, in light of the fact that it contains refutations of non-Jain positions. The ensuing discussions should show the possibilities involved. On the title, see Kapadia 1940-47:2: xxxiv.

15 [Translation by William A. Graham:]

> the principle deities of the Brāhmaṇical pantheon are reviewed with their attributes of violence and cruelty, and thus set against the Jina, immaculate and dedicated solely to the good of all creatures. Although a certain polemic spirit predominates in this section, the basic message is: the various theories should be examined without preconceptions and the best one followed. Fairness of judgement is summarized in verse 40:
>
> "Honor to him in whom no fault is found who possesses
> all the virtues, be he Brahmā, Viṣṇu, or Maheśvara,"
>
> but is in essence contradicted by the preceding exposition and by the discussion included in the second part.

16 All of this points up the need for more care with such terms as *devatā*; it might also reflect the Jain tradition's attitude toward the Jina, another matter that is in dire need of exploration.

Having heard the words and good works of each in detail, wishing to share his excellent qualities, we take refuge in the Vīra.

I have neither partiality toward the Vīra, nor dislike for
Kapila and the others;
Whose words are proven by argument,
his are fit to be accepted.

Further, to interpret such verses as a sign of great tolerance (as which they are very often quoted) or even impartiality may miss the mark. When the importance of *devatā* as part of *tattvārthaśraddhāna* is seen, Haribhadra's remarks take on a rather different tone. When *tattvas* become important, so does *āptatva*, and thus *devatā*.

The foregoing helps to explain the use of *devatā* in the *Ṣaḍdarśanasamuccaya* (especially in regard to such a specific point as the use of the terms to speak of the Buddha), but the issue of *devatā* also serves as a point of reference in the larger framework of *darśana* marks and *samyaktva*. What is here being discussed within the limits of the compendia is part and parcel of a larger process in the Jain tradition, of which *devatā* as a mark of *samyaktva* is a striking symptom. No longer are there only *samyak* and *mithyā* states of the *jīva*, as in the karmic setting for *samyagdarśana*. With the presence of *tattvārthaśraddhāna* and its outside sources there comes the problem of *āptatva*, the problem, in short, of true *devatā* and false *devatā*, of true *tattva* and false *tattva*. In this connection the six-fold non-abodes of *samyaktva* given above are very instructive. The separation of *samyak* and *darśana* means in effect that *samyagdarśana* and *mithyādarśana* no longer imply only the absence of each other. Both are specific entities, with characteristics—marks—that are shared with other viewpoints. The *darśana* marks in the compendia point to this process.

III. *The Ṣaḍdarśanasamuccaya of Rājaśekhara*

Rājaśekhara's *Ṣaḍdarśanasamuccaya* follows Haribhadra rather closely in some respects. The text itself is in meter, and at 180 verses, considerably larger than Haribhadra's work. According to number and distribution of manuscripts, this compendium ranks a distant second to Haribhadra's in popularity, but still far outstrips other Jain compendia (Velankar 1944:402-3).

Rājaśekhara also uses a set of marks, as given in the verse quoted above. In addition to the *devatā* and *tattva* marks, he makes use of mark (*liṅga*, the symbol or object associated with a particular school), dress, conduct (ascetic praxis), teacher (guru), *pramāṇa*, *mokṣa* (the school's teaching on the nature thereof), and *tarka*, which he takes to refer to the actual works composed by members of the school. This makes nine marks in all. While the marks that Rājaśekhara uses include those of Haribhadra, the order in which he takes up the schools varies considerably:

Haribhadra:	Rājaśekhara:
Bauddha	Jain
Nyāya	Sāṃkhya
Sāṃkhya	Jaiminīya (including Vedānta)
Jain	Śaiva (Nyāya)
Vaiśeṣika	Vaiśeṣika
Jaiminīya	Bauddha
Lokāyata	Lokāyata

Rājaśekhara's *devatā* statements are generally lengthier and more detailed than Haribhadra's, and are followed by clear statements as to who is the *guru*, the latter quite clearly separated from *devatā*. This seems to reflect the separation of *devatā* and *guru* in some of the *samyaktva* schemes, a separation that in turn makes Rājaśekhara's descriptive principle more understandable. It might, moreover, indicate that Rājaśekhara's borrowings, or materials in common with Haribhadra, reflect some sense of choice and a principle that is to be followed.

This latter possibility does not arise simply because certain verses are shared by the two compendia. In fact, almost the whole of the content of Haribhadra's work is in Rājaśekhara's, but only some of it is duplicated word-for-word. The reason is simple. Rājaśekhara has, in addition to *devatā* and *tattva*, the marks *guru, pramāṇa*, and *mokṣa* into which much of Haribhadra's material can better be put. In short, there is virtually nothing in Haribhadra that is not also present in Rājaśekhara, but with the difference that the *devatā* and *tattva* marks have been limited and refined, and the rest of Haribhadra's material has been re-stated and re-distributed over the additional marks of *guru, pramāṇa*, and *mokṣa*. What Rājaśekhara discusses under *liṅga*, dress, conduct, and *tarka*, and here and there adds to the other marks, is not duplicated from Haribhadra, but rather constitutes his own contribution.

This characteristic of the shared material is so clear that it nearly demands the conclusion that Rājaśekhara saw the principles active in Haribhadra's work, saw where to refine them, and used the material judiciously to achieve that aim. This borrowed and re-worked material is then surrounded by a host of additional information, mostly descriptive and bibliographic, concerning the schools in question.

However, the additional marks used by Rājaśekhara also raise a question concerning the structure and rationale of the whole. Given the variety shown in the *samyaktva* schemes, his additional marks need not necessarily be considered additions that have about them no sense of the original whole. Yet it might be argued that by introducing these marks Rājaśekhara betrays a lack of understanding of them as the marks of *darśana*.

This impression is somewhat reinforced by the fact that whereas the order of the schools in Haribhadra is in perfect parallel with the descending presence of the *darśana* marks in those schools, the order in Rājaśekhara does not follow such a pattern. With nine marks involved, such a descending order becomes obscured, for where one mark may be less strong or missing, the others are generally present. This shows quite clearly when one compares Rājaśekhara's treatment of the Mīmāṃsā with Haribhadra's.

Along with this, one should consider another point, which consists of Rājaśekhara's own statement about the nature of a *darśana*. According to verses 2-3, *dharma* is that which the six *darśana*s all declare, and all also hold that *mokṣa* comes about by means of the eight-fold *yoga*. The differences between them consist in the nine marks. Then, in verse 4, where he lists the schools, Rājaśekhara adds the remarkable statement that *nāstika* is not a *darśana*.[17] This statement is best evaluated in light of Haribhadra's position on this point. Verses 77b-80 of the latter's compendium read:

> Thus is complete the summary-statement of the *āstikavāda*s.
>
> Others do not hold with separating the Vaiśeṣika from the Nyāya doctrine;
> In their opinion, there are only five *āstikavādī*s.
>
> Indeed, in their opinion the six-*darśana*-number (*ṣaḍdarśanasaṃkhyā*)
> Is made replete (*pūryate*) by including the Lokāyata doctrine; thus
> that doctrine is now recounted.
>
> The Lokāyatas teach thus: there is no *jīva*, nor release (*nirvṛtti*);
> *dharma* and *adharma* do not exist, nor the fruits of merit and demerit.

The introduction of the terms *āstikavāda* and *āstikavādī* is intriguing, for these terms for describing schools of thought are quite absent elsewhere in Haribhadra. That they should occur here as implied synonyms for schools possessing *darśana* marks is a point worth noting, though the unreflective nature of the text and the absence of any old commentary make it necessary to excercise some caution. But the *darśana* marks have such influence elsewhere in Haribhadra that, despite the absence of an explicit statement in the text, one may be justified in saying that this brief statement shows that for Haribhadra, the presence of *darśana* marks is the equivalent of *āstika*-ness.

Rājaśekhara's direct statement about what is not a *darśana* is stronger than anything that Haribhadra explicitly says. Yet, according to verses 158ff., where Rājaśekhara discusses the *nāstika*s (given the proper name Cārvāka in verse 164), their not being a *darśana* has to do with denial of *dharma*, karma, and the

---

17 Nāstikaṃ tu na darśanam.

self. Nowhere is there anything to indicate that the *darśana* marks have a role to play in it, a point at least implied in Haribhadra. At the same time, Rājaśekhara's discussion of the *nāstika*s does set them off sharply from the other schools, for he pays no attention to the marks that might be mentioned, such as teacher, dress, or practice. He concentrates on refuting their position, which is the only refutation in his compendium (while the Lokāyatas are not refuted in Haribhadra).

Several preliminary conclusions seem possible. First, the denial of *darśana* status to the *nāstika*s and the subsequent unique treatment given to them might indicate that Rājaśekhara, despite factors that seem to indicate the contrary, is still operating with a sense that there are certain qualities that are indispensable in a *darśana*. Nonetheless, his sense of the qualities inherent in a *darśana* seems to be different from that which Haribhadra's compendium exhibits. Rājaśekhara's marks themselves have a different thrust, and the structure of the compendium does not seem to conform to what is implied by the notion of *darśana* marks. Further, there are his overt statements in the introductory verses, which seem to subordinate his own marks to *dharma* and *yoga*.

This apparent difference in the conception of *darśana* marks is important, and it has to do with the general phenomenon of the compendium and its relationship to such marks. Rājaśekhara appears, on the whole, to be operating within a model that he knows as a model, but which has an internal structure that he does not grasp. These general impressions of his work can be sharpened by examining briefly another compendium.

IV. *The Vivekavilāsa of Jinadatta*

Jinadatta's *Vivekavilāsa* consists of 1323 verses, out of which verses 238-302 present a compendium-like discussion that the text itself calls "the examination of the six *darśana*s." The text of the whole was not available for this study, nor was any detailed survey. These remarks are based solely on the text of the compendium section printed in R. G. Bhandarkar's *Report for 1883-84*.

While Jinadatta discusses the same schools as Rājaśekhara and Haribhadra, he does not follow the order that either of the others uses, and his work shares hardly any verses with the other two. Most notable is the fact that he makes a single topic out of Nyāya and Vaiśeṣika, and explicitly gives *nāstika* as one of the six *darśana*s when he states his purpose in verse 238:

> The Jaina, Maimāṃsaka, Bauddha, Sāṃkhya,
> the Śaiva and the Nāstika:
> Let the six *darśana*s be known
> according to the distinction of each one's *tarka*.

Jinadatta does not, even in the *nāstika* section, indulge in any refutation, though the out-of-context nature of the available text makes it difficult to use this fact in any crucial argument. Nonetheless, his *nāstika* account is quite different from any of the others. He uses the Lokāyatas' insistence on *pratyakṣa* (direct perception) as an occasion to give terse statements of the other *pramāṇa*s; then the available text concludes with a ringing statement of *pratyakṣa* alone as useful.

In light of what has been said above concerning the nature of a *darśana* in Haribhadra and Rājaśekhara, this is rather striking. At first glance it might seem that Jinadatta has lost sight of the function of *darśana* marks, since his opening verse specifies that the *darśana*s are to be known according to their respective *tarka*s. But this does not prove to be the case, for whatever his use of *tarka* in that verse means, it is *devatā* and *tattva* that give his summary its pattern. This comes across clearly in the verses that introduce the sections within the text, and it even holds for the *nāstika*, save that *devatā* is not mentioned. Thus Jinadatta can hardly be accused of ignoring the *darśana* marks.

It is also valuable to see that since Jinadatta uses these two marks in the way that he does, despite the lack of much shared material, his approach might indicate a certain amount of familiarity among Jains with this approach to schools of thought. Most of all, Jinadatta's treatment of the *nāstika*s demands attention, because it raises and sharpens an issue within the whole arena of *darśana* marks, one toward which this entire discussion has been moving.

Let me recount what has gone before. The *mokṣamārga* formulation gives to *samyaktva* the crucial burden in establishing *samyagdarśana*. The Jain tradition illustrates this well by the presence of overt discussions of *samyaktva*. In essence, one might say that this whole process involves nothing more or less than the evolution of *samyaktva* out of *samyak*, a process of which the matter of *devatā* is an excellent indicator.

But there is also a corollary to this, which is the status of *darśana*. Its position within the discussions of *samyaktva*—indeed, within the development of *samyaktva*—seems somewhat ambiguous. What the compendia appear to illustrate is a resolution, of sorts, of this ambiguity. It cannot be claimed that the compendia initiate the use of *darśana* for schools of thought; something on this order is already present in the later *Sūtrakṛtāṅga*, as shown earlier, and in many other texts. A much more ambitious survey of texts would be required before one could be certain of the status of this usage. But the compendia do show clearly what is implicit in this usage, and in the separation of *darśana* from *samyaktva*, which is that any position can be called "a *darśana*."

On this point, Jinadatta is more radical than the other two authors. Both Haribhadra and Rājaśekhara have seemed to exclude the *nāstika*s from the *darśana* arena, but Jinadatta goes to the heart of the matter by including them, and treating them as if they, too, possess *darśana* marks. He considers the classic Lokāyata position—that there are only the four basic elements out of which all things are built up, and that direct perception is the ony valid means of knowledge—as if this, too, is a *tattva* mark.

Jinadatta's isolated text cannot be considered trend-setting, and there is always the possibility that he is simply mistaken, for at certain points—notably the Buddhist account—his compendium is rather muddled. Without a full study of the complete *Vivekavilāsa*, a strong *caveat* must be entered. But if one reflects on the matter of *samyaktva* and *darśana*, one sees that Jinadatta's position, for whatever reason it is held, is a step beyond the status of *darśana* in the works of Haribhadra and Rājaśekhara.

This is so because the latter two still exclude the *nāstika*s on grounds that do not actually have to do with the absence of *darśana* marks, but rather with the quality of those marks. This is why their explanatory words about the *nāstika*s do not quite ring true. In other words, Jinadatta's position represents a full emancipation of *darśana* from *samyak* and *mithyā*. In effect, it grants to *darśana* a full sense of *darśanatva*, *darśana*-ness, that does not depend on the quality of its marks, but simply on their presence.

There is more information that can be brought to bear on this issue from the remaining two compendia, but before they are considered, it is important to emphasize the way in which the three that have been examined illustrate what may be called the development of *darśanatva*. This development is implicit in the *mokṣamārga*; in fact, it might be viewed as the end product of the formulation of the *mokṣamārga*. This handling of *darśana*, this transformation of "faith" into "a faith," is an extraordinary point in the Jain view of others.

V. *The Sarvasiddhāntapraveśaka*

Because of the isolated nature of Jinadatta's text, it seems risky to base a conclusion about the appearance of what can be called *darśanatva*, or the notion that there is a *darśana*-ness independent of "right" and "wrong," on it alone. Fortunately, there is another compendium that can assist in formulating and demonstrating this conclusion. This is the anonymous *Sarvasiddhāntapraveśaka*. It, again, is something of an isolated text, but in its case there is not the same contextual problem posed by the partial availability of the *Vivekavilāsa*. The *Sarvasiddhāntapraveśaka* also appears to contain a notion implicit in *samyaktva* and *tattvārthaśraddhāna*, somewhat parallel to the *darśanatva* just discussed. This notion could be called *tattvatva*, for reasons having to do with the text and its background, but its thrust is the same as that of *darśanatva*, i.e., that the possession of certain marks extablishes a *darśana*.

The *Sarvasiddhāntapraveśaka* and its background represent something of a separate line of development within the general framework of *darśana* marks. Part of this separateness has to do with the form of this compendium. The *Sarvasiddhāntapraveśaka* is in prose, and thus shares no material with the texts just examined. Its title avoids the word *darśana*. Still, it presents the same six schools as are in the others, and it does not refute them. But its mode of presentation is very much unlike that of the others; it consists simply of statements of the basic *tattva*s of the schools, carried out largely in the words of texts belonging to the schools. Muni Jambūvijaya (the editor) has identified a large portion of the body of the text as consisting of verbatim reproductions of various *sūtra* and commentary sources within the various schools. These reproductions are accompanied by a minimum of comment, so that the whole has the flavor of being simply a concise, anthological introduction to the schools in question.

This in itself might be said to account only for a difference in approach, but this approach contains a point that is most significant. The *Sarvasiddhānta-praveśaka* presents the Lokāyatas as if they, too, had a set of basic *tattva*s; at places the text is even so composed as to be quoting sources, on the model of the other school accounts. The sole difference between the treatment of the Lokāyatas and the others is that in the Lokāyata account, an objector is given a number of questions to ask. But these are not refutations, and the Lokāyata answers are permitted to stand. Nor does the objector make his only appearance in the Lokāyata-section; he merely makes a more extensive appearance. Thus the presentation of the Lokāyatas in the *Sarvasiddhāntapraveśaka* bears a striking resemblance to Jinadatta's positive discussion of the *nāstika*s.

Another feature which sets its presentation apart from the three other compendia is its exclusive focus on *tattva*. Its *maṅgala* verse reads:

> Having made obeisance to Lord Jina,
> author of all things,
> I declare that which is the definition
> of the *tattva*s admitted in all the texts.
>
> This is taught for the sake of revealing
> the sum of *pramāṇa* and *prameya*
> in all the *darśana*s.

Aside from *tattva*, there is no other *darśana* mark in its structure, save that its *tattva* presentation lays a heavy emphasis on *pramāṇa*, as the *maṅgala* indicates. But the *tattva*s and the matter of *pramāṇa* are closely related at all times, the former often being treated as *prameya*; thus it would be difficult to argue that they are separate marks, as in Rājaśekhara. There is no mention of *devatā* or the associated problem of *āptatva*. Yet this difference can actually serve to place the *Sarvasiddhāntapraveśaka* clearly into relationship with the other compendia, and it also points to the background against which it should be seen.

This background, of course, is the matter of *tattva* in the *mokṣamārga*; but this is a subject so large as to make it nearly impossible to explore in a limited, orderly way the *Sarvasiddhāntapraveśaka*'s relationship to it. Fortunately, there are two signposts around which the discussion can be organized: Śīlāṅka's (ninth century C.E.) comments on *Sūtrakṛtāṅga* I.12, and the summary found in Siddharṣi's *Upamitibhavaprapañcākathā*, part IV. But even given this signpost, some earlier background is necessary, if only because the *Sūtrakṛtāṅga* passage on which Śīlāṅka comments requires it.

The actual *Sūtrakṛtāṅga* verse in question is I.12.21:

> He who knows the tortures of hell-denizens, who knows influx (*āsava*) and stoppage (*saṃvara*), who knows sorrow (*dukkha*) and the decay (*nijjara*) [of karma]—he is worthy to expound the *kriyāvāda*.

The presence of this verse of three of the items found in the Jain set of seven (or nine) *tattva*s is the occasion for Śīlāṅka's comments, and here the important and complex issue of the *tattva*s must be examined once more.

The Jain tradition, in the course of its development, faced few problems as interesting and complex as the task of making, in its systematic thought and language, a radical shift away from an analytical approach dominated by karma to one that sought to begin with a set of categories and means of valid knowedge (*pramāṇa*). The formulation of the *tattva*s is crucial to this entire process. The group of *tattva*s that became standard in the Jain tradition bears certain resemblances to other Indian *tattva* formulations. K. K. Dixit (1971:5) goes so far as to say that the formulation of the Jain *tattva*s "was patterned after the Nyāyasūtra talk of twelve *prameyas* (knowables)."[18] Indeed, the *Tattvārthādhigama* (I.6) does treat the *tattva*s partially under the rubric of *prameya*, and the Jain list is heterogenous in nature, mixing ontological and other categories, like the Nyāya list.

Dixit's implied claim of direct imitation, besides being chronologically a bit dubious, is in need of far more documentation than is provided by a certain similarity between two occurrences, and involves issues that need more careful consideration. But this much is clear: however the *tattva* formulation came about, it produced an upheaval of sorts in the Jain tradition. Yet in addition to producing changes in Jain thought, the *tattva* approach to analysis is also a symptom of change. A primary indication that this is the case is that the *tattva*s and other novelties associated with them appear in earnest in later Prakrit texts

---

18 The twelve Nyāya *prameya*s are found in the *Nyāya Sūtras* at I.9.

and in the first systematic Jain efforts in Sanskrit. The *Tattvārthādhigama* is an example of the latter; it also belongs among the first Jain efforts in *śāstra* composition. The formulation of the *tattva*s, then, occurs in a period of great change in Jain thought, a period and process that require close scrutiny before all of its ramifications can be seen.

With this in the background, then, the compendium in question and its related texts can be taken up, the *tattva*s being the primary point of reference. *Sūtrakṛtāṅga* I.12.21 seems to belong to an early phase of the use of elements that would later be part of the full *tattva* list, for the three items that it contains (*āsrava, saṃvara, nirjarā*) are known from early, somewhat different formulations that seem to preclude the *tattva* lists.[19]

The mention of these items is taken by Śīlāṅka as a reference to the full set of *tattva*s, and as an occasion to discuss *tattva* as a problem. The explicit framework of the discussion is that the *tattva*s have been associated with *kriyāvāda* in the verse. Thus Śīlāṅka is forced to disassociate *kriyāvāda* from the Jain position. This he does by insisting that the text means that only a *kriyāvāda* that knows and accepts these *tattva*s in toto is correct. He does not elaborate on the *kriyāvāda*, but instead has a questioner ask, "Well, then, why isn't one to see correctness of teaching in the fact that other *darśana*s have and acknowledge categories?"[20]

This question is the jump-off point for a discussion and refutation of the *tattva*s of the other schools as is found in the *Sarvasiddhāntapraveśaka*, one that consists primarily of the reproduction of statements to be found in the texts of the other schools. The major difference between Śīlāṅka and the *Sarvasiddhāntapraveśaka* rests simply in the fact that after each citation, Śīlāṅka enters a refutation. For example, in his discussion of the Vaiśeṣikas, Śīlāṅka first lists the Vaiśeṣika *padārtha*s (*dravya, guṇa, kriyā, sāmānya, viśeṣa, samavāya*); then lists the nine *dravya*s and discusses how it is that *dravya* is not a proper category; then does the same with *guṇa*; and finally does the same for the rest in turn. Śīlāṅka's attack is not radically different from non-Jain attacks. The Indian tradition is alive with hot debates over whose system of *padārtha*s is adequate or inadequate, and reasons much like Śīlāṅka's are given in such debates. Śīlāṅka's refutation would not be particularly startling were it not for the setting in which they occur: the role of the *tattva*s in the *mokṣamārga*.

When Śīlāṅka's comments are seen against the backdrop of *tattvārthaśraddhāna*, the issues that he raises concerning categories take on a new note of importance. His discussions are, in effect, the other side of the issue of *devatā*

19 Dixit 1971:5. There may be four elements here, for *dukkha* can be taken as a synonym for *bandha*.

20 Nanu ca aparadarśanoktapadārthaparijñānena samyagvāditvam kasmān na abhyupagamyate?

discussed above. The essential problem there was that the *devatā* in any system needed to be unsullied and free from flaw before that system could claim *āptatva* for itself and its source. Here, what Śīlāṅka is clearly driving at is that the *tattva* in each system must make proper sense before it can play the crucial role demanded of it.

That this is part of the same process that has been traced above receives further confirmation from the pattern of Śīlāṅka's remarks, for in them, as in Haribhadra, the Mīmāṃsā and Lokāyata are treated as if they possess the least claim to acceptance. This seems quite clear in Śīlāṅka's closing comment, when he simply says, "The refutation of the *tattva* proposed in the Mīmāṃsaka and Lokāyata opinion is to be done by your own wits; since they have recourse to categories that are repugnant to all men, no direct statement of them is made [here]." In Haribhadra it was less overtly clear; but his first verse on Mīmāṃsā (68) stresses at once that no omniscient (or otherwise qualified) *devatā* exists according to this school, which implies that the Mīmāṃsā thus stands apart from the others. Haribhadra's treatment of the Lokāyatas also submits readily to this interpretation. In addition, Mīmāṃsā and Lokāyata come last in both texts.

There is further confirmation of this pattern, and of the importance of *tattva*, in Siddharṣi's *Upamitibhavaprapañcākathā*. In this immense allegory, as Jacobi (1899-1914:xiv) puts it, "Siddharṣi proposes to explain the mundane career of the Soul *(jīva)* under the name of Saṃsārajīva from the lowest stage of existence up to final liberation." Saṃsārajīva's career involves a great many ups and downs and in its gradual progress through numerous births, in the course of which the mundane characters in the tale constantly change while Saṃsārajīva, who, of course, remains the same, is accompanied by other unchanging characters who are personifications of such forces as *moha*, *mithyādarśana*, etc.[21] In the fourth of the eight books in the text, his life as Prince Rūpidāraṇa forms the framework of the narrative. Within this framework, there occurs a long sermon by a Jain sage named Vicakṣana, and within this sermon there occurs the narrative of one Vimarśa and his nephew Prakarṣa, and their quest for knowledge. This quest takes them at one point to the top of Mt. Viveka ("discrimination"), from where they can see into the city named Bhavacakra ("wheel of birth"). The city is under the rule of King Karmapariṇāma, whose vassal is King Mahāmoha. The latter's chief minister is Mithyādarśana, whose wife is Kudṛṣṭi. Jacobi (1899-1914:lxvi) summarizes the story as follows:

> Prakarsha asked permission to see the working of Mithyādarśana and his wife Kudṛshti, and Vimarśa pointed out to him six wards in Bhavacakra: Naiyāyika, Vaiśeshika, Bauddha, Mīmāṃsaka, and Lokāyata [and Sāṃkhya, which Jacobi

21 The summary given here is based on Jacobi's summary in the introduction to his edition of the text.

> mistakenly omits]. . . . Without counting the Mīmāṃsakas, five of the remaining belong to the six Darśanas or philosophical systems. For the Mīmāṃsā, as Vimarśa explained, was founded in recent times in order to defend the Vedas against the attacks of other sophists. The town Jaina on the peak Apramattatva ["vigilance," "carefulness"] of mount Viveka is commonly counted as the sixth Darśana. The people of this town are not so harassed by Mithyādarśana as those of the wards at the foot of the mountain. For though the inhabitants of all wards except of Lokāyata constructed roads to reach the town of Nirvṛti [i.e., *mokṣa*] which lies beyond the power of Mithyādarśana, . . . only the Jainas know the true road.

Prakarṣa asks what these "roads" consist of, and Vimarśa then gives a concise account of the *tattva*s of the schools, once again presenting a bare-bones account of the categories in the words of texts belonging to the various schools.[22] Each section of his account is prefaced and concluded by the statement that what is given is the "road" built by the school in question, save that the Lokāyatas are said to deny the existence of the city of Nirvṛti, and that the "road" statements are missing altogether from the Mīmāṃsā summary.

After these concise summaries, which contain no criticism, there follows a section that offers brief refutations of the non-Jain positions. Notably, it groups these refutations into three parts. First, it offers a rather superficial critique of the place of the self in the first four schools that have been summarized, Nyāya, Vaiśeṣika, Bauddha, and Sāṃkhya; then it subjects the Lokāyatas to a harsh critique in general terms, for preaching doctrines that cause evil; finally, the Mīmāṃsā is soundly denounced for its denial of *devatā*.

The *Upamitibhavaprapañcākathā* actually contains a great many observations on non-Jains at various points, and thus it cannot be said without qualification that this account of the *darśana*s is representative of the whole work of Siddharṣi. Still, what is significant is the pattern of the presentation and its mode. Once again, the Mīmāṃsā and Lokāyata have been singled out and treated separately from the others, and once again, a presentation of bare statements of categories has occurred. In several cases, this presentation duplicates word-for-word the brief summaries in both Śīlāṅka and the *Sarvasiddhānta-praveśaka*.

It must be admitted that there are inconsistencies between the presentation that Siddharṣi makes and the others that have been surveyed here. Siddharṣi does not, as Śīlāṅka does, criticize the non-Jains on the basis of their *tattva*s. His refutations are rather a mixed bag. Further, he does reckon the Lokāyatas as one of the six *darśana*s, even speaking at one point (p. 670) of the *nāstikadarśana*. His curious reason for excluding the Mīmāṃsā—that it is a recent creation—is not consistent with his later refutation of it on the basis of *devatā*. Also, while

---

22 This portion of the *Upamitibhavaprapañcākathā* begins at p. 664 of Jacobi's edition, and continues through p. 670.

this curious treatment might be motivated by a desire to have six *darśana*s, it is not at all clear—either from the exposition or refutation—why the *nāstika*s should be included ahead of the Mīmāṃsā.

It is not comfortable to have to dismiss these problems without a real solution.[23] The best that can be offered is that Siddharṣi's account of the six *darśana*s is something wedged into a context that contains a great many other elements. Not least in importance would be Siddharṣi's view of the *raison d'être* for such schools. This can perhaps be extrapolated from his account of the rulers of Bhavacakra, given above. That account actually reveals nothing other than a classic older view of non-Jain positions: karma, causing delusion (*moha*), causing *mithyādarśana*. At the very least, one can say that this *darśana* account is being used in a framework that is not the same as that of the compendia with respect to the causes of *mithyādarśana*.

This notwithstanding, the presence of the pattern for handling the schools and the mode of presenting their doctrines are important, for they add coherence to the background of the *Sarvasiddhāntapraveśaka*, which can now be examined directly. The first things to note concerning the *Sarvasiddhāntapraveśaka* are its points of resemblance to Śīlāṅka. The order in which schools are discussed is as follows:

Śīlāṅka	Siddharṣi	*Sarvasiddhāntapraveśaka*
Nyāya	Nyāya	Nyāya
Vaiśeṣika	Vaiśeṣika	Vaiśeṣika
Sāṃkhya	Sāṃkhya	Jaina
Buddhist	Buddhist	Sāṃkhya
Mīmāṃsā	Lokāyata	Buddhist
Lokāyata	Mīmāṃsā	Mīmāṃsā
	Jaina	Lokāyata

A further major point of similarity is the amount of shared and parallel text. All three sources have been described as giving accounts of the schools that consist of straightforward statements of the schools' *tattva*s. Yet even given the fact that there is thus an outside source (the texts of those schools) for their remarks, the text parallels are striking.

23 There is an ancillary point that may deserve mention. Siddharṣi, by his own admission, held Haribhadra in high esteem. Jacobi (1899-1914:v) felt that Siddharṣi was speaking of Haribhadra, in those places in his writings where he mentions him, as if Haribhadra were his actual teacher. Jacobi modified this conclusion when he later accepted Muni Jinavijaya's eighth century date for Haribhadra, but the strong references to Haribhadra remain. Yet, given the discrepancies between Siddharṣi's presentation of the *darśana*s and that of Haribhadra's *Ṣaḍdarśanasamuccaya*, one might doubt that Siddharṣi is referring to the author of the latter.

It seems likely that the shared patterns of presentation point to a body of information within the Jain tradition that was held to be a set of thumbnail sketches of the non-Jain schools. But it would be a serious error to say that this is all there is to the matter. What is more important than the discovery of such a body of material is the way in which the *Sarvasiddhāntapraveśaka* differs from Śīlāṅka and Siddharṣi. Where the other two subjected the various *tattva*s to criticism of one sort or another, the *Sarvasiddhāntapraveśaka* takes a remarkable step. Not only does it not offer any refutations, it goes so far as to imply that the presence of *tattva*s is alone significant to establish a school of thought. It does so by presenting the Lokāyata position as one that contains *tattva*s on an equal footing with the others.

This was pointed out earlier, and it is now time to re-emphasize the parallel that this shows with Jinadatta's approach. With respect to Jinadatta, it was argued that this step represented the complete separation of *darśana* from *samyaktva*. The *Sarvasiddhāntapraveśaka* can be seen as confirming that conclusion.

Further, this is not so only because of the parallel between the two texts themselves. It is also confirmed by the parallel between the companion text of the two and their treatment of the schools, a parallel that exists despite the fact that Śīlāṅka and Siddharṣi present refutations while Haribhadra and Rājaśekhara do not. This is because the parallel consists in the fact that the companions of Jinadatta and the *Sarvasiddhāntapraveśaka* all differ from the latter two in that they treat the legitimacy of a school on the basis of both the presence and the quality of its marks. In other words, "a *darśana*" is still in some sense linked with *samyaktva*, save in Jinadatta and the *Sarvasiddhāntapraveśaka*.

One might say that those texts which still seem to consider the quality of a school's marks reveal a certain ambiguity, or tension, in the status of *darśana* in the compendia. This tension is perhaps inherent in the relationship betwen *darśana* as "faith" and *darśana* as "system," a relationship that now seems well-established. One could not be certain about this relationship were it not for the qualitative force of the marks, which puts its stamp on the patterns and approaches in the compendia, and it should be stressed again that to speak of one's own and others' "faith/school" is something quite extraordinary.

To be quite certain about the relationship in the compendia between the two senses of *darśana* is to see something more significant than the absence of refutations. This use of *darśana* cannot, however, be fully evaluated by itself. To judge the full significance of it, one must also see that this "faith/school" usage, which will be called the "unitive" usage of *darśana*, is not necessarily representative of the Jain tradition. What is more common is actually what might be called a "dual" *darśana*, something well-illustrated by the final compendium to be considered, Merutuṅga's *Ṣaḍdarśananirṇaya.*

VI. *The Ṣaḍdarśananirṇaya of Merutuṅga*

Merutuṅga is by no means the only Jain author to indicate the presence of a dual *darśana*, but since he does so in a compendium-like setting, the contrast between the dual and the unitive *darśana* becomes very clear when his usage is examined. By "dual" is meant the use of *darśana* as a term for both "system" or "school" and "faith," but not in the sense in which the other compendia use it for both. Here there are two referents as well as two *darśana*s, as it were. Just what is meant by this becomes much clearer in Merutuṅga's work.

The *Ṣaḍdarśananirṇaya* is the only one of the five compendia being considered that actually argues against the non-Jain positions, and it is the only one that does not consider the *nāstika*s. Yet it preserves direct links with the texts that might more properly be called compendia, particularly in that its discussions of other schools are very distinctly framed by the marks of *devatā* and *tattva*, and in that it has a framework that is related to the marks of *samyaktva*. The text itself is the latest of the group of five (ca. 1390 C.E.), standing relatively close to Rājaśekhara (ca. 1350 C.E.). These two texts, in fact, are chronologically the closest of any two of the five. Further, it will be argued here that the two of them share the dual *darśana*, and the observations that can be made concerning this shared aspect will be helpful in drawing some conclusions concerning the significance of this use of *darśana*.

The first indication of the status of *darśana* in Merutuṅga's work is the variety of marks and their uses. Though the text uses *devatā* and *tattva* as its internal guideposts, it fits these marks into a framework made up of the marks enunciated by Hemacandra: *deva, guru,* and *dharma*. Then, in his introduction, Merutuṅga adds yet another set of criteria. These are set into his general statement of purpose, in which he undertakes to explain why there should be apparent variety in such arenas as *varṇa, āśrama*, and *darśana*. His explanation is that the differences that produce the four *varṇa*s for *āśrama*s, and six *darśana*s are due to man's reliance on externals rather than on the essential nature of the things in question. His introductory paragraph to the discussion of *darśana*s reads:

> Also, there are six *darśana*s, divided into the Bauddha, Mīmāṃsaka, Sāṃkhya, Naiyāyika, Vaiśeṣika, and Jain. Therein, even though it is generally held that they are true *darśana*s (*saddarśana*s) in that they declare the existence of the self, merit, demerit, heaven, etc., still one may ask why they accept one thing and reject another, each elevating its own position and degrading the others.

This introduces a set of marks by which to judge *darśana*s similar to those spoken of by Rājaśekhara as the common goals of the schools.

Thus Merutuṅga's text seems to be rather a hodge-podge of marks. The internal marks—*devatā* and *tattva*—seem to function within a body of material held in common with the other compendia, save for the refutations that Merutuṅga adds, though the order of presentation is not like any of the others. The function of these marks appears to be strictly formal, which is already a point of note.

The other two sets of marks, however, seem to work directly at cross-purposes. After Merutuṅga has presented his material on the other schools and has entered his refutations, he sums matters up thus:

> Therefore, leaving aside attachment to particular names and other inessentials, all the *tattva*-knowers grant authoritative status to the *tattva*s *deva*, *guru*, and *dharma* solely on the basis of extolling [the *tattva*s'] good qualities. The result is as follows: *deva* is the venerable, all-knowing *arhat*, the Blessed One who has conquered passion, whose nature is that of the highest self. The *guru* is the one possessed of self-restraint, who has attained worthiness through knowledge and *tapas*. *Dharma* is that which arises as the result of the declaration of the all-knowing one. Rightness (*samyaktva*) is knowledge and faith in these three alone.

The remainder of the text consists of diverse quotations from various sources, designed to prove his point.

It is quite clear that there is a conflict between Merutuṅga's opening statement and its set of criteria, and this framework into which he casts matters at the end. Where in the beginning Merutuṅga regarded a "true *darśana*" as one that simply contains a number of basic marks, at the end it is the *samyaktva* of the marks that is crucial. That these exist together in the same text might lead one to think that Merutuṅga is merely a polemicist posing as a compendium author.

Perhaps, but this is not really the whole of it. Merutuṅga's usage actually illustrates precisely the difference between the unitive and dual uses of *darśana*. In his text, the term seems quite clearly to have two referents. Yet where one would expect a conflict, Merutuṅga sees none; he even uses the term *saddarśana*s ("true *darśana*s") to speak of schools. Nor does a lack of tolerance explain the approach that he takes at the end. The point of seeing this is to see that Merutuṅga actually illustrates the more common Jain usage of *darśana*, which is the dual usage. In one breath it means "faith," in the next "system."

This usage also helps to clarify the nature of Rājaśekhara's work, which uses, one will note, much the same sort of criteria for *darśana* as "school" as is present in Merutuṅga. This, more than anything else, points to the source of the discomfort that one feels concerning Rājaśekhara's use of the *darśana* marks. Therefore one can divide the compendia into two groups: (1) those that use *darśana* unitively—Haribhadra, Jinadatta, the *Sarvasiddhāntapraveśaka*; and (2) those that use it in a dual sense—Rājaśekhara and Merutuṅga.

But this dual usage also points to a problem, which arises because it is the case that the criteria presented by Rājaśekhara and Merutuṅga simply are not Jain as such, but are terms drawn from the Indian tradition as a whole. Further, these are terms that the wider tradition could and did use to exclude the *nāstika*s, a use to which these two Jain authors also put them. In sum, the general sense of "a *darśana*" in these two authors' works seems to owe little or nothing to the specific sense of "*darśana*."

A possible explanation for this would be that, since the criteria for "a *darśana*" are here drawn from the Indian tradition as a whole, this dual usage points to a wholly different way of interpreting the compendia and their use of *darśana*. This possibility must be faced squarely. Thusfar, this study has proceeded as if the general use of *darśana* were an extension of the Jain term to other schools. But, given the lack of data on general Indian usage (what is wanting is a serious study of *darśana* as "system" in the wider tradition) one must admit the possibility that the non-Jain tradition also evolved the use of *darśana* as "system" and that the Jains may have found themselves sharing a term with the wider tradition, or that they 'borrowed' this sense of the term—a possibility noted at the outset of the discussion of *darśana*.

This possibility does call for a response, and there is a prima facie case to make against such an interpretation. It has been shown above that the term *darśana* itself undergoes a process of development in the Prakrit texts, in which it appears to move from its early sense of an internal property of the *jīva* to a sense of being a general, abstract element. This development and the subsequent changes induced by the *mokṣamārga* have, it would appear, been shown to carry in them the potential for *darśana*'s capacity to refer to "school."

Therefore, in order to explain the possibility of the dual usage in Rājaśekhara and Merutuṅga it is not necessary to resort at once to some notion of borrowing. At the same time, one must note that some six centuries separate these two authors from the probable date of the first known compendium, and that by the time of Rājaśekhara and Merutuṅga the term *darśana* for school of thought is clearly in use in the larger Indian tradition. Therefore, as concerns these two authors, a definite solution would have to be reserved until such time as the non-Jain Indian uses of *darśana* have been more carefully explored.

But even granting this does not mean that it is a useful solution to attribute the wider Jain use of *darśana* as school to the larger tradition. What one must rather do is try to see into the process whereby the dual *darśana* could come to be. Only by focussing on the process, and on the factors operating in it, can this be seen. It was not obvious without a good deal of investigation that *darśana* in the compendia was, in fact, unitive; and it should not be presumed that because "system" and "faith" are different referents, the Jains could not possibly use the same term for both in the dual sense.

VII. *Conclusion*

The dual *darśana* would appear to be a product of the two factors of commonality and separateness, factors that, though apparently contradictory, are both the product of a reflective process. The temptation to begin by trying to explain this process of reflection itself is almost overwhelming. One can hazard the theory that it is a shift away from karma that is the basic cause, for *darśana* moves away from karma as the Jain view of non-Jains becomes more structured.

The difficulty with such a guess within the limits of this study is that it produces a chicken-and-egg situation. A tradition's view of others is clearly related to its view of itself; it is perhaps even a function of a tradition's self-awareness. In that respect, to write an analysis of the Jain view of others almost becomes an exercise in writing an 'inside-out' history of the Jains. This is not said in order to duck a difficult issue; rather, its purpose is to essay that the reflective process and its results do say something about the Jains' view of themselves as well as of others, even though the discussion is cast in terms of others. Where the issue at hand is concerned, then, the Jains' reflective view of non-Jains should not be seen as an effect in need of a cause. It is more likely both cause and effect, and although the remainder of this essay sets the discussion in terms of the view of others, the overtones of self-awareness will be present constantly.

Behind the identical terms for "system" and "faith" lie the same factors, and the same sometimes puzzling result: the coexistence of commonality and separateness. In the developing Jain view of non-Jains, these two elements seem to appear and work in tandem.

At first glance, this may seem to be a most elementary sort of conclusion. From a certain point of view, this tandem operation is obvious. If one wants to refute others, one must do so on common ground, but giving such common ground immediately requires an intensification of one's own defenses. Further, if one finds oneself on common ground with others, the same result ensues.

The latter point is raised because it does happen that in the shift away from karma, the Jains find themselves on common ground with the larger Indian tradition. This can submit to a number of interpretations, but one should be very cautious about claiming that this shift away from karma is either the cause or the effect of the common ground. It would seem wiser to say that such common ground, and the tandem phenomenon of the sense of commonality and separateness, are not linked to some one specific event, but rather to the general process a largely unknown element. Within the Jain tradition, it has a diffuse character. Outside of it, in the Indian tradition as a whole, it is generally kept in the arena of (visual) perception (from its root, *dṛś*). When it is used of schools of thought, this etymology is often trotted out and put through its paces so as to show that an Indian school of thought is not a mere set of ideas, but a transforming vision, or *Weltanschauung,* or something similar.

Its use in Jain texts requires special attention because when *darśana* occurs in most Jain settings it is commonly translated as "faith"; this is the overwhelmingly dominant Jain sense of the term. Yet in the Jain philosophical compendia, or when it is used in speaking of schools of thought, it is commonly translated as "system" or "viewpoint." This apparent discrepancy in the meaning of a common term is part of what makes the compendia seem isolated from other Jain materials. Finding a solution to the problem of this discrepancy will be the first and primary task of this essay.

An obvious solution to the problem posed by the apparently different uses of *darśana* in the Jain tradition is to presume that in the compendia the Jains are using terminology whose setting is the wider Indian tradition, which, when introduced into the Jain tradition, produces some confusion. Such a process is far from uncommon in the history of Jain thought. In fact, the wider Indian use of *darśana* as "system" does enter into and confuse matters in some of the Jain compendia. Yet in this case the obvious solution is not the most fruitful. Indeed, the task of this essay is to show that the *darśana* of the Jain system proper and the *darśana* of the Jain compendia are related to each other. This cannot be shown directly, for one of the most frustrating features of the Jain compendia and their use of this term is that they never explain it. Yet the connection between the two seems demonstrable, though it consists of a number of elements that must be pieced together.

When considering *darśana* within the Jain tradition, one is likely to be drawn first to the classic statement of the *mokṣamārga*, or way to release, i.e., that it consists of right faith, knowledge, and conduct.[3] However, even within the tradition the term plays at least one major role in addition to the one translated here by "faith." This additional role is its function in the process of perception, where it is often translated as "intuition," though any single word is hard-put to cover its senses. In any case, ordinary visual perception is only a sub-type of it.

The Digambaras and Śvetāmbaras took up somewhat different positions in relation to *darśana* as a part of the process of perception. Nathmal Tatia (1951:70ff.) has gone into this point in some detail, and only a summary is necessary here.[4] The Śvetāmbaras by and large developed the notion of percep-

3 Samyagdarśanajñānacāritrāṇi mokṣamārgaḥ. *Tattvārthādhigama Sūtra* I.1.

4 See also Jacobi 1906:291.

of seeing an orderly structure in the existence of other views and one's relationship to them. This point is raised because of the importance of the shift away from karma in Jain thought, which can lead one to overestimating its effect.

It would seem, in any case, that the Jain tradition's view of others in various settings is informed by this tandem operation of commonality and otherness, and that such a tandem operation is the process within which the dual *darśana* is to be understood. Moreover, some of the seeming frailness of this conclusion is removed when it is applied to the larger goal of gaining some further understanding of the internal process involved in one movement's attitudes toward others.

In this connection, the dual *darśana* is as important a discovery as the remarkable achievement of the unitive *darśana*, for in attempting to see more clearly the problem of relationships between movements, it is important to get beyond the level of the Jain view of non-Jains that might be charaterized as tolerant. In this respect, it is important to see the dual *darśana* over against the unitive *darśana*, for they inform each other.

The one thing, as has often enough been noted, that commonly marks off the compendia as 'tolerant' is their lack of refutations. But to point to this without seeing a further implication is to lose sight of the real significance of the compendia. This real significance lies in the fact that the compendia do not pose complete commonality. Their 'tolerance' is not the opposite of separateness. The opposite of separateness would be the use of *darśana* in only one of the senses in which it is used in the dual *darśana*, and the result would be the complete subsuming of all other positions under one's own—as in the *nayavāda* and in Merutuṅga. This is all too often, in fact, labelled 'tolerance' and held up as significant.

To make this clear, one needs to refer to a term introduced above to characterize the truly striking feature of the compendia. That feature was characterized by the notion of *darśanatva, darśana*-ness. The dual *darśana*, whatever its mode of expression in the Jain tradition, never succeeds in expressing *darśanatva*. There is either "faith" or there is a "system."

At first glance this seems sophistic. But it actually does reveal the way in which commonality and separateness can be generated from one source, and can exist side by side without resolution. It also reveals something of the real significance of the compendia, something that stressing tolerance because of the absence of refutations cannot reveal. *Darśanatva* is more than the absence of refutation, an absence that might be explained by positing in those authors an inexplicable, kindly sentiment that flashes to the fore, and it is more than mere commonality.

Perhaps the latter point is the most important one for gaining an insight into the compendia. Commonality might be said to be the sphere of tolerance as it is all too often posited in order to explain relationships, but that tolerance very often implies nothing more than that the tolerant position simply regards all others as being subsumed under it. What explains such tolerance best is that it is the commonality sketched out here, the commonality that implies and operates in tandem with separateness.

The fact that these principles, working in this way, underlie certain aspects of the Jain tradition may also make those aspects—such as the *nayavāda* (see chapter 14, below)—more explainable. Better still, seeing the compendia in this light permits one to say that they represent more than mere tolerance. They are a case where a few Jain thinkers seem to have taken hold of a problem and made a genuine discovery. That it did not become dominant, or perhaps even prominent, is not something that must necessarily be mourned, so long as its lesson is not forgotten. When the difference between the unitive and the dual *darśana* is seen, one can see more clearly than would otherwise be possible the dynamic process that is involved in one movement's view of others.

Before entering into a final brief observation, a point having to do with language needs mention. Had the unitive *darśana* of the compendia maintained itself more widely, one might feel constrained to find some new term in English in order to translate it. But given the dual status of *darśana*, it is perhaps more appropriate to do what is already de facto the case in translated Jain texts: translate the one as "system" or the like, and the other as "faith." Also, since it seems an injustice to translate *darśana* as either in the texts that do preserve the unitive *darśana*, it may be best to leave it untranslated.

Finally, although this chapter has at several points entered the caveat that the larger Indian tradition would need much more exploration before the points developed here could be generalized very widely, it seems appropriate to point in the direction of one larger issue. That direction is indicated by the dual *darśana* and its limitation to being either *darśana* or "a *darśana*." Its status calls to mind the varying connotations, in the West, of 'religion' and 'a religion.' It may be worthwhile to point out that these two also co-exist in a curious relationship, and that commonality has here, too, given rise to one of the most sharply defined cases for Christian separateness, that of Karl Barth. One cannot yet maintain that there is a full parallel here, but it does seem to be true that the Western awareness of other 'religions' has led to something not unlike the dual *darśana*. Perhaps here, too, commonality and separateness go hand in hand.

9

SAMOSARAṆA: THE JINA AT THE CENTER*

One of the problems that must be treated in order to gain a full picture of Jain religious life in addition to the philosophical and philological portraits of the Jains that currently exist is how the Jain Tīrthaṅkara can serve as the focus of a cultus. Despite the regularly enunciated dogma that, strictly speaking, no savior-saved relationship between the Tīrthaṅkara and the devotee is possible, there is a cultus and a fairly ancient iconographic and monument-building tradition associated with the Tīrthaṅkara. Further, there is not, so far as is known, anything resembling a 'great vehicle' tradition in Jainism. The cult of the Tīrthaṅkara, then, appears to be a promising arena for examining the relationship between the paradigmatic figure of the enlightened teacher and religious cult-forms.

This chapter focuses on a point of striking similarity between the cult of the Buddha (which poses similar, if not identical, problems) and that of the Tīrthaṅkara, namely, the *stūpa*. Some work has been done on the Jain *stūpa*s, but little attention has been paid to the *samosaraṇa* (Skt. *samavasaraṇa*), or "[cosmic] gathering," which is the mythic version of the Jina's first sermon as portrayed in the Jain Prakrit texts. This *samosaraṇa* shares, in many striking ways, mythic and structural features with the Buddhist *stūpa*. The chapter's

* Paper read at the American Academy of Religion Annual Meeting, October 1976. Incorporates material from dissertation, pp. 188-90.

principal aim is to essay an interpretation of these features as possible aids to understanding the relationship of worshipper and Tīrthaṅkara.

The start of this paper does not conform immediately to the topic, but sets the stage for a specific instance illustrative of larger issues. We start by asking a basic question. Is Jainism in and of itself 'a religion'? This is a rhetorical question filled with rather ill-defined terms, yet it is not without force, for the Jain tradition poses a set of problems related to how to understand saviors, salvation, and religious structures.

There are two components, two doctrinal anomalies, to the general problem. First, the Jain Tīrthaṅkara cannot 'doctrinally' be an object of worship, but the Tīrthaṅkara is, all the same, the center of a cultus. Second, the Jain lay community also carries out a variety of 'religious' practices in addition to the worship of the Jina.

In terms of the arena of a savior, or a salvation figure, or salvation, we need to explain a dissonance between the Jain view of salvation and the path to it, and the 'religious' practices of the Jains. To put the dissonance most bluntly: there can be no savior-saved relationship, yet there is a great deal of cultic and ritual life in Jainism.

This has created a problem in understanding Jain religious life. There is a sort of vacuum here—a ringing "yes" to the initial rhetorical question is missing—and, on the negative side, both of the two 'doctrinal anomalies' mentioned above are often casually set aside as being due to extraneous influence on the Jain community. Thus the question, "is Jainism really 'a religion,'" however poorly phrased for the Indian context, or for the study of religion as a whole, is my way of pointing to a problem. In this chapter I hope to open a door to a partial solution of this problem just a tiny crack. This chapter will focus on the cult of the Tīrthaṅkara, but these introductory remarks should also serve to remind us that the other arena, of other lay 'religious' practices, also *badly* needs attention.

How can we approach this cult? Prefigured above is an often-used answer, that it can be attributed to the influences of the surrounding culture. A second answer is that it is a concession of 'popular' spiritualism, and thus not an *essential* part of Jainism. This argument more often is used to explain the *śāsana-devatās*, or minor temple deities, who may be called on for aid in earthly circumstances, than to explain the actual worship of the Jina. Also commonly found is the explanation that the worship is, at heart, 'one-way,' or a meditative tool.

Only the third of these comes close to being an affirmative answer to our over-arching question. But it has, somehow, a 'false' ring to it, for it rests on a very narrow definition of 'worship.'

The need to stick with the third answer has, of course, a basis in the Jain view of the nature of the path to *mokṣa*, and the nature of the goal. The Jain understanding of *mokṣa* is such that it automatically produces a non-bridgeable gulf between the realm of *siddha* and the ordinary person. Thus the Tīrthaṅkara becomes an *exemplar* alone, apparently. And the image-cult probably should be granted the status stated above. But is this the only function of the Tīrthaṅkara? And *can* this be the only basis for a cult? There *is* an image cult, which Mathurā votary tablets point to as being very early, and other significant non-household rites include pilgrimages to sites of various classes. I think there is another dimension to the Tīrthaṅkara than being an exemplar, and it rests on a second major cultic area. Does the cult, rather than providing only a sign of 'concession' or of 'influence,' give us some key to another function for the Tīrthaṅkara? There is a crucial component of the cultus, historically, and this is the *samosaraṇa*.

There are two major aspects of Jain cultic life. On the one hand, there are the many household and *saṃskāra* rites.[1] On the other hand, there is the 'worship' of the Tīrthaṅkara, in terms of both an image cult and a 'temple' cult.

With respect to all of these, as we have stated above, studies of the Jains often imply or state overtly that they are (1) influences from the larger Hindu religious culture; (2) concessions to popular spirituality (the *śāsana-devatās* who can be "called on"); or (3) based upon a one-way relationship, with 'worship' being a 'meditative' prop, and the Jina being only an exemplar. All of these explanations are sometimes true, at least in part. But take care! The first two explanations I shall not explore in this chapter, except to point out that some *very* sophisticated study is needed of the household and *saṃskāra* rites in particular.

Let us then look at the 'worship' of the Tīrthaṅkara. There is evidence of an image-cult from the second century B.C.E. The textual explanation of the image-cult is as an engagement with an exemplar. It should be *bhāva-pūjā*, at heart, and not just *dravya-pūjā*.[2]

But this is quite incomplete, for we have left before us a 'temple-cult,' which I wish to explore by focusing on a particular feature of the Jain tradition: the *samosaraṇa*. The *samosaraṇa* is portrayed by the later Jain tradition as W. Norman Brown (1941:5) has summarized:

> Whenever a Jina . . . obtains perfect knowledge, the gods appear, cleanse the earth for a space of a yojana round about, scent it, and ornament it. They build three

---

1 [Editor's note.] See Jaini 1979:292-95; Sangave 1980:243-52; Williams 1963:274-87.

2 [Editor's note.] *Bhāva-pūjā* refers to worship employing only hymns and mental concentration, whereas *dravya-pūjā* refers to worship employing the actual offering of physical objects. See Williams 1963:187, 216.

> walls, the innermost of jewels, the middle of gold, and the outer of silver, and each wall has four jewelled gates facing the four cardinal directions. In the center is a pedestal with a tree, and under the tree are four lion thrones. The Jina sits on the throne facing the east, and reproductions of him sit on the others. There the Tīrthaṅkara preaches to gods, men, and animals, who have joyously assembled to hear his initial discourse on the great Truth which he has acquired.

The *samosaraṇa* is found repeatedly in temples. In some cases it is a painting or a two-dimensional plaque on a wall, in some cases a small three-dimensional model, and in a few cases is a large three-dimensional replica. It is used so much that P. S. Jaini (1979:196) has described the Jain temple as often being a replication of the *samosaraṇa*.

Now it is worth noting that the *samosaraṇa*, as the celebration of the Jina's attainment of *kaivalya*, is apparently *not* present in the tradition from the very beginning. But it is at least as old as the image cult, from the evidence of its portrayal on votary slabs.

The oldest (presumably) versions of the life of Mahāvīra (in the *Ācārāṅga Sūtra*) and of Mahāvīra and the other Tīrthaṅkaras (in the *Ācāradaśāḥ*, in the portion thereof called the *Kalpa Sūtra*) make no mention of any such extraordinary happening at the point of the Jina's attainment of *kaivalya* and first sermon. The oldest *samosaraṇa* portrayal seems to be in the *Aupapātika*, one of the *Upāṅgas*. Here, in a *once separate* text (E. Leumann 1882:2), is portrayed a *samosaraṇa*.

Other *samosaraṇa*-portrayals in the Śvetāmbara canon rely on the *Aupapātika*, according to Ernst Leumann (1882:2):

> Der erste Theil des Aup. S. nun enthält . . . eine Art Wallfahrtsgeschichte, und zwar ist dieselbe Schema für alle Jaina-Texte, indem in diesen stets nur auf die im Aup. S. gegebene Schilderung verwiesen wird.[3]

Leumann's conclusion is based on the use of *varṇakas* (key-word stereotyped descriptions) in other texts; these are perhaps only a key to the order in which particular texts were put into written form, and not to actual age. However, the use of the *varṇakas* means that the canon's vision of the *samosaraṇa* is essentially that of the *Aupapātika*, and this is sufficient for now.

The most striking difference between the older version, as presented in *Aupapātika*, and the later version summarized above is that the later version restricts the *samosaraṇa* to the occasion upon which the Jina first preaches his message, while the *Aupapātika* version presents it as an occasion that might occur more often. (More in the sense of Jacobi's [1895b:315] explanation: "This

---

3 [Editor's Translation.] The first chapter of the *Aupapātika Sūtra* includes . . . a kind of pilgrimage narrative, and indeed is the model for all Jain texts, in that they were always derived from the descriptions given in the *Aupapātika Sūtra*.

word [*samosaraṇa*] and the verb samôsarai are commonly used when Mahāvīra preaches to a meeting [*mêlâpaka*] gathered around him.")

There are other differences that separate the early and later *samosaraṇa*. The earlier form lacks nearly all the ensignia and royal trappings present in the later version. The *Aupapātika* version tends, in fact, to speak of it not as the event, but as the assembly of people. Accordingly, it occurs at a holy place,[4] rather than a place created for it. The setting is a grove, with an Aśoka-tree at its center;[5] present, but only briefly described, are rings of vegetation (shrubs and trees) growing around the Aśoka-tree.[6] Although certain extraordinary features are supplied by another, apparently secondary recension of the text (Leumann 1882:25), the whole is largely bereft of the details present in the later form. As to the audience, it consists largely of holy men of four sorts, a king and his party, and townspeople. Six classes of divinities are also present, but no mention is made of the presence of animals.[7]

The *samosaraṇa* itself appears, if the earlier and later versions are compared, to have undergone something of a process of evolution. Unfortunately, it has not been the subject of a thorough-going study. In that light, what is said here must be conjectural to a certain extent. However, the later *samosaraṇa* clearly exhibits a sense in which the Jina's teachings are seen as universal in impact.

Moreover, that structure bears a startling resemblance to the formal characteristics of the Buddhist *stūpa*. The Jains are not overwhelmingly *stūpa*-builders, nor do they, save for pilgrimage sites, commemorate in particular the attainment of *nirvāṇa* by the Jinas, or have a relic cult. This makes the structural parallel even more interesting, for it might help us clarify the place of the *stūpa* in the Buddhist cult, a place not really adequately explained by relic-cult, funerary mound, or other particular theories. *And*, it would seem that a case can be made that the Jain *samosaraṇa* is not just something 'borrowed' from the Buddhist *stūpa*.[8]

---

4 *Aupapātika* 2 (Leumann 1882:22) gives the place as Puṇṇabhadda.

5 *Aupapātika* 3-5 (Leumann 1882:22-24).

6 *Aupapātika* 6-9 (Leumann 1882:24-25).

7 *Aupapātika* 23-28 (Leumann 1882:34-50).

8 [Editor's note.] Folkert, in the margin to this chapter, made a note to the *divya-dhvani* and the *Lotus Sutra*, presumably as another point of comparison between the Jain *samosaraṇa*, and the Buddhist *stūpa*. The *divyadhvani* is the "miraculous sound" or "divine sound" emanating from the Jina seated in the *samosaraṇa*. According to P. S. Jaini (1979:42), "Whereas Digambaras imagine the divyadhvani as a monotone—like the sound oṃ—which only the gaṇadharas [the leaders of the mendicant community] are able to comprehend, Śvetāmbaras suggest that the Jina speaks in a human language that is divine in the sense that men of all regions, and animals, can benefit from hearing it."

In the *Lotus Sutra* (*Saddharmapuṇḍarīka*) rather than an emphasis on divine sound we find an emphasis on divine light. For example, in chapter 1 (Hurvitz 1976:4) is the following:

Rather, what we have here is, like the *stūpa*, an imago mundi, a constructive symbolic portrayal of the cosmos, of the totality of the world focused on the Jina at the center. The development and persistence of this image, in cultic practice, in art form, and otherwise in the Jain tradition is noteworthy. But detecting this does not itself solve the problem of its significance for Jains, or for studying the Jains.

But let me attempt a working generalization from all this. First, two elements in Jainism can be seen as significant elements in cult-life: the image-cult, and the *samosaraṇa*/temple cult. These two elements parallel, and perhaps directly express, two polarities in Jainism as a 'religion': the Jina as exemplar, an essentially a-religious pole; and the Jina as focus of 'religious' life. This two-fold parallel extends still one step further. At one pole is the Jain path as a-dharmic, a-social, anti-worldly; at the other pole is the dharmic, social, and worldly community that sustains the tradition.

Bearing all this in mind, then, we can see in the *samosaraṇa* a key to an additional vital dimension of the Tīrthaṅkaras. The Tīrthaṅkara not only exemplifies the transcending of the world (pole #1), he also provides the focal point around which the world is constituted (pole #2).

This is seen in the tradition's vision of the lives of early Tīrthaṅkaras, who were 'culture-founders' in many ways. The Tīrthaṅkara not only shows the way to transcend the world—he or she also *establishes* it. This is explicitly the case with Ṛṣabha, who is described as a culture-founder.[9]

Seen thus 'in the round,' the Tīrthaṅkara and the 'religious' life of the Jain community make a whole that is integrated and legitimate. This helps us understand the Jains, and may help us understand such figures as the Tīrthaṅkaras as well.

> At that time the Buddha emitted a glow from the tuft of white hair between his brows that illuminated eighteen thousand worlds to the east, omitting none of them, reaching downward as far as the Avīci (the lowest) hell and upward as far as the Akaniṣṭha (highest) gods. In these worlds there could be fully seen the six kinds of living beings in those lands. There could also be seen the Buddhas present in those lands, and the *sūtradharmas* preached by those Buddhas could be heard.

In terms of the divine sound, comparison should be made to *The Teaching of Vimalakīrti* (*Vimalakīrtinirdeśa*), where we find the following: "The Blessed One expresses himself in a single sound (*ekasvareṇodāharati*) and beings, each according to his category, grasp its meaning; each one says to himself that the Blessed One speaks his own language; this is an exclusive attribute (*āveṇikalakṣaṇa*) of the Victorious One (*jina*)" (*Vimalakīrtinirdeśa* 1.10.12). Lamotte (1976:12-13n52) gives an extensive footnote on the subject of the Buddha's teachings, with references to theories that the Buddha taught in many languages, taught the entire teachings with a single sound (*ekasvara*), did not speak at all, or taught by other means besides or in addition to words.

9 [Editor's note.] See Jaini 1979:288-29.

10

THE *GACCHA* AND JAIN HISTORY*

General accounts of the Jains, both historical and doctrinal, have commonly been written without giving significant weight to the existence of numerous 'schools'—called *gaccha*s, among other terms—within Jainism. The *gaccha*s are occasionally given a negative value, i.e., the survival of Jainism (in contrast to Buddhism) is sometimes attributed to the absence within Jainism of a "schism" of a serious nature after the early division into Śvetāmbara and Digambara. But they are most commonly simply passed over lightly, at least until ca. 1500 C.E., when more modern Jain 'sects' begin to appear. The purpose of this paper is to sketch the available evidence concerning the nature of the *gaccha*s, to examine ways in which the role of the *gaccha*s in Jainism can and cannot be elucidated by more careful inquiry into their functioning as institutions within Jainism, and to propose a re-evaluation of some of the usual patterns for historical treatment of Jainism.

I will summarize what is known of the *gaccha*s, including different terminologies and the development of *gaccha* as a general term for 'school.' Differences in socio-historical setting as well as chronological development, are examined. The paper then inquires into the role of the *gaccha* under three major headings: (1) the *gaccha* as a means whereby its 'founder's' influence on the Jain community is secured; (2) the *gaccha* as a 'carrier' of doctrine and tradition within Jainism; and (3) the *gaccha*'s role in providing Jainism with an 'identity'

* Paper read at the American Oriental Society Meeting, 1978.

within the larger Hindu tradition. It is recognized that these categories do not exhaust the possibilities of inquiry. I will also survey the usual treatment of Jain history in the period from ca. 1000 C.E. to the present. The focus is upon the treatment accorded 'sects' such as the Loṇkāśā, Sthānakavāsī, and Terāpanthī, with an eye toward re-examining the role that these 'sects' are seen as playing in the development of Jainism. In brief, scholarship has given these more 'modern' sects far greater status than the *gaccha*s of preceding centuries. There is the problem of how to distinguish, in these 'modern sects,' between that which may be an 'extension' of the *gaccha*, and that which makes them truly different. It is appropriate to inquire into the roles that they play in Jainism in comparison with the roles of *gaccha*s in general, and into the validity of our usual view of them in that light.

I.

The Jain Rājaśekhara, as part of his *Ṣaḍdarśanasamuccaya* (ca. 1350 C.E.), gives the following description of the Śvetāmbara-Digambara division within the Jain tradition:

20. There are two wings to the Jain doctrine:
    Śvetāmbara and Digambara;
    The Śvetāmbaras were discussed above,
    and now the Digambaras are told.

21. There are four divisions among Digambaras,
    all following the vow of nakedness:
    The Kāṣṭhasaṅgha, Mūlasaṅgha,
    and the Māthura and Gopyaka Saṅghas.

22. In the Kāṣṭhasaṅgha, the broom is ordained
    to be made of the yak's tail.
    In the Mūlasaṅgha, the brush is made
    of peacock feathers.

23. The broom has never been an issue
    in the Māthura Saṅgha.
    The Gopyas sweep with peacock feathers;
    their greeting is "*dharma lābha*."

24. The rest greet with "*dharma vṛddhi*."
    The Gopyas declare release for women;

The three Saṅghas other than the Gopya
declare that women cannot attain it.

25. Neither the other three nor the Gopyas
hold that an omniscient takes food;
There is no release for one wearing monk's garb,
though he keep the vow well.

26. There are thirty-two obstacles
and fourteen impurities in mendicancy;
How to avoid them
is found in their *āgama*.

27. For the rest, they are like the Śvetāmbaras
in matters of conduct, deity, and teacher;
They accept the logic-treatises
composed by the Śvetāmbaras.

28. Theirs are mostly of the same nature,
illuminated by knowledge of the *syādvāda*;
The *Paramāṣṭasahasrī*,
that moon to the *nyāya*-lotuses;

29. The *Siddhāntasāra* and the other logic-books
are very difficult;
Each word of them is capable
of imparting victory.

30. These divisions in Jain practice, etc.
will presently be obscured in the Kali-age;
And then these present things, taught here,
will have to be learned from the Jain *āgama*.[1]

There is some familiar material here, but also much that seems obscure. I begin with Rājaśekhara's verses because the thesis underlying this brief study is that the prophecy of verse 30 has come very near to fulfillment as concerns our understanding of Jain history and the divisions within the tradition.

What Rājaśekhara relates is either accepted in our conventional view of the Jains, but without very profound understanding on our part, or is by and large overlooked. We accept, and have made part and parcel of our view of the Jains, a Śvetāmbara-Digambara split. But we largely overlook the matters that occupy much of Rājaśekhara's account of the Digambaras: the references to internal

1 [Editor's note.] Folkert's translation.

divisions within the Digambara movement and the details of their differences. Perhaps our understanding of the Jain tradition would be better, and our concerns over continuity and division more creatively shaped, if we were to concentrate on the smaller divisions within the tradition, and make them part and parcel of our understanding of the Jains, and if we were less willing to treat the Śvetāmbara-Digambara split as informing all of Jain history.

The reason for this submission is as follows: the smaller divisions within the tradition, though commonly overlooked or passed over lightly, have been present from very early on. These smaller divisions, known in Digambara circles as *saṅgha*s (as in Rājaśekhara's verses) and in Śvetāmbara circles as *gaccha*s, and both of which possess further sub-divisions as well, have actually been the basic units of the tradition, the units by means of which 'Jainism' has functioned as a living faith in India. To study them fully would require a long-ish monograph; in this essay, I will point out the importance of the *gaccha*s for an adequate understanding of the history of the Jains.

The general development of the Jain tradition is commonly portrayed as containing the following major features:

(1) The ancient period: Pārśva, Mahāvīra, and early followers.

(2) A relatively early division into the Digambara and Śvetāmbara movements, complete by the first century C.E.

(3) A period, partially overlapping the division into Śvetāmbara and Digambara, in which two major developments occur:
   (a) regional spread and development, encompassing the growth to full dimension of the Prakrit 'scriptures' and the rise of a Sanskrit *śāstra* literature in both Digambara and Śvetāmbara circles;
   (b) considerable vernacular literary activity, and an 'accomodation,' both literary and social, between lay Jains and Hindus.

(4) A period of some decay, including regional retrenchment in south and central India and some turmoil in western and northwestern India (in part due to the Muslim presence there), leading eventually to 'reform' and the appearance of 'modern' sects such as the Sthānakavāsīs.

Most of our understanding and study of the Jains occurs against a backdrop provided by this generally accepted periodization, including in particular the roles assigned to internal divisions, namely, the Śvetāmbara and Digambara movements and the 'modern sects.' These internal divisions are an integral part of our understanding of the Jains. At the same time, we perceive the tradition as possessing a basic doctrinal unity.

The Jains are commonly portrayed as a unified religious tradition, at least in terms of doctrine. In this generally accepted periodization, we tend to be aware of internal groups—schools, orders, etc.—in Jainism at only two points: first, the major division into Śvetāmbara and Digambara, and second, the 'modern' schools.

My work on the Jains has led me to be concerned with these internal groups or 'orders'—a feature of Jainism that I first began to grapple with in trying to understand the Jain 'canon' of scripture, especially as it was conceived of by the newer 'schools.' This raised questions in my mind about the 'schools' in general, and our perception of them, and I remain particularly concerned with our treatment of the newer 'orders.' But this has begun to lead me willy-nilly into the jungle of the *overall* history of these internal movements. Though we 'see' them at only certain points, these 'orders' are a pervasive feature of the Jain tradition.

The rise of the 'modern' schools is antedated by Rājaśekhara's verses, but the division into Śvetāmbara and Digambara is part and parcel of our perception of the Jains, and we would expect Rājaśekhara to discuss it. What is more unfamiliar to us in his account are the references to the divisions of the Digambara movement and their points of difference. These subdivisions, and a host of others like them in the Śvetāmbara camp as well, have indeed become obscured in our view of the Jains, for reasons both good and bad. Our understanding of the Śvetāmbara-Digambara divisions is also relatively superficial, even though we all know that the Jains are divided into two major groups, ostensibly over whether a monk should be clothed or not. This brief essay attempts to re-focus our attention on these matters on the off-chance that our general ignorance of the divisions among Jains, including the smaller units of Jains commonly known as *gaccha*s, has kept us from better understanding Jain history as a whole.

II.

The good reason for our ignorance of these divisions is that the Jain tradition is indeed remarkably unitary as concerns fundamental doctrines. Leaving the *gaccha*s aside, one is even hard-pressed to find major doctrinal differences between the Śvetāmbaras and Digambaras. Rājaśekhara is not significantly overstating matters in verses 27 and 28. The major points of difference between the two movements are as he states them:

(1) whether the Jina, having attained omniscience, engages in normal human activities (Śvetāmbara), or not (Digambaras hold that the Jina takes no food, etc., and preaches by means of a "divine sound");[2]

2 [Editor's note.] See Dundas 1985.

(2) the role of nudity in monastic life;
(3) whether women are capable of attaining release (Śvetāmbara) or not (Digambara);[3]
(4) some specifics of begging practice.

Points (1) and (3) have led to occasional, rather dense pieces of metaphysics; but none of these matters that separate Śvetāmbara from Digambara can be traced to fundamental difference in doctrine. As P. S. Jaini (1979:88) has put it:

> [The Śvetāmbaras and Digambaras] have been very alike . . . in their remarkable unwillingness to depart from their basic doctrines and practices. . . . [T]he basic Jaina doctrines thus show extraordinary uniformity through the centuries; indeed, it is possible to consider them as a coherent whole, with little reference to questions of interpretation or chronology.

Certainly these points are not satisfactory for explaining the origins of the different Orders. They do not account for the early divisions, and may in fact obscure our view of the *gaccha*s. The nudity issue in particular seems to be an oversimplification of Jain history, and may also obscure our sense of the development of the Śvetāmbara-Digambara split. To construct a full thesis in place of these is well beyond the scope of this paper. But perhaps we can contribute something to understanding both major and minor divisions by simply looking more closely at the actual subdivisions, using Rājaśekhara as a jump-off point.

Beyond the major divisions, neither the *gaccha*s nor the rise of the more modern divisions can be adequately accounted for in doctrinal terms. Our relative unawareness of many of the divisions among Jains does not come, then, from a misperception on our part of Jain doctrinal differences.

At the same time, it must be admitted that the doctrinal unity is a bit like the modern hot-dog: its substance will hardly bear a moment's reflection. A great many unknown ingredients make up the final unitary product, and to pass over this lightly ignores two important matters. First, the Jains' internal religio-philosophical debates have been lively and often very creative; the impression of unity should not lead one to think that Jain religious philosophy is a stagnant pond. Second, the existence of such unity itself presents an intriguing puzzle. The Jains preserve no record of doctrinal councils. There are certain doctrinal texts (a prime example being Umāsvāti's *Tattvārthādhigama Sūtra*) that, taken with their commentarial traditions, provide something of a normative doctrinal tradition, but there is disagreement over the 'scriptures.' In short, the doctrinal

---

3 [Editor's note.] See Jaini 1991.

unity of the Jain traditions is not well-understood in terms of its causes, though the unity itself appears undeniable.

At the same time, perversely enough, we appear to have allowed doctrinal unity to draw our attention away from the existence of a multitude of divisions within the Jain tradition. These divisions are *not* only just now coming to light.[4] Helmuth von Glasenapp, in the first comprehensive Western study of the Jains (1925:346), was able to observe:

> The Jains do not represent a unified religious community, but rather are splintered into a great number of sects. Divisions have been the order of the day since the earliest times.[5]

One need plunge only briefly into a variety of studies to have the point amply demonstrated. The common term for these monastic 'orders' in the Śvetāmbara tradition is *gaccha*. This term is, however, not uniformly used or understood; and numerous sub-orders and terms for them also exist. *Gaccha* as a term, which may be glossed "way" or "method" of a particular group, appears to have replaced, roughly over the span of time covered by the growth of the basic scriptures of Jainism (600-700 years, quite conservatively) the earlier term *gaṇa*, though the two terms co-existed for many centuries. Schubring (1918:78) notes the change from *gaṇa* to *gaccha* in his study of the *Mahāniśītha*, a canonical text, and the term appears regularly in later canonical material. *Gaṇa* is glossed by *gaccha* in commentaries on canonical texts that date to the ninth century C.E. and before. A thorough study of the transition is in order, and is not known to me; an account could be pieced together once the layers of canonical texts and their commentaries are made fully available to scholars. However, there are other basic sources for the history of the *gaccha*s. These are the *paṭṭāvalī*s, or lists of heads of the 'orders.'

The *Sthavirāvalī* in the *Kalpa Sūtra*, translated by Jacobi (1884d), is a common starting point for surveying the divisions and subdivisions of the Jain movement. In that text, the lineage of all the monks is traced bach to Mahāvīra's disciple (*gaṇadhara*) Sudharman: "The Nirgrantha Śramaṇas of the present time are all (spiritual) descendents of the monk Ārya Sudharman, the rest of the Gaṇadharas left no descendents" (*Sthavirāvalī* 2; Jacobi 1884d:287). The divisions are spoken of as *gaṇa*s, *kula*s, and *śākhā*s. The first of these terms, generally meaning "company" or "assembly," is familiar to us in virtue of the 11 *gaṇadhara*s who are given as the primary disciples of Mahāvīra, and who oversaw the 9 *gaṇa*s of monks. *Kula* generally has a more generically restrictive sense, referring more to an organic unit: family, clan, etc. The classic Vedic

4 [Editor's note.] See the several articles on these divisions published in *Indian Antiquary* in the late nineteenth century: Burgess 1884; Hoernle 1890, 1891, 1892; Klatt 1882, 1894.

5 [Editor's note.] Folkert's translation.

usage of *śākhā* comes perhaps close to being translatable as "school," though within texts it usually has more the meaning of "limb" or "branch."

The rank of these early terms for Jain subdivisions is not clear in the *Kalpa Sūtra* lists of *sthaviras*; but J. G. Bühler (1963:32-33, 37-47), in the course of arguing for the historical verity of the Jain texts translated by Jacobi, pointed to a number of dedicatory inscriptions on Jain statues at Mathurā. Besides confirming in part the lists of teachers in the *Kalpa Sūtra*, the inscriptions appear to rank the early divisions as follows: *gaṇa, kula, śākhā*. They also add a final subdivision not attested in the *Kalpa Sūtra*, the *bhatti* (Sanskrit *bhakti*), perhaps referring to a group of monks who ate together. It is perhaps not quite correct to understand these terms as forming a hierarchy strictly speaking. *Gaṇa* seems clearly to stand at the top; but *kula* apparently (but not always) refers to a line of teachers, not necessarily a division of monks; *śākhā* refers to a "branch" of the *gaṇa*. A clear hierarchical sense does not seem to exist. Their relationship is problematic from the texts, as indicated by Jacobi (1884d:288n2).

The point of this little dose of early Jain material is to establish that 'orders' and 'suborders' within the Jain tradition are an early feature of the movement. Steady reference in the Śvetāmbara canon indicates their continuing presence, though I wish to be the first to admit—even to point out—that the status of the 'orders' throughout this period of Jain history is sorely in need of review. Surveys by U. K. Jain (1975), Nahar and Ghosh (1917), and others,[6] show textual or inscriptional evidence for more than 120 Śvetāmbara *gacchas*, and again as many *kulas* and *śākhās*. Let me point out here, though, that the vast majority of these are not attested to prior to the eighth-ninth centuries C.E. The eventual number of *gacchas* is indeed large, large enough for Śvetāmbara sources to refer to them as beyond counting, or assign the number 84 to them.

We have spoken thus far of Śvetāmbar 'orders'; we must also observe the Digambar pattern, which differs. The term *gaṇa* and *gaccha* are also in use in Digambara circles. But they are for the most part subordinated to the term *saṅgha*, which ususally describes the basic Digambara form of the 'order'; and *gaṇa* and *gaccha* are sometimes present as subdivisions of the same *saṅgha*.

In brief, the Digambaras look back to a Mūla Saṅgha, said (though in *very* late texts) to have been divided by Arhadbali very early on, near the turn of the era, into four new *saṅghas*: the Deva, Sena, Siṃha, and Nandi. The core is the Kundakunda *anvaya* ("succession") in the South, which is attested to by a copper-plate from 466 C.E.; the notion of this succession was perhaps collapsed with the Mūla notion. More reliable accounts, such as that of Devasena in his tenth century *Darśanasāra* (*Daṃsanasāra*), tell us of other basic divisions: the Kāṣṭha, Mathurā , Gopya (Yāpanīya), and Drāviḍa/Dramila Saṅghas. Devasena

---

6 [Editor's note.] See footnote 4, above.

does *not* mention the Mūla Saṅgha; it 'appears' in the north. The Kāṣṭha Saṅgha was founded in the late first century B.C.E. by Loha; he had been leader of the group of monks who remained in the area of Bihar at the time of the great famine which lead to the rise of the Śvetāmbaras, but he had to go elsewhere to start up a new group when the main group of monks returned. The Mathurā Saṅgha was founded in the tenth century C.E. The Gopya or Yāpanīya Saṅgha was founded in the seventh century C.E.;[7] many of their practices and tenets are closer to the Śvetāmbaras, and their status vis-à-vis the two major traditions is unclear.[8] The Drāviḍa, with its headquarters in Madurai, was founded in 583 C.E., as the result of a split over the eating of certain plants, and the allowance of cold-water bathing. The first three plus the Mūla are mentioned in Jain compendia (*darśanasamuccayas*) in the centuries after Devasena and after the appearance of the Mūla Saṅgha in the North. Within these *saṅghas*, as noted, occur *gaṇa, gaccha*, and *śākhā,* plus other terms for subdivisions not attested to in Śvetāmbara sources. The contemporary Digambar community, at least in the north, is divided into two major subdivisions. These are the Bīspanthīs ("20-ers"), and the Terāpanthīs ("13-ers," not to be confused with the Śvetāmbara Terāpanthīs). The latter is an anti-*bhaṭṭāraka* reform group, which also has no image cultus.[9] In general, there seem to have been fewer subdivisions among the Digambaras than among the Śvetāmbaras, a puzzle which is not to be addressed or solved here.

Now, within these two large arenas of material dealing with 'orders,' there is much more detail, deserving more careful generalization than I have given it, and in need of much more work. But I present this survey in order to make a point. Briefly put, by all accounts, there is a remarkable—almost tenacious—unity in Jainism as we have come to know it. Yet the tradition is pervaded by these internal 'orders.' Dealing with this division within unity, i.e., coming to grips with the role of these 'schools' or 'orders' in Jain history is, I believe, a major problem in Jain historiography.

To sum up: the interesting problem that faces us is to try to understand how the Jain tradition can be so thoroughly divided and subdivided, both into larger movements and into subdivisions, and at the same time present a unified teaching to those who study it. The presentation of the problem thus far has indicated that we are both relatively ignorant of the smaller divisions within the tradition, and are also faced with a doctrinal unity that makes even the prominent split into Śvetāmbara and Digambara something of an anachronism.

---

7 [Editor's note.] This according to von Glasenapp (1925:356), who gives the date of the founding of the Yāpanīya Saṅgha as 659 C.E., but questions the date. Upadhye (1933:225), citing the *Darśanasāra*, gives the date as exactly five centuries earlier, in 159 C.E.

8 [Editor's note.] On the Yāpanīya Saṅgha, see Upadhye 1933, 1974.

9 [Editor's note.] On the Digambara Terāpanthīs, see Lath 1981:xxiv-lxiv.

III.

If, then, there is both doctrinal unity and a simultaneous and persistent multitude of divisions within the Jain tradition, is this phenomenon simply to be explained by observing that, once again, a feature of the larger Hindu tradition can only be properly understood in terms of praxis? It is worth observing that, of the matters that separate the Śvetāmbaras and the Digambaras, two (the role of nudity and the begging practice) are overtly matters of praxis, and a third may be (since the capacity of women to attain *mokṣa* is denied by Digambaras at least partly on the grounds that it would be impossible for them to practice true monastic renunciation, i.e., go about naked). It is further notable that the intra-Digambara divisions described by Rājaśekhara also involve matters of praxis.

It is possible to live with such an explanation, and most accounts of the Jains do so, for one cannot ignore the division into Śvetāmbara and Digambara, regardless of doctrinal unity. Moreover, it is possible to see the Digambara-Śvetāmbara disagreement over practice of nudity as reflecting deeply felt convictions about the true nature of practicing renunciation (Jaini 1979:12-13).

There is available, as well, a conceptual framework for dealing with the presence of the smaller divisions, the *gaccha*s, and some of the patterns in their presence. The most common solution is to treat them as 'reform' movements. There is some reason for this. The great proliferation of Śvetāmbara *gaccha*s *does* occur beginning in a period (ninth-tenth centuries C.E.) marked by some falling away from the demanding norms for monastic behavior stated in the 'scriptures.' There was a decay marked by sharp internal criticism, which eventually focussed on the rising power of *caityavāsī*s—religious and social leaders of Jain communities who made 'temples' (*caitya*s) their seats of power, lived well from temple endowments, and gathered monastic followers around them. From this controversy spring the most significant of the extant Śvetāmbara *gaccha*s, the Tapā and Kharatara Gacchas. Further, the most notable of the 'modern' Śvetāmbara groups, the Loṅkā Gaccha founded by Loṅkāśā, and its descendants the Sthānakavāsīs and the Śvetāmbara Terāpanthīs did arise in response to monastic laxity and other points where divergence from older norms appeared to be present, e.g., image veneration. The most notable modern Digambara groups can also be seen in this light, particularly the Digambara Terāpanthīs, who objected to the Digambara *bhaṭṭāraka*s, counterparts of the Śvetāmbara *caityavāsī*s, and to image veneration.

It is in the sphere of praxis that I believe lie important dimensions of the 'orders.' This points to a deleterious result of the emphasis on 'reform.' If we understand it doctrinally, it tends to draw our attention away from the continuous presence of 'orders' in the Jain tradition, and, second, away from the 'life' of that tradition.

It is important to see that 'orders,' though over and over again they may spring from disagreement over praxis, perform a variety of important unifying functions within the Jain tradition that a 'doctrinal unity' alone could not accomplish. In fact, the 'orders' enable that unity by providing working units for study and transmission of learning within the tradition. This is virtually a truism, but one often overlooked.

Second, the 'orders' were early on—see canonical texts and commentaries —regarded as important for proper monastic life and discipline. To be "outside a *gaccha*" is not good. In a note to his translation of the canonical *Ācārāṅga Sūtra*, Jacobi (1884c:47n2), apparently paraphrasing the commentary composed by Śīlāṅka in 876 C.E., notes that *gacchanirgata* ("having left the *gaccha*") seems to be a denigrated condition, and the discipline of submitting to the *ācārya* and to the *gaccha* appears to be extolled. This is duplicated in the rules for the Paryuṣaṇa, the rainy season retreat, found in the *Kalpa Sūtra*. The idea that monks should live in groups (often of 3)—sometimes still called *gaṇa*s—persists to the present day.

In addition, a matter to which the many city- and region-based names of the orders and suborders point, the orders were to some extent the living, operational units of the Jain tradition. In this context we need to see the *caityavāsī*s and *bhaṭṭāraka*s as important *positive* features of Jainism, in that their role as socio-religious 'governors' in some places was vital to the continuity and flourishing of the tradition.

Speaking of the orders in general, Walther Schubring (1962:60-61) wrote, "the teaching proper was scarcely affected by any of them. . . . The new formations which developed . . . are nearly exclusively concerned with formalities."[10] I think that our own notions of what a religious tradition is made of can cause us to pay more attention to images and scriptures as features of 'reform,' for these have 'doctrinal implications.' I seek no cheap parallel here; this is rather by way of stating that our interest in these 'reforms' has tended to focus on 'doctrine,' and not on praxis.

The side-effect is this: the reform thesis draws our attention to a particular phase of, and a particular motivation for, the development of 'orders' in Jainism. This has two deleterious results:

(1) A limit in phase. We pay attention to 'orders' only in the period in question.

(2) A limit in motive. For, leaving aside the *caityavāsa* issue, it has been the case that certain dimensions of the 'modern' orders' concerns may have been overstated, in particular, the aversion to image-veneration, and the Loṅkāśā and Sthānakavāsī acceptance of 31 and 32 canonical books, respectively (as opposed

10 A word of caution concerning the English translation of "formalities."

to the 45 texts usually found in Śvetāmbara circles—though this opens up a whole new chapter).

Aside from these two matters, 'modern' orders are often not considered with care, and recent orders that are neither anti-image nor involved in the controversy over scriptures are often short shrift. When this happens, there is a misapplication of the 'reform' thesis, for it *is* the case that 'orders' that fall outside of this modern reform period were very often formed because of disagreement over practice not involving the 'modern' points.[11]

I wish to hazard the thesis that our scholarly predelictions have something to do with this emphasis on certain motives in the development of 'orders.' Therefore, at the very least, we should understand 'reform' as a function of these orders in the Calvinist sense of ecclesia reformanda.

This entire last matter—the manifold functions of 'orders' as a whole—is a most difficult matter to push beyond the relatively simplistic levels that I have enunciated. But I believe that it must be done; and in doing so, we will serve the Jains well by remembering the continuous vigor and motion within a tradition that we often see as unitary, nearly monolithic, and will perhaps make better judgements concerning the modern 'reform' movements.

IV.

Our basic hypothesis is this: the development of the Jain tradition, even including some dimensions of the eventual Śvetāmbara-Digambara division, is best understood by seeing the tradition as a collection of subdivisions, *gaccha*s and the equivalent. As I said earlier, even to begin to do justice to every known *gaccha*, and to demonstrate the hypothesis fully, would require a large-ish monograph. But to assist us in this task, we can consider how these sub-units represent typical developments in the organizational history of religious movements. It must be admitted that sociological analysis has hardly said the last word in such matters, and so the use of such organizational analysis must be tentative. But it can nonetheless be of value in examining our hypothesis.

The organizational analysis to be used is that presented by Joachim Wach in his *Sociology of Religion*, in particular his analysis of "Specifically Religious Organization of Society" (Wach 1944:109-205). Wach lays out "The Founded Religion" as one of the forms of religious life that falls under the heading "Specifically Religious"; and as Buddhism (with occasional references to Jainism) is one of the exemplars chosen for this part of his study, it is appropri-

11 See *Darśanasāra* of Devasena.

ate to expand Wach's analysis to see whether it can assist us in understanding the Jains at a level that he does not discuss, namely, the *gaccha*.

Wach's position is that a "Founded Religion" is characterized by three general patterns of organization which commonly succeed each other, but which may also co-exist in competition or which may recur as a result of change within the tradition. The first pattern is that of the "circle of disciples" (1944:133ff.). This pattern is present during and shortly after the life of a founder, and consists of those persons personally attached to him. In Wach's (1944:136) words:

> The circle is not strictly organized, but the variety of individualities and the differences in age are harbingers of future differentiation of function among the members. Even in the early days the outstanding disciples enjoy special priveleges and join the so-called "inner circle."

The next pattern is that of the "brotherhood" (1944:137ff.). It is occasioned by the death of the founder, and it replaces the circle of disciples loyal to an ideal (either the figure of the founder or his messenger or both) and to one another (although the remaining personal disciples gain considerable authority). Wach points out that such "brotherhoods" vary considerably in their visions of themselves and their functions, and that a crucial point in their development is the formation either of one large group or of local independent bodies (1944:138-39). This, he notes, is not necessarily a conscious decision, and may be a source of considerable friction.

In any case, increasing complexity and the passage of time produce the following situation:

> Charisma and seniority have now become insufficient for authority. A reorganization sets in, discipline is established, and the period of brotherhood is ended, to be succeeded by a type of new organization, the ecclesiastical body (1944:141).

This new organization develops, according to Wach, in two stages: there are a series of developments within the first, with the second stage being characterized by "the establishment of a constitution to sustain the now stable organization." Wach details this latter occurence as follows:

> The oral tradition is written down, the written tradition is collected and standarized, the doctrine is redefined, and hereafter all deviations and opinions at variance with the officially accepted teachings are classed as heresy (1944:143).

Finally, this "constitutional" stage may be either "minimal" or "maximal" in development, these two terms roughly translating into egalitarian and decentralized or hierarchical and centralized respectively, and representing opposite ends of a spectrum of "constitutional" order (1944:145ff.).

It is difficult to do justice to Wach in such a brief summary of his detailed analysis, and much has had to be omitted. However, the basic features of his stages are sufficient to permit us to see how the inner structures of the Jain tradition might be analyzed according to it.

11

THE JAIN *SĀDHU* AS COMMUNITY BUILDER*

This paper explores the historical and regional development of the role of the Jain *sādhu* ("monk") vis-à-vis the community of Jain laypeople. The general monastic rule of the Jains is reasonably well-known and stated in Jain scholarship, and this rule is commonly taken to be the norm for all Jains. However, the Jain layperson also leads a richly varied religious life, one that is not directed at withdrawal from worldly affairs in the way that the monastic rule demands.

Scholarship has not fully explored the lay community's life, nor, more important, the ways in which the two contrasting life styles are accommodated within a single tradition. This paper explores two religious focal points at which some clarification of this accommodation might be sought: (1) the monastic rain retreat, and (2) the institutionalization of religious activities in the temple, community, and family. The data surveyed leads to the conclusion that the assigning of distinct functions to *sādhu*s, and their exclusion from day-to-day religious activities, has permitted the Jains both to accommodate themselves to the larger Hindu society and to preserve a strong monastic tradition which, by means of the rain retreat, serves at the same time as a major force of continued distinctive communal identity.

The research underlying this paper is largely historical and textual, but it is supplemented by field observations, both personal and reported by other scholars. The textual research has focussed on two groups of sources. The first

---

* Paper read at the American Academy of Religion Annual Meeting, November 1980.

group is a set of texts dating to the early centuries C.E. which describe the monastic rule governing the Jain *sādhu*. In particular, the research looks at those portions of the texts which relate to monastic visitation in Jain communities during the rainy season (July-September), which is the only time when a *sādhu* may stay in one community for more than a week. Specific rules concerning the *sādhu*'s duties to his host community, and vice-versa, have been grouped according to type of activity, so as to portray the variety of religious functions that are enhanced by the *sādhu*'s presence. Commentaries on the texts from later centuries and specific geographic regions show regional interpretations of the rules, and indicate the seriousness with which the rules were observed as the Jain community spread and changed.

The second major group of sources are texts which describe the non-monastic religious functionaries in Jain communities, i.e., temple priests, family astrologers, family priests, religious teachers, and the like. These texts, dating from 900 to 1100 C.E., show the ways in which these non-monastic religious functions are distinguished from those duties which are assigned to the *sādhu*s, and the rationales given for the distinction. Again, later commentaries indicate regional emphases and changes in the structure of Jain religious institutions.

The objectives of the research are to delineate, more clearly than has been the case in prior scholarship, the specific institutional modes by which the Jains have sought to encompass in a single religious community both a radically world-denying religious asceticism (i.e., the monastic orders) and a set of religious values that promote communal solidarity and the continuity of day-to-day human activities. It is hoped that the work will contribute both to historical studies of the Jains and to comparative understanding of the co-existence of monastic and lay values in other religious traditions, e.g., the Roman Catholic and Eastern Orthodox Christian churches.

This paper is situated within two contexts. The first is the classic Brāhmaṇa-*śramaṇa* model of Indian civilization, and the resultant uneasiness that 'order' monasticism causes this model. The second is the eternal question of what to do with the Buddhists and the Jains in discussing the relationship between the *sādhu* and the community in India.

How are we best to consider the many roles of Jain *sādhu*s under this heading of the 'power of sacred persons'?[1] If we take the classic Brāhmaṇa-*śramaṇa* division, then they belong in the latter. Their institutional role in Jainism bears this out: they are *not* the *pujārī*s (temple officiants) of Jainism. Yet they relate themselves in ritual and critical ways to the life of the lay Jain, in ways such that it is not inappropriate to speak of their having 'powers' of both spiritual and communal sorts.

---

1 [Editor's note.] This was the title of the panel of which this paper was part.

But before addressing the communal role of the Jain *sādhu*, I want to address several framing events first. There are, of course, obvious large questions of definition behind the presence of 'Jainism' in the 'Hinduism' section of the American Academy of Religion. None of these questions should be ignored, but most of them are not the burden of my presentation.

The specific concern in the study of 'Hinduism' that wants mention at the outset is this: Where do we place the *sādhu* (Hindu, Jain, Buddhist) in the process of speaking of or defining Hinduism? I don't want to belabor the obvious, but this question much bedevils a student of the Jains, and it has also occurred to me that it bedevils me in the general teaching and study of 'Hindu' religion. The *sādhu* poses a problem in defining 'Hinduism.' This problem can be seen in three phases. In phase one, we let the *sādhus* themselves define it. In this phase, Hinduism is the Uttaramīmāṃsā, and Jainism the school of Syādvāda. In phase two, sociological and anthropological (and other?) concerns lead us to the praxis, the 'communal' forms of Hindu life. In phase three, we begin to see the great, complex middle ground in popular Hindu religion between *śramaṇa* and Brāhmaṇa. (See, for example, the work of W. D. O'Flaherty 1976.)

Let me now address the 'spiritual' and 'communal' powers of a Jain *sādhu*. For a long time we have defined Jainism by the 'spiritual' side of its *sādhus*. A somewhat (to say the least) idealistic picture has emerged from this, of Jainism as an *essentially śramaṇa* movement. We usually focus on the rigorous austerities of the Jain *sādhu* as the benchmark of 'true' Jainism. One might add that this results in a highly 'impersonal' portrayal.

The lay community in this picture provides us with a problem. The classic treatment has been to see the *sādhu* as the model for the layperson, standing in a parallel relationship to that of the Jina, or Tīrthaṅkara, in 'worship,' as the ideal toward which the layperson strives. The Jains themselves, of course, have provided us with grounds for this. The textual tradition that describes the lay life sets it out as follows: eleven *pratimās*, from right "faith" up to virtually *saṅnyāsa*, and a series of *vratas*. The eleven *pratimās* are; (1) right faith, (2) taking the twelve *vratas*, (3) practicing *sāmāyika*, (4) practicing the *poṣadha* fasts, (5) purity of nourishment, (6) celibacy by day, (7) absolute celibacy, (8) abandonment of household activity, (9) abandonment of acquisitiveness, (10) abandonment of approval of activities connected with household life, and (11) renunciation of specially prepared food and approximating the conduct of a *sādhu*. The twelve *vratas* are: five *aṇuvratas* (limited vows) of (1) refraining from causing harm, (2) refraining from false speech, (3) refraining from theft, (4) refraining from illicit sexual activities, and (5) limiting one's possessions; three *guṇavratas* (vows which strengthen the *aṇuvratas*) of (6) geographical restriction of activities, (7) restriction of objects of enjoyment, and (8) refraining from unwholesome activities; and four *śikṣāvratas* (vows of spiritual discipline) of (9) attainment of equanimity through meditation, (10) further geographical restrictions, (11) performing the *poṣadha* fast, and (12) performing charity. (See P. S. Jaini 1979:157-87 and R. Williams 1963:55-181.)

One also finds among the Digambaras descriptions of six lay rituals known as *karmans* (actions), recommended as lay versions of the six monastic *āvaśyakas* (obligations). As given by Jinasena (840 C.E.) and Somadeva (959 C.E.), the six *karmans* are: (1) *devapūjā* (temple worship), (2) *guru-upāsti* (visiting and venerating mendicant teachers; this is replaced by Jinasena with *vārtā*, following an honest profession), (3) *svādhyāya* (study), (4) *saṃyama* (restraint), (5) *tapas* (austerities), and (6) *dāna* (charity). The six *āvaśyakas* on which these are based are: (1) *sāmāyika* (equanimity, the same as the ninth *vrata*), (2) *caturviṃśati-stava* (veneration of the 24 Jinas), (3) *vandanaka* (reverent salutation, a specific dimension of *guru-upāsti*), (4) *pratikramaṇa* (confession of past transgressions; later texts tend to put it on an annual basis as Saṃvatsarī, its special rainy season form), (5) *pratyākhyāna* (resolution of avoidance of future sins, and practice to that end, often using fasting as a basic device), and (6) *kāyotsarga* (abandonment of the body for a limited time). (See P. S. Jaini 1979:189-91, W. Schubring 1962:268-69, and R. Williams 1963:184-85.)

In this picture the lay life is seen as preparation for sādhuhood. How very much this is like the 'fourths' in 'Hindu' circles![2] This picture has been, on the whole, unreflectively considered by scholars. It is very interesting to say that by evolving the *śrāvaka* (ideal layman) image of the *pratimās*, *vratas*, and *karmans*, the Jains drew the lay and monastic paths together. But the truth seems more rough and tumble. As I will discuss below, the Paryuṣaṇa institution may be a more revealing nexus to observe the communal powers and roles of the Jain *sādhu*.

And so, I would say, we are still at the first stage described above. We let the *sādhus* define our picture of the tradition. But this has left us with a problem: can this fully define the Jain community? On the other side, though, we have begun to discover and take more seriously the praxis of Jainism. At most, at present, we are reluctant to define that praxis in other '*sādhu*' terms. For example, we say that Jains are merchants and bankers because there is the least *hiṃsā* in such occupations. But a serious study of the karma texts has convinced me

---

2 [Editor's note.] Folkert here refers to the life-stage (*āśrama*) of world-renunciation (*saṅnyāsa*) which comes as the fourth after those of student (*brahmacarya*), householder (*gṛhastha*), and retired forest dweller (*vanaprastha*), and to the goal (*puruṣārtha*) of liberation (*mokṣa*) which comes as the fourth after the three interrelated goals of righteousness (*dharma*), wealth (*artha*), and enjoyment (*kāma*).

that we need to be more careful. *Hiṃsā* does *not* produce the worst kinds of karma. One is led by this and other observations to a deep suspicion of that pat answer about the socio-economic status of the Jains, and to suggest that a host of other reasons, not very ideal ones, can better account for it.

To carry a bit further, one notes that the actual lay life does not conform to the lay version of the monastic *vrata*s, nor necessarily to the gradual progression through the *pratimā*s. In fact, in ideal terms, the Jain lay person's life is not even supposed to be *sādhu*-dominated in areas of basic religious activity such as temple worship and the *saṃskāra*s (rites of passage).

The *sādhu* is not the *pujārī*. (There are significant differences between the Digambara and the Śvetāmbara *pujārī*s. The former are themselves Jains, whereas the latter tend to be salaried servants belonging to 'Hindu' castes such as Brāhmaṇa, Gardener, or Peasant.) Nor are the rites of passage in a Jain's life presided over by *sādhu*s. These rites probably are not even 'Jain' in origin. The classical description of them, in Jinasena's *Ādipurāṇa*, is most likely after the fact.

In sum, what we have among the Jains, I would like to propose, is in actuality a lovely and increasingly fascinating case of the following problem: what has the Brāhmaṇa to do with the *sādhu*? And I ask it here because it has often seemed to me that in 'Hinduism' as a whole we are only beginning to learn how to answer that question.

Having asked that question, I want to pose two cases that can help us understand this Jain problem. (How readily they can be extended to more specifically 'Hindu' contexts I won't venture to say.) One answer requires that we do some re-conceptualizing of Jain history; the other answer requires that we take better note of a particular part of Jain religious life.

When one looks more carefully at the actual history of Jain asceticism, one sees that the Jains have been far more willing to be '*maṭhavāsī*s,' or temple dwellers,[3] than our standard sketches indicate. The ideal portrait of the Jain *sādhu*, eternally wandering, staying no more than a day or two, must be adjusted.

This seems to have been the case both in the west and in the central south. The latter provides us with the best case studies because there the tendency to become stationary is often associated with a particular group, the Yāpanīyas, who (in a Digambar dominated region) advocated a temple dwelling life style so as to *be* more part of the community. Certainly in the medieval Deccan (see Nandi 1973 and R. B. S. Singh 1975), and perhaps elsewhere, Jainism was far

---

3 [Editor's note.] *Maṭhavāsī* is a term coined by Folkert, meaning "a resident of a monastery." The term used in Jain circles, and by Folkert further on, is *caityavāsī*. The best discussion of the tension in Jainism between "temple-dwelling" (*caityavāsī*) and "forest-dwelling" (*vanavāsī*) *sādhu*s is Premī 1956:478-95.

more predominantly a monastery-dwelling askesis than is often given out. We hypothesize that this was more a Digambara than a Śvetāmbara phenomenon; but even there, the pattern is mixed. Modern groups, especially the Terāpanthīs, have sought to break this pattern. The very name of the Sthānakavāsīs indicates their stress on residence in halls as opposed to temples (see Jaini 1979:310).

The point is that as popularly conceived, and bedeviled by the perceived split between the *sādhus* and the community, this phenomenon has commonly been portrayed as 'decay' in the Jain community. I would propose that it was more likely an innovation that put and kept the community and the *sādhus* together in ways that, had there been no *caityavāsīs*, they would not have been bonded. One must note here the specific place this institution allows for a prolonged lay-guru relationship, and the place here of the guru-preceptor, a relationship that clearly hints at devotion to a swami-holyman. Perversely enough, the alteration of the romantic ideal probably seemed to keep alive the 'spiritual' role of the *sādhu* in the community by enabling regular lay-*sādhu* contact, and by keeping the teacher-preceptor in a position to keep Jain 'Brāhmaṇism' distinctive.

The former 'solution' works well in certain settings, not in others. By and large it works in larger population centers, where 'charity' on a large scale makes *maṭhavāsī* life possible. But what of the small towns and villages?

Here, I would like to propose, the rain retreat works especially well. David Knipe (1975) has already shown the locus of lay-monastic interaction in towns and cities, in, among other contexts, the attention paid by laypeople to the preaching and teaching of *mokṣa*, with emphasis on the rainy-season retreat. This is a time of protracted lay-monastic contact, which is attested both in canonical sources and independently as a hoary tradition since at least Satavāhana times (first to third centuries C.E.).

The basic term here is Paryuṣaṇa (Prakrit Pajjosavaṇā), from *pari* + the verbal root, *vas*, meaning "to stay put, to stay in one place." Broadly speaking, Paryuṣaṇa refers to the entire rain retreat. The *Paryuṣaṇakalpa* (translated by Jacobi 1884d:296-311 as "Rules for Yatis"), one of several appendices to the *Kalpa Sūtra* (part eight of the *Daśāśrutaskandaḥ*, one of the Cheda Sūtras), gives the general rules that apply to it. The whole focus of this appendix is on monastic discipline, part of a tremendous concern for the proper mendicant life (see also *Ācārāṅga Sūtra* II). The description of the Paryuṣaṇa is based on the rain retreat in the classic lives of the Jinas (Schubring 1962:261). The full season of the rain retreat is four months. The opening date is regionally varied, and canonically even in dispute; but the principle appears to be that wandering must stop at once, while the full retreat rules do not take effect until one-and-a-half months (actually, one month and twenty days) later. As a classic focal point for the interaction of the lay and monastic communities, Paryuṣaṇa has undergone two parallel changes. It has changed from a solely monastic discipline to one that is a lay discipline as well, and it has changed from a monastic exercise to a communal experience.

More specifically, Paryuṣaṇa-parva is the 'fast' that ends the year, occupying a specific time-frame within the whole rain retreat. It lasts eight to ten days, or longer. Śvetāmbaras begin in Śrāvaṇa (12th dark), and end in Bhadrapāda (4th bright), while Digambaras observe it for ten days in Bhadrapāda. Von Glasenapp (1925:433-34) describes this fast as modeled on the *poṣadha* fast; alternately, one can say that a 'special edition' of the *poṣadha* fast is used in the Paryuṣaṇa-parva. The *poṣadha* is a special fast performed on four special days (*parva*) in each month. Stevenson (1915:259-60) points out how *poṣadha* has largely become this once-yearly event. Saṃvatsarī is the closing day of Paryuṣaṇa-parva, and of the religious year.

Paryuṣaṇa has two major functions. First, it guarantees a protracted monastic presence, and keeps the community in a lively relationship with the *sādhu*s. Different congregations compete to invite certain *sādhu*s. Here there is a significant 'personalizing' of the *sādhu* as well. Second, it sets off an annual *poṣadha* observance that appears to be the most significant contemporary example of lay people living the monastic ideal in modified form. It thus preserves a 'spiritual' lay ideal, and results in a mutual strengthening of the lay and monastic ideals.

Beyond that, it has bonded the Jain community in intriguing ways. There are the physical re-visits to lay communities by certain *sādhu*s. Von Glasenapp (1925:132-33) discusses *vijñapti*-letters ("declarations") written on the occasion of Saṃvatsarī. These are letters to acquaintances and gurus, sometimes highly crafted on literary models, and often are of value as historical documents. Mrs. Stevenson (1915:159-60) says of these *vijñapti*-letters, "The writer used to be bewildered by receiving letters from Jaina friends and pandits . . . asking her forgiveness in case they had unwittingly vexed her." We can see how such letters help to bind the Jain community across geographical distances.[4] Saṃvatsarī is thus a communal 'Yom Kippur' and, by the *vijñapti* mechanism, a bonding process in its own right.

The rain retreat is fascinating because it shows the spiritual and communal role of the *sādhu*s so tightly intertwined. Such ideal portraits of the *śrāvaka* as that of the *dinacaryā* (daily conduct) found in Hemacadra's twelth century *Yogaśāstra* (see Williams 1963:182-84) are importantly preserved in actuality in Paryuṣaṇa. This annual event has become the significant mechanism for preserv-

---

4 [Editor's note.] In his text, Folkert indicates that in his oral presentation he here related the home-coming dimensions of Paryuṣaṇa in the village of Beḍā, as people who have left the village for business reasons return for Paryuṣaṇa.

ing the important *śrāvaka* ideal by its admitting and regularizing of order in lay-monastic contact.

In conclusion, the *sādhu*-lay relationship in Jainism is much more complex, more rough and tumble, than we popularly portray it. This complexity has consequences beyond just the Jain tradition, however, for in unraveling this puzzle a bit, we are faced with a perennial question in terms of the 'models' we use for understanding the ideals and structures of 'Hinduism' as a whole.

Illus. 2
Three *sādhvīs*
Photograph by Kendall W. Folkert

Illus. 3
Two *sādhvīs* doing scholarly work in an *upāśray*
Photograph by Kendall W. Folkert

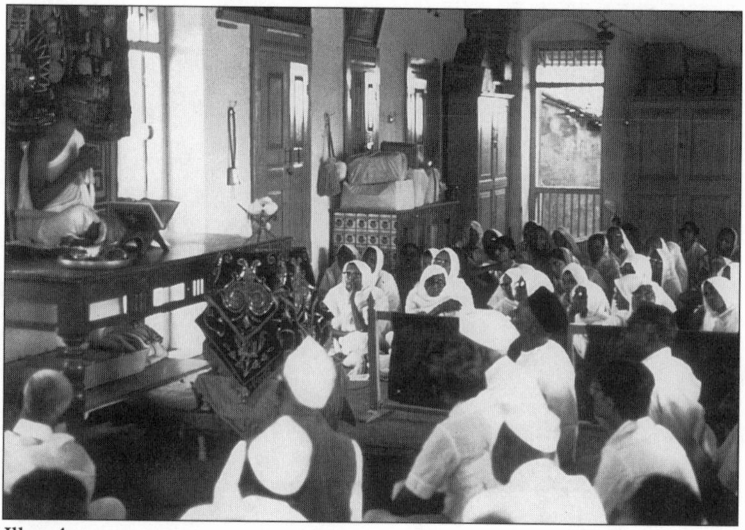

Illus. 4
Muni Jambūvijay delivering a *vyākhyān*
Photograph by Kendall W. Folkert

Illus. 5
Layman bowing in veneration at feet of a *sādhvī*. In return she is blessing him by sprinkling sandalwood powder (*vāskep*) on his forehead
Photograph by Thomas A. Zwicker

12

MONASTIC IDEALS AND THE LAY COMMUNITY IN RELIGION*

INTRODUCTION

In historical terms, the Jains trace their movement to two teachers and exemplars, Pārśva (ca. 800 B.C.E.) and Mahāvīra (599-527 B.C.E.). Both men were radical ascetics, and the core teachings of Jainism are ascetic. Pārśva and Mahāvīra taught that the person (or any living thing) consists of (1) an immortal, essentially perfect soul, called the *jīva*, and (2) a material body whose association with the *jīva* has been generated and continues to be generated by karma. In other words, the embodiment of the *jīva* is the result of every sort of activity carried out in the physical world. The ultimate objective for the human being is to free the *jīva* from this material embodiment. In Jain teaching, this can only be done (1) by radical renunciation of all physical comforts and worldly attachments, and (2) on one's own, for there is no concept here of a 'salvation' granted by a deity. Both Pārśva and Mahāvīra lived lives of such exemplary renunciation that they attained 'release' from physical existence, and they, along with twenty-two predecessors dated far back into prehistoric times by Jains, are venerated as Jinas, i.e., "conquerors" of material bondage.

The religious model for the Jains is, therefore, mendicant poverty, and the core of Jainism is a community of wandering monks and nuns who own no

* Edited from two separate grant proposals from 1982 and 1984.

property, do not live in monasteries, and beg all food. In general terms, the Jain ascetic seeks to detach himself (or herself—because of the view that the *jīva* is of equal nature and status in all living things, women have historically been a significant presence in the movement) from all karma-generating activity. In practical terms, this means that the mendicant lives according to the following five great vows (*mahāvrata*):

(1) to commit no violence;

(2) to practice celibacy;

(3) to speak the truth;

(4) to own no property and live in no fixed place; and

(5) to use nothing not given to one.

From its beginning, then, the Jain tradition has been led by monks and nuns who, following the examples of Pārśva and Mahāvīra, renounce marriage and all sexual activity, do not engage in any livelihood other than self-discipline, and practice mendicant monasticism, living in no one place, and wandering from village to town to city, begging each day's food for that day alone, and sleeping and staying in monastic guest-houses for only brief periods. This pattern changes only in the rainy season (July to November), when the ascetic stay in one place.

While most 'literate' or 'great' religions have contained such monastic or ascetic movements within them, the Jains are of special interest because their basic teachings explicitly require the ascetic life-style in order for the human being to attain liberation or salvation. There is no hope of salvation for anyone living outside of monastic orders. This monastic focus for the tradition notwithstanding, the majority of Jains are and have been lay persons who do not enter orders. The Jain community has from very early on also consisted of lay-persons, men and women who live ordinary lives, venerate the Jinas, follow specific lay rules, and ostensibly await some future life when they will feel led to take full ascetic vows and live as monks and nuns. This points to the basic analytical framework of this study: how to understand the relationship between monasticism and lay life in a religion that teaches an ascetic ideal.

This problem in Jain history is part of a general problem in religious history: the rise of monastic movements and their relationship to lay communities. Most scholarship on this problem has treated monasticism basically as a movement of internal "reform" in religions, or as a movement that seeks to capture a particularly ideal or pristine religious experience, a rarified version of what is available in the religion as a whole. (See Wach 1944:109-205 for a general account of this view and a summary of major earlier scholarship.)

It is noteworthy that few significant studies of monasticism as a variety of religious social structure in India post-date that of Wach, much of whose work is built on that of Max Weber. More recently major scholars of Indian religion and society (for example, Milton Singer 1972, David Mandelbaum 1972, and Louis Dumont 1980) have focused almost exclusively on caste and hierarchy in Indian society, so that the ascetic movements are seen largely in terms of their anti-caste, anti-social function, i.e., as mechanisms for individuals to transcend caste limitations that may affect them.

In the sense in which one might argue that Indian ascetic movements represent a 'pure' religion, i.e., a religious life dominated by personal, individual experience and not by the social functions of religion, some Hindu monastic movements might fit the general thesis that monasticism seeks a more pristine or ideal form of religion. This appears to be the working hypothesis that underlies recent scholarship. The thesis itself raises significant questions about definitions of religion, but even if its working value is granted, it does not readily fit Jainism. In Jainism, historical evidence clearly establishes the monastic and ascetic life as the ideal and the older model. A systematically organized lay community does not appear until nearly 500 years after the founding of Jainism (see P. S. Jaini 1979:157-87) This is clearly different from the way in which the monastic and lay ideals appear to have developed in most other religions. The study of Jainism thus is an occasion for exploring and re-evaluating this basic feature of major religions, and the way that it has been explored by scholars.

THE STHĀNAKAVĀSĪ JAINS

Even granting the unusual nature of the Jain case in general, there are occasions in the history of Jainism that cast the problem into sharper relief. This project will examine one such case, which should make possible some better understanding of the situation in Jainism as a whole, and of the general thesis cited above. The particular case is the rise of an internal Jain reform movement called the Sthānakavāsīs in the sixteenth and seventeenth centuries C.E. in the area around Ahmedabad in Gujarat.

Beginning in the early centuries C.E., as the lay community in Jainism became more systematically organized, a Jain temple cult and other lay rituals had developed. The origins of this cultus are not clear. To some extent, it appears to have been the case that the Jain lay community simply followed Hindu socio-religious practice in such areas as rites of passage, and that these ritual complexes only slowly evolved into distinctive Jain forms. It also appears that the temple cult evolved as a distinctively Jain form of the (at that time) growing Hindu tendency toward theism and devotional religion.

What is notable is that this cultus evolved outside the sphere and control of monastic orders. Temple officiants were laypersons, and lay rituals (including rites of passage) did not involve a monastic priestly class. This is not altogether different from the basic Hindu pattern, as Hindu ascetics are by-and-large outside of the Hindu temple system (the latter being controlled largely by Brāhmaṇ priests). But it is very different from the pattern of Buddhist development, where Buddhist monastic orders came to control the temples. It is the latter comparison that is telling, for Buddhism, like Jainism, initially had an essentially ascetic and monastic orientation, and, like Jainism, faced the problem of integrating a lay community into an anti-social religious ideal.

In Buddhism, this integration occurred by means of doctrinal evolution. The way of salvation (*nirvāṇa*) was opened to laypersons in the Buddhist teachings of the Mahāyāna, the "Greater Vehicle," which taught that ascetic withdrawal from everyday life was no longer necessary for salvation. But in Jainism no such doctrinal evolution occurred; the general thesis, accepted by Jain scholars, is that the lay person's identification with and loyalty to the Jain ideals was cemented by the existence of a set of distinctively lay institutions, which gave the Jain community a point of self-identity and solidarity.

However, by the fourteenth and fifteenth centuries this lay cultus had been significantly 'invaded' by monastic/priestly specialists who had begun to control the temples and cultic life to a significant degree. This development was partly due to decreased observation of the rules governing Jain ascetics, which neither permit them to live in fixed places nor mention any 'priestly' role for them. But it was also due to the growth of the temples as foci of the life of the Jain community, and thus the monks, though ascetic laxity was doubtless present, were also responding to the strength of the temples by using them as an avenue for lay-ascetic interaction.

The sum of this shift in institutional structures was a growing unease in both lay and monastic circles, and out of this setting came the Sthānakavāsī movement. The Sthānakavāsī 'reform' began with a layperson named Loṅkā Śāha. According to P. S. Jaini (1979:309), "Loṅkā Śāha considered the institution of the temple...with its great concentration of wealth and power, to be the main source of corruption and the rituals performed there as totally irrelevant to the [ascetic] path set forth in [the Jain] scripture." Thus the Sthānakavāsī reformers struck at what they perceived to be the root of the problem, the temple, by dissociating themselves from it and its rituals. They focussed instead on an institution known as the *upāśray* ("sanctuary"), a center for study and meeting that ostensibly houses no ritual cultus. Other important subsequent features of the reform included a renunciation of the cult of images in the temples as an aberration from original Jain teachings, and the development of a distinctive canon of scripture with its own commentary tradition.

When Jainism came to the attention of Indologists in the nineteenth and twentieth centuries, it was these latter two features of the Sthānakavāsī movement that particularly caught Western attention (see especially Stevenson 1915 and von Glasenapp 1925). Overlooked in this view of the Sthānakavāsīs was what is historically and methodologically the more interesting and important feature of the reform, namely the loss, by abolition, of a major lay institution, the temple. It is this feature of the Sthānakavāsī movement that is the focal point of this project.

As noted above, the general thesis in Jain scholarship is that the temple provides the lay community with an important point of institutional identity, since laypersons do not participate directly in the ideal form of the tradition, namely the monastic career. This being so, the way in which the Sthānakavāsī community bonds itself together and identifies itself in the absence of the temple is in need of exploration, and such exploration should also be the occasion for re-examination of the general thesis concerning the place of the temple in the Jain lay community.

Although the temple is not part of Sthānakavāsī life, other institutions (such as the *upāśray*) and rituals (such as rites of passage) remain. A clear account is needed of the role of these institutions and rituals in Sthānakavāsī life. The original impetus for the Sthānakavāsī reform appears to have been a desire to revive the original ideal of Jainism's ascetic goals. Thus the Sthānakavāsīs also sought to draw the lay community into closer direct contact with the monastic ideal. However, studies of the Sthānakavāsīs have not clearly explored the actual mechanisms for such closer contact. This project seeks to collect data and write an account of the specifics of Sthānakavāsī lay-ascetic interaction.

As noted above, earlier scholarship has focused on the Sthānakavāsīs' rejection of the cult images and development of their own scriptural canon. This study should enable a re-evaluation of the importance of these two matters. Beyond these specific contributions to the study of Jainism, the project should enable some testing of general scholarly approaches to the study of monastic movements within religious traditions. At the very least, it should clarify the place of Jainism in such theses, and it should also be a contribution to the development of better typologies for understanding monastic and ascetic movements in India, including the early history of Buddhism.

MONASTIC-LAY INTERACTION IN A SAMPLE OF JAIN COMMUNITIES IN GUJARAT

The long history of the Jain community of ascetics and laypersons, its steadfast adherence to its austere discipline, its vast literature, and its influence on the larger Hindu culture have drawn scholars' attention to the Jains since the early 1800s. Yet most scholarship has focused on literary expressions of the tradition, and few students of Indian religion have conducted field observation of the community. This project is generally oriented toward filling that gap, not only because the gap is there, but because its existence has left unsolved a cluster of vital questions about how the community actually functions and has maintained itself for so long.

The project focuses on observation of, and data collection concerning, a set of Jain communities in Gujarat. Its ultimate outcome will be a description and analysis of those communities that will allow conclusions to be drawn concerning one of the most intriguing, yet least well-understood dimensions of Jain life: the lasting bond between the community's two components, the lay persons and the ascetics.

This work will be done among Śvetāmbara Mūrtipūjaka Jains. Interpretive conditions that arise from this choice of subjects for the study will be touched on below. In general terms, the project will consist of observing interaction between wandering ascetics and settled lay persons in two social contexts: (1) a collection of eight to twelve villages in north-central Gujarat; and (2) the Jain communities within the new, south-western section of the city of Ahmedabad, Gujarat.

The lay-monastic interaction to be observed in these contexts has several dimensions, including the religious organizational structures of the lay communities. Hence an associated task is to describe those communities as clearly as possible. This should yield results sufficient to contribute a good deal to such general portraits as exist of Jain communities and their contemporary life, in addition to its specific contribution to understanding lay-monastic interaction.

It has been stated above that Jain lay-monastic interaction is both intriguing and poorly understood. It is worth observing that this project's broadest scholarly context is the role in India as a whole of ascetics, or 'renouncers' of the socio-religious practices and structures of the majority population. In general, the practice of ascetic renunciation in Hindu religion becomes relatively visible around the time of Mahāvīra and the Buddha, i.e., the sixth century B.C.E. In its earlier stages, such renunciation was seen as a critical stance vis-à-vis religious orthopraxis and socio-religious hierarchies. Hindu religious law-books of somewhat later times (ca. 200 B.C.E.) sought to regularize the practice of renunciation, making it a final stage in the life-cycle and thus seeking to integrate it into orthopraxis (see Kane 1968-77:II:416-26, 917-75). But this ideal has continued to be overshadowed by the practice of renouncing ordinary social and religious values earlier in life, making the whole of one's life an ascetic career.

Hindu ascetic practice in contemporary times has been described and analyzed most recently by Miller and Wertz (1976) and by such Indian scholars as G. S. Ghurye (1964). Such studies show that while the *sādhu*, or ascetic or holy man (stereotyped in the Occident as the yogi or fakir on his bed of nails), is perhaps more visible in India than in any other culture, his status in the culture remains ambivalent: ascetics are respected as figures who have, so to speak, the courage of their convictions, and they may at times become near cult-figures. Yet as visible critics of the majority's practice and religiosity, they are also the objects of suspicion and occasional outright hostility.

Within the Jain tradition, however, this picture changes. Because Jain teachings as a whole are critical of the standard values of engagement in social and economic life, one would not expect to see the ascetic viewed in such ambivalent fashion as is true for Hindu culture as a whole. The question of the validity of this expectation, and of its possible full dimensions, raises the specific context of this project.

Such scholars as have examined, mostly on the gounds of literary evidence, Jain ascetic-lay relationships (for example, Jaini 1979 and Williams 1963) have portrayed the situation as follows: the Jain layperson conceives of him or herself as being located on a continuum of spiritual development that ultimately embraces the ascetic career. No ambivalence or hostility obtains, therefore, between layperson and ascetic, and lay life is seen as a preface to asceticism (even if the latter occurs in a subsequent life) and as being penetrated by ascetic values.

The question must be raised, however, of whether or not these portrayals based on literature are subject to the same idealism as the Hindu law books appear to be in their effort to regularize renunciation. A further issue raises itself simply in that the Jains, even at the village level in Gujarat, are a minority population, so that their day-to-day relationship with ascetics is subject to a variety of variables and can hardly be easily isolated from the attitudes of the majority populace that surrounds them.

The project proposed here seeks to focus, then, on the question of validating the ostensible contrast between the Hindu and Jain status of ascetics, and on the general need for the literary portrait of the relationship to be completed by carefully structured field observation. The following specific plan of observation and information-gathering is proposed:

(1) In the village context, to follow the route, from village to village, of a specific small group of Jain monks during the 'wandering' portion of one annual cycle of monastic life; to observe the level and type of interaction between the

group of monks and lay Jains in each village; and to compile a basic profile both of the group of monks and of the lay institutions and general character of the Jain community in each village.

(2) In the city of Ahmedabad, to observe and record the pattern of visits by monastic groups to a specific cluster of Jain communities in one part of the city; to note the size and type of each visiting group; and to complete a basic profile of the lay institutions and the character of this community.

Within these two contexts, a series of issues and tasks can be enunciated, as follows:

(1) Based on specific data from a defined sample, to study the observable level of lay-monastic interaction in Jain communities, as measured by the number of villages, and their Jain population, visited by a specific group of monks; the frequency of daily contact between monks and visitors while the monks are in a given village; and the role of the monks vis-à-vis the on-going religious institutions of the village.

(2) To ascertain whether any dominant factors determining the 'itinerary' of a monastic group can be detected. Hypothetical possibilities in this category include:

   (a) Monastic 'lineage.' Jain monks have, since before the Christian era, organized themselves into lineages, called *gaccha*s. A *gaccha* consists of followers (kept track of over many centuries) of a particular monastic teacher. Although the *gaccha*s have been researched extensively from literary sources (see, for example, Deo 1956 and Sen 1931), the role of a monastic group's *gaccha* is not known insofar as it might affect its patterns of movement. (See also item 5, below.)

   (b) Prior association. It is not known from existing studies whether groups of monks frequently revisit particular villages or, if they do, what time intervals between visits are involved.

   (c) The Jain festival calendar. An important issue for clarifying the nature of the relationship between monk and layperson is the question of whether the monks visit villages in a more or less random pattern as concerns timing, or whether village and family communal occasions prompt their 'schedule.' The greater the validity of the 'ideal' portrait, the less likely this would be.

   (d) Level of activity. Is it in any sense notable that the level of a village's response to the monks prompts them to stay for longer or shorter periods of time?

(3) To see whether differences in any or all areas of observation can be detected between patterns of interaction in villages and in cities. It is vital that this

point be explored because, while the Jain community as a whole has been the subject of a fair degree of urban-rural comparative study (see especially Sangave 1980), no account has been attempted of the survival or modification of traditional patterns of mendicancy in such comparisons.

(4) To note the character of the religious organization of lay communities. Jain laypersons in a single community are usually organized into a *saṅgha* ("association"). The nature of these *saṅgha*s has not been explored by scholars to any extent, and specific questions need to be answered in several areas:

 (a) the general range of the *saṅgha*'s duties and tasks;

 (b) the nature of its organization (offices, division of labor, etc.);

 (c) its role as title-holder to communal properties (temple, monastic guest-house, other properties);

 (d) in light of the foregoing, its role in dealing with visiting groups of monks.

(5) To investigate the relationship of the *saṅgha*s to the *gaccha*s. Lay Jains also consider themselves to be connected loosely with these monastic lineages, and the nature of that connection and the relationship of *gaccha*s to *saṅgha*s within a single community is not clear from existing data. This matter must be explored in order to understand what may be one of the critical factors in the way that monastic groups choose villages to visit (see item 2a, above), and because it appears to be the case that urban Jain communities tend to forego *gaccha*-determination association and form large-scale communal *saṅgha*s. This latter point must be confirmed and analyzed.

(6) In order to accomplish the dual purpose of making the portrayal of lay-monastic interaction as concrete as possible, and to give a specific setting to the data concerning the communities, an effort will be made to map each community observed, and to provide a detailed map itinerary of the movement of the group of monks that is being followed. This is particularly important because of the Jains' status as a minority community; i.e., a full picture of the lay communities and their status is needed to complete the entire portrait.

This research should generate a defined sample and sufficient data to make a significant contribution to knowledge and understanding of the lay-monastic relationship in the Jain tradition beyond the portrayal available in the existing analyses. The final stage of the entire process will involve comparison of the portrait that emerges from this study with the 'ideal' portrait discussed above. The following general outcomes are expected:

(1) The literary portrait of the lay-monastic relationships will be clarified and concretized.

(2) Where a contemporary portrait of the relationship makes the ideal appear less realistic, I will be able to show this clearly.

(3) If the ideal portrait is demonstrably not reliable, it will be possible to point to other factors and mechanisms to account for the remarkable durability of the Jain lay-monastic relationship, and so lay the foundation for a new general explanation of the phenomenon.

As noted earlier, this research occurs within a mainstream Śvetāmbara Mūrtipūjaka setting. Similar studies of other Śvetāmbara settings and of the Digambaras would be required before generalizations for the entire tradition would be possible.[1]

---

1 [Editor's note.] For two subsequent studies that begin to address the issues Folkert raises here, see Carrithers 1989 and Cort 1991a.

Illus. 6
Muni Jambūvijay
Photograph by Kendall W. Folkert

13

NOTES ON PARYUṢAṆ IN SAMĪ AND VEḌ*

[Editor's Introduction]

These research notes constitute Folkert's last writings on the Jains. Fieldwork notes are by their very nature dense and cryptic. They are not meant for public reading, but rather to serve as a memory aid to the researcher. Rituals and texts which are known to the researcher are not explained, nor are people or places introduced. I have added footnotes and translations to aid the reader, while at the same time striving to keep the critical apparatus to a minimum so that Folkert's voice is not lost, and so that the reader can sense the excitement and satisfaction that come from fieldwork. Except where noted, all footnotes are mine. The following description of Paryuṣaṇ (see also chapter 11, above) is designed to provide the reader with background information needed to understand the context of Folkert's notes.

Paryuṣaṇ is the most important annual religious festival of the Śvetāmbar Jains. It falls on eight days during the months of Śrāvaṇ and Bhādrapad (August-September) in the middle of the four-month rainy season period (*comāsu, cāturmās*) when all *sādhus* (male mendicants) and *sādhvīs* (female mendicants) cease their travels and stay in one place. This is therefore a time of heightened lay-mendicant interaction, and Paryuṣaṇ is the most heightened period. Many Jains perform total or water-only fasts for all or part of Paryuṣaṇ, as fasting is

* In *Center for the Study of World Religions Bulletin* 16:2 (1990), 54-73.

believed to be the most efficacious way to cleanse the soul of karma, and a holy time like Paryuṣaṇ is believed to hasten this process. The principal daily activity during Paryuṣaṇ is sermons given for two to three hours every morning and afternoon by the *sādhus*. The subjects of the sermons for the first three days are the five duties for Paryuṣaṇ and the eleven annual duties enjoined upon all lay Jains.

On the afternoon of the third day, a copy of the *Kalpa Sūtra* is taken in a procession from the *upāśray*[1] to the house of the layman, who has successfully bid an auction to perform this rite, and there the book is worshiped. The *Kalpa Sūtra* is among the most important religious texts of the Śvetāmbar Mūrtipūjak Jains. It contains (1) the biographies of Vardhamāna Mahāvīra and the other twenty-three of the Jinas ("Spiritual Victors") or Tīrthaṅkaras ("Congregation Establishers") of this era, (2) the *Sthavirāvalī*, the lineages of *sādhus* from Mahāvīra until the time of the redaction of the text in the fifth century C.E., and (3) the rules for mendicant conduct, including the performance of Paryuṣaṇ. On the morning of the fourth day the *Kalpa Sūtra* is returned, again in a procession, to the *upāśray*, where it is worshiped by the assembled congregation. The sermons on the next four days consist of the public recitation of the *Kalpa Sūtra* along with the vernacular translation of a Sanskrit commentary on the text. In the course of this recitation, on the afternoon of the fifth day the *sādhu* comes to the portion describing the birth of Mahāvīra, and his mother's seeing of fourteen auspicious dreams at the time of his conception. This is known as Mahāvīr Jayantī, "Mahāvīr's Victory."[2] It is celebrated with great fanfare, as will be seen below. Silver replicas of the dreams are lowered from a ceiling of the *upāśray*, received, garlanded, and placed on a table. The rite to perform each of these actions is auctioned to members of the congregation, and the large amount of money raised on this day is used for the restoration and building of temples. After this dramatic representation of the viewing of the fourteen dreams, the rights to garland and swing the cradle of the infant Mahāvīra are also auctioned. Then the *sādhu* reads the relevant verse and the day's celebrations come to a close.

The recitation of the *Kalpa Sūtra* continues for two more days. On the morning of the eighth and final day, the *sādhus* recommence the recitation of the *Kalpa Sūtra* from the beginning, only this time they recite as fast as they can

---

1 A building in which mendicants stay during their travels, and for the four months of the rainy-season retreat. It is also used for sermons by the mendicants, and for the performance of rites such as the recitation of the *Kalpa Sūtra* and *pratikramaṇa*.

2 The final short "a" of Sanskrit and Prakrit words is not pronounced in Gujarati; hence Sanskrit and Prakrit Mahāvīra is pronounced "Mahāvīr" in Gujarati. As a scholar of classical India, Folkert was used to writing words with final short "a's," such as Jaina and Mahāvīra; as a fieldworker he was used to writing words as pronounced, such as Jain and Mahāvīr.

only the Prakrit root text, without its commentaries. Since the root text consists of just over 1,200 metrical units, the text as recited on this occasion is known as the *Bārasā Sūtra* ("Twelve Hundred Verses"). On the afternoon of the eighth day, all of the laity assemble in the *upāśrays*—men and women in separate buildings with *sādhus* and *sādhvīs*, respectively—for the performance of the annual Saṃvatsarī Pratikramaṇa. Since the performance of *pratikramaṇa* [3] involves the taking of a formal vow of temporary mendicancy, everyone is considered to be a mendicant until roughly one hour after sunset the next morning. The next day also sees public felicitation of all those who have performed fasts for all or part of Paryuṣaṇ. This public felicitation is repeated several days later by a large, loud parade through town.

For other notes on this same Paryuṣaṇ, see the fieldwork notes of Thomas Zwicker in the archives of the University of Pennsylvania Museum. For a fuller discussion of Paryuṣaṇ, see Cort 1989:157-83, 444-49, and 1991b.

Illus. 7
Kendall W. Folkert in Māṇḍaḷ. Spring 1985
Photograph by Thomas A. Zwicker

[3] *Pratikramaṇa* is a rite in which the individual, through the recitation of a series of Prakrit and Sanskrit texts and the performance of a series of bodily gestures, dissociates him or herself from any intention behind all of the wrong, karma-producing actions since the previous performance of *pratikramaṇa*. There are five forms of the *pratikramaṇa* rite: daily moring, daily evening, fortnightly, four-monthly, and annual. All of these are performed by Jain mendicants as part of their six obligatory rites. Jain laity are less strict in their observance; most laity perform only the annual (Saṃvatsarī) *pratikramaṇa*, and some of the others on special occasions. See also chapter 6 above.

Paryuṣaṇ program (conference with Tom Zwicker and John Cort, 9.ix.85)

lunar	*solar*		
Śrāvaṇ Vad 11[4]	Day 1	Wed. Sept. 11	
Śrāvaṇ Vad 12	Day 2	Thurs. Sept. 12	
Śrāvaṇ Vad 13	Day 3	Fri. Sept. 13	*Kalpa Sūtra* procession to house[5]
Śrāvaṇ Vad 14	Day 4	Sat. Sept. 14	*Kalpa Sūtra* returned to temple
Bhādrapad Sud 1	Day 5	Sun. Sept. 15	Mahāvīr Jayantī celebration
Bhādrapad Sud 2	Day 6	Mon. Sept. 16	
Bhādrapad Sud 3	Day 7	Tues. Sept. 17	
Bhādrapad Sud 4	Day 8	Wed. Sept. 18	*Bārasā Sūtra* (breakneck-speed reading) Saṃvatsarī
Bhādrapad Sud 5	Day 9	Thurs. Sept. 19	Fast-breaking

Friday, 13 September
(Day 3)

Not seen by us, because of mistaken impression that there were no activities, were the following:

(1) a *bolī* (auction) to determine who would take the *Kalpa Sūtra* into his home; and
(2) removal of the *Kalpa Sūtra* from *upāśray* to home.

Saturday, 14 September
(Day 4)

We arrived in Samī at 8:30 or shortly before. We met Muni Jambūvijay[6] on the steps of the *upāśray*, and other people coming out of the *daherāsar* (Jain

[4] The lunar month in Gujarat is divided into a bright (Sud) fortnight from the new moon to the full moon, followed by a dark (Vad) fortnight from the full moon to the new moon.

[5] [Folkert's note.] Cf. Fischer & Jain 1974:46 [1977:15-16]; n.b. additional eighth-day remarks about the *bārasā-sūtra*, its being read, and other treatments of it as "heiliges Buch" ("holy book").

[6] Muni Jambūvijay is the *sādhu* with whom Folkert was studying the performance and history of *pratikramaṇ*. He was in Samī for the 1985 rainy-season retreat.

temple). We left the motorcycle at H.'s house, and went to the *vāḍī*[7] for *nāsto*,[8] after going into the temple for *darśan*.[9] The central *mūrti* (image) is of Mahāvīr; there is also a neat Maṇibhadra,[10] at the side entrance.

Not seen by us was a morning *pūjā*[11] to the *Kalpa Sūtra*, at the home where it was kept, attended by Jambūvijay.

At 9:00, we went to the *upāśray* for the *vyākhyān* (sermon). As explained later by Jambūvijay, this day begins the reading, with explication, of two sections per day of the *Kalpa Sūtra*. The version used is that with the *Subodhika-ṭīkā*,[12] which is divided into nine sections.

We were urged to sit well forward, among those who were doing *poṣadh*.[13] They were in *dhotī*s (man's wrapped lower garment), with mats,[14] etc. (I later got the impression that they took the vow of *sāmāyik*[15] before the *vyākhyān*, which then served as their *dhārmik sajjhāy*.[16]) This meant that we had only the bare floor to sit on.

The *vyākhyān* lasted until shortly before noon—it was *very* long, and it became very hot in the room. Jambūvijay began with some general discussions on the rainy season and on *Kalpa Sūtra*, then started with the beginnings of *Kalpa Sūtra*. The initial discourse was so long that we thought he'd begun with the *Samācārī*,[17] and felt rather lost throughout, having only Lalwani's (1979) edition and translation to look at.

At 11:00, there was an interruption for announcements concerning activities, fasters, etc. (I need to check this with Tom.) The pandit stands and runs this sort of thing.

General impressions: there was a slow but steady increase in the number of persons present; more women at first than men, but the entire room ultimately was full. Pigeons were nesting in the canopy,[18] clumsily coming and going

---

7 Hall owned by the Jain congregation, used for public feasts.

8 Breakfast or other snack.

9 The rite of viewing an image.

10 Maṇibhadra [Vīr] is an unliberated deity whose role is to protect Jain temples, *upāśray*s, and other institutions. He is particularly associated with the Tapā Gacch lineage of Mūrtipūjak mendicants. His images are frequently unfashioned pieces of stone that have been thoroughly covered with red *sindūr* paste.

11 Rite of worship, involving offerings such as flowers, incense, and food.

12 A Sanskrit commentary on the *Kalpa Sūtra*, composed in 1640 C.E. by Vinayavijaya.

13 Rite in which the individual takes a vow to follow the mendicant life-style for one to eight days.

14 As part of the rites of *poṣadh* and *sāmāyik*, the individual must sit on a special mat.

15 Rite in which the individual takes a vow to meditate for 48 or 96 minutes. *Sāmāyik* is essentially a short form of *poṣadh*.

16 "Religious study," the focus of meditation during *sāmāyik*.

17 The third part of the *Kalpa Sūtra*, sections 224-291, giving the rules of conduct for mendicants.

18 The canopy (*candarvo*) is the cloth hung above a Jina *mūrti* or a mendicant. It serves to protect the *mūrti* or mendicant from defilement, and also serves as a sign of respect.

throughout. People became restless toward noon, as Jambūvijay seemed to be dragging the exposition. I *cannot* follow his Gujarati.

Illus. 8
Muni Jambūvijay delivering a *vyākhyān*
Photograph by Kendall W. Folkert

After the *vyākhyān*, we went to the *vāḍī* for lunch. Then Tom and I played mad dogs and Englishmen, walking around the northeast side of Samī, past the big house, out the now-demolished gate, around to the bus stand, and back to the bazaar. On the way, we got hailed into a shop by an advocate, who was wondering about the presence of foreigners.

We took a bit of rest at N.'s. (Was there tea?) Then at 2:00 the *Kalpa Sūtra* was taken in a procession through the bazaar, *apparently* starting from the *upāśray*, but we missed the very beginning, so I don't know whether the book came from the house where it had been, or what.

Actually it was a nondescript procession: one drummer, a few boys and young men, and a cluster of girls and young women round the one young woman who carried the *Kalpa Sūtra* on her head. The book (the word *pustak*[19] was used whenever it was referred to) was carried in a *thāḷī* (metal tray), the latter having an embroidered cloth laid over it. The book was in a muslin wrapper, had been decorated (with a *svastik*[20]? I can't recall) and sprinkled liberally with sandalwood powder;[21] some rupees and coins were in the *thāḷī* with it.

The procession went straight down the bazaar, from the "temple arch"[22] to the demolished gate, and back. All noise was silenced in the stretch by the big house, both going and coming. We were later told there was a *masjid* (mosque) nearby—I *think* the word *masjid* was used. On the return, the *Kalpa Sūtra* was carried by the girl into the *upāśray* and deposited with Jambūvijay—I lost track of it thereafter. Sloppy work—I guess I was too hot (sweating profusely) to care or to think clearly.

At this point we discovered all that we'd missed, as noted above. This ticked me off, for being so careless about information at second-hand. In any case, the procession simply ended then—there was really very little, if any, notice taken of the *Kalpa Sūtra*'s arrival in the *upāśray* by those persons who were present there.

At 3:00, there was a *vyākhyān* again. This time, we sat on the edge of the floor mat. We'd thought it would be brief. It got started, after more announcements, at about 3:10, and went until a bit after 5:00, with one pause between 4:00 and 4:30. The tone and mood were much the same as in the morning, but it was not a very lively presentation by Jambūvijay. There was much more audience response and presentation in the morning, here only a few noises of assent, or chuckles at various points. The crowd was smaller, but still more or less a roomful.

After the *vyākhyān*, we had to wait 'til after 5:30 to get to Jambūvijay. He was at work, as when the *Kalpa Sūtra* arrived, on the *āmantraṇ*,[23] reading proofs and correcting them with his usual obsession for the details of proofs.

---

19 *Pustak* is the Gujarati word for any book, in contrast to words such as *granth* or *śāstra* which refer only to religious books.

20 The *svastik* is a holy Jain symbol. The four arms of the *svastik* symbolize the four realms of rebirth: those of heavenly creatures, humans, animals and plants, and infernal creatures. The three dots represent the Three Jewels of the Jain path to liberation, right faith, right knowledge, and right conduct. The crescent moon and dot represent liberation.

21 Sandalwood powder (*vāskep*) is used to bless objects and people.

22 A temporary wooden arch erected for Paryuṣaṇ.

23 Printed invitation to a public function.

Note: Jambūvijay and Dharmacandravijay[24] had both plucked their hair[25] since Tom last saw them—we need to narrow this down.

Then J. hoiked us off for tea. Then we were urged into the *upāśray* for *nāsto*. Finally, at 6:35 or so, we left for Veḍ, rolling toward Bospā in post-sunset twilight. We stopped at the Sarasvati bridge for a cigarette. Down the *kaccha* (unpaved) road in near-darkness. After one more stop, we finally jounced into Veḍ, at 7:45 or so.

Most folks were at *pratikramaṇ*—only J. and a few others were about. No *bījḷī* (electricity).[26] Electricians were at work in S.'s house. We sat on a charpoy (rope cot) there for a while, had tea and *savā*,[27] waited for the *pratikramaṇ* to finish. We went up to Y.'s shop and sat there for a bit. Warm greetings from B. Then we went to the new *upāśray* as everyone came out. A really fine sense: this whole group was doing *pratikramaṇ* twice daily, even though there are no *sādhu*s or *sādhvī*s present.

We went to the temple for *darśan*, then onto the courtyard verandahs for the *svapna-bolī*[28] (also *bolī*s for *āratī*,[29] both five-wick and *maṅgaḷ-dīp*,[30] and for the next morning's *pūjā*s). There was closeness and warmth, joking and give-and-take in the *bolī*. Then we went into the *daherāsar* for *āratī*. A *stavan* (hymn) was sung with each—boys and men playing instruments on the right. Women sat out on the entry porch, coming up the center 'aisle' for *āratī*s. The second *āratī* was done by two boys. After the *āratī*, there were *bhāvanās*[31] for about 45 minutes, including pipe-stick dancing.[32] H. was there and taking part. S. played on the harmonium. (Note: I really must work through this 'priest-less' religion with Tom.) It finished with "He Śaṅkheśvar Svāmī."[33] B. was looking great, tending to things, closing up at the end. B. and I beat out rhythms on my knee.

---

24 Muni Dharmacandravijay is the *sādhu* who is disciple and assistant to Muni Jambūvijay.

25 Śvetāmbar Murtipujak mendicants pluck out all their head and facial hair twice annually as part of their austerities.

26 Electricity had come to Veḍ only a few months previously.

27 A kind of seed, eaten as a snack.

28 The *svapna-bolī* ("dream auction") is the auction for the rights to garland, display, swing, etc., the silver representations of the 14 dreams seen by the mother of Mahāvīr. See below.

29 Offering of a lamp (usually with five wicks) before a Jina image.

30 "Holy lamp," a single wick *āratī*.

31 Devotional hymns, done to generate the spirit (*bhāvanā*) of devotion (*bhakti*) in the singers.

32 Pipe-stick dancing is a traditional Gujarati folkdance, in which the dancers hold a wooden stick in each hand, and rap the sticks against those of the other dancers in time with the rhythm of the dance.

33 "He Śaṅkheśvar Svāmī" is a Gujarati hymn to Śaṅkheśvar Pārśvanāth, one of the most popular *mūrtis* in North Gujarat. See Cort 1988.

Illus. 9
Laymen pipe-stick dancing during a procession in Veḍ. Spring 1985.
Photograph by Thomas A. Zwicker

Off to S.'s, where we sat on charpoys, a million stars overhead. There was much scrambling for some tea, as there was no cooking done at S.'s. Tea came from elsewhere, and when it arrived, we got a big *nāsto* to go with it.

We went upstairs to set up in the room, for sleep. A cool night wind blew in through the window.

At J.'s, Tom said, "Back in Veḍ!" I could hardly absorb it, and still can't.

Sunday, 15 September
(Day 5)

We were awakened before 7:00 by S. coming for the *loṭā* (metal water pot). The remembered morning routine. Then the photos and the pen came out—S. had asked about the pen the night before. To my enormous dismay, the pen had no innards. We were off to B.'s to look at pictures and talk and drink tea. Then we went to M.'s, for more tea and *nāsto*, and for an embroidery showing. All over, there were signs of electricity (e.g., M.'s radio-cabinet).

By 9:45 we were back on the way to Samī, after the front and rear tires had been pumped up by B. We stopped beyond Gajdinpur to sit under a tree; Tom wrote some notes. Pairs of bullocks were in fields; one young man came by to check us out.

We arrived in Samī by 11:00, just in time for the flag-replacing.[34] We hurried up to the roof of the temple, where the *pujārī*[35] was just removing the old flags. New ones were carried up in a *thāḷī*, unfolded and taken by three men (need names and background on this—Tom?), who climbed up the three *śikhars* (temple spires) and attached them, and added *kesar* (saffron-sandalwood paste) to what was already on them. A *stavan* was sung when all three were hung. It took about 20-25 minutes for all this.

Illus. 10
Laymen replacing the flags atop the temple
Photograph by Thomas A. Zwicker

[34] Every Jain temple has a distinctive flag, usually a red-and-white striped banner, flying from a pole atop the central spire. It is replaced annually on the anniversary of the initial consecration of the main image of the temple.

[35] Non-Jain salaried temple servant.

Downstairs, the *āṅgī*[36] of the central *mūrti* was being covered with gold leaf. I later heard some fantastic version of how much.

After lunch, I rested a bit, and Tom took off for Veḍ. At 2:30 I went up to the *upāśray* for the *svapna* session. The *pāraṇu* (creche) and *svapnas*[37] were all laid out before the lectern table. By 3:00, most were assembled. H.'s stentorian summons got the rest to start coming inside in earnest. The *bolī* was conducted by H. and B., the latter drenched in sweat by 3:30. It was an active *bolī* for the creche, less so for its small pieces. It was not an active *bolī* for the *svapnas*. There were surprisingly few dynamics (the Panjabi man was allowed the lion and the sun—no praise or big deal), just routine competitive bidding, no singling out that I could detect, but I'm not fully attuned to dynamics. A much more spirited and, on the surface, fun-filled *bolī* was held for the *varghoḍo* [38] and its various roles, with the playing off of B. against a crew of younger men clustered along the *daherāsar*-side windows.

Illus. 11
Silver creche and images of 14 dreams laid out on table before enactment of seeing dreams by Mahāvīra's mother and of birth of Mahāvīra
Photograph by Kendall W. Folkert

36 The ornamentation of an image, often elaborately done with flowers, colored powders, and silver and gold leaf on a silver shield that covers the front of the image.

37 The silver representations of the 14 dreams.

38 Literally "men and horses," a *varghoḍo* is a procession to celebrate the successful completion of Paryuṣaṇ.

All of this took an hour and twenty minutes, while the women, children, and I simply sweltered. Toward 4:30, three garlands of five coconuts were strung on the suspended bar before Jambūvijay. Then a silver chain was put up through the small pulley in the ceiling. Children of winners came forward to catch and garland the *svapnas* as they were quickly hoisted and lowered. All this was done in ten minutes or so. The presiders had to be reminded to get the *svapnas* in order.

Then Jambūvijay, after silence had been restored with difficulty, began to read the birth account.[39] About two-thirds of the way in, a group in the temple-side corner jumped the gun; coconuts began to be thumped on the floor, and bedlam ensued. I have never so much wished for a tape recorder. Silence was never restored. A small circle around Jambūvijay listened to him finish the reading, and then the whole room exploded into coconut cracking and rice throwing. There was a rush to rock the cradle, and to toss a piece cut from a coconut into it. (In an aside, Jambūvijay said that all the focus on the cradle has to do with belief in such activity's capacity to bring progeny.) The floor was a sticky sea of coconut juice and rice. Within ten minutes, the place was emptying rapidly.

I was called back to photograph the nine-year-old who was on an eight-day fast, so I didn't clearly see the giving of sweets to 'beggars.' This was basically done under the archway, where charpoys had been set up to control entry to the lane. This part was relatively disorderly, and needs follow-up questions.

I went to J.'s for tea, then to B.'s for same, plus *līmbu* (lime water)—a way to settle who would give me tea. I had a pleasant time with the latter—some rapport, unspoken, that felt good. *Nāsto*. I went to the temple to see the gold-covered *āṅgī*, which generated a request that I photograph the *mūrti*—and, so far as I could understand, *not* photograph the people in the temple. So, with 400 ASA film, I *think* I got it.

At 7:00, on the way to the temple, I bumped into the cradle-procession coming from the *upāśray*. I followed it to C.'s house, where things were getting set up for *bhajans* (songs) later. During evening *pratikramaṇ*, the boys testing the loudspeakers had to be shushed regularly. I went over there right after *pratikramaṇ*, and saw and photographed the set-up in the house. At that point, only kids and a singer had settled into the lane—and I just wasn't up to staying to see how big a deal it ultimately became. I did not hear, from N.'s, any amplified music after 11:00 p.m.—but I don't know what sort of *darśan*, visitation, etc., process may have been going on, or for how long.

---

39 *Kalpa Sūtra* 93.

Illus. 12
Temple images decorated for Paryuṣaṇ. The word in flowers before the central image is *kṣamāpanā* ("foregiveness"), one of the central virtues underlying Paryuṣaṇ
Photograph by Thomas A. Zwicker

Thereafter, I simply went up into the *upāśray* to watch *pratikramaṇ*. There was a big group, with the room nearly full, though not crowded. Sweltering. It was a memory-test to follow along in the dark. There was a *long sajjhāy/stavan*,[40] especially by the pandit, who began repeating himself and losing his place, and got some hints in various forms to cut it short. I was desperately hot and sleepy by that point.

By 9:30 p.m. it was finished. I was too tired to make myself visible, so I retreated to N.'s to rest up for the 6:30 bus.

Monday, 16 September
(Day 6)

In Ahmedabad.

Tuesday, 17 September
(Day 7)

I left Ahmedabad at 12:30, on the Radhanpur double express. We stopped for tea at Dasādā, and arrived at Samī a bit before 4:00. Tom arrived from Veḍ ca. 4:45. The *vyākhyān* was still happening, but more people were about and in

40 *Sajjhāy* ("study") and *stavan* ("hymn") are often used interchangeably, as the composition or recitation of a *stavan* is a form of study.

houses than had been there on Saturday. (We did not actually go and size up the crowd.) We saw Jambūvijay briefly, then had *nāsto*. The evening we spent walking and then chatting with J.: Tom reviewing the *bolī* list with him, and other desultory topics. At 5:30, we had settled with Jambūvijay that we would do Saṃvatsarī[41] with the proper clothes, etc. We also met and chatted briefly with Dr. S.—many tales of dysentery, malaria, and a death in Rafu from gastro-interitis, in one S.'s household. That should be B.'s in-laws, but no chance to clear this up absolutely. Tom says that Dr. S. is not on intimate terms with the *saṅgh* (congregation). We were told later, by N., that the Dr. comes to the temple for *darśan*, not *pūjā*, but that this is because he is busy; his wife is always regular in *pūjā*. Yet there are some dynamics—cf. the Saṃvatsarī *bolī*.

We did also go to *ārati*. Tom should have notes on the *pūjā*-book. We made a bit more contact with the Kutch Mitra Maṇḍaḷ,[42] in the temple.

Wednesday, 18 September
(Day 8)

Tom went out early to check out the temple, but nothing particular was afoot early. After *nāsto*, we went back to the temple. S. from Maṇḍaḷ and his son were doing the first *pūjā* after the *āṅgī* were removed and the *mūrti* washed. We just generally observed things.

At 9:00 we went to the *upāśray* for the reading of the full *Kalpa Sūtra*, with no commentary (n.b. John Cort's pick up of the phrase "short *Kalpa Sūtra*" in Pāṭaṇ to describe this). Jambūvijay was in his *muhpattī*.[43] A boy held up illustrated pages. Jambūvijay read the *Mahāvīra Caritra*[44] (or most of it), then Dharmacandravijay continued the reading, after donning his *muhpattī*. The crowd was small at first, but grew steadily. After the *Sthavirāvalī*,[45] there was a pause for announcements and for gifting to *tapasvins*,[46] which I got to do as distinguished elder foreigner. I need terminology and clarification on this—I sort of stumbled through it. Then the *Samācārī* with things finishing at about 12:00. All were given rice by H., to throw at Jambūvijay, Dharmacandravijay, and the *Kalpa Sūtra* at the finish.

---

41 Saṃvatsarī is the annual *pratikramaṇ* on the last day of Paryuṣaṇ; see below.

42 Jain association of devotees of Muni Jambūvijay from Kutch (Kacch) in western Gujarat, an area where Jambūvijay spent several years in the 1970s.

43 Cloth held over the mouth to prevent violence through inhalation and exhalation to invisible organisms in the air.

44 The first part of the *Kalpa Sūtra*, sections 1-147, which gives the biography of Mahāvīra.

45 Sections 201-223 of the *Kalpa Sūtra*, giving the lineages of *sādhus* from the time of Mahāvīra until Devardhigaṇi Kṣamāśramaṇa, under whose direction the *Kalpa Sūtra* was redacted in Valabhi in the fifth century C.E.

46 A person performing a fast.

Illus. 13
Muni Jambūvijay wearing a *muhpattī*, recites the *Kalpa Sūtra*. The boy in front is holding up illustrations to the text for viewing by the audience
Illustration by Thomas A. Zwicker

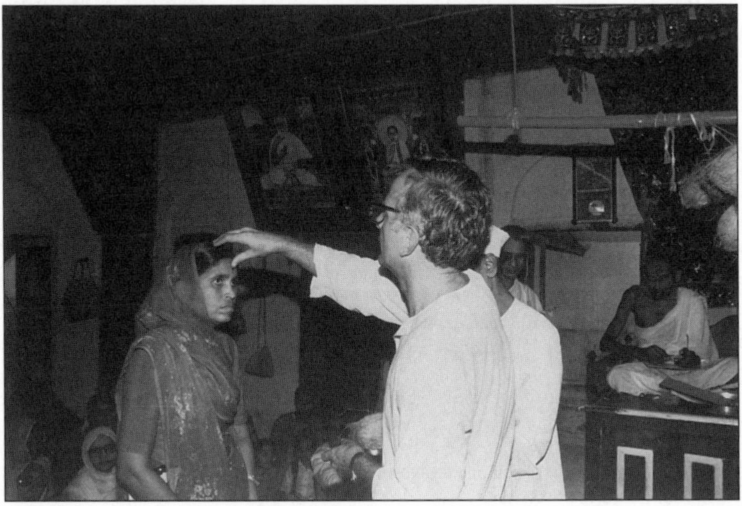

Illus. 14
Gifting to *tapasvin*s. Folkert is making a red mark (*cāndlo*) on the *tapasvin*'s forehead as a sign of respect
Photograph by Thomas A. Zwicker

We missed, thereafter, a procession of a *mūrti* 'round the town, drummers leading, with a few women, some men, and Jambūvijay and Dharmacandravijay—*caitya-paripāṭī*.[47] Lazy for a second time.

I took a rest—hot, sweaty sleep—after lunch. We had been told to come to the *vāḍī* at 3:00 for tea, but it was deserted. So we went down into the bazaar for tea at a Muslim teashop. J. had mats and *muhpattī*s for each of us. We changed clothes[48] in Dharmacandravijay's side-room, and settled in with my *vidhi*-book[49] in front of us. First, a *bolī* was held to see who would 'buy' the various recitations. Dr. S. took the majority (need a count from Thomas). Then Saṃvatsarī began.

Once into the swing of it, I could follow and do about as well as most of the lay people. We got hints and directions from all sides. The pandit generally shouted out the duration of the *kaüssaggs*.[50] The pandit did the *Vaṅdittu Sūtra*[51] the second time, and someone else did it the first time. With the exception of these, the *Sāta Lākha* [52] and *Aḍhāra Pāpasthānaka*[53] (done by the pandit), and the *Ajita-Śānti* [54] (done beautifully by one of the older men, back to my left), only shorter things early on were actually *done* by *śrāvaks* (laymen). Jambūvijay and Dharmacandravijay did the rest. Side note: a roiling noise of kids at play came up from the temple-side right in the middle of *Ajita-Śānti*, and the whole was marvelously and incongruously punctuated by J.'s shouting down to the street for the women to hush up the kids.

One other moment: about one-third of the way in, with daylight turning to late afternoon, a crow cawing outside, a general silence except for the recitation then going on. I was simply seized by the moment, by being there, and by my own thoughts of what the past year of research in Gujarat had been in my life.

Late in the *vidhi* people got tired, especially during the long recitation done by only the *sādhu*s that *śrāvak*s simply have to wait out. There were no

---

47 Literally "procession of temples," a *caitya-paripāṭī* is either a procession to the temples in town, or, as in this case, the procession of a mobile metal *mūrti* through the town. It is one of the five duties (*kartavya*) for Paryuṣaṇ enjoined upon every lay Śvetāmbar Mūrtipūjak Jain.

48 For the performance of *pratikramaṇ*, men wear only a *dhotī* and an unstitched upper robe.

49 A *vidhi* is a rite; a *vidhi*-book containing both the text to be recited and a description of the actions to be performed.

50 Literally "abandonment of the body," this is a rite within *pratikramaṇ*, in which the person stands erect, with arms hanging down at the side and palms facing inwards, for the duration of a certain number of recitations of one of several fixed texts.

51 A hymn of veneration in which one disavows intention behind violation of the twelve vows of a layperson and similar rules of conduct.

52 A text in which one disavows intention behind harm caused to 8,400,000 different types of beings. The title is the first two words of the text, literally "700,000."

53 "Eighteen forms of unwholesome action," a verse in which one disavows intention behind eighteen forms of unwholesome actions.

54 A Prakrit hymn to the second and sixteenth Jinas of the current era, Ajitanātha and Śāntinātha, attributed to Nandiṣeṇa.

sneezes.[55] There were many yawns. I have to say that such a sense of general solemnity as prevailed before 5:30 or so had been rather replaced by an air of fatigue, which was finally broken by the shouted recitation of Haribhadra's *stuti*'s fourth stanza.[56] By then, the end is in sight. At the end, by the time we'd changed, the *upāśray* had pretty much emptied.

We stayed to tell Jambūvijay of our plans to leave early, and he remonstrated vigorously. We had to stay for the fast-breaking in the morning at 7:30. I stayed noncommittal, and was irked, probably unreasonably so. It was my first clash this trip between linearity and Jambūvijay's insistence. In a bit of a funk, we walked out beyond the bus-stand, looked at the setting moon and at the stars, and smoked some illicit cigarettes, having had to walk a gauntlet of Jains sitting in the bazaar, and then having to extract ourselves from a celebration at the fasting kid's house. I'm afraid we were not very gracious. I don't know what to think about such moments.

We went back to N.'s for a big *loṭā* of water; then I went up to bed. Tom chatted a bit longer.

Thursday, 19 September

We were awake before 6:00; Tom went out in time to see the fasters depart for *darśan* at Shankheshvar. We walked out to and around the *taḷāb* (pond), waiting out the hour 'til 7:15.[57] We got back for tooth-brushing; then *nāsto* at 7:30—good strong tea and lots of *nāsto*. We finished up just as the jeep returned from Shankheshvar at 7:45. We followed it to the temple, where the *tapasvin*s went in for a second *darśan*. One of them, at least—the older woman, who looked really worn—did something of a *pūjā* to one of the *mūrti*s. My attention was distracted by one C., of Ahmedabad, who with his wife and friend was doing a short and miniature Siddhacakra-*pūjā*,[58] in the center of the temple. His wife was one of the most active women participants in various settings—now I can't recall just what, but I kept noticing her in the *upāśray*. He informed us that

---

55 It is a bad omen if anyone sneezes during *pratikramaṇ*, necessitating the repetition of an extensive part of the rite.

56 Haribhadra's *stuti* is the *Saṃsāra Dāvā*, a short four-verse hymn in veneration of the Jinas, the Jain scriptures, and the goddess who presides over the scriptures. As a matter of popular custom, the fourth verse is always shouted out.

57 People who have performed *pratikramaṇ* the evening before cannot break their fast (or brush their teeth) until 48 minutes after sunrise, lest in the dim light they unwittingly swallow or otherwise harm some minute living organisms.

58 The Siddhacakra-*pūjā* is a rite of worship of the Siddhacakra ("Circle of Perfection"), a *yantra* (cosmogram) containing nine sacred symbols: the five Supreme Lords of the (1) Jina, (2) Siddha (other liberated beings), (3) Ācārya (mendicant leader), (4) Upādhyāya (mendicant teacher), and (5) Sādhu, the Three Jewels of (6) Right Faith, (7) Right Knowledge, and (8) Right Conduct, and (9) Right Asceticism. These nine contain the totality of the Jain spiritual hierarchy and the principles of the Jain path to liberation.

he had done this Siddhacakra-*pūjā* daily for twenty-two years. He lives near the Air India Jain temple, and gave the impression of wanting us to call on him.

Illus. 15
Layman performing private Siddhacakra-*pūjā* in the temple in Veḍ. Spring 1985
Photograph by Thomas A. Zwicker

Then we went out to follow the *tapasvins*. Jambūvijay and Dharmacandravijay also went out. We went first to the fasting kid's house, where they were breaking their fast. Then to G.'s house, where the main event was. We were hustled in by B. The women *tapasvins* were brought into a downstairs room, and some went upstairs. (I did not see the latter—Tom did.) The men, apparently some of those who had done *upvās* (fast) for Saṃvatsarī, were seated on the verandah of the courtyard.

The first event was the ceremonial *dān* (gifting) of food to Jambūvijay and Dharmacandravijay, beginning with almonds. Jambūvijay told me that the widow of the household-head had had no sons, and that her husband's relatives were there to do things. These included Veḍ people (need names and background on this household from Tom). I got urged into eating—should have resisted—and here missed the upstairs scene. My food included fast-breaking *laḍḍus*[59] —incredibly hard to get down. We finally just left the whole scene at 8:45 or so. As I have not seen fast-breaking before, I should scold myself for being so impatient. I did get some view of the women downstairs being spoon-fed by relatives.

Illus. 16
Muni Jambūvijay blessing *tapasvins* by sprinkling sandalwood powder (*vāskep*) on their heads
Photograph by Thomas A. Zwicker

59 A sweet ball of deep-fried chickpea flour.

A final note: as we had our *nāsto* at 7:30, the Kutch Mitra Maṇḍaḷ was breaking its fast(s) in the *vāḍī*. One of them is M.'s brother. They have adjacent businesses in the grain market in Bombay, and come regularly to Shankheshvar and to see Jambūvijay—but not at *pūnam*.[60] It is too crowded then, they say. They told us that M. was in Bombay—his grandmother had come to see him (we saw her in Veḍ in February) and had insisted he stay on a bit. This group shows promise as people I need to get to know and know about.

I am sure that there are bits and pieces missing from this—but they are more impressionistic—though a joint review with Tom would probably summon up a few more items.

Illus. 17
Kendall Folkert being given a red mark (*cāndlo*) on his forehead as a sign of public respect
Photograph by Thomas A. Zwicker

60 The day of the full-moon, a popular time to go on pilgrimage to a temple or a mendicant.

Bids for Paryuṣaṇ *bolīs*.

A. Creche of Mahāvīra:

1.	Putting up the gateway (*toraṇ*) of coconuts (*śrīphaḷ*)	15 *maṇ*[61]
2.	Taking the cradle of the Lord (Mahāvīra) home	111 rupees
3.	Making the cradle (*pāraṇu*)	21 *maṇ*
4.	Offering the coconuts	16 *maṇ*
5.	Putting the cloth (*rūmāl*) on the Lord	10 *maṇ*
6.	Shaking the Lord's rattle	1 *maṇ*
7.	Putting the gold chain on the Lord	???
8.	Swinging the Lord the first time	15 *maṇ*
9.	Swinging the Lord the second time	12 *maṇ*
10.	Swinging the Lord the third time	7 *maṇ*
11.	Swinging the Lord the fourth time	9 *maṇ*
12.	Swinging the Lord the fifth time	5 *maṇ*

B. Dreams of Mahāvīra's mother

Dream		*Maṇ*
1.	Elephant	2 1/2
2.	Bull	2
3.	Lion	3
4.	Lakṣmī Devī	101
5.	Garland of flowers	1 1/2
6.	Moon	3
7.	Sun	3
8.	Temple ensign	2 1/2
9.	Full pot	4
10.	Lotus Lake	6
11.	Milky ocean	5
12.	Heavenly vehicle	5
13.	Heap of jewels	5
14.	Flame	14

C. *Varghoḍo*

1.	Flower garland	1 1/4	*maṇ*
2.	Sitting in the *rath* (chariot) taking the Lord	1,001	rupees
3.	Charioteer (*sārthi*) of the Lord's *rath*	1,401	rupees

61 For the purposes of the bidding, one *maṇ* (maund) of *ghī* is valued at eight rupees. Since one *maṇ* is roughly eighty pounds, this price is clearly several centuries old.

4. Sitting on the elephant carrying the Lord (1) .... 551 rupees
5. Sitting on the elephant carrying the Lord (2) .... 401 rupees
6. Sitting on the elephant carrying the Lord (3) .... 401 rupees
7. Sitting on the elephant carrying the Lord (4) .... 451 rupees
8. Sitting on the elephant carrying the Lord (5) .... 551 rupees
9. First seat on the horse-drawn cart (*bagī*)............................ 901 rupees
10. Sitting on the right side of the Lord .... 601 rupees
11. Sitting on the left side of the Lord .... 301 rupees
12. Sitting below (in front of) the Lord.. 201 rupees
13. Fifth seat.. 131 rupees
14. Sixth seat (next to driver) .... 161 rupees
15. Indra *dhaj* (flagpole).. 111 rupees
16. Indra *dhaj* (2)... 101 rupees
17. Indra *dhaj* (3)... 101 rupees
18. Indra *dhaj* (4)... 111 rupees
19. Indra *dhaj* (5)... 111 rupees
20. Indra *dhaj* (6)... 131 rupees
21. Indra *dhaj* (7)... 161 rupees
22. Indra *dhaj* (8)... 121 rupees
23. Carrying the *dīvo* (lamp)... 25 1/4 *maṇ*
24. Carrying the silver and gold sticks .... 211/4 *maṇ*
25. Carrying the *cāmar* (whisk)... 5 1/4 *maṇ*
26. Banging the *thālī* .... 7 1/4 *maṇ*
27. Banging the *ghaṇṭ* (bell).. 5 1/4 *maṇ*
28. Taking the Lord's cradle .... 51 1/4 *maṇ*
29. Receiving (*poṅkhaṇu*) the Lord.. 5 1/4 *maṇ*
30. Carrying on one's head Lakṣmī Devī.................................. 11 1/4 *maṇ*
31. Carrying on one's head the *Kalpa Sūtra* .... 31 1/4 *maṇ*

No *bolīs* for carrying 14 dreams

D. Other

1. Buying tins of peppermint chocolates for boys in *pāṭhśāḷā* (religious school): eight bought 2 1/2 tins each.
2. To lower dreams from above: no amount entered.
3. *Āṅgī* on Mahāvīr on Mahāvīr Jayantī (Mahāvīr's Birthday, Day 5): 1,000 rupees. No *bolī* for *āṅgī*; pay cost. Those who do *āṅgī* can do *āratī*.
4. No *bolī* for *snātra pūjā* (special bathing *pūjā*.).
5. Daily *bolīs* for parts of pūjā:
   a. water

b. *brās* (camphor water)
c. *kesar* (saffron-sandalwood paste)
d. *fūl* (flowers) - only if there are flowers
e. *mugaṭ* (crown)

Part II

A JAIN APPROACH TO NON-JAINS: THE 363-ACCOUNT

14

The Problem of Attitudes*

INTRODUCTION

There has been a great deal said and written about the matter of relationships between schools of thought in the Indian tradition. It is an arena already crowded with conceptions and preconceptions, prior studies, and the outlook of the Western world's approach to the problem. The best way to begin seems to be to admit these influences and to attempt to isolate and understand them. There are several issues involved in the problem of relationships and attitudes in India.

First, most of the attempts to account for intra-Indian attitudes and relationships have amounted to a search for Indian equivalents for such terms as orthodoxy, heterodoxy, and heresy. It is important to note that these are not the only terms that may be used to express one tradition's view of another. Yet rarely (if ever) do scholars use such terms as infidel, apostate, or heathen to describe the relationships between Indian movements or schools of thought. The terms that are generally used are those that more commonly apply in the Christian context to intra-Christian relationships. There may be some sense here that the Christian and Indian traditions are both wholes, and thus require the same basic descriptive terms for phenomena within them. Yet one does not see this point being made by scholars, despite the fact that an important limitation has been imposed on the search of equivalent terms.

* From dissertation, pp.13-38.

Second, for better or for worse, various Indian terms and concepts have been used to correspond to these Western notions, notably the terms *āstika* and *nāstika* as correspondents for orthodoxy and heterodoxy.[1] There the process seems to have ended, save for various attempts at refining the correspondence. What is not being tested is the actual correspondence of the phenomena themselves.

The point is that the Western terms in question are relational terms, subjective in significance. Heterodoxy does not regard itself as heterodox. Yet in the common usage of students of religion these terms come to express an abstract, objective notion, not unlike "mainstream" and "that which is outside of the mainstream."[2] In their transplantation into the Indian context, these terms have transmitted this fixed, objective sense to the Indian terms that they translate or gloss. Terms that properly describe views of relationships have come to describe relationships.

For the student of Indian religion, what is lost in this process is entrée to one of the vital aspects of the Indian (or any other) tradition. That aspect is the actual dynamic process by which any religious movement both identifies its own vision and deals with the fact that there are other visions, or at least with the fact that there exists an "otherness" that does not conform to that vision. Thus when such notions as orthodoxy and heterodoxy are taken to be static, descriptive terms for the relationships between schools of thought in India, the student is first of all shut off from the key to understanding such terms, that key being their subjectivity itself. Orthodoxy and heterodoxy in their current sense do not describe the phenomenon, i.e., the view itself; yet this is rarely recognized as being the case. Further, and more significant, one can rarely gain insight into the process whereby the view developed.

At this point a third issue must be raised. The study of these matters has been carried out by scholars in a discipline that is terribly sensitive and defensive on the very subject involved in such notions as orthodoxy and heterodoxy,

---

[1] Or, occasionally, *nāstika* is given as equally heretic. Both scholarship and common usage nowadays seem to fail to recognize the significant difference between heterodoxy and heresy. This is particularly sad because early English usage is much more careful about this than are some other languages.

The *Oxford English Dictionary* (p.1294) gives this etymology for "heresy": "a. Gr. [*haeresis*] taking, choosing, choice, course taken, course of action or thought, 'school' of thought, philosophic principle or set of principles, philosophical or religious sect. . . . " This is reflected in the third definition given for the word: "Opinion or doctrine characterizing particular individuals or parties; a school of thought; a sect." However, the status of current usage is clearly shown by the fact that the remainder of the definitions of "heresy" are indistinguishable from all those given for "heterodoxy," which originally means "[of] another opinion."

[2] In fact, if one will reflect for a moment on the dictionary definitions, all of which stress heterodoxy and heresy as being that which is opposed to the accepted position, one will see that this is what they, too, express. They do not add the qualification that the terms are relational.

namely, the claim of any religious movement that its vision is complete. Western students of religion tend to be uncomfortable with the fact that religious movements practice both inclusion and exclusion. This discomfort, it can be argued, leads to very little emphasis being placed on the fact that religious movements do engage in a process of excluding other views, such activities being commonly described as "sectarian" or "polemic." Neither of these carries a positive connotation in current usage.

The reasons for this attitude lie both in the history of the study of religion, which was early on involved with the notion of the essential oneness of religion, and in Western scholars' sensitivity to Christianity's exclusivity. The result of all this was, particularly around the turn of this century, a complex notion that tolerance was a part of understanding man's religiousness. The vestiges of that notion are still present in the study of religion.

With respect to India, the matter is further complicated in many cases by the general notion—whose origins are also very complex and not altogether separate from the general idea of tolerance in the West—that the Indian tradition is extremely tolerant of conflicting viewpoints. In fact, this nebulous idea of India's tolerance is the only tool that actually functions at times to describe views of relationships in India, and not relationships themselves. Yet it, too, fails to convey the subjectivity that should be expressed in any statement of those views, though this is less a fault of the term than of its unreflective application.

The Jain tradition contains certain elements particularly suited to the study of attitudes between religious movements. One element consists in the fact that the Jain tradition has produced a great deal of literature that deals with the Jain view of non-Jains. A second element is that the Jain philosophical system in the *nayavāda*, or doctrine of standpoints, contains what would appear (and has appeared to scholars) to be a tool for dealing with the presence of other viewpoints. The issue to be raised here concerns a particular interpretation of that philosophical tool, according to which a notion of 'intellectual *ahiṃsa*' is developed, i.e., a notion that "non-injury" includes a fair and tolerant attitude toward opposing schools of thought.

THE JAIN ACCOUNTS OF NON-JAINS

Western scholarship has often been attracted to a class of Indian texts that may be called compendia, of which the Jains appear to have authored some of the earliest examples. These compendia are a group of texts that contain brief summaries of the Indian schools of thought. Of all these works by Jain and non-Jain authors the best known is a non-Jain text, Sāyaṇa Mādhava's *Sarvadarśanasaṃgraha* (fourteenth century C.E.). These compendia are of interest because they are for the most part independent (i.e., not part of other works) descriptive works that are occasionally very close chronologically to particular developments that they describe.[3]

For the moment, however, it is not their potential usefulness as historical sources that is of interest. The interesting point is that here is a class of literature whose major purpose is to deal with the existence of a multiplicity of viewpoints. Moreover, some of the Jain compendia give accounts of the Jain position and the views of other schools without presenting any refutation of the non-Jain positions. This alone makes them of particular interest for any attempt to understand the matter of attitudes. This is particularly so in light of what was said above concerning tolerance, for it has not been unusual for certain scholars (most often Jains) to point to the compendia as striking examples of tolerance in the Indian tradition. Indeed, the absence of refutations is striking; but, as noted, one concern is to see whether the ready use of tolerance to describe such a phenomenon does justice to the materials themselves.

The compendia, however, are not the first systematic efforts by Jains to come to terms with other schools of thought. One of the major difficulties in assessing the compendia is the fact that previous scholarship has failed to relate the compendia to other accounts of various schools of thought. Another major Jain attempt at dealing with the existence of other viewpoints is what can be called the 363-account. It is a complex structure by means of which it is possible to calculate the number of possible philosophical and religious stances, the total number of which is reckoned to be 363. The connection between the 363-account and the compendia is not always clear. In fact, the two seem at first glance to have virtually nothing in common. The 363-account seems to function according to rules of its own making, and to be concerned largely with calculating hypothetical possibilities; the compendia seem to be empirical, descriptive accounts of existing schools. The 363-account seems only to account for other schools in terms of Jain categories, whereas the compendia seem to aim at presenting the actual content of the non-Jain systems.

---

3 [Editor's note.] In his dissertation, Folkert discussed the following five compendia:

Title	*Author*	*Date*
Ṣaḍdarśanasamuccaya	Haribhadrasūri	ca. 750 C.E.
Sarvasiddhāntapraveśaka	unknown	ca. 1150 C.E.
Vivekavilāsa	Jinadatta	ca. 1200 C.E.
Ṣaḍdarśanasamuccaya	Rājaśekharasūri	ca. 1350 C.E.
Ṣaḍdarśananirṇaya	Merutūṅga	ca. 1390 C.E.

He also included the commentaries to Haribhadra of Somatilaka (ca. 1335 C.E.) and Guṇaratna (ca.1400 C.E.).

The dates are based on Dalsukh Malvania's conclusions in his introduction to M. K. Jain's edition of Haribhadra's *Ṣaḍdarśanasamuccaya* (Malvania 1969:12-16), and on Nagin J. Shah's introduction to his edition of Merutuṅga's *Ṣaḍdarśananirṇaya*, pp. 1, 10-11.

Even more important, at first glance, is that the 363-account seems bent on distinguishing incorrect viewpoints from the correct, i.e., Jain position, while the compendia do not for the most part engage in refutations. Thus the connection between the two would not seem to be straightforward. The compendia simply do not seem to be related to what has gone before them, at least not to the 363-account. In fact, their apparent striking departure from the other ways of dealing with non-Jain positions is one of the things that have made it very difficult to assess the compendia properly.

The 363-account itself possesses a feature that sets it apart from other Jain accounts of non-Jains: the development of the 363-account reveals an attempt to explore the fact that other positions exist, not merely to refute them. This is an extremely important point, directly related to the earlier remarks concerning the notions of orthodoxy and heterodoxy. The 363-account represents the Jains' most ambitious early account of the existence of a multiplicity of non-Jain positions. This is importantly different from an account of other views that seeks merely to refute them. Of the latter sort the Jains also produced a great many, the vast number of occasions on which Jain texts undertake refutations of other positions makes it impossible to present even a brief study of them here. The 363-account, however, deals not only with specific points of disagreement between Jain and non-Jain positions, but also with the fact that such differences exist.

Thus it does not merely express the simple and basic relativity involved in the notions of orthodoxy and heterodoxy, i.e., the fact that any position is orthodox to one who occupies it. The 363-account also reaches into the further arena that the static uses of orthodoxy and heterodoxy veil: the arena where a particular movement not only expresses the relationship between itself and others, but also expresses its viewpoint of that relationship, i.e., attempts to consider why there should be such a condition, or just what constitutes it. This is the matter with which the 363-account is occupied.

THE DOCTRINE OF STANDPOINTS (*NAYAVĀDA*)

There are enough general accounts of Jain philosophy to make it unnecessary to do more here than provide a few remarks on the whole, so that the setting of the *nayavāda* is clear, and to add to these some remarks on problems related to the *nayavāda* in particular. Jain philosophy is realist, in both senses in which Western thought knows the term. It accepts the reality of the knowable world external to the perceiving self, and it accepts the actuality of universals.[4]

[4] On this point, where the Jains developed a peculiar position, see Mookerjee 1944.

The general term most often applied to Jain thought is *anekāntavāda*, which is often translated as "relativism," but for which "non-absolutism" is perhaps a better translation. It is not uncommon for the appellation *anekāntavāda* to be applied only to Jain logic,[5] i.e., to that area of Jain analytical thought which deals with propositions and judgement. This is not, strictly speaking, correct; a system that is as avowedly realist as is the Jain system must hold that the external world is the arbiter, in the end, of correct judgement, and that it is the multi-faceted nature of the world that necessitates multi-faceted judgements concerning it.

This is not a trivial or obvious point. The failure to see the world as it is constitutes *ekāntavāda*, or what the Jains would call erroneous, one-sided judgement. Unless this is clearly borne in mind, it is too easy to say that *ekāntavāda* implies merely the human shortcoming of thinking that partial knowledge is the sum of knowledge, or to fall into a hopeless subjectivism, where each cognition of the world is shut off from all others. In the Jain view, both the world and the business of making judgements about it are *aneka*, multi-faceted.

With this in mind, one can begin to consider *anekāntavāda* as expressed in Jain philosophical writings. It must be emphasized that any statement about the actual content of Jain philosophy that is not carefully related to historical developments is something of a compromise, since Jain thought went through such drastic development in its early periods that everything of importance was challenged, debated, and altered in some way. This is particularaly true of the *nayavāda*.

The *nayavāda* is actually one of several components of the formal, analytical side of Jain thought. However, with the passage of time and the debates and changes just mentioned, it became one of two major elements in Jain logic, and took on a fairly standard outline. It was constantly reworked, but its generally accepted form is as follows.

Naya is usually etymologized as coming from *nī*, "to lead, to take, to conduct,"[6] and it is generally translated as "standpoint" or "viewpoint," though the nuances of such a translation are hard to control. In its classic form, the *nayavāda* is seen to consist of seven *naya*s, which are often grouped under two headings. For easy reference, here is a schematic statement:

A. *dravyāstika*	B. *paryāyāstika*
1. *naigamanaya*	4. *ṛjusūtranaya*
2. *saṃgrahanaya*	5. *śabdanaya*

[5] See, for example, Burch 1964.

[6] "Since they lead to, i.e., obtain, cause, enable, bring about, illuminate, grasp, manifest [etc.] the categories of *jīva* and the rest, they are *naya*s." Autocommentary (*Svabhāṣya*) to *Tattvārthādhigama Sūtra* I.35.

3. *vyavahāranaya*
6. *samabhirūḍhanaya*
7. *evambhūtanaya*

Careful translation of these terms is rendered difficult by the fact that different Jain thinkers have understood specific aspects of each one in different ways. Also, the division into two groupings was pioneered by Siddhasena Divākara (who may be as early as C.E. 400 or as late as C.E. 700), who then treated the individual *naya*s very differently, emphasizing the group to which they belong rather than their particular characteristics (Dixit 1971:89-91). Thus this scheme, though it conforms to current general presentations, is actually a composite picture of sorts, the result of a long and checkered development.

The two general headings correspond roughly to such divisions as substance/accident, general/particular, etc. The *naya*s grouped under each are, in effect, standpoints or viewpoints that primarily take into account the general (substantial) or the particular (accidental) aspects of the thing perceived, though the separation of the two realms is not as sharp as the scheme would make it appear. The entire group of seven, further, stands in descending order from general to particular. It can also be divided four/three, in that the first four *naya*s deal with perceived objects and the latter three with the relationship of language to object.

It is in the perception of the seven *naya*s and their exact functions that scholars disagree the most. Therefore, hardly any two accounts of the *naya*s are exactly alike. The English equivalents for the terms also vary, naturally. These variations would require a lengthy discussion to explore fully; here a set of compromise terms is given, again for the sake of easy reference.

naigamanaya : the viewpoint from which the general and particular properties of the object are inadequately distinguished; a commonsense, concrete way of looking at an object.

saṃgrahanaya : the viewpoint that takes primary account of the generic properties of the object.

vyavahāranaya : the viewpoint that regards an object only in light of one's practical experience of it, i.e., in terms of "false particulars."

ṛjusūtranaya : the viewpoint that takes account only of the present mode of an object, or sees it only as the present agglomerate of particulars.

śabdanaya : the viewpoint concerned with the relationship of word to object in general, i.e., the question of synonyms and their significance.

samabhirūḍha naya : the viewpoint concerned with the etymological relationship of word to object.

evambhūtanaya : the viewpoint that holds that language must conform to the function of an object at the moment in which a word is used of an object.

These seven *naya*s are actually abstractions from what some Jain thinkers held to be an incalculable number of possible *naya*s.[7] In G. Hanumanta Rao's (1963:196) words, "Reality is many-faced (*anantadharmātmakam vastu*) and intelligence is selective. There are, therefore, as many ways of knowing (*nayas*) as there are faces to reality." In this light, the disagreements and re-workings that constantly surround the *nayavāda* should not be seen as affecting the fundamental notion or its sphere of operation. Therefore, the *nayavāda* can best be understood as a descriptive and analytical tool by which the ususal approaches to knowledge can better be understood. The long (and continuing) debate over its constituent elements actually centers, then, on whether the two-fold or seven-fold version (or yet some other) is more adequate to the problem being analyzed, namely, the problem of understanding human judgement.

This does, however, leave unresolved the matter of to what ultimate end such an analytical tool was developed. The simplest answer to this is to say that the *nayavāda* both illustrates the complexity of perception and judgement, and provides a means to making it whole and correct. In other words, each *naya* is taken to represent a basic possible assessment of the thing perceived, each possible assessment being quite correct within its own sphere. Under this view, a *naya* that is understood to be limited is, despite that limitedness, a proper *naya* (*sunaya*), while a *naya* that is taken to be the only possible or only correct assessment is an improper *naya* (*durnaya*), simply in virtue of being held to the exclusion of the others. The whole truth, then, is only present when the object is understood to be properly perceptible under all seven *naya*s, or is considered from all seven viewpoints.

An alternative to this is the notion that, in addition to being correct in a limited sense, each *naya* can also be incorrectly used, i.e., that error can be present in a *naya* not only because it is held to be the only correct viewpoint, but also because it is actively misused. A wrongly used *naya* is referred to as *nayābhāsa* (a "fallacious" *naya*), which is meaningfully different from *durnaya* as just

7 See, for example, Siddhasena Divākara, *Sammaïsuttam* III. 47.

described. This difference in possible understandings of the *naya*s is what makes brief statements of them, as above, very difficult to formulate. Those given, in fact, waiver between being statements of *durnaya*s and expressing *nayābhāsa*s.

It appears that these two views of the *nayavāda* were both involved in the on-going Jain debate. Under the former, one needs to be aware of the extent (or potential extent) of the whole in order to be able to reach the whole, and the *nayavāda* becomes much less a tool of descriptive analysis and more a means to the whole. Under the latter view, the *nayavāda* offers the first stage in the process of obtaining knowledge, a process that it cannot in itself complete, but for which it can—if properly used—provide a proper basis.

It is not possible at present to untangle this problem, which is related to the relatively poor information available on the development of Jain thought. What should be pointed out here is that most secondary discussions of the *nayavāda* try to resolve the problem of the two interpretations of the *naya*s by emphasizing one or the other, often by relating the *nayavāda* to some other aspect or feature of *anekāntavāda*. G. B. Burch (1964:73ff.), for example, takes up the first view of the *naya*s and subordinates the second to it; Y. J. Padmarajiah, (1963:303-4, 309ff.), G. Hanumanta Rao (1963:196ff.), and M. L. Mehta (1971:177ff.) fit the *nayavāda* into larger structures. Padmarajiah holds that it and the *syādvāda* (the Jains' seven-fold truth-value model) stand in a correlative relationship, the *nayavāda* serving to analyze and investigate, and the *syādvāda* acting as a synthesizing model, permitting the harmonizing of the varied viewpoints. He notes the ambiguity within the Jain tradition on the question of what constitutes the notions *sunaya, durnaya*, and *nayābhāsa*, but does not force the issue. Hanumanta Rao (who is ultimately very critical of the capacity of the *syādvāda*'s to provide a genuine synthesis) follows essentially the same approach, but he avoids altogether the problem of error. Mehta treats the *nayavāda* almost as a supplement to the *syādvāda*, or as a parallel method; he leans toward the first view of the *naya*s, i.e., as partial truths, and he defines *nayābhāsa* only in terms of claims to exclusiveness, i.e., as equivalent to the first view's notion of *durnaya*.

The significance of this *nayavāda* problem for an understanding of the 363-account rests on the known fact that Jain authors who discussed and developed the *nayavāda* did illustrate certain *naya*s by referring to certain non-Jain philosophical stances. This has generally been reported very unreflectively by scholars, and it should be apparent from the foregoing that how one interprets the *naya*s would have a bearing on how one understands the use of non-Jain schools to illustrate them. Furthermore, it is clear that the Jains themselves put different constructions on the *nayavāda*, and this too is bound to have some bearing on the significance of such illustrations. This matter enters into this study, at least at the outset, because the *nayavāda* has been given a very radical interpretation by some scholars along lines that have to do with the problem of tolerance. This interpretation must at least be accounted for in any study of the Jain view of non-Jains.

'INTELLECTUAL AHIṂSĀ'

The phrase that heads this section occurs in G. B. Burch's (1964:71) assessment of the *syādvāda*; he apparently got it from A. B. Dhruva.[8] It is a radical statement of what has been hinted above concerning the relationship of *ahiṃsā* to accounts of other viewpoints, i.e., that a part of "non-injury" consists in treating fairly and without acrimony the tenets and stances of other thinkers and schools.

The fact that the *naya*s can be interpreted differently plays a role in the notion of 'intellectual *ahiṃsā*.' Two interpretations of the problem of error in the *nayavāda* have been mentioned: first, that *naya*s err in being incomplete; second, that they are susceptible to active misuse. Under the first interpretation, when a *naya* is illustrated by a school of thought, it is possible to draw the conclusion that each school of thought contributes or partakes in a valid, though limited, view of matters, and that if these limited viewpoints can be synthesized one will have the means of understanding matters in their multi-faceted real status. Thus schools of thought are simply extensions of the fact that any one judgement is limited, and no odium need be attached to the various schools of thought except that they are one-sided while the Jain position is not.

Under the second interpretation, where *naya*s are capable of being fallacious as well as limited, matters would be very different. What causes the existence of various schools of thought is not only the fact that judgements tend to be partial, but also that there can be error in those judgements. Thus it is not merely wrong-headed insistence on a particular viewpoint that lies behind the existence of various schools, it is also error itself.

Both of the basic interpretations of the *naya*s exist, as noted, in the Jain tradition. Further, the use of the first interpretation in relation to schools of thought cannot be altogether attributed to the world of scholars. Perhaps the best-known Jain source for such an understanding of the *nayavāda* and its relationship to schools of thought is the following verse by Hemacandra:

> As, because of being alternatives and counter-alternatives
> one to another
> the other prime doctrines are jealous;

8 See Dhruva 1933:lxxiv. Dhruva is wrongly cited as A. D. Dhruva by Burch.

Not so is Thy [the Jina's] religion, in desiring the
Methods [*naya*s] in totality
Without distinction, given to partiality.[9]

Clearly implied is the idea that various schools are each exponents of one or another *naya*, a situation avoided by the Jain system which, as a result, is not "jealous," i.e., exclusionist.

When there is added to this interpretation the practice in Jain texts of illustrating individual *naya*s by specific non-Jain schools, the conclusion seems inevitable that the *nayavāda* can function to resolve the conflict between viewpoints. Burch's statement on the *naya*s reflects both his interpretation of them and this extension of the scope of their activity (Burch 1964:73, quotation from Dhruva 1933:lxxiv):

> We should distinguish a theory in general (*naya*), which is a point of view; a wrong theory (*durnaya*), which in comprehending one point of view rejects all others; and a right theory (*sunaya*), which recognizes its own limitation as valid only somehow (*syat*) and the alternative validity of other points of view. The various non-Jaina philosophies are *durnaya*, rejecting all theories but one. Only *sunaya* gives true knowledge (*pramana*). Jainism, therefore, "visualizes the whole truth," while other philosophies "possess only the gleam of the broken light."

Dhruva is not quite so radical, but clearly holds to the same general position:

> Jainism is par excellence *the* doctrine of ahiṃsâ—ahiṃsâ not only of physical life, but also of intellectual outlook (darśana). In the latter, moreover, it did not stop short at a mere negative attitude of toleration towards other schools, but took the positive step of investigating *how* each of those schools erred. As a result it came to the conclusion that the errors of those schools were only *partial truths* as seen from particular angles of vision—that none of them was wholly wrong, and if each of them would see things from the point of view of the opponent as well as from their own, there would be perfect harmony all round.

Dhruva, it should be noted, appears to hold that the *nayavāda* took shape with constant reference to the stances of various schools of thought. Burch, on the other hand, seems to take it as a possible application of a pre-existing doctrine. Both presumptions are also found in the works of numerous other scholars, Jain and non-Jain, who express some notion of *anekāntavāda* in general and *nayavāda* in particular as holding a key of sorts to the resolution of differences among schools of thought. Burch and Dhruva are quoted here because they clearly exemplify the assumptions behind such an idea.

The *nayavāda* may, indeed, imply a way of explaining, or even resolving, the differences between schools of thought. But in itself it would seem to be a more or less neutral analytical approach, and it certainly claims superiority for

---

9 *Anyayogavyavacchedikādvātriṃśikā*, translated by F. W. Thomas, p. 164.

the Jain position. It requires a considerable interpretive step before Dhruva can speak of "harmony all round"; and such a statement proceeds not only from a particular interpretation of the *nayavāda*, but also, one suspects, from the scholar's predisposition toward seeing tolerance in the *nayavāda*.

Nor is this possible predisposition limited to the *nayavāda* and studies of it. Nathmal Tatia has also put forth something of a case for the existence of 'intellectual *ahiṃsā*.' Beginning with the undoubted emphasis in the early Jain tradition on *ahiṃsā*, Tatia (1951:21) notes the Jain concern for "cautiousness in speaking," and notes instances where the Jain scriptures include warnings against categorical assertions and invoke the use of conditional expressions as part of their teachings on careful speech. The kernel of his argument reads (Tatia 1951:22):

> One should not hurt the feelings of others. If there are different doctrines, there must be reasons for their origin. It is the duty of a patient thinker to find out the sources of these doctrines. Non-violent search for truth should inspire the enquiries of a thinker. He should not be prejudiced by preconceptions. It is this attitude of tolerance and justice that was responsible for the origin of the doctrine of Non-absolutism (*Anekānta*). Out of universal tolerance and peace-loving nature was born cautiousness of speech.

Tatia's argument has the virtue of beginning with *ahiṃsā* and a known interpretation of it, namely, careful speech. But the whole of his argument is highly interpretive, and proceeds from a presumption of tolerance that cries out for broader verification.

Dayanand Bhargava (1968:106ff.) has put forth another argument, one based on the relationship of *bhāva* (the internal state of the self) and *dravya* (external forces and substances, including karma, that affect the self). Jains have often debated the question of *bhāva* as "intent" and its role in the karmic consequences of activity. Yet when Bhargava (1968:108ff.) takes the notion of *bhāvāhiṃsā*, of not possessing even the internal state related to actually doing harm, and extends it into tolerance for the viewpoints of others, he clearly is on his own.[10] Though the interpretation seems to be possible, there appears to be little evidence for its earlier presence in the tradition. Bhargava's argument, too, seems to begin with a presumption of tolerance and to proceed from it, and it is in leaving such presumptions unconsidered that claims of the existence of 'intellectual *ahiṃsā*' fail to justify themselves.

With regard to the *nayavāda* itself and its relationship to the Jain view of others, several observations are in order. First, the preceding pages have attempted to show the problems involved in interpreting the *nayavāda* itself, and

---

10 Note that the notion of *bhāva* and *dravya* as "intent" and "act" is only one possible interpretation of the pair.

how those problems relate to understanding it as a tool for dealing with the existence of other views. To a certain extent, the elucidation of these two problems makes up a whole. That, however, would require a separate study.

A second important point is that the *nayavāda*, either by name or structure, does not enter in any way into the 363-account, though it does occur in the work of one major commentator on the 363-account. One would not expect this if the *nayavāda* were intimately related to the problem of conflicting viewpoints. Nonetheless, a great many discussions of the *nayavāda* do contain accounts of non-Jain schools; therefore it seems unfortunate not to include *nayavāda* more fully. But the state of Jain scholarship also puts obstacles in the way. For example, Mallavādin's *Dvādaśāranayacakra* is a major piece of evidence concerning the *nayavāda* as a tool for dealing with opposing schools of thought;[11] but the work itself is still in the process of being made fully accessible to students of the Jains.[12] Other texts also remain unedited, or unavailable in this country.

The point at which the *nayavāda* actually enters into the 363-account, in the commentary tradition, requires that some attention be given to it. However, its absence from the other Jain attempts to account for other viewpoints, and the difficulty of assessing it properly without devoting a full study to it, mean that the *nayavāda* does not hold a prominent position in this study of the 363-account. Nonetheless, since it presents so important a possible source of information of Jain attempts to deal with others, a full study of it must remain a desideratum.

---

11 It is, in fact, the major basis for Burch's article.

12 After two less-than-successful attempts at editing this text had been made by other scholars, Muni Jambūvijaya has produced an excellent edition. The text itself has had to be reconstructed largely on the basis of Siṃhasūri's commentary on it; therefore the flaws in the earlier editions were not merely matters of editorial decision. See also Frauwallner 1957.

15

THE 363-ACCOUNT: KEY ELEMENTS*

INTRODUCTION

Two tasks are involved in examining the 363-account. First, there exists no single text that is completely devoted to expounding the 363-account. Rather, references to it, and versions of it, are scattered throughout a great many textual loci. Only by paying considerable attention to these varied references can a proper picture of the account be pieced together. Second, this picture must also include some attention to other Jain mentions of non-Jain positions. In my opinion, the 363-account is not only an account of the differences between Jains and non-Jains, but also an attempt to deal with the fact of such differences. This is the element that differentiates it from other accounts; however, in order to see this, one must take note of other sorts of accounts, and see the 363-account in relation to them.

First to be given attention are the process of locating the 363-account in the great mass of Jain literature, and the full account itself. Thereafter the issue of differentiating it will be taken up. It should also be stated that this discussion of the 363-account has both a negative and a positive task to perform. The negative task is to correct an impression given by earlier studies of this account, which have tended to treat the 363-account as a static entity. The positive task is to

* From dissertation, pp. 59-82.

look for its peculiar nature. In the first part of what follows, the negative task may seem at times to dominate the positive, but it is nonetheless necessary.

THE 363-ACCOUNT: PRIOR STUDY

The matter of locating this account in the mass of Jain literature is considerably simplified by the fact that it has caught the attention of several scholars. F. Otto Schrader, Benimadhab Barua, and Amulyacandra Sen have made a generally thorough search of Jain texts, seeking references to this and other accounts. Other scholars, such as Gopinath Kaviraj, have studied aspects of the Jain accounts of others. In general, however, the major interest of these scholars has been in reconstructing the non-Jain systems, not in understanding the complex of issues and attitudes that might enter into constructing such an account.

Several studies by these scholars form the major basis for this chapter's selection of sources. The earliest of the works in question is Schrader's 1902 *Über den Stand der indischen Philosophie zur Zeit Mahāvīras und Buddhas*. It, like almost every other work of this sort, refers at its ouset (Schrader 1902:iii) to Hermann Jacobi's remarks in the Introduction to his second volume of translations of canonical texts, where Jacobi says (Jacobi 1895a:xxvii):

> The records of the Buddhists and Jainas about the philosophical ideas current at the time of the Buddha and Mahāvīra, meagre though they be, are of the greatest importance to the historian of that epoch. For they show us the ground on which, and the materials with which, a religious reformer had to build his system.

Schrader relates his work directly to Jacobi's position, and in the course of stating his own goals, he provides some information relevant to his sources and to the general availability of materials (Schrader 1902:iii-iv):

> Dieser Ausspruch brachte mich, nachdem ich schon früher durch Herrn Professor Leumann auf das zu besprechenden System der dreihundertdreiundsechzig Darśanas aufmerksam gemacht worden war, auf den Gedanken, nach jinistischen, buddhistischen und wenn möglich auch brahmanischen Quellen eine Schilderung der zu Mahāvīras und Buddhas Zeit besonders vertretenen philosophischen Richtungen zu geben. Zwar musste ich mir sagen, dass zu einem solchen Unternehmen eigentlich die Zeit noch nicht gekommen sei, indem die vollständige Erschliessung der jinistischen Litteratur voraussichtlich noch manche wichtige Aufschlusse geben wurde. Aber je mehr ich . . . von dieser Litteratur kennen lernte, um so mehr drängte sich mir die Überzeugung auf, dass, wenn nicht ein unerhörter Zufall uns noch in Besitz des, speziell von den philosophischen Ansichten handelnden, verloren gegangen zwölften Aṅga bringen sollte, kaum irgendwelche

Nachrichten zu Tage treten werden, die nicht von unseren Hauptgewährsmännern, Malayagiri und Śīlāṅka, in ihren Kommentaren verwertet worden sind.[1]

Barua's contribution to the study of the 363-account is found mainly in his *A History of Pre-Buddhistic Indian Philosophy*. This work has a different scope than Schrader's. While Barua describes his goal as the general delineation of Indian philosophical thought in the period when the Buddhist and Jain movements arose, and names as his most important sources the Buddhist and Jain scriptures and the *Mahābhārata*, the weight of his work is on interpreting and clarifying Buddhist references to non-Buddhists, and where possible seeing a unified portrayal in them. This has some effect on his interpretation of Jain materials, as will be seen. He, too, refers to Jacobi's statement (Barua 1970:viff., 188).

Sen's efforts are found in a work whose title (*Schools and Sects in Jaina Literature*) is more direct and limited, as are his aims; the literature in question is really only that of the Śvetāmbara canon (Sen 1931:1). He states his general purpose as follows (Sen 1931:3-4):

> It will . . . be our task to examine the many references throughout the canon with a view to find out what views each of them upheld and whether any of them can be identified with schools whose doctrines we are familiar with. This will serve a double purpose of showing in the first place what was the historical background of the Nirgrantha doctrine, what views they felt called upon to refute and thereby establish the superiority of the Nirgrantha creed, and secondly of showing though in an indirect manner, the condition of many doctrines of the time by means of the light thrown by the Jainas regarding the philosophical and religious atmosphere of India of that period . . . . It is to be remembered that this work is not intended to be a history of the philosophies of the time. The principal object is to get as clear an idea as is possible to the tenets, as they appeared to the Nirgranthas, of other schools and sects in those ancient days with a view to create a suitable background for the study of Jainism.

Other scholars take much the same tack that is evident in these statements. The general intent in all cases has been to use the Jain sources either for straightforwardly historical purposes or for the purpose of creating the backdrop

---

1 [Editor's Translation.] This position [of Jacobi] inspired me, upon reflection, when Professor Leumann called my attention to the above-mentioned system of 363 *darśana*s, to give a description, according to Jaina, Buddhist, and whenever possible Brahmanical sources, of the representative philosophical schools of thought at the time of Mahāvīra and the Buddha. I must admit that the time for such an undertaking has actually not yet come, for the complete exposure of Jaina literature will probably reveal several important discoveries. But nonetheless . . . the more I came to know this literature, the more convinced I became that even if an astonishing stroke of luck someday put us in possession of the lost twelfth Aṅga, which dealt especially with philosophical matters, hardly any information would come to light which had not been evaluated by our principle authorities, Malayagiri and Śīlāṅka, in their commentaries.

for an understanding of the Jains (or Buddhists). There is little sense of the Jain accounts of non-Jains as something more (or less) than an inchoate attempt at historiography.

This being the case, it is not too surprising that the Jain accounts, both in general and in the specific case of the 363-account, are not treated very reflectively. Schrader deserves great credit for having gathered the assorted sources for a study of the 363-account out of a mass of poorly explored Jain literature. At the same time, his uncritical use of those sources leaves two false impressions. First, he does not make it clear that not all sources treat the 363-account in the same way. Second, he treats the variations that he does note as if they were of little consequence. Both of these impressions should be corrected by the evidence presented in the following chapters.

Barua's approach is perhaps less important for study of the Jain accounts of non-Jains than for its attempts to clarify the background of early Buddhism. In the course of these attempts, Barua regularly does violence to the Jain accounts. His approach tends to take the Buddhist accounts of non-Buddhists as normative and then to claim that the Jain accounts state essentially the same thing. This often results in outright distortion.

Sen's work on the 363-account is only a presentation of the full account, but this is at least true to the Jain sources. Unfortunately, that part of Sen's book which deals with the 363-account is nothing more than a paraphrastic translation of part of Guṇaratna's commentary on Haribhadra's *Ṣaḍdarśanasamuccaya*. Sen has collected a good deal of useful data in other parts of his study, but the section of the book that presents the 363-account does nothing to advance one's knowledge of its history or significance (Sen 1931:29-37).

What must be said in general is that all of these studies have significantly failed to assess seriously the meaning of such accounts, and most of them have treated the sources less than carefully. Nonetheless, without their prior work of searching through the mass of Jain literature, this study could not hope to advance beyond a most insignificant sampling of sources. Given the base provided by these prior studies, this study can treat seriously the significance of the 363-account and the specific element in it that differentiates it from other Jain accounts, namely, the fact that it is an attempt to deal with the existence of non-Jain viewpoints. It is in this respect that a re-examination of the 363-account can best hope to serve some purpose.

THE 363-ACCOUNT

The full 363-account can best be presented at the outset of the analysis of it, since it is fairly complex. In its final form, it is highly schematic, and contains instructions for calculating the number of various types of philosophical positions. These instructions were translated into a diagram by Schrader (1902:3-4), which is given here for reference in the discussions that follow.

kriyāvāda:	jīva								
	ajīva								
	āsrava						kāla		
	bandha		sva		nitya		īśvara		
	saṃvara		para		anitya		ātman		
	nirjarā						niyati		
	puṇya						svabhāva		
	apuṇya								
	mokṣa								
	9	x	2	x	2	x	5	=	180

akriyāvāda :	jīva							
	ajīva				kāla			
	āsrava				īśvara			
	bandha		sva		ātman			
	saṃvara		para		niyati			
	nirjarā				svabhāva			
	mokṣa				yadṛcchā			
	7	x	2	x	6	=		84

ajñānavāda :	jīva				
	ajīva		sattva		
	āsrava		asattva		
	bandha		sadasattva		
	saṃvara		avācyatva		
	nirjarā		sadavācyatva		
	puṇya		asadavācyatva		
	apuṇya		sadasadavācyatva		
	mokṣa				
	9	x	7	=	63
			sattva		
	utpatti		asattva		
			sadasattva		
			avācyatva		
	1	x	4	=	4
				=	67

vinayavāda :			sura		
			nṛpati		
	kāya		yati		
	vāc		jñāti		
	manas		sthavira		
	dāna		adhama		
			mātṛ		
			pitṛ		
	4	x	8	=	32
				=	363

It should be readily apparent that the materials used in constructing this scheme draw heavily on the formal categories of Jain philosophy. Headings one through three begin with the basic categories of Jain analytical thought, though it must be noted that these categories themselves have a history of development within the Jain tradition, and are regarded as being either seven or nine by the Jains themselves. *Jīva* (soul, self) and *ajīva* (not-soul) sum up between them all existents. This basic division is complemented and paralleled in Jain thought by other means of categorizing existent entities, though as the tradition developed, this basic division plus the other five (or seven) categories came more and more to be the standard way of stating the Jain *tattva*s.

The remaining categories actually belong to the process by which the *jīva* is bound by karma and achieves release. *Āsrava* is the influx of karma-particles toward and onto the *jīva; bandha*, the resulting bondage; *saṃvara*, the stoppage of influx; *nirjarā*, the decay of already present karma*; mokṣa*, the result of *saṃvara* and *nirjarā*, the return of the *jīva* to its pristine state. *Puṇya* and *apuṇya* are often given as *dharma* and *adharma*. The Jains appear to have first understood *dharma* and *adharma* as the media of motion and rest. Their later appearance in Jain thought in the sense in which Hindu India understood them is a point of some interest, which will be touched upon subsequently.

Sva and *para*, as well as *nitya* and *anitya*, are also related to basic premises in Jain thought, but are not generally present as actual categories. However, the items *kāla, īśvara*, et al., occur in a number of places in Indian thought as a whole. They apparently represent a commonly used method of attempting to classify schools of thought according to their acceptance of different basic ideas of causality. What is known of them will be introduced below.

In the third heading, *sattva, asattva*, etc., are the seven constituents of the *syādvāda*, the Jains' multivalent logic-model; this, too, is taken up in detail below. Although most of this material is readily identifiable, the elements within the fourth heading, *vinayavāda*, and the names of the headings themselves (*kriyāvāda*, etc.) are not part of the Jain analytical tradition. This discrepancy, as well as the history of the more familiar elements, provide certain points of departure for the analysis of the account in chapters 16 and 17. In the meantime, it is useful first to examine the working of the scheme and the pattern of its occurrence in Jain literature.

The ideal operation of the 363-account would proceed thus: the *kriyāvādī* (who, according to the commentators, teaches the existence of world and soul) has 180 options. Each Jain category (*jīva, ajīva*, etc.) can be viewed in two ways: as unique (*svataḥ*) or relative (*parataḥ*). The resultant 18 are each, then, subjected to another dual possibility: eternal (*nitya*) or transient (*anitya*). The 36 possibilities that are then present are further subject to five options in the realm of causality, i.e., the view that time (*kāla*) or one of the other four is the agent of creation or causality in general. This results in 180 options, any of which would be a *kriyāvāda*. The standard compact presentation of the first option is: *asti jīvaḥ svato nityaḥ kālataḥ*. This form of expression nearly defies translation, but it might be given as: "There exists a soul (*jīva*) that is unique (*svato*), eternal (*nityaḥ*), and subject to time (*kālataḥ*)"[2] The second of the 180 options would be put: *asti jīvaḥ svato nityaḥ īśvarataḥ*, and so on, until all had been covered.

The *akriyāvādī* takes what is basically the opposite position. His options are formulated: *nāsti jīvaḥ svato kālataḥ*, and so on. Since the *jīva*, et al., do not exist, there is no question of their being eternal or non-eternal; thus *nitya* and *anitya* are absent from the scheme under this heading. However, since *sva* and *para* have to do with knowledge as well as existence, they remain. Chance (*yadṛcchā*) is added to the list of causal agents, and the whole works out to 84 options.

The *ajñānavādī* (agnostic/sceptic, also given as *ajñānikavādī*) has 63 possible options with respect to knowledge of the Jain categories. This heading is quite peculiar, and is discussed fully in chapter 16. The *vinayavādī* (which the commentators take as "one who teaches respectful service") can show respect through four means toward eight objects, and thus has 32 options open to him. The end result of all of this is 363 philosophical stances.

It is quite obvious that this scheme actually makes little logical sense when it is worked out option by option, especially if one insists that each of the

---

2 Concerning the translation of *svataḥ* and *parataḥ* as "unique" and "relative," respectively: I reach this conclusion because of the remarks of the commentators, who take the two terms to indicate not necessarily ontological independence or dependence, but rather whether or not the nature of the *jīva*'s being (and its being known) has any relationship with the nature of other entities on these two points. Schrader (1902:7) quotes Śīlāṅka on the point: *tatra svata iti svenaiva rūpeṇa jīvo 'sti na paropādhyapekṣayā hrasvatavadīrghatva iva.* This simple gloss is used by all commentaries subsequent to Śīlāṅka, and is discussed again below, in chapter 16.

options must function within the four larger headings as they relate to each other. The cumbrousness of the scheme shows up particularly in the commentarial literature, where authors are given to the revealing practice of referring to *kālavāda*, *īśvaravāda*, etc., as if these were the basic headings rather than *kriyāvāda*, etc. Their discussions are based on what seems to be a more concrete understanding of *kālavāda*, etc., and one gets the distinct impression that, despite the instructions for building the scheme and the order in which it is laid out, it does not bear a distinct relationship with any concrete content for the whole.

Schrader (1902:6-8) himself attempted to work the system out in another way, also using *kālavāda*, etc., as the starting point. His various attempts include methods of calculation not attested in the commentaries, and he does not press the issue when the sense of the whole escapes him (Schrader 1902:6-8). In fact, his interest lies far more in *kālavāda*, etc. (which are more widely known in Indian thought), than in the scheme itself.

This is most definitely not the case. Although the presentation of textual references by Schrader (and others) does not make any differentiation among the sources, most of the individual textual loci do not present the entire system as he diagrams it. In fact, the sources present a thoroughly heterogenous picture, and the primary impression is that the full-fledged 363-account is a late product, indeed.

In order to make this clear, the whole mass of sources that refer to the 363-account can best be viewed schematically before they are analyzed. Chronology is an issue, and thus the following list presents them in that way. Included in the list are sources that mention the 363-account in whole or in part, mentions of the latter sort being those that refer to its major components (e.g., *kriyāvāda*) and thus were occasions for commentators to refer to the whole. This list is drawn from the works of the scholars mentioned above, certain other secondary sources, and further perusal of the texts. It is weak in that the very early Digambara texts are not available for study, nor were they examined by the scholars whose works were consulted.[3]

[3] The major secondary sources are: Schrader 1902:2; Sen 1931:29ff.; Malvania 1969:13; Weber 1883-85:20[259].

List of sources:

Date B.C.E./C.E.	Śvetāmbara texts	Digambara texts
300	*Ācāraṅga* I.1.1	
	Sūtrakṛtāṅga I.1.2.24	
200	*Sūtrakṛtāṅga* I.10.16-17	
	Sūtrakṛtāṅga I.6.27	
100	*Sūtrakṛtāṅga* I.12	
	Uttarādhyayana XVIII.23ff.	
0	*Ācāradaśāḥ* VI	
	Sūtrakṛtāṅga II.1 passim	
100	*Sūtrakṛtāṅga* II.2.79ff.	
	Sūtrakṛtāṅga Niryukti 117b-121	
200	*Sthānāṅga* IV.4	
	Bhagavatī XXX.1	
300		Kundakunda, *Bhāvapāhuḍa* 135, 140
400	*Tattvārthādhigama Svabhāṣya* VII.18, VIII.1	
500	*Nandī* 88	
		Pūjyapāda , *Sarvārthasiddhi* on *Tattvārthādhigama* VIII.1
600		
700	Haribhadra on *Nandī* 88	Akalaṅka, *Tattvārtharājavarttika* on *Tattvārthādhigama* VIII.1
	Haribhadra on *Āvaśyaka Niryukti*	
800	Siddhasenagaṇi on *Tattvārthādhigama* VII.18, VIII.1	
	Śīlāṅka on *Ācāraṅga* I.1.1	
900	Śīlāṅka on *Sūtrakṛtāṅga* passim	
1000	Abhayadeva on *Sthānāṅga* IV.4	Nemicandra Siddhāntacakravartin, *Gommaṭasāra*, Karmakāṇḍa VII
	Abhayadeva on *Bhagavatī* XXX.1	
1100	Nemicandra on *Uttarādhyayana* XVIII.23ff.	
	Malayagiri on *Nandī* 88	Bhāskaranandin, *Sukhabodha* on *Tattvārthādhigama* VIII.1

1200	Malayagiri on *Rājapraśnīya*	
1300	Somatilaka on Haribhadra, *Ṣaḍdarśanasamuccaya*	Śrutasāgara, *Tattvārthavṛtti* on *Tattvārthādhigama* VIII.1
1400	Guṇaratna on Haribhadra, *Ṣaḍdarśanasamuccaya*	
1500		

It is not possible to portray dates with precision in a table like this, but the general picture should be clear. Precise dates are discussed below, when individual texts come under scrutiny.

The major criticism made above concerning the other studies of this material was that those studies had not treated carefully the variations in the way that the sources present the 363-account. As noted, the full account as diagrammed and discussed by Schrader may be comparatively late. It cannot be found, in fact, in any sampled source earlier than Haribhadrasūri's commentaries on *Āvaśyaka Niryukti* and *Nandī Sūtra*, ca. 750 C.E. The earlier sources present parts of the scheme, and statements about the number of schools in it, the four major headings (*kriyāvāda*, etc.), and the number of schools in those headings; but no sample text prior to Haribhadra gives the means for calculating the totals, or any categories other than the four major headings.

Despite the caution necessitated by the fact that the list of sources cannot be called absolutely complete, there appears to be a definite chronological pattern in the way that the sources present the account. To show this pattern clearly, the list is presented again, broken into the following groups of sources: (A) those that give only the four headings (or one or more of them); (B) those that give the four headings plus the number 363 or its subtotals (180, etc.); (C) those that present the method of calculating and describing the stances under each heading (or appear to know of that method without giving it).

A. Sources giving the four headings alone (300 B.C.E. - 200 C.E.)

Ācārāṅga I.1.1
Sūtrakṛtāṅga I.1.2.24
Sūtrakṛtāṅga I.10.16-17
Sūtrakṛtāṅga I.6.27
Sūtrakṛtāṅga I.12
Uttarādhyayana XVIII.23ff.
Ācāradaśāḥ VI
Sūtrakṛtāṅga II.1 passim
Sthāṇāṅga IV.4
Bhagavatī XXX.1

B. Sources giving the headings plus number (0 - 1350 C.E.)

Sūtrakṛtāṅga II.2.79ff.
Sūtrakṛtāṅga Niryukti 117b-121
Bhāvapāhuḍa 135, 140
Tattvārthādhigama Svabhāṣya VII.18, VIII.1
Nandī 88
Pūjyapāda, *Sarvārthasiddhi* on *Tattvārthādhigama* VIII.1
Akalaṅka, *Tattvārtharājavarttika* on *Tattvārthādhigama* VIII.1
Bhāskarandin, *Sukhabodha* on *Tattvārthādhigama* VIII.1
Śrutasāgara, *Tattvārthavṛtti* on *Tattvārthādhigama* VIII.1

C. Sources giving the calculation-method (700 - 1450 C.E.)

Haribhadra on *Nandī* 88
Haribhadra on *Āvaśyaka Niryukti*
Siddhasenagaṇi on *Tattvārthādhigama* VII.18, VIII.1
Śīlāṅka on *Ācārāṅga* I.1.1
Śīlāṅka on *Sūtrakṛtāṅga* passim
Nemicandra Siddhāntacakrvartin, *Gommaṭsāra*, Karmakāṇḍa VII
Abhayadeva on *Sthāṇāṅga* IV.4
Abhayadeva on *Bhagavatī* XXX.1
Nemicandra on *Uttarādhyayana* XVIII.23ff.
Malayagiri on *Nandī* 88
Malayagiri on *Rājapraśnīya*
Somatilaka on Haribhadra, *Ṣaḍdarśanasamuccaya*
Guṇaratna on Haribhadra, *Ṣaḍdarśanasamuccaya*

With both the general chronology and these groups in mind, one can begin to delve more deeply into the components of the 363-account. It appears that there are three major components in the full account, corresponding to the groups just given. The first consists of the four main headings, *kriyāvāda*, etc. The second consists of the number 363 and the subtotals that make it up. The third is the method of calculation plus the various other internal categories and headings.

Of the three components, two consist of material that is not only older than the full 363-account, but apparently also independent of it, i.e., they are not merely its first nascent parts. These two are the four headings, and the number 363. In the case of the four headings, the distinction between *kriyāvāda* and *akriyāvāda* appears to have been used very early in both Jain and Buddhist sources to describe a fundamental division between philosophical stances. *Kriyāvāda* is understood by the commentators as "the teaching concerning activity," or "the activity of the on-going self" or "responsible activity"; and *akriyāvāda* as "the teaching concerning non-activity," or "the self as non-agent" or "action not implying a self." There is no doubt that these terms had a broad, independent role outside of the 363-account. The bulk of the sources given in group A, above, are independent references using *kriyāvāda* and *akriyāvāda*.

The other two major headings—*ajñānikavāda* and *vinayavāda*—are less prominent outside the 363-account. However, the few isolated references that are known would indicate some independent status for them. This surmise is buttressed by the fact that they occur in certain Digambara accounts of non-Jains where *kriyāvāda* and *akriyāvāda* do not. These four headings and their significance are discussed later. The point at issue here is that these major components of the 363-account appear to have had independent roles outside of the account. In the context of the difference between the 363-account and accounts that seek merely to refute non-Jain views, the discovery and examination of these outside roles can play an important part in evaluating the special nature of the 363-account.

The second component, the number 363, was likely also an independent factor. Within it as a factor are the subtotals that make it up. It is worth noting that the total and its subtotals may be two separable elements, though they are placed together in the source-groups given above. The chronology of the existing sources would indicate that the number 363 occurs alone before the subtotals begin to appear. Its first appearance in a canonical text is in *Sūtrakṛtāṅga Sūtra* II.2.79 (the second book of *Sūtrakṛtāṅga* is generally held to be later than the first book). It also occurs independent of the subtotals in *Bhāvapāhuḍa* 140, and in *Tattvārthādhigama Sūtra Svabhāsya* VIII.1. Since the former contains, in verse 135, a reference to the subtotals, it is not terribly strong evidence; but the latter's reference to 363 is quite isolated from any subtotals.

Sūtrakṛtāṅga Niryukti, which is at least somewhat later than even the second book of *Sūtrakṛtāṅga* itself, appears to be the earliest extant statement of the subtotals of the number 363, each attached to the proper heading. The verse in *Sūtrakṛtāṅga Niryukti* (119) that contains them is duplicated (or quoted) in virtually every text that refers to the 363-account once the subtotals are present. It is impossible to tell for certain whether or not a verse from another source was incorporated into the *Niryukti*, but it is at least possible to say that it is the oldest known source that not only refers to the total (363) but also to the subtotals that belong to the headings.

Whether or not the subtotals were independent of the total number may seem to be a rather inessential matter. However, when we take up the analysis of the contents of the 363-account, the importance of the point should become clear. For the moment, the independence of the number 363, both from the full 363-account and from its subtotals, can be attested in at least one other way.

Albrecht Weber has presented certain information regarding the number 363 and its use in similar contexts. A note to his discussion of *Āvaśyaka Niryukti* XX reads as follows (Weber 1883-85:137[75]):

> . . . a letter of [Anton] Schiefner to me . . . contains the following statement extracted from the introduction of a Thibetan work edited by Wassiljew: 'there are 363 different schisms in the religion of India.' Since I found nothing of the kind in the introduction of Tāranātha, which was doubtless referred to here, I had recourse to Wassiljew himself. . . . I received from him the following kind reply:—'I cannot inform you definitely in which of my works 363 Indian schools are mentioned, if at all; but it is certain that this number is frequently mentioned in Thibetan works. In Djandja Vatuktu's Siddhānta . . . I find the following: "In the sūtras are mentioned 96 darsana papantika . . . , 14 dijakrita muluni . . . , 62 injurious darsana, 28 which do not permit salvation, and 20 which are ruinous." In Bhania's [*sic*] work Tarkadjvala all the darsanas are enumerated in 110 species. . . . According to my hasty count there are more than 120 names, probably because the same school is mentioned twice, i.e. in Sanskrit and Thibetan. And at the end, after mention of all 110 (—120), we read:—*in all 363 darsanas*.'

The reference by Vaisl'ev [Wassiljew] to the *Tarkajvālā* and its preservation of the number 363 as the total number of systems is certainly significant, as is his testimony to the number's occurrence elsewhere. Unfortunately, the text of the *Tarkajvālā* remains inaccessible to most scholars, since it is preserved only in Tibetan.[4] Its date—the sixth century C.E. (Gokhale 1958:165)—does not make it a primary source equal to *Sūtrakṛtāṅga*. However, its use of the number 363 in relation to a different list of schools than that provided by the Jain model is of some importance.

It would be of prime significance to recover from various sources the rationale behind the use of the number 363. However, the scope of the problem is truly overwhelming, especially as no immediate source within the Jain tradition for such a number presents itself. A few suggestions are taken up later, in the analysis of the account; but for the moment the point is not to solve the number puzzle but to see that the number 363 itself can be and has been of use in other settings that discuss schools of thought. It has also apparently been used with other subtotals. This argues strongly for the likelihood that 363 and the subtotals attached to it in the Jain account are separable elements, and that the whole matter of number was originally quite separate from the headings and their internal elements.

---

4 V. V. Gokhale (1958:165ff.) gives a general introduction to the *Tarkajvālā*, including a review of the various names that have been given to the author. Bhavya is his choice out of the many, a list that does not include Bhania. Five of the eleven chapters of the *Madhyamakahṛdaya* (of which a Sanskrit text has been found), to which the *Tarkajvālā* forms an autocommentary, have been explored by the various Japanese and Indian scholars. See Karl H. Potter 1983:108-110. [Editor's note.] See also Quarnström 1989.

Only when the third component, the calculation, is added to the first two elements, i.e., the headings and the numbers, does the full-fledged 363-account emerge. It is found only in the texts in group C, above. The most effective way of showing the relationships, chronological and structural, between the various elements in the full account is to present a final schematic outline of the development of the 363-account.

Schematic outline:

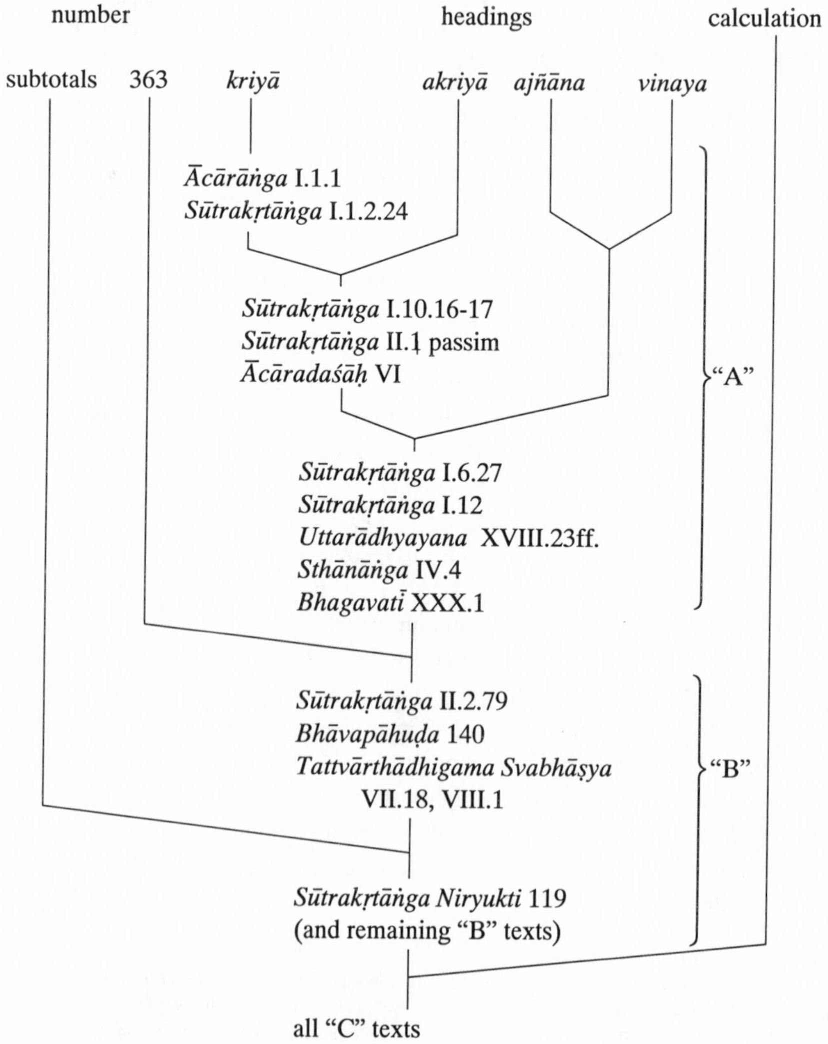

Once again, a general chronological pattern holds true; and the important point to note is that the end of this complex process is the first point at which the sources tally with Schrader's presentation. In order to make the system work, a number of further elements are introduced in group C. They are: (for *kriyāvāda* and *akriyāvāda*) the list of *kāla, īśvara*, et al.; and the *nitya/anitya* and *sva/para* pairs; (for *ajñānikavāda*) the seven modal statements that make up the *syādvāda*; (for all three) the Jain *tattvas*; and (for *vinayavāda*) the four instruments of proper behaviour, *vāc*, et al., and the eight objects to be treated properly, *sura*, et al.

None of these groups of items ever occurs in texts in goups A and B. Yet it seems very unlikely that Haribhadra, the author of the oldest text in C, should have undertaken to draw together all of these additional disparate elements and weld them into a whole. This is a point that could spark endless debate. It is obvious that the full 363-account has to have begun somewhere, and it is perhaps foolish to argue circumstantially against its first discoverable occurrence being its first actual occurrence.

However, the issue is not merely one of abstract probability. There are other factors. First, Haribhadra's commentaries are the earliest known Sanskrit commentaries on the Prakrit scriptures. This is an argument that can cut two ways. First, one might argue that the shift to Sanskrit comment is a likely point for the introduction of new elements; and it is true that the Sanskrit commentaries broke away from the sub-commentary model shown by the Prakrit commentaries. On the other hand, one might properly argue that at present, in the almost complete absence of real data from the *bhāsa* (*bhāṣya*) and *cuṇṇi* (*cūrṇi*) layers of the Prakrit tradition, one cannot assume anything when confronted by such a multi-faceted development as the calculation-method. This point gains in importance in that certain of Śīlāṅka's comments on the 363-account quote verses that summarize some parts of the calculation.

The latter point makes it seem likely that something approaching the full 363-account was developed in the Prakrit commentaries. There is one further possibility: that the scheme received some development in Digambara texts prior to the *Bhāvapāhuḍa*, though this argument is weakened by the fact that the Digambara *Tattvārthādhigama Sūtra* commentaries contain no hint of the calculation method. In sum, though, it seems unlikely that Haribhadra's commentaries do more than introduce the full 363-account into the realm of Sanskrit comment and analysis.

Left aside for a bit has been the increasing dominance of the 363-account, which runs parallel to the growth of the account out of several elements. This matter of dominance must also be taken up here, for it also has to do with the special nature of the 363-account as an attempt not only to refute, but also to treat the existence of other viewpoints.

The existence of other Jain accounts of non-Jains has been mentioned before. Of particular importance is the presence in the extant Śvetāmbara literature of one text whose major purpose is the exposition of non-Jain doctrines. That text is the *Sūtrakṛtāṅga Sūtra*.[5] Although it contains sections on subjects not related to non-Jain doctrines, the bulk of it is given over to accounting for various theories concerning the creation of the universe, the nature of the self, causality, and the like. The character of these expositions is generally polemic; therefore the *Sūtrakṛtāṅga* itself does not share the 363-account's concern for the problem of the existence of other viewpoints.

However, numerous passages in *Sūtrakṛtāṅga* are given above as sources for the 363-account. This chapter has been at some pains to show that, contrary to the impression given by prior studies, the 363-account does not exist in its full form until relatively late. At this point, however, the issue becomes more than a question of the growth of the account; it also has to do with the question of how and why the scattered elements of the account begin to be used to treat other viewpoints in a way that amounts to more than refutation.

Until the nature and function of those elements is more clearly shown, the particular character of the 363-account will not become clear. Yet it must be observed here that the scattered occurrences of the elements do not serve a purpose other than refutation. It is not until there are four headings, in *Sūtrakṛtāṅga* I.12 and the sources grouped with it in the diagram given above, that one can see something other than refutation becoming the function of these elements of the 363-account.

The fact that there is a detectable process here, a process that also involves a shift in the use of those elements, is an extremely important point in understand-

---

5 The lost twelth *Aṅga* has often been an object of speculation as to its content. Its title—*Dṛṣṭivāda* (*Diṭṭhivāya*)—has often led to conjecture that this *Aṅga* contained accounts of non-Jain doctrines. Albrecht Weber (1883-85:15[248]), 56-57[349-52]) raised the issue early on, based on the fact that the Jain tradition holds that certain portions of the *Dṛṣṭivāda* did indeed deal with certain heterodox groups. The fact that *diṭṭhi* is commonly used in Buddhist texts to denote heterodox positions undoubtedly played a role in such conjectures. The Jains hold that the *Dṛṣṭivāda* also contained the fourteen *Pūrva*s (*Puvva*s), the oldest statements of the Jina's teachings; according to the Jain accounts cited by Weber, the presence of accounts of heterodox doctrines are not the prime *raison d'être* of the *Aṅga*. The loss of the *pūrva*s is held to have spurred the collection and ordering of the remainder of the *Aṅga*s (see above, chapter 4), but this entire matter remains unclear. The notion that the *Dṛṣṭivāda* was a repository for heterodox opinions was advanced again by Schubring (1962:77-78) whose conclusions were restated and re-advocated by Alsdorf (1938:287). The upshot of their arguments was that *pūrva* may have originally stood for *pūrvapakṣa*; and Alsdorf in particular held that the loss of the *Aṅga* had to do with the later tradition's desire not to preserve heterodox opinions. This thesis is soundly denounced by Kapadia (1941:75ff.). For the purposes of this study, it seems quite fruitless to raise the issue again, especially as no new data can be brought to bear on it. [Editor's note.] See also Alsdorf 1973.

ing the 363-account. This process, furthermore, involves more than the account by itself. It also involves the striking fact that by the time of *Nandī Sūtra* (ca. 500 C.E.) the 363-account was used to characterize the whole of *Sūtrakṛtāṅga*. *Nandī Sūtra* includes a listing of the Śvetāmbara scriptures, with brief accounts of each; its account of *Sūtrakṛtāṅga*, itself examined below, uses the 363-account to summarize it.

This development especially points out the growing dominance of the 363-account, for it here replaces the entire catalogue of refutations in *Sūtrakṛtāṅga*. This implies, further, an important point concerning the particular nature of the 363-account. It must be asked whether it is sufficient to speak merely in terms of domination, or whether the growth in the account's importance does not also reflect a shift in the overall way in which non-Jain positions were viewed. In other words, does the growing influence of the 363-account reflect a process whereby the Jains no longer viewed other schools merely as positions to be refuted, but also as posing a larger problem of why other viewpoints should exist? The full answer to this question can only emerge from detailed study in the following two chapters.[6]

---

6 See chapter 18 for a presentation of the texts themselves.

16

THE 363-ACCOUNT: THE FOUR MAIN HEADINGS*

INTRODUCTION

The major goals of the preceding chapter were to show that the full 363-account is made up of a number of separate elements, and in so doing to show that this particular account came to exercise great influence in the Jain tradition as an account of other viewpoints. It seems quite clear from the evidence presented that the whole is a structure made up of various elements that enter into it at various points, and that the 363-account was being widely used to summarize non-Jain viewpoints. Its influence is perhaps nowhere better revealed than in the fact that the *Sūtrakṛtāṅga* is summarized, by the time of the *Nandī Sūtra*, solely in terms of the 363-account. In other words, the major Jain catalogue of other viewpoints is regarded by ca. 500 C.E. as having the 363-account as its major thrust.

This process of expansion and growing influence is the single major aspect of the 363-account that has escaped the other studies of it. As discussed at the beginning of the preceding chapter, these other studies have in effect treated the 363-account as a source of information for the period of Indian thought out of which it sprang. In so doing, they have undertaken little analysis of the account itself. It has been treated as if its contents were static, objective material, or as if

* From dissertation, pp. 119-72.

much of what it contains is pure polemic, and thus not worth attention. Prior study of the 363-account has rarely looked upon it as a phenomenon in its own right, and this failure to take it seriously in its own right has led to the overlooking of its dynamic aspects.

The previous chapter also sought to point out the varied elements themselves that come together to make up the full 363-account. Where that chapter stressed the independence of various elements, this chapter will examine the process by which those elements come to be a systematic whole. The analysis will focus on the elements in the account, namely, the four main headings (*kriyāvāda, akriyāvāda, ajñānikavāda, vainayikavāda*), and the elements within those headings. Once these elements have been discussed, the next chapter will re-examine the structure and the orientation of the entire account, including its terminology. The result should be a better understanding of this particular Jain attempt to come to grips with the existence of other viewpoints.

This examination of elements in the 363-account has two layers of material with which to work. The first layer is the four major headings themselves, and the second is the elements within those headings. It is the structure of the account as revealed in the preceding chapter that is the backdrop for this discussion. It has been shown that a general chronological pattern holds for the three elements—headings, number, and calculation—that make up groups A, B, and C. To quickly review the relationships between and within those groups: (A) Certain texts show *kriyā* alone, certain others *kriyā* coupled with *akriyā*. When all four headings begin to occur together, *ajñāna* and *vinaya* enter the scheme together. (B) The number 363 first occurs in relation to all four, and has no subtotals attached to it. Thereafter the subtotals appear, first in *Sūtrakṛtāṅga Niryukti*. (C) The calculation method adds the elements within the headings, which complete the full account.

Further, there is the larger framework of the development of the 363-account, which gives a crucial direction to this analysis. As has been noted earlier, the full account appears to concern itself not only with the refutation of other viewpoints, but also with reflection on the existence of other viewpoints. The latter factor does not appear to be present in the separate elements. This means that the elements that become the 363-account play two roles in the history of the full account: one as a tool for refutation, the other as part of a more general consideration of the existence of other views. In this chapter, these roles are referred to as roles outside of and within the 363-account, and in the difference between these roles lie significant clues to the peculiar nature of the full account.

This distinction of roles does not rest only on the perception of a peculiar nature or purpose in the full account. The material within the headings, as was seen when the whole 363-account was presented earlier, consists largely of categories and items from within the Jain tradition. The headings and numbers, as can be seen from the analysis in the last chapter, consists of materials that were once independent of the final, full account. Thus both layers of material do have roles both inside and outside the 363-account.

One can observe preliminarily that the existence of the elements within the headings in their non-363-account roles is something that is relatively easy to demonstrate and analyse. Therefore, one is readily able to see how they work in the scheme over against their functions in other settings. The existence of the four main headings outside the scheme is more problematic; their non-363-account roles are far more difficult to account for.

For simplicity's sake, the material can be handled in three blocs. *Kriyāvāda* and *akriyāvāda* have nearly identical forms in the account, and their roles outside the account are more visible. Thus they form one focal point. The other two headings—*ajñānikavāda* and *vainayikavāda*—differ from each other and from the first two both in terms of their structure within the account and their roles outside the account. Futher, their functions within the scheme do not receive much in the way of clear or useful justification from Jain authors. Because of these factors, each of these receives separate treatment.

These latter two headings appear to be the most artificial constructs in the entire 363-account. In fact, they seem to be the result of the need for a specific number of viewpoints and the search for some way of reaching that particular total. This artificiality shows clearly in the internal categories within the *vainayikavāda* heading. The former is treated first.

THE *AJÑĀNIKAVĀDA* HEADING

The internal elements in this heading, as found in the full 363-account, consist solely of formal categories from Jain thought, except for one: *utpatti*, origination. The remainder are simply the nine-fold version of the Jain *tattva*s and the seven elements of the *syādvāda*. Nine multiplied by seven equals 63; in order to make up the remainder, so as to have 67 *ajñānikavāda*s, *utpatti* is considered under four of the seven *syādvāda* elements.

The option under this heading can readily be made out: *asti jīvaḥ, nāsti jīvaḥ, astināsti jīvaḥ*, etc., applying each of the seven *syādvāda* elements to each of the nine *tattva*s, and the first four elements to *utpatti*. One possible interpretation of this way of presenting the *ajñānikavāda*'s options is to say that this is a defensible way of presenting the varieties of *ajñāna* that are possible. Two factors militate against this explanation. First, the problem of finding some way of adding four factors so as to reach a total of 67 is so inelegantly solved that one is led toward the conclusion that the number 67 was important enough to justify a bit of contortion. Second, the explanation of *ajñānikatva*, of the heading itself, that is generally given by the commentators is not related to the schematic presentation. Thus both layers of material—the heading and its internal elements—present points of interest that should be examined as concerns their roles inside and outside of the account.

First, in order to make up four additional options, the first four *syādvāda* elements—*sat, asat, sadasat, avaktavya*—are applied to *utpatti*. The commentators take various approaches to the implicit question of why only the first four elements should be applied to *utpatti*. Haribhadra does not explain this point at all.[1] Śīlāṅka on *Sūtrakṛtāṅga* I.12.1 says that the other three elements apply to parts of already existent things, but that the discussion here concerns origination itself, and thus only the first four apply.[2] Śīlāṅka's *Ācārāṅga* comment on this point is a bit different, but its thrust is the same. Abhayadeva on *Sthānāṅga* IV.4 and Malayagiri on *Nandī* 88 also raise the parts-versus-wholes point (Abhayadeva doing so with reference to the *Ācāraṭīkā*), but neither of them actually limits the discussion to *utpatti*. Instead, both of them discuss it with reference to the wider question of how the *syādvāda* functions.[3]

This point concerning the application of elements one through four only to wholes is true of the *syādvāda*'s function with relation to all entities (see Mehta 1971:170ff.); but this leaves the *utpatti*'s peculiar status quite unexplained. Even if one were to grant that *utpatti* is somehow a unitive element in a way that the other *tattva*s are not (a point that Schrader [1902:48] suggests might be reached by understanding the other three *syādvāda* elements as applicable to modes instead of to parts), one is left with the question of why *utpatti* should have been used to find the three extra options, and not something else.

The only readily apparent reason is that origination, in terms of causal principles, is an important feature of the *kriyāvāda* and *akriyāvāda* headings (as will be shown shortly), and thus an attempt was made to include it in this heading as well. However, there is still a distinct air of arbitrariness about this choice, since the Jain accounts of origination do not resemble the way that *utpatti* is used here;[4] and thus *utpatti* is still an odd element in the heading, since the other elements in it function within the scheme much as they do outside of it. Thus it is not only difficult to account for the fact that *utpatti* should involve only four options, but also difficult to account for its presence at all. This combination must make one very suspicious; the net effect is to heighten the impression that

---

1 See the translation in chapter 18.

2 See the translation in chapter 18.

3 For a fuller discussion of this commentary tradition on *utpatti* and the *syādvāda*, see Schrader 1902:47ff.

4 Cf. *Tattvārthādhigama* V.29(Ś), V.30(D), and the commentaries thereon.

the number 67 was a major factor in the development of the internal workings of this heading.

The second factor that makes it unlikely that the 67 options are simply a way of showing the varieties of *ajñāna* is the way that the commentators explain the heading itself. They are all given to the revealing practice of glossing the 67 positions in this way: "Who knows that the *jīva* (*ajīva*, etc.) exists (does not exist, etc.)? And what use is that knowledge?"[5] These glosses provide a particular vision of *ajñānikatva*, which is that *ajñāna* is not 67 varieties of error, but rather a certain attitude toward the problem of knowledge.

To make this point, i.e., to say that there is no use in knowing something, does not in any way require the 67-option structure. The only reasonable use of the structure would be to illustrate faulty knowledge. Yet this is the one explanation of *ajñāna* to which the commentators give the least attention. More than that, not one of them observes that the addition of the particle *syāt* to the 67 propositions would make them all correct in Jain terms; nor is there any hint that it is the unequivocal statement of any one option that makes it false.

From Haribhadra onward, two basic explanations are given for the *ajñāna* heading: (1) that *ajñāna* is equal to knowledge that is of poor quality, or faulty (*kutsitaṃ jñānam*), and thus that *ajñānika*s are those who possess such faulty knowledge; and (2) that *ajñānika*s are those who hold *ajñāna* to be a virtue, both because the quest for knowledge produces only confusion, contradiction, and bad feelings, and because acts that are done unreflectively do not carry resultant karma-bondage. Thus there are two positions within the latter explanation: scepticism and agnosticism.

The two basic explanations (ignorance and scepticism/agnosticism) are clearly very different from one another. Haribhadra is the only commentator to give much of an explanation of the former, i.e., of *ajñāna* as faulty knowledge, and he does so only in relation to a grammatical problem.[6] The others merely state the first possibility,[7] and then go on to carry out virtually the entire discussion of *ajñānikatva* in terms of the latter interpretation, i.e., in terms of *ajñāna* as scepticism or agnosticism. This is in direct contrast to the nature of *ajñāna* as presented in the older texts where it is discussed as part of the problem of other viewpoints, i.e., to *ajñāna*'s role outside the account. *Sūtrakṛtāṅga* I.1.2 and I.1.3 contain references to *ajñāna*, and of course *Sūtrakṛtāṅga* I.12 considers it as one of the *samosaraṇa*s. In all of these passages, *ajñāna* means ignorance or

---

5 See the translations of Haribhadra and Śīlāṅka in chapter 18.

6 See the translation in chapter 18.

7 It is notable that Malayagiri on *Nandī* 88 solves the grammatical problem that troubled Haribhadra by referring to a *sūtra* in Hemacandra's grammar. The implication is that he saw only grammatical ramifications in the problem, and none of the significance of the distinction between the two explanations of *ajñāna*.

error at base, compounded by the inability or unwillingness to see beyond such error.

This means that only the commentators' explanation of *ajñāna* as false or faulty knowledge is related to the sort of *ajñāna* that is presented in the texts themselves. The notion of *ajñāna* as ignorance is also presented in the Digambara *Tattvārthādhigama* commentaries excerpted in chapter 18. They show that there is fairly widespread occurrence of *ajñāna* as ignorance in Jain accounts of other viewpoints. Thus there is a distinct discrepancy between the role of *ajñāna* inside and outside the 363-account.

This discrepancy is one of the greatest incongruities in the 363-account. Jacobi, Schrader, and Barua have all taken much the same approach to the puzzle. All three have taken the position that the *syādvāda* is actually either the Jain response to sceptic opponents (Jacobi 1895a:xxvii ff.; Barua 1970:318ff.) or the result of outright borrowing from them (Schrader 1902:50-51). The internal elements in the *ajñāna* heading are seen as representing an actual sceptical viewpoint, and they are said to resemble the *syādvāda* because the latter is derived from that viewpoint. It has often been observed that the *syādvāda*'s seven propositions bear a distinct resemblance to the equivocating responses put into the mouth of Sañjaya Belaṭṭhiputta in the Buddhist accounts of the six arch-opponents of the Buddha. Jacobi (1895a:xxviiff.) is the most forthright exponent of the notion that Mahāvīra's response to Sañjaya was to take the latter's sceptical equivocation and turn it into a logical tool. (This is the actual context of Jacobi's oft-quoted remark, given at the outset of chapter 15, above.)

Barua is more ambitious, for he seeks to develop a full picture of scepticism in early Indian thought. He understands Sañjaya as a precursor who failed to carry his critical inquiry far enough, leaving to Mahāvīra and the Buddha the transformation of scepticism into critical inquiry (Barua 1970:331ff.). In the course of arguing these points, both Barua and Jacobi overlook certain important matters. First, as Schrader (1902:51) correctly observed, the Jain canonical texts do not present the *syādvāda* except in nascent terms. Nor, as has been noted, is the *ajñāna* of the older accounts of other viewpoints related to scepticisim; rather, it is error. Schrader does not relate the *syādvāda* directly to Sañjaya, as do others,[8] but he is still subject to the criticism that he failed to note that it is only the later commentary tradition that relates scepticism to the *syādvāda*, the formal element in Jain thought that resembles Sañjaya Belaṭṭhiputta's equivocation.

---

[8] Barua (1970:318) remarks, "Mahāvīra's expression Aṇṇāniya or Ajñānika has reference to Sañjaya and his school." The sole piece of evidence for this is the brief passage in *Uttarādhyayana* XVIII, given in chapter 18 of this study, where King Sañjaya is asked about the four headings. King Sañjaya is in no way a sceptic. Barua does not mention in any way the thinness of the evidence that he cites, and one must regard this Jain connection between *ajñāna* and Sañjaya as proving absolutely nothing.

Barua (1970:328-29) buttresses his connection between the *syādvāda* and Sañjaya by quoting the Buddhist account of the Amāra-*vikkhepa*s, or "Eel-wrigglers," which does bear a resemblance to portions of Śīlāṅka (and later commentators) on the issue of *ajñānikatva*. However, he omits those portions of the Jain commentaries that do not parallel the Buddhist version. The two traditions are alike in regarding sceptics as those who see no use in *jñāna*, but rather only increased argumentation and strife. However, the Jains go on to include agnosticism proper in the definition, i.e., *ajñāna* as not mere scepticism, but also a virtue in avoiding karma-bondage. This point is altogether overlooked by Barua. Indeed, it does not fit his notion of scepticism as the precursor and antithesis to critical inquiry.

The crucial point here is that the notion of *ajñāna* as a virtue, however expressed, is not something that the scheme of 67 options serves to illustrate. It is clear that the three scholars' treatments of *ajñāna* do not take into account the fact that the full 363-account is late, nor the fact that *ajñāna* as a heading in the 363-account appears to have existed before there was a need or a means for making out 67 varieties thereof. It is this need for 67 types of *ajñāna* that best explains the occurrence under this heading of the seven-part *syādvāda* and the other, clumsy elements in it, not any direct connection between the heading and the *syādvāda*, such a direct connection being the major premise of the other treatments.

To summarize, the internal elements in the *ajñāna* heading appear to have only one role in the 363-account itself, which is to permit the creation of 67 options. As to the original sense of the heading alone, the best guide seems to be the usage of *ajñāna* in other Jain texts, where the word means error, and the explanation of *ajñāna* that is given in other Jain accounts such as the five-fold scheme in the *Tattvārthādhigama* commentaries. This original sense and the commentary tradition's introduction of scepticism and agnosticism into it in the 363-account will be treated more fully in the next chapter. For the moment, analysis of the structure of the heading has at least clarified the roles of its various elements and cleared the way for further study.

One more observation is important. It has been noted that since the scheme of 67 options represents the *syādvāda* minus *syāt*, one might expect that somewhere some commentator would raise the issue of unequivocalness versus equivocalness as a basic difference between *ajñāna* and *jñāna*. Yet this occurs nowhere. One might expect that, since a set of seven categories was needed here in order to construct the scheme, the *nayavāda* might have been introduced. This may be a fairly useful point in the debate over how and to what extent the *nayavāda* was understood as a tool for dealing with non-Jain viewpoints.

THE *VAINAYIKAVĀDA* HEADING

It was pointed out earlier that the categories in the *vainayikavāda* heading are the major index to its artificiality, though its outside role is also problematic. The character of this heading is very different from the other three in that its constituent elements are not familiar categories or groups of categories from within the Jain tradition. As given in chapter 15 above, the *vainayikavāda* consists of 32 options. Four means of *vinaya* exist: voice, body, mind (*manas*), and charity. There are eight proper objects for *vinaya*: deity, ruler, ascetic, sage, elder, inferior, mother, and father. These multiplied by each other yield 32 options.

The commentators explain this heading more briefly than any other, and take the view that its flaw is its claim to be the only means to release. This explanation is consistent with the fact that the heading and its options are not negatively formulated, in contradistinction to the *ajñānikavāda*. Beyond this, it is difficult to analyze, or to find a *raison d'être* for, this heading, or a role for it outside the 363-account.

Within the Jain tradition, the term *vinaya* is not given a prominent place in formulations of monastic and lay disciplines, though *Uttarādhyayana* I and *Sūtrakṛtāṅga* I.14 discuss it quite fully in a sense that has nothing to do with it as an alternative viewpoint or school of thought. Umāsvāti considers *vinaya* briefly as one of the six types of internal austerities that are part of the assorted means to achieving *nirjarā*, or decay of karma already associated with the *jīva*.[9] Umāsvāti also gives four objects for *vinaya: jñāna, darśana, cāritra*, and *upacārāḥ*.[10] The first three are the basic categories of the Jain *mokṣamārga*. The sense of *vinaya* in relationship to them is generally taken to mean sincere dedication.[11] The fourth object is glossed by the *Svabhāṣya* and by Pūjyapāda and others to mean the general practices involved in doing homage to the leaders of the Order and to other such prominent persons.[12] This sense of *vinaya* begins to encroach on the next element in the list of internal austerities, which is *vaiyāvṛttya*, or respectful service.[13] Here one finds lists of objects that correspond more to those given in the *vainayikavāda* heading. But these are not the objects of *vinaya* proper.

---

9 *Tattvārthādhigama* IX.20; the term for internal austerity is *uttara tapas. Nirjarā* is the step after *saṃvara*, the point where the influx of karma is stopped or slowed. See above, chapter 15. Cf. von Glasenapp (1925:208ff.), where the term used for internal austerity is *ābhyantaratapas*.

10 *Tattvārthādhigama* IX.23.

11 See Pūjyapāda's comments (S. A. Jain 1960:264).

12 *Tattvārthādhigama Svabhāṣya*, p. 202; Pūjyapāda, *Sarvārthasiddhi* on *Tattvārthādhigama*, p. 338.

13 *Tattvārthādhigama* IX.24.

Within the realm of lay-prescriptions, *vinaya* is expanded and elaborated, generally in close relationship to *vaiyāvṛttya*; both are often placed within the notion of *vātsalya,* which serves as a general rubric for the services and respect paid to each other by all the members of the Jain community, monastic and lay alike (see Williams 1963:241ff.). However, in none of the elaborations of *vinaya, vaiyāvṛttya*, or *vātsalya* does there occur a list of objects or modes that matches the items in the heading as given in the 363-account.

The four means by which *vinaya* may be done also are not matched anywhere in the standard discussions. The triad of voice, body, and mind occurs constantly in the Jain tradition; nor can one doubt the importance of charity (*dāna*) for the Jains, for on this relationship between members of the tradition rests the whole life-style of the Jain monk. But these items do not occur as a tetrad in the standard expositions of *vinaya*, or of *dāna*, or in cases where the voice-body triad is prominently used.

Thus one cannot find a direct correspondence between *vinaya* in the 363-account and in the general discussions of it as it pertains to the ordering of the Jain community. However, there is one further notion of *vinaya* to be found in Jain texts, which is the one expressed in the Digambara commentaries on *Tattvārthādhigama* VIII.1, which are given in chapter 18, below. There the *vinaya* is given as one of five varieties of *mithyādarśana*, and the commentaries understand it to mean not differentiating between faith in one or another deity of teaching. This occurrence of *vinaya* seems quite anomalous, and the commentators do not relate it to the discussions that have to do with the community.

The thrust of these observations is that the heading itself, *vinaya*, as an alternative viewpoint, has only the slimmest of connections with the larger Jain tradition—that connection being the problematic Digambara comments just mentioned. Further, this is not at all the sense given to the heading by the Śvetāmbara commentaries on the 363-account. The commentators' understanding of *vinaya* appears, rather, to conform to *vinaya*'s general sense as subsumed under *vaiyāvṛttya* and *vātsalya*. But if that be the case, one wonders why the internal elements of the heading bear little relationship to the categories used in the standard expositions. In the end, there would seem to be no external justification for the limits put onto the instruments and objects of *vinaya* save for the requirements that the whole total 32.

Yet even though one might be satisfied that the internal workings of this heading are arbitrary, there remains the riddle of the existence at all of this fourth heading. This point is not spoken to by the commentators, nor by the texts themselves, nor have other studies of the 363-account been able to explain it even in the way that they attempted to account for the *ajñāna* heading. The texts themselves provide virtually no clues. Aside from the inclusion of *vinaya* in the usual listings of the four headings, the only text that provides any hint of its content is *Sūtrakṛtāṅga* I.12.3-4. The passage in question is almost impossible to translate, simply because it is unclear just what the referents of the terms are. Jacobi and Schubring have produced very different versions.

Jacobi 1895b:316:

> Believing truth to be untruth, and calling a bad man good, the various upholders of Vinaya, asked about it, explain their tenet. (3)
>
> Without perceiving the truth they speak thus: this object (viz. Moksha) is realised by us thus (viz. by Vinaya). [4a]

Schubring has radically amended the text, and translates so as to attach the first part of verse three to the *ajñānikavāda*, which is described just prior to the verses on *vinaya*.

Schubring 1926:150; bracketed inserts are his:

> 3a. indem sie das Wahre für unwahr ansehen [und] das Schlechte gut nennen.
>
> 3b. [c.] Welche Leute [aber] ferner, als die nicht wenigen Verfechter der frommen Lebensführung, wenn [von Ungutem] auch nur berührt, [ihr] Wesen in der Tat zu frommer Art erzogen haben, 4a. die sagen: "'[ihr sollt] keine Neu-Sāṃkhya [sein]', so spricht diese Frage [der Weltanschauung zu uns]."[14]

Schubring's translation seems cumbersome, and his use of the notion of neo-Sāṃkhya[15] in order to make sense of the passage seems a bit farfetched, given the point on which it turns, particularly in a textual tradition as problematic as that of *Sūtrakṛtāṅga*. Further, the linking of verse 3a to *ajñāna* is not necessary save for his own understanding of the heading. After the analysis that follows, it should seem reasonable to take the verse as Jacobi does.

---

14 [Editor's Translation.]

> 3a. in that they consider what is true false [and] call what is bad good.
>
> 3b. [c.] The people who [however] moreover, as the many advocates of the pious way of life, even if only touched [by something which is not good], have trained [their] being in fact in a pious manner, 4a. say: "'[You should] not be Neo-Sāṃkhya,' thus this question [of worldview] speaks to us."

The text reads:

> saccam asaccam iti cintayantā, asāhu sāhutti udāharantā jeme jaṇā veṇaiyā aṇege, puṭṭhāvi bhāvaṃ viṇaiṃsu ṇāma (3)
>
> aṇovasamkhā iti te udāhū, aṭṭhe sa obhāsai amha evam (4a)

15 Schubring (1926:150): "*aṇovasaṃkhā* [in text] ist auf *anaupasāṃkhyāḥ* zurückzuführen, nicht mit Śīl. auf *anupasaṃkhyā*, und auch nicht mit Jacobi =*anupasaṃkhyāya* zu setzen. 'Neu-Sāṃkhya,' unserm Worte 'Neu-Buddhisten' nachgebildet, will Anhänger der philosophischen Theorie im Gegensatze zu solchen der frommen Praxs bezeichnen, als welche die Vainayika gelten wollen."

[Editor's Translation.] *aṇovasaṃkhā* [in the text] is to be derived from *anaupasāṃkhyāḥ*, not following Śīlāṅka from *anupasaṃkhyā*, and also not following Jacobi as equivalent to *anupasaṃkhyāya*. "Neo-Sāṃkhya," our imitation of the term "Neo-Buddhist," is intended to denote a follower of the philosophical theory in contrast to the religious practice, as indicated by Vainayika.

Jacobi's only real attempt to explain the heading comes in the parenthetical glosses in his translation. Here he is simply relying on Śīlāṅka.[16] Schrader (1902:12-13) also goes no further than to reproduce the opinions of Malayagiri and Śīlāṅka (the latter likely being Malayagiri's source). Śīlāṅka does quote a verse in connection with the calculation, which is discussed below.

Barua, as with *ajñāna*, is more ambitious. He equates the Jain *vinayavāda* with the Buddhist *sīlabbata*, and extends the general notion of proper conduct as an alternative viewpoint into the entire Indian corpus of writings on *dharma*, *nīti*, and *kāma* (Barua 1970:332ff.) Whether this *tour de force*, based almost exclusively on Buddhist materials, is successful or not is not the issue here. The point is that Barua's approach says nothing about the *vinaya* heading in the 363-account.

The crux of the problem with regard to *vinaya* is, then, two-fold, involving both layers of material. First, as has been seen, the internal components of the heading do not square with the categories in the Jain discussions of *vinaya*. They can, and likely should, be explained by the fact that the number 32 was a desideratum. The heading itself, however, is more of a problem. Again, the Digambara commentaries on *Tattvārthādhigama* VIII.1 deserve notice in that they preserve a notion of *vinaya* that may have some connection with the laconic passage in *Sūtrakṛtāṅga* I.12, but this is all the purely Jain evidence that there is at present.

Outside of the Jain texts, however, there does exist a major piece of evidence attesting the independent existence of a notion of *vinaya* that has to do with other viewpoints. This evidence is drawn from several Pali Buddhist texts, notably *Dīgha Nikāya* I.4-5 (*Brahmajāla Sutta* 9) and its parallel at *Majjhīma Nikāya* III.49, and from *Dīgha Nikāya* III.135, 175 (*Pāsādika Suttanta* 28, and *Lakkhaṇa Suttanta* II.25). The first of these comes from within the section also known as the *Sīlakkhanda*, which is an important source for Barua's inferences concerning the *sīlabbata*; but Barua has failed to note that the term *vinayavādī* also occurs in this passage.

Moreover, the term is placed, here and in other sources, within a list of terms that have apparently foiled the various translators of the texts. The terms are: *kālavādī*, *bhūtavādī*, *atthivādī*, *dhammavādī*, and *vinayavādī*. Two of these are immediately recognizable as items from within the 363-account. *Bhūtavādī* also occurs in some other Jain accounts of other schools. So far as the present sources are concerned, *atthivādī* and *dhammavādī* are not directly attested, although *atthivādī*, in the absence of direct evidence to the contrary, can be read *astivādī*, perhaps in the sense of *Sūtrakṛtāṅga Niryukti*'s gloss of *kriyāvādī*.[17]

---

16 See the translation in chapter 18.

17 See translation of *Sūtrakṛtāṅga Niryukti* 118, in chapter 18.

The various translators of the Pali texts have generally taken *atthivādī* to be *arthavādī*, and have paraphrastically translated the remainder of the terms. T. W. Rhys Davids (*Dīgha Nikāya*, p. 5) translates:

> Gotama the recluse . . . [speaks] in season . . . , in accordance with the facts, words full of meaning, on the disciple of the Order.

I. B. Horner (*Majjhima Nikāya*, p. 97) makes it:

> He is one that speaks at a right time, in accordance with fact, about the goal, about *dhamma*, about discipline.

T. W. and C. A. F. Rhys Davids (*Dīgha Nikāya*, pp. 126-27):

> [He] is a prophet of the hour, a prophet of fact, a prophet of good, a prophet of the Norm, a prophet of the Discipline.

It is clear that the translators had no more reference within the Buddhist tradition to what these terms might mean than has this study within the Jain tradition for the meaning of the term *vinaya*. Nor has the Buddhist commentary tradition any more help to offer than the Jain. Yet it seems clear that these terms do not mean what they are translated to mean. It seems quite clear that they all have reference to alternative teachings. This inference is supported primarily by the fact that they duplicate, in three cases, terms that have such a meaning within the Jain tradition.

The settings of the Buddhist passages are also important to this conclusion. *Dīgha Nikāya* I.4-5 (and its parallel) occurs in a discussion of what a non-Buddhist might say of the Buddha; the phrase at issue here is just such a statement by an outsider. The passage is apparently understood by the Buddhist tradition and by the translators (T. W. Rhys Davids and Horner) as being a case of an outsider saying things that are true, but not really descriptive of the Buddhist position. This is the framework that the *Dīgha Nikāya* provides for the statement and the larger series of remarks of which it is a part (see Barua 1970:334).

Dīgha Nikāya III.135 is even more intriguing, for it is part of a Buddhist discussion of how the Jains fared after Mahāvīra's death. It discusses the qualities of a teacher, of his knowledge, and of the art of his teaching, and then ranges into the details of proper teachings, including spells and prophecies. (This is surely the context in which T. W. and C. A. F. Rhys Davids, above, chose to translate *-vādī* by "prophet.") The important point is that this passage again has as its larger setting the discussion of one viewpoint by another. *Dīgha Nikāya* III.175 is a discussion of the characteristics of great persons, in which the phrase is once again translated by "prophet" (T. W. and C. A. F. Rhys Davids, *Dīgha Nikāya*, p. 163). The translators, in their introduction to the passage, note that this is a thoroughly heterogenous text, where old materials have been gathered into a new setting (T. W. and C. A. F. Rhys Davids, *Dīgha Nikāya*, pp. 132ff.).

It is certainly hazardous to guess at what layers of material may be incorporated into various Pali texts, but the phrase itself certainly seems to be a separable element, and it does not seem unlikely that it is older than the final texts into which it is set. It is even more striking that the texts should share so common a general context, namely, the discussion of other viewpoints. These references alone provide a valuable confirmation of the independent existence of *vinayavāda* as a category in such discussions, and make it likely that the heading did not first spring into existence at the points in *Sūtrakṛtāṅga* and elsewhere where it and *ajñāna* join *kriyā* and *akriyā* to make up the full set of four 363-account headings. However, its settings in the Buddhist texts still do not provide any real further information on the significance of the term.

Yet there is one further set of Buddhist texts from which some further help might be gotten. The passages in question are found at *Aṅguttara Nikāya* IV.172ff. (*Aṅguttara Nikāya, Mahā-Vagga* XI-XII), and in certain parallel passages, some of which will be discussed shortly in another connection. In these passages the context is again striking. Two dialogues are involved. In the first, a Brāhmaṇa from Verañjā comes to see the Buddha and asks him about the truth of a number of things that are said of him. In the second, Sīha, a Jain layman, goes to the Buddha and puts one question to him, also asking if certain statements concerning his teachings are true. In reply, the Buddha gives nearly the same statement to each man. In sum, the general context is once again the statements concerning one viewpoint that might be made by outsiders.

The issues raised by the Brāhmaṇa are: (1) that the Buddha shows no respect to venerable and aged Brāhmaṇas; (2) that the Buddha is *arasarūpa*, which the translator, Hare (p. 118), takes to mean "lacks taste," roughly in the sense of taking no pleasure in things, though both he and the commentary tradition clearly find the term hard to explain; (3) that the Buddha is *nibhoga*, which is taken to mean that he lacks property or social status; (4) that the Buddha is *akiriyavādo*, which is truly of interest and will be taken up shortly; (5) that the Buddha is an *ucchedavādo*, which is taken to mean "annihilationist" in the sense of one who teaches that the self perishes with the body; (6) that the Buddha is *jegucchī*, i.e., that he feels abhorrence; (7) that the Buddha is a *venayiko*, the point of particular interest for this discussion; (8) that the Buddha is a *tapassī*, one given to rigorous ascetic praxis; and (9) that the Buddha is *apagabbho*, which is taken to mean that he opposes the notion that proper behavior leads to rebirth in higher stations.[18]

---

18 For more details on these, see Hare, *Aṅguttara Nikāya*, pp. 117ff.

Sīha, the Jain, raises the question of whether the Buddha is an *akiriyavādo.* In reply, the Buddha speaks to (1) *akiriyavādo,* (2) *kiriyavādo,* (3) *ucchedavādo,* (4) *jegucchī,* (5) *venayiko,* (6) *tapassī,* (7) *apagabbho,* and (8) *assattho* (the latter taken to mean a "doctrine of consolation").[19]

Both of these passages will figure again in the discussion of *kriyā* and *akriyā*; for the present, they once again testify to the prior existence of *vinaya* in the context of attempts to deal with other viewpoints. In neither of them, however, is it readily possible to make out the content of the term, although they may make possible an hypothesis, as follows.

It has been noted above that the more common Jain approach to the term is that it signifies an attitude of respectful service to co-religionists. Also noted was the existence of *vinaya* as respect and discipline in the sense of possessing proper *darśana, jñāna,* and *cāritra.* Finally, the sole textual gloss of *vinaya* (*Sūtrakṛtāṅga* I.12.3-4) seems to state that it is the inversion or absence of certain values, as when one holds untruth to be truth and unholy to be holy (taking the verse as Jacobi takes it). The Digambara *Tattvārthādhigama* commentaries seem to hew to this line, calling it a position that does not differentiate between viewpoints and deities, while the Śvetāmbara commentary tradition seems to be able to deal with it only in that it is held by some to be the only way to *mokṣa.*

The Buddhist reference to *vinaya* and *venayiko,* above, appear to have been understood by Buddhaghoṣa—and thus by the translators—as meaning the abolition of social values and morality.[20] The Buddha's response to the allegation that he is a *venayiko* is ambiguous; Hare takes the term to mean "abolitionist," and translates the Buddha's answer as follows (Hare, *Aṅguttara Nikāya,* p. 119; elipses his):

> '. . . Brāhman, I preach the doctrine of abolishing lust, hatred and infatuations; I teach the Dhamma of abolishing all evil and sinful conditions. Rightly might one say . . . : "The recluse Gotama is an abolutionist," but not in the way you mean.'

If one takes *Sūtrakṛtāṅga* I.12.3-4 as Jacobi takes it, associating the inversion of values with the *vainayika*s, one can perceive a glimmer of common ground between this Jain category and the (perhaps) garbled notion that the Buddhist tradition preserves of the term *venayiko.* The version presented by the Digambara commentaries is then one step removed from this, in that it perceives the *vinaya* type of *mithyādarśana* to be the absence in the realm of deity and principle. It is possible, though not certain, that the Digambara notion may

19 See Hare, *Aṅguttara Nikāya,* pp. 125ff.

20 Hare, *Aṅguttara Nikāya,* pp. 119; Barua 1970:333 (where he passes an unsubstantiated judgement on Buddhaghoṣa). For Buddhaghoṣa's interpretation, s.v. *vinaya, venayika* in Rhys Davids and Stede: 1921-25:623, 648.

belong in the same general arena as the Buddhist and *Sūtrakṛtāṅga* notions of *vinayavāda*.

More important than this hypothesis concerning the content of the term is the point observed before, that the Buddhist tradition provides confirmation of the existence of *vinayavāda* as a category for discussing opposing viewpoints. This explains the presence of *vinaya* in the four headings far better than can the Śvetāmbara commentary tradition, which seems to know only the sense of "reverential service," and which further seems to have constructed the internal elements in such a way as to create 32 options, with little regard for the significance of the heading.

Again, these must be regarded as tentative conclusions; but they are certainly more useful than what the commentaries supply. In sum, this puzzling heading in the 363-account gains a good deal of intelligibility viewed in this light. How it relates to the whole, however, remains to be taken up. This cannot be done without reference to the structure of the whole and its settings, and these aspects will be explored after the other two headings have been anaylyzed.

THE *KRIYĀ*- AND *AKRIYĀVĀDA* HEADINGS

As was shown in the schematic diagram of the 363-account and in the texts presented in chapter 15, these two headings comprise the earliest textual references that the later tradition saw as referring to the 363-account. An early notion of a distinction between viewpoints as *kriyā*- or *akriyāvāda*s thus seems to be indicated by the pattern of the sources, a dual notion that seems to procede the four-fold pattern that emerges when *ajñāna* and *vinaya* enter the picture.

The previous discussions in this chapter have revealed a distinction between the functions of *ajñāna* and *vinaya* outside of and within the full 363-account, largely by means of examining the roles of internal elements and the headings themselves. Here the same approach can be used fruitfully, again for both layers of material. But in this case it is more valuable to begin with the headings and to devote more attention to them, because these two headings are known outside of the four-fold scheme as tools for evaluation and refutation. This creates a different sort of problem than was presented by the other two headings.

Chapter 15 noted five sources that mention only *kriyāvāda* or only it and *akriyāvāda*:

> *Ācārāṅga* I.1.1 (*kriyā* alone)
> *Sūtrakṛtāṅga* I.12.24 (*kriyā* alone)
> *Sūtrakṛtāṅga* I.10.16-17 (*kriyā* and *akriyā*)
> *Ācāradaśāḥ* VI (*kriyā* and *akriyā*)

Sūtrakṛtāṅga II.1 passim (*kriyā* and *akriyā*)

All remaining texts in groups A and B mention all four headings. (One, *Uttarādhyayana* XVIII, preserves mention of all four and mention of *kriyā* and *akriyā*.)

The first point to note is that except for *Sūtrakṛtāṅga* II.1 the texts in this group are uniform on one crucial point: they all speak of *kriyāvāda* as a correct view. (The apparent exception posed by *Sūtrakṛtāṅga* II.1 will become clear later.) The first two texts in the list contrast *kriyāvāda* with assorted other views; the next two contrast it with *akriyāvāda*. Since these texts are the older sources, it would appear that before *kriyā* and *akriyā* were part of the larger four-fold pattern, they functioned as a basic way of stating the difference between Jain and non-Jain positions.

The texts that mention all four headings are not uniform on this point. In some cases, *kriyāvāda* is presented as the correct view and the other three are treated as incorrect. In others, all four headings are regarded as non-Jain positions. Those that either implicitly or explicitly retain the notion of *kriyāvāda* as correct are:

Sūtrakṛtāṅga I.6.27
Sūtrakṛtāṅga I.12
Uttarādhyayana XVIII
Bhagavatī XXX.1
Sthānāṅga IV.4
Sūtrakṛtāṅga Niryukti 117b-121

Those that reject all four headings are:

Sūtrakṛtāṅga II.2.79
Bhāvapāhuḍa 135, 140
Tattvārthādhigama Svabhāṣya VII.18, VIII.1
Nandī 88
Pūjyapāda, *Sarvārthasiddha* on *Tattvārthādhigama* VIII.1
Akalaṅka, *Tattvārthavastika* on *Tattvārthādhigama* VIII.1
Bhāskaranandin, *Sukhabodha* on *Tattvārthādhigama* VIII.1
Śrutasāgara, *Tattvārthavṛtti* on *Tattvārthādhighama* VIII.1

The texts in group C, where the full 363-account first occurs, uniformly reject, explicitly or implicitly, all 363 as being non-Jain positions. Since this group of texts includes some commentaries on sources that do not reject all the headings, the commentators are often involved in the task of explaining or overcoming a contradiction. The one most directly faced with the problem was Śīlāṅka, who wrote the extant comments on the texts that most directly present *kriyāvāda* as a correct position. His way of solving this problem is very important for an understanding of the 363-account and of other Jain attempts to deal with the existence of non-Jain viewpoints. For the moment, it is simply useful to note that while the texts commonly present *kriyāvāda* as correct, Śīlāṅka does not see it as correct; and since Jacobi was relying on Śīlāṅka, this fact caused considerable confusion in his translations, as may be seen in his notes to the *Sūtrakṛtāṅga* and *Uttarādhyanana* passages that mention *kriyāvāda*.[21]

Based on this significant discrepancy alone, one can already say that a difference between the roles of the headings inside and outside of the full 363-account has been discovered. However, the matter is not so simple that it can be left at that, since the early sources for the notion of *kriyāvāda* apparently give the term a certain content. Thus one is faced with the difficulty of explaining how this notion could cease, in the later sources, to be understood as referring to the Jain position. Solving this problem requires a very careful look at those sources and at the apparent meaning of the term in them. In *Ācārāṅga* I.1.1, *Sūtrakṛtāṅga* I.1.2.24, and *Sūtrakṛtāṅga* I.10.16-17, *kriyāvāda* apparently means the following: the self exists, is involved in activity, and is ultimately responsible for its acts; in fact, it suffers karma-bondage in consequence of careless activity. *Akriyāvāda* is basically the reverse, on one or more points, of this general position.

It certainly must be admitted, however, that such a concise definition of *kriyāvāda* owes a good deal to etymology and careful reading of the context in which the term occurs. The term itself is seldom glossed, and when it is, the sense is not altogether clear. *Ācārāṅga* I.1.1, for example, is genuinely concerned with the existence of an on-going self; but the term *kriyāvādī* merely occurs in that context, and is not explained. *Sūtrakṛtāṅga* I.1.2.24 says that *kriyāvāda* has been declared before (or, "of old"), and that according to it, those who pay no heed to karma stay longer in *saṃsāra*. *Sūtrakṛtāṅga* I.10.16-17 only mentions *kriyā* and *akriyā* in the context of the various opinions of men, though by stretching the context, *kriyāvāda* can be understood as opposing a notion of the self as inactive. However, *kriyāvāda* is not actually set into opposition to that notion. A similar setting is presented in *Sūtrakṛtāṅga* II.1.17, 24, 28, and 32, where *kriyā* and *akriyā* are paired in a list of options. *Uttarādhyanana* XVIII.33 only says that a wise man accepts *kriyā*, not *akriyā*. *Ācāradaśāḥ* VI, which would appear to be rich in content, is a problematic source. As noted in chapter 15, Schubring thinks that it is an interpolation. Its context and content do not match the others, and though it is important in other ways, it does not seem wise to use it as a source for the meaning of *kriyā* and *akriyā*.

Texts that mention *kriyāvāda* and *akriyāvāda* as part of the four headings add a bit more. *Sūtrakṛtāṅga Niryukti* 118 glosses the two by *atthi* (*asti*) and

21 See especially Jacobi 1895b:83, 319.

natthi (*nāsti*), but says no more. *Sūtrakṛtāṅga* I.12, which is the longest exposition of the headings, gives the most information, summing up *kriyāvāda* and *akriyāvāda* in fairly concrete terms. *Akriyāvāda* is said to entail the denial of karma and its transmission, and the general view of an *akriyāvādī* is put thus in verse 7:

> There rises no sun, nor does it set; there waxes no moon, nor does it wane; there are no rivers running, nor any winds blowing; the whole world is ascertained to be unreal.[22]

Kriyāvāda is then summed up in terms of acceptance of karma and *saṃsāra*, of non-injury, of proper behavior, and finally, in verse 21, in terms of knowing certain things, three of these being Jain *tattvas*: *āsrava, saṃvara*, and *nirjarā*. The age of *Sūtrakṛtāṅga* I.12 will be considered shortly, though it can be said here that it is apparently younger than the other passages. In any case, it is more an exposition of common Jain doctrines than of the notions embodied in *kriyāvāda*, or in a doctrine whose chief feature one would expect to be "activity."

The other early sources have little or nothing to add to these bits of information. If one adds all of this together, one can arrive at the general definition given above, which corresponds to the definition usually found in the later sources. However, it is certainly not concise nor carefully delimited, and its multi-faceted nature was one of the factors that allowed the commentators to solve the discrepancy between *kriyāvāda* as correct and an incorrect view. (To a large extent, in fact, it is the case that the commentators supplied the general definition. Their ability to work with and around it must, then, be examined with some care. Just how the various aspects of *kriyāvāda* were interpreted by the later tradition will be seen more clearly in the next chapter, where the commentators' solutions are examined.) There appears, then, to exist a paradox of sorts, in that the sense of *kriyāvāda* seems to have been altered radically in the course of the Jain tradition.

Such a conclusion, however, requires a particular premise, that *kriyāvāda* is actually synonymous with the Jain position. It has been shown that, so far as content is concerned, a rough equivalence can be made out, but that the earliest sense of *kriyāvāda* is very difficult to pin down. But more important than the bits of content supplied by the early sources is the fact that *kriyāvāda*'s role is what changes, not its content.

That this is the case can be shown in stages, again with the aid of Buddhist sources. In the first stage, *kriyāvāda* appears as one of a number of ways of describing the position. In the second, it is contrasted with *akriyāvāda*, though

---

22 Jacobi's (1895b:317) translation; cf. Schubring 1926:151.

neither it nor its opposite always occurs alone. In the third stage comes the final transformation, where *kriyāvāda* becomes the Jain position. Only after this is it rejected in the later tradition.

For the first stage, Jain sources are scanty, but Buddhist texts aid considerably. *Kriyāvāda* as one of several terms used of a proper position occurs in the first text introduced in chapter 15, *Ācārāṅga* I.1.1. There this summary statement occurs: "Such a one is an *ātmavādī*, a *lokavādī*, a *karmavādī*, a *kriyāvādī*." This appears to be a stylized statement,[23] as most of it is not closely related to the discussion in which it is set. Only "*ātmavādī*" actually follows from what has been said in that section of *Ācārāṅga*.

At this point, Buddhist texts can assist, for this impression of *Ācārāṅga* passage as a formula is re-inforced by a passage from the *Soṇadaṇḍa-Sutta* of the *Dīgha Nikāya* (I.115), where the Brāhmaṇa Soṇadaṇḍa praises the Buddha by saying, "Indeed, the *śramaṇa* Gautama is a *karmavādī*, a *kriyāvādī*; he puts not-doing-ill foremost in his teachings to Brāhmans." The *Vinayapiṭaka, Mahāvagga* I.38.11 adds another such statement when it describes the procedures to be followed when certain types of persons seek admission to the Order. It states that if Aggikas or Jaṭilakas seek admission, they are to be given the *upasampāda* ordination (to full privileges in the Order), and no *parivāso* (probationary period) is required. It then reads (*Vinayapiṭaka, Mahāvagga* I.38.11): "What is the reason for this? O Bhikkus, they are *karmavādīs*, *kriyāvādīs*."[24]

There is yet another formula-statement in the Buddhist scriptures, this time put into the mouth of the Buddha himself in the *Aṅguttara Nikāya* (*Tika Nipāta, Yodhājīva Vagga*). Here, a contrast is expressed between the *kriyāvāda* of the Buddha and the *akriyā*-doctrine of Makkhali Gosāla:

> O monks, Makkhali—that infatuated man—proclaims thus, holds such a view: there is no deed (karma), there is no action (*kriyā*), there is no virtue (*vīrya*) . . .
>
> O monks, all those who in the past were *arhat*s, fully enlightened ones, exalted ones all—they were all *karmavādīs*, *kriyāvādīs*, *vīryavādīs* . . .
>
> O monks, I myself, who am now an *arhat*, a fully enlightened one, I am a *karmavādī*, a *kriyāvādī*, a *vīryavādī*.[25]

The classic Buddhist statement on Makkhali (*Dīgha Nikāya, Sāmaññaphala Sutta*) does not set up such a contrast; it rather emphasizes the antinomian fatalism more commonly associated with the Ājīvika teachings.

---

23 Schubring, in his edition of the *Ācārāṅga* (p.1) sets the text of this particular statement as a separate paragraph, without divulging the reasons for doing so; this is not, however, the sole reason for regarding this as a separable element.

24 Translation: T. W. Rhys Davids and Oldenberg, *Vinayapiṭaka*, pp. 190-91. The identification of the proper names in the passage does not seem to be possible at present.

25 *Aṅguttara Nikāya* I.286-287 (middle paragraph omitted).

The combined effect of the *Ācārāṅga* passage and the Buddhist texts is to confirm the broader role of *kriyāvāda* outside the 363-account, and to raise the possibility that the term had something of a stylized role in the description of a proper stance, be it Buddhist or Jain. It is very important to bear this in mind, for scholars have often overlooked this possibility, and have regarded *kriyāvāda* as expressing only the Jain position. Therefore, when one comes to the second stage mentioned above—*kriyā* paired with *akriyā*—it has often been taken for granted that the pair refers exclusively to Jain and non-Jain stances, respectively. Barua (1970:196, 383, et passim) is quite unequivocal on this, as is Schrader (1902:6-7 et passim). Some interpreters of the Buddhist tradition have also laid heavy emphasis on *kriyāvāda* as the quintessence of the Jain position, often giving it a sense approaching "salvation by works," (see, for example, E. J. Thomas 1949:207).

However, the Jain texts that pair the two are not so clear on this point. Recall the following: *Sūtrakṛtāṅga* I.10.16-17 places the pair in the context of the various opinions that men hold; *Ācāradaśāḥ* VI is not a clear source; *Sūtrakṛtāṅga* II.1.17 (and parallels) gives this pair along with five other pairs of terms; *Sūtrakṛtāṅga* II.1.30 pairs them alone, but in a *niyativādī*'s *pūrvapakṣa*; *Uttarādhyayana* XVIII pairs them alone, but in a verse with a very general thrust, not one that identifies them as referring to Jain and non-Jain positions.

Thus the temptation to see *kriyāvāda* and *akriyāvāda* in the way that Barua and the others have viewed them should be avoided. In fact, there is further evidence against such an identification, particularly against the notion that the Jain position is equivalent to the *kriyāvāda*, although it has commonly been interpreted to buttress such an identification. This evidence has to do with the tale of Sīha, the Jain layman who wishes to question the Buddha, which was introduced earlier in connection with *vinaya*. When Sīha expresses his desire to Mahāvīra, the latter's response is:

> Sīha, how is it that you, who profess *kriyā*, wish to go and see the *śramaṇa* Gautama, who is an *akriyāvādī*? Sīha, the *śramaṇa* Gautama is an *akriyāvādī*; he teaches a law of *akriyā* and trains followers according to it.[26]

When Sīha later confronts the Buddha, he repeats these allegations verbatim.

Before taking up the Buddha's response, one should note that this passage would tend, by itself, to re-inforce the standard view of the terms in question. However, the same response that Mahāvīra gives to Sīha is given by an unnamed group of teachers to the householder Meṇḍaka when he sets out to see the Buddha, in *Vinayapiṭaka, Mahāvagga* VI.34. The text in the two cases is identical. Meṇḍaka is nowhere associated in any way with Mahāvīra. Therefore, while

---

26 *Aṅguttara Nikāya* IV.180. Cf. the parallel passage at *Vinayapiṭaka, Mahāvagga* VI.31.

the appellation *akriyāvādī* is here applied to the Buddha, the possibility must be admitted that its opposite is not necessarily to be associated with the Jains, since Meṇḍaka, like Sīha, is called a *kriyāvādī*. When this fact is added to the testimony of the Buddhist texts where the Buddha calls himself a *kriyāvādī* (above), it does not seem proper to insist that the two terms refer to the Jain and Buddhist in a fixed way, or that *kriyāvāda* means *the* Jain position.

The point can be explored further by examining the Buddha's responses, both to Sīha and on other occasions. His reply to Sīha is as follows:

> There is a way, Sīha, in which one who wishes to speak correctly concerning me could say that the *śramaṇa* Gautama is an *akriyāvādī*, that he teaches a law of *akriyā* and trains followers according to it . . .
>
> And what, Sīha, is [that] way . . . ? I . . . teach *akriyā* in respect of misconduct in body, voice, and mind. I teach *akriyā* with respect to the multitude of evil and impure conditions.[27]

Immediately noteworthy is the fact that the Buddha also speaks to Sīha concerning the fact that someone might call him a *kriyāvādī*:

> There is a way, Sīha, in which one who wishes to speak correctly concerning me could say that the *śramaṇa* Gautama is a *kriyāvādī*, that he teaches a law of *kriyā* and trains followers according to it. . . .
>
> And what, Sīha, is [that] way. . . ? I . . . teach *kriyā* in respect of good conduct in body, voice, and mind. I teach *kriyā* with respect to the multitude of pure conditions.[28]

To these answers should be added the Buddha's description of his teachings in the *Aṅguttara Nikāya* (*Samacitta Vagga*), where an unnamed Brāhmaṇ comes to question him; the Brāhmaṇ simply asks what it is that the Buddha teaches, and the Buddha replies; "O Brāhmaṇ, I am both a *kriyāvādī* and an *akriyāvādī*." The Brāhmaṇ asks how this is so, and the Buddha's further response is identical to the passages just given.[29]

In addition to these occasions upon which the Buddha speaks of himself in relation to both *kriyā* and *akriyā*, there are a few others that deal only with *akriyā*. Discussed earlier in relation to *vinaya* was the passage immediately preceding the tale of Sīha in the *Aṅguttara Nikāya*, where the Brāhmaṇ from Verañjā speaks with the Buddha. As will be recalled, he casts a number of reproaches at the Buddha, including the accusation that the latter is an *akriyāvādī*. The Buddha's response to this particular point duplicates the *akriyā*-portions of the passages just given.[30] The same statement concerning *akriyā*

---

27 *Aṅguttara Nikāya* IV.182, 183.
28 *Aṅguttara Nikāya* IV.182, 183. This duplicates the above passage, save for use of antonyms.
29 *Aṅguttara Nikāya* I.62.
30 *Aṅguttara Nikāya* IV.174.

occurs at *Vinayapiṭaka, Suttavibhaṅga* I.1.3. At *Aṅguttara Nikāya, Catukka Nipāta, Kamma Vagga*, a Brāhmaṇ named Sikha Moggallāna also accuses the Buddha of *akriyā*; the Buddha again denies it in this case, but not in the stock phrases of the other passages.[31]

When the tale of Sīha is viewed in the context of these passages that parallel or duplicate the crucial portions of the Buddha's remarks to Sīha, and even Mahāvīra's statement to Sīha, the cumulative effect would seem to be that in the matter of *kriyā* and *akriyā* the Buddhist sources do not preserve a sense of *kriyā* as the Jain position, nor of the Jains' alone using *akriyā* to contrast their position with that of the Buddha. This is an important corroboration of the possibility raised earlier concerning the early sense of *kriyāvāda* in the Jain sources, namely, that the specific content and attributions associated with the term are more the product of the later Jain tradition.

An attempt to disentangle an "original" meaning for this pair of terms would likely not succeed. However, some speculation concerning their sense in this variety of settings may be in order. It would seem that the Buddha's protestations to both Sīha and the Brāhmaṇ from Verañjā may make better sense than the translators of the texts in question have heretofore thought. Woodward (*Aṅguttara Nikāya*, p. 57) and T. W. Rhys Davids and Oldenberg (*Vinayapiṭaka*, p. 110) have tended to treat the Buddha's statements on *kriyā* and *akriyā* as plays on words, shrewd answers, perhaps. The necessity of explaining them in such a way arises partly from the notion that *kriyā* and *akriyā* represent fixed theoretical positions that belong to particular schools, as when *kriyā* is absolutely identified with the Jains.

The contexts of the Buddhist statements are also important for understanding the terms. In the several cases given, the Buddha's answer is part of a longer statement concerning a number of things that might be said of him. The same, it must be noted, is the case with respect to the formula-like statements in which the term *vinaya* was earlier found to be located. The same also holds for the early passage in *Ācārāṅga* and for the several passages in *Sūtrakṛtāṅga* II.1 where *kriyā* and *akriyā* form part of a list of pairs. Thus the early Jain sources share this important feature with several of the Buddhist texts that mention *kriyā* and *akriyā*. The conclusion seems inescapable that these terms are part of a larger 'vocabulary' of sorts that was used to characterize points of view, one's own and others, particularly since the one common thread that unites virtually all of the texts in question—both Jain and Buddhist—is that they stand in contexts where opposing viewpoints are being discussed.

To attempt to interpret them as having specific referents is, then, not a fruitful path to take. It would seem that any school of thought could use at least

31 *Aṅguttara Nikāya* II.232.

some of these terms in order to speak of others, although some of them do appear to refer to more specific positions. It is also possible that such terms were used to refer to any number of non-Brāhmaṇic viewpoints, including in that case both the Jains and Buddhists.

In this respect, it is certainly valuable to bear in mind the Brāhmaṇic usage of both *kriyā* and karma, a usage that has a specific context in Vedic ritual activity and speculation concerning it. If the uses to which *kriyā* and *akriyā* are put in these early Jain and Buddhist sources are seen against such a backdrop, the terms gain immense depth and significance. A *kriyā-* or *karmavādī* might then be not merely a propounder of a certain doctrine of *kriyā* or karma. Rather, such a one might be seen as standing within the bounds of the Brāhmaṇic tradition, or better, his viewpoint has a connection with *kriyā* and karma as the larger Brāhmaṇic tradition understands and uses the terms and notions. An *akriyāvādī* is one who denies these basic elements.

For the further light that these terms might shed on the problematic relationship between the Brāhmaṇa and *śramaṇa* positions in the period of early Jain and Buddhist thought, this point deserves a full separate study. For the immediate purpose of tracing the development of their role in the 363-account, one can at least draw the following conclusion concerning the first stages of use of *kriyā* and *akriyā*. Each is one of several ways of expressing the fact that a viewpoint is correct or incorrect. They appear to possess a certain amount of content, particularly when seen against a Brāhmaṇic backdrop, but they are not to be identified with one or another position. They function in a general sense, not as expressions of the particular theoretical stance of the school using the terms.

In the third stage, however, matters change. Here the *kriyāvāda* seems to become quite explicity the Jain position. To this stage would belong *Sūtrakṛtāṅga* I.12, *Sūtrakṛtāṅga Niryukti* 117b-121, *Bhagavatī* XXX.1, and *Sthānāṅga* IV.4. (*Sūtrakṛtāṅga* I.6.27 and *Uttarādhyanana* XVIII.23 are ambiguous; they do not reject *kriyā*, but only give it as one of the four headings that comprise all systems without explicity placing the Jain position outside or inside of those four.[32]) Of primary importance is the fact that this group of sources is made up of texts that are closely related. As noted in chapter 15, *Sūtrakṛtāṅga Niryukti* 117b-121 is the *niryukti* portion attached to *Sūtrakṛtāṅga* I.12, and the *Bhagavatī* and *Sthānāṅga* passages share with *Sūtrakṛtāṅga* I.12 and the *niryukti* the term *samosaraṇa*, a term absent from other 363-account

[32] *Uttarādhyayana* XVIII.33 explicity approves of *kriyā*; thus one can presume that when *kriyā* is given as one of the four in verse 23 it is not being condemned. This does not necessarily mean that *kriyā* is *the* Jain position; but the derogatory tone of Jacobi's translation of verse 23 (Jacobi 1895b:83) seems wrong. Hence I translate as I do in chapter 18.

texts. These few are the only sources that present the *kriyāvāda* as equalling the Jain viewpoint.

Of these passages, *Sūtrakṛtāṅga* I.12 appears to be the oldest. There is a prima facie case for this conclusion in its obvious precedence over the *niryukti*, and the case is bolstered by the facts noted in chapter 15 concerning the *Bhagavatī* passage (namely, that it occurs in the apparently younger portion of the text) and the composite nature of *Sthānaṅga* as a whole. Further, *Sūtrakṛtāṅga* I.12 appears to be younger than other portions of *Sūtrakṛtāṅga* I. This conclusion need not be based only on the pattern of *kriyā*-usage or on the general structural growth of the 363-account. There is other evidence for its age, in particular a sign of grammatical development that is found in I.12.21, in the form of the infinitive used. In this verse the infinitive in *-ium* appears: so *bhāsium arihai kiriyavādam* ("he is worthy to expound the *kriyāvāda*"). According to L. A. Schwarzschild (1960-61:211), this *-ium* infinitive appears in Middle Indo-Aryan subsequent to the more common form, which ends in *-ttae*.

This is a useful corroboration of the general patterns shown in chapter 15 concerning the 363-account as a whole, and a valuable point in detecting the stages in the uses of *kriyā* and *akriyā*, for it is *Sūtrakṛtāṅga* I.12 that makes the most unequivocal connection between *kriyāvāda* and the Jain position. This enhances the importance of the fact that the sources exhibiting this identification are related to each other. This relatedness is further strengthened by another common element, which is the term *samosaraṇa*, which first appears in the 363-account in *Sūtrakṛtāṅga* I.12 and recurs in the other texts in this group. This particular term in this usage (i.e., as referring to schools of thought) is confined to this group of sources.

The most important thing to come to light when one sees this narrow group of texts as the purveyors of the *kriyāvāda* as the Jain position is the very limited arena affected by this notion of equivalence. When this is seen, it becomes even more clear that it will not do to claim that *kriyāvāda* is synonymous with the Jain point of view. Rather, the term is adjectival in the great majority of the cases, and those which regard it as equally the Jain view are the exceptions, not the rule.

Given this discovery, the door is at least open to understanding how Śīlāṅka and others have treated *kriyāvāda* as an incorrect position, for when *kriyāvāda* is seen from this perspective, one does not have to account for an apparent rejection of the earlier Jain tradition on the part of the later tradition. Still, there remains an important shift to be accounted for, since even if the *kriyāvāda* does not actually equal the Jain position, nonetheless it is not a perjorative adjective in the early sources. The process by which it became a non-Jain position thus remains unexplained, even if it is now clear that for the most part it was not *the*

Jain point of view. There is a possible solution for this problem, which will be presented in the next chapter in connection with the commentators' rejection of *kriyāvāda*.

For the moment, in the narrower terms of this study, it is extremely useful to see the broader setting and wider range of possible understandings of *kriyā* and *akriyā*, for they allow one to understand better how it should be that within one school of thought the same term—*kriyāvāda*—could seem at one point to be one thing and at another later point another thing. If one sees the specific content of the term as something attached to it in the course of later understandings of the term, one is spared the difficulty of explaining such a discrepancy.

What emerges then is the likelihood that the notions of *kriyā* and *akriyā* was not so much being given new content or undergoing an active process of reversal of content. Rather, the terms seem to be in the process of being narrowed and specified. In effect, the Jain commentary tradition was giving them a specific content where, perhaps, little or none existed before, and was now treating terms that had a general significance of some sort as referring to specific theoretical stances.

With this preliminary conclusion, this examination of *kriyā* and *akriyā* themselves will stop. However, the internal elements of these headings have not yet been scrutinized; they will be examined before the chapter concludes, particularly so as to examine the purpose(s) of their arrangement in the calculation model.

As was shown in chapter 15, the elements within the *kriyā* and *akriyā* headings cannot be attested as part of the 363-account prior to the commentaries, i.e., the texts in group C. They do, however, play detectable earlier roles outside of the 363-account, though these roles are less easy to find in the case of some of the elements. *Sva/para* and *nitya/anitya* are pairs of notions that play fairly vital roles in Jain analysis of the existence and knowledge of the world and the self, though none of them remains visible as a 'category' proper in later Jain thought. As a result, it is not easy to isolate or describe them in great detail. The Jain *tattva*s require the least searching and explanation. The elements *kāla*, *īśvara*, etc., are widely known, and only their particular role in the 363-account needs some analysis.

Sva and *para* were briefly discussed earlier, when the full 363-account was presented and the problem of translating the formulae using these terms was discussed. Given there was the basic gloss of *sva* (or *svataḥ*, as it is used in the scheme) that Śīlāṅka and later commentators provide. It should be observed at once that none of these commentators argues this point in any way, nor do any of them provide lengthy or argumentative statements concerning *sva* or *para*. The glosses of the latter are somewhat more lengthy than those for *sva*, but even the most complete statement of both is far from sophisticated. This most complete statement occurs in Śīlāṅka on *Ācārāṅga* I.1.3, and it is slavishly followed by the subsequent commentary tradition. Put together, Śīlāṅka on both *sva* and *para* reads as follows:

> Therein, "unique" means that the *jīva* exists in a form of its own, one having no reference to another factor as in the case of shortness and longness. . . . How then is the "relative existence" of the self to be understood? . . . In this world, the distinguishing of the nature of all existents occurs in relation to the nature of other existents, in the way that the distinguishing of shortness occurs in relation to longness and of longness in relation to shortness. In this same way, having considered things like pillars and pots, which are not-self, there arises the awareness of the self as something distinct from that; thus that which is the true nature of the self is ascertained relatively, not uniquely.[33]

It seems quite clear that both the existence and knowledge of the self (and the other *tattvas*) are involved in the use of the terms. Schrader (1902:7) considers these glosses to have been written with the *syādvāda* in mind; though this is chronologically possible, it does not establish *sva* and *para* as existing early on for the purpose of evaluating non-Jain schools. In fact, there are no glosses in Haribhadra on *Nandī* 88, which is the earliest source for the full 363-account.[34]

That such a pair was an early part of Jain thought is also doubtful. As to the possibility of its representing an early form of the *syādvāda*, K. K. Dixit's investigations of the beginnings of this logical tool have turned up a passage in *Bhagavatī* that antedates the appearance of the *syādvāda* in recognizable form, but which does discuss the problem of variable predication. According to Dixit (1971:26), the passage "declares that everything . . . is a 'self' from the standpoint of its own properties, a 'not-self' from the standpoint of alien properties, indescribable from the standpoint of both."[35] This passage has a certain bearing on the problem of knowledge and existence as it developed in the *syādvāda*, but it has little to do with the problem of ascertaining the nature of the self and other entities as expressed in the gloss above. This use of *sva* and *para* does little more than express an epistomological cliché that is hardly unique to the Jain viewpoint. Were there more to it, one would not expect the commentators to settle for such simple glosses. As it is, the glosses seem to be post hoc explanations of items that are present in the 363-account for other reasons.

Much the same is true of *nitya/anitya*, though this pair has a far stronger pedigree in the history of Jain thought. It might be viewed as a forerunner of the

33 Śīlāṅka on *Ācārāṅga* I.1.3. Cf. Schrader 1902:7-8. Since the *Āgamasaṃgraha* edition of *Ācārāṅga* is a very poor text, I have relied heavily on Schrader to reproduce it here.

34 See the translation in chapter 18.

35 Dixit unfortunately cites an edition of *Bhagavatī* not available to me, citing it furthermore by page number and not by passage.

full Jain notion that an object possesses three fundamental characteristics, origination, decay, and permanence (*Tattvārthādhigama* V.29[Ś], V.30[D]). M. L. Mehta (1971:166) points out another *Bhagavatī* (VII.2.293) passage, which he holds to foreshadow the *syādvāda*, and which he translates as follows:

> O Gautama! from one point of view the soul is permanent; from another point of view, the soul is not permanent. From the point of view of substance, the soul is permanent; from the point of view of modes, the soul is not permanent.

Here one can see a reasonable connection between an actual early Jain approach and the use of *nitya/anitya* in the 363-account, save that the 363-account version has nothing to do with substance and mode.

It is impossible to guarantee that nothing like the 363-account uses of *sva/para* and *nitya/anitya* occurs in actual Jain discussions of the problems of existence and knowledge. But secondary studies reveal nothing closer than the examples cited; and while one can say that they are in some senses related to the expressions in the 363-account, and can even say that it would not be unreasonable to expect a Jain account of non-Jains to use such categories, it is hardly necessary that it do so. The uses to which these two pairs are put do not appear to serve much more than a numerical purpose, i.e., the reaching of certain desired totals. This is made quite likely by one fact alone: even if these concepts do come from some earlier stage of Jain thought, it seems hardly necessary to preserve such crude and unsophisticated tools in a scheme where something as refined as the full seven-membered *syādvāda* is also present (in the *ajñānikavāda* heading). This argument would falter if it were discovered that the full *kriyā* and *akriyā* headings (i.e., the headings inclusive of internal elements) were older than the others, but the present evidence shows nothing of the sort.

The likelihood that there is numerical juggling involved becomes even more apparent when one examines the uses made of the Jain *tattva*s and the elements *kāla*, etc. With regard to the *tattva*s, their history as either seven or nine in number was alluded to in chapter 15. It will be recalled that the items that cause the variation are *puṇya* and *apuṇya*, or *dharma* and *adharma*. Both versions of the list of *tattva*s are present in the early stages of the formulation of the Jain position in terms of *tattva*s, a form in which it did not occur until relatively late. *Tattvārthādhigama* I.4 lists only seven; *Uttarādhyayana* XXVIII.14, which is apparently another early piece of systematization (Dixit 1971:21), lists the ninefold version.

Since both versions are present at an early stage in Jain analytical thought—present, in fact, in two of the earliest texts to give the *tattva*s in this (later standard) form—the presence or absence of *puṇya* and *apuṇya* in lists of *tattva*s should likely be seen as part of the general process by which the Jains sought to formulate their position in terms of *tattva*s. This development in Jain thought is a very important and complex matter. For now, it is sufficient to observe that the presence or absence of these items in the *tattva* lists has nothing to do with the existence or non-existence of *jīva*, *ajīva*, etc. Rather it appears to arise from a problem in thinking out the role that *bhāva*s (internal states of the *jīva*)[36] play in determining the auspiciousness or inauspiciousness of *āsrava*, karma-influx (see Mehta 1971:76). The later Jain tradition continued to be troubled by the question of *puṇya* and *apuṇya*, for, strictly speaking, any karma-influx is unsatisfactory, be it good or bad. Yet the process of finding a mode of expression for its analytical thought that would share the vocabulary and concerns of the larger Indian tradition must have required that the Jains deal with the problem. Thus whether or not these items are present or absent has a reason fully independent of the 363-account, and of the attempt to deal with other views.

Furthermore, given the way in which the alternatives in the 363-account are formulated, the difference between *kriyāvāda* and *akriyāvāda* depends on the affirmation or denial of the existence of the *tattva*s; this question should (as Schrader [1902:8] has pointed out with some asperity) include all items in both cases. Given this combination of factors, the conclusion seems called for that numbers were the primary determinant in organizing the groups of *tattva*s within the headings.

The final group of internal elements consists of *kāla*, etc. It has been noted that the commentators tend to fasten onto these as the most concrete entities in the whole of the 363-account.[37] There appears to be good reason for this, in that these items found wide currency in a great variety of Indian texts as a way of summarizing various viewpoints. These are likely the least artificial of all the elements in the entire 363-account. It is thus not surprising that the commentators should have tended to focus on them, and to preserve—in the form of verses and other quotations—evidence of their existence outside of the 363-account.[38] These elements, partly because of their wide currency, have been studied by a number of scholars. Thus a full review of all of them is not needed. Only one point requires attention, and it again has to do with numerical totals.

As to other studies, Schrader (1902:17-46) provides a detailed review of all those mentioned in the 363-account. Barua (1970:198-212) goes into detail only on *kāla*, but provides a rich list of other sources for these items. An excellent account of a number of them has been given by Gopinath Kaviraj (n.d.:45-71). The general approach to them, though the individual treatments may vary, is summed up by Kaviraj (n.d.:46):

---

36 See chapter 18.

37 See above, chapter 15.

38 Verses summarizing *kālavāda*, etc., occur at various places. Śīlāṅka's commentary on *Sūtrakṛtāṅga* I.12.1 has collected them in one place; see the translation in chapter 18.

> Many of these had been in vogue in independent forms, and as interrelated, long before the rise of Buddhism. And there seems to be good reason to believe that in the course of centuries, with the systematisation of schools, some of these doctrines lost their independence altogether and came to be affiliated to the systems *newly built up*.

Given these other studies, the items in question need not be passed in review. Of greater importance is the fact that the testimony of the various sources indicates that the number of items in this group may vary. According to Barua's (1970:198) list of sources, the following are some of the prominent versions of this group of elements:

Śvetāśvatara Upaniṣad I.2:	*kāla, svabhāva, niyati, yadṛcchā, bhūta, yoni, puruṣa, ātman*[39]
Suśruta I.7:	*svabhāva, īśvara, kāla, yadṛcchā, niyati, pariṇāma, prakṛti*
Mahābodhi Jātaka 528:	*ahetuvāda, issarakāraṇavāda, pubbekatavāda, ucchedavāda, khattavaijjāvāda*[40]
Aśvaghoṣa, *Saundarānanda Kāvya* XVI.17:	*kāla, svabhāva, niyati, yadṛcchā, bhūta, puruṣa, īśvara, prakṛti*

One should also note the brief formula containing *kāla*, *bhūta*, etc., that occurs in the Buddhist texts cited above. Barua (1970:198) cites several other sources that duplicate lists given here, and Kaviraj (n.d.:45-46) adds still others. Without listing all of them the point should be clear: there is a core of items in these lists, around which can occur numerous variations. The number of items in the list does not appear to be fixed in any way, and thus the lists of elements in the 363-account do not appear to be subject to any standard list of these items. Once again, it seems quite likely that the 363-account's calculation method and its requirements dictate the number of items in the lists in the account.

This point, coupled with the earlier observations on the way in which the number of Jain *tattva*s is varied between the *kriyā* and *akriyā* headings, and the dubious relevance of the *sva/para* and *nitya/anitya* pairs, should serve as a final piece of evidence for the conclusion that numerical elements lie behind the internal structure of these two headings as well as the *ajñāna* and *vinaya* headings.

---

39 Two of these are controversial. Deussen (1897:291-92) and Hume (1931:394) disagree over whether *yoni* is to be taken as a separate element. Hume takes it thus, Deussen does not. *Ātman* is usually taken as standing in opposition to all the others in this verse; but since it occurs as part of the group in other settings, I list it with them here.

40 Masatoshi Nagatomi (personal communication) informs me that this list of elements appears to be incomplete. I am relying here on Barua, and have been unable to consult the text.

CONCLUSIONS

One final point remains with respect to the subtotals and the structure of the 363-account. As was noted in chapter 15, one really cannot determine whether the various subtotals antedate the four means of calculating them, or whether the number 363 and the desire to express 363 options led to the development of the subtotals. This problem will exist until the mass of Prakrit commentaries that lie between the *niryukti*s and the Sanskrit commentaries has been fully explored. Still, the internal elements of the 363-account may shed some light on this problem, although chronological considerations make a firm conclusion hard to sustain.

According to what is thus far known, the *Sūtrakṛtāṅga Niryukti* is the first to present the subtotals (though they may exist even before this). Dating the *niryukti*s is difficult, but the latest likely date for a *niryukti* on an older *Aṅga*, such as *Sūtrakṛtāṅga*, would seem to be ca. 200 C.E. (see Schubring 1962:84-85). Thus one might maintain that the subtotals are at least as early as that.

As to the internal elements themselves, it is possible that the *Tattvārthādhigama* and chapter XXVIII of *Uttarādhyayana* belong to about this period, and it is in these texts that the early statements of the Jain *tattva*s are found. However, the seven elements of the *syādvāda*, which are so prominent in the *ajñāna* heading, seem not to be present in this form much prior to Siddhasena Divākara's *Sammaïsuttam*. It would require very incautious dating to place the *Sammaïsuttam* as far back as the *Sūtrakṛtāṅga Niryukti*. Although a great range of dates is suggested for Siddhasena, the general consensus places him not earlier than 450 C.E., though some scholars are willing to push this date back to 350 C.E.[41]

The use made of the *syādvāda* in constructing the *ajñāna* heading would indicate that this is not a notion in the throes of development, as it certainly would have to be if the calculation method were as old as the *niryukti*. The best that one can say is that it seems highly unlikely, then, that the full calculation model is as old as the subtotals themselves. This has the effect of making it even more likely that the elements within the headings are shuffled about with the calculation in mind, for it would be a more exacting task to reproduce four subtotals than to come up with the 363 options.

With these observations on number and the structure and uses of the internal elements in the four headings, the negative task involved in considering the 363-account may fairly be regarded as concluded. Its primary aim has been to shatter the image of the 363-account as an homogenous whole, and in so doing to reveal the process that produced the whole out of many elements. At the same time,

41 For the range of dates, see A. N. Upadhye 1971:*3-*72.

certain points have already been raised that have to do with its special character as a tool for reflection upon the existence of other viewpoints. In particular, these are the shift in the sense of *ajñāna* from ignorance to scepticism and even agnosticism, and the discovery that *kriyā* and *akriyā* undergo an important shift in roles when they become part of the four headings.

The positive task now is in exploring how the 363-account works to reflect on the existence of multiple viewpoints. This task, and the problem of how these separate elements came to be a whole, are the subjects of the next chapter.

17

THE 363-ACCOUNT: THE STRUCTURE OF THE WHOLE*

In the first two portions of this chapter, the dissected 363-account of chapter 15 and 16 will be examined more as whole. The particular concern that most occupies this chapter is the appearance of *kriyā, akriyā, ajñāna*, and *vinaya* as a group of four headings, and the implications of the appearance of these four as a group for the significance of the 363-account as a whole. In addition, this chapter will essay a preliminary statement concerning the peculiar character of the 363-account, namely, its function in analyzing the existence of non-Jain positions, not merely refuting them. The chapter concludes with a brief examination of the problem posed by the *nayavāda*.

THE FOUR-FOLD ACCOUNT

The 363-account has been left in a rather broken-apart condition as a result of the 'negative' task carried out in the two preceding chapters. The concern here is to attempt to see how it might be put back together, so to speak, and therefore to see how it might have evolved in the Jain tradition. This means, in light of the last chapter's discoveries, that the object of this examination is to see

* From dissertation, pp. 173-225.

how certain items out of a larger field, or 'vocabulary' as it has been called, come to represent some sort of totality.

The focus of this totality is the four headings. Chapter 15 has shown that the four headings certainly precede the full calculation-model; the closing pages of chapter 16 have argued that even the subtotals may have preceded the calculation-method; and chapter 15, again, has argued briefly that the number 363 may be independent of the four headings.

Thus it would seem wisest to presume that the presence of four headings is to be considered apart from specific numerical totals, i.e., that there did not come to be four headings because they were useful in reaching a certain total number. Certainly the evidence of chapter 16 indicates that the elements within the calculation model do not bear a strong relationship to the headings unless numbers are associated with the latter. Therefore it seems proper to examine the headings themselves first. This problem can be broken into two parts: the matter of why there should be four headings, and the question of why the particular four headings of the 363-account should be there. Neither of these is easily solved.

Four Headings

The development of four headings is a problem because the last chapter has shown that in the larger 'vocabulary' of terms used in discussing opposing viewpoints there is no particular predeliction toward limiting the terms to four in number. Further, in the growth of the 363-account as discussed above, there is an abrupt and unexplained shift at the point where *ajñāna* and *vinaya* are linked with *kriyā* and *akriyā*. Nothing can be detected in this process that could be pointed to as indicating a slow process of selection moving toward the use of these four items.

Further, it appears quite certain that the use of these four headings is a later development. This emerges from the texts themselves. Where the group of four appears, the ages of the texts (as discussed above with respect to *Sūtrakṛtāṅga* I.12, *Bhagavatī* XXX, and *Sthānāṅga*) point to the strong likelihood of its being later.

Moreover, there is another piece of textual evidence that points both to the later occurrence of these four headings and to a certain significance for the number four itself. The source in question is *Sūtrakṛtāṅga* II.1, which is a self-contained prose segment (part of the heterogenous second book of *Sūtrakṛtāṅga*[1]) entitled "The Lotus."[2] In "The Lotus," Mahāvīra relates how four men come, one from each of the cardinal points, to a pool filled with lotuses, at

1 On *Sūtrakṛtāṅga* II, see Schubring 1962:87.

2 "The Lotus" is translated in full by Jacobi (1895a:335-55) and Schubring (1926:27-41). [Editor's note.] See also Bollée 1977-88:I:131-64.

the center of which is one particularly large and beautiful specimen. Each man wades into the pool, seeking to pluck the lotus at the center, but each becomes mired in the mud-bottom of the pool and none succeeds in reaching the center. In the end, a monk well-advanced in ascetic practice comes to the edge of the pool and summons the lotus, which flies up to him.

Mahāvīra's summary interpretation of the elements in the tale is not altogether without contradictions (*Sūtrakṛtāṅga* II.1.12, 60), but the attainment of the lotus at the center of the pool is clearly equivalent to attaining *mokṣa*, and the four men from the cardinal directions are teachers of the views (1) that *jīva* and body are the same, (2) that all consists of only the five basic elements (*mahābhūtas*), (3) that *īśvara* is the cause of all, and (4) that *niyati* is the cause of all things.

Three of these four positions are recognizable as members of the group of *vādas* that occurs in the 363-account and other sources. That they are grouped as four is important, but it is also important to note that "The Lotus" contains two occassions where *kriyā* and *akriyā* are given as a pair. On the first such occasion (II.1.17, with parallels at verses 24, 28, 32), *kriyā* and *akriyā* are part of a longer list of pairs, the others being working good or ill, merit or demerit, purity or impurity, release and non-release, and going to hell or not. On the second occasion (verse 30), the pair occurs in a statement put into the mouth of the *niyativādī*:

> Indeed, in this world are two [sorts of] men. Some men admit *kriyā*, some men do not admit *kriyā*.

Chapter 16 has discussed how these occurrences of *kriyā* and *akriyā* are involved in understanding the terms themselves. Here the important point is that while *kriyā* and *akriyā* occur only as a pair, the passage itself uses a four-fold scheme to portray non-Jain viewpoints. This would seem an important point in considering the role of the number four itself, as opposed to its being associated with four particular headings.

On this point, the way in which the headings are portrayed is also notable, in that they are associated with the four cardinal directions. The use of the directions is a constant motif in Jain texts where a totality, or universality, is to be portrayed. (The intermediate points may also be mentioned.) Within the same chapter (*Sūtrakṛtāṅga* II.1.13) a passage occurs in which the four directions are used simply as a means of saying "all men." Other such passages are so numerous as to make citing them all unnecessary, and the point of the usage itself does not need belaboring.

It must be admitted that "The Lotus" and its presentation of four positions in a mode commonly used to depict a totality are hardly sufficient to do more than point to a possible way of understanding the emergence of the four 363-account headings. The actual role of the number four is, in the remaining sources, very much involved with the content of the four headings. Yet it is important to note that, regardless of content, the four are understood as presenting the sum of possible viewpoints. This comes across very clearly in several of the sources that first present the four, especially *Sūtrakṛtāṅga* I.6.27, *Uttarādhyayana* XVIII, and *Sūtrakṛtāṅga* II.2.

Sūtrakṛtāṅga I.6.27 expressly states that in knowing the *kriyāvāda*, etc., Mahāvīra had mastered all *vāda*s. The verses following *Uttarādhyayana* XVIII.23 several times speak of Sañjaya's exposition in relation to all other positions, which are expressed in verse 23 as the four headings. *Sūtrakṛtāṅga* II.2.80, immediately after the statement of the four in connection with the number 363, has all the propounders form a circle in order to teach the lesson that *ahiṃsā* is a principle immediately understandable from every viewpoint.

Neither in "The Lotus" nor in these examples is there any hint that the four headings represent only some part of the possible stances. The contexts, if not the statements themselves, make it quite clear that a totality is being expressed. This sense of totality also plays a role in the use, in certain texts, of the term *samosaraṇa*; but this usage has other implications that make it more useful to consider it at a later point. The immediate issue is that four positions, out of many more, begin to express the sum of all positions. Even though it is not possible to pin down with precision the exact point at which this begins to occur, it is quite essential that this point be noted. Making it stand out in sharp relief was one of the purposes behind the dissection of the 363-account in the last chapter.

Its importance cannot be overlooked, because the appearance of this sense of totality—possibly linked with the number four itself—marks a turning point in the Jain consideration of other viewpoints. No more are the viewpoints a jumble of assorted positions with no fixed limit. With the appearance of four headings, a structure is seen in the existence of those other viewpoints. The existence of many positions becomes subject to a rationale of sorts.

One will have noticed, however, that the four positions presented in "The Lotus" do not themselves seem to submit readily to some sort of rationale. Nor has it been readily possible to see how far the four headings in the 363-account express some sort of rounded whole, save in that they are four in number. However, the analysis in the previous chapter was primarily concerned with the relationship between the headings and the calculation-model. The headings alone, as expressing a totality, can and should be considered apart from their internal elements. This separation may make possible some vision of them as expressing a rational whole, the sum of all viewpoints.

The Four Headings

As shown in chapter 16, *kriyā* and *akriyā* are present as a pair (though sometimes in larger groups of pairs) before they become part of a set of four. Their presence as a pair also represents something of a process of selection, since they are each present in longer lists of adjectives that may be applied to correct or incorrect positions. Once again, the actual process of selection cannot be pin-pointed at various stages. However, a number of Jain sources present what may be traces of such a process, and these may help in getting some view of *kriyā* and *akriyā* as emerging from their respective larger settings.

In order to see these traces, it is necessary to recall the suggestion made in chapter 16, namely, that properly understanding *kriyā* and *akriyā* may rest on seeing them against a backdrop of Brāhmaṇic usage and understanding. The several texts that are useful in seeing into the Jain use of *kriyā* and *akriyā* as a pair are also better understood against such a backdrop. The prominent sources involved are texts that present the pair alone, those that give some sort of gloss of the significance of the pair, and some remarks in the later commentaries.

Those that present *kriyā* and *akriyā* alone (i.e., not as part of a longer list of pairs), or that gloss them in a significant way are *Sūtrakṛtāṅga* I.10.17, *Uttarādhyayana* XVIII.33, *Sūtrakṛtāṅga* II.1.30, the *Sūtrakṛtāṅga Niryukti*, and *Ācāradaśāḥ* VI. In the first three sources, *kriyā* and *akriyā* clearly stand for two basic options. *Sūtrakṛtāṅga* I.10.17 is neutral as to their value; *Uttarādhyayana* XVIII.33 states that a wise man chooses *kriyā*. *Sūtrakṛtāṅga* II.1.30 makes the clear statement that the world is divided into *kriyā* and *akriyā*. Compared with the Jain and Buddhist sources in which *kriyā* and *akriyā* are part of larger groups of items, this reduction to two basic positions already marks a significant change.

In *Sūtrakṛtāṅga Niryukti* and *Ācāradaśāḥ*, the two items are glossed in terms of *asti* and *nāsti*. The glosses in *Sūtrakṛtāṅga Niryukti* 118 have commonly been taken to mean that "the *jīva* exists." But neither the verses nor *Sūtrakṛtāṅga* I.12 (to which the *niryukti* passage is attached) actually says this. The restriction of *asti* and *nāsti* to the *jīva* appears to be the doing of the later tradition, as has been discussed earlier. As to the lengthy glosses in *Ācāradaśāḥ* VI, it is the opinion of Schubring (1962:110, 1966:14) that the content of the passage is the result of an outright borrowing of the notions of *āstika* and *nāstika* from elsewhere, since the glosses in this passage seem to be making *kriyā* and *akriyā* the equivalent of those terms.

However, given that *kriyā* and *akriyā* need to be seen against a Brāhmaṇic backdrop, this suggestion of borrowing may be unnecessary. It seems more likely that what is occuring here, in the presentation of only two options and in the *asti*/*nāsti* glosses, is a process of selection and clarification that to some extent shares in the terminology of the larger Indian tradition. In making his suggestion, Schubring is presuming the existence of a fixed notion of *āstika* and *nāstika*, one that the Jains could borrow. J. C. Heesterman, however, considers that *nāstika* has merely the basic sense of "one who refutes," the term's referent being he who took the negative side of a ritualized debate in the setting of Vedic sacrifice-related disputations. According to Heesterman (1968-69:171), *nāstika* thus has a sense, in its early settings, of being "a role, a party in the game of disputation free from any specific doctrinal content, both parties being bound by the rules of the game that unites them, and not by any doctrine that separates them."

Both the setting and Heesterman's observations are important, for the setting would also make sense of *kriyā* and *akriyā* if this study's earlier surmise is at all correct. These early Jain pairings of the terms, and their glosses, may actually provide a glimpse from the Jain side into a process whereby schools of thought began to organize themselves and others around a point that did not have to do with specific doctrines, but rather with their general willingness to accept, to say "yes" to what they perceived to be the basic orientation of the religious activity of the time. Viewed in this way, even *Ācāradaśāḥ*'s long glosses of *kriyā* and *akriyā* would not seem strange.

The notion that *kriyā* and *akriyā* have something to do with *asti* and *nāsti* persists even into the earliest Sanskrit sources for the 363-account. Haribhadra's commentary on *Nandī* may show this, for in the last sentence on *akriyāvāda*, Haribhadra declares that the calculation results in a total of 84 *nāstika*s.[3] The term is not used for any of the other headings. That in certain Jain circles the *akriyāvāda* by itself was regarded as encompassing the sum of incorrect positions is also revealed by a passage in *Sthānāṅga* VIII, which lists eight types of *akriyāvāda*.[4] No connection is made between this approach and the four-fold statement in *Sthānāṅga* IV.4, nor does the commentator, Abhayadeva, make any. *Akriyā* here is not related merely to the notion that the *jīva* does not exist, but rather includes a lengthy statement of non-Jain views.

This list, as Barua (1970:197) has pointed out, bears a striking resemblance to the Buddhist classification presented in the *Brahmajāla Sutta*.[5] The question of whether the Jain list is borrowed is perhaps academic, since this eight-fold *akriyāvāda* is known to occur only at this one point in the Jain tradition. The point of mentioning it is to show that *akriyā* is here seen as a general category for the incorrect, not one limited to a specific doctrinal position.

---

3 See the translation in chapter 18.

4 Text: Āgamasaṃgraha edition 484b-486b (including commentary).

5 The *Sthānāṅga* passage is incorrectly given as IV.4 by Barua. For a full account of the eight, see Schrader (1902:54-57).

It seems reasonably clear that at one point in the Jain tradition, *kriyā* and *akriyā* stood as a pair, expressing correctness and incorrectness, and that the emergence of this pair reflects a certain process of selection. This does not by itself shed direct light on the group of four, but this pair of terms seems to have undergone a further process of reflection that may help to make the four headings intelligible.

This process is not reflected clearly in the 363-account sources themselves. It is found, rather, in a few scattered texts that are involved in elaborating the *nayavāda*. The latter will be examined by itself at a later point; here only its bearing on *kriyā* and *akriyā* is at issue.

The early history of the *nayavāda*, as K. K. Dixit has shown, is filled with various attempts at formulating the number and types of possible standpoints. Among these early attempts, a small corner is occupied by one that focussed on *kriyā* and *jñāna* as two basic positions. This approach seems to have had no impact on the later tradition's dealings with the *naya*s. Its chief source is the *Āvaśyaka Niryukti* (I.407-408) (Dixit 1971:76), and it is elaborated briefly in Jinabhadra's *Viśeṣāvaśyakabhāṣya* (3591), which Dixit (1971:123) translates:

> *Jñānanaya* says that everything depends on *jñāna*, while *kriyā* is useless; *kriyānaya* says that everything depends on *kriyā*. The correct position is to accept both.

These shadowy references are very slim evidence, and would be useless were it not for a feature of Śīlāṅka's commentary on *Sūtrakṛtāṅga*. Śīlāṅka is given to the perhaps revealing practice of saying that *kriyāvādī*s are those who rely on ritual action alone, while *akriyāvādī*s rely on knowledge. This gloss is rather at odds with the definitions that he must provide in connection with the 363-account calculation-model, where he takes the better-known position that *kriyāvāda* refers to the existence of the self, *akriyāvāda* being the reverse thereof.[6]

This leads one to speculate that *kriyā* and *akriyā*, in addition to being a Jain variety of the notion of *āstika/nāstika*, received a certain amount of elaboration in terms of action versus knowledge. If this hypothesis is correct, then it is possible to see how *ajñāna* and *vinaya* could be grouped with *kriyā* and *akriyā* to make a totality that was also four-fold.

This need not be as hypothetical as it sounds. The previous chapter has pointed out at some length that *ajñāna* and *vinaya*, as headings, do not bear a direct relationship to their internal constituents, and that the earliest occurrences of the terms do not jibe with the commentators' definitions. Those early versions do, however, provide direct counterpoints to *kriyā* and *akriyā* if the latter pair be understood as referring to action and knowledge.

---

6 See the translation in chapter 18.

The early sense of *ajñāna*, both independent of and within the four-fold set of headings, is ignorance. This point has been shown above. Even in its later transmutation into scepticism or agnosticism, it would provide a perfect counterpoint to the notion of *akriyā* as knowledge. The later point of view might in fact be an attempt to sharpen up such a counter-position, but an argument to that effect is not necessary.

The early sense of *vinaya*, in Buddhist sources, in the Digambara commentaries on *Tattvārthādhigama*, and in *Sūtrakṛtāṅga* I.12 (the sole point where it is at all explained in Śvetāmbara sources prior to the commentaries), has been more difficult to elucidate. But it has been suggested that in all of these cases it refers to activity that is destructive or in contradiction of basic norms of proper behavior.[7] If this is seen to be the case, it then provides a proper counterpoint to *kriyā* as action that is correct.

However, it is much harder to explain the later version of *vinaya* as "respectful service" whose flaw lies only in exclusive reliance thereon. The only point of assistance is this: the later version of *vinaya* seems to get its content solely from its constituent internal elements, which are determined by numerical requirements. The problem of interpreting *vinaya* in the later tradition may have been made more complex by the fact that the Jains (like the Buddhists) hold to a notion of *vinaya* that is quite unlike that presented in the accounts of other viewpoints. Thus some confusion (again, as in the Buddhist sources) was perhaps inevitable, the result being that *vinaya* was interpreted in terms of its later, more popular meaning, and the flaw of excessive reliance on it would then be the only one that could be found. Thus it is possible, though not in a strikingly conclusive manner, to account for *vinaya* as well.

These four—in senses that persist almost only in shadowy forms and traces—do present a four-fold picture that is a totality: proper action, knowledge, wrong knowledge, destructive action. It is surely significant that these four are compatible with the only early gloss of all of them in *Sūtrakṛtāṅga* I.12, and that difficulty in seeing them as a totality arises only in the later tradition, at the point where the calculation model occurs.

The significance of this totality has alrady been commented on, but it is worth stressing again. Here, out of the welter of viewpoints catalogued in *Sūtrakṛtāṅga* and elsewhere, there comes to be a synthetic view of the whole. This is a remarkable point in the Jain view of the existence of many viewpoints, for the existence of viewpoints is seen to have some structure. But the viewpoints have not yet a reason for being, and on this point there is not unanimity.

---

7 See especially the translations and meanings proposed by the translators of the Pali texts, in chapter 16, above.

Two basically different approaches to this point emerge in the history of the 363-account, *samosaraṇa* and *mithyādarśana.*

SAMOSARAṆA AND *MITHYĀDARŚANA*

The two terms in the title of this section sum up the two different approaches. The latter is more briefly treated here. The former is more complex, and has in it the seeds of still further studies. It is taken up first.

Samosaraṇa

This term is applied to the four headings, as a general term applicable to all four, in only a few of the 363-account sources. Yet in those sources, the use of the term seems to be both a response to the totality expressed in the four headings and an answer to the question posed by their existence. The earliest use of the term appears to occur in *Sūtrakṛtāṅga* I.12.1. With this passage are associated three others that use the term: the *niryukti* on *Sūtrakṛtāṅga* I.12, *Sthānāṅga* IV.4, and *Bhagavatī* XXX. It is quite significant that these texts are among the first to use the four-fold set of headings. The importance of *samosaraṇa* is certainly enhanced by the fact that its introduction accompanies the turning point in the Jain view of others that is represented by the four-fold headings.

Sūtrakṛtāṅga I.12.1 states that there are four *samosaraṇa*s:

> These are the four positions (*samosaraṇa*s) that the propounders each declare: they state action (*kriyā*), inaction (*akriyā*), respectfulness (*vinaya*) as the third, and agnosis (*ajñāna*) as the fourth.

Just how to take this term in this usage has been a problem. Jacobi (1895a:315) translates it as "creed," and explains it thus:

> This word and the verb samôsarai are commonly used when Mahâvîra preaches to a meeting (mêlâpaka) gathered round him.

Schubring (1926:150) uses "Platform," and explains it as follows:

> Nach *āhaṃsu* zu schliessen, versteht der Dichter *samosaraṇa* als "Predigt." In der Jaina-Kunst ist es die göttlich bereitete Stätte, wo der Kevalin lehrt, bei Śīl die Versammlung der Gläubigen aus solchem Anlass (*melāpaka*). Zur Deckung aller drei Begriffe sei der parlamentarische Ausdruck "Plattform" gestattet.[8]

---

8 [Editor's Translation.] To conclude from *āhaṃsu* [in the text], the author understands *samosaraṇa* as "sermon." In Jaina art it is a divinely constructed place where the Kevalin teaches. According to Śīlāṅka, it is the gathering of believers (*melāpaka*) for that purpose. The parliamentary term "platform" applies to cover all three conceptions.

Neither scholar explains, or tries to explain, how it is that this particular term should come to be used of non-Jain positions. There are, in fact, no obvious explanations for this fact. The *samosaraṇa* itself is an interesting feature of the Jain tradition's view of the work of the Tīrthaṅkara. The later tradition portrays it as W. Norman Brown (1941:5) has summarized:

> Whenever a Jina . . . obtains perfect knowledge, the gods appear, cleanse the earth for a space of a yojana round about, scent it, and ornament it. They build three walls, the innermost of jewels, the middle of gold, and outer of silver, and each wall has four jewelled gates facing the four cardinal directions. In the center is a pedestal with a tree, and under the tree are four lion thrones. The Jina sits on the throne facing the east, and reproductions of him sit on the others. There the Tīrthaṃkara preaches to gods, men, and animals, who have joyously assembled to hear his initial discourse on the great Truth which he has acquired.

In this form, i.e., as the occasion on which the Jina preaches his first sermon, the *samosaraṇa* is a constant feature of the later tradition's accounts of the lives of each Tīrthaṅkara. However, where the *samosaraṇa* is portrayed in older texts, both its form and purpose appear to be rather different. An early version may be the one preserved in the *Aupapātika*, the first of the *Upaṅga*s. Other *samosaraṇa* portrayals in the Śvetāmbara canon rely on the *Aupapātika*, according to Ernst Leumann (1882:2):

> Der erste Theil des Aup. S. [*Uvav.*] nun enthält . . . eine Art Wallfahrts-geschichte, und zwar ist dieselbe Schema fur alle Jaina-Texte, indem in diesan stets nur auf die im Aup. S. gegebene Schilderung verwiesen wird.[9]

Leumann's conclusion is based on the use of *varṇaka*s (key-word stereotyped descriptions) in other texts; these are perhaps only a key to the order in which particular texts were put into written form, and not to actual age. However, the use of the *varṇaka*s means that the canon's vision of the *samosaraṇa* is essentially that of the *Aupapātika*, and this is sufficient for now.

The most striking difference between the older version, as presented in *Aupapātika*, and the later version summarized above is that the later version restricts the *samosaraṇa* to the occasion upon which the Jina first preaches his message, while the *Aupapātika* version presents it as an occasion that might occur more often (more in the sense of Jacobi's explanation). As an event in the career of the Tīrthaṅkara, the *samosaraṇa* is, in fact, altogether absent from the *Ācārāṅga* and *Ācāradaśāḥ* (*Kalpa Sūtra*) versions of the life of Mahāvīra, which one can presume are fairly old versions.

---

9 [Editor's Translation.] The first chapter of the *Aupapātika Sūtra* includes . . . a kind of pilgrimage narrative, and indeed is the model for all Jain texts, in that they were always derived from the descriptions given in the *Aupapātika Sūtra*.

There are other differences that separate the early and later *samosaraṇa*. The earlier form lacks nearly all the ensignia and royal trappings present in the later version. The *Aupapātika* version tends, in fact, to speak of it not as the event, but as the assembly of people. Accordingly, it occurs at a holy place,[10] rather than a place created for it. The setting is a grove, with an Aśoka-tree at its center;[11] present, but only briefly described, are rings of vegetation (shrubs and trees) growing around the Aśoka-tree.[12] Although certain extraordinary features are supplied by another, apparently secondary recension of the text (Leumann 1882:25), the whole is largely bereft of the details present in the later form. As to the audience, it consists largely of holy men of four sorts, a king and his party, and townspeople. Six classes of divinities are also present, but no mention is made of the presence of animals.

The *samosaraṇa* itself, if the earlier and later versions are compared, appears to have undergone something of a process of evolution. Unfortunately, it has not been the subject of a thorough study. In that light, what is said here must be conjectural to a certain extent. However, the later *samosaraṇa* clearly exhibits a sense in which the Jina's teachings are seen as universal in impact. This is overtly shown by the makeup of his audience.

Further, the point is symbolically re-inforced by many of the features of the later *samosaraṇa* which, in finished form, exhibits nearly all of the cosmic symbols commonly found in another major Indian imago mundi, the *stūpa*. It may even share aspects of the conception of the Vedic fire-altar as presented in the *Śatapatha Brāhmaṇa*.[13] Prominent among the features that point to cosmic representation in the *samosaraṇa* are: (1) the gods' preliminary activity in clearing and securing a space;[14] (2) the pedestal, tree/parasols, and the platform at the center, which parallel very closely the features of the *yūpa*, or mast, at the center of the *stūpa* (which is apparently related to the *yūpa*—sacrificial stake—associated with the fire-altar);[15] and, (3) the gates at the four cardinal points.[16] The circular walls, enclosing grades of beings in the Jina's audience, might even be assimilable to the grades of attainment associated in the Buddhist tradition with successive *pradakṣiṇā*s of the *stūpa*.[17]

---

10 *Aupapātika* 2 gives the place as Puṇṇabhadda.

11 *Aupapātika* 3-5.

12 *Aupapātika* 6-9.

13 For great assistance in discovering and analyzing these parallels, I am indebted to Nancy E. Falk.

14 Cf. *Śatapatha Brāhmaṇa* 2.1.1.8-10, and Sylvain Lévi 1966:48.

15 See Paul Mus 1935:113-17 and Jean Przyluski 1935:199-210.

16 This cosmic symbol, and its associations with the number four, are prominent in all later *samosaraṇa* representations.

17 See Susumu Nakamura 1951:348-51.

These parallels surely point the way for a thorough study of the *samosaraṇa* in relation to the *stūpa*. Such a point can hardly be taken on here, but a significant and prominent point seems established: the sense in which the *samosaraṇa* is a portrayal of totality, of universality.

The earlier *samosaraṇa* does not seem to have pointed so much in this direction. It conforms much more to the term's etymology: *sam-ava-sṛ*, a gathering together. But between it and the later form there is clearly indicated a process in which the term and occasion are invested with a much more complex notion, and it seems reasonable to consider the occurrences of *samosaraṇa* in relation to the four headings as falling somewhere in this process. This may show more clearly in a closer examination of the texts.

Sūtrakṛtāṅga I.12 by itself has done only one thing; it has associated the term *samosaraṇa* with the four headings. In so doing, it uses the term in the plural, as if to say that these are four "assemblies" that have gathered around four positions. This usage, taken at face value, would seem much closer to the earlier *samosaraṇa* than the later (which makes chronological sense), save that it implies that a *samosaraṇa* is more than just any gathering to hear a teaching, but is rather *the* gathering, *the* audience, *the* group of followers associated with a particular teaching.

Next, in the group of texts apparently associated with *Sūtrakṛtāṅga* I.12, *samosaraṇa* takes on an interesting dimension, for in all of them it is used as a means of classifying existent things. The *Sūtrakṛtāṅga Niryukti* passage translated in chapter 18 begins at verse 117b, where the actual discussion of *kriyā*, etc., begins. In the immediately preceding verses, the *niryukti* has dealt with *samosaraṇa*. The discussion is based on the distinction in Jain thought between *dravya*s, or external conditions, and *bhāva*s, or internal states.

In verses 116-117a,[18] the *niryukti* states that the *samosaraṇa*s are to be understood as six-fold, according to the fact that there are three conditions into which *dravya* falls: conscious, unconscious, and mixed. Each can vary by time (*kāla*) and place (*kṣetra*), giving rise to six types of *dravya*, which are the six *samosaraṇa*s. In 117a, the term *samosaraṇa* is also applied, on the same six-fold model, to *bhāva*. Verse 117b then goes on as translated in chapter 18: "Also, there are *kriyā*, *akriyā*, *ajñāna*, and *vinaya*."

It is difficult to say just what is involved in the use in the *niryukti* of *samosaraṇa* in this classification process. The terms *kāla*, *kṣetra*, *bhāva*, and *dravya* are items that are commonly used, in various configurations, in early Jain texts that are occupied with the classification of existents (see Dixit 1971:24). *Samosaraṇa* does not figure in these early patterns. The obvious solution would be to say that this *niryukti* is simply falling back on familiar terms in order to

[18] These are numbered as vv. 118-119a in the Āgamasaṃgraha edition.

interpret an anomalous occurrence, but the context makes this seem unlikely, for *Sūtrakṛtāṅga* I.11 (the preceding chapter) contains a discussion of the six classes of beings, and the *niryukti* appears to build on this in its handling of *samosaraṇa*. Thus the six-fold scheme is not necessarily out of place, though the term *samosaraṇa* is strange to it. Yet once it has made these statements, the *niryukti* simply continues on, summarizing briefly the contents of *Sūtrakṛtāṅga* I.12, and giving no hint as to why *samosaraṇa* should here have been put into the arena of classifying existent things.

Whatever the significance of the *niryukti*'s approach, Śīlāṅka's commentary on the *niryukti* verses in question makes nothing of it whatsoever. His comments[19] begin with a gloss of the term, in which he speaks of *samosaraṇa* simply as a gathering (cf. Jacobi's explanation, above), after which he goes into great detail on various classifications of *bhāvas*, including classifications that take note of the presence of "right faith" (*samyagdarśana*) and "wrong faith" (*mithyādarśana*) in the *jīva*. Despite the fact that the *niryukti* (and *Sūtrakṛtāṅga*) considers one of the *samosaraṇas* to be a correct position, and despite the fact that *samosaraṇa* is being used as a term for a viewpoint, Śīlāṅka makes no connection at all between this and the material that he presents in his comments. The term *samosaraṇa*, in fact, is not mentioned again once its gloss has been presented.

Śīlāṅka is not, however, necessarily a good indicator of the status of *samosaraṇa*, since his understanding of the text is directed at a different issue (which will be discussed later). The other texts—*Sthānāṅga* and *Bhagavatī*—that make use of *samosaraṇa* (and which are likely much earlier than Śīlāṅka, though perhaps later than the *niryukti*) provide a better standpoint for interpreting the term. In both *Sthānāṅga* and *Bhagavatī*, the passages that use *samosaraṇa* also occur in settings where the different classes of beings are under discussion. Once again, however, the texts themselves do not reflect on the term *samosaraṇa*.

Of the two passages, that in *Sthānāṅga* IV.4 is the more laconic—this being quite in keeping with the overall nature of *Sthānāṅga*. It is set in a section that describes classes of men under various four-fold headings. After giving the short statement quoted in chapter 18, the passage interprets the four *samosaraṇas* as another four-fold way of classifying men, save that it goes on to include the *nārakas* as well. Without elaborating on the latter point, it then concludes its coverage of the subject.

Bhagavatī XXX is far more discursive, and chapter XXX even bears the title *samosaraṇa*. The classificatory nature of the chapter and those surrounding it was noted earlier. The discussion of the *samosaraṇas* opens chapter XXX, with

---

19 Pp. 210b-211 of the Bhavnagar edition and pp. 446-47 of the Āgamasaṃgraha edition.

the lines given in chapter 18 being the first words of the section. It then goes on to relate the *samosaraṇa*s to other modes of classification. The focus of this effort is the notion of *leśyā*s, or "hues" of various *jīva*s in various states of karmic activity. This is extended to the classes of beings according to number of external sense-organs, and other Jain methods of classification; each of these better-known classifications is viewed here through the eyes of the term *samosaraṇa*, so to speak.

The particularly interesting aspect of the discussion in both texts is the distinction that is made among the four *samosaraṇa*s. As in the *Sūtrakṛtāṅga Niryukti*, *kriyāvāda* is clearly understood to be a correct position, and the other three are seen as incorrect. This distinction holds throughout the process of examining other modes of classification, even to the point where the status of future births is considered in relation to *samosaraṇa*. Thus *samosaraṇa* is here being used in full conjunction with other Jain models for considering the variegated nature of all existent things, though once again there is no overt reflection on the process or, as noted, on the term.

This absence of reflection means that the point of the use of the term in such discussions and classifications simply cannot be clearly extracted from the texts themselves. However, in the *Bhagavatī* treatment of the term, the *samosaraṇa*s are clearly seen and used as a means of discussing the possible conditions of the *jīva* with respect to how deeply it is enmeshed in karma. The general significance of *samosaraṇa* in the Jain tradition has already been discussed, and its cosmic, or universal, features pointed out. How could this classificatory use of it relate to the more general usage?

The earliest use of *samosaraṇa* in the 363-account, that in *Sūtrakṛtāṅga* I.12, does not participate heavily in the sense of totality or universality. But perhaps the *niryukti* and certainly *Bhagavatī* use the term to analyze all beings in terms of the condition of the *jīva*. This comes very close to being a position that is only implicit in the later *samosaraṇa*, namely, that the Jina's message reaches each hearer in a way consistent with the hearer's status. This is a position from which it would be possible to conclude that the different conditions of creatures account for the varying viewpoints in the world. This is the direct implication of the *Bhagavatī* passage.

In considering this problem, it is also important to take cognizance of another development that is unique to the texts that use *samosaraṇa*, which is the inclusion of the Jain position within the four-fold set of headings, something that happens nowhere else. The point at which the Jain position is included is under *kriyāvāda*; this inclusion happens already in *Sūtrakṛtāṅga* I.12. The problems that this raises have been discussed at length in chapter 16. Here the matter must be viewed somewhat differently. For purposes of understanding this fact it is doubly unfortunate that the *samosaraṇa* has not been fully studied, and still more unfortunate that *Bhagavatī* does not reflect on its use of the term. But the implication of *Bhagavatī* XXX's entire discussion is clear: the four *samosaraṇa*s exist as part of the karma-caused variety in the world, and the correct, Jain viewpoint therefore is part of a spectrum of viewpoints.

This approach, veiled though the point may be, contains within it not merely a structure for handling many viewpoints, it also accounts for their existence. They are the result of karma, and karma is what differentiates them from the Jain position. Hidden in these few texts that use *samosaraṇa* and include the Jain position in the four is, then, another remarkable point in the process of dealing with other viewpoints.

But it fell far short of carrying the day. Śīlāṅka was clearly not in sympathy with it—in fact, he seems not to have seen at all what might be implied. Abhayadeva, the commentator on the *Bhagavatī* passage that is perhaps the farthest extension of the notion, also seems not to have known quite what to do. He simply says, "Although these are elsewhere all considered wrong views, here the first [i.e., *kriyāvāda*, as opposed to the other three headings] is to be seen as containing right views."[20] Thereafter he restricts himself to explaining the text. Aside from this raised eyebrow, so to speak, he does not tangle with the issues involved.

What would those issues be? The emergence of a four-fold scheme out of its larger background has already been noted for its significance. Now, using a term that is usually restricted to a Jina's own teachings, the four headings are seen to include the Jain position. Further, this step accompanies, in at least one set of texts, the beginnings of the use of the four headings. Thus the emergence of a structure for viewing other positions seems almost to call forth this *samosaraṇa* approach to explaining their presence.

The potential significance of this point can be seen looking at what the next step might have been, but apparently never was: the use of *samosaraṇa* in the singular in this context. In all of these texts, the plural continues to be used, as if to say that each viewpoint is a closed circle. But the same term is applied to all, a term that the tradition also applies to a Jina's teaching and to those who hear it. Where the later tradition presents the *samosaraṇa* in the singular, it includes all classes of creatures. Where the *Bhagavatī* chapter applies it in the plural, it includes all classes of creatures.

The difference between the two would seem to imply an important notion about the nature and source of the difference between the Jain and non-Jain positions. In these texts, where *samosaraṇa* is used in the plural, the non-Jain positions appear to have been granted a status that is equal to, yet distinct from,

20 *Bhagavatī*, p. 1837a.

the Jain stance; this impression is re-inforced by the fact that the Jains are included in the four-fold scheme. This is notably different from the use of the four-fold scheme only as a means for dealing with other viewpoints; for, though the latter has introduced a structure into the non-Jain viewpoints, it has not re-defined the relationship between Jain and non-Jain. *Samosaraṇa*, in the limited arena where it is used, does re-define that relationship and make explicit the reason for the existence of other positions.

Yet, as stated, *samosaraṇa* did not become the standard approach. Nor did this vision of the relationship between Jain and non-Jain positions become standard. What apparently did become the norm is summed up in Abhayadeva's aside: "These are all considered wrong views." This development is next to be considered.

Mithyādarśana

The use of the term *mithyādarśana* to cover this approach raises some problems that are treated more thoroughly elsewhere (see chapter 8 above). Yet it must be raised here in order to explore the dominant approach of the 363-account sources, which is that the four headings all stand for incorrect, non-Jain points of view, and do not include the Jain position. Chapter 16 has discussed the fact that the early uses of *kriyāvāda* need not be taken as equivalent to the Jain position, although the term has a positive sense. The *samosaraṇa* texts do take it as being the Jain stance, while the remaining texts take what is perhaps an even more perplexing step: they turn a non-perjorative term into a negative one.

This development cannot be downgraded in any way, for it perhaps represents another important part of the development of the self-awareness of the Jain—or any—tradition, namely, the process whereby one's own position is detached from those of others. Where the *samosaraṇa* approach seems to regard the Jain position as describable by the notion of *kriyā*, and even (as in *Sūtrakṛtāṅga* I.12) gives *kriyā* a specific Jain content, the more dominant approach in the 363-account seems to have been to detach the Jain position from *kriyā*. This line of analysis must, as with the others, be hypothetical at some points. But to ignore the fact that the Jains' perception of *kriyā* also altered itself in a negative direction would be to ignore something fully as important as the *samosaraṇa* approach.

One can begin to explore the negative understanding of *kriyāvāda* by recalling the suggestion made in chapter 16 that the Jain handling of *kriyāvāda* is a case where a less than specific term becomes more specific. It would seem wise to presume that this process lies behind both the positive and negative approaches to *kriyā*. Even so, the positive understanding is in many ways easier to understand, since the term's original sense is positive. The rise of the negative approach is more difficult to get at.

The process by which this came about is detectable, though complex. A major key to understanding it lies in the end-product, as exemplified by the *Tattvārthādhigama* commentaries, which most strongly present the four headings as all being wrong views. The instructive point is the context in which they do so, for the discussion of the four occurs under the general rubric of *mithyādarśana*, while introducing a particular understanding of this important notion.

Mithyādarśana is regarded by the Jains as the product of karma of a specific sort. This karma has the effect of beclouding the *jīva*'s innate quality of *darśana* and, as such, of leading it to hold false views. This karma-context for non-Jain views is in itself not at all far removed from the general direction of the *samosaraṇa* approach discussed above. But in the *Tattvārthādhigama* commentaries it is given a particular twist in relation to the 363-account, for in these sources the schools of thought are not considered under the heading of *mithyādarśana* that results from karma, but rather under *mithyādarśana* that results from the teachings of others.

This discussion is clearly drawn in each commentary translated in chapter 18. Two sorts of *mithyādarśana* are postulated, one that is inborn and one that comes from others' teachings. The inborn variety is said to arise in virtue of the working of karma, and in all these texts it is sharply differentiated from that which arises from outside, through the teaching of others.

Even this differentiation seems to have undergone a process of sharpening. The *Svabhāṣya* on *Tattvārthādhigama* describes *mithyādarśana* as being of two sorts, either *abhigṛhīta* or *anabhigṛhīta*. In chapter 18 these terms are translated as "active" and "passive" because the *Svabhāṣya* does not make explicit the external source of the former. It does say that "active" *mithyādarśana* consists in the reflective choice of one of the 363 "faulty teachings," but it cannot be said whether this "active" form of *mithyādarśana* rests primarily on the final choice itself or on the state in which the choice is made. Nathmal Tatia (1951:145) makes a firm statement on this point:

> Umāsvāti divides *mithyādarśana* into two categories viz. *abhigṛhīta* (firmly held) and *anabhigṛhīta* (lightly held). The acceptance of a wrong view and obstinate tenacity for it is *abhigṛhīta* and the opposite of it is *anabhigṛhīta*. The difference between the two is determined by the degree of the intensity and tenacity of the adherence to perversity.

Tatia's statement seems to err a bit in the direction of emphasizing the state in which the choice is made, but it reflects a possible interpretation of the *Svabhāṣya*'s terse statement.

While the *Svabhāṣya* may be ambiguous, the other *Tattvārthādhigama* commentators are not. They interpret the two types of *mithyādarśana* in terms of source, using terminology different from that of the *Svabhāṣya*. In place of *anabhigṛhīta* there occurs *naisargika*; and in place of *abhigṛhīta*, *paropadeśa-pūrvaka*. This terminology occurs in the commentaries of Pūjyapāda, Akalaṅka, Bhāskaranandin, and Śrutasāgara. Even Siddhasenagaṇi, who retains the terminology used in the *Svabhāṣya* because of his close following of that text, gives an interpretation that differentiates the two types of *mithyādarśana* more in terms of their sources.

This shift in terminology reflects a genuine change in the perception of non-Jain positions. It is the end-product of a process whose middle stages are somewhat difficult to detect, for it involves not only a shift from the approach of the *Svabhāṣya,* but also a sharp shift from the early discussions of various viewpoints in *Sūtrakṛtāṅga*. In those early accounts, other teachings are commonly referred to as *micchādiṭṭhī* (Sanskrit *mithyādṛṣṭi*), the teachings of those under the influence of *mithyādarśana*. Hence there is nothing new in the use of the terms to speak of others in the *Tattvārthādhigama* commentaries; what is new is the distinction of two types of *mithyādarśana*, one that springs from karma and one that springs from others' teachings.

In this connection, a brief survey of terminology is in order, for there are signs in the terminology that point to the process whose end-point is the position taken in the *Tattvārthādhigama* commentaries. To begin, there follows a list of terms specifically applied to non-Jain positions in *Sūtrakṛtāṅga,* drawn from those chapters in which the discussions of non-Jains are concentrated.

Sūtrakṛtāṅga passages	Terms for non-Jains
I.1.1.10	*mandā* (dull-witted)
I.1.1.14	*mandā, vāiṇo* (*vādī*s)
I.1.1.17	*bālā* (fools)
I.1.1.20-25	*vāiṇo*
I.1.2.4	*bālā, paṇḍiamāṇiṇo* (those who fancy themselves learned)
I.1.2.5	*pāsatthā* (see below)
I.1.2.10	*micchādiṭṭhī* (those possessed of *mithyādarśana* *aṇāriyā* (unworthy ones)
I.1.2.11	*mūḍhagā* (deluded), var. *micchāgā*
I.1.2.13	*micchādiṭṭhī, aṇāriyā*
I.1.2.16-17	*annāṇiyā* (ignorant ones)
I.1.2.32	*micchādiṭṭhī*

I.1.3.13	*pāvāuyā* (propounders)
I.1.4.1	*bālā, paṇḍiamāṇiṇo*
I.3.4.1	*mando*
I.3.4.9	*pāsatthā, aṇāriyā, bālā*
I.3.4.13	*pāsatthā, micchādiṭṭhī, aṇāriyā*
I.6.27	*thāṇam, vāyam*
I.11.28, 31	*micchādiṭṭhī, aṇāriyā*
I.12.1	*samosaraṇa, pāvāduyā*
II.1.12	*annautthiya* (see below)
II.2.79	*pāvāduyā*

The terms listed show an overwhelming emphasis on ignorance, delusion, dullness, and the like. There is nothing in most of them or in most of the discussions from which they are drawn that emphasizes the 'otherness' of the teachers of non-Jain positions. In general, it can be said that the wrongness of the views refuted in *Sūtrakṛtāṅga* rests on error. This means, given the early Jain emphasis on karma as the single most important differentiation factor in the universe, that these wrong views are by implication the result of karma, and not of others' teachings.

Only two specific terms for non-Jains occur in *Sūtrakṛtāṅga*, but their presence is an indication of what might be the middle stages in the process that culminates in the *Tattvārthādhigama* commentaries; for the occurrence of such specific terms, whose point of reference is not karma-induced error, should indicate a shift in perception of non-Jain teachings. These terms are *pāsattha* and *annautthiya*. The former term has puzzled both commentators and translators. Jacobi (1895a:240), following Śīlāṅka, says:

> Pāsattha, usually translated pārśvastha 'outsider,' those who do not acknowledge true arguments; another rendering is pāśastha 'held in bondage.'

Schubring (1926:124) suggests that those described by this term may be "eccentric" (*eigenbrödlerisch*) followers of the Jain way, perhaps implying that *pārśvastha* has the sense of "followers of Pārśva," Mahāvīra's predecessor, between whose followers and Mahāvīra a certain degree of tension is occasionally hinted at; but Schubring does not elaborate. In any case, *pāsattha* is not a common term in later Jain sources.[21]

Annautthiya, however, is noteworthy both for its context here and for its later popularity, particularly in canonical texts. The Jains Sanskritize the term both as *anyayūthika* and *anyatīrthika*, the former meaning "one who belongs to

21 [Editor's note.] On this term, see also Dundas: forthcoming.

another Order," the latter, "another founder [of an Order]."[22] The common context of *annautthiya* is the standard warnings to Jains against associating with non-Jains or following their teachings. It is accompanied in such warnings by another term of great popularity, *parapāsaṇḍa*. Statements containing these terms are found in numerous loci, classic versions being those in *Upāsakadaśāḥ* I.44 and 58. I.44, as translated by Hoernle, reads:

> At this point . . . the blessed Mahāvīra . . . spoke . . . thus: "Truly, O Āṇanda, a disciple of the Samaṇa . . . must know and avoid the following five typical offenses against the law of right belief; viz., scepticism, unstableness, distrustfulness, praising of heterodox teachers [parapāsaṇḍapasamsā], and intimacy with heterodox teachers [parapāsaṇḍasamthave]."

Upāsakadaśāḥ I.58, again in Hoernle's translation, reads:

> Then the householder Āṇanda . . . spake . . . thus: "Truly, Reverend Sir, it does not befit me, from this day forward, to praise and worship any man of a heterodox community [reading *anyayūthika*], or any of the devas of a heterodox community, or any of the objects of reverence of a heterodox community."

The exact content and intent of these terms is not always easy to make out. The Jain tradition itself does not provide many clues, and until the lexicography of Jain Prakrit and Sanskrit usage advances considerably, it is not likely that one will be able to say concisely what is involved in the two terms. They are not always used interchangeably in Jain texts, but the tradition seems to have been groping, almost, for a precise way of differentiating between them. A statement that might shed some light on this point occurs in Haribhadra's commentary on the *Āvaśyaka*:

> One should avoid and not honor *annautthiyas*, i.e., wandering students (*carakas*), mendicants (*parivrājikas*), begging monks (*bhikṣus*), madmen (*bhautas*), etc., as well as avoid and not honor the deities of *annautthiyas*, Rudra, Viṣṇu, Sugata, etc., or the objects reverenced by *annautthiyas*, i.e., *caityas*, images of *arhats*; or the things reverenced by *bhautas* . . . ; also the things reverenced by the *boṭikas*. There are 363 *parapāsaṇḍas*, which are to be distinguished from *pāsaṇḍas*, who are guided by an omniscient one.[23]

Haribhadra then goes on to give the verse that occurs at *Sūtrakṛtāṅga Niryukti* 119, and to give the standard calculation-model.

---

[22] On the problem of which Sanskrit form is the more correct, see Weber (1883-85:36[299]), and Leumann 1882:95. Leumann holds out for *anyatīrthika*, an opinion followed by others. [Editor's note.] On this term, see also Deleu 1970:38-44 and 1977.

[23] The text on which this translation is based is available in this country only in Weber 1886-92:784-85. Even this text consists only of excerpts, which makes the deciphering of particular terms very difficult. *Boṭika* is used in Jain texts as a term for the Digambaras, but even that usage is unclear. See Leumann 1885:91-135.

Haribadra's remark on *parapāsaṇḍa*s is certainly significant, and should be supplemented by Hoernle's (1885-90:22) observation on the term:

> The word *pāsaṇḍa* has, with the Jains, no bad sense. It means generally 'the adherent of any religion,' especially of their own. Hence, with the Brāhmans, it came to mean 'an adherent of a false or heterodox religion'; with them *pāsaṇḍa* is equal to the Jain *para-pāsaṇḍa*.

Hoernle's observation is a bit simplistic, and should certainly be checked against a wider variety of Jain sources (e.g., Kundakunda's *Bhāvapāhuḍa*, translated in chapter 18, uses *pāsaṇḍa* without the *para*-prefix). In any case, because of the term's significance in Sanskrit,[24] the Jain use of the term should be examined.

This brief excursion into these terms can have, so far as the terms themselves are concerned, only the effect of showing avenues for future work. Within the scope of this study the point is less ambitious, but not less telling. Based on what has been unearthed here, an important observation is in order. The appearance of these specific terms, stressing as they do the 'other' and its role in *mithyādarśana*, would appear to mark a significant shift in the Jain view of the non-Jain, a shift that would logically culminate in the division between "inborn" and "received" *mithyādarśana* as presented in the *Tattvārthādhigama* commentaries.

Yet there is an important factor in *annautthiya* and *parapāsaṇḍa* that must be stressed. The presence of these terms does introduce a sense of 'otherness'; yet they also present a sense of commonality between the Jains and the others, a commonality clearly expressed in both terms. It is important to see this as a mode of expression quite different from that which becomes standard in the *Tattvārthādhigama* commentaries. In the latter, 'otherness' comes altogether to the fore and commonality all but vanishes, something that shows clearly in that 'otherness' is not treated on the basis of karma.

That this represents a process of sorts is borne out by the chronology of the texts. *Annautthiya* does not appear until the later portion of *Sūtrakṛtāṅga*, and does not become common until such texts as *Upāsakadaśāḥ*, which are agreed to be later than *Sūtrakṛtāṅga* on the whole. Also, the full sense of 'otherness' in the *Tattvārthādhigama* commentaries appears to postdate the more common use of *annautthiya*.

If a genuine development has been detected here, then the change in the understanding of *kriyāvāda* may also become more intelligible. In those texts, especially Śīlāṅka's commentaries, where *kriyāvāda* must be explained as being wrong, it is not clear just where the flaw in it lies. Its chief fault appears to be its

---

24 Wendy Doniger O'Flaherty (1971:272) gives great prominence to this term in her discussion of heresy, calling it "the Sanskrit term most closely corresponding in negative tone as well as in denotation to the English 'heretic.'"

non-Jain-ness. Thus *kriyāvāda* might most adequately be seen not as a term whose content has been altered, but rather as the victim, as it were, of a growing Jain separateness from everything 'other.' The same may well hold true for the shift in the meaning of *ajñāna*. The additional senses of scepticism and agnosticism make quite good sense when seen in this context of 'otherness' and separation of wrongness from karma-caused error.

One additional feature of the *Tattvārthādhigama* commentaries may both explain and be explained by this approach to the problem: the long lists of names. These lists, as noted in chapter 15, have been explored by Schrader, but no distinct patterns of school-affiliation or the like have emerged from these studies of the lists. This seems a very curious circumstance, for one would expect the names of the various teachers to be grouped in some way corresponding to the character of the headings. Yet this does not seem to be the case, certainly not in light of Akalaṅka's brief excursion into the question of why certain teachers should be put under certain headings. Akalaṅka does not know why, or does not care.

The important point in understanding these lists is that they occur in texts that make a strong distinction between "inborn" and "received" wrong faith. Thus one might not be far wrong in suggesting that the lists of names serve no other purpose than to stress and document the 'otherness' of the four headings. More than anything else, the lists appear to be a hodge-podge of every teacher or sage that might have been known or associated with some text or school. Viewed as part of the process of stressing 'otherness,' the names both shed some light on the process and may themselves be best explained by it.

363 AND SOME PRELIMINARY CONCLUSIONS

This approach to the positive and negative sense of *kriyāvāda* and the other three headings may well grant some new insight into the terms and their settings, and into the Jain tradition's self-understanding. Yet it leaves unexplained the complex and artificial structure of the 363-account in its full version. Further, it must be admitted that none of the currently available sources sheds any real light on the purpose behind the evolution of this grandiose structure.

It would be of prime significance to recover from various sources the rationale behind the use of the number 363. Yet none of the calculation schemes ever refers to an external rationale for the number, and the scope of the problem is truly overwhelming, especially as no immediate source within the Jain tradition for such a number presents itself. Schrader (1902:8) notes that in a few sources a certain king was paid tribute by 363 cities. This isolated reference can only attest to a certain currency for the number, but cannot explain it. It is perhaps also noteworthy that according to *Uttarādhyayana* XXXIV. 20, the total of the various degrees of *leśyā*s (the "hues" of the *jīva*) equals 363. However, the number 363 is reached only by totalling numbers that are not totalled in the source itself, and the commentators do not take any note of a relationship between the possible number 363 here and in the 363-account (see Charpentier 1910:21ff., and Jacobi 1895a:198-99). One other direction for the inquiry presents itself: the number 363 is so tantalizingly close to the 360-day Indian year that one can hardly dismiss this possibility, with all its symbolic implications. Yet once again an utter absence of external verification stymies any attempt to follow up this line.

Later sources within the Jain tradition are no better informed. Śīlāṅka, commenting on *Sūtrakṛtāṅga* II.2.79, states, "all these propounders—the basic divisions and their followers—are given because this is the customary way of stating the matter." In his comments to *Sūtrakṛtāṅga* I.12, he quotes a series of short verses that give the method for calculation; another set of verses is either presented or preserved in Nemicandra's *Gommaṭasāra*.[25] But the evidence of chapter 16, where it has been shown that the details of the calculation considerably postdate the early existence of the four headings, renders it highly improbable that the verses preserved in either of these later sources represent any older traditions. Nor does Nemicandra present any rationale whatsoever for the number 363.

The best that one can conclude, then, would seem to be that the internal structure of the 363-account is artificial and some distance removed from the earliest senses of the headings, which it actually serves to obscure at a number of points. Yet one must concede a certain as yet unexplained force for the number 363, and perhaps even for the subtotals, a force sufficient to evolve such a complex and artificial structure.

In the absence of a full explanation for this structure, one must also ask what effect certain solutions might have on the conclusions drawn in this study. It is certainly true that any set of symbolic values for these numbers would open up new avenues of explanation, particularly if such values might account for the Jain view of the origins of schools of thought. But the greatest safeguard against such a development has already been pointed out. This is the fact that the Jain tradition itself did not overtly preserve any sense of the numbers' significance. To guess at what automatic associations they might have borne seems dangerous and fruitless. The conclusions reached here, then, seem reasonably safe.

In sum, the 363-calculation cannot be regarded as without significance, and the door must be left open for some future discovery. But on the whole, the final version, in which the calculation model appears, should not be allowed to

[25] For both, see chapter 18.

obscure the important early stages in the account and their significance. Two matters of great importance can be seen in the developing account. The first is the positive interpretation of the *kriyāvāda*; the second, the negative. When seen in tandem, the two make an important statement about the matter of relationships between schools of thought. The two interpretations of the single term can be seen as illustrating two sides of a process of growing self-consciousness on the part of the Jains. Both interpretations originate from the same point, from the general 'vocabulary' for speaking of acceptable and non-acceptable positions. The positive interpretation reflects one development of that vocabulary; the negative, another.

The positive understanding seems to affirm a commonality between the Jain position and others, a commonality reflected in the use of the term *samosaraṇa* and the implicit understanding that it is karma that causes the variety of schools of thought. Yet, as noted, this affirmation of commonality, of the Jain position as one among a number of like positions, did not come altogether to the fore. The negative interpretation, with its stress upon 'otherness' and the non-karmic source for schools of thought comes to be more dominant, with such terms as *annautthiya* and *parapāsaṇḍa* perhaps representing an intermediate step.

In tandem, the two seem to illustrate a dual process. The sense of commonality is still present in the negative process, and the sense of separateness is present in the positive. The point of this observation is that the evolving Jain sense of the relationships between their own and other positions seems to participate in an understanding of themselves as being both like others in crucial respects and yet quite separate from them.

Where the study of the relationship between schools of thought is concerned, both of these understandings carry strong significance. In what sense religious movements understand each other in such terms—as alike, yet separate—actually might be said to underly the whole of the study of one movement by another, in the sense that such study may be no more than an extension of the basic way in which movements perceive each other. If this were the only point to be drawn from a dissection and analysis of the 363-account, it would already be of value. As it is, however, the Jain tradition offers yet another arena for investigation, the philosophical compendia. The discovery of the two directions present in the earlier accounts are of significant help in understanding the compendia, and the latter can shed still more light on the general problem of relationships.

ŚĪLĀNKA AND THE NAYAVĀDA

This study will conclude with a brief examination of the one point where the *nayavāda* enters into the 363-account. This particular case is examined here because it helps to raise and clarify the matter of how the 363-account represents an attempt to consider the existence of other viewpoints, not merely refute them.

It is important to examine this specific case of the *nayavāda* and the 363-account in this light. In chapter 14, the *nayavāda* and its potential as a tool for dealing with the existence of a multiplicity of viewpoints were introduced and discussed at some length. Certain limitations on the possible study of the *nayavāda* were noted there, and what follows here is not conceived to be an exhaustive investigation. However, the *nayavāda* enters into the commentary level of the 363-account at one point, and the use to which it is put raises certain questions concerning it. This discussion seeks to touch on those questions without raising the entire complex of issues surrounding the *nayavāda*.

The point at which the *nayavāda* becomes a feature of the history of the 363-account is Śīlāṅka's commentary on *Sūtrakṛtāṅga* I.12. This problematic passage has already been explored from several angles; the crucial point in Śīlāṅka's commentary is his handling of the identification made in the text between the *kriyāvāda* and the Jain point of view. Śīlāṅka does not see the *kriyāvāda* as a correct position, and this presents him with a problem that he solves by using—at least indirectly—the *nayavāda*.

Śīlāṅka asserts that the *kriyāvāda* is correct only when one accepts all the possibilities comprised under that heading. At first glance this seems quite striking, for the two processes pointed out in the preceding section might seem to be combined here. One's own position subsumes in it all other positions; thus both commonality and otherness co-exist in one structure. The *nayavāda*, in fact, exhibits just this potential, and its possibilities in this direction should be seen as lying behind the approaches to it that were discussed in chapter 14.

However, as presented by Śīlāṅka, this approach does not really make sense of the 363-account, for he applies the *nayavāda* only to the *kriyāvāda*, and does not see the other three headings as also being part of the correct stance, subsumed under the Jain position. This is the first significant sign that Śīlāṅka's use of the *naya*s is less than fully creative or effective.

Śīlāṅka's full statement (presented in chapter 18) does not, in fact, center on the *kriyāvāda* itself or mention the other three headings. He focusses completely on the items in the 'causal' list within the *kriyā* heading: *kāla, niyati, svabhāva,* etc., and puts his final conclusion in terms of those items:

> In this way, seeing all these—time, etc.—as having causal power, and admitting the self, merit, demerit, other-worldly things and the like, the *kriyāvādī* is to be seen as possessing the quality of right faith (*samyagdṛṣṭitva*).[26]

Śīlāṅka then has an objector raise the question of how correctness could reside in an aggregate of several things that are individually incorrect. His response is, in essence, that the whole is more than the sum of its parts, and to buttress his response he quotes eight Prakrit verses. It is only in these verses that the term *naya* occurs; it is not used by Śīlāṅka in any part of the body of his comments. The verses read as follows.

1. Viewing unequivocally as the cause of all
   one out of time, self-nature, necessity, prior deeds,
   human effort:
   This is erroneousness; but viewed as a whole
   they make up correctness.

2. Indeed, all of these—time and the rest—
   are causal forces as a collection in this world;
   Linked in this way alone are they properly
   part of every effort.

3. But not simply through time, etc., individually
   arises anything at all;
   In this world even cooking *mudga* and the like
   has the collection of all these as its causes.

4. Just as cat's-eyes and other jewels of various quality,
   when not joined together
   Are not given the name "necklace,"
   though they be valuable;

5. Even so, the teachings of individual parties,
   though they be thoroughly convinced,
   Mutually ignoring other positions, do not—
   all these *nayas*—attain to being called
   right faith.

6. Again, just as those jewels, tied together into order,
   according to their different qualities,
   Are called a necklace, and lose
   their individuality;

26 For the full statement, see the translation in chapter 18.

7. Just so all these *nayavādas*, when explained
   according to their separate states,
   Do not attain to being called right faith
   when they exist separately.

8. Therefore, all the *nayas* are erroneous views
   when limited to their own position;
   But when they are determined to be interrelated
   their nature is correctness.

Six of these eight verses also occur in Siddhasena Divākara's *Sammaïsuttam*: verse one at *Sammaïsuttam* III.53, verse eight at I.21, and verses four through seven at I.22-25. These parallels both help to explain certain features of Śīlāṅka's remarks, and raise certain issues concerning the *nayavāda* and non-Jain schools of thought.

As concerns Śīlāṅka's use of the verses, it has been noted by Schrader that Śīlāṅka replaces *īśvara* and *ātman* in the 363-account list of items with *purākṛta* (prior deeds) and *puruśakāra* (self-exertion). However, Schrader does not note that in the process of explaining the calculation of the 363 options Śīlāṅka uses the standard 363-account list. Schrader's explanation of how Śīlāṅka's alterations came about ("Denn selbstverständlich wurde von den Jainas die Existenz der *ātman-brahman* und vor allem die des *īśvara* durchaus negiert"[27]) is rather weakened thereby.[28] The point would rather seem to be that Śīlāṅka's alterations were made with the quoted verses in mind, and that the problem lies in the introduction of these verses into a context that they do not precisely fit.

Śīlāṅka's problem arises from his need to subjoin a version of the 363-account that takes a positive view of the *kriyāvāda* to one that does not. The solution to the problem appears to have presented itself in the form of the quoted verses. These Śīlāṅka introduces without extending the principle inherent in them to include all four headings. Thus his use of the verses appears to function as a solution to his problem alone, and not as part of a new theory or vision of the 363-account or of the relationship between the Jains and other positions. When this is seen to be the case, the potential significance of this passage in Śīlāṅka fades considerably.

As concerns the *nayavāda* itself, it would seem quite clear that Śīlāṅka is not aware of it as offering a strong alternative to the 363-account's approach to multiple viewpoints. This does testify indirectly to the status of the *nayavāda* on this point. However, since the verses are not quoted in the exact order in which

27 [Editor's Translation.] "It was self-evident to the Jainas that the existence of *ātman-brahman* and above all *īśvara* was denied."

28 For his remarks on this problem, see Schrader 1902:6-7.

they occur in the *Sammaïsuttam*, it cannot be said for certain that Śīlāṅka is quoting from this highly important work in the history of the *nayavāda*. Therefore, the presence of these verses in *Sammaïsuttam* requires comment, in the course of which a few observations on the *nayavāda* itself are in order.

Since the verses contain material (the items *kāla*, etc.) commonly found in discussions of non-Jain views, they themselves represent a case where the *nayavāda* seems to be involved in the problem of handling other positions. As concerns the items in the verses, chapter 16 has already shown that lists containing *kāla*, etc., may vary widely, so that the *Sammaïsuttam* verses are not necessarily deviations from any set standard. Of more significance is the question of what one might be able to conclude concerning the *nayavāda* itself, based on how this list of items is used in *Sammaïsuttam*. This, in turn, raises the issue pointed out in chapter 14: what sort of relationship exists between the *nayavāda* and the problem of non-Jain viewpoints?

The development of the *nayavāda* has been admirably traced by K. K. Dixit in his *Jaina Ontology*, and the following remarks rely largely on his observations. Dixit (1971:24) points out that the doctrine first makes recognizable appearances in *Anuyogadvāra, Āvaśyaka Niryukti, Ṣaṭkhaṇḍāgama*, and *Tattvārthādhigama*, all of which are texts that exhibit a fair advance over the early Jain theories of predication and judgement. In most of these texts (e.g., *Tattvārthādhigama* I.6, 33[D]; I.6, 34-35[Ś]) its form is not yet the standard seven-fold variety presented above, though the notion that there are seven, and the usual names for the seven, do occur in these early sources (Dixit 1971:69-70, 78). In all these texts, the import and thrust of the doctrine is undergoing a steady process of evaluation and experimentation, so that even though the later standard form is recognizable at places, it is surrounded by alternative approaches and formulations (of which the *Tattvārthādhigama* passages are excellent examples).[29]

In light of this general picture of the beginnings of the *nayavāda*, it is useful to consider Dixit's (1971:88-89) general assessment of the early *nayavāda* and its relationship to non-Jain schools:

> It can plausibly be argued that the seven *nayas* . . . represented so many non-Jaina ways of looking at things, ways with which these theoreticians had become acquainted in the course of their day-to-day missionary work. But the argument is weak and the fact seems to be that the advocates of 7 *nayas* [i.e., the non-Jaina positions] are almost . . . "men of straw." . . . In any case, no Āgamic text ever mention [*sic*] a well-established non-Jaina school of philosophy as an upholder of this

[29] Among such alternative formulations is the two-fold division of the *nayas* into *kriyānaya* and *jñānanaya* that was discussed earlier. This division appears with a slightly different thrust at *Sammaïsuttam* III.68. Though of interest for this study, this alternative appears to have had little or no lasting influence on the *nayavāda*. See Dixit 1971:78.

> *naya* or that. Of course, this does not mean that the doctrine of 7 *nayas* was formulated in utter isolation from the contemporary development taking place within . . . Indian Philosophy in general. . . . What is being emphasised is that even while developing the doctrine of 7 *nayas* the Āgamic texts make no explicit reference to a non-Jaina school of philosophy, nor can it be made out that such a reference is implicitly there.

Dixit's term "Āgamic" refers to the texts given above (*Tattvārthādhigama* et al.), and his point is valuable in forming a tentative judgement concerning the early *nayavāda* and non-Jain views. Beyond this, however, Dixit sees the texts of the later Jain thought being much more aware of and concerned with the existence of other schools. Of Siddhasena and others of his time (which Dixit places somewhat after the period to which the above texts belong) he says (Dixit 1971:111):

> It seems that the Jaina theoreticians of the period had somehow come to the conclusion that the so many non-Jaina philosophical views are just so many one-sided expressions of truth and that their task simply was to point out how this or that philosophical view was actually a one-sided expression of truth.

This is the atmosphere in which he places the later *nayavāda*.

The point of this, however, is not that the *nayas* were conceived as a tool for explaining multiplicity in schools of thought, but rather that they served very well as tools for refutation. This, in fact, is the way in which the above-noted division into *kriyā* and *jñāna* is used at *Sammaïsuttam* III.68. Siddhasena uses these two basic *naya* formulations simply as instances of incorrectness.

This is the general tone of Siddhasena's discussion of the *nayas* in relation to other viewpoints. There does not seem to be a sense of the *nayavāda* as explaining or accounting for the existence of other schools of thought; only their wrongness is accounted for. In this respect, several verses from *Sammaïsuttam* III are instructive. In III.47-49, Siddhasena comes close to making a summary statement about *nayas* in relation to schools of thought:

47. There are as many *nayavādas* as there are ways of speaking;
and there are as many different doctrines as there are *nayavādas*.

48. Kapila's *darśana* is to be stated as one of [the] *dravyāstika* [*naya*];
In the Buddha-*naya* there is purely the *paryāya*-aspect.[30]

49. Though the Ulūka position be supported by both [basic *nayas*],
It is false, for since each puts itself forward, they are independent.[31]

---

30 On *dravyāstika* and *paryāyāstika*, see above, chapter 14.

31 I follow Dixit 1971:111 on the translation of several points,.

Siddhasena then reviews several absolutist positions concerning the existence of the self, in the course of which comes a verse that also occurs in Śīlāṅka:

> 53. Viewing unequivocally as the cause of all
> one out of time, self-nature, necessity, prior deeds,
> human effort:
> This is erroneousness; but reviewed as a whole
> they make up correctness.

Thereafter, in verses 54-55, Siddhasena enumerates six constituents of a correct position or an incorrect one, the crucial point being one-sidedness. No more mention is made of specific schools or views. Verse 53 that lists *kāla*, etc., is not systematically related to an exposition of viewpoints, but is rather a self-contained illustration of the folly of partial views. It and those that mention the other schools of thought seem to have little or no systematic or intrinsic connection with the structure of the *nayavāda* itself. Furthermore, verse 47 that introduces the mention of specific schools would certainly seem to undercut any contention that the *nayavāda* sees some structure or order in the crowd of non-Jain positions.

The context of Siddhasena's mention of specific schools is also instructive. A major thrust of *Sammaïsuttam* III is that *dharma*, or true teaching, consists of two parts, *hetuvāda* and *āgama* (III.43ff.). The *nayavāda* is part and parcel of the former, and in Siddhasena's view:

> 46. The proper *nayavāda* is support of the *āgama*;
> But wrongly put it undoes both parts [*hetu* and *āgama*].

Here, then, is the point of departure for his consideration of non-Jain viewpoints. The sum of the whole is more or less that the *nayavāda*, as a tool, will support the *āgama* position; and where there is disagreement with that position, i.e., disagreement with the Jain position, the reason for it is the misapplication of the *nayavāda*. Siddhasena clearly does see the *naya*s as a way of accounting for the differences between views; but although some of his statements come very close to it, he does not seem to see beyond the level of refutation.

From one point of view, this is so slightly removed from being a genuine consideration of why there should be many points of view that it does not seem reasonable or easily possible to maintain that anything is lacking. To some extent, this is due to the nature of the *nayavāda* itself, for implicit in it is the notion that the correct position is the sum of a number of positions. But as Siddhasena seems to understand the *nayavāda*, especially as revealed in verse 47 of *Sammaïsuttam* III, the schools of thought that are introduced seem to serve only an illustrative purpose. The *nayavāda*'s *raison d'être* lies elsewhere than in seeing some structure in the existence of these viewpoints, even though it may be applicable thereto.

So far as the history of the *nayavāda* is concerned, this logical tool does not itself seem to have been shaped by the need to express a totality of viewpoints, though it certainly represents an attempt to grasp the number of possible approaches to making judgements concerning objects and propositions. This implicit totality in the *nayavāda* is what makes it tempting to conclude that it is what the scholars discussed in chapter 14 say that it is; but one must beg, given the evidence at hand, to disagree.[32]

This is a somewhat disappointing conclusion, for the *nayavāda* can be seen as participating in the dual process identified in the last section of this chapter, i.e., the vision that one's own and other positions are alike in crucial repects, yet different. Yet when it is used to discuss others, the *nayavāda* appears to exemplify the sort of approach shown in the later 363-account, where a radical separation of 'others' from one's own position overwhelms the commonality that is understood to exist between one's own stand and the others. The possibility that—even in Śīlāṅka—the *nayavāda* might represent a new fusion of commonality and self-awareness was mentioned above. But it has also been shown that a truly new expression of the relationship between the Jains and the others did not emerge.

The *nayavāda*, rather, seems more to stress 'otherness,' and not to move toward the commonality implicit in it. Nowhere is this more clearly shown than in Hemacandra's *Anyayogavyavacchedikādvātriṃśikā*, which was composed some 400 years after Śīlāṅka. This work, quoted in chapter 14, contains a striking statement linking the *naya*s and schools of thought. But despite the fact that other schools, as representing various *naya*s, would implicity be related in some way to the Jains, Hemacandra never explores or expresses that commonality. He, too, uses the *nayavāda* only as a handy tool for refutation.

The *nayavāda*, then, can guardedly be said not to exhibit the crucial characteristics of the four-fold core of the 363-account, despite all its tendencies in that direction. It certainly cannot be said that the *nayavāda* deserves no further exploration along these lines, but such exploration is far beyond the limits of this study.

---

32 Mallavādin's *Nayacakra*, which was also touched upon in chapter 14 as being the source for much of the scholars' opinion of the *nayavāda*, might well prove to be an exception to this disagreement. But the history of Mallavādin's work itself would argue that the *nayavāda* did not function in such a way, for this work seems to have been left aside by much of the subsequent Jain tradition.

18

THE 363-ACCOUNT: TEXTS*

Since references to the 363-account occur in so many scattered loci, brief remarks on context accompany the passages that are presented. The texts are given in groups, according to the divisions introduced in chapter 15. This should enable the reader to link the specific texts to the general scheme of development and dominance that has been described in this section. All translations are mine.

GROUP A

These sources are all Śvetāmbara canonical texts, and general remarks on them have been made by various scholars. Brief introductions are given here, both for each text as a whole and for the specific passages in question.

Ācārāṅga Sūtra as its title (Skt. *ācāra*) indicates, is composed of teachings on proper behavior. In the passage in question, the terms *kiriyāvāī*, *āyāvāī*, and *logāvāī* are used to describe one who accepts the existence of an on-going self and patterns his behavior accordingly. No other passage in *Ācārāṅga* bears on the 363-account.

Ācārāṅga Sūtra I.1.1.3b-4a:

* From dissertation, p. 82-118.

> In the same way, some have the knowledge: "There is in me an on-going self; and this 'I' arrives [when born] from this or that cardinal or intermediate direction out of all the cardinal and intermediate directions."
>
> Such a one is an *ātmavādī*, a *lokavādī*, a *karmavādī*, and *kriyāvādī*.

Sūtrakṛtāṅga Sūtra is a different matter. Its title is always explained as meaning that the text gives accounts of one's own and other doctrines, though the etymology of the title itself is unclear. Its Sanskrit form (*Sūtrakṛtāṅga*) is likely false, since *sūya* is not the Ardhamāgadhī equivalent of *sūtra*. Schubring (1935:62; 1962:87) hazards the guess that *sūya* equals the Sanskrit *sūci*, perhaps in the sense of "array" or even "vision" (*dṛṣṭi*). The false Sanskritization is found early in the Jain tradition. In any case, *Sūtrakṛtāṅga* is a catalogue of accounts of non-Jain views, and it is not surprising that a large number of sources are found in it, both for the 363-account and for other accounts referred to in later chapters.

Two of the *Sūtrakṛtāṅga* passages given here (I.1.2.24 and I.10.16-17) are apparently to be understood in the same general light as the *Ācārāṅga* text, that an on-going self exists, and is responsible for its actions and their consequences. *Sūtrakṛtāṅga* I.6.27 is part of a list of Mahāvīra's qualities, and it is notable only for giving all four headings. *Sūtrakṛtāṅga* I.12.1, which introduces a full chapter on the four headings, is much more important. The title of the chapter is *samosaraṇa*, a term whose meaning and origins have been discussed in chapter 17. It should be noted here that as a term for the schools represented by the four headings, it is extremely important for understanding the peculiar character of the 363-account. The chapter consists of twenty-two verses, and breaks down as follows: verses 2-10 very tersely summarize the tenets of *akriyāvāda*, *ajñānikavāda*, and *vinayavāda*; and verses 11-22 are an exposition of *kriyāvāda*, from which it appears that the Jains considered themselves *kriyāvādī*s.

This particular chapter, forming as it does a whole devoted to the exposition of the four headings, may fairly be considered the locus classicus of this scheme in *Sūtrakṛtāṅga*, and one of the most significant passages on this point in the canonical texts. This conclusion is buttressed by the fact that the verses in *Sūtrakṛtāṅga Niryukti* that summarize the four headings are intended as memorial verses for this chapter. Given these factors, the materials in *Sūtrakṛtāṅga* I.12 must be weighted accordingly when they are used in discussions of the 363-account.

Sūtrakṛtāṅga Sūtra I.1.2.24:[1]

> Also, there is the previously stated faith of the *kriyāvādī*; [It declares] increased *saṃsāra* for those who put aside thinking on karma.

---

1 The 1950 Bhavnagar edition of the first book of the *Sūtrakṛtāṅga* is superior to the 1880 Āgamasaṃgraha edition, and so is used where possible.

Sūtrakṛtāṅga Sūtra I.10.16-17:

Some in this world, indeed, [hold that] the self is not involved in activity; questioned by one of these, [the monks] explain self-restraint. Those who are involved in destructive acts are enmeshed in the world; they do not know the law that brings release.

Men here, verily, have different opinions; they declare action (*kriyā*) and inaction (*akriyā*). For a mortal fool who pampers the body without restraint there is increased karma bondage.

Sūtrakṛtāṅga Sūtra I.6.27:

Having considered the stance of the *kriyāvāda, akriyāvāda, vinayavāda*, and *ajñānika*, having thus mastered all the teachings, he [Mahāvīra] lived with restraint all his life.

Sūtrakṛtāṅga Sūtra I.12.1:

These are the four positions that the propounders each declare: They state action (*kriyā*), inaction (*akriyā*), respectfulness (*vinaya*) as the third, and agnosis (*ajñāna*) as the fourth.

Sūtrakṛtāṅga Sūtra II.1.17 (parallels: II.1.24, 28, 32):

Such as these cannot inform one concerning activity (*kriyā*) or inactivity (*akriyā*), doing good or doing ill, merit or demerit, purity or impurity, attainment or non-attainment [of release], hell or its absence.

Sūtrakṛtāṅga Sūtra II.1.30 (partial):

Indeed, in this world are two [sorts of] men. Some men admit *kriyā*; some men do not admit *kriyā*.

These last two *Sūtrakṛtāṅga* passages require a further word of explanation. Both occur within a chapter that is a parable, discussed in chapter 17, concerning types of non-Jain views. The latter passage is taken from a *pūrvapakṣa* that expresses the views of an upholder of Necessity (*niyati*), so its striking use of *kriyā* and *akriyā* must be tempered a bit. These two passages conclude the presentation of *Sūtrakṛtāṅga* sources in group A.

The next passage comes from *Uttarādhyayana Sūtra*, where, in contrast to *Sūtrakṛtāṅga*, the focus is generally on the life of the ascetic, not on doctrine. The *Uttarādhyayana Sūtra* text itself is filled with tales of pious men, and the commentary tradition associated with this text adds a great many such tales of its own. Chapter eighteen is devoted to the tale of King Sañjaya and his conversion to the Jain way of life. Verse 23 is a question addressed to Sañjaya by another ascetic; verse 33 is part of Sañjaya's reply. Jacobi's translation differs from this in that he puts verse 23 into Sañjaya's mouth; this puts a very different tone onto his translation of the remaining verses in the passages. The reasons for taking the verse as given here are discussed above in chapter 16.

Uttarādhyayana Sūtra XVIII.23, 33:

> O great sage, [there are] activity (*kriyā*), inactivity (*akriyā*), respectfulness (*vinaya*), and agnosis (*ajñāna*); what does a wise man say concerning these four things?
>
> One who stands firm would affirm *kriyā*, [and] put aside *akriyā*; one who has faith must practice the difficult law according to the faith.

No other *Uttarādhyayana Sūtra* passage bears on the 363-account.

Ācāradaśāḥ, in which the next source is located, contains ten sections on monastic and lay practices. The eighth of these, as the texts are presently constituted, is the *Kalpa Sūtra* edited and translated by Jacobi. Part six contains a brief discussion of *kriyā* and *akriyā* as part of an account of the eleven lay-*pratimās*, or vow-stages. Part of the passage given here duplicates parts of *Sūtrakṛtāṅga* II.2, but the duplicate portions are not concerned with *kriyā* and *akriyā*. Schubring holds that the text given below is an interpolation, since it fits its context a bit poorly and is not duplicated in other discussions of the *pratimās*. This point, and its bearing on *kriyā* and *akriyā*, are discussed below.[2]

Ācāradaśāḥ VI (partial):

> In this world, verily, eleven vow-stages for laymen are declared by the blessed elders. What, indeed, are the eleven vow-stages for laymen . . . ? These, verily, are . . . , as follows:
>
> He who is an *akriyāvādī* [is] a *nāstikavādī*; he [is] *nāstika*-minded; [his is the] *nāstika*-view. He is not a declarer of truth; he does not declare what is unchanging; he declares that "there is nothing beyond this world"; that there is neither this world nor another; that there is neither mother nor father, neither *arhant*s nor *cakravartin*s, neither *bāladeva*s nor *vāsudeva*s, neither the nether-worlds nor their denizens. There is no distinction between the effects of the fruits of doing good or ill. There is neither good action nor good results, neither evil action nor evil results. Doing good and doing ill are fruitless. Souls are not reborn; there is neither hell nor the abode of bliss. The one who declares thus, is thus-minded, has such a view, stands firm attached to such opinions—he is a man of many desires. [The remainder duplicates *Sūtrakṛtāṅga* II.2.61-68, through: He will not easily attain true vision in the future.] Such a one is an *akriyāvādī*.
>
> Of what sort is a *kriyāvādī*? [The answer duplicates the above, with the negative particles removed, up to:] though a man of great desires, his is the northern [auspicious] netherworld, the bright fortnight; he will easily attain true vision in the future. Such is he who is a *kriyāvādī*. Though he be devoted to the whole law, for one [who does not reach this first *pratimā*, where error is removed] the whole of the

2 See Schubring 1962:110 and 1966:14. On the *pratimās*, see R. Williams 1963:172-81.

> vows previously begun is not correct. This is the *darśana*-lay-vow, the first lay-vow-stage.[3]

The last two sources in group A are from *Sthānāṅga Sūtra* and *Bhagavatī Sūtra*. Given here are only those passages that present the elements in the 363-account. Each one rests in a large, complex context, and the full passages are discussed in chapter four. The short passages are given here so as to introduce their terminology. The full sources are different from most of the others in group A, though the difference will become fully evident only in the later discussion.

Sthānāṅga Sūtra IV.4 (partial):

> There are declared to be four teaching-positions: *kriyāvādīs*, *akriyāvādīs*, *ajñānikavādīs*, [and] *vinayavādīs*.[4]

This *Sthānāṅga* source must first be judged in terms of the nature of the text in which it is found. *Sthānāṅga* consists of ten chapters, which are devoted to accounts—mostly non-analytical—of objects that occur singly, in pairs, in triads, etc., up to groups of ten. Thus this passage occurs in chapter four, since it treats a group of four items.

It is also noteworthy that the context of the verse is quite different from the contexts of such sources in *Sūtrakṛtāṅga*. The passage given is followed by one that relates certain classes of beings to certain doctrinal views. This approach to the *raison d'être* of variety in doctrine deserves some scrutiny; but here it must be viewed in light of its occurrence in a text devoted to classification, or even to explanation by classification (a feature of a good many Jain texts, early and late).

An additional note of caution is needed regarding items found in *Sthānāṅga*. Scholars are united in regarding a text of this sort as being highly susceptible to interpolation, since additional items or groups of items can easily be added to a particular chapter. The unsystematic nature of the text plus this possibility requires additional care in interpreting this particular source. Fortunately, it can be interpreted in the light of a parallel source in *Bhagavatī*.

Bhagavatī XXX.1 (partial):

> [Gautama:] Master, how are the teaching-positions known?
> [Mahāvīra:] Gautama, the teaching positions are known as four-fold: *kriyāvādīs*, *akriyāvādīs*, *ajñānikavādīs*, and *vinayavādīs*.

Bhagavatī's 40 chapters are divisible into two groups: 1-20 and 21-40. The first group contains older material, much of it concerning Mahāvīra's life and activities, cast for the most part into loosely organized collections of legends and tales. This literary form breaks off after chapter 20, though the remaining

3 Emendations to the text itself by Schubring; bracketed English inserts mine. The translation of the next to the last sentence omits a number of technical terms.

4 I have slightly emended the text, based on the commentary.

chapters are generally kept in dialogue-form, as above. What is more striking is the organization of the material in the second part of the book, chapters and groups of chapters being organized around specific topics.

The method according to which these topics are approached is centered around classificatory principles, having to do largely with karma, its varieties, and its effects on existents. Of immediate importance is the similarity of this passage to *Sthānāṅga* IV.4, a similarity that extends even to the immediate context of the two passages, i.e., the types of creatures belonging to various types of doctrine.

This concludes the presentation of the texts in group A. It should be very clear that they stand at a great distance from the full 363-account, and that this distance must be given more attention than has been accorded it up to now.

GROUP B

These texts take the four headings and add to them the notion that there are 363 different schools, of four different types. Only two canonical texts are included here, plus the *niryukti* on one of them. These three sources are presented first, as a group, despite the fact that they do not occur together in the lists given above. This is done because they present less problems than some of the other sources in B, and because they are somewhat interrelated.

A few introductory remarks are in order concerning these sources. *Sūtrakṛtāṅga* II.2.79 is the only *Sūtrakṛtāṅga* passage to link the four headings and the number 363. It stands in a part of the book that is younger than the part containing the texts in group A. The *Nandī* passage comes from the part of *Nandī* that lists the various Śvetāmbara texts and summarizes them. The passage given is, in fact, the *Nandī* summary of *Sūtrakṛtāṅga*. Thus it is reduced somewhat in status as an independent source. However, it is important in another sense, for it shows that *Sūtrakṛtāṅga*—the catalogue of non-Jain positions—was closely linked with the 363-account by the time that the *Nandī* summary was composed. The *Sūtrakṛtāṅga Niryukti* passage, which is attached to *Sūtrakṛtāṅga* I.12, is not in itself a sign of such development in the view of *Sūtrakṛtāṅga*. However, the great currency of its verse 119 (or the source of that verse) in later accounts adds to one's picture of the dominance of the 363-account.

Sūtrakṛtāṅga Sūtra II.2.79 (partial):

> There are reckoned to be 363 propounders, as follows: *kriyāvādī*s, *akriyāvādī*s, *ajñānikavādī*s, and *vinayavādī*s.

Sūtrakṛtāṅga Niryukti 117b-121:

Also, there are *kriyā, akriyā, ajñāna*, and *vinaya*.
Kriyāvādīs declare "It is," *akriyāvādīs* "It is not,"
ajñānīs [declare] agnosis, *vinayavādīs* adherence to *vinaya*.
There are 180 [types of] *kriyā*, and 84 of *akriyā*,
67 of *ajñānika*, and 32 of *vinaya*.
Their doctrinal conclusions are declared in detail in this chapter;
And the positions are stated by it, their true natures being determined.
The *kriyāvādī* has a correct view, while the rest are false;
having abandoned wrong teaching, give service to this true teaching.

Nandī Sūtra 88 (partial):

> What is the *Sūtrakṛtāṅga*? By it is explained the world, the non-world, the world-and-non-world; souls are explained, non-soul and that which is soul and non-soul. One's own doctrine is explained, and other doctrine, and that which is of both. In the *Sūtrakṛtāṅga*, the host of 363 propounders—180 *kriyāvādīs*, 84 *akriyāvādīs*, 67 *ajñānikavādīs*, 32 *vinayavādīs*—having been shown, one's own doctrine is established.

The other texts in group B are more problematic than these three canon-based sources. This is largely so because the bulk of them are from Digambara works, many of which have been studied very little. Even Umāsvāti's *Tattvārthādhigama Sūtra* and its commentaries have not been analysed in depth. For a study such as this one, this raises the difficulty of avoiding distortion of a source's significance, since the source is only a very small part of a poorly known text. Thus the introductory remarks to the remaining texts in B are often rather lengthy.

The first of these is the *Bhāvapāhuḍa* of Kundakunda. This text is not generally considered to be one of Kundakunda's major works; his authorship of it is, in fact, doubted by some scholars.[5] Nonetheless, even the reckoning to his

[5] The *Bhāvapāhuḍa* has commonly been taken as one part of a six-part composition, *Chappāhuḍa* (or *Ṣaṭpāhuḍa*) because Śrutasāgara (ca.1500 C.E.) wrote a commentary on it and five other *pāhuḍas* as a group. At times, two other *pāhuḍas* are added to these and the whole entitled *Aṣṭapāhuḍa*, but this is not commonly the case. According to A. N. Upadhye (1935:xxxvi), each *pāhuḍa* should be considered an independent text. This is supported by the fact that when they are listed in the order in which Śrutasāgara grouped them, they do not present any standard Jain order for the topics covered.

While scholars do not rate the *pāhuḍas* very highly, some of this may be due to very imperfect acquaintance with them. F. W. Thomas (1935:xviii-xix), who appears to reckon only with the *Aṣṭapāhuḍa* setting of the texts, gives *Bhāvapāhuḍa* 137 as the locus of the mention of 363 systems, and gives the number of *kriyāvādīs* as 80. (Since I have had no recourse to the edition of the text used by Thomas, the latter two points are tentative judgements; but Thomas makes no mention of any alternatives.)

In the matter of authorship, when Winternitz (1933:577) casts doubt on Kundakunda's authorship, he refers to and probably relied on W. Denecke 1926:160-68. Denecke (1926:163), on linguistic grounds, holds that the *Chappāhuḍa* cannot be by the author of the major works attributed to Kundakunda; he also holds that the individuality of the various *pāhuḍas* points to a heterogenous origin. Upadhye does not agree. I cannot adjudge this.

[Editor's note.] See also Schubring 1957.

account of any aspect of Jain thought must be seen as having some degree of significance, both in view of the high esteem accorded his other works (they are included in the four Digambara *anuyogas*[6]) and because Kundakunda stands at the very beginning of Digambara philosophical activity.

According to Upadhye (1935:xxxiv, xxxvii), the *Bhāvapāhuḍa* is not so much a systematic consideration of its subject as it is a compilation of items related to it, with little if any elaboration of technical points. *Bhāva* here refers to the states of the *jīva*, which are of various sorts depending on the level of the activity of karma. In this role as a state of the *jīva, bhāva* is strongly contrasted with the notion of *dravya*, or "substance," in this particular text. The point of this contrast in most Jain thought is that *bhāva*, the state of the *jīva*, is that which makes it possible for *dravya*, in the form of karma, to affect the *jīva*. According to Upadhye (1935:xxxii), this particular text regards *bhāva* itself as a positive force, *dravya* as negative; *bhāva* as internal purity, *dravya* as external practice.

One may tentatively say that here the various doctrines belong in the sphere of *dravya*. Again according to Upadhye (1935:xxxii), "various virtues, religious practices, austerities, scriptural study and knowledge: all these are simply a farce in the absence of *bhāva*," according to the way in which the *Bhāvapāhuḍa* presents the matter. It is against this background that the *Bhāvapāhuḍa* sources for the 363-account should be seen.

Bhāvapāhuḍa 135, 140:

There are 180 *kriyāvādīs*, and 84 [declarers] of *akriyā*;
There are 67 [sorts of] *ajñānī*, and 32 of *vainayika*.

There are 363 divisions of heresy; having got rid of the wrong path,
Set your mind on the Jaina way; what use these declarers of untruth?

Verse 135 is virtually identical with *Sūtrakṛtāṅga Niryukti* 119; verse 140 has no known parallel.

As noted above, Śrutasāgara has commented on the *Bhāvapāhuḍa*. His commentary on *Tattvārthādhigama Sūtra* VIII.1 is included in the sources in group B, and is given below. His comments on *Bhāvapāhuḍa* 135 and 140 show no knowledge of the calculation method; but the comment to 135 has interesting features, and is thus given below, following the *Tattvārthādhigama* comment. He merely glosses verse 140.

The next texts given, Umāsvāti's *Tattvārthādhigama Sūtra* (usually dated to ca. 300 C.E.[7]) and its commentaries, present still another challenge. Umāsvāti is acclaimed by both the Śvetāmbaras and Digambaras, and this particular work

---

6 See chapter 4 on the Digambaras' authoritative works.

7 Umāsvāti's exact date is a constant subject of debate. The fourth century C.E. is a compromise dating; he was apparently roughly contemporary with Kundakunda, whom the Digambaras hold to have been his teacher.

has more than twenty commentaries, major and minor, that are known to be extant.[8] The *Tattvārthādhigama* text on which the commentaries are based varies somewhat, and the variations follow sectarian lines—Śvetāmbaras using one version, Digambaras another.[9] It is worth noting that the Digambara textual tradition is more uniform than the Śvetāmbara.

Digambara commentaries outnumber Śvetāmbara by more than five to one. One of the Śvetāmbara commentaries, further, is a source of considerable controversy. The Śvetāmbaras hold that it is Umāsvāti's autocommentary (*Svabhāṣya*), while the Digambaras reject his authorship of it, principally because it interprets certain *sūtra*s in a way that follows Śvetāmbara teachings. Most Western scholars have taken for granted the common authorship of the *sūtra*s and the *Svabhāṣya*; the Digambara rejection of the *Svabhāṣya* has generally led the scholars to conclude that Umāsvāti was actually a Śvetāmbara, with the qualification that the distinction between the two sects at his time was likely not very clear.[10]

The Digambaras have their own traditions concerning Umāsvāti—which are not unanimous, but do have an inscriptional basis (see Jacobi 1906:287ff. and J. L. Jaini 1920:vii)—and their claims should perhaps be re-examined on the basis of R. Williams's (1963:1-2) discovery that at least on certain critical points related to the prescriptions regarding the life of the layman the *sūtra*s set the model for the later Digambara tradition, while the *Svabhāṣya* is in accord with later Śvetāmbara works.[11] The overall relationship between *sūtra*s and *Svabhāṣya* also presents contradictory or ambiguous evidence, and so the problem of the latter's authorship remains unsolved.[12]

Alongside these unsolved issues there is the fact that the great mass of commentary literature has been only rudimentarily explored. The number of these commentaries that has been printed is small, only nine.[13] These nine, however, are those written by the more influential figures among the many commentators. The available printed texts are examined here, with the exception of Vidyānanda's *Ślokavārtikālaṅkāra*. (The latter breaks totally with the traditional pattern of comment, and provides no source material for the 363-

---

8 See Velankar 1944:154ff., and J. L. Jaini 1920:xviii-xix.

9 For a comparison of the two text traditions, see J. L. Jaini 1920:204-210.

10 See Jacobi 1906:287ff., von Glasenapp 1925:105-6, and Winternitz 1933:579. The latter two clearly rely on Jacobi.

11 Note that there is no sectarian textual variation in the passages cited by Williams.

12 See Jacobi 1906:240-91. H. R. Kapadia (1926-30:2:36-40, 47) presents what seems to him to be conclusive evidence of harmony between *sūtra*s and *Svabhāṣya*. However, P. S. Shastry, in the introduction to his edition of Pūjyapāda's commentary on the *Tattvārthādhigama*, advances evidence that he feels proves the contrary. [Editor's note.] The issue of the relationship of the *Tattvārthādhigama* and the *Svabhāṣya* has been the subject of much recent scholarship. See Bhatt and Tripathi 1974; Bronkhorst 1985; Ohira 1982; and Zydenbos 1983:9-13.

13 See Potter 1983:82-84. His listing omits Pūjyapāda's *Sarvārthasiddhi*.

account.) Those covered here are the disputed *Svabhāṣya*, Siddhasenagaṇi's *Ṭīkā*, Pūjyapāda's *Sarvārthasiddhi*, Akalaṅka's *Tattvārtharājavārttikālaṅkara*, Bhāskaranandin's *Sukhabodha*, and Śrutasāgara's *Vṛtti*.[14]

Of these, the *Svabhāṣya* and Siddhasenagaṇi's commentary represent the Śvetāmbara tradition (the *Svabhāṣya* is in group B, Siddhasenagaṇi's work in group C); the rest are all Digambara commentaries. The latter are all closely related to each other in content and style, and the relevant comments all occur at the same point in the *sūtras*. Thus the Digambara comments are presented first, followed by the *Svabhāṣya*.

Tattvārthādhigama VIII.1 is the *sūtra* under which the Digambara commentators chose to include in their remarks some mention of non-Jain schools of thought. The *sūtra* reads:

> The causes of bondage are: wrong faith, non-abstinence, negligence, the passions, and being involved in activity.[15]

The context of the *sūtra* is Umāsvāti's broad discussion of the seven Jain *tattvas* that represent the fundamental factors in the process of the soul's bondage and eventual release. Bondage, *bandha*, is the fourth item in the standard list of *tattvas* (*Tattvārthādhigama* I.4). The first of the causes of bondage, "wrong faith," *mithyādarśana*, is the point at which non-Jain systems are mentioned by the commentators. The Digambara commentaries will now be presented, in chronological order.

Pūjyapāda's commentary, the *Sarvārthasiddhi*, is usually dated to the sixth century C.E.,[16] and his version of the *sūtras* themselves is the one usually followed by the subsequent Digambara tradition. His remarks on VIII.1 are fairly lengthy, but of considerable interest for this study. He divides "wrong faith" into two varieties: (1) that which is "inborn," i.e., derived from the action of karma on the self; and (2) that which arises in consequence of the teachings of others. Of the former he has little to say (though what he does say is significant,

---

14 The two printed commentaries to which I had no access are Yaśovijaya's *Bālāvabodha* (which falls well outside the period covered by this study, belonging to the seventeenth century C.E.) and the *Laghuvṛtti* begun by Haribhadra and completed by his student Yaśobhadra. The portion attributed to Haribhadra extends only to the mid-sixth chapter, and thus contains none of the passages examined here. Nevertheless, Yaśobhadra's testimony would be of great value. Unfortunately, the text appears not to be available in any U.S. library.

15 There is no sectarian variation in the *sūtra* or its numbering.

I have translated *kaṣaya* as "the passions." Though *kaṣāya* is often translated as "stain" or "impurity," it has a different meaning in Jain texts. *Tattvārthādhigama* VI.4 and Pūjyapāda's comments thereon are a good example of a Sanskrit-writing Jain's understanding of the term and its relationship to the more common meaning. *Tattvārthādhigama* VIII.9 presents a more systematic statement of the passions, which are anger, pride, deceitfulness, and greed. See S. A. Jain 1960:223-24.

16 See Potter 1983:99, and Williams 1963:17.

and is discussed below, along with other Digambara statements on this point); the latter receives a much fuller treatment.

Pūjyapāda, *Sarvārthasiddhi*, on *Tattvārthādhigama Sūtra* VIII.1 (partial):

> Wrong faith is two-fold: that which is inborn and that which is occasioned by others' teaching. Thereunder, inborn [wrong faith] is that which is characterized by lack of firm conviction concerning the true nature of things, arising in virtue of the presence of karma that causes error, without others' teaching. [Wrong faith] occasioned by others' teaching is four-fold, in virtue of the options of the *kriyāvādī*, the *akriyāvādī*, the *ajñānika*, and the *vainayika*. Or, wrong faith is five-fold, being absolutist wrong faith, contradictory wrong faith, doubting wrong faith, moralist wrong faith, and agnostic wrong faith. Of these, the claim that a substrate and a quality are "only this" or "only thus" is absolutist [wrong faith]; or that everything is eternal, or momentary, or that it all consists only in the Lord. Contradictory [wrong faith] is [holding] that [a monk] who has possessions is possessionless, that an omniscient takes morsels of food, that a woman attains [*mokṣa*], and the like. Doubting [wrong faith] does not decide whether or not "right faith, knowledge, and conduct are the path to release." *Vainayika* wrong faith [holds] that faith is the same in the case of all deities and all systems. Agnostic [wrong faith] consists in the incapacity to determine what is beneficial and what is not. It has also been said:
>
> There are 180 [sorts] of *kriyā*, and 84 of *akriyā*,
> Of *ajñānī*, 67, and 32 of *vinaya*.[17]

It is clear that Pūjyapāda gives at least equal weight to a five-fold account of other viewpoints. This five-fold account occurs in each of the commentaries in the Digambara series, and a part of the reason for presenting them all here is to show how the 363-account, devoid of any mention of a calculation method, is treated alongside this five-fold account.

The three remaining Digambara commentaries, taken by themselves, reflect a heavy dependence on Pūjyapāda. They follow not only his version of the *sūtras*, but also his comments. There is only one deviation from Pūjyapāda's comments in the texts that follow, but it is a striking one. Both Akalaṅka and Bhāskaranandin attach groups of proper names to the four headings in the 363-account. This is a total departure from the mode of all other sources of the account; it is duplicated by Siddhasenagaṇi alone on the Śvetāmbara side.[18]

Unfortunately, the name assignment is not only a point for possible speculation about the function and development of the 363-account. It also raises a set of vexing problems, which center on the fact that Akalaṅka apparently

---

17 This and other texts given in this chapter are from editions that are not, in many cases, well-edited. Emendations on my part have often been necessary. These are generally minor, and I have not, therefore, provided an apparatus.

18 According to Schrader (1902:15), the same name assignments are made in Haribhadra and Yaśobhadra *Laghuvṛtti* on *Tattvārthādhigama*, which would mean that Yaśobhadra was the author who supplied the names, since he would have written the comments on *Tattvārthādhigama* VIII.

attaches two subtotals to two headings in a way different from the other sources. The problem is compounded by what appears to be a corrupt text tradition.

The issue will become clearer after the texts are presented. In the excerpts that follow, the full lists of proper names are given only in the translation. There they are given according to Schrader, who investigated them individually and clarified the textual variations in the lists. There are many minor variations in the Sanskrit forms of the names; since this study does not propose to examine the individual names, it will not advance beyond Schrader's work. Hence it seems of little value to reproduce here the lengthy and varying Sanskrit lists.

The first of the available commentaries written after Pūjyapāda is that of Akalaṅka (now dated 720-780 C.E.). He follows Pūjyapāda closely except for the name assignment and a shift in the structure of his comments. The full title of Akalaṅka's work is *Tattvārtharājavārttikālaṅkāra*, and it is divided into brief *vārttika*-comments and Akalaṅka's own comments on them, the *alaṅkāra*, or elaboration. The *vārttika* portion of the commentary is followed by Bhāskaranandin, whose date is ca. 1100 C.E. The translation omits the *vārttika*-portions, which are duplicated in the *alaṅkāra*.

Akalaṅka, *Tattvārtharājavārttikālaṅkara* VIII.1 (partial):

> Wrong faith is established as two-fold. How? By division into what is inborn and that which is caused by others' teaching.
>
> Thereunder, it is established that inborn [wrong faith] is that which, characterized by lack of firm conviction concerning the true nature of things, arises in virtue of error-karma aside from others' teachings.
>
> Wrong faith caused by others' teaching is to be known as being four-fold. How? In virtue of the options of *kriyā-* and *akriyāvāda*, *ajñānika* and *vainayika* doctrine.
>
> In virtue of the doctrine-options of Kokkula, Kāṇṭheviddhi, Kauśika, Hariśmaśru, Māṇṭhanika, Romaka, Hārīta, Muṇḍa, Aśvalāyana, etc., the *kriyāvāda*s are to be seen as being 84-fold.
>
> In virtue of the division between the systems of Marīci, Kumāra, Kapila, Ulūka, Gārgya, Vyāgrabhūti, Vādvali, Māṭhara, Maudgalyāyana, etc., the number of *akriyāvāda*s is to be recognized as 180.
>
> From division into the views of Śākalya, Bāṣkala, Kuthumi, Sātyamugri, Rāṇāyana, Kaṇva, Madyandin, Mauda, Pippalāda, Bādarāyaṇa, Sviṣṭakṛt, Aitikāyana, Vasu, Jaimini, etc., the number of *ajñānikavāda*s is to be known as 67.
>
> From division into the ways of Vasiṣṭha, Parāśara, Jātukarṇa, Vālmīki, Romaharṣiṇi, Satyadatta, Vyāsa, Ailāputra, Aupamanyava, Indradatta, Ayasthūla, etc., the *vainayika*s are reckoned as 32. These are the 363 divisions of wrong teaching.
>
> At this point it is said: How is it that [you attribute] agnosis (*ajñānikatva*) to Bādarāyaṇa, Vasu, Jaimini, etc., who are upholders of action (*kriyā*) enjoined by *śruti*? [To this] it is said; Because they put forth the killing of living beings as bringing about *dharma*; and indeed, since killing living beings is a cause of demerit, it cannot be admitted as having the quality of bringing about *dharma*. . . .

Such are the options of wrong faith occasioned by others' teaching; others are also conjectured to be properly enumerable. They are innumerable from the aspect of the evolute-options, and their division into sub-classes is endless. That which is inborn wrong faith is also multi-faceted, because it includes the unconscious one- two- three- and four-sensed beings, and the conscious five-sensed creatures, barbarians, hill-people, savages, etc.

Also, a five-fold wrong faith is to be known: absolutist wrong faith, contrary to wrong faith, doubting wrong faith, *vainayika* wrong faith, and *ajñānika* wrong faith. Thereunder, asseveration that a quality and substrate are "this alone" or "thus only" is absolutist [wrong faith], or that "all this is *puruṣa* only" (*Ṛgveda* 10.90), or that all this is simply eternal or simply non-eternal. Contrary [wrong faith] consists in such affirmations as that [a monk] who has possessions is possessionless, that a *kevalin* eats bits of food, that a woman attains [release], and the like. Doubting [wrong faith] consists in being divided in opinion as to whether or not right faith, knowledge, and conduct constitute the path to release. *Vainayikatva* consists in the same faith toward all deities and all doctrines. *Ajñānikatva* is being incapable of distinguishing what is beneficial and what is not.

Bhāskarandin, *Sukhabodha* on *Tattvārthādhigama Sūtra* VIII.1 (partial):

Wrong faith is established as two-fold. How? By division into that which is inborn and that which is caused by others' teaching. Thereunder, *nisargaḥ* is said to be the natural state [of something]. That which arises naturally is said to be inborn (*naisargika*). The sense [of this] is that the [wrong faith], characterized by lack of firm conviction concerning the true nature of things, which arises without others' teaching, in virtue of the rise of internal error-karma, is inborn [wrong faith]. The wrong faith that is caused by others' teaching is four-fold; this is in virtue of the options of the *kriyā-* and *akriyāvādī*, and *ajñānika* and *vainayika* opinions. Thereunder, there are 84 *kriyāvāda*s, from division into the opinions of Kokkula, Kāṇṭheviddhi, Kauśika, etc. There are 180 *akriyāvāda*s, in virtue of the doctrine-options of Marīci, Kumāra, Kapila, Ulūka, Gārgya, Vyāgrabhūti, etc. The *ajñānikavāda*s number 67, from division into the systems of Śākalya, Bāṣkala, Kuthumi, Sātyamugri, etc. But the *vainayika*s are 32 in number. How? From division into the doctrines of Vasiṣṭha, Parāśara, Jātukarṇa, Vālmīki, etc. These divisions of wrong teaching are, in sum, 363. Such are the options of wrong faith occasioned by others' teaching. By men who know these, others too can be listed; and they are innumerable from the aspect of their evolute-options, and from the distinction of their subdivisions an endless number arises. That which is inborn wrong faith is also multi-faceted, because it includes the unconscious one- two- three- and four-sensed [beings] and the conscious five-sensed creatures, barbarians, savages, hill-people, etc. Or, one may understand that wrong faith is of five sorts: absolutist wrong faith, contrary wrong faith, doubting wrong faith, *vainayika* wrong faith, and *ajñānika* wrong faith. Thereunder, the asseveration that a quality and a substrate are "this alone" or "thus only" is absolutist [wrong faith], or that "all this is *puruṣa* only," or that all this is simply eternal or simply non-eternal. Contrary [wrong faith] consists in [such affirmations as] that though [a monk] have possessions, he is possessionless, that a *kevalin* takes bits of food, that a woman attains [release], etc. Doubting [wrong faith] consists in swaying between two positions, namely, whether or not right faith, knowledge, and conduct are the path to release. *Vainayika* [wrong faith] consists in the same faith toward all deities and all doctrines. *Ajñānika* [wrong faith] is being incapable of distinguishing what is beneficial and what is not.

The close link between these last two texts should be obvious. Bhāskaranandin tends to use only Akalaṅka's *vārttika* plus a bit more. He gives, for example, a few names beyond those in the *vārttika*. His section on the five-fold variety of wrong faith is almost word-for-word repetition of Akalaṅka. However, he omits one of the striking features of Akalaṅka's remarks, which is the debate on the suitability of assigning certain names to the *ajñānika* heading. Not that Akalaṅka does not question the matter of assigning names in general, though his is the earliest known text to use these lists. He only debates the particular assignments under one heading, and his answer is not so much aimed at *ajñānikatva* as it is at sacrificial killings. Further, Akalaṅka is the only author who debates the assignments at all.

The other feature of both these accounts that can hardly be overlooked is that both of them state that there are 84 *kriyāvāda*s and 180 *akriyāvāda*s. M. K. Jain, from whose edition the above is translated, introduces alternate readings at crucial points so as to make the headings and numbers conform to the more common model that was given above. However, he offers no textual evidence for those alternate readings, nor does he give any explanation of his emendations. It is likely that the alternates are his own suggestions. That they are not supported by the textual tradition is made likely by two facts. First, Bhāskaranandin reproduces the version of the account that has the numbers switched. Second, Schrader's manuscript sources, at least in part, had the numbers switched;[19] and G. L. Jaina's edition of the commentary shows no variants.

It is furthermore not possible to solve the problem by referring to the particular names assigned to the headings and not the numbers. Siddhasenagaṇi, as will be seen below, gives the group of 180 (which he calls *kriyāvādīs*) as headed by Marīci, etc., and the group of 84 (which he gives as *akriyāvādīs*) as headed by Kokkula, etc. In other words, the names and numbers are the same as in Akalaṅka and Bhāskaranandin. But while Siddhasenagaṇi has the names, numbers, and headings all aligned, Akalaṅka and Bhāskaranandin have switched the headings. Granted that an alpha-privative can easily be lost in a textual tradition, there is yet another piece of evidence that makes it seem that the Akalaṅka-Bhāskaranandin version may simply be an error on their part. This is the fact that neither of them quotes the Prakrit verse (*Sūtrakṛtāṅga Niryukti* 119)

19 Schrader 1902:15. He claims to be reproducing Akalaṅka at that point, but parts of his text differ radically from the printed editions, except for the names and the number-switch.

that gives the headings coupled with the numbers commonly associated with them.

Now, to say that a portion of the Digambara tradition may have made an error on this point is perhaps to prejudge the case, for a good deal of the foregoing has been devoted to showing that the 363-account in its full form is not very old. Possibly certain Digambara circles put the scheme together differently, but this is not very likely. The problem has been raised, and it must be left at that for the present, for the evidence is not strong enough on either side—textual corruption or error by the authors—to compel a conclusion, although the later discussion of the significance of the name assignments in general may shed a bit more light on the possibilities involved.

The one remaining Digambara commentary to be presented here, that of Śrutasāgara, returns almost completely to Pūjyapāda's model. One additonal Prakrit verse is added, a verse not duplicated in other printed commentaries. Śrutasāgara's date (not earlier than 1400 C.E.) means that he stands a great chronological distance from the commentary on which his is modelled; one must presume something of an intervening tradition.

Taken alone, Śrutasāgara's comments might seem to imply that, in the interval, the conceptions of *kriyāvāda, akriyāvāda, ajñānikavāda*, and *vinayavāda* have become drastically altered. Śrutasāgara's comments on *Bhāvapāhuḍa* 135, which are given after his *Tattvārthādhigama* comment, make quite clear what he understood by these headings. This understanding is quite at variance with the way in which the headings are presented in the full discussions of the 363-account in group C. However, it is not necessarily true that Śrutasāgara (or the intervening tradition) lost sight of the original. The differences may point to another issue, the full implications of which are discussed in chapters 16 and 17.

Śrutasāgara, *Tattvārthavṛtti* VIII.1 (partial):

> Therein [in the *sūtra*], wrong faith has two modes, from division into that which is inborn and that which is caused by others' teaching. Thereunder, inborn wrong faith, characterized by lack of firm conviction concerning the true nature of things, arises even without others' teaching, in virtue of the rise of error-karma. Marīci, the son of Bharata,[20] is to be seen as an example of this. Wrong faith caused by others' teaching is to be known as having four modes; this comes from division into that of the *kriyāvādī, akriyāvādī, ajñānika*, and *vainayika*. Wrong faith is also five-fold: absolutist, contrary, doubting, *vinaya*, and *ajñāna*. Thereunder, absolutist wrong faith consists in maintaining that in the matter of quality and substrate "this alone" or "thus only" is the case, or that all this is self (*pumān*) only, or only eternal or only non-eternal. Contrary wrong faith is saying that [a monk] who has possessions is

20 The Marīci in question is one of the figures in the Jain accounts of the early history of the world. [Editor's note.] See *Triṣaṣṭiśalākāpuruṣacaritra* I.6.1-52 (English Trans. Vol.I, pp. 327-30).

possessionless, [or] that a man or woman who eats food is a *kevalin*; another name for it is inverted wrong faith. [With regard to doubting wrong faith] this has been said:

Śvetāmbara, Digambara, Buddhist, and others too—
Purified alike as selves, they attain release, no doubt.

Doubting wrong faith is the not choosing of a position on the issue of whether or not right faith, knowledge, and conduct are the path to release. *Vainayika* wrong faith consists in saying that all gods and all doctrines are to be viewed as equal, are to be praised only, and are not to be disparaged. *Ajñānika* wrong faith is being unable to distinguish wherein lies benefit and harm. A verse makes clear the previous divisions:

There are 180 [sorts of] *kriyā* and 84 of *akriyā*,
67 of *ajñānika*, and 32 of *vainayika*.

Śrutasāgara on *Bhāvapāhuḍa* 135:

There are 180 *kriyāvādīs*, Brāhmaṇas who esteem the *śrāddha* and other rites. There are 84 divisions of doubting wrongness, i.e., of *akriyāvādīs*. They are mostly Śvetapaṭas, from the Indracandra and Nāgendra *gaccha*s, who resort to the rice-water and boiled-water practices; they are pretenders, of multi-faceted deceitfulness. There are 67 who hold that release comes through *ajñāna*, followers of the doctrines, made up of followers of ascetic practices, who reckon on release by means of deference to mother, father, ruler, mankind, etc. In this way there are 363 wrong teachings that should be rejected; this is the sense [of the verse].

There remain only two brief texts in group B. These are the disputed *Tattvārthādhigama Svabhāṣya*'s comments on *Tattvārthādhigama* VII.18 and VIII.1. Siddhasenagaṇi, who follows the *Svabhāṣya*, also makes relevant comments at both of these points. The comment to VII.18 centers on the *aticāra*s, or transgressions, of *samyaktva*, or correctness of faith. There are five of these, the last two of which are admiring adherents of other views, and praising adherents of other views.[21] It is in glossing the phrase "other views" that the *Svabhāṣya* introduces the comment relevant for this study.

Tattvārthādhigama Sūtra Svabhāṣya VII.18 (partial):

He says "other views" meaning a view that is different from the *arhat*-(Jaina) teaching. That is two-fold, active and passive. Admiring and praising those attached thereto—*kriyāvādīs*, *akriyāvādīs*, *ajñānikas*, and *vainayikas*—are transgressions against *samyaktva*.

This comment forms the basis of the *Svabhāṣya*'s comment on VIII.1, which is little more than a brief gloss.

Tattvārthādhigama Svabhāṣya VIII.1 (partial):

Thereunder, wrong faith is the opposite of right faith. [Wrong faith] is two-fold, active and passive. Therein, the choosing of incorrect faith after reflection, i.e., the

21 For full discussion of these, see Williams 1963:46-47.

choosing of the 363 faculty teachings—agnosis, etc.—is active [wrong faith]. The rest is passive.

This concludes the lengthy presentation of texts in group B. Despite the long introductions that have often been necessary, the texts as a group should stand out as being very different in many respects from group A, and yet not at all like the texts in C, which present the full 363-account as diagrammed earlier.

GROUP C

The principal characteristic of texts in this group is their presentation of the method for calculating the full 363-account. Since this method and its workings have been diagrammed and detailed above, not all of the texts that present it are given here. Two texts that do present it and are given in translation are Haribhadra on *Nandī* 88, and Śīlāṅka on *Sūtrakṛtāṅga* I.12.1. The calculation itself alters hardly at all through the whole mass of sources. However, the details that accompany it provide much material for analysis. Thus sections above draw on the sources in C for two things: (1) the components of the full 363-account, and (2) the remarks that Jain authors saw fit to add to the account itself.

Haribhadra's comment on *Nandī* 88 represents the oldest known full account of the method for calculating the 363 options in the 363-account. It is very terse, compared with the efforts of later commentators on this point. The basic pattern of such a presentation does not alter in the course of the lengthy commentary tradition. The later commentators added embellishments and sometimes more information; an example of an expanded comment is provided by Śīlāṅka's commentary on *Sūtrakṛtāṅga*, which is the next item translated here. Other later commentators, like Abhayadeva and Malayagiri, produced comments very much like that of Śīlāṅka. Such remarks are also incorporated into Guṇaratna's commentary on the *Ṣaḍdarśanasamuccaya* of Haribhadra.

The translation omits certain parts of the commentary. Each section begins with a grammatical gloss of the passage in question, which would be expected in a very early commentary in Sanskrit on a Prakrit text. These grammatical glosses have been paraphrased or omitted. The *Nandī* passage itself is translated above.

Haribhadra on *Nandī Sūtra* 88 (partial):

> Those whose practice it is to declare that activity is inherent in the self, averring that "without an agent activity is impossible," are *kriyāvādīs*. Further, those who are characterized by this affirmation of the existence of the self, etc., are to be known as being 180 in number by this means: Having arranged in order the nine categories—*jīva, ajīva, āsrava, bandha, saṃvara, nirjarā, puṇya, pāpa*, and *mokṣa*, under the *jīva* category one should place this pair: *sva* and *para*. Under them, [place] the pair *nitya* and *anitya*. Again, under them place [these] five: *kāla, īśvara,*

ātman, niyati, svabhāva. Now, the alternatives are to be constructed thus: "There is a self, unique, eternal, and subject to time." This is one alternative. Here is the sense of the alternative: the *kālavādī*s declare that there exists, indeed, a self, in a form of its own, that is eternal. Through the same stated formula [is expressed] the second alternative, that of those who hold that *īśvara* is the cause of all; and the third alternative, that of the *ātmavādī*s, who declare that "all this is *puruṣa* only," etc.; the fourth alternative, that of the *niyativādī*s; and the fifth alternative, that of the *svabhāvavādī*s. In this way, keeping the word "unique" (*svataḥ*), one gets five alternatives. By using the word "relative" (*parataḥ*) one also gets five alternatives. [Thus] by using [the rubric] eternality, one gets these ten alternatives. In the same way, under non-eternality one gets ten alternatives; [and so] twenty are gotten by means of the category *jīva*. There being twenty alternatives in each of the other eight [categories] as well, gotten in the same way, one thus gets twenty multiplied by nine, or 180 *kriyāvādī*s.

There are 84 *akriyāvādī*s. [gloss omitted] *Akriyāvādī*s are those who declare that activity cannot occur in any category [i.e., any basic existent] whatsoever that does not persist [i.e., that is momentary], and that this being so [i.e., the categories being momentary], the absence of activity is established. Also, some of them declare:

All the *saṃskāra*s are momentary.
How can there be activity in unenduring things?
Their origination alone
is called both activity and agency.

Those who are characterized by the denial of the existence of the self, etc., are to be seen as being 84 [in number] by this means: Removing *puṇya* and *apuṇya* from among them, the categories—now seven—are put down. Under *jīva* the pair *sva* and *para* is placed (because of the non-existence of the self, there is no *nitya-anitya* division). Under the five—*kāla*, etc.—a sixth is placed, namely, *yadṛcchā*. Thereafter, the alternative is stated: there is no self, unique, subject to time. That is one alternative. By doing the same with *īśvara*, etc., ending with *yadṛcchā*, there are in all six alternatives. Then by stating that there is no self, relative, subject to time, etc., one gets [another] six alternatives, twelve in all. In the same way, one gets twelve alternatives for each of the other six—*ajīva*, etc. Thus there are twelve multiplied by seven, or 84 *nāstika*s.

There are 67 *ajñānikavādī*s. *Ajñāna* means knowledge that is of poor quality; those whose knowledge is thus are called *ajñānikavādī*s. [Here Haribhadra enters into a gloss of *ajñānika* in which he has an objector ask why the *taddhita*-suffix (-*ika*) is necessary. In the course of justifying the use of the suffix, Haribhadra states that *ajñāna* by itself is only the opposite of *jñāna*, the result of *mithyādarśana*; but the suffix makes it possible to speak of *ajñānikatva*, "ignorant-ness," as opposed to "ignorance."] Or, *ajñānika*s are those who live according to *ajñāna*, or who make it their goal. They are characterized by their assertion that the bondage which ensues from unpremeditated deeds is without effect, and the like. They are to be known as being 67 in number by this means; having put down, as before, the nine categories—*jīva*, etc., and having placed *utpatti* at the end [of the list of nine], one should place under these the following seven items: (1) existence, (2) non-existence, (3) existence and non-existence, (4) inexpressibility, (5) existence and inexpressibility, (6) non-existence and inexpressibility, and (7) existence, non-existence, and inexpressibility. For each category—*jīva*, etc.—[there are] seven alternatives, thus nine multiplied by seven, or 63. But for *utpatti* there occur only the first four alternatives: existence, non-existence, existence and non-existence, and inexpressiblity. These added to 63 make 67. One alternative would be: who knows that the self exists? And what is the use of such knowledge? In the same way one should state [the matter] for non-existence, etc. Also for *utpatti*: does it arise from the existent, the non-existent, both, or something inexpressible? Who, indeed, could know this? No one at all. This is the meaning [of the *ajñānika*-heading].

There are 32 *vainayikavādīs*. [gloss omitted] Therein, *vainayikas* are those who live according to *vinaya*, or who make it their goal. They, characterized by the assertion of a *vinaya* in teachings that consist of respectfulness whose hallmark is its absoluteness, are to be known as being 32 in number by this means: [they declare that] respectful service is to be done at the proper place and time, with voice, mind, body, and through charity, to each of the following: deity, ruler, sage, ascetic, elder, younger, father, and mother. The four means [voice, etc.] in the eight occasions [for service], deity, etc., yield in all the sum of 32.

Haribhadra does not comment in detail on the remainder of the passage.

The portion of Śīlāṅka's comments presented here is actually a part of his remarks on *Sūtrakṛtāṅga Niryukti* 117b-121. The verses in the *niryukti* were presented above. Here they are given again, as they occur in the commentary. Just prior to this section, Śīlāṅka has been discussing the term *samosaraṇa*. Those remarks are also discussed, in chapter 17. Also contained in the comments given here are three verses that give the way of calculating the options in three of the 363-account headings. These were discussed in chapter 16.

The translation opens with Śīlāṅka already discussing verse 117b of the *niryukti*.

Śīlāṅka on *Sūtrakṛtāṅga Sūtra* I.12:

Also, there are *kriyā, akriyā, ajñāna*, and *vinaya*. (117b)

Those whose practice it is to declare that the *jīva* and other categories exist, etc., are *kriyāvādīs*. Their opposites are *akriyāvādīs*. Also, the *ajñānīs* teach mistrust [or: concealment] of knowledge (*jñānanihnava*), and the *vainayikas* act according to *vinaya* or for its sake. . . . Now, making clear their true nature by showing the real meaning of their names, he [the *nijjutti*-author] says:

> *Kriyāvādīs* declare "It is," *akriyāvādīs* "It is not,"
> *ajñānīs* [declare] agnosis, *vinayavādīs* adherence to *vinaya*. (118)

Those who recognize activity (*kriyā*) and that only, in that they say "the *jīva* and the other categories simply exist"—those are the *kriyāvādīs* that the text refers to in the words "It is," etc.; and because they so declare matters, they are in a state of wrong faith (*mithyādṛṣṭāyaḥ*). Thus: If it is claimed that "the *jīva* simply exists," then, because of the limitation [i.e., "simply exists"], since it is not held that in some ways it does not exist, it would result that entities of another nature would posess the existence that is the *jīva*'s own nature; and thus the universe would not be variegated. But this is neither seen nor desired.

Further: those who declare that the *jīva* and the other categories simply do not exist are *akriyāvādīs*; because they propound non-existence, they are altogether in a state of wrong faith. Thus: When there is the unequivocal denial of the existence of the *jīva*, there will be the absence of an agent; then, from the act of saying "It is not" there will follow the absence of this denial [of the *jīva*'s existence]; and because of its absence, the existence of all things becomes unavoidable.

Further: those who hold that there exists not knowledge, that is to say, non-knowledge, are *ajñānīs*. They declare that non-knowledge alone is desirable. They too are altogether in a state of wrong faith. Thus: Without knowledge it is not possible to state that non-knowledge alone is desirable; and since they do state this, they must certainly admit knowledge.

Further: The *vainayikas*, who would have the obtaining of heaven and release result from *vinaya* alone, are in a state of wrong faith, because the obtaining of release is not to be had without both knowledge and activity.

Both the nature of the *kriyāvādī* and the others, and the refutation of the same, have been propounded in detail in the *Ācāraṭīkā*, and thus are not dwelt upon here.

He now says, in order to portray the number of their subdivisions:

> There are 180 [types of] *kriyā*, and 84 of *akriyā*,
> 67 of *ajñānika*, and 32 of *vinaya*. (119)

The *kriyāvādīs* are 180; this is according to the following method. The nine categories—*jīva*, etc.—are put down in order. Under them is put the dual division *sva* and *para*; under this another dual division, *nitya* and *anitya*; and under this, in order, the five words *kāla, svabhāva, niyati, īśvara*, and *ātman*. Then the method is put to use as follows: "There exists a self, unique, eternal, subject to time"; and again, "There exists a self, unique, non-eternal, subject to time." In this way a double option is also gotten by using "relative" (*para*), and in all, four options are obtained by using *kāla*. Four options apiece are also obtained from *svabhāva, niyati, īśvara*, and *ātman*. Four multiplied by five equals twenty, and this many are gotten through the *jīva*-category. In this way, each of the [remaining] eight—*ajīva*, etc.—yields twenty; and thus there are nine multiplied by twenty, or 180 *kriyāvādīs* altogether.

Now, of *akriyāvādīs*, who hold that the *jīva* and the other categories simply do not exist, the number is 84, as follows: having put down the seven categories, *jīva*, etc., the dual option *sva* and *para* is put under them, and then under that are placed six words; *kāla, yadṛcchā, niyati, svabhāva, īśvara*, and *ātman*. This is the method for establishing the divisions: "There does not exist a self, unique, subject to time"; and again, "There does not exist a self, relative, subject to time." In this way, each one—*yadṛcchā, niyati, svabhāva, īśvara*, and *ātman*—yields two divisions; in all there are twelve. They, further, multiplied by the seven categories—*jīva*, etc.—equal 84. As has been said:

> From *kāla*, *yadṛcchā, niyati, svabhāva, īśvara*, and *ātman*
> arise 84 [options];
> In the opinion (*mata*) of the *nāstikavādīs*, elements (are said)
> not to be, either unique or relative (to others).

Now, 67 sorts of *ajñānika*s, who seek to establish the desired end by means of *ajñāna* alone, who perceive that though knowledge exists, it is useless because of many faults, are to be understood in this way: Having set down in order the nine categories—*jīva*, etc., under them are to be placed the following seven elements: (1) *sat*, (2) *asat*, (3) *sadasat*, (4) *avaktavya*, (5) *sadavaktavya*, (6) *asadavaktavya*, (7) *sadasadavaktavya*. This is how [the options] are declared: (1) Who knows that the *jīva* exists? And what use is there in knowing? (2) Who knows that the *jīva* does not exist? And what use is there in knowing? (3) Who knows that the *jīva* both exists and does not exist? And what use is there in knowing? (4) Who knows that the *jīva* cannot be expressed? And what use is there in knowing? (5) Who knows that the *jīva* exists and cannot be expressed? And what use is there in knowing? (6) Who knows that the *jīva* does not exist and cannot be expressed? And what use is there in knowing? (7) Who knows that the *jīva* exists, does not exist, and cannot be expressed? And what use is there in knowing? In this way the seven elements are also used with *ajīva*, etc.; in all, there are 63. Also, there are four other headings, as follows: (1) Who knows that there exists an originating cause for all beings? And what use is their in knowing? (2) Who knows that there does not exist an originating cause of beings? And what use is there in knowing? (3) Who knows that there exists and does not exist an originating cause of beings? And what use is there in knowing? (4) Who knows that the originating cause of beings cannot be expressed? And what use is there in knowing? In all, there are 67. The other three elements have reference to portions of existent things, and are not applicable to the case of origin itself; so they are not set down here. It has been said:

> The doctrine of the *ajñānikavādī* has the nine—*jīva*, etc.—
> sevenfold, [by means of] *sat*, etc.
> [Also,] who knows whether an originating cause exists or not,
> or is both, or inexpressible?

Now, the 32 *vainayika*s, who would have the other world result from *vinaya* alone, are to be reckoned in the following manner: Four kinds of *vinaya* may be observed—that of mind (*manas*), voice, body, or charity—toward god, ruler, ascetic, sage, elder, inferior, mother, or father. In all, there are eight multiplied by four, or 32. It has also been said:

> The *vainayika* doctrine consists in *vinaya* to be performed
> with mind (*cetas*), voice, body, or charity,
> At all times toward god, ruler, ascetic, sage, elder, inferior,
> mother, or father.

All these—the *kriyāvādī*s, *akriyāvādī*s, *ajñānī*s, and *vainayika*s—put together equal 363 opposing doctrines (*prāvādukamata*s).

Having thus shown the number of teachings, now, in order to show their place in this chapter [*Sūtrakṛtāṅga* I.12], he says:

> Their doctrinal conclusions are declared in detail in this chapter,
> And the positions are stated by it, their true natures being
> determined. (120)

[Omitted here is Śīlāṅka's gloss of this verse, which is only a routine explanation in some detail, perhaps because he is writing a Sanskrit commentary on a Prakrit text.]

Now, in order to show how there is a distinction among these teachings as regards the state of being a correct teaching and the state of being a wrong teaching, he says:

> The *kriyāvādī* has a correct view, while the rest are false;
> Having abandoned erroneous teaching, give service to this true teaching. (121)

"Correct" (*samyak*) means non-contrary (*aviparīta*); "view" (*dṛṣṭi*) means vision (*darśana*); that view is a correct view which possesses an accurate determination of the categories (*padārthas*).[22] [Someone asks:] "Which one is that?" One says: [It is] the *kriyāvādī*, whose practice it is to declare matters by saying "It is." The term *kriyāvādī* was made known above, where it is said: "*kriyāvādīs* declare 'It is.'" Now, we shall take up this word again, so as to furnish a definition of the state of being a correct view, for the correct view has not yet been made known. [This view is] thus: That there is a distinction between the world and what is not the world; that there is a distinction between good and ill; that there is a self; that there is the fruit of good and ill, defined as the reaching of heaven or hell.

There is time (*kāla*) as the cause of all the universe, seen in its effects: origin, growth, maintenance, and destruction, as well as in the cold and hot seasons, in tree, flower, fruit, etc. As it has been said, "Time matures creatures," etc.[23] There is also self-nature (*svabhāva*) as the cause of all the universe. It [the word] is formed from "self/own" (*sva*) and "being/becoming" (*bhāva*), because all things conform to their own nature, whether sentient or insentient, capable of release or not capable thereof, in visible form or not, even as *dharma*, *adharma*, *ākāśa*, *kāla*, etc. each take the particular forms of motion, rest, pervation, distinction, non-distinction, etc. As has been said: "What [makes the sharpness] of thorns," etc. Also, necessity (*niyati*) is regarded as having causal capacity, for whenever existents (*padārthas*) are fixed [as they are] it is because of necessity. As has been said: "What is to be attained [comes] through connection with the power of necessity," etc. Also, previously done [acts] that are pure and impure are the cause of results that are desirable and undesirable. As has been said:

> Whatever fruits of previously done acts are stored up
> arise in this world,
> Just as perception arises pursuant on the prior lighting
> of a lamp.[24]

Also:

> Every man is born possessed of his former deeds;
> He is swept along by them, and not according to his wishes.

---

22 Here is a clear case where the dual sense of *darśana* as both "faith" and "system" renders translation difficult. Śīlāṅka's definition of *samyagdṛṣṭi* is clearly different from the standard Jain definition of "right faith"; this is why I translate as above.

23 This and other quotations that follow in this commentary are commonly found in Indian discussions of the causal factors.

24 This translation is problematic; the text appears to be corrupt.

and so on. Also, human effort is a causal factor, since nothing at all is attained without it. As has been said:

> Do not think, "It is all fate," and put effort
> away from yourself;
> Without effort, who could even get oil out of sesame seeds?

Also:

> By exertion, O beautiful-limbed one, a man sees
> good fortune;
> By exertion even a lowly worm
> destroys giant trees.[25]

In this way, seeing all these—time, etc.—as having causal power, and admitting the self, merit, demerit, other-worldly things, and the like, the *kriyāvādī* is to be seen as possessing the quality of correct vision (*samyagdṛṣṭitva*). But the other teachings—*akriyāvāda, ajñānavāda, vainayikavāda*—are to be seen as erroneous teachings (*mithyāvāda*s). Thus: The *akriyāvāda* is an utter (*atyanta*) *nāstika*, denying all the perceptibly established categories—*jīva*, etc; and thus he is simply in a state of wrong faith. And the *ajñānavādī* who, when there are five types of *jñāna*—*mati* and the rest—that tell us what to accept and what to reject,[26] nevertheless teaches that *ajñāna* is the good—how could he be anything but mentally disordered? Also, the *vinayavādī*, who proposes that the attainment of things to be [properly] achieved through knowledge and activity comes absolutely solely from *vinaya*, is to be rejected. In this way, these possessors of wrong views are to be regarded as teaching things in a way that is contrary.

[Objection:] But the *kriyāvādī* too, although in his 180 varieties he here and there admits *kāla* and the others, has been set down [elsewhere than in the *niryukti*] as holding a false view. How then is he now said to hold a correct view? [To this] it is said: There is error here because, while the one who says, in unqualified fashion, that "the *jīva* simply exists" [is holding this position], at the same time he regards time alone as the cause of all this universe, or just self-nature, or just necessity, or just one's prior deeds, or just self-effort; making time or one of the others the cause quite independent of all else. Thus, if the *jīva* exists in unqualified fashion, then whatever there is, by its synopticity, would become simply the *jīva*. Accordingly, correctness is spoken of when there is recourse to a qualified assertion.[27]

Correctness also arises here from taking the position that causality is present in the mutually dependent collection of time and the rest. [Objection:] Well then, how is it that there is correctness in time, etc. taken together, when they are erroneous if taken independently? For it is not true that things which are not something individually are capable of it as an aggregate. [Your proposal is] like [getting] oil from sand. Nor can you say that when they are seen in that way, this is something like an irrelevant name [added to their individual status].

As has been said:

---

25 The party addressed in the verse is likely a deer.

26 This is a reference to the five Jain classes of knowledge.

27 I am indebted to Daniel H. H. Ingalls for help with this paragraph.

1. Viewing unequivocally as the cause of all
   one out of time, self-nature, necessity,
   prior deeds, human effort:
   This is erroneousness; but viewed as a whole
   they make up correctness.

2. Indeed, all of these—time and the rest—
   are causal forces as a collection in this world;
   Linked in this way alone are they properly
   part of every effort.

3. But not simply through time, etc., individually
   arises anything at all.
   In this world even cooking *mudga* and the like
   has the collection of all these as its causes.

4. Just as cat's-eyes and other jewels of various quality,
   when not joined together
   Are not given the name "necklace,"
   though they be valuable;

5. Even so, the teachings of individual parties,
   though they be thoroughly convinced,
   Mutually ignoring other positions, do not—
   all these *nayas*—attain to being called
   correct vision.

6. Again, just as those jewels, tied together into order,
   According to their different qualities,
   Are called a necklace, and lose
   their individuality;

7. Just so all these *nayavādas*, when explained
   according to their separate states,
   Do not attain to being called correct vision
   when they exist separately.

8. Therefore, all the *nayas* are erroneous views
   when limited to their own position;
   But when they are determined to be interrelated
   their nature is correctness.

Śīlāṅka goes on, after this gloss of the *niryukti* verses, to comment on the individual verses of *Sūtrakṛtāṅga* I.12, where he generally repeats what he has already said here concerning *kriyāvāda*, etc.

In general, the texts in group C are a tradition, in the older sense of the word. Each commentator draws on his predecessors, and what one gets here is a steadily accumulating mass of information. Yet there are some important distinctions to be made within this final group of sources for the 363-account.

First, Nemicandra's commentary on *Uttarādhyayana* is part of a somewhat separate commentary tradition. The *Uttarādhyayana*, with its account of monastic life and achievement, became the core of a rich series of commentaries that are mainly devoted to compiling and re-telling tales related to those in the text proper. Thus there is a series of several large Sanskrit commentaries on *Uttarādhyayana* that actually consists mostly of tales related in Prakrit (though some of the commentators saw fit to put these into Sanskrit). The first commentary in this series is that of Śāntisūri (or Śāntyācārya), ca. 1025 C.E. This commentary was apparently eclipsed by that of Nemicandra (whose pre-*dīkṣā* name, Devendra, is occasionally given with this text), ca. 1075 C.E. Other notable later commentaries are those of Kamalasaṃyama and Lakṣmīvallabha. Because of the peculiar nature of this commentary tradition, it is not analyzed in detail in this study. Nemicandra's text shows that he knows of the calculation-method, as does Kamalasaṃyama's, but these authors do not elaborate on the 363-account at all.[28]

Another special case in C is the *Gommaṭasāra*, the only Digambara work in the group. Composed ca. 1000 C.E. by Nemicandra Siddhāntacakravartin, it is a veritable encyclopedia of Digambara speculation. Its hundreds of verses of classification and calculation cover two major headings, *jīva* (all the classes of beings) and karma (all the workings of all the types of karma). Included under the latter heading are the 363 schools of thought. The Karmakāṇḍa section of the book thus includes an account of the calculation-method, and so the verses devoted thereto are given here. One should mark the fact that this Digambara source—a very prominent Digambara text—is quite unlike the Digambara *Tattvārthādhigama* commentaries in group B.

The following verses are interspersed among verses that present the *kālavāda*, etc. (A number of these verses duplicate verses quoted in Śīlāṅka and elsewhere in such discussions.) As sources of the 363-account calculation-model they are not likely very old. Here they are as numbered as in the text.

876. There are said to be 180 [types of] *kriyā*, and 84 of *akriyā*,
 67 of *ajñānī*, and 32 of *vainayika*

877. The divisions [of *kriyā* are thus:] the nine *tattva*s
 are affirmed to exist uniquely, relatively,

[28] Neither Śāntisūri nor Nemicandra is available in printed form in this country. My account of Nemicandra is based on two Harvard manuscripts, H 676 and H 804. Horace I. Poleman (1938:365) assigns the number 6804 and 6805 to these. There are occasional difficulties, but the text can be gotten reasonably from these two. Another Harvard manuscript (H 1024) is said by Poleman (1938:365, manuscript no. 6806) to be Śāntisūri's commentary, but the manuscript's colophon matches none of the known manuscripts of Śāntisūri, and the identification appears to be based only on the title given in the colophon: *Śiṣyahitā*.

eternally, non-eternally,
And in relation to *kāla, īśvara, ātman, niyati*, and *svabhāva*.

884. In that (1) the seven categories—*puṇya* and *pāpa* being removed—
are said not to exist, either (2) uniquely, or (3) relatively,
And (4) subject to *kāla*, etc., there arise 70
[types of *akriyā*] out of four factors.

885. Also, out of three factors—the seven categories, said not
to exist subject to necessity and time—
Arise fourteen non-existence-varieties; and [thus there are]
84 [types of] *akriyā*.

886. Who knows the nine categories' existence, non-existence,
both, or inexpressibleness,
Or [the first three] linked with inexpressibleness? Thus
the nine multiplied by seven make 63.

887. Also, indeed, four questions arise from the aspects
of existence: as pure being, or origination,
Or both or neither; thus there are 67 [types of]
ajñānī.

888. *Vinaya* of mind, voice, body, and charity, toward
god, king, sage, ascetic, elder,
Younger, mother, and father: this is to be done,
and thus there are eight four-fold, [or 32 *vinaya*s].

889. By those whose views are self-serving, 363 alternatives
of error are propounded;
They snare the minds of the ignorant.

One should note the somewhat variant calculation model that is presented here, bearing in mind the fact that this is the only known Digambara source to present the model. Without more material than is available concerning author and text, it does not seem wise to speculate concerning the variations. Therefore no attempt was made in the body of this study to draw any conclusions based on them.

The final text given here is Siddhasenagaṇi's comment on *Tattvārthādhigama* VIII.1. Siddhasena is included in group C because of his comment on *Tattvārthādhigama* VII.18, which is an early standard account of the calculation method. His comments on VIII.1 are notable in that he includes the lists of proper names that are given by Akalaṅka, his near contemporary (latest date for Akalaṅka is 780 C.E.; earliest date for Siddhasena, 800 C.E.). Note that

Siddhasena's assignment of numbers to headings follows the Prakrit verse (*Sūtrakṛtāṅga Niryukti* 119), though he does not quote it, while his assignment of names to numbers is the same as Akalaṅka's. Except for Guṇaratna's commentary on Haribhdara's *Ṣaḍdarśanasamuccaya*, this is the only known source in Śvetāmbara texts that makes use of these lists.

Siddhasenagaṇi on *Tattvārthādhigama Sūtra* VIII.1 (partial):

> "Therein" means: of the two sorts of wrongness, active and passive. The explanation of active is this: "[something] assented to." Active wrongness is the assertion as the one and only truth of that which is arrived at by active acceptance of wrong faith, active acceptance of incorrect faith when one is somewhat acquainted with *matijñāna*, etc. [the Jaina types of knowledge]. He declares the many divisions of that sort of faith: "of the *ajñānika*s, etc." *Ajñānika*s means those of whom there is said to be *ajñāna*; or they are those who live according to it or praise it. They claim that *ajñāna* alone brings about man's goals, that no one can know an entire thing truly. And these adherents of the *ajñāna*-party, being of 67 varieties as their doctrine is differentiated by some particular issue, just as there are 18 schools of Buddhists, all teach plurality [i.e., the manifoldness, and thus unkowableness of things]. Confused by the errors of such views, the sages Śākalya, Bāskala, Kuthumi, Sātyamugri, Rāṇāyana, Aitikāyana, Vasu, Jaimini, etc. have popularized this false faith. By the word "etc." [in the *Svabhāṣya*] are indicated the *kriyāvādī*s, *akriyāvādī*s, and *vainayika*s. Thereunder, the *kriyāvādī*s are divided into 180: the teachers Marīci, Kumāra, Kapila, Ulūka, Gārgya, Vyāgrabhūti, Vādvali, Māṭhara, Maudgalyāyana, etc., all holding separate doctrines. The *akriyāvādī*s have 84 varieties, whose doctrines have been spread by such teachers as Kokkula, Kāṇṭheviddhi, Kauśika, Hariśmaśru, Māṇṭanika, Romaka, Hārīta, Muṇḍa, Aśvalāyana, etc. The *vainayika*s are of 32 varieties; Vasiṣṭha, Parāśara, Jātukarṇa, Vālmīki, Romaharṣiṇi, Satyadatta, Vyāsa, Ailāputra, Aupamanyava, Indradatta, Ayasthūla, etc. are the sages who have taught the *vinaya*-expositions. . . . "Bad teachings" means teachings that are reproachable because whatever they say is possessed by the demon of unequivocalness; that is the meaning.[29]

In addition to the basic features that permit the division of these texts into groups A, B, and C, there are a number of other points of interest and lines along which they might be divided. Easy access to these other points of interest and making clear the characteristics of the groups have been the major reasons for this lengthy text-presentation.

One further important observation must be made concerning the texts in group C. The bulk of these are commentaries, and both the development of the peculiar nature of the 363-account, and its growing dominance, can be seen in that fact. If one reflects on the process that is revealed in the sources, one can see that it is precisely because the commentary tradition saw something, because it read something into the scattered elements in the earlier sources, that the 363-account emerged in full form.

---

29 Proper names according to Schrader 1902:15-16.

Part III

FOUR JAIN PHILOSOPHICAL COMPENDIA

19

INTRODUCTION TO THE COMPENDIA*

The Jain philosophical compendia discuss schools of thought and various issues that are known features of Indian thought. The approach of the compendia can be described as descriptive, even historical. Most of the Jain compendia contain no refutations of the positions of which they give an account. The positions are simply stated, in summary style, without any argumentation to the contrary. This is true of all but one of the works translated here.

In general, the compendia have gotten short shrift from scholars. This may be partly because they seem to spring full-blown into existence, so that their place in Indian thought is hard to assess. But more commonly, they are rather taken for granted. They have not been studied to any great extent as a phenomenon in their own right. Students of Indian thought have tended to see in these works some corroboration of an extraneous notion. Those interested in tolerance find the Jain compendia highly interesting as a confirmation thereof, because of the absence of refutations. Another common conclusion is that these compendia represent the beginnings of some notion of a history of philosophy.

The tendency to see the compendia in the light of what one is seeking is perhaps the single outstanding characteristic of most studies of them. Visions of

* From dissertation, pp. 227-331. See also chapter 8. In the dissertation, Folkert also included K. Satchidananda Murty's translation of Haribhadra's *Ṣaḍdarśanasammuccaya*. Folkert (1975:327) noted, "a new English translation of this text is in order," but for various reasons did not provide such a new translation in the dissertation. There are indications in his papers that he intended to translate this text, but never did so.

them as a whole, as a problem unto themselves, are rare. This has left a great many loopholes in the current view of these compositions.

One of the few analyses of the Indian compendia themselves has been made, in an abbreviated way, by A. K. Warder. In "The Description of Indian Philosophy," Warder (1970) examines a number of Indian accounts of the various schools of thought. He is actually looking for a way of isolating a particular Indian term or set of terms that might correspond to the English "analytical philosophy." Without judging the success or failure of this part of Warder's work, two points can be abstracted from it.

First, Warder's fairly cursory survey reveals that two prominent unsolved issues exist with respect to these accounts of schools. One is the number of schools, which is given in a great many places as six. The other is the terminology used of the schools. Of the first issue, Warder (1970:8) says, "The number six seems to be popular, whilst there is a general consensus of opinion as to which the six primary schools are, if not exact agreement." This statement quite adequately sums up the state of scholarly knowledge about the number and particular schools included in the compendia. As to the matter of terminology, Warder is content to treat such terms as *tarka*, *mata*, and *darśana*—all terms with wide currency in the texts that he surveys—as basically synonymous. These two issues are points of great interest for an overall view of the compendia; their unresolved state is the first striking thing about Warder's brief survey.

The second striking thing is the way in which Warder's treatment of the sources reveals the lack of scholarly awareness of them as a whole. This point requires a bit of elaboration. Warder finds a number of ways in which the various schools of thought are enumerated, and focuses on the distinction of *ānvīkṣiki* into six *tarka*s (Jain, Buddhist, Lokāyata, Sāṃkhya, Nyāya, and Vaiśeṣika) in Rājaśekhara's *Kāvyamīmāṃsā*. It is important to note that his presentation does not seriously touch the question of whether such a model for distinguishing schools of thought might also involve a statement about why there should be various schools.

Warder (1970:5-7) presents the fact that Rājaśekhara places *ānvīkṣikī* in the arena of *pauruṣeya śāstra* ("human" learning), along with *purāṇa, mīmāṃsā, sāhityavidyā*, and some others such as *daṇḍanīti*. Opposed to the general category into which these fall is *apauruṣeya śāstra* ("non-human" learning), which, according to Rājaśekhara, consists in the Veda: *mantra, brāhmaṇa upaveda*, and the *vedāṅga*s; while over against the two *śāstra* arenas stands *kāvya*.

Implicit in Rājaśekhara's scheme would seem to be an accounting for the actual existence of various schools, for the six *tarka*s are the products of *ānvīkṣikī*, which is part of the *pauruṣeya* side of *śāstra*. Warder (1970:7) goes so far as to say:

> It is this secular and critical approach, either rejecting revelation such as the *Veda* or leaving it aside, which distinguishes these six schools from the Mīmāṃsā metaphysics of Vedic investigation.

Thus there is present in Rājaśekhara some attempt at accounting for the origin of schools of thought, in that the *tarka*s occupy a position with a specific rationale. But one must work between the lines of Warder's analysis in order to see this.

It is at such a point that one feels sorely the lack of some perception of the compendia and like texts as phenomena in their own right. What does an attempt at classification such as Rājaśekhara's imply? It will not do simply to let such texts stand as "historical" documents of some sort. Granted that Warder does not treat the texts as signs of openness or tolerance, nor tout them as "histories," he nonetheless grants to their discussions of various viewpoints an unreflective, descriptive character that cannot properly be assumed to exist without further investigation of the texts and what they represent.

With this general theoretical problem in mind, the first striking feature of Warder's account can be taken up again: the matter of the number six and the terminology. Dealing with these problems is less than simple because the number six and the term *darśana* have become part and parcel of the now standard way of enumerating and regarding Indian schools of thought. This fact often seeps back into historical study of earlier groupings and terminology, though it is not necessarily well-founded in early sources. It is intriguing that the Jain compendia rely heavily on the term *darśana* and present six schools of thought. This is apparent from the titles of three of them. In fact, it would appear that the Jain compendia, compared to other Indian sources, tend more toward using the term *darśana*, at least early on. As to the number six, it has not been possible to find a specific source for its widespread use in Jain texts. The Jain compendia do not provide any overt clues concerning their predilection for this number, nor can one do more in the end than hazard a theory. But this is not such a cul-de-sac as might at first seem, for the investigation of the term *darśana* in chapter 8 sheds a surprising amount of light onto this particularly vexing problem.

20

SARVASIDDHĀNTAPRAVEŚAKA

INTRODUCTION

As discussed in chapter 8, the *Sarvasiddhāntapraveśaka* is both like and unlike the other texts being translated here. It is in prose, and thus shares no material with the other texts translated. Its title avoids both the word *darśana* and the number six. Still it presents the same six schools as are in the others, and it does not refute them. The order in which they are presented is different from the others, and its mode of presentation is very much unlike that of the others. The presentation of the schools in the *Sarvasiddhāntapraveśaka* consists simply of statements of the basic *tattva*s of the schools, carried out largely in the words of texts belonging to the schools.

The order in which schools are discussed bears a strong resemblance to the presentations by Śīlāṅka in his commentary on *Sūtrakṛtāṅga Sūtra* I.12 and Siddharṣi in his *Upamitibhavaprapañcākathā*:

Śīlāṅka	Siddharṣi	*Sarvasiddhāntapraveśaka*
Nyāya	Nyāya	Nyāya
Vaiśeṣika	Vaiśeṣika	Vaiśeṣika
Sāṃkhya	Sāṃkhya	Jain
Buddhist	Buddhist	Sāṃkhya
Mīmāṃsā	Lokāyata	Buddhist
Lokāyata	Mīmāṃsā	Mīmāṃsā
	Jain	Lokāyata

These parallel lists should make it clear that the *Sarvasiddhāntapraveśaka* follows the same general pattern as that in the other two texts.

The actual date of the *Sarvasiddhāntapraveśaka* is uncertain. Muni Jambūvijaya in his "Introduction" (*Upakrama*) to the text (p.11) notes that the oldest manuscript with which he worked dates to ca. 1145 C.E. According to the number of known copies, it does not seem to have been a widely-known text (Velankar 1944:428). In a way, then, it suffers from some isolatedness. Yet its importance is not diminished thereby.

The translation presented here is based on the edition of the text prepared by Muni Jambūvijaya. The work itself and its date have been discussed above in the Introduction. As mentioned there, this particular compendium consists to a great extent of quotations taken from the texts of the schools being described. Muni Jambūvijaya's edition contains identifications of these sources; those identifications are contained in the translation, but credit for tracing them belongs solely to the editor of the text.

The following abbreviations are used to designate the sources of quotations:

BS	*Bṛhaspati Sūtras*; see footnote 10 below.
JS	Jaimini, *Mīmāṃsā Sūtras*
NB	Dharmakīrtri, *Nyāyabindu*
NS	Gautama, *Nyāya Sūtras*
NV	Uddyotakara, *Nyāyasūtrabhāṣyavārttika*
PBh	Praśastapāda's *Bhāṣya* (*Padārthadharmasamgraha*) on VS
SK	Iśvarakṛṣṇa, *Sāṃkhyakārikas*
VS	Kaṇāda, *Vaiśeṣika Sūtras*

TRANSLATION

Having made obeisance to Lord Jina,
  author of all things,
I declare that which is the definition
  of the *tattva*s admitted in all the texts;

This is taught for the sake of revealing
  the sum of knowledge and its object
  in all the *darśana*s.

Naiyāyika darśana. Now in the Naiyāyika *darśana* there is this: "*pramāṇa*, *prameya*, doubt, purpose, illustrative instances, accepted conclusions, parts of the syllogism, argumentation, ascertainment, debate, wrangling, cavil, fallacies of the middle term, quibble, refutations, and points of defeat; from knowledge of the true nature of these comes attainment of the highest [i.e., release]." [NS 1.1.1]

Now the comment to this: *pramāṇa* is that by which something is known (*pramīyate*). Also, there is this common definition for it: *pramāṇa* is the cause of the perception (*upalabdhi*) of an object. Also, perception is the judgement that [an object] is to be rejected, etc. [i.e., rejected or sought after]. It [*pramāṇa*] is four-fold, as follows: "*pratyakṣa, anumāna, upamāna*, and *śabda* are the *pramāṇas*." [NS 1.1.3] Thereunder, *pratyakṣa* is as follows: "*pratyakṣa* is the knowledge (*jñāna*) that arises from the contact of sense and object, being inexpressible, unerring, and definitive." [NS 1.1.4] Here is the explanation of this: The senses are the olfactory and the like; objects are pots and the like; the contact between them is their relationship; and from this contact it [the knowledge] arises. It is not simply manifested, and thus this [Nyāya position] differs from the Sāṃkhya opinion. By the word "knowledge" (*jñāna*) it is distinguished from joy and the like. And since knowledge when expressed is indissoluble from words, "inexpressible" is stated [as a characteristic of primary perception]. Also, this same knowledge might still be erroneous; therefore the definition here says "unerring." "Definitive" means being definite by nature; thus it is differentiated from dubious knowledge. Thus is *pratyakṣa* to be defined in detail.

Now *anumāna*: "*anumāna* is preceded by it, and is three-fold: *pūrvavat, śeṣavat*, and *sāmānyato dṛṣṭa*." [NS 1.1.5] "Preceded by it" means preceded by perception. Three-fold refers to division in terms of *liṅga* [the "mark" in the inferential process]. *Pūrvavat* means inference of effect from cause, such as [inferring] that there will be rain from seeing clouds building up. *Śeṣavat* means inference of cause from effect, in the way that one concludes from a particular sight of a full river that "there has been rain upstream." That [inference] named *sāmānyato dṛṣṭa* is like this: Having noted that in the case of Devadatta and others, they come to be in another place by having moved, one concludes the same in the case of the sun and the like.

"*Upamāna* is the means of establishing that which is to be proven by means of something well-known that has the same nature." [NS 1.1.6] The cow is well-known; since, along with the cow, the *gavaya* [wild ox] is of the same nature, i.e., has the quality in common with it of possessing hump, hoof, horns, etc., *upamāna* is the means of establishing from this common nature that which is to be proven, namely, [that what is seen is] a *gavaya*; so that one says, "As a cow is, so is a *gavaya*." Now then, what is accomplished here by means of *upamāna*? The purpose of *upamāna* is to understand the relationship between a name and the thing named.

Now, what is *śabda*? "*Śabda* is a reliable person's assertion." [NS 1.1.7] Indeed, "a reliable person" means one who possesses the quality of having had direct experience; and that teaching which is presented by such a person is reliable teaching, it is *āgama*, and thus it is the *pramāṇa* called *śabda*.

What, then, is the collection of things to be known (*prameya*) through this valid knowledge (*pramāṇa*) by a person desirous of release? To this it is said: "The self, the body, sense, object, knowledge, mind, action, fault, death, fruits, sorrow, and release are to be known." [NS 1.1.9]

Now this is doubt (*saṃśaya* [the third category]): doubt is knowledge that is of the nature of uncertainty, e.g., "this is something (or other)." For example, in very dim light, in a place appropriate to either, upon seeing a post or a man, one thinks: "It may be a post, it may be a man."

Now purpose (*prayojana* [the fourth category]): purpose is that which, when one is engaged in it, something is undertaken.

Now example (*dṛṣṭānta* [the fifth category]): an example is something that has come to be the object of no objection [i.e., is commonly accepted], such as, in the realm of non-eternal objects, pots, etc.; and ether, etc. [in the realm of eternal things].

Next: accepted conclusions (*siddhānta* [the sixth category]). They are fourfold, as follows: *sarvatantrasiddhānta* (conclusions accepted by all parties), *pratitantrasiddhānta* (conclusions accepted by one or more parties and opposed by some), *adhikaraṇasiddhānta* (conclusions upon whose acceptance other conclusions naturally follow), and *abhyupagamasiddhānta* (opponents' conclusions that are hypothetically granted, but whose consequences are then refuted, thus putting the opponent in a bad light).

Now, the parts of the syllogism (*avayava* [the seventh category]): "Proposition (*pratijñā*), mark (*hetu*), example (*udāhraṇa*[1]), application (*upanaya*), and conclusion (*nigama*) are the parts of the syllogism." [NS 1.1.32] Therein, [for example] "sound is non-eternal" is the proposition. "Because it possesses the quality of having been produced" is the mark. "Like a pot" is the example. In this world, whatever has the quality of having been made, that is seen to be non-eternal, as in the case of a pot; [in this way] a universal law (*vyāpti*) is in accordance with the example.[2] And thus, "sound has the quality of having been produced" is the application. The conclusion is: "therefore, because it has this quality of having been produced, sound is non-eternal." Also, even in the case of a dissimilar example (*vaidharmyodāharaṇa* [an example showing negative invariable concomitance]) e.g., "whatever is in this world is not non-eternal, that does not have the quality of having been produced, like ether, etc.; nor does sound have the quality of not having been produced," the conclusion

---

1 The text reads *udāraṇa*.

2 An alternate reading omits this sentence.

remains "therefore, because it has this quality of having been produced, sound is non-eternal."

Argumentation (*tarka* [the eighth category]) is the state of considering what must be the case, subsequent upon doubt; for example, "This must be a person or a post."

Ascertainment (*nirṇaya* [the ninth category]) is the condition of determination that is subsequent to doubt and argumentation.

There are three kinds of colloquy: debate, wrangling, and cavil. Debate (*vāda* [category ten]) occurs when teacher and student take up position and counter-position for the sake of practice.

"Wrangling (*jalpa* [category eleven]) is finding fault with [another's] thesis by means of quibble, [pointing out or introducing] apparent errors, and [using] points of defeat"; [NS 1.2.2] and it is carried out with an opponent.

Cavil (*vitaṇḍa* [category twelve]) is argument without the establishing of any position of one's own.

Flaws of the middle term (*hetvābhāsa*s [category thirteen]) are the indeterminate (*anaikāntika* [where the mark and the thing to be proven are in relationship of only partial pervasion]), etc.

Quibble (*cchala* [category fourteen]) is saying such things as "Devadatta has nine (or: a new [the word *nava* meaning both of these]) blanket(s)."

Refutations (*jāti*s [category fifteen]) are instances that have the appearance of error [which one may use in debate to confuse an opponent].

Points of defeat (*nigrahasthāna*s [category sixteen]) are points that give one a victory over another, for example: "the opponent's giving up his own thesis, shifting his thesis, contradicting his thesis, disclaiming his thesis, changing the mark, changing the topic, talking nonsense, using jargon, incoherence, getting things out of order, omitting essential points, belaboring the obvious, repeating himself, failing to answer, failure to follow the argument, making an insufficient response, evasion, admitting defeat while claiming a flaw in the opponent's position, overlooking error, claiming an error where none exists, deviation from an accepted conclusion, and fallacies of the middle term." [NS 5.2.1]

Thus the Naiyāyika *darśana* is concluded.

Vaiśeṣika darśana. Now, in order to summarize the Vaiśeṣika position, one says: The attainment of the ultimate goal (*niḥśreyasa* [i.e., *mokṣa*]) comes from knowledge of the true nature of substance, quality, action, universal, particularity, and inherence. Thereunder, there are nine substances: "Earth, water, fire, air, ether, time, space, self, and mind (*manas*) are the substances." [VS 1.1.4]

Therein, earth is [defined] by its possession of earth-ness. It is two-fold: eternal and non-eternal. The eternal is characterized by [being in the form of] atoms; the non-eternal is that which has the character of being a product. Earth is fitted with fourteen qualities, in that it possesses the qualities of color, taste, odor, touch, number, dimension, severalty, conjunction, disjunction, proximity, distance, weight, fluidity, and velocity.

"Water is [defined] by its association with water-ness." [PBh 14] It possesses color, taste, touch, number, dimension, severalty, conjunction, disjunction, proximity, distance, weight, natural fluidity (*svābhāvikadravatva*), viscosity, and velocity. Its color is white only, its taste is sweet only, and its touch cool only.

"Fire is [defined] by its association with fire-ness." [PBh 15] It possesses eleven qualities, namely, color, touch, number, dimension, severalty, conjunction, disjunction, proximity, distance, induced fluidity (*naimittikadravatva*), and velocity. Therein, its color is glowing white, and its touch is hot.

"Air is [defined] by its association with air-ness." [PBh 16] It possesses nine qualities, namely: touch that is neither hot nor cold, number, dimension, severalty, conjunction, disjunction, proximity, distance, and velocity. Support (*dhṛti* [e.g., of leaves borne on the wind]), trembling [of leaves, etc.], and the like are marks of it, as are sound, the absence of odor, and a touch that is neither hot nor cold.

"Ether" (*ākāśa*) is a name adopted by convention, because of its one-ness.[3] It possesses six qualities: number, dimension, severalty, conjunction, disjunction, and sound; and sound is [its] mark.

"Time is the cause of the perception of the relationship of prior and posterior, simultaneity and nonsimultaneity, slow and quick." [PBh 26] It possesses the five qualities of number, dimension, severalty, conjunction, and disjunction.

"The mark of space (*dik*) is the notion that one thing is directionally related to another." [VS 2.2.12] Specifically, [notions like] "this is to the East of that," or "this is to the North." It possesses five qualities: number, dimension, severalty, conjunction, and disjunction; and its name is adopted by convention.

"Self is [defined] by its association with self-ness." [PBh 30] It possesses fourteen qualities: knowledge (*buddhi*), pleasure, pain, desire, aversion, volition—its mark—, *dharma, adharma, saṃskāra* [the capacity of acquiring modification through experience], number, dimension, severalty, conjunction, and disjunction.

---

3 This statement, based on Praśastapāda (see text, p. 7) must be explained by referring the reader to the formulation of the other introductory definitions, where the definition of a particular substance (*dravya*) is based upon the relationship of the individual to its class. The process, in Vaiśeṣika thought, of stating (or better, defining) the categories and their members is more than the cataloguing of basic existents. It is also part of the process of explaining how these existents are to be known. For this latter purpose, the defining of any specific substance depends on the relationship of individual to class; but in the case of ether, time, and space (*dik*), which are unitive elements, this relationship is not possible. Thus it cannot be part of the definition, and hence the pattern is broken at this point.

"Mind is [defined] by its association with mind-ness. It is the cause of ordered knowledge. It possesses eight qualities: number, dimension, severalty, conjunction, disjunction, proximity, distance, and velocity."

Such is the substance-category.

Now the qualities: Color, taste, odor, and touch are *viśeṣaguṇa*s [qualities that distinguish certain substances]. Number, dimension, severalty, conjunction, disjunction, proximity, distance—these are the *sāmānyaguṇa*s [qualities common to a number of substances]. The qualities of the self are knowledge, pleasure, pain, desire, aversion, volition, *dharma, adharma, saṃskāra*. Weight is a quality of earth and water; fluidity of earth, water, and fire; viscosity of water alone. *Saṃskāra* in its form of momentum (*vega*) occurs only in substances capable of motion. Sound is the quality of ether. Quality is [defined] by its association with quality-ness. Similarly, there are subordinate universals [within the category], e.g., color is [defined] by color-ness, taste by taste-ness, and so on.

Such is the quality-category.

Now the category of action: The actions are impelling upward, impelling downward, contraction, expansion, and motion [in general]." [VS 2/1/7] Action is [defined] by its association with action-ness. By the word "motion [in general]" is included gyration, flow, sinking, rising, etc.

Such is the action-category.

"Universals are two-fold, superior and subordinate." [PBh 164] Thereunder, the superior universal is existence (*sattā*) alone, because it is the cause of the notion "existent" that accompanies [every instance of our cognizing] substance, quality, and action. For it has been said: "From whence we cognize that 'it is' concerning substance, quality, and action—that is existence." [VS 1.1.7] Also, the subordinate [universals] are substance-ness, quality-ness, action-ness, etc. Therein, substance-ness is present only in substances, quality-ness only in qualities, action-ness only in actions.

Thus the universals-category.

"Particularities (*viśeṣa*s) are final, and reside in eternal substances." [PBh 4] Eternal substances are the four-fold atoms [i.e., the atoms of the first four substances: earth, water, fire, and air; their atomic form being their eternal form], emancipated selves, and emancipated minds.[4] Particularities [exist, or are so-called] because they possess the quality of causing the knowledge of the basic distinctions [among things].

Thus the particularity-category.

4 This is a curious point. First, the list is not complete, for it omits other eternal, non-atomic substances (ether, time, and space). Also, the addition of the adjective "emancipated" to self is an oddity.

"Inherence (*samavāya*) is that relation which causes the knowledge that one entity is in another, [a relation] between receptacle and that which resides in it [like that between a cloth and the threads in it] when they are inseparably joined." [PBh 5, 171]

Thus the inherence-category.

If we are to declare *pramāṇa* according to the Vaiśeṣika doctrine, [it is thus:] they say that there are only two *pramāṇa*s, *anumāna* and *pratyakṣa*, because of the inclusion of the remaining *pramāṇa*s therein.

Thereunder, showing what inference (*laiṅgikaṃ pramāṇam* [*anumāna*]) is, they say: "This is the effect of that"; "This is the cause of that"; "This is related to that"; "This is related to the same thing as that is"; and "This contradicts that." Where [the mark] is the effect of something, one infers, for example, rain because of a special flooded state of a river. Where [the mark] is the cause of something, one infers, for example, that there will be rain because clouds are building up. [In the first case, the mark is the effect—the river in flood; in the second, the mark is the cause—the clouds.] The mark that is a relation is two-fold: conjuctive and inherent. The conjunctive mark is like the conjunction between smoke and fire. The inherent mark is like the inherence between horn and cow. The mark that inheres in the same thing as that which is to be known is of two kinds: where one infers an effect from another effect, and where one infers a cause from another cause. In the former case, one may infer color from touch; in the latter, one may infer hand from foot. The contradictory mark is of four kinds: where one infers something existent from something non-existent, where one infers something non-existent from something existent, where one infers something non-existent from something non-existent, and where one infers something existent from something existent. Thereunder, one infers the existence of the wind blowing away the clouds from the non-existence of rain. Next, one infers the non-existence of wind blowing away clouds from the existence of rain. Next, one infers that a pot has not been in contact with fire from the non-existence of any blackness on the pot. Finally, one infers the existence of a breach in a dike from the existence of a flood. Similarly, other types of mark may be understood: for example, the clearness of water implies that Canopus has risen; the rising of the moon implies neap tide and the blossoming of the water-lily; and such like. This is indicated by the words "this is the effect of that"; because the purpose of this *sūtra* is to illustrate inferential marks, not to furnish a definitive set.

If one asks, "What is the definition of *pratyakṣa*?" they say, "That which arises from contact of self, sense, mind, and object, and is other than those." [VS 3.1.13] The comment to this is: the self is yoked to mind, mind to sense, and sense to object. From this four-factored contact comes knowledge of pots, colors and the like. From a three-factored contact [i.e., self to mind to sense, because of the peculiar nature of sound] comes knowledge of sound. From a two-factored contact [i.e., self to mind] come pleasure and the like. Thus *pratyakṣa* is also declared.

Thus the Vaiśeṣika *darśana* is concluded.

Jaina darśana. Now, the following is furnished in order to set out clearly the true nature of *pramāṇa* and *prameya* according to Jaina doctrine. Now someone says: "If this is so, then declare what is that *pramāṇa* and *prameya*." [Response] Therein, *prameya* is: "The *tattva*s [that] are *jīva, ajīva, āsrava, bandha, saṃvara, nirjarā*, and *mokṣa*." [*Tattvārthādhigama Sūtra* 1.4] Therein, the *jīva* is characterized by the evolution of pleasure, pain, knowledge, etc. Its opposite is *ajīva*. "Wrong faith, incontinence, carelessness, passion, and activity are the causes of bondage (*bandha*)." [*Tattvārtha* VIII.1] "Activity consists in the acts of body, voice, and mind." [*Tattvārtha* VI.1] "Influx (*āsrava*) consists of it [it meaning karma, or the activities just mentioned]." [*Tattvārtha* VI.2] "Pure [influx] consists of merit"; [*Tattvārtha* VI.3] its opposite of demerit. The effect of influx is bondage. Stoppage (*saṃvara*) is the opposite of influx. Decay (*nirjarā*) is the fruit of stoppage.

Next, *pramāṇa* is *pratyakṣa, anumāna,* and *āgama*. Thereunder, *pratyakṣa* is determinate, non-erroneous knowledge occasioned by the sense-organs and *manas*. This is the common definition of *pratyakṣa*; from the point of view of closer determination [of its nature], limited (*avadhi*) and other [sub-types of perception are present]. *Anumāna* is knowledge of a thing possessing a mark, by means of the mark, which does not occur elsewhere [than in concomitance with the thing to be known], such as knowledge that there is fire by means of [seeing the mark, namely,] smoke. *Āgama* consists of such things as [the teaching that] "Heaven comes from doing penance" and such like, because it brings about determinate and uncontroverted knowledge, as do the eyes, etc.

Thus the introduction to the Jaina doctrine is complete.

Sāṃkhya darśana. Now, the following is furnished in order to show the Sāṃkhya opinion. Therein /are *prakṛti, puruṣa,* and their contact (*tatsamyoga*)./[5] *Prakṛti* is the state of equilibrium among *sattva, rajas,* and *tamas*. / Evolution (*pariṇāma*) is its unbalanced state, when / from this *prakṛti, mahān* arises; from *mahān, ahaṃkāra*; and then from *ahaṃkāra*, the eleven organs: five sense-organs (*buddhendriya*s), five action-organs (*karmendriya*s), and mind (*manas*). Then, from the same *ahaṃkāra*, when *tamas* predominates, [arise] the five *tanmātra*s, as follows: the *tanmātra*s of sound, touch, color, taste, and smell. And from them, respectively, come the elements (*bhūta*s): ether, air, fire, water, and earth; and the aggregations of elements: bodies, trees, etc.

---

5 An alternate reading omits the portions enclosed by //, in this and the next-but-one sentence.

If we are to state the character of *sattva*, etc., [according to Sāṃkhya, it is thus:] they say that the effect of *sattva* is clarity, lightness, stimulation, affection, joy; the effect of *rajas* is dessication, suffering, disjuntion, disturbance, aversion; the effect of *tamas* is obstruction, weariness, loathing, depression, heaviness.

> *Sattva* is light, illuminating, agreeable;
> *rajas* is motion and excitement;
> *Tamas* is heavy and obscuring; their actual operation
> is like [the oil, wick, and flame of] a lamp. [SK 13]

Thus far the discussion of *prakṛti* in its gross and subtle forms.

Now, what is the true nature of *puruṣa*? The true nature of *puruṣa* is consciousness (*caitanya*). There is conjunction between *prakṛti* and *puruṣa* for the sake of enjoyment, a relationship like that between a blind man and a cripple. Enjoyment means the perception of sounds and the like, and the perception of qualities and other *puruṣa*s. If one asks, "Is the *puruṣa* one or many?" they say that is is many. What, then, is the reasoning behind this? *Puruṣa* is many because we see that the causes of birth and death follow fixed rules, and because of the varied states [of individuals] in *dharma* and *adharma*. It [*puruṣa*] is called the *ātman*.

Now *pramāṇa* is to be declared. On this they say: *pratyakṣa, anumāna*, and *āgama* [are the *pramāṇa*s]. Therein, [this is] *pratyakṣa*: *pratyakṣa* is the functioning of the auditory sense, etc. Functioning means the objectivizing, that is, the transformation [into objects] of the auditory, tactile, visual, taste, and olfactory [senses], presided over by *manas*, as they operate in the perceiving of objects—sound, etc.

Now *anumāna*: "*anumāna* is the proof of what remains [to be proven], arising from a single perception, because of a [universal] connection."[6] "Because of a connection" means that [the result arises] from a mark, because of a relation that is invariable, like that between smoke and fire.

"*Śabda* is the assertion of a reliable person." [NS 1.1.7[7]] Whoever does not do bad deeds, and is well-versed in something, he is reliable on that point. The teaching that is given by him is reliable, such as "There are *apsaras*s in heaven" or "The Kurus live in the North." Thus there are these three *pramāṇa*s only, because of the inclusion of the remaining *pramāṇa*s in them.

Thus the Sāṃkhya doctrine is completed.

Bauddha darśana. Now this is said by way of showing the Bauddha opinion. Therein, the categories (*padārtha*s) are the twelve *āyatana*s, as follows:

---

6 This appears to be a quotation from NV. It is given as such in a note to the text, p. 16. Hence it is marked here in the translation as a quotation.

7 The source is given in the text, p. 17, as NS 1.7.

the sense of sight, the sense of smell, taste, touch, hearing, *manas*, color, flavor, odor, tactility, sound, and *dharma*. *Dharma*s are pleasure, etc.

One says, "What, then, is the means of discriminating among them?" [The response is:] *pramāṇa*; it is two-fold: "*pratyakṣa* and *anumāna*; therein, *pratyakṣa* is non-erroneous [and] prior to mental construction (*kalpanā-poḍha*)." [NB 1.3, 4] Mental construction consists in joining name, universal, etc. [to the object]. Therein, the construction of name is [the source of] thought, "It is a cow" and the like. The construction of quality is [the source of] the thought, "It is white" and the like. The construction of activity is [the source of] the thought, "[Someone is] cooking," "[Someone is] teaching" and the like. The construction of substance is [the source of] the thought, "He is a staff-holder," or "It is horned" and the like. *Pratyakṣa* not informed by such construction is called *pramāṇa*.

Now *anumāna*: *anumāna* is knowledge, born of a three-fold mark, of the thing bearing the mark. This three-fold mark is: (1) sharing a quality with the minor (*pakṣadharmatva*), (2) existence in the minor (*pakṣa*), and (3) non-existence outside the minor. *Anumāna* is knowledge of a property-possessor [e.g., a fire-possessing mountain] as possessed of that property which is the major term [e.g., fire], because it possesses the middle term [e.g., smoke] which has the three-fold validity. Thus there are only two *pramāṇa*s, because of the inclusion of all the remaining *pramāṇa*s therein.

Thus the Sugata doctrine is complete.

Mīmāṃsaka darśana. In the Mīmāṃsaka doctrine, the desire to know *dharma* is to be put into effect after Veda-study. Since that is so, one should examine the cause of *dharma*. That cause is scriptural injunction (*codanā*), for it is said: "*dharma* is the goal of that which is defined as injunction." [JS 1.1.2] And "injunction" is said to be a statement that is a stimulus to activity, such as "A man who desires heaven should perform the *agnihotra* [sacrifice]. *Dharma* is to be defined in this way, and not through *pratyakṣa*, etc.[8]

Someone says: "How is it that *pratyakṣa* is devoid of causal force [in leading one to *dharma*]? [Response:] Because it is of this nature: "That which is *buddhi*-born when the self's senses are active upon an existent entity (*satsamprayoga*) is *pratyakṣa*; it is without causality because it has the nature of being [only] perception of that which exists at the moment." [JS 1.1.4] In this way, *anumāna* is also without causality, because of its being subsequent to *pratyakṣa*; and *upamāna* is also without causality, because in it, when one grasps the similarity of nature between cow and *gavaya*, the thing that is known (*prameya*)

8 This opening paragraph duplicates the statement on the Mīmāṃsā in the *Upamitibhavaprapañcākathā*. See chapter 19 above .

is simply "cow."[9] So also [without causality] is *arthāpatti*, which is two-fold: from seeing and from hearing. That which comes from hearing is like being told a fat man, named Devadatta, does not eat in the daytime; the conclusion, accordingly, is that he eats at night. Herein, the *prameya* is the statement that he eats at night. That which comes from seeing is like knowing (*pramīyate*) that fire has the capacity to burn from seeing something turned into ashes. In this way other applications can be stated, by reference to the texts. *Abhāva* is also without causality, because its object is a nothing. Therefore, *dharma* is to be defined [or known] only on the basis of injunction, and not otherwise. Also, significance—the quality of causing perception of meaning—lies only in the *varṇa*s (articulate sounds); and this has reference to external objects only, not otherwise. For it is said: "[The word *gauḥ*] is made up of the *ga*-sound, the *au*-sound, and the *visarga*: thus says the blessed Upavarṣa." [*Śābarabhāṣya* 1.1.5] The conjunctions and disjunctions of the air impelled by the speaker and reaching the ear of the listener are what manifests the *varṇa*s, *ga*, etc. And those manifested sounds are alone signficant, and none other. The connection between words and objects is eternal; nor is there for the Mīmāṃsakas such a thing as a word (*pada*) or sentence apart from the *varṇa*s, for the working of word and sentence rests in the *varṇa*s alone.

Thus the Mīmāṃsaka doctrine is complete.

Lokāyata opinion. By way of describing in brief the true nature of *pramāṇa* and *prameya* as laid down by the followers of the Bṛhaspati doctrine, one says as follows. Therein, to describe *prameya*, one says: "The principles (*tattva*s) are earth, water, fire, and air."[10] Someone says: "In addition to the principles, though there are body, senses, etc." [Response:] These are not in addition to the principles, because "the aggregates of those [principles] are called body, senses, and objects." The body is an aggregate of elements, as are the senses and their objects. Therfore, there are only four principles. If someone objects that knowledge is an additional principle, the response is that this is not so, for it is said: "Consciousness comes from these [principles]." The sense is that it is only a quality of them, like the power of intoxication in the constituents of wine. If objected: "Well, then, the self is an additional principle"; that also is nonsense, because the *sūtra* author says: "The *jīva*s are like water-bubbles," and "The self is a body qualified by consciousness." [Objection:] "Well, then, the goal of man

---

[9] An alternative reading would be translated that the *prameya* is only that a *gavaya* is like a cow; see the text, p. 19. But the reading translated here gives the correct sense of the Mīmāṃsā understanding of the function of *upamāna*, which is that it really has reference to the previously seen cow, not to the *gavaya* that is being seen. Hence its result is not new knowledge.

[10] The source-like passages enclosed in quotation marks are identified by the editor of the text as *Bṛhaspati Sūtra*s, and are drawn from a number of sources. However, the author writes as though they were from a particular text and author.

would be some additional principle." To refute this, one says: "The goal of man is pleasure, to be attained by doing [that which leads to it] and not doing [that which does not lead to it]." It is also "sensual pleasure only"; release, etc. is naught other than this. [Objection:] "Well, then, surely there must be some other self that is the seat of judgement." [Response:] That is nothing but the abandonment of what is seen and conjecturing about what is not seen. Therefore, this is established: there are only four principles.

Now *pramāṇa*: This is the common definition of it: *pramāṇa* is the distinguishing of an object hitherto unperceived. The means to this is the contact of sense and object, etc. "*Pratyakṣa* is knowledge of an object as it actually is, when that object is in close proximity." This is the definition of *pratyakṣa*; and in this doctrine "*pratyakṣa* is the sole *pramāṇa*." [Objection:] "Well, then, it is also said [in your *sūtras*] that '*anumāna* is [knowledge] of an object not in contact [with the senses].'" [Response:] But that [is said] according to another doctrine, not in reference to our own doctrine. Thus is established in brief the true nature of the Lokāyatas' *pramāṇa* and *prameya*.

Thus the Lokāyata doctrine is complete.

This completes the *Sarvasiddhāntapraveśaka*; the Naiyāyika, Vaiśeṣika, Jaina, Sāṃkhya, Bauddha, Mīmāṃsaka, and Lokāyata doctrines are completed in summary.

21

RĀJAŚEKHARA, *ṢAḌDARŚANASAMUCCAYA*

INTRODUCTION

The *Prabandhakośa* of Rājaśekhara (ca. 1349 C.E.) is one of the major sources of information on the life of Haribhadra. Although there are scholars who do not assign the *Ṣaḍdarśanasamuccaya* and the *Prabandhakośa* to the same author,[1] the general position of Jain scholars is that the two are by the same man.[2] This point seems to be strengthened by the fact that Rājaśekhara's compendium follows Haribhadra's *Ṣaḍdarśanasamuccaya* rather closely in some respects, and by the fact that certain features of Rājaśekhara's work are more readily understandable if it is viewed as the work of the *Prabandhakośa* author.

The text itself is in meter, and at 180 verses, considerably larger than Haribhadra's work. According to number and distribution of manuscripts, this compendium ranks a distant second to Haribhadra's in popularity, but still far outstrips other Jain compendia (Velankar 1944:402-3).

Rājaśekhara's text shares large blocs of material with Haribhadra's, and it is valuable to note what material is duplicated in the two compendia:

1 See Potter 1983:198, 311.

2 See Malvania 1969:15, and Sandesara and Thakar 1962:41.

school	Haribhadra vv.	Rājaśekhara vv.	mark
Jaina:	[45-46	8]	*devatā*
	47	12	*tattva*
Nyāya:	[13	90-94]	*devatā*
	14	97	*tattva*
	15	98	
Sāṃkhya:	34a	42a	*devatā*
	35a	45b	
	36	46	
	37	47	
	38	48	*tattva*
	39	49	
	40	50	
	41	51	
Jaiminīya:	[68	63b]	*devatā*
	69	64	
	70	65	*tattva*
	71	66	
Vaiśeṣika:	[59	130-131]	*devatā*
	60	116	
	61	117	
	62	118	
	63	119	*tattva*
	64	120	
	65	121	
	66	122	
Bauddha:	[4	133b-136a]	*devatā*
	5	139	
	6	140	*tattva*
	7	141	

Of all the texts presented here, this compendium contains the greatest number of curious pieces of information. Many of these cry out for further exploration. The translation that follows seeks to be as accurate as possible, given the presence in the text of some rather odd specific items and at least one major digression (verses 36-41) that seems to be out of place. The only text available is that edited by Pandits Haragovinda Dāsa and Becara Dāsa, in the Yaśovijaya Jaina Granthamālā; it gives little or no help at problematic loci.

TRANSLATION

1. Having bowed with devotion to my teachers,
   having reverenced Lakṣmī,
   What is to be said concerning all the systems
   Rājaśekhara declares.

2. *Dharma* is beloved in all the world;
   let the six systems declare it.
   Among them, in mark, dress, conduct,
   deity and teacher,

3. In *pramāṇa* and *tattva*, release and logic (*tarka*),
   one perceives difference.
   This is their common declaration:
   release comes through the eight-fold *yoga*.

4. Jaina, Sāṃkhya, Jaiminīya,
   Yoga and Vaiśeṣika,
   And Bauddha: these are the systems;
   but *nāstika* is not a system.

* * *

5. Therein, in the Jaina doctrine the mark
   is first of all the broom
   And the mouthshield; and the dress
   and is known as the loin-cloth, etc.

6. The details in the matter of dress, etc.
   are to be known from the mass of *niryukti*s;
   Conduct is characterized by the five *samiti*s
   and the three-fold *gupti*.

7. Wandering, careful speech, proper eating,
   sitting for meditation, careful evacuation:
   So are known the five *samiti*s; the three *gupti*s
   involve avoiding contact with women.

8. The Tīrthaṅkaras are twenty-four,
   Vṛṣabha and the rest;
   They are the illuminating suns of complete knowledge,
   being freed from the eight karmas' afflictions.

9. The teacher is said to be the keeper
 of the great vow, constant,
 Knower of the secrets of all the *āgama*s,
 conqueror of passion, self-esteem, etc., possessionless.

10. Two *pramāṇa*s are held herein,
 pratyakṣa and *parokṣa*;
 Thereunder, *prameya* is regulated by the *syādvāda*,
 and consists in six substances.

11. *Dharma, adharma*, ether, time,
 matter, and consciousness:
 These are known as the six substances;
 their subdivisions are found in the *āgama*.

12. *Jīva, ajīva*, merit and demerit,
 influx and stoppage,
 Bondage, decay, and release: nine *tattva*s
 are held by the *arhat*s.

13. *Jīva* is characterized by consciousness;
 ajīva is what is other than that.
 Merit consists of agglomerates of good karma,
 demerit of agglomerates of bad.

14. Influxes are held to be passions, activity,
 eternal objects, and the like;
 That which causes cessation of influx
 is known as stoppage.

15. Bondage is regarded as the acquisition
 of pure and impure karma;
 The removal of the mass of previously gotten karma
 is known as decay.

16. The fixation of the true nature of the *jīva*
 through destruction of karma is release (*śivam*).
 It is obtained through faithful conduct
 in accord with these nine *tattva*s.

17. The venerated Śvetāmbaras
 use the "*dharma lābha*" greeting;[3]

---

[3] This form of greeting, roughly "May you attain *dharma*," recurs in verse 23; verse 24 contains another, roughly "May your *dharma* increase."

They beg food, etc., from door to door,
like bees going from flower to flower.

18. The well-known *Pramāṇamīmāṃsā*,
a collection of *pramāṇa*-discussions;
The *Nayacakravāla tarka*,
and the *Syādvādakalikā*;

19. That sun to the *prameya*-lotus, the *Tattvārtha*,
the means to all things;
The *Dharmasaṃgrahaṇī*, etc.—this is the mass
of logic-material in the Jaina teaching.

20. There are two wings to the Jaina doctrine:
Śvetāmbara and Digambara;
The Śvetāmbara were discussed above,
and now the Digambaras are told.

21. There are four divisions among Digambaras,
all following the vow of nakedness:
The Kāṣṭhasaṅgha, Mūlasaṅgha,
and the Māthura and Gopyaka Saṅghas.

22. In the Kāṣṭhasaṅgha, the broom is ordained
to be made of the yak's tail.
In the Mūlasaṅgha, the brush is made
of peacock-feathers.

23. The broom has never been an issue
in the Māthura Saṅgha.
The Gopyas sweep with peacock-feathers;
their greeting is "*dharma lābha*."

24. The rest greet with "*dharma vṛddhi*."
The Gopyas declare release for women;
The three Saṅghas other than the Gopya
declare that women cannot attain it.

25. Neither the other three nor the Gopyas
hold that an omniscient takes food;
There is no release for one wearing monk's garb,
though he keep the vow well.

26. There are thirty-two obstacles
and fourteen impurities in mendicancy;

How to avoid them
    is found in their *āgama*.

27. For the rest, they are like the Śvetāmbaras
    in matters of conduct, deity, and teacher;
They accept the logic treatises
    composed by the Śvetāmbaras.

28. Theirs are mostly of the same nature,
    illuminated by knowledge of the *syādvāda*;
The *Paramāṣṭasahasrī*,
    that moon to the *nyāya*-lotuses;

29. The *Siddhāntasāra* and the other logic-books
    are very difficult;
Each word of them is capable
    of imparting victory.

30. These divisions in Jaina practice, etc.
    will presently be obscured in the Kali-age;
And then these present things, taught here,
    will have to be learned from the Jaina *āgama*.

31. One who takes pleasure in the eight-fold *yoga*,
    having known correctly the Jaina doctrine,
Having made his karma small,
    will obtain uninterrupted bliss.

* * *

32. Now we declare the Sāṃkhya doctrine:
    they carry the single and triple staff;
The loin-cloth is their clothing,
    and they are clad in *dhātu*-red.

33. With shaven head, using a deerskin seat,
    eating in the houses of the twice-born,
Some follow the practice of taking only five swallows;
    they mutter the twelve syllables.

34. "*Oṃ namo nārāyaṇāya*," say their devotees
    in return.
They also say this when doing obeisance,
    but they stop at *namo*.

35. In Bhārata the wooden mouthshield
    is called the *bīṭa*;
Its *raison d'être* is compassion, for it prevents
    ingesting creatures through the mouth.

For they declare:

36. Through the expelling of a single breath
    from the nose,
Creatures are killed; a thousand, O Brāhmaṇa,
    by speaking the least syllable.

37. Out of pity for water-creatures,
    they make use of a filter;
They constantly explain these teachings
    to their devotees [in this way]:

38. Thirty-six finger-breadths long,
    twenty finger-breadths wide,
A sturdy filter one should make;
    it would strain out many creatures.

39. Water-creatures born to saltwater
    die from sweet water,
But others die from saltwater;
    therefore, one should not mix them.

40. In one drop of the thread
    that falls from a spider's mouth
Are subtle creatures; if they were each beesized,
    the three worlds could not hold them.

41. As if it were filled with saffron,
    water filled with subtle creatures
Cannot be strained clear
    even by a strong filter.

42. Some Sāṃkhyas have no *īśvara*,
    and some have *īśvara* as their deity;
Those [just described] are without *īśvara*,
    and the others take refuge in Nārāyaṇa.

43. The learned ones in the Sāṃkhya-teaching
    exalt Viṣṇu;

Their teacher is said to consist
in the words spoken by Caitanya.

44. The *pramāṇa*-triad is *pratyakṣa*,
anumāna and *śabda*;
They argue that the remaining *pramāṇa*s
are included therein.

45. The number of *tattva*s held by these men,
learned in Sāṃkhya, is twenty-five;
The triad of qualities is to be known as
sattvam, rajas, and *tamas*.

46. Indeed, *prakṛti* is said to consist
in equilibrium among these three;
It is to be called by the names *pradhāna* and *avyakta*;
it is eternally like unto itself.

47. From it arises *buddhi*,
which is called *mahān*;
from that in turn the *ahaṃkāra*,
from that, the group of sixteen:

48. Touch, taste, smell, sight,
and hearing as the fifth,
They declare to be the five sense-organs.
There are also the motor-organs:

49. Anus, genitals, voice, hand, and foot
are stated, and *manas* as well;
The other five items are the *tanmātra*s,
and thus there are sixteen.

50. From *rūpa* comes fire; from *rasa*, water;
from *gandha*, earth; from *svara*, ether;
From *sparśa*, wind. In this way arise
five elements from the five *tanmātra*s.

51. Thus *prakṛti* is declared in the Sāṃkhya doctrine,
in the form of twenty-four *tattva*s.
Also, there is the non-agent *puruṣa-tattva*,
eternally conscious, quality-less, enjoyer.

52. Formless, conscious, enjoyer, eternal,
everywhere present, devoid of activity,

Not-doer, without quality, subtle:
such is the self in the Kāpila system.

53. Separation from *prakṛti* is release;
when it is subdued, the self finds its true form.
Prakṛti is involved in bondage and release,
but not *puruṣa*.

54. The doctrinal spokesmen among the Sāṃkhyas
are Kapila, Āsuri, the Bhārgavas,
Ulūka, and Pañcaśikha; and Īśvarakṛṣṇa
is the author of the *śāstra*.

55. His logic books, Maṭhara's commentary,
and the *Tattvakaumudī*,
Gaudapāda and Ātreya, plus the seventy *Sāṃkhya Sūtras*:
these are the major authorities.

56. There are many of them in Kāśī,
many keeping the one-month-fast.
The learned ones follow the smoke-path,
but these follow the sun-path.

57. Since they are devoted to the Veda,
the learned ones follow the sacrifice-path;
Rejecting the Vedic *hiṃsā*, etc.,
the Sāṃkhyas are *adhyātmavādī*s.

58. They declare the greatness of their
own doctrine [thus]:
If one is devoted to the Sāṃkhya doctrine,
then there is release without effort.

59. Laugh, drink, play, eat, enjoy always;
take as much pleasure as you wish.
If you know the doctrine of Kapila, then
you will speedily attain release and bliss.

* * *

60. Now I declare the Mīmāṃsā-following;
it is also called the Jaiminīya.
The Jaiminīyas also carry the single or triple staff,
like the Sāṃkhyas.

61. The Mīmāṃsakas are two-fold:
karma- and *brahma*-Mīmāṃsakas.
The Vedāntins hold with *brahman*,
while Bhaṭṭa and Prabhākara choose karma.

62. They are clad in *dhātu*-red,
and sit on a deerskin;
The Bhāṭṭas and Prābhākaras are shaven,
and carry a water-pot.

63. The only practice accepted by them
is *vedānta* meditation;
In their doctrine there is no deity
distinguished by omniscience, etc.

64. Therefore, because there is no actual perception
of things beyond the senses,
Certainty about the actual state of things
comes from the eternal words of the Veda.

65. Thus Veda-study is to be done assiduously
at the outset;
Then the desire to know *dharma*, which is
the means to *dharmas*, should be acted upon.

66. *Dharma* is of the character of impulse,
but it is said to be the word
That leads one to action, as in:
"Desiring heaven, one would perform the *agnihotra*."

67. The Veda alone is their teacher;
there is no other declarer at all.
Thus they say to themselves [and not to a *guru*],
"I have renounced, I have renounced."

68. Having washed the sacred thread
they drink that purified water.
According to dress, they are all Sāṃkhya-followers,
but concerning *tattva*s there is a great difference.

69. The Bhāṭṭas adhere to six *pramāṇa*s;
I will now declare their names:
Pratyakṣa and *anumāna*, together with
śabda and *upamayā*,

70. *Arthāpatti* and *abhāva*. These are known
as the six *pramāṇa*s of the Bhāṭṭas.
In the Prabhākara doctrine there are five;
they do not accept *abhāva*.

71. A principle of great import is
that *brahman* is one only, without a second.
Pillars, pots, etc. are only manifestations;
in their teachings they have no import.

72. "A Mīmāṃsaka is like a twice-born";
therefore they shun the food of *śūdra*s.
Since they are received through transmission,
the Vedas are not authored by men.

73. There are four divisions of Mīmāṃsakas;
therein are the Kuṭīcara,
And the Bahūdaka, the Haṃsa,
and the Paramahaṃsaka as well.

74. The Kuṭīcara dwells in a *maṭha*
and accepts patrons;
The Bahūdaka bathes at the river-bank,
and eats bland alms-food.

75. The Haṃsa wanders in many places,
his body sere from *tapas*.
Of him who is a Paramahaṃsa
the conduct I now declare:

76. Going in a northerly direction,
as far as his strength will take him,
There he keeps a fast,
devoted to *vedānta* meditation.

77. The last of these groups is the best;
their patrons are Brāhmaṇas.
Like the Sāṃkhyas, in their doctrine
the self's release is separation from *prakṛti*.

These *śloka*s are in the *Gārgīyasmṛti*:

78. He who carries the triple staff, with tufted tonsure,
wearing the sacred thread, homeless,

Who eats once a day in a patron's house—
who behaves so, he is a Kuṭīcara.

79. One who has the appearance of a Kuṭīcara,
who begs from Brāhmaṇas, having subdued the need to eat,
He is to be known as a Bahūdaka,
devoted to repeating Viṣṇu's name.

80. One without sacred thread and tonsure,
clad in yellow-red, carrying a staff,
Who stays one night in a village
and three nights in a city,

81. Asking alms from Brāhmaṇas, at wise men's houses
at hours when no cooking is being done,
Such a one is a Haṃsa,
who dwells in a hut.

82. When knowledge arises in a Haṃsa,
then he becomes the best, a Paramahaṃsa;
He takes food from all castes,
and carries a staff or not, as he wishes.

83. The *Prapañcamithyā* and the *Kaṭhavallikā*,
the everywhere-known *Bhāgavatapurāṇa*:
These and other books of theirs are many,
but in this world their movement is small.

* * *

84. Now I declare the Yoga-doctrine;
another name for it is the Śaiva.
They carry the staff,
and wear the tucked-in loin-cloth.

85. Wearing a woolen cloak,
with a mass of knotted hair,
Practitioners of ash-smearing,
taking tasteless food,

86. Carrying the *tumba*-gourd under the arm,
usually dwelling in the forest,
Devoted to works of hospitality,
eating tubers, roots, and fruit,

87. They may be married or without wife;
among them, the unmarried rank higher.
They are devoted to the five-fire *tapas*;
they carry the *prāṇaliṅga* in their hands.

88. Having cleaned their teeth,
having washed feet, hands, and mouth,
Thrice daily they besmear their limbs with ashes
and devote themselves to Śiva-meditation.

89. When a patron greets them,
doing *kṛtāñjali* to them,
He says: "*oṃ namaḥ śivāya,*"
and the Śaiva replies: "*śivāya nama.*"

90. Śaṅkara is their deity,
the agent of creation and dissolution;
His principal *avatāra*s number eighteen,
which are worshipped by them.

91. I now declare their names:
Nakulīśa, then Kauśika,
Gārgya, Maitrya, and Kauruṣa;
Īśāna is said to be the sixth;

92. The seventh is Pāragārgya, then
Kapilāṇḍa and Manuṣyaka,
Aparakuśika, Atri, Piṅgalākṣa,
then Puṣpaka;

93. Bṛhadācārya and Agasti;
Santāna is known as the sixteenth;
Rāśikara is the seventeenth,
and the other is Vidyāgururatha.

94. The eighteen Tīrtheśas
are worshipped by them at every occasion.
Worship and meditation before these eighteen
are to be known from their *āgama*.

95. Akṣapāda is their teacher;
thus they are called Ākṣapādakas.
Having attained the highest state of restraint,
they go about naked.

96. The *pramāṇa*s are four:
pratyakṣa, then *anumāna*,
upamāna and *śabda*; the results
are different for each.

97. The *tattva*s herein are sixteen,
pramāṇa, etc., as follows:
Pramāṇa, prameya,
saṃśaya, prayojana,

98. *Dṛṣṭānta*, then *siddhānta*
avayava, tarka, nirṇaya,
Vāda, jalpa, vitaṇḍa,
hetvābhāsa, and *cchala*,

99. *Jāti*s and *nigrahasthāna*s;[4]
their application is very difficult.
Release is said to be
the endless separation from pain.

100. The *nyāya*-logic [book] written by Jayantācārya
is extremely difficult;
Another author is Udāyanācārya,
veritable architect of a palace of books.

101. Bhāsarvajña is the author
of the logic *sūtra*s named *Nyāyasāra;*
On this logic treatise there are
eighteen lucid commentaries.

102. But the commentary named the *Nyāyabhūṣaṇa*
is very famous among them;
And is of particular note,
since they recite it in assemblies.

103. Having kept the twelve-year Śiva-*dīkṣā*,
one is indeed released;
Be that one even a male or female servant,
he reaches *nirvāṇa*.

104. The steadfast ones among these
present exegetical teachings;

4 These untranslated terms are all discussed above, in the *Sarvasiddhāntapraveśaka*.

Therein there is this verse,
which shows the path of release:

105. Not the river from heaven, nor serpents,
nor the garland of skulls,
Nor the sickle-moon, nor Pārvatī,
nor matted locks, nor ashes;
Where there is nothing other at all,
that form of the Lord,
Honored by the ancient sages,
we adore.

106. He alone is to be served by *yogīs*;
but the *yogī* who is not steadfast on that one
In meditating, he will be visited by desires
for royalty and such pleasures.

And it is said by them in their own *yogaśāstra*:

107. The *yogī* who thinks on the passionless one
gets passionlessness;
For the man who thinks on the impassioned one
the passion is sure.

108. With whatever form
the soul is linked,
It thereby takes on that form,
like crystal that shows all colors.

109. The Naiyāyika doctrine was declared by me
according to the scriptures;
The learned may see different things
in these same texts.

110. Their patron
is the Lord of Sutārā's heart,
The speaker of truth, Hariścandra,
born before Rāma and Lakṣmaṇa.

111. In the keeping of the *bharaṭa*-vow
is no caste-distinction whatever;
That vow-keeper who is devoted to Śiva
is a *bharaṭa*.

112. Among all these leaders,
the *bharaṭa*s alone are the priests;
The rest give honor to them,
but this is not to be done face-to-face.

* * *

113. Now I declare the Vaiśeṣika;
another name for it is Pāśupata.
Their mark, etc., is like the Yoga [Nyāya];
they even have the Tīrthakaras.

114. In the matter of *pramāṇa* and *tattva*
there is division between Vaiśeṣika and Yoga;
In this doctrine there are two *pramāṇa*s:
pratyakṣa and *anumāna*.

115. It is held by them
that all remaining *pramāṇa*s are included therein.
The *tattva*s are just six,
including substance, etc.

116. Substance, quality, action,
and universal as the fourth;
Particularity and inherence:
these are the six *tattva*s in their doctrine.

117. Thereunder, substance is nine-fold:
earth, water, fire, ether, air,
Time, space, self, *manas*;
quality, on the other hand, is twenty-five-fold:

118. Touch, taste, color, smell, sound, number,
conjunction and disjunction,
Dimension and severalty,
proximity and distance,

119. Knowledge, joy, sorrow, desire,
merit, demerit, volition,
Saṃskāra, aversion, viscosity, weight,
fluidity and velocity: these are the qualities.

120. Upward impulse, downward impulse, contraction
and expansion, and general motion:

These are the five types of action;
universals are two: greater and lesser.

121. Thereunder, the highest is that called "being";
substance-ness, etc. are the lesser.
Then there is particularity; it is called "final"
because of its distinguishing force, when
residing in eternal substances.

122. Inherence is the cause of knowing
in this world the connection
Between things that are essentially united,
in the relationship of receptacle and resident.

123. The same practices are found in general
in the texts of Yoga and Vaiśeṣika;
The teacher is Śaṅkara,
the one named above.

124. Their logic treatises are:
the *Kandalī*, in 6000 words,
Composed by *ācārya* Śrīdhara;
the commentary of Praśastakara,

125. In which are 700 sections;
and the *sūtra*s number 300;
There is the commentary written by Vyomaśiva,
known as the *Vyomamati*;

126. It is in 9000 words;
and another is the *Kiraṇāvalī*
In 6000 words, woven together
from the teachings, by Udāyana.

127. The commentary composed by Śrīvatsācārya
is known as the *Līlavatī*;
It is in 6000 words. And there is
one work, the *Atreyatantraka*,

128. That is at present lost,
since the disciples were lacking in diligence.
They are wise in conduct and custom,
in works of atonement as well.

129. Release is known as the final separation
of the self from sorrow;
So it is also stated concerning the Yoga,
since they are generally alike.

130. Śiva, in the form of an owl,
before the sage Kaṇāda,
Declared this doctrine;
therefore it is called the "*aulūkya*."

131. But because the Yoga doctrine
was composed by the seer Akṣapāda,
It is known as the Ākṣapāda;
the two doctrines are in general the same.

* * *

132. Now I will declare the Buddhist doctrine.
The tonsure, wearing of skins, and water-pot
Are their characteristic marks. Their clothing is red,
and they are much concerned with purity.

133. Dharma, Buddha, and Saṅgha comprise
their doctrine of three jewels;
Tārā is their deity,
destroyer of all obstacles.

134. They have seven Tīrthaṅkaras,
marked on their necks is a triple stripe:
Vipaśyī, Śikhī, Viśvabhūḥ,
Krakucchandas, Kāñcana,

135. And Kāśyapa; the seventh
is Śākyasimha, Arkabāndhava,
Also called Rāhulasūḥ, Sarvārthasiddha,
of the family of Gautama.

136. Son of Māyā and Suddhodana, and elder brother
of Devadatta was he.
The teachers are held to be
Śauddhodani, Dharmakīrti, and the rest.

137. In their doctrine there are two *pramāṇas*,
pratyakṣa and *anumāna*;

It is the declarer of the four noble truths:
sorrow and the rest.

138. In this doctrine the Buddha is all-knowing;
he declares the four knowables:
These *tattvas* are sorrow, its arising,
the way, and cessation.

139. Sorrow consists in the transient *skandhas*,
and they are declared to be five:
Vijñāna, vedanā, saṃjñā,
saṃskāra, and *rūpa.*

140. That whence the whole of passion, etc.,
in this world arises,
Known to be of the nature of "me" and "mine,"
is what is called "arising."

141. All the *saṃskāras* are momentary,
and the knowing that it is so
Is here to be known as the way.
Cessation is said to be release.

142. The clearness of knowledge that belongs to him
who is attached to Sugata's practices
Is held by some Buddhists to be release;
for others, release is destruction of consciousness.

143. They do not accept the self,
but accept knowledge alone.
It, consisting in a momentary series,
goes alone into another birth.

144. There are four divisions among Buddhists;
their devotional practice is different in each case.
They are to be known from this verse,
which sets forth their doctrines:

145. By the wise Vaibhāṣika it is held
that knowledge is the link with the object;
By the Sautrāntika it is held
that the mass of external objects is known by *pratyakṣa*;
By the followers of Yogācāra it is held
that judgemental knowledge has forms;

And, verily, the wise Madhyamas believe
that the highest knowledge is pellucid.

146. The *Tarkabhāṣā, Hetubindu, Nyāyabindu,*
and also the *Arcaṭa,*
Kamalaśīla's *tarka,*
and the *Nyāyapraveśaka;*

147. And the *Jñānapāramitā*, etc.:
in their doctrine the books are ten.
Their assembly-halls are round;
they are known as *buddhāṇḍaka*s.

148. A soft bed; something to drink
upon arising in the morning;
A meal at midday;
and something to drink in the afternoon;
Treacle and sugar
at midnight;
This ends in release
as seen by Śākyasiṃha.

* * *

149. The distinctions of mark, etc., have been declared
for the systems devoted to the good,
But not their details; and this has been stated
to the best of my knowledge.

150. So as to accomplish the eight-fold *yoga,*
the devotees concentrate on the marks.
All declare it as having eight parts;
I will now state its true nature.

151. Non-injury, truthfulness, non-theft,
and holy poverty comprise *yama.*
Niyama consists in purity, contentedness,
study, and penance.

152. Then, *āsana* is sitting properly,
doing meditation on the deity;
Prāṇāyama is suspension of breathing,
stoppage of exhalation and inhalation.

153. *Pratyāhāra* is withdrawal of the senses
from external objects;
Dhāraṇā is the momentary, steady fixation
of one's consciousness on the object of meditation;

154. *Dhyāna* is a series
of separate thoughts on that object;
And *samādhi's* nature is the appearance
of that very object alone.

155. Thus is *yoga* held to be eight-fold,
consisting in the eight parts that are *yama*, etc.
The *yoga* that is the means to release
is of the nature of knowledge, faith, and conduct.

156. *Dharma* consists in cessation
in the systems that seek the highest good;
But it consists in activity for householders
desiring the pleasures of royalty, etc.

157. *Dharma* that is cessation is bereft of all objectionable things;
it leads to attaiment of release.
Dharma that is activity consists in charitable works;
it leads to earthly reward.

158. The followers of the systems know the soul
to be the agent of *dharma* and *adharma*.
The *nāstika*s do not accept it;
their face is set away from merit and demerit.

159. They declare thus before assemblies:
there is neither soul nor karma;
Dharma and *adharma* are not found. Thus
what could be their fruits?

160. This world consists only in as much
as falls in the realm of the senses.
My dear! Look at the [false] wolf-track
that the unlearned are excited over.

161. Drink and eat, beautiful lady! What is dead,
O beautiful-bodied one, concerns you not.
O timid one! What is gone does not return.
All this is just an aggregate.

162. There is a tetrad of elements:
earth, water, fire, and air.
Therein, the knowable is only
that which results from sensual perception.

163. Just as the body, etc., come together
out of the collection of elements—earth, etc.,
So is the nature of consciousness
like intoxication coming from the constituents of liquor.

164. When there is rejection of that which is seen,
there is a turning toward the unseen;
This is the folly of the world:
so the Cārvākas declare.

165. In the successive demolition of their doctrines,
let us first consider the soul.
By means of such conceptions as
"I am sad" and "I am happy,"

166. And "I know a pot," a triad
manifests itself:
Object, activity, and agent.
What will refute [the existence of] this agent?

167. If you say that the body alone is the agent,
then there is no agent, for the body is not sentient.
If you say that sentience arises from contact between
elements and consciousness, that is crudely put.

168. "By me it is seen, heard, touched, smelled,
tasted"—in this
How do those who make the above declaration
account for the fact of a single agent?

169. Since it is shown by self-knowledge
that there is a conscious self in one's own body;
And then shown by inference
that this is also so in other bodies,

170. The existence elsewhere of the conscious activity
perceived in one's own body
Is proven by virtue of *pramāṇa*; thus
consciousness is not to be refuted.

171. These unseen things being shown,
karma-bondage is easily
Established through various apprehensions,
since it binds without beginning.

172. Karma, made up of merit and demerit,
accumulates or dissipates;
In virtue of this come joy and pain,
and not, indeed, by chance.

173. Existence and non-existence always
arise in dependence on another cause;
For variety among creatures
arises from this dependence.

174. The desire to suckle at the breast,
which is present immediately in infancy,
Is an impression from a previous birth,
since it has not been learnt in this one.

175. Therefore, it is not proper
to take pleasure in the sayings of the *nāstika*s;
Let the self, wise, separate from karma,
other-worldly, be known.

176. And it, by means of the eight-part *yoga*
having totally rooted out karma,
Attains release; indeed, therein
it intensely enjoys bliss.

177. The states of having a beginning, endlessness,
incomparableness, flawlessness, and natural felicity
Having attained, it rejoices,
free, experiencing all knowledge.

178. For those who are always inoffensive,
who desire the welfare of *guru* and god,
Who are of little passion,
release is close at hand.

179. Release comes as the necessary consequence
of time, nature, destiny, consciousness,
And other actions, when they are ripe,
and in no other way.

180. For the sake of instructing the young, Maladhārisūri
 Śrī Rājaśekhara, having first learnt
Correctly, from his teacher, what is found in the chief
 logic-treatises,
 has declared in brief the six systems.

22

MERUTUṄGA, *ṢAḌDARŚANANIRṆAYA*

INTRODUCTION

The *Ṣaḍdarśananirṇaya* is the only text translated here that actually argues against the non-Jain positions, and it is the only one that does not consider the *nāstika*s. The text itself is the latest of the group (ca. 1390 C.E.), standing relatively close to Rājaśekhara (ca. 1350 C.E.). These two texts, in fact, are chronologically the closest of any two.

This translation is based on the text edited by Nagin J. Shah, published in his *Collection of Jaina Philosophical Tracts*. Most of the identification of quotations in the text was done by the editor. Where identifications are supplied that are not in the edited text, they are placed in brackets. Verse numbers in quotations traced to the *Mahābhārata* are given according to the Poona critical edition. Many of the untraced quotations are to be found in other works translated here, often given there as quotations as well. To cross-reference these has not seemed necessary.

TRANSLATION

Honor to the highest self, whose true nature
is to be sought in meditation,

In whose single nature are knowledge and bliss,
who sets aside all misfortune.

Verily, in this world there have arisen four *varṇa*s, four *āśrama*s, and six *darśana*s; in this and other ways, the variety of all things is established. Yet the prideful sense that "I am the highest of all these," which arises in the nature of things, is very hard to restrain, and, viewed from the highest standpoint, wrong. If you ask why, the answer is as follows.

Indeed, there are four *varṇa*s: the *brāhmaṇa*, *kṣatriya*, *vaiśya*, and *śūdra*. Although the common view is that the *brāhmaṇa* is pre-eminent and best, *brāhmaṇa*-ness—whose chief characteristics are truthfulness, doing *tapas*, sense-control, and other things of *brahman*-nature—is chief over it. It was determined by the ancient enlightened teacher (*bauddhācārya*) that the *brāhmaṇa-varṇa* would not everywhere exist based only on the other *varṇa*s' acceptance, investiture with the sacred thread, etc. Therefore, it is said in scripture:

Brahman is truth, *brahman* is *tapas*, *brahman* is sense-restraint,
brahman is compassion toward all creatures; this
is the definition of *brāhmaṇa*.
A *brāhmaṇa* becomes one by living the *brahmacarya*, just as
one becomes skillful by practicing a craft;
else there is only the name, as in the case of the firefly.

And *brahman*, whose form is truth, etc., can be found being born in all *varṇa*s, in the form of selves whose nature is pure.

There are *cāṇḍala*s in all *jāti*s; there are *brāhmaṇa*s
in all *jāti*s;
Even among *brāhmaṇa*s there are *cāṇḍala*s; and among
*cāṇḍala*s, *brāhmaṇa*s.

—thus according to the authority of scripture.

Further, *brahmacarya*, householdership, forest-dwelling, and mendicancy are the four *āśrama*s. Therein, the former two *āśrama*s consist of those who abide in dwellings, and the latter two of those who wander about (*yati*s). Also, although according to custom only those who wander are to be reverenced by those who abide in houses, *yati*-ness is higher than that. It consists in freedom from desire, not in forest-dwelling, wearing bark-garments, eating flowers, leaves, and fruit, etc. Even though those who live in the forest may do all of that, still that does not make them *yati*s, because deer and the like do not achieve that state though they dwell on the earth, live by gleaning, bear cold and heat, etc. Nor does it come by ceasing to pamper one's body, etc., because we see that even in the case of cattle, etc. Nor does it come from begging food, fasting, etc., for then it would arise when there is famine. Nor does it come from possessing nothing, for then even the unfortunate would be *yati*s. Therefore, *yati*-ness consists in thrusting out love and hate, and making equanimity (*samatā*) one's own; for it is said:

> Even in the forest arise the faults of passion, etc.;
> even in the house there is the *tapas* of five-sense-control;
> The house of one who has cast out passion,
> and does irreproachable works, is an ascetic's grove.
> —*Hitopadeśa*

Further:

> If love and hate are present, what use is *tapas*?
> And if those two are absent, what use is *tapas*?

Also, there are six systems, divided into the Bauddha, Mīmāṃsaka, Sāṃkhya, Naiyāyika, Vaiśeṣika, and Jaina. Therein, even though it is generally held that they are true systems (*saddarśana*s) in that they declare the existence of the self, merit, demerit, heaven, etc., still one may ask why they accept one thing and reject another, each elevating its own position and degrading the others.

Herein, the Bauddhas have the Buddha as their deity (*devatā*) and proclaim the four noble truths: sorrow, etc. Thereunder, the five *skandha*s, *vijñāna*, etc., and the twelve *āyatana*s comprise sorrow. Arising (*samudaya*) consists in the cause of passion, etc., which is called condition of "my-ness" (*ātmīyabhāva*). The way (*mārga)* is the knowing that all of this is momentary. Release is the cutting-off of the series of knowledge-moments. The meaning of this is that release is annihilation (*nirodha*). There are two *pramāṇa*s: *pratyakṣa* and *anumāna*.

It being so, if the definition of Bauddha-ness includes the statement that "the Buddha is the *devatā*," then in that case is the Buddha beyond *saṃsāra* or not? If he is not beyond *saṃsāra*, then through being stained by passion, etc., like us he is not divine (*na devaḥ*). If he is beyond *saṃsāra*, is he momentary or not? If momentary, then he is not beyond *saṃsāra*, for there is no release [for him], since there is no cutting-off of the series, because of the momentariness. If he is not momentary, does he exist or does he not? If you say that he exists, that is wrong, because it contradicts the argument that "whatever exists is momentary." If you say that he does not exist, you have no valid means of knowing [him], because as in the case of the [non-existent] ass's horn, there would have to be valid knowledge of non-being. Thus, how can it be said that "the Buddha is the *devatā*" by these declarers of absolutistic momentariness (*ekāntakṣanikatvavādīs*)?

Moreover, when it is maintained that everything is momentary, there could be no prescription of the means to release, for there would be no enjoyment of the fruits of the release, since there is the destruction without a trace of the momentary knowledge of all things. You may say: let there not be the maintaining that release consists of the cutting-off of the series of knowledge-moments; even so, who is there to enjoy the fruits of release [i.e., why quibble about release, since there is no on-going self]? In that case, because there would be the cutting-off of the knowledge-series in every creature, simply naturally at the time of death, there would be release for each; and there would be no fruitfulness in performing particular actions. If you say: since that very knowledge-series enters another body somewhere else, there is not the problem of release at the time of death, that is wrong. This is because of the illogic of this [notion of] energy into another body, as follows: a lamp-flame that has no lamp-pot as its locus cannot enter another lamp-pot; just so, a thought-series without a supporting body cannot enter another body. If you say that it enters by the force of karma, that is wrong, because the act done by a knowledge-moment in a previous body [according to your doctrine] consumes its own karma and is destroyed. So then, by what karma does the knowledge-moment that is about to arise elsewhere gain another body? If you say: by the karma done by the preceding knowledge-moment, that is wrong; for then everything would totter, since one would do the act and another enjoy the fruit.

Some [Buddhists] hold that release is the arising of knowledge that is purified of all confusion and free of all forms of various external objects, when all impressions (*vāsanās*) have been cut off. But that, too, is improper; because, while an impure knowledge-moment has the power to create its like, it has no power to create a knowledge-moment that is pure and unlike it. Thus there would be an accidental cutting-off. Therefore, all this is not momentary. Rather, the self is eternal, and has substantiality in that it is always the receptacle of qualities such as knowledge, etc. As said:

> As a man puts off worn garments and puts on new ones,
> So the self puts off worn bodies and enters other new ones.
>
> —*Bhagavadgītā* 2.22

Also, the *jīva*, having destroyed all karma, having taken on endless knowledge, attains its true nature: release. As said:

> The *jīva* is bliss, bliss is the *jīva*;
> the *jīva* is not separable from bliss.

The *jīva* may be bound by karma,
but it is other than karma, and always bliss.

Now, for the Mīmāṃsakas there is no ominiscient one at all, nor any *āgama* declared by such a one. The only authority is the Vedas, which are eternal in that they are not of human origin. In this system, *dharma* is characterized as that which, in the form of instigating words, impels one to ritual action, such as sacrifices, etc. There are six *pramāṇas*: *pratyakṣa, anumāna, āgama, upamāna, arthāpatti,* and *abhāva*. For those of them who are *brahmādvaitavādīs*, release consists in the self's dissolution into the *ātman.*

Now, they are to be examined in this way. This omniscient one that you reject—is his nature knowledge or ignorance? If he possesses knowledge, how do you refute the existence of reliability in his teachings? If you say that he is of an ignorant nature, that is wrong, because it is not possible to refute non-knowledge, even of pots, etc. Moreover, when you say that there is no omniscient one, do you mean that there is none in this time and place, or in all times and all places? In the first case, we also accept that alternative. In the second case, anyone who actually knows that there is no omniscient one in all times and places is himself ominiscient. Therefore, how is it that there is no omniscient one? Since the omniscient one is thus shown to exist, the *āgamas* declared by him are also established as authoritative, because of the reliability of [his] teachings.

Also, it is wrong to say that the Vedas are not of human origin, since the *śāstras* consist of words, and words cannot in any way be gotten without the operation of the human palate, lips, etc. Next, because of the absence of non-human origin, the Vedas are not eternal. Moreover, if the Vedas were eternal, would they then be naturally perceptible (*upalabhyasvabhāva* [i.e., in and of themselves perceptible]) or not naturally perceptible? Here there is a flaw in both alternatives. When they are eternal, there is the problem of their constant perception or non-perception. On the other hand, if innate perceptibility is rejected, non-eternality ensues. Thus the Vedas are neither non-human nor eternal, and thus they are not a valid source of knowledge. [Also,] there is the authority of scripture [on this point]: "The Vedas are not the *vedas*; the Sacrifices are not the sacrifices." In the *Gītā* it is also said:

Fools propound that
which is flowery words,
O son of Pṛthā; they rejoice in Vedic teaching,
saying that there is none other.

Those whose nature is desire, whose goal is heaven,
are turned toward that which gives rebirth as karma's fruit,

Toward that which consists of many specific rituals,
toward the fruits of pleasure and lordship.

Robbed of wit by the Veda's teachings,
clinging to pleasure and lordship,
Their intelligence has the nature of effort;
it is not exercised in contemplation.

The sphere of the Vedas is the three *guṇas*.
Be free of the three *guṇa*s, O Arjuna,
Free of opposites, eternally abiding in *sattvam*,
Free of fret over wealth, self-possessed.

—*Bhagavadgītā* 2.42-45

Moreover, how do the ambrosia-eating gods come to eat the flesh of cows, etc., when they are being sacrificed too with the cow-sacrifice, etc.? Therefore, because that flesh is not given to them, the ritual activities of the sacrifice, etc., are not the causes of heaven's bliss.

The post cut, the victim bound, the bloody flesh slashed—
If this is the way to heaven, what is the way to hell?

Thus the words of Bhaṭṭārakaśrīśuka. Therefore, the sacrifice of the self—through non-injury, restraint, and asceticism—is the only way to heaven, etc. It has also been said:

The senses made the victims, *tapas* the altar,
Let *ahiṃsā* be the given oblation; this is the eternal sacrifice.

In the Sāṃkhya opinion, the self (*puruṣa*) is the agency-less, quality-less enjoyer. *Prakṛti* is the state of balance among the *guṇa*-triad. It can also be called by the designations *pradhāna* and *avyakta*. From *prakṛti* arises *mahat*, which means *buddhi*; from *mahat* arises the *ahaṃkāra*. From the *ahaṃkāra* comes a two-fold creation (*sṛṣṭi*), eleven-fold and ten-fold. Thereunder, this is the eleven-fold one: the five sense-organs, the five action-organs, and the *manas*. This is the ten-fold group: sound, color, smell, taste, and touch; and out of them, ether, fire, earth, water, and air—the five elements. These are the twenty-five principles; and from knowledge of these arises release. As has been said:

One who knows the twenty-five principles,
and takes pleasure in whatever his state,
With shaven head or tufted tonsure,
he attains release, no doubt.

Also:

Release is the separation of *puruṣa* and *prakṛti*;
The three *pramāṇa*s are *pratyakṣa, anumāna*, and *śabda*.

Now, there is the following examination [of this doctrine]. If *prakṛti* is insentient, how does *buddhi*, whose nature is intelligence, arise from it? If you say that *prakṛti* produces *buddhi* when led to do so by *puruṣa*, then is the sentient *buddhi* a quality of *puruṣa* or a quality of *prakṛti*? If it is a quality of *puruṣa*, how is it that it arises out of *prakṛti*? If it is a quality of *prakṛti*, how can it be that out of *prakṛti*, whose nature is insentient, there comes this *buddhi*-quality, whose nature is knowledge? There is a contradiction here, since you cannot say that when light is being produced from the sun, there arises the quality of darkness. Furthermore, if *puruṣa* is not an agent, when one says, "I will perform *dharma*" or "I will perform *adharma*," who brings about the actual attempt? If you say that it is *prakṛti*, that is wrong, because it is insentient. If you say that it is *puruṣa*, that is wrong, because you admit the doctrine of its non-agency. Therefore, the [correct] principle is that *saṃsāra* is beginningless, as is the karma-bound *jīva*; for there is the authority of the teaching that "There never was a time when this universe was not as it is now." Moreover, there cannot be release for anyone at all through knowledge of principles alone, without action; for without the fruition of action it is improper to posit satisfaction through the knowledge of principles. As has been said:

Action is the giver of fruits,
not by any means knowledge alone;
For, though one know of the enjoyment of women and food,
from the knowledge alone comes not pleasure.

In the Naiyāyika opinion, Śiva, all-pervading, all-knowing, eternal, agent of creation and destruction, is the *devatā*. There are four *pramāṇa*s: *pratyakṣa, anumāna, upamāna*, and *āgama*. The sixteen principles are: *pramāṇa, prameya*, doubt, purpose, illustrative instances, accepted conslusions, parts of the syllogism, argumentation, ascertainment, debate, wrangling, cavil, fallacies of the middle term, quibble, refutations, and points of defeat. The attainment of release comes from thorough knowledge of these. The self's release is the cessation of pain, [which condition is] unlimitedly qualified by bliss and eternal knowledge. Now, they [i.e., these teachings] are to be examined in the following way. Now, Śiva is eternally existent; does he bring about creation and destruction through a single innate capacity, or a dual one? Therein, it cannot be said, first, that this comes about through only a single nature, because the natures of creation and destruction stand in extreme contradiction, like light and dark. If you say that [one of them is brought about] through another nature, then he [Śiva] is not eternal, because this [possibility] is contradicted by the characterization of him as eternal, i.e., as being of an unchanging, unborn, established single nature. Therefore, saying that only the Blessed One is eternal, and creates and destroys as he will, is wrong, because it is impossible for a desire [to create or destroy] to arise in one who is free of the six-fold impulse-mass whose nature is desire, anger, greed, trickery, pride, and pleasure. Moreover, does this omniscient one create enemies for himself? A wise one does not exert himself when the result is the cutting-off of the path of purity. Now, if you say that those favoring him were created first, and thereafter the enemies, in that case he is not onmiscient, because of his ignorance of the [future] existence of his as yet unborn foes. Also, if the universe has the Lord as its maker, the one must still wonder whether the Lord has a maker. Now, are you not talking out of both sides of your mouth when you say that beginningless destruction is the established self-nature of the Blessed One, and that the nature of this universe is such that it has none other as its maker? Moreover, it is not the case that the one form of the eternal Śiva has three divisions—Brahma, Viṣṇu, and Maheśvara—because it is improper to think that a triple division into the separate qualities of majesty, etc. could occur in something unitive and eternal. Also, if this one is omniscient and all-pervading, then wherever the *jīva* is, there is Śiva, for there is the teaching that "All the universe, indeed, consists in Viṣṇu"; would it not also be the case that, as all creatures are pervaded by him, so they would all also possess omniscience? Also, if there is this state of consisting completely in Śiva or consisting completely in Viṣṇu, then men would be confused about the status of worshipper and object of worship, free and bound, etc., in this universe. Therefore, these sayings:

> The soul of things is only one, occuring in each body;
> That which is one appears multiple, like the moon in the pool.

and:

> The universe is like a clod of dirt . . .

and others like them are to be understood as teaching that an untainted intellect, such as Śiva's, is in each creature. Nor does Śiva enter into various creatures like droplets of quicksilver, for, because of the teaching that "weapons do not cut him" (*Bhagavadgītā* 2.23), it is improper to posit that a *jīva* can be fragmented. Nor is it to be said that he enters into various activities in that his activities are multiple by nature, from having inborn divisions; for then those divisions would have to be distinct from one another or not distinct from one another. If they are distinct, then there is the flaw of fragmentation. If they are not distinct, then when one of them is joyful or sorrowful, all would have to be joyful or sorrowful. Therefore, Śiva is undivided, not master of creation and destruction, all-knowing, and standing in the highest station. As has been said:

> Whose nature is singularity, devoid of all qualities,
> Beyond the six-fold impulse, that form declare the wise;
> Bereft of *saṃsāra's* bondage, unsullied by stain or sorrow.
> —*Nyāyamañjarī*, Navamāhnika

and such like. Elsewhere it is also said:

> Not the heavenly Ganges, nor the hooded serpents,
> nor even the garland of skulls;
> Not the sickle-moon, nor Pārvatī,
> not matted locks or ashes;
> Where there is nothing other at all,
> that form of the Lord,
> Honored by the ancient sages,
> let us adore.

Śiva is also the *devatā* of the Vaiśeṣikas. There are six categories [according to them]: substance, quality, action, universal, particularity, and inherence. *Pratyakṣa* and *anumāna* are the two *pramāṣa*s. Release is said to exist when there is endless separation from the nine *viśeṣaguṇa*s: knowledge, pleasure, pain, desire, aversion, volition, *dharma, adharma*, and *saṃskāra*. These [teachings] are to be tested in the following way. Now, the *āgama*s are either sources of valid knowledge or they are not. If they are not, how is it, then, that authoritativeness is granted to the ordering of things into the six categories, etc., on the strength of *āgama*? If the *āgama*s are the sources of valid knowledge, why are there only two *pramāṇa*s? Therefore, *āgama, arthāpatti*, etc., are also to be considered *pramāṇa*s; otherwise, all commonsense understanding would be contradicted. Moreover, release being the cutting-off of the *viśeṣaguṇa*s, there is in that case no difference between the *jīva* and that which is *ajīva*, space, etc., because of the absence of omniscience and pleasure in the *jīva*. Thus in your doctrine, the knowledge that distinguishes *jīva* and *ajīva*—which is there when release has been obtained through knowledge of principles, etc. [not through knowledge alone]—is cut off at the roots. There is also this: just as the light of the sun, when it is hidden by a cloud that is gradually going away, becomes brighter and brighter until, when the cloud is completely gone, there is light everywhere, just so the knowledge that is in the *jīva*, covered with karma, becomes clearer and clearer as karma is gradually destroyed, until at the moment of release, when all karma is destroyed, it arises as complete, total knowledge. Nor is there any separation from knowledge. Moreover, the *yogī*s see the true nature of the highest self; while [you say that] it is the cessation of all known objects, what is seen [by the *yogī*s] is ever greater and greater supremely blissful joy. Therefore, if at the moment of release there is this cessation [that you declare], how do you deal with this supremely blissful joy [that the *yogī*s see] occurring? As has been said in the *Nyāyasāra*:

> Wherefore, release should be known indeed
> as unending joy,
> Beyond the senses, to be grasped by the *buddhi*,
> hard for the unripe self to attain.

In the blessed Jaina system (*darśana*), the *devatā* is the blessed highly pre-eminent, omniscient Jina, who is free of all desire and aversion. *Jīva, ajīva*, etc., are the nine principles. The two *pramāṇa*s are defined as *pratyakṣa* and *parokṣa*. The sphere of *pramāṇa* is every multi-faceted object, embraced in the *syādvāda*. The path to release consists of right faith (*samyagdarśana*), knowledge, and conduct. This [doctrine] is to be tested in the following way. Now, does the triple path to release—right faith, knowledge, and conduct—consist of three separate elements, the three combined, or both separate and combined? Thereunder, they are not separate, because many have possessed, or possess now, or will possess—in detail or in brief—firm conviction (*śraddhāna*), i.e., faith, and awareness (*avabodha*), i.e., knowledge, regarding the nine principles, *jīva*, etc., as they really are; but without conduct they did not, do not, and will not attain release. And conduct, which is defined according to the *āgama* as renunciation of all that is objectionable, is not present in those who behave improperly; thus they have not, do not, and will not attain [release]. Therefore, the path to release does not consist of separate elements. Nor are they combined, because of the attainment of release by the Cakravartin Bhārata and others who only practiced [proper behaviour] in kingship. Nor are they both separate and combined [in different cases], because the Blessed One's mother, and Marudeva [the patriarch] and others attained release, though it is impossible for knowledge, etc., to arise alone or jointly in the absence of a Tīrthakāra. Therefore, the only true form of the three jewels, right knowledge, etc., is the self that has reached full development in all the conditions of purity and brightness. And that alone is release. It is said:

> The self consists only in faith,
> knowledge, conduct—indeed, that
> Which in a *yati* is made up of these
> is the controller of the body.

This self alone is there, free of the senses,
    when *saṃsāra* is destroyed;
It alone, the conqueror of the senses,
    do the wise call release.

Therefore, leaving aside attachment to particular names and other inessentials, all the *tattva*-knowers grant authoritative status to the principles of deity, teacher, and *dharma* solely on the basis of extolling [the principles'] good qualities. The result is as follows: the deity is the venerable all-knowing *arhat*, the Blessed One who has conquered passion, whose nature is that of the highest self. The teacher is the one possessed of self-restraint, who has attained worthiness through knowledge and *tapas*. *Dharma* is that which arises as the result of the declaration of the all-knowing one. Rightness (*samyaktva*) is knowledge and faith in these three alone. For it is said in the *Viṣṇu Purāṇa*:

Through study and restraint
    he is seen to be the highest self;
The means to attainment therein—
    that is declared to be this *brahman*.
—*Viṣṇu Purāṇa* VI.6.1

Therein, concerning the deity it is said:

That which is unmanifest, undecaying,
    inconceivable, unborn, immutable,
And whose nature cannot be portrayed,
    of whose hands, feet, etc., it is improper [to speak],

The true nature of that highest self
    is designated by the term "*bhagavat*";
The word "*bhagavat*" is the denomination
    of that primeval, undying self.

Highest of the high, in whom no flaws abide,
    Lord over finite and infinite,
Lord of all, omnipresent, omniscient, omnipotent,
    known as the Highest Lord;

That knowledge by which he is conceived,
    contemplated, and known,
Knowledge undefiled, complete, supreme, pure, one—
    that is knowledge; all else is ignorance.
—*Viṣṇu Purāṇa* VI.5.66, 68ff.

It has also been said by Viśvakarman:

Not obtained by the senses,
    eternally pure in total knowledge,
Gone to the highest station, calm amidst the worldly flow,
    dwelling, indeed, at the limits of the world;

Whose form there is composed of light,
    who exists here in human form,
Who has subdued passion and aversion,
    He is that Highest Lord.

It is also said by the Bauddhas:

By whom was shattered Māra's strength,
    crushed the cage of being,
Attained the state of *nirvāṇa*,
    to that Buddha I bow down.

It is also said in the *Yogaśāstra* [of Hemacandra]

Omniscient, conqueror of the flaws of passion, etc.,
    worshipped in the three worlds,
Declarer of things as they are,
    such is the divine *arhat*, Lord of all.

Also, in the *Yogasāra*:

Silent, free of worldly ties, tranquil,
    all-knowing, virtuous, strong,
He alone is to be known as the Blessed One,
    divine, untainted.

Whose nature is like the sky, protector of all,
    beyond activity, time, and quality;
Free of *saṃsāra* and origination,
    glowing with every lustre;

Filled with fullest knowledge,
    abode of fullest bliss,
In all the systems, the divine Lord
    is perceived by total meditation.

Thus this is the principle [as concerns the *devatā*]:

In whom there is conquest of passion, etc.,
which are the seed and sprout of existence,
Brahmā or Viṣṇu or Hari or Jina,
to him be obeisance.
—Hemacandra, *Mahādevastotra* 44

The teacher is the man of equanimity who is the seat of knowledge and *tapas*. For it is said:

Not through total knowledge,
or even *tapas*, comes worthiness;
But where there is proper conduct,
there, indeed, a worthy one is said to be.
—*Yajñavalkyasmṛti* 1.200

Also:

Those who are patiently forebearing,
whose deeds are full of knowledge,
Who have conquered the senses
and ceased from harming creatures,
Whose possessions are restricted
to what the hand can hold,
They are *brāhmaṇa*s,
worthy of leading others.
—*Vyāsasmṛti* 4.58

Also:

The sage who is free of all attachments,
firm as the sky,
Self-contained, alone, wandering, tranquil,
him the gods look upon as a *brāhmaṇa*.

Who is as chary of multitudes as of a snake,
of the esteem of the gods as of a hell-creature,
Of women as of a corpse,
him the gods look upon as a *brāhmaṇa*.

Whose life has *dharma* as its goal,
whose qualities are aimed at knowledge,
Who is satisfied with little for the sake of merit,
him the gods look upon as a *brāhmaṇa*.

[Thus it is said] in the *Śāntiparvan*. Also:

Hearthless [unmarried], houseless,
stopping only one day in each dwelling,
Free of attachments; him having seen,
our fathers called him a sage.

[Thus it says] in the *Mārkaṇḍeya Purāṇa* (87.2), *Rucistotra*. Also:

He who performs *ahiṃsā* and declares the truth,
whose face is turned away from all attachment,
Who lives the *brahmacarya*, reverenced by all,
that monk is a teacher according to the Bauddha doctrine.

Therefore, this is the quintessence [of the teacher-mark]:

Those who observe the greater vows, who are firm,
who live only on alms,
Who are absorbed in tranquility and are teachers of *dharma*,
they are considered to be teachers.
—Hemacandra, *Triśaṣṭiśalākāpuruṣacaritra*, *Śāntināthacaritraparvan* 2.3.896

Also, *dharma* is declared by the omniscient one to be ten-fold, in the form of tranquility, gentleness, rectitude, release, asceticism, equanimity, truth, purity, non-possession, and *brahmacarya*. Also:

Ahiṃsā, truthfulness, non-theft,
purity, sense-control,
Charity, compassion, self-control, tranquility—
these bring about *dharma* for all men.
—*Yajñavalkyasmṛti* 1.122

Also:

Harmlessness to all creatures is held
to be of all duties the highest.

If in the context of sacrifices,
firewood, and sacrificial stakes,
Men foolishly eat meat,
not in this is *dharma* revealed.

Wine, fish, honey, meat, alcohol,
mixed boiled rice and sesamum:

This has been declared by knaves. Their use
is not proper [for those dwelling] in forests.

Those are declared in the world
because of delusion and desire;
*Brāhmaṇa*s realize the presence of Viṣṇu
in every sacrifice.
His worship, it is held, should be made
with the rice and milk of a pure mind.

To sacrifice with fire-wood
is prescribed in the Vedas;
Yet whatever is done by pure,
wise, cleansed men,
And whatever else is noble,
that is worthy of [being offered to] the deity.

Thus it says in the *Mahābhārata, Śāntiparvan* [2.257.6b, 8-11]. Also:

Be not censorious; speak what is true and innocent,
Without deceit, not harsh, not malicious, not slanderous.

Also:

Brahmacarya and *ahiṃsā*: that is said
to be bodily *tapas*;
Control of mind and voice, equanimity: that is said
to be mental *tapas*.

Also:

Mildness, tranquility, peace,
ahiṃsā, truth, rectitude,
Non-maliciousness, humility, modesty,
steadfastness and self-control:
These are *brahma*-conduct; by these
one attains that highest One.

Thus [it says] in the *Śāntiparvan*.

Thus having seen the correct nature of the three principles—deity, teacher, and *dharma*—held in common by all the systems, and having left behind the rest, which is naught but attachment to inessentials, the wise man should know, believe, and practice this triple quintessence of all knowables; thus he will attain great increase in all good and blessed things.

This has been composed by Merutuṅgasūri, of the Añcalagaccha.

23

JINADATTA, *VIVEKAVILĀSA* 238-302

INTRODUCTION

Jinadatta's *Vivekavilāsa* consists of 1323 verses, out of which verses 238-302 present a compendium-like discussion that the text itself calls "the examination of the six *darśanas*." The text of the whole was not available for this study, nor was any detailed survey. The translation is based solely on the text of the compendium-section printed in R. B. Bhandarkar's *Report for 1883-84*. In his report, Bhandarkar (1887:156) proffers the following summary of the whole:

> The author proposes to present his readers with a short quintessence of all the previous Śāstras. The subjects with which it deals range from precepts of the highest morality to the interpretation of dreams and such advice as that about reading the Vātsyāyanasūtra, taking care not to spread a knowledge of it promiscuously. So in one place the author gives short metrical summaries of the tenets of six systems of philosophy, vis., the Jaina, Maimāmsaka, Bauddha, Sāmkhya, Śaiva and Nāstika. . . . Two of these summaries, those of the Jaina and Bauddha doctrines, have been quoted in the Sarvadarśanasaṃgraha, the first under the name of the author and the second under the name of the work.

As to the author and date, the information available has not advanced beyond that also given by Bhandarkar (1887:156):

> Jinadatta was a pupil of Rāsila and Jīvadeva, who were of the Gachchha that flourished in the town of Vāyaḍa. He wrote his Vivekavilāsa for the gratification of Dhanapāla, the adopted son of Devapāla of the Vāyaḍa family who was the trusted

minister of Udayasimha of the Chāhumāna (or Chāhvāna) dynasty, the lord of Jāvālipura.

Based on this information from the colophon, and on the identification of the Udayasimha mentioned there as having lived in the first half of the thirteenth century, Bhandarkar places Jinadatta between 1200 and 1250 C.E.[1]

The translation presented here is based solely on the version of the text printed in R. G. Bhandarkar's *Report for 1883-84*, pp. 458-63. Other printed editions of the text were not available. As noted in the discussion of this text in chapter 8, the fact that these few verses out of a work of 1323 *śloka*s are all that is available makes drawing conclusions about the work somewhat risky. Nonetheless, the existence of this portion of the work, bearing the resemblances that it does to other Jain compendia, has made its inclusion valuable despite the risks involved.

The translation itself has been hard to make, save for the few verses that are duplicated in other texts. The text presented by Bhandarkar indicates numerous variant readings, some of which are incorporated here, but most of which are not helpful. The text is poor, and some points in it are utterly unclear or corrupt. Thus the translation has certain spots in it that are almost conjectural.

TRANSLATION

Now begins the examination of the six *darśana*s:

238. The Jaina, Maimāṃsaka, Bauddha, Sāṃkhya,
 the Śaiva and the Nāstika:
Let the six *darśana*s be known
 according to the distinction of each one's *tarka*.

Now the Jaina:

239. The [five] hindrances that arise from both taking and giving
 things for occasional and repeated use;
Also, sleepiness, fear,
 ignorance and abhorrence;

240. Laughter, concern about comfort and discomfort,
 passion and aversion, incontinence, yearning,

1 [Editor's note.] On this text and its author, see also R. Williams 1963:14-15.

Sorrow, and erroneousness—in whom
are not present these eighteen flaws,[2] he

241. Is the divine Jina, the teacher,
the one who propounds correctly the *tattva* knowledge.
Jñāna, darśana, and *cāritra*
are the road to heaven.

242. [There are] also the *syādvāda*, and the two *pramāṇas*,
pratyakṣa and *anumāna*.
This entire universe is eternal and non-eternal;
there are either nine or seven *tattvas*:

243. *Jīva* and *ajīva*, merit and demerit,
influx, and also stoppage,
Bondage, decay, release;
the comment to these is now stated.

244. *Jīva* is characterized by consciousness;
ajīva is what is other than that.
Merit consists of agglomerates of good karma;
demerit is the opposite.[3]

245. Influx means association with karma;
stoppage is the hindrance of karma.
Bondage arises from being bound with karma;
its [karma's] removal is decay.

246. Destruction of the eight karmas is release.
By some is made the inclusion here
That when there is stoppage, it comes from merit;
and when influx, from demerit.

---

2 Verses 239 and 240 are one of the more problematic portions of the text. The eighteen flaws listed here are not found in the standard discussions of the qualities of a teacher, or in the prescriptions for lay and monastic life, as a group of eighteen. The first *pada* of verse 239, moreover, appears to be corrupt. As given by Bhandarkar, p. 458, it reads: *balabhogopabhogānām*. I translate this as "[of] things for occasional and repeated use." The Jaina tradition includes among the vows for laymen a vow that places limitations on *bhogopabhoga*, or on *paribhoga* and *upabhoga*, the two being understood as items to be used repeatedly (beds, houses, furniture, and the like) and items to be used only once (food and drink, primarily). See Bhargava 1968:130ff.; and Williams 1963:102ff. for full discussions of this. *Balabhoga* (var. *bālābhoga*) is not found as a version of these terms, though there is always the possibility that some part of the Jaina tradition made such a use of the term. That my translation is correct would seem to be the case, particularly as the general vow concering limiting the two sorts of items is subject to five transgressions; and this number added to the individual flaws given in the two verses totals eighteen.

3 This verse is identical with verse 13 in Rājaśekhara, save for the fourth *pada*.

247. The irreversible release declared by the Jina,
 coming when there is the destruction of the eight-fold karma,
 Is the self's abiding at the top of the universe,
 having attained the state of four-fold bliss.

248. Avoiding women, eating alms-food,
 with plucked-out hair,
 The Śvetāmbaras forbear in purity,
 being unattached Jaina saints.
 Keeping the vows of purity, involved in *tapas*,
 followers of the triple *gupti*,
 Having no *siddhānta*, always wandering,
 their senses conquered,[4]

249. Hair plucked-out, peacock-broom in hand,
 using the hand as a bowl, the Digambaras
 Remain standing when in the house of a donor;
 they are the other Jaina seers.

250. A *kevalin* does not eat, nor a woman attain release—
 thus the Digambaras
 Declare this great difference [between the sects];
 they are [actually] the same as the Śvetāmbaras.

Thus the Jaina *darśana*; now the Maimāṃsaka:

251. The Mīmāṃsakas are two-fold:
 karma- and *brahma*-Mīmāṃsakas.
 The Vedāntins hold with *brahman*,
 while Bhaṭṭa and Prabhākara choose karma.[5]

252. *Pratyakṣa*, *anumāna*, and the Vedas,
 along with *upamā*,
 Arthāpatti and *abhāva*:
 these are Bhaṭṭa's six *pramāṇas*.

253. In the Prabhākara doctrine these are five,
 because of the exclusion of *abhāva*.

---

[4] Bhandarkar notes that this verse is written in the margin of one of his manuscript sources. Its observation on the lack of a *siddhānta*, plus the fact that it is apparently not a part of the original text, is of some interest. One might conclude from it that the matter of a Digambara *siddhānta* was not of much import at the time of Jinadatta, but that at some later date a copyist or commentator felt it necessary to insert an observation on the point.

[5] This verse is identical with verse 61 in Rājaśekhara.

But the *advaita*-declaring Vedāntin
accepts either [set of] *pramāṇas*.

254. For the Vedāntin teachers of *advaita*,
all this universe is that *brahman*;
Dissolution into the *ātman*
is held to be release in Vedāntic opinion.

255. Not doing reprehensible deeds, performing the six allowable acts,
avoiding the food of *śūdras*, etc.,
Wearing the sacred thread, a twice-born,
a Bhaṭṭa [follower] may be a householder.

256. But in the Vedānta *darśana*, the twice-born
are called "blessed ones";
These teachers of *brahman* eat in Brāhmaṇa-houses
and do not wear the sacred thread.[6]

257. There are four divisions of "blessed ones":
the Kuṭīcara, Bahūdaka,
Haṃsa and Paramahaṃsa,
each more excellent than the preceding.

Thus the Maimāṃsaka opinion; now the Bauddha:

258. For the Bauddha, Sugata is the deity,
and everything is a momentary flux;
Their *tattva* tetrad, called the noble truths,
is ordered as follows:

259. There is sorrow, and the basis (*āyatana*);
from it is held to come the arising (*samudaya*);
There is also the way (*mārga*); let be heard
the explanation of this, in this way:

260. Sorrow consists in the transient *skandhas*,
and they are declared to be five:
Vijñāna, vedanā, samjñā,
saṃskāra, and *rūpa*.

Now the *āyatanas*:

---

6 Verses 255-256 are not easy to understand or translate. Their thrust is somewhat the same as verses 72ff. in Rājaśekhara.

261. The five senses—auditory, etc.,
the five objects [of the senses], *manas*,
And the *dharma-āyatana*; these
are the twelve *āyatana*s.

Now the arising:

262. That from which, in the heart of men,
arises the mass of passion, etc.,
Known to be of the nature of "me" and "mine,"
that, indeed, is the arising.

Now the way:

263. All the *saṃskāra*s are momentary,
and the firm knowing that this is so—
That is to be known as the way,
and that is laid down as *mokṣa*.[7]

264. There is also the *pramāṇa* pair:
pratyakṣa and *anumāna*.
There are four Buddhist sects (*prasthānika*s),
called the Vaibhāṣika, etc.

265. By the Vaibhāṣika it is verily held
that the [external] object is reached by knowledge;
The Sautrāntika position is that the object
grasped by *pratyakṣa* is not external.

266. The conclusion of the Yogācāra
is that judgement (*buddhi*) is the possessor of forms;
Indeed, the Madhyamas consider
that what is known is solely self-contained.

267. The occurrence of the cutting-off, when there is knowledge
[that all is just] a stream of knowledge-moments
[born of] passion, etc.—
This is proclaimed to be release
in all four Buddhist [sects].

---

[7] Verses 260-263 share a number of *pada*s with verses 5-8 in Haribhadra and verses 139-141 in Rājaśekhara. The text is quite corrupt.

268. The wearing of skins, the water-pot, the tonsure,
tattered garb, a meal in the forenoon;
The Order, and the ochre robe
are employed by the Buddhist mendicants.

Thus the Buddhist opinion; now the Sāṃkhya:

269. By some Sāṃkhyas Śiva is held to be the deity;
by others, Nārāyaṇa.
For both, all the other *tattva*s, etc.,
are held in identical fashion.

270. For the Sāṃkhyas there are the three *guṇa*s:
sattvam, rajas, and *tamas*.
Prakṛti, then, is a state of equilibrium
among these three.

271. From *prakṛti* comes first *mahān*,
then from the latter arises *ahaṃkāra*,
And the five sense-organs,
the eye, etc.; and the five

272. Motor organs; voice, hand, foot,
genitals, and anus;
And *manas*; as well as the five *tanmātra*s:
sound, color, taste,

272a. Touch and smell; and from these comes
the pentad of earth, etc.
This is *prakṛti*. But *puruṣa*
is held to be other than it.[8]

273. In the Sāṃkhya opinion, the universe
is eternal and consists of twenty-five *tattva*s.
There is here a triad of *pramāṇa*s:
pratyakṣa, anumāna, āgama.

274. Whenever there occurs the separation
of *prakṛti* and *puruṣa*,
Then, the Sāṃkhyas say, there is release,
and it is called *khyātiḥ*.

---

8 The verse is so-numbered in Bhandarkar's edition of the text.

275. A Sāṃkhya's tonsure may be tufted,
shaven, or matted; he is clad in red, etc.
For the Sāṃkhya there is no abiding in a dwelling;
to the *tattva*, indeed, is his great attachment.

Thus the Sāṃkhya opinion; now the Śaiva:

276. In the *darśana* of Śiva there are two *tarka*s,
the Nyāya and the Vaiśeṣika;
The Nyāya's *tarka* consists of sixteen *tattva*s.
The Vaiśeṣika has six.

277. Because of their mutual inclusion of each's principles,
a division between them may or may not exist.
Śiva is the deity of both,
the eternal one, agent of creation, etc.

278. There are four *pramāṇa*s
for the Naiyāyikas:
Pratyakṣa and *āgama*, and also
anumāna and *upamāna*.

Now the *tattva*s:

279. *Pramāṇa* and *prameya*,
and doubt and purpose;
Illustrative instances, and also accepted conclusions,
syllogism-elements, argumentation, and ascertainment;

280. Debate, wrangling, cavil,
middle-term fallacies, and quibble,
Refutations and points of defeat:
such are the sixteen *tattva*s.

Now the Vaiśeṣika:

281. First, in the Vaiśeṣika opinion
there is a *pramāṇa*-triad:
Pratyakṣa and *anumāna*,
and the third one is *āgama*.

282. The six *tattva*s are substance, quality,
also action, universals, and particularity,

Along with inherence; their explanation
is now declared.

283. Substance is declared to be nine-fold:
earth, water, fire,
Air, ether, time,
space, self, and mind as well.

284. [The first] four are eternal and non-eternal,
depending on their state as cause or effect;
But mind, space, time, self, and ether—
these five are eternal.

Now the qualities:

285. Touch, color, taste, odor,
number, and dimension,
Severalty, conjunction, disjunction,
and distance, verily;

286. Proximity, knowledge, number,
sorrow, desire, aversion, volition,
Merit, demerit, *saṃskāra*,
weight, and also fluidity;

287. Viscosity, and sound—the qualities
are thus four and twenty.
Now the actions will I declare,
according to each one's designation.

288. Being propelled upward and downward,
contraction, expansion,
And general motions—thus the actions
are declared to be five in their *āgama*.

289. Universals are of two sorts:
greater and lesser as well.
Particularities (*viśeṣa*s) abide in atoms;
they are eternal.

290. Inherence is the cause of apprehending the relationship
that obtains in this world
Between things known to be inseparably joined,
existing as receptacle and that which resides in it.

291. From the absence of the occurrence
of pleasure and pain, in object, sense, and knowledge
Comes the condition of the self
held by the Naiyāyikas to be release.

292. But the Vaiśeṣikas' release
is the cutting-off of knowledge, etc.,
Which are the nine internal *guṇa*s
among the twenty-four Vaiśeṣika-*guṇa*s.

293. [The Śaiva] ascetics—ash-wearers,
loin-clothed, with matted locks,
Wearing the sacred thread—are four-fold,
divided according to practices, *mantra*s, etc.

294. Śaivas, Pāśupatas,
Keepers of the Great Vow,
And fourth, Kālamukhas: these are
the main divisions of ascetics.

Thus the Śaiva; now the *nāstika*:

295. That which exists is made up of five elements,
and *pratyakṣa* is the source of valid knowledge
In the doctrine of the *nāstika*. The self if not
another [element] wherein might reside good and bad.

296. *Pratyakṣa* is uncontroverted knowledge
within the sphere of the senses.
Knowledge inferred from a mark,
like establishing fire from smoke,

297. Is *anumāna*; it is three-fold:
pūrva, śeṣa, sāmānyata; as in
[Inferring that there will be] crops from [seeing] rain,
[inferring that there has been] rain from [seeing] full rivers,
[and inferring] motion from [seeing] the sun set in the West—

298. [So *anumāna*] is known. *Upamā*, or similarity,
comes from commonality in thing known and thing to be shown,
As in that a *gavaya* is like a cow, since both
have the quality of possessing a dewlap, etc.

299. Also, *āgama* is the assertion of a reliable person;
it is said to be present when there is trustworthiness
And experience of the thing in one's assertions about something.
Finally, there is *arthāpatti*:

300. A fat chap does not eat by day;
thus the conclusion is that he eats at night.
Since there is the absence of the capacity
to establish things in the five *pramāṇa*s,

301. Each teacher establishes his own opinion
on the basis of valid knowledge of principles (*tattvapramāṇataḥ*);
But that a principle exists ultimately—
that *pramāṇa* cannot show.

302. Begone, all *śāstra*s,
and all your secrets!
One alone—sensual perception—is correct;
nor is study [using it] fruitless.

BIBLIOGRAPHY

TEXTS AND TRANSLATIONS

Abhidhānacintāmaṇi of Hemacandra.

1847 Sanskrit text ed. and trans. O. Böhtlingk and C. Rieu. St. Petersburg: Kaiserlichen Akademi der Wissenschaften.

Ācāradaśāḥ (Ācāradasāo).

1966 Prakrit text ed. W. Schubring. French trans. C. Caillat. In *Drei Chedasūtras des Jaina-Kanons: Āyāradasāo, Vavahāra, Nisīha.* Hamburg: Cram, De Gruyter & Co. Alt- und Neu-Indische Studien 11.

Ācārāṅga Sūtra (Āyāraṅga Sutta).

1880 Prakrit text, with Sanskrit *Ṭīkā* of Śīlāṅka and Sanskrit *Dīpikā* of Jinasiṃhasūri, Prakrit *Nijjutti* of Bhadrabāhu, and Gujarati *Bālāvabodha* of Pārśvacandrasūri. Calcutta: New Sanskrit Press. Āgamasaṃgraha 1.

1882 Ed. H. Jacobi. London: Oxford University Press for the Pali Text Society. Pali Text Society Text Series 3.

[1884] 1968 Trans. H. Jacobi. In *Jaina Sūtras* 1:1-213. Oxford: Clarendon Press. (Reprint Delhi: Motilal Banarsidass. New York: Dover Publications.) Sacred Books of the East 22.

1981 Ed. and trans. Yuvācārya Mahāprajñā. Ladnun: Jaina Vishva Bharati. Jain Canonical Text Series 1.

Anekāntajayapatākā of Haribhadrasūri.

1940-47 Sanskrit text with Sanskrit *Svopajñā Vyākhyā* of author and Sanskrit *Vivaraṇa* of Municandrasūri, ed. H. R. Kapadia. 2 vols. Baroda: Oriental Institute. Gaekwad's Oriental Series 88, 105.

Aṅguttara Nikāya.

[1885] 1888 Pali text ed. R. Morris. Vol. 1: *Ekanipāta, Dukanipāta, and Tikanipāta.* Vol. 2: *Catukka Nipāta.* London: Oxford University Press for the Pali Text Society.

1899 Ed. E. Hardy. Vol 4: *Sattaka-Nipāta, Aṭṭhaka-Nipāta, and Navaka-Nipāta.* London: Oxford University Press for the Pali Text Society.

1932-33 Trans. F. L. Woodward as *The Book of the Gradual Sayings (Anguttara-Nikāya) or More-Numbered Suttas.* Vol. 1: *Ones, Twos, Threes.* Vol. 2: *The Book of the Fours.* London: Oxford University Press for the Pali Text Society.

1935 Trans. E. M. Hare as *The Book of the Gradual Sayings (Anguttara-Nikāya) or More-Numbered Sayings.* Vol. 4: *The Books of the Sevens, Eights, and Nines.* London: Oxford University Press for the Pali Text Society.

Antakṛddaśāḥ (Antagaḍadasāo).

1907 Trans. L. D. Barnett as *The Antagaḍadasāo* and *Aṇuttarovavāiyadasāo.* London: Royal Asiatic Society. Oriental Translation Fund (n.s.) 17.

1932 Prakrit text, with Prakrit *Antakṛddaśāvṛtti* of Abhayadeva, ed. and trans. M. C. Modi as *The Antagaḍa-dasāo and the Aṇuttarovavāia-dasāo.* Ahmedabad: Gurjar Granth Ratna Karyalay. Prakrit Granthamala 1.

[n.d.] Prakrit text ed. and trans. N. V. Vaidya as *Antagaḍadasāo, Aṇuttarovavāiyadasāo,* and *Bambhadatta.* Poona: the editor.

Anuttaraupapātikadaśāḥ (Aṇuttarovavāiyadasāo).

1907 See *Antakṛddaśāh.*

1932 See *Antakṛddaśāh.*

[n.d.] See *Antakṛddaśāh.*

Anuyogadvāra Sūtra (Aṇuogaddārāiṃ).

1970 Trans. T. Hanaki. Vaishali: Research Institute of Prakrit, Jainology, and Ahimsa. Prakrit Jain Institute Research Publications Series 5.

Anyayogavyavacchedikā of Hemacandra.

1933 Sanskrit text with Sanskrit *Syādvādamañjarī* of Malliṣeṇa, ed. A. B. Dhruva. Bombay: The Department of Public Education.

1960 With *Syādvādamañjarī* of Malliṣeṇa, trans. F. W. Thomas as *The Flower-Spray of the Quodammodo Doctrine.* Berlin: Akademie-Verlag.

Aupapātika Sūtra (Uvavāi Sutta).
1882 Prakrit text ed. E. Leumann. Leipzig: F. A. Brockhaus. Abhandlungen für die Kunde des Morgenlandes 8:2.

Āvaśyaka Sūtra (Āvassaya Sutta).
[1916-17] 1982. Prakrit text with Prakrit *Nijjutti* attributed to Bhadrabāhu and Sanskrit *Ṭīkā* of Haribhadrasūri, ed. Ācārya Sāgarānandasūri. Bombay: Āgamodaya Samiti. Siddhānta Saṃgraha 1. (Reprint in 2 vols. Bombay: Śrī Bherulāl Kanaiyālāl Koṭhārī Dhārmik Trust.)

Bhagavatī Sūtra (Bhagavaī Sutta) or *Vyākhyāprajñapti (Viyāhapannatti).*
1882 Prakrit text with Sanskrit *Ṭīkā* of Abhayadeva, Sanskrit *Anuvāda* of Rāmacandragaṇi, and Gujarati *Bhāṣāṭīkā* of Megharāja, ed. Ṛṣi Nānakacanda. Banaras: Jaina Prasāraka Press. Āgamasaṃgraha 5.
1865-66 See Weber.
1970 See Deleu.
1973-85 Trans. of *śataka*s 1-11 by K. C. Lalwani. 4 vols. Calcutta: Jain Bhawan.

Bhāvapāhuḍa of Kundakunda.
1921 Prakrit text ed. P. Pannālāla Sonī. In *Ṣaṭprābhṛtādisaṃgraha*. Bombay: Jaina Grantha Ratnākara Karyālaya. Māṇikacandra Jaina Granthamālā 17.

Bṛhatkalpa Sūtra.
1905 Prakrit text ed. and German trans. by W. Schubring as *Das Kalpa-sūtra, die alte Sammlung jinistischer Monchsvorschriften*. Leipzig: G. Kreysing.
1910 Trans. of 1905 by M. S. Burgess in *Indian Antiquary* 39, 257-67.

Candravedhyaka (Candāvijjhaya).
1971 Prakrit text ed. and French trans. C. Caillat. Paris: Institut de Civilisation Indienne.

Catuḥśaraṇa (Caüsaraṇa).
1974 Prakrit text ed. and trans. K. R. Norman. In *Brahmavidya* 38, 4-59.

Darśanasāra of Devasena.
1934 Prakrit text ed. A. N. Upadhye. In *Annals of the Bhandarkar Oriental Institute* 15:198-206.

Daśavaikālika Sūtra (Dasaveyāliya Sutta).
1932 Prakrit text ed. E. Leumann and trans. W. Schubring. Ahmedabad: Anandji Kalianji.
1973 Trans. K. C. Lalwani. Delhi: Motilal Banarsidass.

Dharmabindu of Haribhadra.

1968 Trans. K. K. Dixit. Ahmedabad: L. D. Bharatiya Samskrti Vidyamandir. L. D. Series 19.

Dīgha Nikāya.

1889 Pali text ed. T. W. Rhys Davids and J. E. Carpenter. Vol. 1. London: Oxford University Press for the Pali Text Society.

1889 Trans. T. W. Rhys Davids. Vol 1. London: Oxford University Press. Sacred Books of the Buddhists 2.

1911 Trans. J. E. Carpenter. Vol. 3. London: Oxford University Press for the Pali Text Society.

[1921] 1957 Trans. T. W. Rhys Davids and C. A. F. Rhys Davids. Vol. 3. London: Oxford University Press. (Reprint London: Luzac & Co. for the Pali Text Society.) Sacred Books of the Buddhists 4.

Dvādaśāranayacakra of Mallavādin.

1966-76 Sanskrit text ed. Muni Jambūvijaya. 2 vols. Bhavnagar: Jaina Ātmānanda Sabhā. Ātmānanda Jaina Grantha Ratnamālā 92, 94.

Gommaṭasāra of Nemicandra Siddhāntacakravartī.

[1927-37] 1974. Prakrit text ed. and trans. S. Prasada and A. Prasada. 3 vols. Lucknow: Central Jaina Publishing House. (Reprint New York: AMS Press.) Sacred Books of the Jainas 5, 6, 10.

Jñātṛdharmakathāḥ (Nāyādhammakahāo).

[n.d.] Prakrit text ed. and trans. of chs. 4-9, 16 by N. V. Vaidya. 2 vols. Poona: editor.

1978 See Schubring.

Kalpa Sūtra (Kappa Sutta) of Bhadrabāhu.

[1847] 1972 Trans. J. Stevenson. In *The Kalpa-Sūtra and Nava Tatva* [sic]. London. (Reprint Varanasi: Bharat-Bharati.)

[1879] 1879 Prakrit text ed. H. Jacobi. Leipzig: F. A. Brockhaus. Abhandlungen für die Kunde des Morgenlandes 7:1.

[1884] 1968 Trans. H. Jacobi. In *Jaina Sūtras* 1:217-311. Oxford: Clarendon Press. (Reprint Delhi: Motilal Banarsidass. New York: Dover Publications.) Sacred Books of the East 22.

1979 Trans. K. C. Lalwani. Delhi: Motilal Banarsidass.

Mahāniśītha Sūtra (Mahānisīha Sutta).

1963 Prakrit text ed., English trans. of chs. 1-3 by J. Deleu, and German trans. of chs. 4-5 by W. Schubring, in *Studien zum Mahānisīha. Kapitel* 1-5. Hamburg: Cram, de Gruyter & Co. Alt- und Neu-Indische Studien 10.

Majjhima Nikāya.

1899 Pali text ed. R. Chalmers. Vol. 3. London: Oxford University Press for the Pali Text Society.

1959 Trans. I. B. Horner as *The Collection of the Middle Length Sayings.* Vol 3: *The Final Fifty Discourses* (*Uparipaṇṇāsa*). London: Luzac & Co. for the Pali Text Society.

Nandī Sūtra (Nandi Sutta) of Devavācaka.

1880 Prakrit text with Sanskrit *Ṭīkā* of Malayagiri and anonymous Gujarati *Bālāvabodha.* Calcutta: New Sanskrit Press. Āgamasaṃgraha 45.

1966 With Sanskrit *Vṛtti* of Haribhadrācārya, Sanskrit *Durgapadavyākhyā* on *Vṛtti* of Śrīcandrācārya, and anonymous Sankrit *Viṣamapadaparyāya* on *Vṛtti*, ed. Muni Puṇyavijaya. Varanasi and Ahmedabad: Prakrit Text Society. Prakrit Text Society Series 10.

Nirayāvalī Sūtra (Nirayāvaliyāo).

1934 Prakrit text ed. with trans. V. J. Chokshi and A. S. Gopani. Ahmedabad: Gurjar Grantha Ratna Karyalaya. Prakrit Granthamala 4.

Pramāṇamīmāṃsā of Hemacandra.

1970 Trans. S. Mookerjee and N. Tatia. Bks. 1-2. Varanasi: Tara Publications.

Rājapraśnīya Sūtra (Rāyapaseṇī or Rāyapaseṇaïjja Sutta).

1880 Prakrit text with Sanskrit *Ṭīkā* of Malayagiri and Gujarati *Bālābodha* of Megharāja. Calcutta: New Sanskrit Press. Āgamasaṃgraha 13.

Ratnakaraṇḍa Śrāvakācāra of Samantabhadra.

1931 Trans. C. R. Jain as *The Householder's Dharma.* 2d ed. Bijnor: The Jaina Publishing House.

Ṣaḍdarśananirṇaya of Merutuṅga.

1973 Sanskrit text ed. N. J. Shah. In *Collection of Jaina Philosophical Tracts*, 1-19. Ahmedabad: L. D. Institute of Indology. L. D. Series 41.

Ṣaḍdarśanasamuccaya of Haribhadrasūri.

1887 *ṢDS (Pullè).* Sanskrit text ed. F. L. Pullè as "Shaṭdarçanasamuccayasûtraṃ." In *Giornale della Società Asiatica Italiana (Firenze)* 1:47-73.

1905 *ṢDS (Suali).* With Sanskrit *Tarkarahasyadīpikā* of Guṇaratna, ed. L. Suali. Calcutta: Asiatic Society of Bengal. Bibliotheca Indica 167.

1908 Luigi Suali. "Matériaux pour servir a l'histoire du matérialisme indien." [Translation of Lokāyata section, with Guṇaratna's commentary.] In *Le Muséon* (n.s.) 9:277-98.

1957 Trans. K. Satchidananda Murty as *Shad-Darsana Samuccaya* (*A Compendium of Six Philosophies*). Tenali: Tagore Publishing House.

1957 *ṢDS (Śāstrī).* With Sanskrit *Laghuvṛtti* of Maṇibhadra, ed. G. D. Śāstrī. Banaras: The Chowkhamba Sanskrit Series Office. Chowkhamba Sanskrit Series 95.

1969 *ṢDS (Jain).* With Sanskrit *Tarkarahasyadīpikā* of Guṇaratna, Sanskrit *Laghuvṛtti* of Somatilaka, and anonymous Sanskrit *Avacūrṇi*, ed. M. Jain. Calcutta: Bhāratīya Jñānapīṭha. Jñānapīṭha Mūrtidevī Jaina Granthamālā Sanskrit Grantha 36.

Ṣaḍdarśanasamuccaya of Maladhāri Rājaśekharasūri.

[n.d.] Sanskrit text ed. Pt. Haragovindadāsa and Pt. Becaradāsa. Varanasi: Śreṣṭhibhūrābhāītanujaharṣacandra Nijadharmābhyudayayantrālaya. Yaśovijaya Jaina Granthamālā 17.

Saddharmapuṇḍarīka.

1976 Trans. from Chinese of Kumārajīva by L. Hurvitz as *Scripture of the Lotus Blossom of the Fine Dharma.* New York: Columbia University Press.

Sammaïsuttam of Siddhasena Divākara.

1971 Prakrit text ed. A. N. Upadhye. In *Siddhasena's Nyāyāvatāra and Other Works*, 171-87. Bombay: Jain Sahitya Vikasa Mandala.

Sarvadarśanasaṃgraha of Sāyaṇa Mādhava.

1904 Trans. E. B. Cowell and A. E. Gough. London: Kegan Paul, Trench, Trübner & Co.

Sarvasiddhāntapraveśaka

1964 Sanskrit text ed. Muni Jambūvijaya. Bombay: Jain Sāhitya Vikāsa Maṇḍala.

Śatapatha Brāhmaṇa.

[1882-1900] 1968. Trans. J. Eggeling. 5 vols. Oxford: Clarendon Press. (Reprint Delhi: Motilal Banarsidass.) Sacred Books of the East 12, 26, 41, 43, 54.

Sthānāṅga Sūtra (Ṭhāṇaṅga Sutta).

1880 Prakrit text with Sanskrit *Ṭīkā* of Abhayadeva and Gujarati *Bhāṣāṭīkā* of Megharāja, ed. Ṛṣi Nānakacanda. Banaras: Jaina Prasāraka Press. Āgamasaṃgraha 3.

Sūtrakṛtāṅga Sūtra (Sūyagaḍāṅga Sutta).

1880. Prakrit text, with Sanskrit *Ṭīkā* of Śīlāṅka, containing the Prakrit *Nijjutti* attributed to Bhadrabāhu, Sanskrit *Dīpikā* of Harṣakula, and Gujarati *Bālāvaboda* of Pārśvacandrasūri. Bombay: Nirṇayasāgara Press. Āgamasaṃgraha 2.

[1895] 1968 Trans. H. Jacobi. In *Jaina Sūtras*, 2:235-435. Oxford: Clarendon Press. (Reprint Delhi: Motilal Banarsidass. New York: Dover Publications.) Sacred Books of the East 45.

1950 With Sanskrit *Ṭīkā* of Śīlāṅka, containing the *Nijjutti* attributed to Bhadrabāhu, ed. Pannyāsa Candrasāgaragaṇi. Bhavnagar: Śrīgoḍīpārśvanātha Jaina Derāsara. Śrīgoḍīpārśvajainagranthamālā 4.

1978 Prakrit text, with Sanskrit *Ṭīkā* of Śīlāṅka, containing the Prakrit *Niryukti* of Bhadrabāhu, ed. Ācārya Sāgarānandasūri, re-ed. Muni Jambūvijaya. Delhi: Motilal Banarsidass. Lala Sunderlal Jain Agamagranthamala 2.

Syādvādamañjarī of Malliṣeṇa.

See *Anyayogavyavacchedikā.*

Tattvārtha (Tattvārthādhigama) Sūtra of Umāsvāti.

1903-05 Sanskrit text with Sanskrit *Svabhāṣya* of Umāsvātī, ed. K. P. Mody. Calcutta: Asiatic Society of Bengal. Bibliotheca Indica 159.

[1906] 1906 Ed. with German trans. H. Jacobi as *Eine Jaina-Dogmatik: Umāsvāti's Tattvārthādhigama Sūtra.* Leipzig: F. A. Brockhaus. (Reprint from *Zeitschrift der Deutschen Morgenlandischen Gesellschaft* 60:287-325, 512-51.)

1915 With Sanskrit *Tattvārtharājavarttika* of Akalaṅkadeva, ed. Pt. G. L. Jaina. Banaras: Candraprabha Press.

[1920] 1974 Ed. and trans. J. L. Jaini. Arrah: Central Jaina Publishing House. (Reprint New York: AMS Press.) Sacred Books of the Jainas 2.

1926-30 With Sanskrit *Svabhāṣya* elucidated by Siddhasenagaṇi, ed. H. R. Kapadia. 2 vols. Bombay: Karnatak Printing Press. Sheth Lalbhai Jain Pustakoddhar Fund series 67, 76.

1944 With Sanskrit *Sukhabodha* of Bhāskaranandin, ed. Pt. A. Shantiraja Sastri. Mysore: Government Branch Press. University of Mysore Library Publications, Sanskrit Series 84.

1949 With Sanskrit *Tattvārthavṛtti* of Śrutasāgarasūri, ed. with Hindi trans. M. K. Jain and assisted by U. Jain. Banaras: Bhāratīya Jñānapītha. Jñānapīṭha Mūrtidevī Jaina Granthamālā Sanskrit Grantha 4.

1953-57 With Sanskrit *Tattvārtharājavarttika* of Akalaṅkadeva, ed. M. K. Jain. 2 vols. Banaras: Bhāratīya Jñānapīṭha. Jñānapīṭha Mūrtidevī Jain Granthamālā Sanskrit Granthas 10, 20.

1960 With Sanskrit *Sarvārthāsiddhi* of Pūjyapāda, trans. S. A. Jain as *Reality: English Translation of Shri Pujyapada's Sarvarthasiddhi.* Calcutta: Vira Sasana Sangha.

1971 With Sanskrit *Sarvārthasiddhi* of Pūjyapāda, ed. Pt. P. S. Shastry. Delhi: Bhāratīya Jñānapīṭha. Jñānapīṭha Mūrtidevī Granthamālā Sanskrit Grantha 13.

Triṣaṣṭiśalākāpuruṣacaritra of Hemacandra.

1931-62 Trans. H. M. Johnson as *The Lives of the Sixty-Three Illustrious Persons.* 6 vols. Baroda: The Oriental Institute. Gaekwad's Oriental Series 51, 77, 108, 125, 139, 140.

Upamitibhavaprapañcākathā of Siddharṣi.

1899-1914 Sanskrit text ed. P. Peterson and H. Jacobi. Calcutta: Asiatic Society of Bengal. Bibliotheca Indica 144.

Upāsakadaśāḥ (Uvāsagadasāo).

1885-1890 Prakrit text ed. and trans. A. F. R. Hoernle. 2 vols. Calcutta: Asiatic Society. Bibliotheca Indica 105.

Uttarādhyayana Sūtra (Uttarajjhāyā Sutta).

[1895] 1968 Trans. H. Jacobi. In *Jaina Sūtras*, 2:1-232. Oxford: Clarendon Press. (Reprint Delhi: Motilal Banarsidass. New York: Dover Publications.) Sacred Books of the East 45.

[1922] 1980 Prakrit text ed. J. Charpentier. 2 vols. Uppsala: Appelbergs Boktryckeri. Archives d'Études Orientales 18. (Reprint in 1 vol. New Delhi: Ajay Book Service.)

Vimalakīrtinirdeśa.

1976 Trans. S. Boin from French tr. by É. Lamotte. London: Pali Text Society.

Vinayapiṭaka.

1879-81 Pali text ed. H. Oldenberg. Vol. 1: *Mahāvagga*. Vol. 3: *Suttavibhaṅga, First Part* (*Pārājika, Saṃghādisesa, Aniyata, Nissaggiya*). London and Edinburgh: Williams and Norgate.

[1881-82] 1964. Trans. T. W. Rhys Davids and H. Oldenberg. *Vinaya Texts*. Part 1: *The Patimokkha and the Mahavagga I-IV*; Part 2: *The Mahavagga V-X and the Kullavagga I-III*. Oxford: Clarendon Press. (Reprint Delhi: Motilal Banarsidass.) Sacred Books of the East 13, 17.

Vipākaśruta (Vivāya Suya).

[n.d.] Prakrit text ed. and trans. V. J. Chokshi and M. C. Modi. Ahmedabad: Gurjar Grantha Ratna Vidyalaya. Prakrit Granthamala 6.

Vivekavilāsa of Jinadatta.

1887 Sanskrit text in R. G. Bhandarkar, *Report on the Search for Sanskrit Manuscripts in the Bombay Presidency During the Year 1883-84*, pp. 156, 458-63. Bombay: Government Central Press.

Vyavahāra Sūtra (Vavahāra Sutta).

1966 French and German trans. C. Caillat in W. Schubring (ed.), *Drei Chedasūtras des Jaina-Kanons*, pp. 49-89. Hamburg: Cram, de Gruyter & Co. Alt- und Neu-Indische Studien 11.

Yogaśāstra of Hemacandra.

1989 Trans. A. S. Gopani. Jaipur: Prakrit Bharti Academy and Mevanagar: Shri Jain Svetamber Nakoda Parshwanath Teerth.

MODERN WORKS

Alsdorf, Ludwig

1938 "A New Version of the Agaḍadatta Story." In *New Indian Antiquary* 1:281-99.

1965 *Les études jaina: État présent et taches futures*. Paris: Collège de France.

1973 "What were the Contents of the Dṛṣṭivāda?" In *German Scholars on India*, vol. I, 1-5. Varanasi: Chowkhambha Sanskrit Series Office.

Barth, Auguste

1880 "Bulletin Critique des Religions de l'Inde." In *Revue de l'Histoire des Religions* 1:239-60.

1881 "Bulletin Critique des Religions de l'Inde." In *Revue de l'Histoire des Religions* 3:72-98.

1889 "Bulletins des Religions de l'Inde, IIe Partie: Bouddhisme, Jainisme, Hindouisme." In *Revue de l'Histoire des Religions* 19:259-311.

1902 "Bulletins des Religions de l'Inde, IV: Jainisme." In *Revue de l'Histoire des Religions* 45:171-85.

1914-27 *Quarante Ans d'Indianisme: Ouvres de August Barth*. 5 vols. Paris: Ernest Leroux.

Barua, Benimadhab

[1921] 1970 *A History of Pre-Buddhistic Indian Philosophy*. Calcutta: University of Calcutta. (Reprint Delhi: Motilal Banarsidass.)

Basham, A. L.

1963 *The Wonder That Was India*. Rev. ed. New York: Grove Press.

Bhandarkar, R. B.

1887 See *Vivekavilāsa*.

Bhargava, Dayanand

1968 *Jaina Ethics*. Delhi: Motilal Banarsidass.

Bhatt, Bhansidhar and Chandrabhal Tripathi.

1974 "Tattvārtha Studies I-II." In *Adyar Library Bulletin* 38:64-83.

Bollée, Willem B.

1977-88 *Studien zum Sūyagaḍa*. 2 Vols. Wieshaden: Franz Steiner. Schriftenreihe des Südasien-Instituts der Universität Heidelberg 24, 31.

Bronkhorst, Johannes

1985 "On the Chronology of the Tattvārtha Sūtra and some Early Commentaries." In *Archiv für Indische Philosophie* 29:155-84.

Brown, W. Norman

1941 *Manuscript Illustrations of the Uttarādhayayana Sūtra.* New Haven: American Oriental Society. American Oriental Series 21.

Bühler, Georg

1878a "The Digambara Jainas." In *Indian Antiquary* 7:28-29.

1878b "The Three New Edicts of Asoka." In *Indian Antiquary* 7:141-60.

1882 "Ueber eine kürzlich für die Wiener Universität erworbene Sammlung von Sanskrit- und Prakrit-Handschriften." In *Sitzungsberichte der Philosophische-Historischen Classe der Kaiserlichen Akademie der Wissenschaften zu Wien* 99, 563-79.

1887a "On the Authenticity of the Jaina Tradition." In *Wiener Zeitschrift für die Kunde des Morgenlandes* 1:165-80.

1887b *Über die Indische Secte der Jaina.* Wien: Kaiserliche Akademie der Wissenschaften.

1888 "Further Proofs for the Authenticity of the Jaina Tradition." In *Wiener Zeitschrift für die Kunde des Morgenlandes* 2:141-46.

1889 "Further Proofs for the Authenticity of the Jaina Tradition." In *Wiener Zeitschrift für die Kunde des Morgenlandes* 3:233-40.

1890a "Further Proofs of the Authenticity of the Jaina Tradition." In *Wiener Zeitschrift für die Kunde des Morgenlandes* 4:313-31.

1890b "Kleine Mittheilungen: New Jaina Inscriptions from Mathurâ." In *Wiener Zeitschrift für die Kunde des Morgenlandes* 4:169-73.

1891a "Kleine Mittheilungen: New Excavations in Mathurâ." In *Wiener Zeitschrift für die Kunde des Morgenlandes* 5:59-63.

1891b "Kleine Mittheilungen: Dr. Führer's Excavations at Mathurâ." In *Wiener Zeitschrift für die Kunde des Morgenlandes* 5:175-80.

1892a "New Jaina Inscriptions from Mathurâ." In *Epigraphia Indica* 1:371-93.

1892b "Further Jaina Inscriptions from Mathurâ." In *Epigraphica Indica* 1:393-97.

1894a "Further Jaina Inscriptions from Mathurâ." In *Epigraphia Indica* 2:195-212.

1894b "Specimens of Jaina Sculptures from Mathurâ." In *Epigraphia India* 2: 311-23.

1896 "Kleine Mittheilungen: Epigraphic Discoveries at Mathurâ." In *Wiener Zeitschrift für die Kunde des Morgenlandes* 10:171-74.

[1898] 1898 "A Legend of the Jaina Stūpa at Mathurā." In *Sitzungsberichte der Philosophische-Historischen Classe der Kaiserlichen Akademie der Wissenschaften,* 1-14. (Reprint *Indian Antiquary* 27:49-54.)

[1903] 1963 *The Indian Sect of the Jainas.* Trans. J. Burgess of Bühler 1887b. London: Luzac. (Reprint Calcutta: Susil Gupta [India] Private Ltd.)

Burch, George Bosworth

1964 "Seven-Valued Logic in Jain Philosophy." In *International Philosophical Quarterly* 3:68-93.

Burgess, J.

1884 "Papers on Śatruñjaya and the Jainas. VII. Gachchhas, Śrîpûjyas, Yatis, Nuns, &c." In *Indian Antiquary* 13:276-80.

Carrithers, Michael

1989 "Naked Ascetics in Southern Digambar Jainism." In *Man* (n.s.) 24:219-35.

Charpentier, Jarl

1910 "The Leśyā-theory of the Jainas and Ājivikas." In *Festskrift tillegnad Karl Ferdinand Johansson,* 20-38. Göteborg: Wald. Zachrissons Boktryckeri A.-B.

1922 See *Uttarādhyayana Sūtra.*

Chatterjee, A. K.

1978-84 *A Comprehensive History of Jainism.* 2 vols. Calcutta: Firma KLM (Private) Limited.

Chaudhuri, Nirad

1974 *Scholar Extraordinary: The Life of Professor the Rt. Hon. Friedrich Max Müller, P.C.* London: Chatto & Windus.

Cort, John E.

1988 "Pilgrimage to Shankheshvar Pārshvanāth." In *Center for the Study of World Religions Bulletin* 14:1:63-72.

1989 "Liberation and Wellbeing: A Study of the Śvetāmbar Mūrtipūjak Jains of North Gujarat." Harvard University Ph.D. dissertation.

1990 "Models of and for the Study of the Jains." In *Method of Theory in the Study of Religion* 2:42-71.

1991a "The Śvetāmbar Mūrtipūjak Jain Mendicant." In *Man* (n.s.) 26:549-69.

1991b "Śvetāmbar Mūrtipūjak Jain Scripture in a Performative Context." In *Texts in Context: Traditional Hermeneutics in South Asia,* 171-94. Ed. J. Timm. Albany: SUNY Press.

Cunningham, Alexander

[1873] 1966 *Report for the Year 1871-72.* Calcutta: Archaeological Survey of India, Vol. III. (Reprint Varanasi: Indological Book House.)

Deleu, Jozef

1970 *Viyāhapannatti (Bhagavaī), the Fifth Aṅga of the Jaina Canon. Introduction, Critical Analysis, Commentary & Indexes.* Brugge: Rijksuniversiteit te Gent.

1977 "Lord Mahāvīra and the Anyatīrthikas." In *Mahāvīra and His Teachings*, 187-93. Ed. A. N. Upadhye, et al. Bombay: Bhagavān Mahāvīra 2500th Nirvāṇa Mahotsava Samiti.

Denecke, W.

1926 "Mitteilungen über Digambara-Texte." In *Beiträge zur Literaturwissenschaft und Geistesgeschichte Indiens: Festgabe Hermann Jacobi zum 75.* Geburtstag, 160-68. Bonn: Kommissionsverlag Fritz Klopp.

Deo, S. B.

1956 *History of Jaina Monachism*. Poona: Deccan College Postgraduate and Research Institute.

Deshpande, Madhav M.

1979 *Sociolinguistic Attitudes in India*. Ann Arbor: Karoma. Linguistica Extranea Studia 5.

Deussen, Paul

1897 *Sechzig Upanishad's des Veda aus dem Sanskrit übersetzt und mit Einleitungen und Anmerkungen versehen.* Leipzig: F. A. Brockhaus.

Dhruva, A. B.

1933 See *Anyayogavyavacchedikā.*

Dixit, K. K.

1971 *Jaina Ontology*. Ahmedabad: L. D. Institute of Indology. L. D. Series 31.

Dumont, Louis

1980 *Homo Hierarchicus*. Rev. Eng. ed. Trans. M. Sainsbury, L. Dumont, and B. Gulati. Chicago: University of Chicago Press.

Dundas, Paul

1985 "Food and Freedom: The Jaina Sectarian Debate on the Nature of the Kevalin." In *Religion* 15:161-98.

Forthcoming "The Marginal Monk and the True Tīrtha." In *Volume in Honour of J. Deleu*. Ed. K. Watanabe. Tokyo.

Fischer, Eberhard, and Jyotindra Jain

1974 *Kunst und Religion in Indien: 2500 Jahre Jainismus.* Wien: Museums für Völkerkunde.

1977 *Art and Rituals: 2500 Years of Jainism in India.* Trans. J. Jain-Neubauer of Fischer and Jain 1974. New Delhi: Sterling.

Folkert, Kendall W.

1975 "Jaina Approaches to Non-Jainas: Patterns and Implications." Ph.D. thesis, Harvard University.

Foy, Willy.

1900 "Vedische Beiträge." In *Zeitschrift für Vergleichende Sprachforschung auf dem Gebeite der indo-germanische Sprachen* 36, N.F. 16:133-38.

Franklin, W.

1827 *Researches on the Tenets and Doctrines of the Jeynes and Boodhists.* London: the author.

Frauwallner, E.

1957 "The Editions of Malavādī's Dvādaśāranayacakram." In *Archiv für Indische Philosophie* 1:147-51.

Freedman, David Noel, and M. P. O'Connor, eds.

1983 "The Bible and Its Traditions." In *Michigan Quarterly Review* (Special Issue) XXII:3.

Geertz, Clifford

1973 *The Interpretation of Cultures.* New York: Basic Books.

Ghurye, G. S.

1968 *Indian Sadhus.* Bombay: Popular Prakasham.

Glasenapp, Helmuth von

1915 *Die Lehre vom Karman in der Philosophie der Jainas.* Leipzig: G. Kreysing.

[1925] 1964 *Der Jainismus: Eine indische Erlösungs-religion.* Berlin: Alf Häger. (Reprint Heldesheim: Georg Olms.)

1942 *The Doctrine of Karman in Jain Philosophy.* Trans. G. Barry Gifford of von Glasenapp 1915. Bombay: Bai Vijibai Jivanlal Panalal Charity Fund.

Gokhale, V. V.

1958 "The Vedānta-Philosophy Described by Bhavya in his *Madhyamakahṛdaya.*" In *Indo-Iranian Journal* 2:165-80.

Guérinot, A.

1906 *Essai de bibliographie jaina.* Paris: Annales du Musée Guimet.

Halbfass, Wilhelm

1979 "Observations on Darśana." In *Wiener Zeitschrift für die Kunde Südasiens* 23:195-203.

Hanumanta Rao, G.

[1927] 1963 "The Jaina Instrumental Theory of Knowledge." In *Proceedings of the Indian Philosophical Congress,* 129-35. Ed. Satichandra Chatterjee. Calcutta: The Calcutta Philosophical Society. (Reprint in *Recent Indian*

Philosophy, Vol. 1:193-200. Ed. K. Bhattacharyya. Calcutta: Progressive Publishers.)

Heesterman, J. C.

[1968-69] 1985. "On the Origin of the Nāstika." In *Wiener Zeitschrift für die Kunde Süd- und Ost-Asiens* 12-13 (Beiträge zur Geistesgeschichte Indiens: Festschrift für Erich Frauwallner), 171-81. (Reprint in *The Inner Conflict of Tradition*, 70-80. Chicago: University of Chicago Press.)

Hoernle, A. F. Rudolf

1885-90 See *Upāsakadaśāḥ*.

1890 "The Pattavali or List of Pontiffs of the Upakesa-Gachchha." In *Indian Antiquary* 19:233-42.

1891 "Two Pattavalis of the Sarasvati Gachchha of the Digambara Jainas." In *Indian Antiquary* 20:341-61.

1892 "Three Further Pattavalis of the Digambaras." In *Indian Antiquary* 21:57-84.

Hopkins. E. Washburn

[1898] 1970 *The Religions of India*. Boston: Ginn & Co. (Reprint New Delhi: Munshiram Manoharlal.)

Hume, Robert Ernest

1931 Trans. *The Thirteen Principal Upanishads*. 2nd rev. ed. London: Oxford University Press.

Hurvitz, Leon

1976 See *Saddharmapuṇḍarīka*.

Jacobi, Hermann

1879 See *Kalpa Sūtra*.

1880 "On Mahāvīra and his Predecessors." In *Indian Antiquary* 9:158-63.

1884a "Ueber die Entstehung der Çvetâmbara und Digambara Sekten." In *Zeitschrift der Deutschen Morgenländischen Gesellschaft* 38:1-42.

1884b "Introduction." In *Jaina Sūtras*, 1:ix-liii. Oxford: Clarendon Press. Sacred Books of the East 22.

1884c See *Ācārāṅga Sūtra*.

1884d See *Kalpa Sūtra*.

1895a "Introduction." In *Jaina Sūtras*, 2:xiii-xli. Oxford: Clarendon Press. Sacred Books of the East 45.

1895b See *Sūtrakṛtāṅga Sūtra*.

1899-1914 See *Upamitibhavaprapañcākathā*.

1906 See *Tattvārtha Sūtra*.

Jain, Jyoti Prasad

1964 The *Jaina Sources for the History of Ancient India.* Delhi: Munshi Ram Manohar Lal.

Jain, S. A.

1960 See *Tattvārtha Sūtra.*

Jain, Uttam Kamal

1975 *Jaina Sects and Schools.* Delhi: Concept.

Jaini, Jagmander Lal

[1915] 1979 *Outlines of Jainism.* Ed. F. W. Thomas. London: Jain Literature Society. (Reprint Indore: J. L. Jaini Trust.)

Jaini, Padmanabh S.

1979 *The Jaina Path of Purification.* Berkeley: University of California Press; Delhi: Motilal Banarsidass.

1991 *Gender and Salvation: Jaina Debates on the Spiritual Liberation of Women.* Berkeley: University of California Press.

Kane, P .V.

1968-77 *History of Dharmaśāstra.* Rev. ed. 5 vols. Poona: Bhandarkar Oriental Research Institute.

Kapadia, Hiralal Rasikdas

1926-30 See *Tattvārtha Sūtra.*

1940-47 See *Anekāntajayapatākā.*

1941 *A History of the Canonical Literature of the Jainas.* Surat: the author.

Kaviraj, Gopinath

[n.d.] [1966?] "Theism in Ancient India." In *Aspects of Indian Thought,* 45-71. Burdwan: University of Burdwan.

Klatt, Johannes

1882 "Extracts from the Historical Records of the Jainas." In *Indian Antiquary* 11:245-56.

1894 "The Samachari-Satakam of Samayasundara and Pattavalis of the Anchala-Gachchha and other Gachchhas." Revised with editions by Ernst Leumann. In *Indian Antiquary* 23:169-83.

Knipe, David M.

1975 *Jainism.* Program 6 in the video series *Exploring the Religions of South Asia.* Madison: WHA-TV.

Lalwani, K. C.

1979 See *Kalpa Sutra*.

Lamotte, Étienne

See *Vimalakīrtinirdeśa*.

Lassen, Christian

1861 *Indische Alterthumskünde*. 4 vols. 2nd ed. Leipzig: L. A. Kittler.

1873 "Papers on Satrunjaya and the Jains." Trans. E. Rehatsek of Lassen 1861:755ff. In *Indian Antiquary* 2, 193-200, 258-65.

Lath, Mukund

1981 *Ardhakathānaka: Half a Tale*. Jaipur: Rajasthan Prakrit Bharati Sansthan.

Leeuw, Gerardus van der

[1964] 1986 *Religion in Essence and Manifestation*. 2nd ed. Trans. J. E. Turner. London: George Allen Unwin. (Reprint Princeton: Princeton University Press.)

Leumann, Ernst

1882 See *Aupapātika Sūtra*.

1885 "Die alten Berichte von dem Schismen der jaina." In Indische Studien 17:91-135.

1905 "Zum siebenten Kapitel von Amitagati's Subhāṣitasaṃdoha." In *Zeitschrift der Deutschen Morgenländischen Gesellschaft* 59:578-88.

1934 *Übersicht über die Āvaśyaka-Literatur*. Ed. W. Schubring. Hamburg: Friederichsen, de Gruyter & Co. Alt- und Neu-Indische Studien 4.

Lévi, Sylvain

1966 *La doctrine du sacrifice dans les Brāhmaṇas*. 2nd ed. Paris: Presses Universitaires de France. Bibliothèque de l'École des Hautes Études LXXIII.

Lüders, Heinrich

1961 *Mathurā Inscriptions*. Ed. K. L. Janert. Göttingen: Vandenhoeck & Ruprecht. Abhandlungen der Akademie der Wissenschaften in Göttingen, Philologisch-Historische Klasse 47.

MacLeish, Archibald

1952 *Collected Poems 1917-1952*. Boston: Houghton Mifflin.

Malvania [Mālvaṇiyā], Pt. Dalsukh

1968 "Jaina Agamas." In *Nandisuttam and Aṇuogaddārāim*, 6-31. Eds. Muni Puṇyavijaya, Pt. D. Mālvaṇiyā, and Pt. A. Mohanlāl Bhojak. Bombay: Shri Mahāvīra Jaina Vidyālaya. Jaina-Āgama-Series No. 1.

1969 "Prastāvanā" to *ṢDS* (*Jain*), 5-21.

Mandelbaum, David

1972 *Society in India*. 2 vols. Berkeley: University of California Press.

Marshall, J. H.

1904 "Introduction." In *Annual Report 1902-1903*, 1-13. Calcutta: Archaeological Survey of India.

Mehta, Mohan Lal

1971 *Jaina Philosophy*. Varanasi: P. V. Research Institute. Parshvanath Vidyashram Series 16.

1975 "Jaina Monastic Discipline." In *Jainism*, 68-77. Ed. G. S. Talib. Patiala: Punjabi University.

Miller, David M. and Dorothy C. Wertz

1976 *Hindu Monastic Life*. Montreal: McGill-Queens University Press.

Mitra, Rajendralal

1876 *Notices of Sanskrit Mss.*, vol. 3. Calcutta: Baptist Mission Press.

Mookerjee, Satkari

[1944] 1978 *The Jaina Philosophy of Non-Absolutism*. Calcutta: The Bharati Mahavidyalaya. (Reprint Delhi: Motilal Banarsidass.)

Müller, F. Max

1873 *Introduction to the Science of Religion: Four Lectures Delivered at the Royal Institution, with Two Essays: On False Analogies, and The Philosophy of Mythology*. London: Longmans, Green.

[1879a] 1965, 1962. "Preface to the Sacred Books of the East." In *The Upaniṣads*, Part 1, ix-xxxviii. Oxford: Clarendon Press. (Reprints Delhi: Motilal Banarsidass. New York: Dover Publications.) Sacred Books of the East 1.

[1879b] 1965, 1962. "Program of a Translation of the Sacred Books of the East." In *The Upaniṣads*, Part 1, xxxix-xlvii. Oxford: Clarendon Press. (Reprints Delhi: Motilal Banarsidass. New York: Dover Publications.) Sacred Books of the East 1.

[1889] 1975 *Natural Religion: The Gifford Lectures Delivered Before the University of Glasgow in 1888*. London: Longmans, Green. (Reprint New York: AMS Press.)

Mus, Paul

1935 *Barabadur: Esquisse d'une histoire du bouddhisme fondée sur la critique archeologique des textes*. Paris: Paul Guenther.

Nahar, Puran Chand, and Krishnachandra Ghosh

[1917] 1988 *An Epitome of Jainism*. Calcutta: H. Duby. (Reprint Delhi: Sri Satguru Publications. Sri Garib Dass Oriental Series 40. Reprint New Delhi: Caxton.)

Nakamura, Susumu

1951 "Pradakshiṇā, a Buddhist Form of Obeisance." In *Semitic and Oriental Studies: Festschrift William Popper*, 348-51. Ed. W. J. Fischel. Berkeley: University of California Press.

Nandi, Ramendra Nath

1973 *Religious Institutions and Cults in the Deccan*. Delhi: Motilal Banarsidass.

O'Flaherty, Wendy Doniger

1971 "The Origin of Heresy in Hindu Mythology." In *History of Religions* 10:268-303.

1976 *The Origins of Evil in Hindu Mythology*. Berkeley: University of California Press.

Ohira, Suzuko

1982 *A Study of the Tattvārthasūtra with Bhāṣya*. Ahmedabad: L.D. Institute of Indology. L.D. Series 86.

Padmarajiah, Y. J.

[1963] 1986 *A Comparative Study of the Jaina Theories of Reality and Knowledge*. Bombay: Jain Sahitya Vikas Mandal. (Reprint Delhi: Motilal Banarsidass.)

Poleman, Horace I.

[1938] 1967 *A Census of Indic Manuscripts in the United States and Canada*. New Haven: American Oriental Society. (Reprint New York: Kraus Reprint Corp.)

Potter, Karl H.

1983 *Encyclopedia of Indian Philosophies, Vol. I: Bibliography*. Rev. ed. Princeton: Princeton University Press.

Premī, Nāthūrām

1956 *Jain Sāhitya aur Itihās*. Bombay: Hiṅdī Granth Ratnākar.

Przyluski, Jean

1935 "The Harmika and the Origin of the Buddhist Stupas." In *Indian Historical Quarterly* 11:199-210.

Quarnström, Olle

1989 *Hindu Philosophy in Buddhist Perspective*. Lund: Plus Ultra. Lund Studies in African and Asian Religions 4.

Redfield, Robert

1956 *Peasant Society and Culture*. Chicago: Chicago University Press.

Renou, Louis

[1953] 1968 *Religions of Ancient India*. London: Athlone; New York: Oxford University Press. (Reprint New York: Schocken Books.)

Rhys Davids, T. W., and William Stede

[1921-25] 1966, 1975. *Pali-English Dictionary*. Chipstead: The Pali Text Society. (Reprints London: Luzac; New Delhi: Oriental Books Reprint Corporation.)

Ricouer, Paul

1979 "The 'Sacred' Text and the Community." In *The Critical Study of Sacred Texts*, 271-76. Ed. W. D. O'Flaherty. Berkeley: Berkeley Religious Studies Series.

Sandesara, B. J.

1962 "Section VII: Prakrits and Jainism." In *Proceedings and Transactions of the All-India Oriental Conference, Twentieth Session, Bhubaneswar, October 1959, Vol. I: Proceedings and Presidential Addresses,* 87-131. Ed. V. Raghavan. Poona: All-India Oriental Conference and Bhandarkar Oriental Research Institute.

Sandesara, B. J., and J. P. Thakar

1962 *Lexicographical Studies in Jaina Sanskrit*. Baroda: The Oriental Institute.

Sangave, Vilas Adinath

1980 *Jaina Community: A Social Survey*. 2nd ed. Bombay: Popular Prakashan.

Schrader, F. Otto

1902 *Über den Stand der indischen Philosophie zur Zeit Mahāvīras und Buddhas*. Leipzig: the author.

Schubring, Walther

1918 *Das Mahānisīha-Sutta*. Berlin: Königl Akademie der Wissenschaften.

1926 (Trans.) *Worte Mahāvīras: Kritische Übersetzungen aus dem Kanon der Jaina*. Göttingen: Vandenhoeck & Ruprecht.

1935 *Die Lehre der Jainas, nach dem alten Quellen dargestellt.* Berlin: De Gruyter.

1957 "Kundakunda echt und unecht." In *Zeitschrift der Deutschen Morgenländischen Gesellschaft* 107:557-74.

1959 "Jinismus." *In Die Religion in Geschichte und Gegenwart,* 3rd ed., 668-70. Tubingen: J. C. B. Mohr (Paul Siebeck).

1962 *The Doctrine of the Jainas.* Trans. W. Beurlen of Schubring 1935. Delhi: Motilal Banarsidass.

1966 See *Ācāradaśāḥ.*

1978 *Nāyādhammakahāo: Das sechste Anga des Jaina-Siddhānta.* Ed. J. Deleu. Mainz: Akademie der Wissenschaften und der Literatur. Abhandlungen der Geistes- und Sozial wissenschaftlichen Klasse Jahrgang 1978 Nr. 6.

Schwarzchild, L. A.

1960-61 "The Indeclinable *JE* in Middle Indo-Aryan." In *Bhāratīya Vidyā* (*Munshi Felicitation Volume*), 20-21, 211-17.

Sen, Amulyachandra

1931 *Schools and Sects in Jaina Literature.* Calcutta: Visva-Bharati Book-Shop. Visva-Bharati Studies 3.

Shah, Chimanlal J.

[1932] 1989 *Jainism in North India: 800 B.C.—A.D. 526*. London: Longmans, Green. (Reprint New Delhi: A. Sagar Book House.)

Singer, Milton

1972 *When a Great Tradition Modernizes.* New York: Praegar.

Singh, Ram Bhushan Prasad

1975 *Jainism in Early Medieval Karnataka*. Delhi: Motilal Banarsidass.

Smith, Vincent A.

[1901] 1969 *The Jain Stûpa and Other Antiquities of Mathurâ*. Allahabad: Archaeological Survey of India. New Imperial Series 20. (Reprint Varanasi: Indological Book House.)

Smith, Wilfred Cantwell

1957 *Islam in Modern History*. Princeton: Princeton University Press.

[1971] 1976 "The Study of Religion and the Study of the Bible." In *Journal of the American Academy of Religion* 39, 131-40. (Reprint in *Religious Diversity: Essays by Wilfred Cantwell Smith*, 41-56. Ed. W. G. Oxtoby. New York: Harper & Row.)

Stevenson, Mrs. Sinclair [Margaret]

[1915] 1970 *The Heart of Jainism.* London: Oxford University Press. (Reprint New Delhi: Munshiram Manoharlal.)

Suali, Luigi.

1905 See *Ṣaḍdarśanasamuccaya* of Haribhadrasūri.

Tatia, Nathmal

[1951] n.d. *Studies in Jaina Philosophy*. Banaras: Jain Cultural Research Society. (Reprint Varanasi: P. V. Research Institute.)

Thomas, E. J.

1949 *The Life of the Buddha as Legend and History*. 3rd rev. ed. London: Routledge & Kegan Paul.

Thomas, F. W.

1935 "Introduction" to Barend Faddegon (tr.), *The Pravacana-sāra of Kunda-kunda Ācārya, together with the commentary, Tattva-dīpikā, by Amṛta-candra Sūri*, xi-xxiv. Cambridge: Cambridge University Press. Jain Literature Society Series 1.

Upadhye, A. N.

1933 "Yāpanīya Saṅgha—A Jaina Sect." In *Journal of the University of Bombay* I:6:224-31.

1935 "Introduction" to *Śrī Kundakundācārya's Pravacanasāra* (*Pavayaṇasāra*), 2nd ed., i-cxxvi. Bombay: Shetha Manilal Revashankar Jhaveri. Rāyachandra Jaina Śāstramālā.

1971 *Siddhasena's Nyāyāvatāra and Other Works*. Bombay: Jain Sahitya Vikasa Mandala.

1974 "More Light on the Yāpanīya Sangha: A Jaina Sect." In *Annals of the Bhandarkar Oriental Research Institute* 55:9-22.

Velankar, Hari Damodar.

1944 *Jinaratnakośa: An Alphabetical Register of Jain Works and Authors. Vol. 1: Works*. Poona: Bhandarkar Oriental Research Institute.

Wach, Joachim

1944 *The Sociology of Religion*. Chicago: University of Chicago Press.

Wackernagel, Jacob

1930 *Altindische Grammitik*. III. Band: *Nominalflexion-Zahlwort-Pronomen*, von Albert Debrunner und Jacob Wackernagel. Göttingen: Vandenhoeck & Ruptrecht.

Warder, A. K.

1970 "The Description of Indian Philosophy." In *Journal of Indian Philosophy* 1:4-12.

Weber, Albrecht

1858 *Üeber das Çatrunjaya Mâhâtmyam: Ein Beitrag zur Geschichte der Jaina.* Leipzig: F. A. Brockhaus. Abhandlungen für die Kunde des Morgenlandes 1:4.

[1865-66] 1866-67. *Uber ein Fragment der Bhagavatî: Ein Beitrag zur Kenntniss der heiligen Sprache und Litteratur der Jaina.* In Abhandlungen der Koniglichen Akademie der Wissenschaften zu Berlin, Phil.- Hist. Klasse. (Reprint Berlin: Königlichen Akademie der Wissenschaften.)

1883-85 "Uber die heiligen Schriften der Jaina." In *Indische Studien* 16:211-479, and 17:1-90.

1886-92 *Die Handschriften-Verzeichnisse der Koniglichen Bibliothek zu Berlin.* 2 vols. Berlin.

1893 *Weber's Sacred Literature of the Jains.* Trans. H. W. Smyth of Weber 1883-85. Bombay: at the Education Society's Steam Press. (Reprint from *Indian Antiquary* 17-21 [1888-92].)

1901 "The Śatrunjaya Mâhâtmyam. Trans. K. S. Godbole of Weber 1858. Ed. J. Burgess. In *Indian Antiquary* 30, 239-51, 288-308.

Welch, Holmes

1957 *The Parting of the Way: Lao Tzu and the Taoist Movement.* Boston: Beacon Press.

Williams, R.

[1963] 1983 *Jaina Yoga: A Survey of the Medieval Śrāvakācāras.* London: Oxford University Press. (Reprint Delhi: Motilal Banarsidass.)

Wilson, H. H.

[1828-32] 1862. "Sketch of the Religious Sects of the Hindus." In *Asiatic Researches* 16-17, 1-136, 169-314. (Reprint as *Works, Vol. 1: Essays and Lectures Chiefly on the Religion of the Hindus, Vol. 1: A Sketch of the Religious Sects of the Hindus.* Ed. R. Rost. London: Trübner & Co.)

Windisch, Ernst

1917-20 *Geschichte der Sanskrit-Philologie und Indische Alterhumskunde.* 2 vols. Strassburg: Karl J. Trübner (vol.1); Berlin: Vereinigung Wissenschaftlicher Verleger, and Leipzig: Walter de Gruyter (vol. 2).

Winternitz, Moriz

1933 *A History of Indian Literature Vol. 2: Buddhist and Jaina Literature.* Trans. S. Ketkar and H. Cohn. Calcutta: University of Calcutta Press.

Zydenbos, Robert J.

1983 *Mokṣa in Jainism, according to Umāsvāti.* Wiesbaden: Franz Steiner Verlag. Beiträge zur Südasien-Forschung, Südasien-Institut, Universität Heidelberg, 83.

GLOSSARY OF SANSKRIT, PRAKRIT, PALI AND GUJARATI TECHNICAL TERMS

abhigṛhīta (active or firmly held type of *mithyādarśana*), 295-96

abhyupagamasiddhānta (opponents' conclusions that are hypothetically granted, but whose consequences are then refuted, thus putting the opponent in a bad light), 348

ācārya (mendicant leaders of the Jain community), 89, 163, 375

adharma (the medium of rest), 234, 273-332, 350-51, 354, 362, 379, 389, 391

advaita (non-dualist school of Vedānta), 403

āgama ('canonical' literature), 78-81, 122, 125, 155, 308, 348, 353-54, 362, 363, 371, 387, 389, 391-92, 405-07, 409

agnihotra (Brāhmaṇic fire-sacrifice), 355, 368

ahaṃkāra (sense of I-ness [Sāṃkhya]), 353, 366, 388, 405

ahiṃsā (non-harm, non-injury, one of the five *mahāvrata*s of the mendicant), xvii, 7-11, 18, 24, 217, 224-26, 282, 396-97

ajīva (not-soul, that which is not sentient, one of the *tattva*s), 7-10, 115, 234-35, 251, 274, 327-29, 353, 362, 391, 401

ajñāna (ignorance or agnosticism), 248-53, 255-59, 261, 277, 279-80, 285-86, 300, 326-28, 331, 333, 336-37

ajñānavādī (propounder of agnosticism), 233, 235

ajñānika (agnostic, sceptic), 251, 321-26, 328-31, 337

ajñānikatva (the state of being agnostic), 250-51, 253, 322, 328

ajñānikavāda (philosophic stance of agnosticism), 235, 240, 243, 248, 273, 312-13, 322-23, 325, 328

ākāśa (ether or space, one of the six existents [*dravya*]), 332, 350

akriyā (inaction, non-activity), 248, 262-63, 266-71, 275, 277, 279-81, 283-86, 290, 313-14, 335-36

akriyāvāda [Pkt. *akiriyavādo*] (teaching concerning non-activity), 223, 235, 239-40, 243, 248-49, 254, 256, 261-67, 284-85, 312-13, 324-25

Akṣayatṛtīya. *See* Index.

INDEX

Reprinted works of Kendall Folkert

Parts of "The Jainas." In *A Reader's Guide to the Great Religions*, 2nd Edition, 231-46. Charles J. Adams, Editor. Copyright © 1977 by The Free Press, a Division of Macmillan, Inc. Reprinted by permission of the publisher.

Review: Padmanabh S. Jaini, *The Jaina Path of Purification*. In *Journal of Asian Studies* 39 (1980), 829-31. Copyright © 1980 by The Association for Asian Studies, Inc. Reprinted by permission of the publisher.

"Jainism." In *A Handbook of Living Religions*, 256-77. Edited by John R. Hinnells (Viking, 1984). Copyright © John R. Hinnells and Penguin Books Ltd., 1984. Reproduced by permission of Penguin Books Ltd.

Parts of "The 'Canons' of 'Scripture.'" Reprinted from *Rethinking Scripture: Essays from a Comparative Perspective*, edited by Miriam Levering by permission of the State University of New York Press. *Rethinking Scripture: Essays from a Comparative Perspective*, 170-79. Edited by Miriam Levering. Albany: State University of New York Press, 1989. Copyright © 1989 State University of New York.

"Jain Religious Life at Ancient Mathurā: The Heritage of Late-Victorian Interpretation." In *Mathurā: The Cultural Heritage*, 103-12. Edited by Doris Meth Srinivasan. Delhi: Manohar and American Institute for Indian Studies, 1989. Copyright © 1989 American Institute for Indian Studies. Reprinted by permission of the publisher.

Photographs by Thomas A. Zwicker © 1989 The University of Pennsylvania Museum Archives.